Business Communication Dynamics

Bobbye Sorrels Persing

Central State University, Oklahoma

Charles E. Merrill Publishing Company
A Bell & Howell Company
Columbus   Toronto   London   Sydney

To my granddaughter Jennifer
who brings new joy to my life

Published by Charles E. Merrill Publishing Co.
A Bell & Howell Company
Columbus, Ohio 43216

This book was set in Optima

Production Editor: Ben Shriver

Cover Design Coordination: Will Chenoweth

Cover Photo: William Holbrook
    Sculpture: Hyatt Regency Hotel, San Francisco

Letterhead Designs: Dan Robinson/Pony-X-Press

Library of Congress Catalog Card Number: 80–84741

International Standard Book Number: 0–675–08153–X

Printed in the United States of America

1 2 3 4 5 6 7 8 9 10—85 84 83 82 81

Preface

The majority of business students take at most only one course in business communication. Therefore, that one course should sweep the full range of the communication requirements of business—sending and receiving written, oral, and nonverbal messages—even as it probes into key communication activities. The one course should sweep and probe in a manner that immediately improves all of the communication arts and skills at the same time that it whets appetites for more power in them—whether that power is gained through self-study or additional communication courses. I have developed this book as a systems approach to meeting these purposes.

The book treats communication as an integrated, whole process and uses a logical organizational plan to unfold that process. It begins with the receiving acts of reading, listening, and receiving nonverbal messages (Chapters 1–3). From that foundation for learning, it moves to theory (Chapter 4), guidelines (Chapters 5–6), and the sending acts of writing, speaking, and sending nonverbal messages (Chapters 7–18).

The book covers just enough theory to establish the groundwork for the business applications that form the core of the book. It features six comprehensive, practical guidelines for developing and receiving messages efficiently. The guidelines stress the importance of defining purposes, understanding participants, identifying channels, controlling interference, sending and receiving messages, using feedback, and evaluating at each stage of the communication transaction. Each major topic in the book includes a reinforcing review of the guidelines as they apply to that topic.

Each chapter includes at least one passage marked so that the reader may time reading speed. In conjunction with the marked passages the book features 23 self-tests and their solutions. It also includes forms for recording speed and comprehension scores for the passages (Appendix A).

Because nonverbal messages carry about 65 percent of the meaning in face-to-face exchanges, this book has an unusually comprehensive survey of nonverbal communication. It deals with both nonverbal receiving and nonverbal sending (Chapters 3 and 16).

Similarly, because oral communication occupies about 75 percent of the business communicator's time, compared to 25 percent for the written, this book includes a thorough summary of oral communication and a realistic emphasis upon listening and speaking in business exchanges (Chapters 2 and 15 and Appendix B).

Even with the appropriate emphasis upon the nonverbal and oral, the book provides extensive coverage of the written as well. It covers general principles of writing as well as teaching the specifics of writing all the major types of messages used in business today.

The final two chapters (17–18) apply and reinforce all of the sending and receiving acts by offering practical coverage of careers and employment.

The book centers on the reader. It contains over 400 exercises and illustrations in comprehensive and varied form. It threads exercises in oral and written activities through all chapters. It includes a vocabulary list, a summary, at least one timed-reading self-test, and a chapter self-test in every chapter. It employs and presents guidelines for the nonsexist communication style (Appendix D). It provides down-to-earth reviews of grammar, spelling, word usage, sentence structure, and other mechanics (Appendix C). Throughout it emphasizes the importance of organizational communication and of group communication activities for business.

Even with the comprehensiveness and thoroughness of its survey, the book is quite containable in one collegiate term. Because many sections and chapters involve extensive self-learning devices, the professor need devote little or no class time to them. Moreover, because of the self-contained nature of many of the chapters and parts, the professor may elect to omit or just skim some of them—particularly when the text is used in a quarter system. The professor may accomplish such reduced coverage without disrupting the continuity of the course. On the other hand, the book contains such a wealth of material and exercises that it will fit a two-term course quite well.

This book is suitable for the basic business communication course offered at the lower- or upper-division level. However, it is mature enough to serve more advanced students equally well. It also makes a good reference source for business communicators.

To acknowledge some of the people who helped make the book possible, my special appreciation goes to my daughter, Lynne Persing (graduate student, The University of Oregon) for her invaluable contributions. Not only did she make creative suggestions, but she developed the first drafts for Appendix C and for many of the examples and exercises for the book, as well as for many of the solutions in the instructor's manual. My appreciation also goes to Thomas H. Inman (Arizona State University), Norman F. Kallaus (The University of Iowa), John M. Penrose (University of Texas at Austin), Marcia K. Shallcross (Palomar College), Betty Sisk (Corpus Christi State University), and Joan Warner (The University of Akron) for their suggestions. Thanks also to my editors at Merrill Publishing, Burton C. Gabriel and Ben Shriver, for their helpful advice; to Jan Tuepker and Martha Perry for their excellent typewriting; and to Colene Maxwell, Cindy Manning, Bridgette Perry, Gratia Bowen, Amorita Sorrels, Evelyn R. Duncan, and Vickie Sage for their contributions. I also appreciate the support of the remainder of my family, friends, and colleagues—especially that of my husband Roland. Without them the task would have been impossible.

Contents

Part a

RECEIVING

Reading

Whatever the approach taken to the study of life, superiority of communication emerges as a principal characteristic that sets humans above the other animals. As a dynamic participant in a kaleidoscope of communication systems, you live your life as a unique example of that superiority.

You speak. You listen. You write, read, touch, sigh, think, smile, and move. Although all of these acts are integral parts of the communication process, they represent but a few of the communication roles you play. You must slip in and out of all the required roles with imperceptible precision and agility—and generally perform several of them simultaneously.

Right now you are participating in at least one communication transaction: You are reading.

As you read, you continually make innumerable decisions about the meanings you are creating for the marks, letters, words, phrases, sentences, illustrations, colors, textures, and other symbols that you observe. The transaction of such meanings between senders and receivers forms the basis of all forms of human communication.

An efficient way to begin this study of communication is to divide the process into its component parts. Begin logically by analyzing the receiving act in which you now participate—reading.

PRINCIPLES OF READING

Average people spend about 16 percent of their waking hours reading. Businesspeople spend significantly more time than that because their work requires it.

People in business depend daily on the information contained in newspapers, periodicals, books, letters, reports, memoranda, and other written material. Thus, the quicker the businessperson reads and comprehends, the more efficiently the business runs.

Obviously, you already read. Perhaps you read well, or perhaps you do not read as well as you would like. You already may have taken some specialized work in reading improvement or speed reading. If you have not, you may want or need to do so now. If reading improvement is your goal, your institution probably has a reading center to aid you.

Whatever your level of ability and experience, however, you will benefit from this review. It will help you sharpen the arts and skills that lead to efficient reading.

Consider two reading categories: (1) speed, comprehension, and efficiency and (2) retention. Then consider some communication guidelines adapted specifically to the reading process.

Speed, Comprehension, and Efficiency

As you review the concepts associated with good reading, you may want to participate in some self-timing and self-testing. If so, locate a stopwatch or a standard watch with a second hand or a digital display of seconds.

To check your reading efficiency, first record how many seconds you take to read a designated passage. Read it carefully for content even as you attempt to read it as quickly as you can. Then take a brief comprehension test provided at the end of the passage.

Mangieri and Baldwin deal with comprehension, speed, and types of reading in the first excerpt which you may want to time. Time yourself on the material that falls between the sketches of a watch.

 Rate of comprehension rather than rate per se should be your primary objective in any reading task. In general, the more complex and expansive the requirements of comprehension, the slower your rate of reading will need to be in order for you to properly absorb information. There are four basic types of reading: careful reading, rapid reading, skimming, and scanning.

Careful reading is the slowest kind of reading, ranging from 50 to 350 words per minute, again depending upon the intricacy of the material. Careful reading is normally employed to . . . [conquer] detail, analyze content, or solve problems. You generally use this style of reading when you are . . . going to be tested on the material read.

Rapid reading can proceed at rates ranging from 300 to 600 words per minute. It is employed when the conceptual burden in the material is light, or when the retention of large amounts of specific information is not especially critical.

Skimming is a subcategory of reading which allows the reader to greatly increase reading rate by sacrificing exposure to detail. The purposes of skimming are to absorb main ideas, to grasp the general nature of the content, or to review previously read material. With practice, people can learn to skim efficiently at rates as high as 1500 words per minute.

Scanning is the fastest kind of reading. It is also the most restrictive in terms of the actual amount of information processed. The purposes of scanning are finite and highly specific. At speeds approaching 3000 words per minute, a reader can search for names, dates, numbers, textbook subheadings, or the answers to specific questions. It should be noted that a person proficient in scanning will see little or nothing other than the information which he [or she] is seeking.[1]

(294 words)
(test on page 5)

---

[1]John N. Mangieri and R. Scott Baldwin, *Effective Reading Techniques: Business and Personal Applications* (New York: Harper & Row, Publishers, Inc., Canfield Press, 1978), pp. 66-67.

Just record your time now; you will calculate your speed and efficiency rating after taking a comprehension test—Self-Test 1.

When taking the self-test, you should not look back at the passage you just read. Write your answers and scores on a piece of scratch paper unless you do not plan to sell this book at the end of the term.

The self-test has two parts: immediate recall (what you remember just after reading) and immediate inference (what you infer just after reading).

Self-Test 1
Excerpt about Types of Reading
(Careful Reading)

A. Recall (10 points each). For each multiple-choice question, select the most accurate answer.

1. The primary objective in any reading task:
   a. Is speed
   b. Depends on the type of reading
   c. Is comprehension
   d. Can be summarized as the rate of reading
   e. Is a good rate of comprehension

2. The four basic types of reading may be called:
   a. Careful reading, rapid reading, skimming, and scanning
   b. Reading for pleasure, for main ideas, for specific information, and for total recall
   c. Slow, moderately fast, fast, and speed reading
   d. Reading for absorption, comprehension, central themes, and review
   e. Problem-solving, analysis, retention, and searching

3. The fastest kind of reading involves:
   a. A great deal of processed information
   b. Speeds approaching 3,000 words a minute
   c. Grasping the general nature of the content
   d. Reading material for broad and unspecified purposes
   e. Seeing everything in the passage, but using rapid eye movement

4. The slowest kind of reading involves:
   a. Speeds ranging from 200–400 words a minute
   b. A light conceptual burden
   c. The need for retention of small amounts of specific information
   d. Conquering detail, analysis, or problem solving
   e. Searching for specific details, while blocking out all other information in the passage

5. The second slowest kind of reading involves:
   a. Material over which a student might be tested
   b. Searching for things like names, dates, numbers, or textbook subheadings, while skipping large chunks of material entirely
   c. Rates from 300 to 600 words a minute
   d. Skipping some sections
   e. Absorption of main ideas and the general nature of the content

6. The second fastest kind of reading involves:
   a. Rates up to 2,000 words a minute
   b. Reading for detail
   c. Grasping the general nature of the content

Self-Test 1 — (continued)

    d. Searching for certain details such as answers to specific questions without considering any other information

    e. Light or pleasure reading

  7. Which one of these lends itself to the fastest reading?

    a. Reviewing previously read material

    b. Searching for predetermined types of information

    c. Analysis

    d. Retention of large amounts of specific information

    e. Complex material

B. Inference (15 points each). For each multiple-choice question, select the most accurate answer.

  1. Mangieri and Baldwin:

    a. Dismiss speed as an unimportant factor in reading

    b. Define the rate of comprehension as the reading rate expressed in number of words a minute

    c. Consider textbook reading to be in the category of the slowest type of reading

    d. Do not classify a process as reading if any of the material is skipped

    e. Do not classify pleasure reading as true reading

  2. The excerpt indicates that:

    a. Mangieri and Baldwin consider only the slowest kind of reading to be appropriate for business situations.

    b. The insertion of an ellipsis or bracketed words cannot slow the reading speed.

    c. Mangieri and Baldwin's views are too old to be considered valid.

    d. The fastest reading rate allows for virtually no information processing.

    e. Mangieri and Baldwin do not favor any one of the four types of reading over the others.

Solution to Self-Test 1
Excerpt About Types of Reading
(Careful Reading)

A. Recall (10 points each)

  1. e   **5.** c

  2. a   **6.** c

  3. b   **7.** b

  4. d

B. Inference (15 points each)

  1. c

  2. e

Check and score your performance on the test over the quoted material. Because the points total 100, your score will be a percentage.

Now that you have recorded your time and comprehension test score (c.t.s.), determine how fast and how efficiently you read. To find the number of words a minute, multiply the total number of words read by 60 (because your time is in seconds). Then divide the product by the number of seconds:

$$\text{words a minute (w.a.m.)} = \frac{(\text{total number of words read}) \times 60}{\text{number of seconds}}$$

For example, if someone read the present excerpt in 86 seconds, the rate would be calculated:

$$\text{w.a.m.} = \frac{294 \times 60}{86} = \frac{17,640}{86} = 205$$

As the passage itself states, speed alone does not give enough information. Comprehension must enter into any proper assessment of reading ability. Therefore, use the concept suggested by Jacobus of calculating a reading efficiency score (r.e.s.).[2] To find that score, multiply the w.a.m. figure by the c.t.s. score:

$$\text{reading efficiency score (r.e.s.)} = \text{w.a.m.} \times \text{c.t.s.}$$

For the preceding 205 w.a.m., if that person made 70 percent on the comprehension test, the efficiency rate would be:

$$\text{r.e.s.} = 205 \times .70 = 144$$

In contrast, suppose that another person read at a rate of 300 w.a.m., but scored only 40 percent on comprehension. That person's r.e.s. would be only 120. If still another person had a reading rate of only 150 w.a.m., but scored 100 percent, the reading efficiency score would be 150.

Were you able to read the excerpt at a rate of 50–350 w.a.m., the appropriate range for careful reading? Did your r.e.s. still fall in the 50–350 w.a.m. range?

The process of including reading tests over useful material is continued throughout this book. Several more times in this chapter and at least once in each subsequent chapter, you will have the opportunity to time and test yourself over a passage marked by two watches. The page number for each comprehension test is indicated. The passages differ in length and difficulty.

If you decide to use the passages and tests, try varying your reading mode (and speed) among the four types. However, you probably will want to emphasize careful reading.

If you should want to time and test yourself over an entire chapter, a full-chapter test appears at the end of each. You may estimate the number of words in a chapter by multiplying the number of pages by 305 (the average number of words on each page).

Before continuing with the analysis of reading as a topic, turn to Appendix A and observe the forms for recording performances on timed readings. The forms include separate sections for the four types of reading. They provide places for the date, the self-test number or material read, the number of words, the number of seconds, the w.a.m., the c.t.s., and the r.e.s. In addition, graphs for each of the four types provide an opportunity for plotting your progress in both speed and reading efficiency.

If you would like to keep a record of your performance through the term, your professor may provide you with full-page copies of the forms. As an alternative you could make photocopies of the forms in the appendix. If you do not intend to sell your book, you may even keep the records directly on the forms in Appendix A.

If you keep a record of your reading improvement throughout the term, view the long sweep of the charts. Avoid accepting isolated changes as absolute signs of

---

[2]Lee A. Jacobus, *Improving College Reading*, 3d ed. (New York: Harcourt Brace Jovanovich, Inc., 1978), p. 334.

general changes. The levels of difficulty, lengths of the passages, kinds of test questions, and other factors will have an impact on your individual entries.

Types of reading

The excerpt you read sets forth the following classification of the types of reading when speed is the issue:

> Careful reading (complex reading) 50–350 w.a.m.
> Rapid reading (simple reading) 300–600 w.a.m.
> Skimming (main-idea reading) up to 1,500 w.a.m.
> Scanning (search-for-specific-facts reading) up to 3,000 w.a.m.

Careful reading   Use the careful reading type when reading for learning-level comprehension and long-term retention of both generalizations and details. Also use it when analyzing, solving problems, proofreading, and checking for accuracy.

Rapid reading   For light or pleasure reading, take in "chunks" of material—even as you cover virtually all of it. Get the essence of the content and continue reading. Do not try to remember every detail.

Time yourself as you use the rapid-reading style to read these paragraphs:

 There are many differences in each person's ability to see. One person may have difficulty seeing objects that are close, while another may find it difficult seeing objects that are some distance away. If you must hold ordinary written material either very close to your eyes or at arm's length in order to read it, if the material you are reading seems blurred, or if your eyes tire easily or hurt, then you should consult an eye doctor. You may need to wear glasses, perhaps only for reading. If you already wear glasses, you may need to have them changed.

Whether or not you wear glasses, you should practice good eye hygiene. Here are a few suggestions:

1. Rest your eyes every half hour or so by looking into the distance or by closing your eyes for a few minutes.
2. Exercise your eyes from time to time, particularly after doing close work. One good eye exercise is to rotate the eyes slowly, without moving your head. Move your eyes far to the right; then to the left; then up; and finally, down. These exercises will help to strengthen your eye muscles.
3. Avoid reading in bright sunlight or while riding in a car, train, or other vehicle.
4. Have eye injuries or sties attended to at once by a doctor. . . .

Poor lighting contributes to eye tiredness and loss of clear vision. Of course, nonglaring daylight provides the best light for reading, and light-colored walls and furnishings permit the best use of daylight. Indirect lighting, rather than semidirect or direct lighting, is the best artificial lighting. Therefore, make certain that there are no glaring light bulbs visible to the eyes or any other glaring or shiny spots anywhere near where you are reading.

For the best reading conditions, sit comfortably in a well-ventilated (not overheated) room that is free from distracting sights and sounds. Above all, do not attempt to do serious reading with the radio, television, or stereo on.[3]

(331 words)
(test on page 9)

[3]Marie M. Stewart, Frank W. Lanham, Kenneth Zimmer, Lyn Clark, and Bette Ann Stead, *Business English and Communication*, 5th ed. (New York: Gregg Division/McGraw-Hill Book Company, © 1978), p. 30. Reproduced with permission.

After recording your time, take Self-Test 2. Then score the test, find your reading speed and reading efficiency scores, and record them.

Self-Test 2
Excerpt about Eyes and Reading Conditions
(Rapid Reading)

A. Recall (16 points each). For each multiple-choice question, select the most accurate answer.

1. You should rest your eyes:
   a. About every 15 minutes
   b. About every 30 minutes
   c. About every 45 minutes
   d. By staring for a few minutes
   e. By rubbing them

2. Good eye hygiene may be practiced by reading:
   a. In bright sunlight
   b. While reading in a car, train, or other vehicle
   c. With ordinary material held at arm's length
   d. With ordinary material held one or two inches from your eyes
   e. By giving eyes a rest occasionally by closing them for a few minutes or looking into the distance

3. Good conditions for reading can be provided by:
   a. Light-colored walls and furnishings because they permit the best use of day-light
   b. Direct lighting
   c. Very bright light bulbs
   d. Semidirect lighting
   e. Shiny spots near where you are reading

4. Which one of these is good for your eyes?
   a. Taking care of eye injuries or sties without seeing a doctor
   b. Going without prescribed glasses at times to strengthen eye muscles
   c. Exercising your eyes by blinking rapidly 15 times
   d. Rotating the eyes slowly, without moving your head
   e. Consulting an eye doctor only when you reach the point that you can no longer see the words

5. For most people, good conditions for careful reading include:
   a. Music playing in the background
   b. A friend in the room doing calisthenics
   c. Sitting in a comfortable chair
   d. A room with no ventilation
   e. Sitting within hearing or vision range of a television or radio

B. Inference (20 points). For the multiple-choice question, select the most accurate answer.

Concerning the eyes and conditions for reading:
a. Eyes can be hurt by too much light, just as they can be hurt by too little.
b. An 85° room is perfect for reading.
c. A room cannot be too cold for reading.
d. Reading is perfectly all right in an airplane.
e. Far-sightedness is more serious a problem than is near-sightedness.

Solution to Self-Test 2
Excerpt about Eyes and Reading Conditions
(Rapid Reading)

A. Recall (16 points each)
   1. b   **4.** d
   2. e   **5.** c
   3. a

B. Inference (20 points)
   a

The book from which the foregoing paragraphs come is a high-school text-book—written at a relatively low level of difficulty. In addition, the content is of such a nature that past experience and common sense help you to read it at a fast pace, yet recall the details. Therefore, you probably were able to establish an efficiency score in the 300–600 w.a.m. range.

Skimming Though your eyes touch all of the material, skimming involves extremely rapid reading. You move past details in order to gain perspective on the whole or the central thesis.

You probably often skim newspapers and magazines. In addition, skimming also serves well in textbook reading, particularly as a preview or a postview technique. It allows you to establish or reconstruct the whole before or after you dwell on the parts during the careful-reading process.

To establish your skimming speed, comprehension, and reading efficiency levels on a preview basis, skim the section titled "Guidelines for Reading" on pages 22-24. Try to skim it in 20 seconds or less. It contains 517 words, and you want to reach for the 1,500 w.a.m. upper limit. Then take Self-Test 3, check it, do your calculations, and record the data on the skimming table and graphs.

Self-Test 3
Excerpt about Guidelines for Reading
(Skimming)

A. Recall (30 points each). For each multiple-choice question, select the most accurate answer.

   1. The guidelines for reading do *not* include:
     a. Use feedback to and from the writer.
     b. Read the messages in light of the purposes, the participants, the environment, the channel, and the interference.
     c. Define your purposes, the writer's purposes, yourself, the writer, and the environment.
     d. Identify and immediately try to correct the problems of the other.
     e. Control potential and actual interference within both you and the writer, and external to both of you.
     f. Evaluate at each stage.
     g. Identify the reading channel.

   2. The focus of the discussion of the guidelines was on:
     a. Public speakers
     b. Poets
     c. Readers
     d. Actors

      e. Report writers
      f. All business communicators
      g. Nonverbal transactions

B. Inference (40 points). For the multiple-choice question, select the most accurate answer.

The guidelines for reading can be rewritten to apply to:
      a. All forms of human communication
      b. Speaking and listening
      c. Verbal communication
      d. Nonverbal communication
      e. a–d
      f. Not a–d

Solution to Self-Test 3
Excerpt about Guidelines for Reading
(Skimming)

A. Recall (30 points each)   **B.** Inference (40 points)
  1. d   a
  2. c

When you later reach the point for carefully reading the section you just skimmed, you should be able to do so more quickly than you would have without the skimming.

Scanning Unlike skimming, scanning does not require that you read every word. Instead, start with a preset mental list of the kinds of facts you want from the material. Then move through it at speeds of up to 3,000 w.a.m., and block out everything other than the facts desired.

You have scanned many times. For example, you have searched for certain data in an encyclopedia. You have skipped through a textbook looking only for certain words or sections. You have scanned a newspaper article to find a dollar amount, a Consumer Price Index, or a date. You have scanned a telephone directory page looking for a name.

To practice scanning, turn to page 89 and time yourself on the section titled "Levels of Communication." Search for just two things: (1) the name used in this book for the communication level that includes the telephone conversation and (2) the name used in this book for the communication level that includes thinking. When you have located them, do two things: Jot down the time it took, and mark the last word that you read. Then return to this section and complete and check Self-Test 4 before calculating your rate.

Self-Test 4
Excerpt about the Levels of Communication
(Scanning)

A. Recall (30 points each). For each of these types of communication, write in the name used for the communication level that includes it.

  1. Telephone conversation: _____

Self-Test 4 — (continued)

2. Thinking: _____

B. Inference (40 points). For the multiple-choice question, select the most accurate answer.

Establishment of the concept of levels of communication:

a. May help me to improve my understanding of the communication process
b. Is important because I can know exactly which class includes each type of communication I encounter
c. Seems more important to communication application than to communication theory
d. Cannot possibly be of importance to the business communicator
e. Occurred hundreds of years ago and has remained unchanged

Solution to Self-Test 4
Excerpt about the Levels of Communication
(Scanning)

A. Recall (30 points each)   B. Inference (40 points)
   1. Medio   a
   2. Intrapersonal

To estimate the number of words you scanned, first count two or three lines to determine the typical number of words per line. Then multiply that figure by the number of lines you scanned. Once you know the number of words, you may proceed with your calculating and recording.

Did you perhaps decide that you had the information needed by the time you had read the first paragraph? If so, you missed the point that the assignment had asked for the names used in this book. Such names might or might not have been the same as those traditionally used. In addition, if you were not actually looking for the words "telephone" and "thinking," or some variation of them, you may not have been scanning.

You will, of course, give a careful reading to the section on communication levels as you move into that material. At this point, though, return to the coverage of reading, with particular emphasis upon how to increase your efficiency—regardless of which of the four types you employ.

Techniques for increasing speed, comprehension, and efficiency

Reading represents a complicated, but whole process. Techniques for improving one aspect of your reading skills—whether speed, comprehension or efficiency—often tend to improve others. Consider these 15 reading-improvement techniques:

1. Select proper reading type.
2. Concentrate.
3. Set time schedules.
4. Be an active reader.
5. Keep eyes moving.
6. Read in logical blocks of words.
7. Read just enough to capture thought.
8. Improve symbol/meaning manipulation.
9. Hold internal speaking apparatus still and quiet.

10. Read quickly.
11. Underline and take notes sparingly.
12. Preview careful-reading material.
13. Review careful-reading material.
14. Control personal and environmental factors.
15. Practice.

Select proper reading type   If you read carefully, when skimming would be suffi-cient, you have wasted time. On the other hand, if you scan some material that should have been read for fuller comprehension, you probably will have to reread it at the proper speed. Thus, you *may* have lost some time in the process. ("May," appears in the previous sentence because previewing a careful-reading passage using one of the faster speeds can sometimes *save* time in the long run.)

Concentrate   Concentrate to serve at least two purposes. First, concentrate upon the content so that you do not have to reread for desired comprehension. Second, concentrate upon keeping moving—keeping up the speed itself.

Consider these suggestions for concentration: Keep your mind from wandering to topics other than your reading. Ignore everything else. Improve your ability simply to remain seated for long periods of time. Provide a setting that will reduce interference.

Set time schedules   Use time schedules to aid reading efficiency. However, set them realistically. If you set too little time for a task, you may not taste success, but only become frustrated and dissatisfied. On the other hand, if you set too much time, you may take all of the time allotted whether you need it or not, thus wasting some time. Have you not dawdled over something simply because you had the time to do so?

You cannot, of course, become a computer—spitting out work at previously established rates down to the fraction of a second. However, because time is such a valuable commodity—whether it is used for work or pleasure—you no doubt can improve your ability to spend it wisely.

Be an active reader   Receiving is just as active and participative a process as is sending. Therefore, be an active reader.

All too often receivers take on the posture of passive or resistant beings—unable or unwilling to participate assertively in the communication process. In effect, this posture reflects an inner attitude that says, "I am under the control of the writer; I have no active role in this communication transaction."

Indeed, however, you do have a great deal of control. By applying the proper techniques, you can exercise it.

Keep eyes moving   Reading involves extremely complex visual and mental processes. Consider a few of the findings about these processes.

First, your eyes make a point fixation. For left-to-right reading, the fixation is a focus just to the left of the symbols to be read. The fixation encompasses a number of words for a duration of about one-fourth of a second.

After each fixation your eyes jump forward to another fixation. The jump lasts only about one-tenth as long as the fixation itself.

The actual transfer from the eyes to the brain occurs during the fixations. However, the stages unfold so rapidly that the eyes seem to move continuously from left to right. Only the sweeping return from the end of one line to the fixation at the beginning of the next seems to interrupt the movement. In truth, the only continuous motion exists within the return itself.

In addition to the fixations, jumps forward, and sweeping returns, the eyes also engage in regressions. Regressions are movements in which the eyes move rapidly back from one point to a fixation to the left of it. As natural, reinforcing acts, regressions can actually improve reading performance—unless overused.

The mental part of reading is, of course, more complicated than the visual part. As your eyes accomplish their work, your mind simultaneously accomplishes its task. It processes visual perceptions already received, receives new ones, and controls the entire operation—including the difficult choices of fixation points. Researchers still do not understand how the mind does what it does; the concept is overwhelming.

Return to the eye movements for a moment. The wider the span of symbols in fixations, the shorter the durations of fixations, jumps, and returns. The fewer the number of unnecessary regressions, the faster the speed and comprehension. Therefore, even though the motion is not a continuous, smooth flow, keep your eyes ever moving.

The general suggestion to keep eyes moving applies to all four types of reading. However, scanning involves such wide fixation spans that it creates a gross downward motion seemingly devoid of left-to-right movement.

Avoid unnecessary regressions and breaks in eye movement. For example, if your mind does not hold any meaning for a given word, you may tend to regress a few times or even stop to locate the word in a dictionary before proceeding. However, before doing so, try to keep moving through the passage. Frequently, the context supplies sufficient clues to permit you to evolve a meaning good enough to allow you to continue without a break.

If you still have to use a dictionary, mark the point at which you stopped reading. Then use the dictionary efficiently and return to the passage with an undiminished eye-movement momentum.

Another way to keep eyes moving in careful reading is to slow to a pace that will reduce the need for regressions and extensive rereading. Even though you read slower, you often make a net gain in speed because you eliminate some rereading.

A serious interruption of eye movement occurs when you stop to underline or make notes. The loss in comprehension is generally much greater than any potential gain from the underlining. Therefore, unless you have absolute control over your pencil (control that prohibits you from underlining too much), avoid using it.

Read in logical blocks of words   To illustrate the importance of reading logical blocks of words, time yourself separately on each of two passages. Read carefully for comprehension, take the tests, and calculate reading efficiency scores. You need not record these scores.

SEGMENT 1:

Order some things. Get towels, pencils, small nails, memo pads, bolts, paper clips, and grass cutters. Also call the office manager, bus driver, chief accountant, florist, receptionist, and hairdresser to remind them of the meetings next Tuesday and Friday.

(39 words)
(test follows immediately)

Self-Test over Segment 1
(Careful Reading)

Recall (50 points each)

1. Which one of these is *not* listed for the order?
   a. Grass cutters
   b. Towels
   c. Bolts
   d. Small nails
   e. Ballpoint pens

2. Which one of these is *not* mentioned in the segment?
   a. A meeting on Friday
   b. Bus driver
   c. Bookkeeper
   d. Receptionist
   e. Office manager

Solution to Self-Test over Segment 1
(Careful Reading)

Recall (50 points each)
1. e
2. c

SEGMENT 2:

 As you complete assignments, make checkmarks beside appropriate instructions. Also count number of requests for new supply catalogue, and report number in memo to shipping room. Write thank-you note for gift. Invite usual participants to my meeting next Wednesday.

(39 words)
(test follows immediately)

Self-Test over Segment 2
(Careful Reading)

Recall (50 points each)

1. Which one of these is *not* part of the segment?
   a. Report number of requests to shipping room.
   b. Count requests.
   c. Complete assignments.
   d. Place checkmarks beside appropriate instructions.
   e. Write to payroll department.

Self-Test — (continued)

2. Which one of these is *not* part of the segment?
   a. Write a thank-you note.
   b. Invite people to meeting.
   c. A supply catalogue
   d. Write a letter.
   e. Meeting next Wednesday

Solution to Self-Test over Segment 2
(Careful Reading)

Recall (50 points each)
1. e
2. d

First, compare your reading rates for the two segments. You probably read Segment 2 more quickly than Segment 1, even though each has 39 words and includes instructions.

One reason for the difference is that Segment 1 includes a series of relatively unrelated words divided by commas. With Segment 2 you had greater opportunity to read logical phrases. If you took advantage of the expanded context, you swept up several words in one eye span or fixation. Segment 1 required you to read much of it a word at a time.

Now compare the scores on the comprehension tests. Again, you probably scored better on the second than the first. Though both segments contain many facts to recall, those in Segment 2 can be digested as natural units of information.

Finally, contrast your reading efficiency scores. If you read Segment 2 by taking in related blocks of words rather than by reading one word at a time, this final score no doubt reflects the superiority of that approach by being higher than that for Segment 1.

One final illustration should serve to emphasize the importance of reading thought units rather than words. Introspectively observe your arrested progress as you read this sentence word for word as marked:

The _ʃ_ efficient _ʃ_ reader _ʃ_ moves _ʃ_ smoothly _ʃ_ from _ʃ_ the _ʃ_ beginning _ʃ_ of _ʃ_ one _ʃ_ word _ʃ_ or _ʃ_ phrase _ʃ_ to _ʃ_ another — _ʃ_ reading _ʃ_ just _ʃ_ enough _ʃ_ to _ʃ_ capture _ʃ_ the _ʃ_ thought.

Now observe the efficiency with which you read the same sentence in logical blocks as marked.

The efficient reader moves smoothly _ʃ_ from the beginning of one word or phrase _ʃ_ to another—_ʃ_ reading just enough _ʃ_ to capture the thought.

Read just enough to capture thought   Consider another rule for increasing speed: Read just enough of a word or phrase to capture the thought. To illustrate, maintain a smooth eye movement as you read this sentence:

Busi_____ communi_____ is noth____ mor__ th__ th_ applica_____ of t__ univers__ princi____ __ hum__ com_____.

As you read, you already no doubt skip past "a," "an," "the," and other such short, relatively unimportant, and transitional words. Make an overt effort to perform the same sort of rapid eye movement as you slide past endings on longer words—or even several words in a phrase. As you practice this approach, your gains in speed will reflect a real growth on your part.

Read another skeleton sentence. Again, keep moving.

To be _ bet__ communi_____, adop_ as ma__ prov__ tech_____ as you c__, as soon __ you ___.

Reading such vacated words and phrases can take on the semblance of playing a game. However, the most important lesson from the game is to learn to skip letters, syllables, and words even when someone has not removed them for you. Make a concerted effort to read normal material in the same way.

Read this final sentence while maintaining the resolve that you will read only enough of the word and phrase beginnings to create meanings in your mind:

As a communication receiving act, reading is one of the most complex and dynamic mental and physical processes in which you will ever participate.

Were you able to truncate some words and phrases after picking up just a few letters?

Do you ever feel that you are "cheating" if you do not read every word, every syllable, every letter? If so, reject that attitude. You only read improperly when you do not take advantage of your mind's awesome ability to fill in the logical gaps you may leave as you bound forward through reading passages.

Improve symbol/meaning manipulation   Reading includes seeing symbols, transferring them to the brain, and giving meaning to the received symbols. The meaning-giving stage draws on both experience and creativity.

For the symbols you have encountered before, the time consumed is minimal. However, when you encounter new symbols, you must manipulate previous, related experiences in order to give meaning to them. Thus, an important device for increasing reading ability is to experience as many symbols/meanings as you can—to build meanings for a vast number of symbols.

Do not consider meanings to be fixed, however. They vary from context to context—and often change with each new experience. Nonetheless, the more times you deal with a certain symbol or set of symbols, the more rapidly you will be able to establish a meaning the next time you encounter it.

A good way to expand your ability to supply meanings for symbols is to read a great variety of publications. With some reasonable priorities, read everything you can find. Read it as rapidly as you can at the reading level you have chosen.

If you follow these suggestions, a productive cycle emerges. One of the best ways to become a more rapid reader is to increase your ability to recognize and supply meanings for symbols. At the same time, one of the best ways to increase that facility is by reading rapidly.

All other kinds of communication also contribute to improving your capability to establish meanings. Every time you listen, speak, write, and observe or create nonverbally, you have an opportunity to expand that capability. The secret lies in being eager to understand and use new symbols.

To this point you have not seen the word "vocabulary"—for two major reasons. First, a vocabulary includes only words, and words are not the only symbols.

Anything can be a symbol; anything can lead you to create meanings about that thing. You create a different meaning for a series of words that form a thought unit than you do if you just string together the meanings for each word taken one at a time. Thus, the unit itself becomes a unique symbol.

You also give meaning to someone waving to you, to a shade tree on a hot day, to punctuation marks, to an embrace, to a cool drink, to a pleasant memory—in short, to everything you sense or think.

The second major reason for delaying introduction of the idea of vocabulary lies in the emphasis that it places upon the words themselves. Instead, the emphasis should be upon the meanings that people create for words.

Only you can generate a meaning for the symbols you encounter. The words themselves have no meanings; they are simply collections of things called "letters." Letters are just marks, and neither letters nor marks have meanings. The meanings arise from your mental manipulation of them.

Once you have put words-as-symbols into proper perspective, however, do use vocabulary lists. Do use word lists, glossaries of terms, dictionaries, and the-sauruses as aids to learning. They are necessary and valuable collections of words coupled with other words attempting to define them as people have verbalized their meanings.

When you encounter a word list, first supply those meanings you already hold. Then check a dictionary for expanded definitions. Look up the words in a thesaurus to determine synonyms and antonyms for as many as you can. Then write several sentences for each, carefully thinking about the meanings they have for you. Deliberately use the words in conversations or writings.

Make your your own vocabulary lists. As you encounter words for which you cannot create satisfactory meanings, jot them down. However—and herein lies the advantage of this approach—copy the entire sentence (or at least the phrase), rather than just the word. Once you have a list of several sentences or phrases, proceed to your reference books.

Partially for the reason that everyone can benefit from exposure to new words, this textbook may include some words you have not seen many times. You may want to identify them as you encounter them. One exercise at the end of each chapter includes a list of some possibly unfamiliar words.

Hold speaking apparatus still and quiet   From the foregoing rather theoretical treatise on symbols and meanings, turn now to a mundane way to increase reading speed: Do not make vocal sounds or movements as you read. If you do, you slow toward oral reading speed—which is much slower than silent reading.

As an example, time yourself as you read the next narrative paragraph aloud. (You may be in a place where you cannot read aloud. If so, simulate the process by moving your throat muscles, tongue, and even your lips as if you are speaking aloud.) Read for your comprehension and for the comprehension of others who may or may not actually be present. (Begin reading aloud now.)

As you read these words aloud, observe how you can still read thought units, but how much slower the overall movement is. Observe also that you cannot read just the beginnings of words and phrases; you must cover everything. Think how, if you can read aloud well, you probably do not engage in regressions as much as you do in silent reading. In contrast, though, notice how you sometimes must regress in order to correct the pronunciation of a word or to place proper emphasis on a phrase. In summary, vocalized reading is much slower than silent reading.

(100 words)

Calculate your reading speed for the preceding paragraph and compare it with your other careful-reading speed(s). Because the content is relatively simple, no comprehension test or reading efficiency score is appropriate here. Even with the simplicity of the material, you probably found that your reading rate was much slower than that for the silent-reading segments.

Read quickly   Somewhat surprisingly, the best comprehension does not necessarily coexist with the slowest speed. Instead, the optimum comprehension usually occurs when your speed approaches the maximum for the range of reading purpose. Therefore, always read as quickly as you can for the selected reading type.

Underline and take notes sparingly   As suggested earlier, many people overuse a pencil. Therefore, the best rule may be to leave it on the table while reading.

If you need a pencil only to make a dash or dot in the margin of an occasional passage to which you may need to return, then keep one in your hand. However, if you mark something every other line or so, you probably should lay it aside.

Excessive marking interferes with the momentum of the reading process. It may also become a crutch for avoiding genuine mental activity.

Even if you make an outline or compile notes after the actual reading, keep them brief. Again, a common inclination is to write too much. Such an inclination perpetuates the myth that copying from one page to another will magically create learning.

Instead of that laborious, time-killing exercise, engage your mind fully in the task of comprehending directly from the pages of the book. Make only skeleton summary notes—and then only if you are sure they help you to recall better than you do without them.

Preview careful-reading material   If your reading requires comprehension and retention of relatively difficult material, preview it before beginning the careful reading. The preview should include scanning, skimming, and/or rapid reading.

For example, in previewing a textbook, you probably should scan for headings, lists of rules or objectives, or similar key points. After the scanning, you might skim the chapter or section for the general ideas contained there. Finally, you may need to read through the material rapidly to pick up whatever information you can before moving into the careful reading.

Your understanding will improve with each additional step that you employ efficiently prior to careful reading.

Review careful-reading material   Just as you preview material to improve comprehension, review it following a careful reading. Again, you may use any or all of the other types of reading to accomplish the review, for you reinforce your learning with each one.

The minimal review would at least include a repetition of your scanning of the subtitles in the unit. It also could include the search for some key points that might be hazy in your mind.

Control personal and environmental factors   Both your own personal characteristics and details of your environment make up the setting in which you read. Your speed, comprehension, and retention suffer if you do not establish these conditions at the best possible level. Three major categories define the setting for reading: (1) personal physical conditions, (2) psychological conditions, and (3) external conditions.

Your physical condition contributes a great deal to your ability to read. Obviously, the major physical feature is your eyes. Care for them.

Also attend to your general state of health. Good health contributes to good reading as much as to any other activity.

Your psychological state has an important impact upon your ability to read well. When you approach a reading situation, first try to separate yourself physically from any persons or places that distress you emotionally. Then, using whatever devices you can bring to bear, concentrate upon the task at hand. Overcome your own psychological obstacles to concentration.

Control external conditions as much as you can. For best reading, try to establish as many of these conditions as possible:

1. Comfortable and pleasant surroundings
2. Good seating at a desk or table
3. Proper lighting
4. Appropriate temperature and ventilation
5. Quietness
6. Reading aids (pencil, paper, dictionary, thesaurus)

Practice   Though implicit in all of the other speed-improvement hints, the final one calls for you to practice. Nothing can possibly do more to help you read better than reading can. Of course, the efficacy of repetition and practice depends on the *quality* of the time spent practicing. Reinforcement of bad habits rather than good ones can be counterproductive.

Retention

To this point, you have concentrated upon reading efficiency focused on the goals of immediate understanding and recall. However, mid-range and long-range recollection of the material you have comprehended also plays an important role in communication.

Some say that everything that has ever been perceived is stored in the brain and can be recalled no matter how much time has elapsed between the storage and the recall. That theory, of course, represents the ultimate in retention. However, if all learning is stored forever, much of it is deeply recessed—so recessed that most people do not seem to be able to recover it without the aid of psychiatry or hypnosis.

The major concern here, however, lies far from such extreme measures. It rests with improving the practical ability to retain information in such a way that it can be recalled even after long periods of time. Though involving some overlapping, five general categories delineate how to accomplish such retention:

1. Use memory aids.
2. Set priorities.
3. Think.
4. Reinforce.
5. Develop resolve.

Use memory aids

Mechanical approaches to retention include developing acronyms, abbreviations, merged words and letters, or special designations for key points. For example, one plan for remembering the structure of persuasive messages uses the acronym AIDA (attention, interest, desire, action). A similar acronym is AICA (attention, interest, conviction, action).

Another acronym aids the recollection of the requirements for granting credit—the three C's (character, capital, capacity). The seven C's of good business letter writing are sometimes listed as courtesy, clearness, completeness, coherence, correctness, concreteness, and conciseness.

If used wisely, memory aids can be effective devices for improving retention. However, if you must go through time-consuming machinations to develop the aids, you probably could learn the material in the same time period without them.

Set priorities

Another approach to retention requires that you set priorities. Although humans may be able to store virtually everything ever perceived, information learned seems to fall into access layers from which the mind must draw. Hence, the closer to the surface that information lies, the easier it is to recall.

To expand your retention ability, then, choose carefully the items which you will place in predominant positions in your mental ordering. For example, unless telephoning is your highest priority, why memorize dozens of phone numbers? Would not your immediate-access data bank be better used for *important* data? Although you may have the capacity to remember the telephone numbers *and* the important material, why clutter the top strata with trivia that can be stored outside of your mind?

Decide what takes precedence over what, and concentrate on retaining the highest-ordered items resulting from the decision. You encounter too much learning—especially as the years pass—to try to maintain all of it for immediate recall.

Think

Closely related to the concept of setting priorities, sheer thinking contributes to retention. To remember things, think about them. Think not only about their level of significance, but about how they relate to other things you know, about how they can help you, and about how important they are to future intake of material.

Though many learning theories attempt to explain thinking, it still remains largely a mystery. Therefore, experiment with your thinking process to learn which methods work best for you. Above all, engage your mind. Improved retention assuredly will result.

Reinforce

Obviously, the one-time-over capture of material would be the ideal way to learn for retention and recall from the standpoint of efficiency. However, you cannot always accomplish that feat.

A useful alternative to capturing information perfectly the first time encountered is to receive and send it several times. Such a process reinforces the learning.

Variations in the avenues of reception probably improve the quality of repetitive input. For instance, you may learn educational material through the performance of several acts. You may read a textbook passage several times and read other publications on the same subject. You may listen to a lecture, participate in a discussion, and view a film. All of these receptive acts may be necessary for full comprehension and retention.

Another way to reinforce learning of material you have read is to summarize it aloud—even if only for yourself. Better yet, talk with someone about it. If you make brief notes or underline, review them periodically. Call the information to your mind's surface.

You also may reinforce by integrating material into other material. Interweave it; do not consider it an end unto itself. Relate it to other topics and other communication situations. Think of it as part of a larger whole and, thus, review it as you combine it with other information.

Of course, each added reinforcement takes time that could be used for another topic, so avoid unnecessary review. Try to accomplish your goals in as few repetitions as possible, but use reinforcement to the full extent that it is profitable for you.

Develop resolve

A final set of procedures for retention involves the resolve—the commitment—to retain knowledge. Some memories are etched so indelibly in your mind that you cannot shake them even if you wish you could. However, many others exist because you overtly decided to have them exist. Recollections involving things learned during formal education often fall into the latter class. Therefore, unless you experience something either so pleasant or so awful that you cannot help but remember it, you need to develop a disciplined will to retain.

The next section ties the receiving/reading act to guidelines for the communication process. You previewed the guidelines in one of your reading-efficiency segments.

GUIDELINES FOR READING

 Six guidelines form the backbone of the communication process as developed in this book. Though development of these guidelines forms the focus of another chapter, briefly review them as they apply to reading:

1. Define your purposes, the writer's purposes, yourself, the writer, and the environment.
2. Identify the reading channel.

3. Control the interference internal and external to you and the writer.
4. Read the messages in light of the purposes, the participants, the environment, the channel, and the interference.
5. Use feedback to and from the writer.
6. Evaluate at each stage.

Define Purposes, Participants, and Environment

As a reader you should define your own purposes for reading and make a vigorous effort to define the purposes of the writer. In addition, define who you are and who the writer is, and understand the environment in which you both operate.[4]

The more carefully you delineate everyone and everything in the communication transaction, the better you will understand. The better you understand, the better you will communicate.

Identify Channel

The channel carries the message and thus influences the communication interaction. As a reader, identify the characteristics of the channel chosen by the writer.

The book you are reading now is an example of one type of reading channel. Other reading channels include letters, notes, memoranda, reports, forms, essays, newspapers, and magazines. Each type has certain advantages and disadvantages.

The further removed a channel is from a face-to-face encounter, the weaker it is. Participants who cannot see each other cannot interact directly. Therefore, the reading channels are among the weakest.

Reading channels do have the power to carry complex messages. In addition, they serve as permanent records of messages—records that can be reread.

Control Interference

Communication interference can exist within or outside of people. Recognize and try to control all potential and actual interference associated with such elements as the people involved, the channel, and the environment.

Use your reading of this book as an example again. Think about the kinds of interference that might occur as you read. Whatever the interference, do your best to overcome it.

Read

For reading, the next guideline involves seeing words and nonverbal symbols and assigning meanings to them in order to create messages in your mind.

At this stage you should take account of the identifications made in the first three guidelines—the purposes and backgrounds of yourself and the writer, the environment, the channel, and the interference—and use them to your purpose or control them.

---

[4]To avoid the awkwardness that accompanies any attempt to indicate that the communication may involve more than one sender or receiver, the singular forms are used consistently in this book.

Use Feedback

The concept of feedback receives special attention in the guidelines. Feedback occurs when the original receiver transmits information about how well the initial message has been received. The more immediate, accurate, and extensive the feedback, the better the communication.

Evaluate

Evaluation of communication can improve it tremendously. Keep a critical outlook throughout all stages of the process and adjust your perceptions according to the results of that outlook.

(517 words, including 30 words in footnote)
(test on page 10)

SUMMARY

Communication is a complex process involving you in shifting transactions in which you act as sender and receiver of written, oral, and nonverbal (wordless) messages. The core of the process has you assigning meanings to the symbols used in the transaction.

Reading forms one of your major receiving activities. Reading speed, comprehension, efficiency, and retention all contribute to the effectiveness of your performance.

Reading rates range from 50 to 350 words a minute (w.a.m.) for careful reading (heavy material), from 300 to 600 w.a.m. for rapid reading (light material), up to 1,500 w.a.m. for skimming (main-idea reading), and up to 3,000 w.a.m. for scanning (search-for-predetermined-data reading).

Comprehension includes immediate recall of the reading matter and inferences drawn from it, with the comprehension test score (c.t.s.) expressed as the proportion of correct answers to questions.

The *reading efficiency score* (r.e.s.) is a composite found by (w.a.m. × c.t.s.). The r.e.s. is a better measure of reading ability than either w.a.m. or c.t.s. alone.

Retention refers to the ability to recall material after a lapse of time.

To increase speed and comprehension, (1) select the proper reading type, (2) concentrate, (3) set time schedules, (4) be an active reader, (5) keep your eyes moving, (6) read in logical blocks of words, (7) read just enough to capture thought, (8) improve symbol/meaning manipulation, (9) hold speaking apparatus still and quiet, (10) read as quickly as you can, (11) underline and take notes sparingly, (12) preview careful-reading material, (13) review careful-reading material, (14) control personal and environmental factors, and (15) practice.

To improve retention, (1) use memory aids, (2) set priorities, (3) think, (4) reinforce, and (5) develop resolve.

Your continuous thread of control over the communication process lies in applying guidelines. The guidelines for reading are:

1. Define purposes, participants, and environment.
2. Identify reading channel.
3. Control interference.
4. Read messages in light of purposes, participants, environment, channel, and interference.
5. Use feedback.
6. Evaluate.

Practice

1. Time yourself as you read a recent *Wall Street Journal* article from an inside page (to avoid having to locate a "continued" portion of the article). Read for main ideas. Upon completion, and without looking back, write down the main ideas. Estimate the number of words in the article by determining the average number of words per line, and multiplying that average by the number of lines. Calculate your speed. Ideally, it will approach 1,500 w.a.m. You can test yourself for comprehension by reviewing the article for main ideas and determining what proportion of them you wrote down correctly. You can then calculate your r.e.s. If you believe that the scores are fairly representative, record them on the tables and charts from Appendix A.
2. Skim the section titled "The Importance of Listening" in Chapter 2 (pages 32-33). Record your time. Complete Self-Test 5.

Self-Test 5
Excerpt about the Importance of Listening
(Skimming)

A. Recall (30 points each). For each multiple-choice question, select the most accurate answer.

   1. A person spends about what percentage of her or his waking time listening?
     a. 5 percent
     b. 95 percent
     c. 85 percent
     d. 45 percent
     e. 15 percent

   2. The ability to listen:
     a. Represents a major element of human relations
     b. Is not important
     c. Is important only to people in management
     d. Is a natural ability only certain people possess
     e. Does not play a role in gaining knowledge

B. Inference (40 points). Indicate whether the following statement is true or false:

Listening can be practiced.

Solution to Self-Test 5
Excerpt about the Importance of Listening
(Skimming)

A. Recall (30 points each)
   1. d
   2. a

B. Inference (40 points)
True

3. Write a short pencil or typewritten draft of a memorandum to be sent to all of the employees in your office. Make up a company name. In the memorandum name and briefly explain the meaning of the six guidelines for communication as they apply to reading. (An example of a memorandum appears on page 377.)

4. Read several paragraphs in one of your textbooks. Consult a dictionary on the words about which you are unsure. After you have read the definitions of the words in question, write sentences using the words. Make a determined effort to use the words appropriately in conversations.

5. Proofread an assignment you have prepared. Time yourself and figure your w.a.m. score. Proofread the assignment again, record your time, and figure your w.a.m. score. Did you miss any errors the first time through? If so, note the types of errors you overlooked. Did you find a pattern to what you overlooked? Practice catching the errors you are most likely to miss.

6. Pretend that you will meet with one of your professors next week to discuss your grade. In preparation for the meeting, answer the following questions:
   a. What are my purposes and the professor's purposes? Who am I in this situation? Who is the professor? What is the environment in which the exchange will take place?
   b. What will the channel be?
   c. What potential internal and external interference exists?
   d. How can I best send and receive messages in light of the purposes, the professor, the environment, the channel, and the interference?
   e. How will I use feedback?
   f. How will I evaluate?

7. Read the letter on p. 281 for comprehension, and time yourself. Then take Self-Test 6.

Self-Test 6
Import Car-Talog Sales, Inc., Letter
(Careful Reading)

A. Recall (30 points each). For each multiple-choice question, select the most accurate answer.
   1. Eleanor Parkins' order:
      a. Will be shipped on time
      b. Will be shipped late
      c. Cannot be shipped
      d. Is in the mail, except for one item
      e. Was lost
   2. Which of the following does the writer offer Ms. Parkins?
      a. A refund
      b. A substitute for the items not in stock
      c. A discount on substitute items
      d. An apology
      e. A free gift

B. Inference (40 points). Indicate whether the following statement is true or false.
   The primary purpose of Y.R. Self's letter to Eleanor Parkins is to thank her for her order.

Solution to Self-Test 6
Import Car-Talog Sales, Inc., Letter
(Careful Reading)

A. Recall (30 points each)   B. Inference (40 points)
   1. d   False
   2. b

8. On your own, write a one-page paper on the importance of improving your reading skills. Then form groups of four or five students. You and every other group member read your papers to the group. You may then want to evaluate each paper and select one from each group to be read before the whole class. This exercise will allow you to review this chapter, practice writing, practice speaking, and practice listening, the subject of the next chapter.

9. You are the training and development director for a major corporation. A new employee tells you that though he is doing well with most of his work in the engineering department, he sometimes has trouble reading what he considers to be difficult material. What advice would you give him?

10. Assume that your professor will give you an examination in one week over the first chapter of this textbook. Your professor suggested that you concentrate on the major concepts set forth in the chapter. The fifty-minute examination will consist of seven essay questions, and you must answer six of the seven. You realize that though you have read the chapter, you can recall very little of its content. You decide that you must read it again. This time you want to retain the important information you read so that you can do well on the examination. You know that to improve retention you may (1) use memory aids, (2) set priorities, (3) think, (4) reinforce, and (5) develop resolve. Now write a one- or two-page plan that answers these questions.

   a. What, if any, memory aids will I use? Why do I believe that they will prove helpful to me?

   b. To what subjects within the chapter should I assign priority status? Why do I believe these subjects are the ones on which I should concentrate my efforts?

   c. How can I assure that I will actively think about what I am reading?

   d. What, specifically, can I do to reinforce the information that I wish to retain?

   e. Most important, what steps can I take to develop my resolve to complete the established study process and to remember what I read?

11. [*Your professor will time this exercise.*] You must study for an examination that will be given next week. You want to find or prepare a good reading environment. Write a paragraph explaining what reading environment you will seek and why you will seek it.

12. Concentration is often difficult to accomplish. Make a list of internal and external devices that have helped you concentrate in the past. Make another list of new devices that might help you concentrate now and in the future. For example, you might always have taken a walk just before you studied, and you might plan to start keeping a glass of water at your study place.

13. You meet a fourth-grader who says that she does not like to read. She says that she finds it "boring and hard." What suggestions would you make that would help her find reading more interesting? What advice would you give that would help her find reading less difficult? Remember, she is both very young and quite dismayed.

14. Develop symbol/meaning interpretations by analyzing these symbols and creating meanings for them. Check your dictionary and thesaurus. Write several sentences for each and use the words in conversation and writing. Return to the list sometime later and give your version of the meaning for each from memory. These are the symbols:

a.	Assessment	j.	Persevere
b.	Efficacy	k.	Pertinent
c.	Explicit	l.	Procrastinate
d.	Helix	m.	Regress
e.	Implicit	n.	Reverie
f.	Interpersonal	o.	Semantics
g.	Intrapersonal	p.	Subconscious
h.	Kaleidoscope	q.	Subsequent
i.	Myriad	r.	Thesaurus

15. Take and score Self-Test 7 over Chapter 1.

Self-Test 7
Chapter 1

A. Recall (15 points each). For each multiple-choice question, select the most accurate answer.

    1. The meanings of words:
        a. Are inherent
        b. Are assigned by people
        c. Do not change
        d. Do not differ among people
        e. Relate to their pronunciation

    2. Which of the following statements does *not* accurately characterize careful reading?
        a. Careful reading involves reading for learning-level comprehension and long-term retention.
        b. Proofreading is one type of careful reading.
        c. Careful reading should be undertaken at 200–1,500 w.a.m.
        d. Mangieri and Baldwin put the range of speeds for careful reading at 50–350 w.a.m.
        e. Careful reading is used in problem solving.

    3. Which of the following is *not* set forth in this book as a major reading classification?
        a. Careful reading
        b. Skimming
        c. Scanning
        d. Fixing
        e. Rapid reading

    4. Which of the following does *not* contribute to efficient reading?
        a. Reading in indirect artificial light or non-glaring daylight
        b. Using a pen or marker to underline many words and phrases
        c. Practicing reading and recording w.a.m. and r.e.s. scores
        d. Reading in a quiet place where distractions are kept to a minimum
        e. Developing the resolve to read without allowing your mind to stray

    5. Which of the following does *not* contribute to increasing reading speed and comprehension?
        a. Selecting the proper reading type
        b. Taking copious notes as you read
        c. Reading as quickly as you can for the reading type chosen
        d. Concentrating
        e. Being an active reader
        f. Reading in logical blocks of words
        g. Improving your ability to manipulate symbols and meanings
        h. Underlining and taking notes sparingly
        i. Previewing careful-reading material
        j. Reviewing careful-reading material
        k. Practicing

B. Inference (25 points). For the multiple-choice question, select the most accurate answer.

The guidelines for reading:
    a. Can be used only when the communicator has fully developed her or his communication arts and skills

b. Are guidelines written specifically for use in business situations
c. Define, in detail, every aspect of the communications process
d. Are known to all managers
e. Are guidelines that can be expanded to apply to all forms of human communication

Solution to Self-Test 7
Chapter 1

A. Recall (15 points each)   **B.** Inference (10 points)
  1. b   **4.** b   e
  2. c   **5.** b
  3. d

2

Listening

To continue the logic of concentrating first upon applications of communication receiving, consider the arts and skills of listening.

Ideally, you would learn more about listening by listening—just as you learned more about reading by reading. However, the nature of the book channel prohibits full implementation of that ideal approach. Therefore, use a combination tactic: Read to gain information about listening, and listen to apply the information gained.

This textbook and your professor will provide several means for directed listening applications. In addition, you participate daily in real-world situations that provide great opportunity to apply listening arts and skills.

Most people spend about 45 percent of their time in communication with other humans doing what should be listening. The reason for writing "what should be" is that people do not always listen; too often they just hear. As with seeing and reading, hearing and listening are different. All listening involves hearing, but not all hearing involves listening. Listening is an active, thinking communication act, whereas hearing is a passive, physical one.

Listening plays such an important role in communication that its neglect in educational realms is shocking. You have studied reading and writing from your earliest school days and possibly have had some formal training in speaking. However, unless you are one of a fortunate few, you have never participated in a formal learning unit related to listening. Rogers and Roethlisberger go so far as to suggest:

> . . . The biggest block to personal communication is . . . [the human's] inability to listen intelligently, understandingly, and skillfully to another person. This deficiency in the modern world is widespread and appalling. In our universities as well as elsewhere, too little is being done about it.[1]

---

[1] Reprinted by permission of the Harvard Business Review. Excerpt from "Barriers and Gateways to Communication" by Carl R. Rogers and F. J. Roethlisberger (July-August 1952), 46ff. Copyright© 1952 by the President and Fellows of Harvard College. All rights reserved.

This chapter will help fill that void. The coverage of listening will give you the opportunity to expand and reinforce what you already know about the subject.

To this point, you have more or less accepted the contention that listening is important enough to warrant considerable study. Now review still more support for that view.

THE IMPORTANCE OF LISTENING

 To finish analyzing an apportionment of the typical person's time among communication acts, examine Table 1.

TABLE 1   ESTIMATED PROPORTIONS OF TYPICAL PERSON'S
TIME SPENT IN VARIOUS COMMUNICATION ACTS

Typical Person	Percent Spent	Percent Spent
Waking Time		
Intrapersonal Communication	30	
Interhuman Communication	70	
Total Communication		100
Interhuman Communication Time		
Speaking and Related Nonverbal Messages	30	
Listening and Related Nonverbal Messages	45	
Total in Oral and Related Nonverbal Message Transactions		75
Writing and Related Nonverbal Messages	9	
Reading and Related Nonverbal Messages	16	
Total in Written and Related Nonverbal Message Transactions		25
Total in Interhuman Communication		100

The sizes of these approximations vary from writer to writer. However, all keep the relative sizes of the proportions about the same. All say that people generally take part in more interhuman than intrapersonal communication, in more oral than written communication, in more reading than writing, and in more listening than speaking.

Like reading, listening allows you to gain knowledge, to take in the ideas and opinions of others, to receive instructions (briefings), to increase your bank of communication symbols, and to improve your ability to use symbols. Listening also reinforces other received messages, gives pleasure, and altogether lets you use your mind in a satisfying way. However, to a greater extent than reading, listening plays a major part in human relations—the social interactions that define a great deal of life itself.

Think of the different kinds of listening you do: You listen as you converse informally—in person, by telephone, or by two-way radio. You listen to the radio, television, stereo, and tape player. You listen to speakers and lecturers in formal situations. You listen as you participate in a dialogue. You listen when someone screams "Fire!" You listen to the instructions of a superior or an instructor. You listen to the cooing of a baby or a symphony orchestra.

Consider the importance of listening to business. First, review the purposes and kinds of listening cited in the preceding paragraphs. Then, in particular, try to visualize how strongly a manager depends upon listening in order to carry out her or his duties. Listening helps the manager know the all-important details about things and people, maintain motivation and morale, and make wise decisions.

Listening is just as important for any other business position. Picture for example the work of a salesperson, a secretary, a computer programmer, an accountant, a stockbroker, a loan officer, a personnel interviewer, an in-service-training instructor, and a collection officer.

(414 words — including table)
(test on page 25)

THE LISTENING PROCESS

Like reading, listening is basically a mental process. It encompasses three broad stages: (1) selection, (2) reception, and (3) symbol/meaning manipulation.

Select

Because you hear much more than you listen to, selection of the listening message initiates the process. That selection involves a deliberate mental act. For example, think of how you function in a room crowded with conversational groups. You hear all the sounds around you, but you selectively listen to only the few people in your immediate circle.

Have you ever so successfully shut out everything else that someone had to call your name several times before you shifted the focus of your attention? Your concentration is often so fixed that such a shift is quite difficult; many times only a shocking or startling event can cause you to redirect it.

Receive

Once you select the sound to which you will listen, the next stage is reception. The complicated hearing mechanism picks up the chosen sound waves and transfers them to the brain. Hearing ability is a critical part of the process.

Engage in Symbol/Meaning Manipulation

The most complicated part of listening requires your mind to take the internal message symbols, interpret them, and convert them into meanings for you. As described in Chapter 1 for reading, only you can create symbol meanings that are right for you. Neither the written nor the spoken word has any inherent meaning.

Speed adds a dimension to listening that differs from the speed concept for reading. People talk at about 125 w.a.m. socially and at about 100 w.a.m. before an audience. However, they think at about 400 w.a.m. Therefore, a great disparity exists—a disparity that creates problems in the ability to concentrate while listening. As a listener, your mind may wander because of such a difference in the capacities for sending and receiving. Speed, then, remains a consideration for listening—but in a different way than for reading.

Comprehension and retention are of key importance in listening as in reading. However, you usually cannot relisten as you can reread. Therefore, the danger of misunderstanding and forgetting is even greater when listening than when reading. The typical person cannot remember half of what he or she just heard, and can recall only one-fourth of it a short time later.

GUIDELINES FOR LISTENING

The guidelines for listening parallel those for reading:

1. Define your purposes, the speaker's purposes, yourself, the speaker, and the environment.
2. Identify the listening channel.
3. Control the interference internal and external to you and the speaker.
4. Listen to the messages in light of the purposes, the participants, the environment, the channel, and the interference.
5. Use feedback to and from the speaker.
6. Evaluate at each stage.

Define Purposes, Participants, and Environment

Determine your purposes for listening and attempt to learn the speaker's purposes for speaking. Begin with your purposes.

Listen with purpose

Reasons for listening run the gamut from sheer survival to human fulfillment. In application, then, purposes for listening relate to satisfying both immediate and long-term human needs and wants. Possibly yours is a very basic need, such as to obtain food, clothing, and shelter; maintain good health; or protect yourself from injury or harm. Possibly your need is a social one, such as to be accepted, liked, loved, respected, or admired. Perhaps you want to experience pleasure, joy, or recreation. Perhaps you need to use your mind in a creative way, gain information or knowledge, or reach conclusions and make decisions. Whatever the reason for listening, try to be aware of it and listen purposefully.

Many times you can establish your purposes well ahead of the listening event. For example, all previously announced lectures, speeches, radio and television shows, meetings, conferences, and interviews offer you such an opportunity. You then can prepare properly to satisfy the purposes you have established.

Determine speaker's purpose

To decide what you think the speaker's purposes are, ask yourself: "Is the speaker talking to me because I can help satisfy her needs? Is she trying to provide me with pleasure or entertainment? Is she simply imparting information? Does she wish to engage in dialogue that will help us both reach conclusions or make decisions? Is she trying to persuade me to do something?"

Though you cannot always grasp the speaker's purposes to your full satisfaction, you still need to try to identify them. Your listening efficiency will improve greatly as you become aware of others' goals.

Define participants

Understand everything you can about yourself and about the speaker. Assess backgrounds, beliefs, values, prejudices, biases, and attitudes as they relate to the subject of the communication. If you fail to understand such characteristics, you have little basis for improving or judging the quality of the exchange.

Define environment

Though closely akin to defining the participants, definition of the environment in which you function warrants some emphasis. In general terms the environment includes everything not a part of the participants themselves. It includes the natural and synthetic surroundings. It even includes other people.

Identify Channel

Different channels have different advantages and disadvantages. Therefore, one of your early responsibilities as a listener is to identify the particular channel at work.

For example, with the telephone you miss the potential for feedback that accompanies an interpersonal, conversational exchange. If you listen to a speaker from the back of a large room, you do not have the advantage the comes with listening to a speaker in a room that holds ten.

Know your channels—their weaknesses and strengths. Understand the interference and feedback capabilities of each.

The oral channels provide more advantages than the written ones in terms of human interplay. However, they have the disadvantage of not yielding a permanent record—unless the participants make a recording. Therefore, do not fall into the trap of automatically assuming that when you are listening you are better off in every way than when you are reading.

Control Interference

Try to control potential and actual obstacles to listening. Prevent their occurrence if you can. If they already exist, seek to eliminate or neutralize them.

Interference may be internal or external to the participants. It may be mental, emotional, or physical.

If your hearing is impaired temporarily or permanently, interference with your listening is inescapable. If you become psychologically defensive about what a speaker says, a barrier to communication rises. Interference occurs when a microphone is not functioning properly, when a telephone connection is bad, when distracting noises cover the voice of the speaker, when a radio has static, or when a speaker has a condescending attitude.

Listen

The decoding stage represents the crux of the process for you as a listener. Decoding is taking the received symbols and converting them into internal meanings.

All that you have done to this point now becomes part of the most critical stage. Understanding yourself, the purposes, the speaker, the environment, the channel, and possible interference does not serve as an end unto itself. Instead, it serves as a backdrop helping you to actually receive and decode the message.

The listening sequence at this stage, then, becomes: Select the message you wish to hear, hear it, and mentally supply meanings for what you hear. However, you may maintain this ideal order of events only when you can look ahead to listening situations.

For instance, if you receive a telephone call from a stranger, you have to make some very quick judgments about the why, who, what, where, and when of the situation. All the while, you must simultaneously be creating meanings for the words and tones you are hearing.

Likewise, even with someone you know, you often must scramble mentally in order to make decisions about the person in any unannounced circumstance. Such an occasion might be a chance meeting, an unexpected expression of opinion during a prescheduled meeting, a drop-in visit by the boss, or a friend's sudden angry outburst over some issue.

Your ability to listen effectively in these spontaneous conversations depends heavily upon your facility in symbol/meaning manipulation. Suggestions for improving this skill form another part of this chapter.

Use Feedback

As an active listener, you should initiate feedback to the original speaker. In addition, you should take account of feedback subsequently initiated by the original speaker in response to your feedback.

With mass-media communication such as radio and television, you have little chance for feedback, and even the little feedback that is possible is delayed. Few radio or television shows feature direct telephone participation or computer hookups. Even these attempts provide limited access to only a few people. In most cases, you have only the written media as avenues for feedback.

When you sit as a member of a large audience listening to a formal speaker, your feedback often counts for little. The speaker often cannot see very many people well enough to detect facial expressions. Concerted applause, silence, laughter, groans, posturing, or restlessness provide about the only feedback for her in those circumstances.

Though the compact setting involving a small audience improves the feedback potential, it still remains restricted. If the speaker allows questions and discussion, however, the situation improves considerably.

Even an intermediary such as a telephone puts severe limitations on feedback from a listener. However, changes in vocal tone and pitch, the use of silence, and the opportunity for questioning represent significant advantages compared to mass-media communication.

When you do have the advantage of being in the physical presence of the speaker, use your feedback opportunities to the fullest. Ask questions. Repeat in different words what has just been said. Use nonverbal messages to indicate your interest in and assessment of what you hear.

Evaluate

Evaluation is the binder of a process that begins with establishment of purposes. Even as you accomplish all of the mental feats previously described, you should still assign one small part of your mind to act as an objective evaluator of the entire process. You should continually monitor how well the communication is going—how well the interchange meets your expectations and even those of the speaker.

If you find part way through a listening situation that your listening is not serving your original purposes, you have several options. You can simply stop listening—but that is often an unwise move. In channels such as conversations, discussions, dialogues, open forums, and meetings (channels that allow for interjected feedback), you can try to correct the communication so that it does begin to serve your purposes. If you cannot correct it, you may choose simply to revise your purposes while you continue to listen.

Evaluation puts you in some control—even of communication that involves receiving. You can get what you want out of it—although you might have to revise what that is after you move into the process.

To review the guidelines in another way, consider some hints and techniques for improved listening comprehension and retention.

TECHNIQUES FOR LISTENING

The suggestions for increasing listening power bear a striking resemblance to those related to reading. Both are receiving acts, though, so quite naturally they have common criteria for accomplishment. Helpful techniques are:

1. Select proper listening mode.
2. Concentrate and think.
3. Be an active listener.
4. Improve symbol/meaning manipulation.
5. Take notes sparingly.
6. Control physical and psychological setting.
7. Listen for retention.

8. Preview.
9. Review.
10. Practice.

Select Proper Listening Mode

 Always try to anticipate or at least make a rapid decision about the kind of listening you will do.

Listening modes and reading types have some similarities and some differences. For example, the four types of reading relate to speed, whereas their counterparts for listening do not. However, consider how your listening may improve if you decide to select one of these listening modes:

1. Careful listening: You want to comprehend and retain not only the general idea of heavy material, but the details as well.
2. Attentive listening: You want to comprehend and retain not only the general idea of light material, but the details as well.
3. Skimming: You want to comprehend and retain only the general idea.
4. Scanning: You want to locate and retain only preset and specific kinds of information.

By being clear about which of the four modes of listening you have elected, you can participate more efficiently in any communication. As developed in Chapter 1, appropriate alignment of mode with situation will greatly improve the communication—and negate wasted effort.

Concentrate and Think

Although its applications for listening differ from those for reading, the time dimension has quite an impact on listening. Again, you think faster than a speaker can speak. For that reason, a potentially dangerous gap exists between the processes—a gap that can play havoc with your power to maintain concentration upon the subject.

If your mind starts to wander while listening because of your excess mental capacity, you may lose the entire train of thought. Therefore, the requirement of concentrative effort becomes even more critical for listeners than for readers. If you drift for a few minutes while reading, you can always go back to the point at which you lost your concentration. With listening you usually cannot.

Following are some tactics for concentrating paraphrased from Huseman, Lahiff, and Hatfield:

1. *Anticipate what the speaker will say next.* Whether or not what you anticipate is confirmed, the act of anticipating serves to focus your attention upon the subject at hand.
2. *Focus on the message.* Weighing the speaker's evidence and pondering the speaker's words for deeper meanings—particularly connotative ones—fill the gap created by the speech-thought rate differential.

3. *Review previous points.* Continually review the major points the speaker has already covered. Reviewing aids the listening and learning process because it reinforces ideas.[2]

Concentration can also be improved through will power, through overcoming barriers, and through proper application of the guidelines and techniques recited here.

Think by analyzing the material. This approach is called critical listening, and it is particularly appropriate for careful listening.

For all kinds of listening, however, you need to be critical to the extent that you evelute not only the content, but the reliability of the speaker as well. Determine the level of rationality of the speaker. Determine the degree of completeness and accuracy of the information being transmitted. Determine the quality and soundness of the speaker's ideas. In addition, look past the the prejudices, deceptions, and emotions into the sheer value of the message and the credibility of the person who is delivering it.

(521 words)
(test on page 47)

Be an Active Listener

Activity as opposed to passivity in listening requires mainly that you follow the six communication guidelines and the other nine hints listed here. However, the concept of activity in and of itself adds critical dimension to the process. Listening actively is based on the recognition that ultimately you alone have the power to listen, and to affect dramatically the quality of the ensuing communication.

If in the receiving state you view yourself as helpless, you do not provide the impetus necessary for communication to flourish. If you listen actively, the speaker will be stimulated to even more activity, and as a result, the communication has a chance to fulfill its potential.

Though empathy contributes to listening, it is not a sufficient substitute for active listening, particularly if it is arrested at a state of quiet understanding of the other. Full-blown listening includes feedback—an open, frank response to the speaker.

As an example, suppose that you have listened intently, politely, and courteously for 20 minutes to a co-worker's grievance against a supervisor. You may even understand and sympathize with his position. However, you will not become an active listener until you translate that understanding and sympathy into feedback from the sought-out listener you are to him.

Your course of action may be to state exactly what you think he should do. You may help him analyze the situation so that he arrives at his own decision. You may simply state your concern for the difficult situation. You may say nothing, but feed back with supportive body language.

---

[2]Richard C. Huseman, James M. Lahiff, and John D. Hatfield, *Interpersonal Communication in Organizations* (Boston: Holbrook Press, Inc., 1976), pp. 113-114.

Whatever your decision, however, you made it overtly. You did not just sit with folded hands and a wandering mind, or at most a polite, distant attitude that says "I feel sorry for you." You entered the arena. You played an active role.

The critical listening approach described in the preceding section also has applications for active listening. As you share responsibility for the exchange, you start to develop a critique. The critique deals not only with the content, the speaker, and yourself, but with the communication process itself. You do so not to subvert the process, but to profit from it.

You may decide through active, critical listening that a speaker at a formal affair may be sincere, but has the facts wrong. You may decide that she makes grammatical errors and has distracting mannerisms. You may decide that you have an innate prejudice against her "type." However, as an effective listener, you can still benefit from the experience.

Analyze how the speaker's development could have been improved. Make notes about the facts you think are wrong so that you can check them for accuracy. Consider in what ways, if you were the speaker, you could improve the communication for this audience. Objectively determine whether your rejection of poor grammar could be a form of snobbishness. Challenge your own dismissal of her words by considering that you might have rejected them because of your prejudgment about her "type."

Whether you need to employ empathy, critique, self-interest, or some other technique, never be satisfied to be merely a receiving spectator at your own communication events. As an initial listener, you are just as much a player as is the initial sender. The toss of the coin simply placed you as the first receiver—but a receiver just as responsible for making the exchange into an exciting game as is the sender.

Improve Symbol/Meaning Manipulation

As suggested, the listening process centers upon the ability to decode—to create meanings for messages comprised of symbols selected by someone else. Therefore, just as for reading, an indispensable technique for effective listening is the development of a broad-ranging internal library of symbols and meanings. It also includes the facility for creating new meanings as you encounter new symbols.

Whereas reading focuses upon words, though, listening focuses upon both words and nonwords. The color, texture, and quality of paper in a reading situation simply do not have the impact of the color, texture, and quality of a voice. Therefore, to become an improved listener, expand your command of all types of symbols.

Recall the suggestions for improving the manipulation of symbols and meanings for reading (pp. 17-18). With only minimal revisions, these techniques apply just as well to listening. Therefore, no repetition of them is necessary here.

Take Notes Sparingly

Again echoing a tactic for efficient reading, take only a few notes during a listening encounter. Unless you can control the tendency to want to write everything you hear, do not take any notes. Used wisely, skeleton notes of major points and key details can reinforce comprehension and retention. However, trying to capture everything usually becomes a distraction. It often proves to be a device that detracts from the concentration necessary for good listening.

Similarly, though recording a presentation can form the basis for relistening for purposes of clarification or reinforcement, it can become a substitute for listening. Therefore, use recording instruments only for particularly weighty presentations and careful-listening situations. Even then, use them only to supplement active listening. Of course you should always obtain from the speaker the permission to record.

Control Physical and Psychological Setting

As a good listener, try to understand and control three important elements of the setting. They are: (1) your personal physical condition, (2) the psychological makeups of both you and the speaker, and (3) the external physical setting in which you are functioning.

Personal physical conditions

Your ears are the basic personal physical equipment in listening. Even if you do not seem to have any particular problems, have your ears tested. Most campuses provide a free or inexpensive hearing clinic for such a purpose. If you find that you have some hearing loss, pursue the matter with a specialist.

Avoid loud noises—particularly repeated earsplitting noises endured over long periods of time. The decibel levels of factories, radios, stereos, and many live music performances cause untold damage to hearing abilities.

Your general state of health and your physical condition at a given time also have an impact upon listening. Therefore, attend to your health not only for good living, but for good communicating.

Psychological conditions

Try to know your own psychological background and present psychological state, as well as those of the speaker. Awareness is the beginning of the solution for any problems in human psychology.

Use positive thinking. Do not allow yourself to become defensive or stop listening simply because a speaker does not suit your tastes in looks, dress, grooming, accent, values, beliefs, or attitudes. Separate content from the distracting features of the person delivering it.

Avoid interrupting the speaker. In addition, try not to think so much about what you are going to say next that you miss much of the speaker's message.

In short, establish an empathetic and knowledgeable view of human psychology—both for you and the speaker.

External conditions

For optimal listening, control both the aural and visual elements of your surroundings. Certainly, the aural is of highest importance. However, to the extent that you can enhance accompanying visual nonverbal cues, that avenue becomes important too.

Sit or stand comfortably but alertly. Locate yourself so that you can see and hear well. Adjust the temperature appropriately and try to have good ventilation. If you have a choice, make the surroundings reasonably attractive and tidy. However, try not to be preoccupied with such factors.

Ward off any foreseeable interference. Avoid sitting by people who whisper to you during oral presentations. Stay away from potential outside noises such as those emanating from a foyer or hall. Try to locate yourself in a spot that provides for good eye contact.

Listen for Retention

With slight transformation, the tactics for retention summarized for reading work just as well for listening. Memory aids, priorities, thinking, reinforcement, and resolve can once again prove useful.

Use memory aids

If the speaker presents an acronym, saying, gimmick, or clever outline, definitely use it to help you remember. However, you probably will not have time to create your own such memory aids during any ongoing listening activity. You might do so later from tapes or notes, though, as an aid to reinforcement.

As you listen to the speaker, make mental lists. Also create mental images from the words you hear. When being introduced to people, try to think of some word association for the name, occupation, home town, address, interests, or other distinguishing characteristics about the person.

Remember a name by associating it with the name of someone you know. Picture the spelling of the name. Say the name aloud several times during the conversation. It not only adds a personal, human touch, but also helps to fix the name in your mind.

Repeat some of the facts that you want to recall and tie them to something familiar. You might find yourself saying, "Oh, you live in New Lenox. I have a cousin who lives there."

Following such a conversation you may want to capture the facts in writing. The writing not only provides immediate reinforcement for your learning, but also forms the basis for additional reinforcement through later reading.

Even if you have made notes, try to remember the information without looking at them. Use the notes only as security in case of forgetfulness, and not as a substitute for retention.

A related device for dialogue is to question or restate in your own words the ideas and concepts spoken by another. Not only does such a process help you remember, it often serves to clarify the intent of the speaker. Consider this skeleton of a sequence that actually occurred in a committee meeting: One member said, "I am absolutely opposed to listing the policy items in a priority order." A second member then said, "No matter what we do, the final implementation depends upon the quality and good faith of the people who implement the policy." A supporter of a priority listing then said to the second speaker, "Do you mean, then, that you do not favor a priority listing?" The second speaker replied, "No, as a matter of fact, I like the concept of a priority listing."

You have undoubtedly participated in just such exchanges—exchanges in which an oral recasting of what one person thought he or she had heard was quite wrong. However, you probably also have accepted countless other statements as you thought you heard them, when actually you misunderstood.

The lesson here is that you should rephrase and question anything and everything that has left even an inkling of confusion in your mind, as far as that is practical. Not only will you have more vivid recall of the interchange, but you may alter the course of the interchange entirely. Moreover, the alteration likely will make the interchange more productive.

Set priorities

As with information gained through reading, you cannot possibly keep everything that you hear at the tip of your fingers. Therefore, determine what is critical for recollection and what is unworthy of it. Then place other elements on a continuum between the two extremes and store everything according to the ranking. Though this process may be slightly more difficult for listening than for reading, it nonetheless can and should be adopted. Your mind can accomplish the feat. It can simultaneously carry an outline of major points, select details for storage, assign value weights according to the relative importance of those details, and store them in keeping with that valuation.

Think

As mentioned in Chapter 1, a good way to remember is to think. As you listen, keep your mind active, and afterwards, continue to think about what was said.

Reinforce

Retention improves as you repeatedly allow into your mind the material you have judged to be important. A repetition of the entire listening sequence can be accomplished if you tape it and replay it. If the material is critical enough, have a typewritten transcript made of the tape. Reinforcement improves if different channels can be used for repeated reception.

If you take notes, review them as soon as possible after completion of the communication. As with the tape recording, you may want to convert the handwritten notes into typewritten form for easier reading.

Develop resolve

All mental activity rests on a foundation of motivation. Unless you genuinely want to store information for ready recall, you probably will not. Only the most startling occurrences—be they good or bad—stay with you without determination on your part. Therefore, your will power, your resolve, and your commitment can do more to improve comprehension and recall than all of the mechanical aids you can devise.

Preview

For a listening situation to have the best possible chance of success, prepare for it well. If you know ahead of time that you will do some important listening, preview that pending opportunity.

Simulate as clearly as possible the upcoming event in your mind. Review any titles, outlines, or agenda provided. Anticipate everything you can about who will say what, preview what questions you might ask, and determine just what points you want to be covered.

Some skeleton notes prepared ahead of time can contribute significantly to your mental organization as you go into the interchange. You might even leave space to fill in your findings during the course of it. Arrange related written material in logical order for ready reference during the session.

Prepare psychologically to concentrate, and to assert control over tendencies to be mentally lazy or intolerant of the speaker. Also steel yourself to comprehend and to retain what you have heard.

Previewing stresses the direct application of the communication guidelines of defining the purposes, participants, environment, channel, and possible interference. In addition, it indirectly considers the remaining guidelines; for even during the preview you are thinking about how you will decode, feed back, and evaluate.

Review

Following a listening encounter, review the content of the exchange. Also review the quality of it. Evaluate to determine whether you accomplished your purposes and whether you performed well in all other aspects of the process. By reliving the experience briefly, you will help fix material in your mind. You also will stand to improve your performance the next time you participate in another listening experience.

Practice

As is a sound idea for any mode of communication, take advantage of every opportunity you have to apply these principles for good listening. Because you spend so much of your interhuman communication time listening, you have untold chances for their application.

SUMMARY

About 45 percent of a person's interhuman communication time is spent listening or hearing. A distinction must be made between the two because all listening involves hearing, but not all hearing is listening. The role that listening plays in the business world is such an important one that everyone should learn what constitutes competent listening and what can be done to improve listening arts.

Listening is a mental process including three stages: (1) selection, (2) reception, and (3) symbol/meaning manipulation. *Selection* is essentially choosing that to which you will listen. *Reception* involves the actual physical hearing process. Then when your mind takes internal message symbols, interprets them, and converts them into meanings, you engage in *symbol/meaning manipulation*.

Guidelines for effective listening are

1. Define purposes, participants, and environment.
2. Identify listening channel.
3. Control interference.
4. Listen to messages in light of purposes, participants, environment, channel, and interference.
5. Use feedback.
6. Evaluate.

Define your *purposes* and those of the speaker. Learn as much as possible about *yourself* and about the *speaker*. Understand the *environment* in which the exchange takes place.

Identify the *listening channel* by determining its characteristics and relative strengths and weaknesses. For example, while a telephone exchange may be convenient, it has some disadvantages compared to the face-to-face conversation.

Control as much *interference* as you can. Static on the radio and a speaker's condescending attitude are two examples of interference.

The crux of the listening process is *decoding* the speaker's message in light of the purposes, participants, environment, channel, and interference. At this stage you must be a conscious listener who is aware of all of the relevant circumstances affecting the transaction.

A productive communication involves the intelligent use of *feedback* to and from the speaker. Without feedback, the exchange of information is practically nil.

By *evaluating* at each stage of the interchange, the listener can monitor how well the communication is going—how well the interchange is meeting the listener's and speaker's expectations.

Ten techniques may be employed toward increasing listening power:

1. Select proper listening mode.
2. Concentrate and think.
3. Be an active listener.
4. Improve symbol/meaning manipulation.
5. Take notes sparingly.
6. Control physical and psychological setting.
7. Listen for retention.
8. Preview.
9. Review.
10. Practice.

Practice

1. Your professor or another student will read a selection from another chapter in this book or play a recording. Apply the techniques you have just reviewed as you listen and take brief notes. Then complete the comprehension test that the professor will administer.
2. Attend a session of another class or ask a colleague to tape a discussion or lecture in one in which you are not a student. Prepare for listening as well as you can, and then listen to that unfamiliar presentation—taking brief notes as you do. Without relistening, write a one-page summary of your findings.
3. Apply the ten listening techniques to one entire session of the class in which you use this book. Write a one-page summary of the session.
4. Apply the ten listening techniques to a meeting of another class in which you are a student. Write a one-page summary of the meeting.
5. Your professor will divide the class into small groups and give each member of the group a short biographical sketch of a hypothetical person. Each then tries to become that person by studying the sketch for a few minutes. Then, each person fully introduces herself or himself as the hypothetical character. After all have spoken, each will tell or write down as much as possible about each of the others. Evaluate how well each person listened to and recalled what each hypothetical character said.

6. Have another student who has some knowledge in a particular business field pretend he or she is your manager at a firm in that field. Ask your "manager" to tell you about the way business is conducted at the firm. Listen and participate, making use of the six guidelines for effective listening. Write a summary of how you answered or employed each of the six guidelines. How could the interchange have been improved?

7. Keep a log on one whole day's communicating time. How does the time you spent listening compare to the time you spent speaking, reading, writing, hearing, and in other forms of communication?

8. Using the techniques for effective listening, prepare for and attend a speech. Write a summary of the speech. Also summarize how you made use of the ten listening techniques.

9. Watch and listen to instructional programs on an eduational network. Practice listening and make a record of what you believe your listening strengths and weaknesses are.

10. You are a member of a local civic organization and must present a light, even humorous, five-minute talk on self-improvement at the next meeting. You choose the topic of listening. Write a one- or two-page presentation. (Your professor may ask some of the class members to present the statements orally.)

11. You are a department manager at the Huge Corporation. You hold weekly meetings with your 32-member staff. At the beginning of each meeting, you give a brief talk on the department's successes and problems and on current issues. After each talk, though, your staff members inevitably ask you questions that you already had answered in your beginning-of-the-meeting speech. You know that you are a good speaker; so you conclude that many of your staff members just do not listen to you or to each other. You now decide to prepare a two- or three-page speech for next week's meeting. The subject of the speech will be the importance of listening and techniques for good listening. Prepare the speech. Remember, your staff doesn't listen, so you will need to include attention-getting devices in your speech.

12. Many people have trouble remembering other people's names. They probably did not listen to the names when the people were first introduced to them. Meet with a group with which you have met before. Without talking, you and each other group member try to recall and write down the names of the other group members. Check your work. Did some of you forget each other's names? Now discuss ways in which you can learn to listen to and then remember people's names.

13. Develop symbol/meaning interpretations by analyzing these symbols and creating meanings for them. Check your dictionary and thesaurus. Write several sentences for each. Use the words in conversation or writing. Return to the list sometime later and give your version of the meaning for each from memory. These are the symbols:

a. Anticipate   g. Manipulate
b. Approximate   h. Mode
c. Clarify   i. Nonverbal
d. Continuum   j. Participative
e. Critique   k. Random
f. Decode   l. Verbal

14. Complete Self-Test 8 over the sections titled "Select Proper Listening Mode" and "Concentrate and Think" (pages 38-39).

Self-Test 8
Excerpts about Selecting Proper Listening Mode
and Concentrating and Thinking

A. Recall (13 points each). For each multiple-choice question, select the most accurate answer.

1. Which of the following is not considered a listening type?
   a. Careful listening
   b. Speed listening
   c. Skimming
   d. Attentive listening
   e. Scanning

2. Concentration is important to listening because:
   a. You think faster than you speak and may lose your concentration on subjects.
   b. You may miss important points of a speech because of lack of concentration.
   c. You speak faster than you think and may lose your train of thought.
   d. Both a and b
   e. Both b and c

3. Critical listening does *not* involve which of the following?
   a. Evaluating the content for reliability
   b. Determining the degree of accuracy of the information being transmitted
   c. Skimming the material and retaining only the general ideas
   d. Determining the quality and soundness of the speaker's ideas
   e. Determining the reliability of the speaker

4. Concentration may be improved by:
   a. Will power
   b. Overcoming barriers
   c. Proper application of listening guidelines
   d. a–c
   e. b and c only

5. Which of the following is a true statement regarding effective listening?
   a. Critical listening cannot improve comprehension.
   b. Concentration is less critical for listening than for reading.
   c. Making a rapid decision about the kind of listening you will do may improve listening ability.
   d. Determining a listening mode will not allow you to participate more effectively in the communication process.
   e. Not a–d

6. Which of the following is *not* a concentrative tactic?
   a. Anticipating what the speaker will say next
   b. Reviewing previous points made by the speaker
   c. Focusing on the message—looking for deeper meanings
   d. Being preoccupied with your own views on the subject
   e. Focusing attention upon the subject at hand

B. Inference (22 points). For the multiple-choice question, select the most accurate answer.

The act of listening:
   a. Is merely a function of hearing a person speak
   b. Is a function of such ongoing processes as concentrating and thinking
   c. Requires the use of little or no acquired skills
   d. Is merely an attitude about what one hears
   e. Can easily be maintained with little or no concentration on the part of the listener

Solution to Self-Test 8
Excerpts about Selecting Proper Listening Mode
and Concentrating and Thinking

A. Recall (13 points each)   **B.** Inference (22 points)
   1. b   **3.** c   **5.** c   b
   2. d   **4.** d   **6.** d

·**15.** Take and score Self-Test 9 over Chapter 2.

Self-Test 9
Chapter 2

A. Recall (15 points each). For each multiple-choice question, select the most accurate answer.

  1. Listening:
    a. Is the same as hearing
    b. Does not involve hearing
    c. Is a passive, physical function
    d. Always involves hearing, though hearing does not always involve listening
    e. Is not a communciation act

  2. The interhuman communication time spent in listening and receiving related nonverbal messages is:
    a. 1 percent
    b. 45 percent
    c. 16 percent
    d. 90 percent
    e. 30 percent

  3. The first broad stage of the listening process is selection. In this context, selection refers to:
    a. Choosing the appropriate channel
    b. Choosing the listening type
    c. Choosing that to which you will listen and tuning out the rest
    d. Choosing the location for the interchange
    e. Not a–d

  4. While listening to a live speech:
    a. Take as many notes as possible.
    b. Try to anticipate what the speaker will say next.
    c. Think about different subjects in order to keep your mind active.
    d. Look up the words you do not understand.
    e. a–d

  5. Which of the following is *not* a guideline for effective listening?
    a. Define purposes, participants, and environment.
    b. Identify listening channel.
    c. Control interference.
    d. Select, hear, and decode speaker's messages in light of purposes, participants, environment, channel, and interference.
    e. Select, hear, and revise speaker's messages in light of personal biases.
    f. Use feedback to and from speaker.
    g. Evaluate at each stage of interchange.

6. Which of the following is *not* a technique for listening effectively?
   a. Practice.
   b. Preview.
   c. Review.
   d. Select proper listening mode.
   e. Concentrate and think.
   f. Be a passive listener.
   g. Improve symbol/meaning manipulation.
   h. Take notes sparingly.
   i. Control physical and psychological setting.
   j. Listen for retention.

B. Inference (10 points). Select the most accurate answer.

Listening:
   a. Requires no real preparation
   b. Can take place only when the speaker is physically present
   c. Is an art and skill that takes considerable effort to develop
   d. Should be practiced by only those people who do not speak very often
   e. Is productive only when both the speaker and listener are in agreement

Solution to Self-Test 9
Chapter 2

A. Recall (15 points each)   **B.** Inference (10 points)
   1. d   **3.** c   **5.** e   c
   2. b   **4.** b   **6.** f

3

Receiving Nonverbal Messages

By now considering nonverbal receiving after reading and listening, you will complete a review of the triad of receiving activities.

Think of the words "nonverbal receiving" as including wordless reception at least through all five known senses. At the same time, understand that nonverbal observation includes more than sheer sensing. Nonverbal observing involves much more than seeing, hearing, touching, smelling, and tasting, for it draws upon at least as much perceptual acuity and mental processing as do reading and listening.

Even as you accept the triad developed for organizational purposes, remind yourself that separation of the communication whole into parts creates an artificial image of the process. That reminder becomes particularly necessary before a study of nonverbal communication.

The nonverbal category can fairly well stand alone as a primitive communication type. However, it also is an integral part of both the writing/reading and the speaking/listening modes.

Think how all of these things communicate without words:

Paintings	The taste of soured milk
Instrumental music	The aroma of baking bread
Dance	A kiss
Photographs	Tears
Lack of punctuality	The roar of the wind
A finger pointed upward	A bugler playing taps
(and the choice of	A poignant silence
finger does matter)	A clenched jaw or fist
A handshake	The wag of a dog's tail

In addition, no verbal communication can occur independently of the nonverbal. Nonverbal messages can replace, repeat, contradict, complement, accent, or regulate verbal communication. Though all these functions are important, think particularly about the contradictory situations.

One common finding is that when verbal and nonverbal messages conflict, many people tend to believe the nonverbal instead of the verbal. People assume, usually subconsciously, that nonverbal messages are more natural and more difficult to manipulate than are the verbal ones. Thus, they place greater trust in them.

Nonverbal messages deal primarily with emotions and attitudes. Nonverbal symbols lack the sophistication needed to carry complex messages.

Some theorists do not even consider the tools of nonverbal communication to be symbols. In this book, however, the word "symbols" is meant to include both words and nonwords used in the communication process.

A major barrier to learning about nonverbal communication is the lack of dictionaries, thesauruses, and grammars cataloging nonverbal symbols. Thus, a nonverbal communicator does not have equal access to the kinds of aids available for verbal communication.

The overriding barrier, however, is the general inattention to nonverbal communication within formal educational patterns. For example, you probably have not encountered a substantial unit on nonverbal communication in your schooling to this point.

The major part of this chapter covers some of the information needed to correct the neglect of nonverbal communication by traditional curricula. First, however, review the relative importance of nonverbal and verbal communication.

THE IMPORTANCE OF NONVERBAL COMMUNICATION

"Actions speak louder than words." "A picture is worth a thousand words." "What people do is more important than what they say." "First impressions [virtually always nonverbal ones] are the lasting impressions." These kinds of sayings illustrate the common understanding of the importance of nonverbal communication.

Indeed, nonverbal communication characterizes a great deal of human behavior. However, reviewing the table of communication proportions (page 32) shows that nonverbal communication is not even included as a separate category, but only in association with verbal activities. Undoubtedly, the estimates need to be revised to treat nonverbal communication in isolation from the others.

Some evidence of the impact of nonverbal communication lies in the findings of Birdwhistell, an acknowledged authority in the field. He estimates that the typical person spends only about 10 or 11 minutes each day in speaking words, with an average spoken sentence of about 2.5 seconds. He also suggests that in a two-party conversation, the nonverbal elements carry 65 percent of the social meaning, leaving only 35 percent to the verbal level.[1]

Other estimates place as much as 80 percent[2] or even 93 percent[3] of the message load on the nonverbal. Whatever proportion holds true for a given situation, the nonverbal elements unquestionably contribute substantially to oral exchanges.

---

[1]From NONVERBAL COMMUNICATION IN HUMAN INTERACTION, Second Edition, by Mark L. Knapp, p. 30. Copyright© 1978, by Holt, Rinehart, and Winston. Reprinted by permission of Holt, Rinehart, and Winston.

[2]Charles U. Larson, *Communication: Everyday Encounters* (Belmont, Calif.: Wadsworth Publishing Company, Inc., 1976), p. 50.

[3]Albert Mehrabian, *Silent Messages* (Belmont, Calif.: Wadsworth Publishing Company, Inc., 1971), pp. 43–44.

For written messages the proportion of the meaning carried by verbal elements is larger than that carried by nonverbal elements. However, the proportion carried by the nonverbal elements still remains significant.

TYPES OF NONVERBAL COMMUNICATION

Researchers and writers suggest many different classifications of types of nonverbal communication. Review only two of the classifying systems here.

Immediacy, Power, and Responsiveness

Mehrabian asserts that nonverbal behavior and related communication occur in only three primary dimensions based on three metaphors: (1) the immediacy metaphor, (2) the power metaphor, and (3) the responsiveness metaphor.[4]

Immediacy

The immediacy metaphor is based on the fact that humans approach the things they like and avoid the things they dislike. For nonverbal communication, then, the like-dislike metaphor deals with both physical proximity and perceptual stimulation. Mehrabian writes, "Approach and immediacy indicate preference, positive evaluation, and liking, whereas avoidance and nonimmediacy indicate lack of preference, dislike, and, in extreme cases, fear."[5]

Positive, physical immediacy between people includes such acts as sitting or standing close to one another, maintaining a face-to-face posture, and touching or leaning toward the other. A lack of immediacy is obvious when opposite behaviors occur.

Power

By equating dominance, strength, or high status with power, the second metaphor emerges. Power generally relates to size, but size involves more than sheer physical bulk. For example, a person who strides or struts exhibits more power than one who takes small steps or shuffles. One who slouches or bows shows much less power than one who stands erect to the full extension of her or his height. The relaxed person who occupies a great deal of physical space shows more status than one who is tense and occupies minimal space.

Through the size and conspicuousness of such things as cars, houses, furniture, jewelry, and clothing, humans reveal much about their relative status—or at least their views of what constitutes status. Similarly, the more relaxed one is, the greater the power. If you lean back in your chair and cross your legs, you demonstrate more power than you do if you sit forward on the chair with your arms close to your body and your legs straight with knees pressed together.

Responsiveness

Responsiveness, probably the most basic way in which you communicate emotion, involves adaptive actions ranging from the comatose to the frenzied. You respond to

---

[4]Ibid., pp. 113, 115, 116.

[5]Ibid., p. 114.

your environment by showing anger, joy, surprise, fear, boldness, happiness, sadness, anxiety, quietude, petulance, pity, or benevolence. With such responses, you enter an arena of the nonverbal that is particularly valuable for human communication transactions.

Nine Nonverbal Classes

For this book, a structure involving nine classes forms the expanded foundation for nonverbal communication types. The structure includes categories rapidly becoming traditional for analysis of the subject: (1) face, (2) eyes, (3) voice, (4) movement, (5) touch, (6) appearance, (7) space, (8) time, and (9) environment.

Face

Theorists suggest that the face reveals more about emotional state and personality than any other human part. For example, some research by Mehrabian led to this formula for communicating any feeling:

$$\text{Total feeling } = \begin{array}{l} 7\% \text{ verbal feeling} \\ 38\% \text{ vocal feeling} \\ 55\% \text{ facial feeling}[6] \end{array}$$

Notice, too, how this formula leads to the earlier reported suggestion that humans receive about 93 percent of any feeling from the two nonverbal components and only 7 percent from the words uttered by the person.

Facial expressions   The face is capable of hundreds of emotional expressions based on different blends of available facial movements. However, researchers have consistently identified only six primary ones: surprise, fear, anger, disgust, happiness, and sadness.

Each person has unique expressions for even the six—and many more for the nuances and permutations deriving from them. Therefore, reading facial expressions can be difficult.

Adding to the difficulty is the great ability of many people to mask emotions. They can feign interest or attention while their minds race on to another subject. They can hide behind expressions that belie the truth.

The face also contributes as it helps to regulate conversations. Flashing the eyebrows, pursing the mouth, and winking often regulate by inviting or starting transactions. These and other facial expressions also help to control conversational turn-taking and culmination.

Paralleling the Mehrabian metaphors, the face contributes to expressions all along the scale between the poles of liking/disliking, dominance/submission, pleasantness/unpleasantness, intensity/control, and action/passivity.

Ekman and Friesen identify eight facial styles exhibited consistently by many people. A summary of the eight styles is:

1. The Withholder—Inhibited, with little facial movement
2. The Revealer—Uninhibited, with a great deal of facial movement
3. The Unwitting Expressor—Limited number of expressions thought to be masked, but not

---

[6]Ibid., p. 44.

4. The Blanked Expressor—Blank face instead of the emotion the person thinks is there
5. The Substitute Expressor—Emotion shown but different than expressor thinks
6. The Frozen-Affect Expressor—Permanent display of a given emotion (e.g., always looks sad because that is permanent feature of facial configuration)
7. The Ever-Ready Expressor—Display of given initial emotion no matter what the stimulus
8. The Flooded-Affect Expressor—Overriding state (e.g., anger) colors all other emotions.[7]

Smiling   Smiling contributes greatly to facial expressions.

McGough describes three major types of smiles. In the first, the simple smile, the lips barely touch, and no teeth show. This smile is a private smile showing happiness, and usually occurs when the person is alone. The upper teeth show in the upper smile which is used when greeting another person, and involves some eye contact. Both the upper and lower teeth show in the third type of smile, the broad smile. The broad smile usually occurs when a person is laughing. Eye-to-eye contact is minimal.[8]

Smiles do not always indicate happiness, though, and often mask true feelings. McGough writes:

> Most of us have seen the oblong, or polite, smile. This smile has no depth to it, although upper and lower teeth show. We may recall disliking the person who flashed this toothy grin at us. This smile conveys condescension. . . .[9]

McGough also identifies a smile that shows that a person feels inferior—the "lip-in" smile. The "lip-in" smile is similar to the upper smile, but the lower lip is drawn over the teeth.[10]

Eyes

The eyes also express a great deal about the person. Many people say that they observe people's eyes before anything else about them.

In review of the nonverbal contribution of the eyes, consider eye gaze and other factors.

Eye gaze   Mehrabian's immediacy metaphor fits the concept of eye gaze well. Research shows that, generally, people's eyes approach what they like and avoid what they do not like. For example, eye contact between a speaker and audience increases the audience's assessment of the speaker as a credible source.

People generally maintain more eye gaze and mutual eye gaze with those whose approval they want, those to whom they bring good news, and those whom they like. They also do so with people toward whom they feel positive, in whom they have an interest, and whom they know and trust.

---

[7]Paul Ekman and Wallace V. Friesen, *Unmasking the Face* (Englewood Cliffs, N.J.: Prentice-Hall, 1975).

[8]Elizabeth McGough, *Your Silent Language* (New York: William Morrow and Company, 1974), pp. 30–31.

[9]Ibid., pp. 31–32.

[10]Ibid., p. 32.

Averted eyes show anger, hurt feelings, and a hesitancy to reveal the inner self. They show a reticence in one who is the bearer of bad news and the avoidance of a competitor, someone who is offensive, or a stranger. They also reveal negativism and the need to increase psychological distance, as in an elevator, waiting room, or other small space.

Eye gaze relates to power also. If a person of status initiates eye contact, the subordinate is expected to maintain it. However, if the subordinate initiates it, the dominant person need not maintain it. The status person may look away or even gaze into the distance.

Dominance generally places the person of status at the head of the table. Such placement puts this powerful individual in a position of flexibility and control over eye contact, yet leaves her or him free to look elsewhere when a subordinate initiates it. Side-by-side seating is unsatisfactory to the person of status because of the difficulty of controlling eye contact.

When subordinates keep their eyes on the dominant individual, their behavior seems to run counter to the approach/avoidance theory, for they approach someone whom they dislike. However, power and responsiveness to it take precedence over liking in such a situation.

A similar exception occurs when a person dislikes another, but fears that person. In these circumstances, the eyes remain riveted on the feared one.

Another implication of the power and responsiveness metaphors is clear: One whom you fear must have some power over you. Therefore, you want to show subordination by honoring the nonverbal "rule" that you maintain eye gaze upon that person of power. By following the "rule," you may curry that person's favor and prevent whatever you fear from that person. In addition, if you maintain eye gaze, you will be more likely to pick up clues to how you should behave in order not to incur the wrath of the feared one.

Eye behavior communicates in many ways. It shows emotions. It establishes conversational regulators. It also monitors feedback. The last category serves as a reminder that the eyes not only supply information, they receive it as well.

Other factors   Many other factors associated with the eyes, eyebrows, and accompanying elements enter into nonverbal communication. Shape, color, eye size, pupil size, position, blinking, wrinkles, and eye movements contribute to the overall expressions that emanate from the eye region. For example, heavy eyebrows unbroken across the nose communicate something quite different than do two thin and distinct eyebrows. Many attribute different qualities to people with blue eyes than to those with dark eyes. People often associate big, open, wide eyes with frankness or naiveté. They often associate narrow, beady, squinted eyes with untrustworthiness.

Voice

Because the voice carries oral verbal messages, its function as the bearer of nonverbal messages often receives less attention than it should. However, paralanguage—the vocal cues that accompany spoken words—contributes significantly to the richness of communication.

Trager suggests that paralanguage includes four major categories: (1) vocal qualifiers, (2) vocal segregates, (3) vocal differentiators, and (4) vocal qualities.[11]

Vocal qualifiers   Ongoing variations in pitch, rate, and volume of the voice are the vocal qualifiers.

A high pitch may indicate nervousness, anxiety, tension, fear, surprise, dynamism, anger, joy, cheerfulness, or impatience. A low pitch may show affection, sadness, boredom, pleasantness, intimacy, or empathy.

The rate of speech also seems to change with emotions or personality types. A slow rate often accompanies intimacy, affection, boredom, or sadness. A rapid or clipping rate of speed seems to go with anger, cheerfulness, impatience, joy, animation, stress, or extroversion.

Voice volume tends to vary with emotional and personality characteristics in the same direction as pitch and rate. Loudness seems to occur in conjunction with anger, cheerfulness, joy, strength, fearlessness, activity, and high status. Softness appears with affection, boredom, sadness, intimacy, empathy, fear, passivity, weakness, and low status.

As you review the associations for the three voice qualifiers, you will observe that low pitch, slow rate, and softness tend to appear together, just as high pitch, fast rate, and loudness do.

Vocal segregates   Sounds, unnatural silences, and meaningless words used only to fill gaps between meaningful words act as vocal segregates. Examples include "uh," "ah," "uh-huh," "um," "er," and even "I mean," "ya know," "man," "OK," and "well." Such fillers often indicate stress and create a negative impact on the receiver.

Vocal differentiators   Specialized vocal sounds communicate along a broad spectrum. Think of the meanings you create when you hear these differentiators:

Yawning	Snoring	Sharp exhaling
Laughing	Yelling	or inhaling
Crying	Clearing the	Spitting
Sucking	throat	Hissing
Belching	Whining	Stretching
Giggling	Coughing	Moaning
Whispering	Sneezing	Groaning
Sniffing	Hiccoughing	Slurping
Swallowing	Sighing	Gurgling

Even though such vocalizations are not words, they communicate nonetheless.

Vocal qualities   The summary tone or quality of a voice is a composition of many factors, including pitch, volume, rate, resonance, rhythm, inflection, and enunciation.

Though temporary changes in pitch, volume, and rate act as vocal qualifiers, the three also serve to characterize the general quality of the voice.

---

[11]G. L. Trager, "Paralanguage: A First Approximation," *Studies in Linguistics* 13 (1958): 1–12.

Resonance (timbre) varies from the fully amplified tones associated with sadness, boredom, and affection, to the thin or blaring tones associated with joy, impatience, cheerfulness, and anger.

Rhythm is the regularity or irregularity—the smoothness or jerkiness—of the vocal pattern. Regularity often expresses confidence, sincerity, satisfaction, fear, activity, surprise, joy, cheerfulness, or affection. Irregularity may express anger or sadness.

Inflection is the rising and falling of the voice. Monotones seem to express boredom. Steady or slightly upward inflection often shows affection, impatience, or satisfaction. Upward inflection usually indicates cheerfulness or joy. Irregular inflection may show anger. Downward inflection can reveal sadness.

Enunciation describes the distinctness with which one pronounces or articulates words. A slurred sound often accompanies sadness and affection, and, to some extent, boredom and satisfaction. At the other extreme, a clipping style frequently belongs to anger and impatience.

Other blending factors contribute to the quality of voice expression—and to the value judgments you make about it. Recall how you react to such voice characteristics as throatiness, thinness, quaking, breathiness, stridency, flatness, dialects, racial differences, accents, and tenseness. Think also of the dramatic messages conveyed by poignant pauses and extended periods of silence in a church, synagogue, funeral home, courtroom, or government chamber.

Consider how combinations of verbal and nonverbal symbols can create inconsistent messages. Positive words can be combined with negative tones of voice, and negative words with positive tones to create double-edged messages. Sarcasm often results. When it does, the ultimate decision about meaning usually tips in the direction of the nonverbal vocal qualities rather than the words.

For example, think about how the tone and emphasis of delivery make the difference in how you react to phrases such as: "You're really weird." "I hate you." "You're so cute." "That was so clever." "You certainly handled that well."

Though verbal/nonverbal inconsistencies occur more often in informal and casual settings, the nonverbal component can contradict the verbal component even in the most formal controlled circumstances.

In the United States, the low-pitched, deep voice is considered to be the "perfect" voice—particularly for those seeking power. How much of the worship of the low voice arises from an instinctual appreciation and how much from socialization is unknown.

Though many Americans work at developing low voices, other vocal cues seem more often to be instinctual than learned. Therefore, they are much more difficult to mask than facial and other nonverbal messages.

Recall how Mehrabian's research suggests that receivers gain 38 percent of the total feeling of a message from vocal cues. The proportion is second only to the 55 percent conveyed by facial expression.

Movement

The nonverbal communication arising from human movement (motile or kinesic behavior) can be grouped in five categories: (1) emblems, (2) illustrators, (3) regulators, (4) adaptors, and (5) postures and gestures. The first four derive from the work of

Ekman and Friesen, who also included affect displays (facial expressions) in their taxonomy.[12]

Emblems   A large number of body movements act as symbols with relatively fixed verbal translations. They often replace verbal messages entirely. Such symbols become emblems.

A large number of body movements act as symbols with relatively fixed verbal translations. They often replace verbal messages entirely. One list includes about seventy of such emblems.[13] Consider only a few examples here:

1. Patting the stomach—"I'm full of food"
2. Nodding the head up and down—"Yes" or "I agree"
3. Patting the adjacent seat—"Sit beside me"
4. Shaking fist—"I'm angry"
5. Yawning—"I'm bored" or "I'm angry"
6. Cupping hand behind ear—"I can't hear you"
7. Clapping hands—"I approve"
8. Placing first finger on lips—"Be silent"
9. Circling the first finger parallel with the side of the head—"That person's crazy" or "That person's stupid"
10. Moving one index finger across the other or smacking the end of the tongue several times against the upper teeth—"For shame"
11. Forming the first and second fingers in the shape of a "V"—"Peace" or "Victory"
12. Shrugging shoulders and raising palms of hands upward—"I don't know"
13. Tapping finger against skull—"I'm thinking"
14. Tapping finger on own chest—"Me"
15. Standing at side of road and pointing thumb in direction of traffic—"I'd like a ride" (hitchhiking)
16. Rolling eyes—"I'm exasperated"
17. Waving—"Hello," "Goodbye," "Come here," "Here I am"

Illustrators   Body movements and gestures that synchronize with and complement words are illustrators. When people "talk" with their hands, they use illustrators. For example, picture someone telling you about the size of a fish he caught. Can you imagine the description using only words?

Consider other kinesic illustrators. Suppose you make the vehement statement, "I will *not* allow this to happen." Would you slap a fist into the palm of the other hand or make a sharp downward motion of one hand as you say the word "not"?

Do you automatically wave an arm as you call "Taxi"?

When you talk about an object in your presence, do you point or gesture toward it as you say words such as: "Take this desk." Do you usually nod your head as you answer "Yes" to a question?

---

[12]Paul Ekman and Wallace V. Friesen, "The Repertoire of Nonverbal Behavior: Categories, Origins, Usage, and Coding," *Semiotica* 1 (1969): 63–70, 82–92.

[13]H. G. Johnson, Paul Ekman, and Wallace V. Friesen. "Communicative Body Movements: American Emblems," *Semiotica* 15 (1975): 346–350.

Regulators   When body motions serve to add instructions or controls to oral transactions, those motions are regulators. Examples of such nonverbal symbols include:

Mutual gazes	Smiles	Embraces
Waves	Forward leanings	Shoulder slaps
Kisses	Knuckles tapping	Handshakes
Head movements	on a desk	Shifts in eye
Head nods	Posture changes	contact
Grooming actions		

Conversational turn-taking is punctuated by such acts as raising and lowering eyebrows, leaning forward and backward, and moving hands. Initiating and breaking away from conversations involve a great deal of nonverbal regulation. For example, have you ever consciously or subconsciously looked at your watch in an attempt to shorten a conversation with someone? Similarly, have you ever slapped your hands on the arms of your chair or on your thighs while rising in order to terminate an exchange?

Adaptors   Adaptors are actions adopted as responses to learning situations. Many of them form in childhood. They tend to be associated with negative emotions. They seem to occur for some instrumental purpose: controlling emotions, getting along with others, or satisfying needs. They often appear as adaptive means for coping with discomfort created by negative feelings about oneself, other people, or the environment.

Examples of adaptors include picking or holding things, scratching, pinching, rubbing, covering eyes, self-grooming gestures, and manipulation of objects.

Though adaptors are not intended to act as symbols, they can reveal something of the emotional state of the individual exhibiting them.

Postures and gestures   Various postural and gestural movements serve as emblems, illustrators, regulators, and adaptors. However, they also combine to serve as collective expressions of attitudes.

Mehrabian provides an excellent summary of the clusters of postures and gestures that relate to his three metaphors.

Portraying the immediacy metaphor, for example, postures that lean toward or open to another tend to show liking or warmth. Those that slouch, lean away, or close off from another tend to reveal disliking and coldness.

In terms of the power metaphor, Henley suggests that certain clusters are associated with a person of power and status in communication with one of lesser status. The clusters of the powerful person include relaxation, informality, close proximity, touching, staring and ignoring, showing emotion, and a nonsmiling expression.[14] In contrast, Henley concludes that the subordinate takes on clusters that include tension, circumspection, distance, nontouching, averting eyes while watching furtively, hiding emotion, and smiling.[15]

An additional important finding made by Henley is that the postures and gestures between men and women often virtually parallel those for status nonequals, with men in the position of power.[16]

---

[14]Nancy M. Henley, BODY POLITICS: POWER, SEX, AND NONVERBAL COMMUNICATION© 1977, pp. 124–150. Adapted by permission of Prentice-Hall, Inc., Englewood Cliffs, New Jersey.

[15]Ibid.

[16]Ibid.

Fitting with the metaphor of responsiveness—of adaptation—people straight-forwardly exhibit many expressions. Such expressions include cheerfulness, affec-tion, pleasantness, joy, fear, anger, nervousness, caution, worry, and defensiveness. They also attempt to hide emotions. Knapp summarizes that clues to deception include:

Shifty eyes	Looking at the	Scissoring legs
Passing hands	ceiling	High-pitched voice
over mouth	Averted eyes	More adaptors and
More uncertain	Fewer illustrators	longer adaptor
hand-shrug		duration
emblems	Less nodding	More speech errors
Tearing at fingernails	Tense leg positions	Frequent leg-
		position shifts
Hand pressed	Drawn-out smile	Hands holding onto
into cheek		knees[17]

Though research into deception cues yields incomplete results, one finding seems to be consistent: "Obviously, failure to perform nonverbal acts which ordi-narily accompany verbal acts is a sign something is wrong."[18]

Touch

Montagu and Matson urge that American adults are deteriorated children because they have been desensitized to the communication possible through the largest human organ—the skin.[19] Though the power of the tactile sense has been subli-mated in this culture, it still can carry a great deal of a message. Touching can show tenderness, affection, encouragement, and the full range of emotions.

The infant begins its communicative life largely through the sense of touch. As the baby is fed, suckled, nuzzled, hugged, kissed, cradled, powdered, changed, cuddled, and stroked, human exchange begins to unfold. The denial of extensive touching can have untold negative impact upon the infant's development.

For children and adults the amount of accepted touching varies with many factors. Some of them are sex, age, culture, environment, the state of a relationship, intimacy, intensionality, power and status, and immediacy.

The greater freedom of the male to touch the female is reported in the preced-ing paragraphs to illustrate differences in power and dominance. Other negative attitudes toward touching in this culture arise from diverse sources. They include the Puritan ethic and attitudes about sex, the emotionalism associating same-sex touching with homosexuality and lesbianism, and the ritualism of handshakes and backslaps.

Touching actions serve as regulators (guiding, attention-getting, accenting) and as both conveyors and elicitors of positive as well as negative feelings. Touching conveys the total range from highly impersonal to highly personal meanings.

If a person touches a portion of another person's body that is considered unavailable at a given stage of a relationship, the reaction likely will be negative.

---

[17]Knapp, *Nonverbal Communication*, pp. 229–232.

[18]Ibid., p. 231.

[19]Ashley Montagu and Floyd Matson, *The Human Connection* (New York: McGraw-Hill Book Company, 1979).

However, if even a nonintimate pats your back as an accompaniment to a compliment, you probably will receive it as a positive stroke.

Controlled research conducted by Fisher, Rytting, and Heslin yielded this discussion of the results:

> . . . a casual touch of a very short duration in a Professional/Functional situation [library clerks checking out books to university students] had positive consequences for the recipient. . . . subjects in touch conditions evidenced more positive responses than subjects in no touch conditions. Further, . . . [the analysis] suggests that while the response to the touch condition was uniformly positive for females, it was more ambivalent for males. . . . It is suggested that females, who have had more experience as recipients of touch from significant others, may be more comfortable than males when receiving momentary interpersonal touches from strangers.[20]

The movement toward sensitivity training, body awareness, and encounter groups seems to indicate the rekindling of an interest in understanding touching. As a wise communicator, you will learn as much as you can about the subject.

Appearance

Your appearance both reflects and creates your own self-image—as well as the image that others have of you.

Three categories can organize a review of the nonverbal communication inherent in appearance: (1) the person, (2) clothing, and (3) accessories.

The person Many human characteristics contribute to one's general appearance. Height and weight carry meaning in people's minds. Body type also has an impact on the perception of others. The three descriptive classes most used are the ectomorph, the mesomorph, and the endomorph. The ectomorph is thin, tall, and fragile; the mesomorph, muscular, bony, and athletic; and the endomorph, fat, soft, and round.

Many people attach personality traits to the three body types—and stereotype them on that basis. Some of the stereotypes include:

Ectomorphic	Mesomorphic	Endomorphic
anxious	dominant	dependent
self-conscious	confident	complacent
precise	energetic	sluggish
shy	determined	placid
awkward	outgoing	affectionate
withdrawn	active	cooperative
cautious	assertive	forgiving
nervous	adventurous	sensitive

Body hair also proves to be a point of judgment about a person. Though the debate has settled somewhat, the length of the hair on the male head has been a major source of contention based on nonverbal perception. Fights, banishments, and even killings have occurred because of the demand from parents that sons have their hair cut.

---

[20]Jeffrey D. Fisher, Marvin Rytting, and Richard Heslin, "Hands Touching Hands: Affective and Evaluative Effects on Interpersonal Touch," *Sociometry* 39 (December 1976): 419.

Hair color—particularly for women—also creates nonverbal messages. Red hair is associated with a fiery temper; blonde, with stupidity; and brunette, with seductiveness.

Moustaches, beards, and sideburns make nonverbal statements to some. Moreover, hair on the male's chest and even on legs and arms is considered to be manly in many quarters. However, facial and body hair for the female is considered unattractive—to the extent that many women shave underarms and legs in order to remove it.

Skin color also bears on judgments about people. Racial stereotypes arise in some cultures, based on variations in skin colors. In addition, many lighter skinned people struggle to obtain deep suntans. The pale look is considered unhealthy and sometimes ugly.

A person's appearance also depends on age, culture, occupation, and sex. General standards exist for how a person should look on the basis of these factors.

The state of grooming and cleanliness also communicate. A common phrase during the height of the debate raging over the length of male hair was, "I don't care how long it is if he'd just keep it combed and clean." Although the statement was not always reflective of true feelings, it did indicate a reliance upon cleanliness and grooming as symbols of a person's values.

Another category of nonverbal personal characteristics deals with general attractiveness. The premium placed upon beauty in this culture has worked in a particularly detrimental fashion toward females. Research has shown, moreover, that unattractive children receive significantly less positive attention from parents and teachers than do their attractive counterparts, and that this lack of attention often results in poorer self-images for the less attractive students.

Handicaps also—unfortunately—communicate nonverbally in a negative way to many people. People who have some abnormality or deformity in face or form—whether from birth, accidents, or disease—too often are discounted as somehow second-rate citizens. This unfortunate assessment of being "different" often drives a wedge, preventing real communication between them and the other participants.

The general carriage and demeanor of a person report something of the importance of that person. Contrast your evaluation of a person who walks firmly with chin held high and one who shuffles with a dejected look. Picture someone you know who has a personal charismatic aura. Do such qualities emanate more from the nonverbal realm than from the verbal one?

Clothing A brief recitation of some words and phrases should illustrate the powerful communicative role that clothing plays. Make mental associations as these types of garb call types of people to mind:

Black leather jackets	White socks	Jeans
Miniskirts	Evening gowns	Fur coats
Polyester knit pantsuits	Cashmere sweaters	Imprinted T-shirts
Bikinis	Tailored suits	Bow ties
Sheer fabrics	Frills	Plunging necklines
Corduroy	Gray flannel suits	Tight-fitting clothing
Earth shoes	Boots	Sandals
Hats	Stockings	Bare legs
Slacks and shirts	Skirts and blouses	Dresses

Choices of clothing speak quite loudly about one's personality, status, power, attitudes, values, behavior, occupation, and confidence. Such importance has been attached to clothing for the business executive that several best-selling books on the subject exist, setting out the kinds of clothing that establish an image of power.

Accessories   Articles other than garments contribute to appearance and dress. Recall the imagery you associate with these examples of such accessories:

Pins	Badges	Emblems	Buttons
Tatoos	Earrings	Other jewelry	Cosmetics
Eyeglasses	Sunglasses	False eyelashes	Scarves
False fingernails	False teeth	Gold inlays	Tinted hair
Billfolds	Umbrellas	Canes	Purses

Space

Like the animals, humans stake out and maintain territories and attempt to control bubbles of space around themselves. This inclination is so strong that encroachment upon another's space can lead to serious miscommunication.

The use of space and territory (proxemics) varies from culture to culture. However, cultures do have many common features. For example, ownership of land and other real property provides evidence of territorial concerns in most of them. Disputes over boundaries between nations tragically form the basis for many devastating breakdowns in communication—wars.

General concepts   Question yourself about some aspects of space and territory. Have you ever:

1.   Held a book or newspaper in front of your face, looked out of a window, pretended to be asleep, or stared into space on public transportation or in a crowded waiting room?

2.   Looked straight ahead or at the floor indicator or averted your eyes so as not to meet those of someone else in an elevator?

3.   Used your toe, a stick, a towel, or a chair to mark boundaries around "your" area on a beach?

4.   Identified a chair, an area on a library table, or a desk as yours—and felt perturbed if someone else occupied it?

5.   Drawn an imaginary line or placed objects down the middle of the back seat of a car to separate quarreling children?

6.   Drawn a line and dared someone to step over it?

7.   Been scolded as a child for sitting in your father's chair?

8.   Talked more to someone across a banquet table than to those close beside you—thus subconsciously trying to ignore their invasion into your territory? If you did talk to someone next to you, turned your body and chair and leaned back in order to create some space?

9.   Sat next to two people on a sofa or in the seat of a car and talked straight ahead rather than consciously acknowledging them as occupying some of your space?

10.   Thought about how sports and games involve competition over terri-

tory—even to the extent of often arranging spectators on different sides of the playing field according to team allegiance?

11.   Been seated in an area such as a bus, office, waiting room, restaurant, library, or classroom and felt threatened by someone sitting down beside you when many other isolated seats were available?

12.   Sat next to someone in a situation such as that described in the last example and observed the person squirm or even move to a new location?

13.   Felt isolated even in crowded circumstances because of the territorial walls erected by others?

14.   Placed a sign on your room door to indicate that it is your zone of privacy—your territory?

15.   Been upset to learn that someone has invaded your home or room in your absence? (Some people who have been robbed state that the loss of material items does not bother them so much as knowing that some unknown person has been there and touched their belongings.)

16.   Walked, jogged, or bicycled into a residential neighborhood and felt or been told that you were not wanted on "their" streets? Been run off the road by a motorist who obviously thought you had no right to the space?

17.   Considered the difference in the amounts of space allocated to first-class and coach passengers on commercial airlines?

18.   Thought of how ownership of a "big" car has spatial and status meanings associated with it?

As you read the questions, you likely thought, "My feelings in the situation depend on other factors as well." If so, you were correct. The reaction to territorial invasion does vary with the circumstances. Knapp suggests:

> Although we often think people vigorously defend their territory, the type of defense is highly dependent on who the intruder is, why the intrusion is taking place, what type of territory is being encroached upon, what type of encroachment is used, . . . how long the encroachment takes, and where it occurs.[21]

Massing of humans   Whether one's space is violated or not can depend on the massing of humans. A mass does not always have a negative impact on communication. Many people regularly seek out and enjoy settings that include large numbers of other people; witness the popularity of dining out. However, overcrowding may create an emotional state brought on by the undesirable presence of too many "trespassers."

Distances   Another refinement calls for distinctions among the types of distances over which people communicate. Hall's writings suggest four such types: public space, formal space, informal space, and intimate space.[22]

Public distance marks off speeches or lectures to an audience where the closest person is about ten or more feet away.

---

[21]Knapp, *Nonverbal Communication*, p. 141.

[22]Excerpt from THE SILENT LANGUAGE by Edward T. Hall, pp. 163–164. Copyright© 1959 by Edward T. Hall. Reprinted by permission of Doubleday & Company, Inc.

Formal distance calls for about four to eight feet of space between participants in such activities as job interviews.

The distance is about three feet—about an arm's length away—in informal settings. It is appropriate for casual conversation.

Intimate distance (about eighteen inches or less) is reserved strictly for those invited into it. Encroachment upon it by a nonintimate often leads to a significant reaction on the part of the person whose space is violated.

Respect for space   People tend to honor the space of others. They avoid violating it and become quite uncomfortable when they must. You probably have apologized many times to people whose territory you have entered accidentally or against your will.

Time

The passage of time divides human life into centuries, decades, years, weeks, days, hours, minutes, and seconds. Time is based on lightness and darkness, the seasons, hormonal and other biological cycles, and the life cycle itself. Time undergirds all communication. However, time also plays direct roles in communication.

You doubtless grasp the sense of an observation such as: "It was Jack Benny's timing that made him a comedic genius." The statement acknowledges that communication involves more than simply projecting verbal and nonverbal messages through space.

Humans have time clocks within them. If you have ever flown across several time zones within one day's time and experienced jet lag, you know how disoriented you become. Similar experiences occur with the switching of work hours among day, swing, and graveyard shifts. Some people even grumble about the two annual adjustments for daylight-saving time.

Other evidence of the time-bound nature of Americans can be found through these vignettes:

1. Workers punch time clocks.
2. Passengers become upset because a bus (plane, train) is late.
3. Transportation schedules include departure and arrival times so precisely as 9:02 A.M.
4. Radio announcers state the time frequently.
5. People place clocks in virtually every room and office in which they live and work.
6. A worker tells everyone who will listen about cutting 4 minutes off the trip to the job that morning.
7. Time-management seminars abound.
8. People admonish others to use time wisely.
9. One of the major analytical approaches to business and economic conditions involves time series.
10. Many producers base pay scales on numbers of pieces produced per hour.
11. Production experts conduct time-and-motion studies.
12. People complain that they do not have the time to do what they want or need to do.
13. People feel complimented or honored when others "take the time" to do something for them.

14. A supervisor reminds an operator, "Time is money."

Preoccupation with time leads to stereotypes about the proper durations of time for given activities. Generally, managers require employees to work five 8-hour days a week, beginning and ending at the same times each day. Many of them resist the four-day week and the concept of flexible working hours. Students become upset if a professor keeps them two or three minutes past the end of class or keeps them the full period on the first day of class.

Movies should be no longer than two hours—including commercials when shown on television. Most television shows should be 30 minutes to an hour long. Though plays may have some flexibility, the two-hour limit, including expected intermissions, prevails. A sermon or a speech should be from 20 to 30 minutes in length.

Even when a lunch break takes only 30 minutes, it is called a lunch hour. Similarly, academic people still call a 50-minute examination an hour exam.

Another type of concern about time relates to what people consider the proper time of day to do certain things. For example, people who eat the main meal of the day near midday, and call it "dinner," are considered somewhat uncouth by those who have dinner at 8 P.M. Equally misunderstood are those who eat the third meal of the day at 4:30 or 5:00 P.M.

How people treat time is important. An applicant late for an interview probably loses any chance for the job. Being late for a party, however, is not considered improper. In fact, people often consider those who arrive exactly on time or, perish the thought, early, to be social novices.

The higher the status, the later one can be for a scheduled beginning time. For example, doctors expect patients to be on time for appointments, but doctors may be late for theirs. Professors may walk into classrooms late, but they expect students to be on time.

(641 words)
(test on page 81)

Environment

The nonverbal environment affecting your communication includes other people, things, and nature.

People   This book deals primarily with communication between or among specifically identified participants. However, other people also indirectly affect transactions. The section on space deals with one of them—the effect of massing.

People enter into the communication process under other circumstances, in the dimension of active or passive outsiders. Their presence often has a negative effect. Recall making a telephone call while other people could see or hear you. Their presence likely made your conversation different than a private call would have been. As long as you felt that the others were passive and did not enter into the process, their impact probably was minimal. However, as soon as you noticed them listening or reacting to your words, your conversation likely shifted from the form it would have taken otherwise.

You no doubt can recreate similar occurrences involving interpersonal conversations in an office, a waiting room, an airplane, a train, or a bus.

A particularly telling experience involves your starting a conversation in privacy and then having someone enter your environment. You can sense the shift in both your and your partner's modes of expression. The interloper has altered your environment by becoming a part of it. Again, the degree of the alteration of your original communication depends upon the activity or passivity of the one who interrupted.

The presence of other humans can have a positive impact upon a given transaction. For example, if you are angry at the other direct participant, the presence of others may lead you to control yourself. The interjection of a third party can also create silences that allow you to collect your thoughts. It can also allow you to end a conversation that you already wanted to terminate.

Think also about the impact of others around you when you read or write. Have you had people read over your shoulder? Have you become irritated or lost concentration as a result? Have you ever felt that someone was eyeing you as you attempted to read a book in a public library? Outsiders in your reading/writing environment usually create interference rather than make any positive contribution.

Things   Consider these characteristics of a *room*:

Size	Shape	Location
Arrangement of	Architectural	Colors
the furniture	design	Decorations
in it	Presence or	Number and location
Draperies or	absence of	of windows
blinds	carpet	Odors
Acoustics	Lighting	Noises
General aesthetics	Temperature	

Research has shown that virtually all of these things have an effect upon human communication behavior.

Have you ever entered a home or office and felt hesitant to touch anything? Have you entered other homes and offices and felt engulfed with warmth and invitation?

As an example in the business world, picture the two kinds of banks. Traditional banks are cold, austere, echoing, uncarpeted, pillared, marbled bastions of clinical finance. Contemporary banks are warm, woodtoned, carpeted, inviting, human places for dealing with money matters.

Function suggests much of the structure and arrangement of buildings, rooms, and contents. However, the shrewd communicator will not allow function to become a dictator that creates negative surroundings.

The *arrangement of furniture* also serves to illustrate the importance of things in the communication environment. First, picture a classroom with the chairs arranged in rows, facing the professor. Contrast that image with a room with chairs in a circle or semicircle. More interplay usually takes place when people face each other than when they line up one behind another.

A desk often serves as a barrier between communication participants. Thus, the placement of a desk becomes an important nonverbal element.

The arrangement of chairs and sofas in a home or office may not facilitate conversation, or at the very least, may alter patterns of conversation from what they otherwise would be.

Bright *lights* stimulate activity. Dim lights contribute to intimacy between intimates, but may create some discomfort between nonintimates.

The *temperature, humidity, and ventilation* of a room can have a significant impact upon the communication that transpires there.

Though not consistently affirmed through research, *colors* do seem to affect people's communicative efforts.

Hues with a possible positive or stimulating influence include yellow, yellow-green, green, blue, violet, purple, red, and orange. Colors with the potential for a negative effect are black, brown, and white.

The *layouts and structural features* of rooms, buildings, and even cities affect communication.

Building design can cause or allow people to encounter or avoid one another. Offset office or apartment doors on either side of a hall lead to less communication than occurs when doors face each other. Offices or apartments near elevators or stairway landings lead to more interchange than do those removed from them.

Locations, sizes, and designs of offices relate to power and status. Generally, the higher the status of an individual, the higher the office is in a multistoried building. The office frequently is large and requires visitors to overcome great distances and barriers to reach it. It probably has an outside wall with windows, with the corner room (most windows) usually occupied by the executive with the most power. It usually has a door. It may be next to a private elevator leading to an exit by the parking space nearest the entrance.

Obviously, the nonverbal accompaniments of power tend to cut the individual off from colleagues with whom communication needs to be an ongoing process. Therefore, the wise executive reserves that bastion of privacy for the kinds of creativity that require it. However, he or she moves out into the other offices, hallways, and workplaces for as much of the day as can be spared. Otherwise, the executive may find that the trappings of status destroy the interactions that allowed that status to develop in the first place.

In many ways the people who work in large, central, open areas have the advantage. Thrown into regular contact with one another, they learn a great deal about business and about human relations.

Fences, walls, dividers—all represent barriers to human communication. Though sometimes desirable, the separation also can be detrimental.

A quick way to establish the impact of *sounds* is to recall a time when you changed environments and had difficulty adjusting to the new set of stimuli. The classic example occurs when a city dweller goes to the country or the country dweller goes to the city. Either finds the unfamiliar mix of noises (or lack of them) to be so disconcerting that he or she becomes edgy and cannot even sleep well.

Research has shown that the type and volume of music they hear communicates nonverbally with people. Plato urged that only martial types of music be played in order to keep people in the tight, militaristic, functional mode. In 1979 music on radios and televisions was outlawed in Iran because it was said that it destroyed the desired religious attitude and had a "numbing" effect on the mind.

Elsewhere, though, music is piped into offices, factories, supermarkets, mental institutions, bus stations, and even dairy barns and chicken houses. The type and the intensity of music relate to the site, the people, the time of day, and the type of activity desired.

Soothing, quiet music is chosen for mental institutions. Office workers may begin the day hearing soft music, but may find it slowly intensified for the times when people tend to tire—particularly just after lunch and near quitting time. Supermarket shoppers often hear fast, upbeat music. The idea is to keep the customers moving and buying.

Any pervasive *aroma* can play a part in the creation of an environment. Think how these aromas might affect your behavior:

Cooking smells	Musty odors from carpets
Fumes from paint or chemicals	or draperies
used in office work	Smells of garbage and
Odor of too many human	pollutants
bodies in a small, hot	Fragrance of flowers
area	and house plants
Room deodorants	Perfumes
Colognes	Shaving lotions

One last example of the importance of odors to human interaction exists in the controversial topic of smoking. Though all of the controversy does not center upon the smell alone, a great deal of it does. The battle between smokers and nonsmokers often creates a severely destructive wedge between communication parties—all from a nonverbal, environmental factor.

The nonverbal surroundings include things that *touch* as well as those that affect the other senses. You feel the textures of the throw pillows, upholstery fabrics, woods, and metals used in construction of chairs, sofas, and other office furniture.

Even through your shoes you experience a different nonverbal sense from a carpeted floor and a tile, concrete, or wooden floor. The extent of the ramifications of floor material can be assessed by considering the person who stands and walks on concrete all day, compared to one who does so on carpet. The tired and aching feet that result from the concrete have a significant impact upon the person who must cope with them.

In similar fashion, the cushioned seat and the hard metal or wooden seat can make the difference in the behavior of the persons sitting on the two types.

Nature   Natural elements create an atmosphere that affects humans. If you work ten miles from home and a blizzard occurs, your well-being is affected—no matter how perfect your immediate environment.

The *weather* has an untold influence on personality undertones for many people. Heat, cold, barometric pressure, humidity, wind, ice, rain, snow, sunshine, and cloudiness all affect moods and performance. Gray, overcast, rainy days put some people into a depression.

In a clearly related way, the *climate* of a region contributes to the undercurrent of general human activity. People in the temperate climates tend toward alertness, activity, and achievement more than those people in the tropical ones. Cold and low humidity serve as stimuli; heat and high humidity serve as depressants.

Variety in the elements of weather and climate also adds a stimulating dimension to human interchange, which is missing in areas in which the weather rarely changes.

Combinations of weather and climate factors have a multivaried effect on human behavior. A 25-mile-an-hour wind has a quite different meaning for someone sailing on a beautiful lake on a warm spring day than for someone standing on a drab street corner in a cold rain waiting for a bus.

Even for fixed people and locations, the seasons of the year can have a dramatic effect. You doubtless can recall emotional lows associated with the starkness of winter and emotional highs associated with the burst of spring.

Consider one more piece of evidence of the importance of temperature: the relationship between summer heat and certain kinds of mass human unrest. Such events as the destructive urban riots of the 1960's relate to such complex factors as the state of politics, the level of the economy, racial discrimination, and ghetto conditions. However, the factors exist all year, and the riots erupted in the heat of summer.

Some research has related *solar and lunar activities* to mood changes or "swings." A great deal of skepticism greets those who claim the relationships; however, some people suggest that behavior is predictably more agitated when the moon is full and that accidents relate to the cycles of both the sun and moon.

GUIDELINES FOR RECEIVING NONVERBAL MESSAGES

Now that you have reviewed the concepts associated with nonverbal communication, apply them through a base provided by the guidelines for all communication receiving. In this context the guidelines are:

1. Define your purposes, the sender's purposes, yourself, the sender, and the environment.
2. Identify the nonverbal channel.
3. Control the interference internal and external to you and the sender.
4. Select, observe, and decode the messages in light of the purposes, the participants, the environment, the channel, and the interference.
5. Use feedback to and from the sender.
6. Evaluate at each stage.

Define Purposes, Participants, and Environment

As a nonverbal receiver, begin to identify your reasons for receiving nonverbal messages. By doing so, you can set priorities and become more selective.

Some examples of nonverbal-receiving purposes—involving decisions both to receive and not to receive—include:

1. Even though crowds of people bother me, I will attend this party because of the business contacts I can make there.
2. My fear of hurricanes nags at me so constantly that I'm going to move from the coast.
3. Though this painting depresses me, I will display it. It would hurt Uncle Charlie if I didn't. I'll avoid looking at it.
4. Alice always gets right in my face when she talks with me, so I will discuss this assignment with Sonia.
5. I'm not going out to lunch with George any more; his unpressed clothes and dirty hair embarrass me.

6. Though Mary's trembling and being in a wheel chair made me uneasy at first, I now kneel, squat, or sit down to meet her at her level. She's an interesting, enjoyable person.
7. I watch Harold's hands when he talks; they often tell me something different than his words.
8. I dislike Dana's habit of scratching her head, so I look away when she does it.
9. I try to stay out of John's path. He seems to think that being male and the boss give him the right to throw his arm around my shoulder any time he wants.
10. I'm going to study Ms. Klaus's face when I tell her the news; I want to see how she takes it.
11. I always try to maintain eye contact with Mr. Metsger, so I can figure out what he really expects of me.

Because so many purposes emanate from the sender's subconscious regions, nonverbal messages can be particularly difficult to identify. For example, as you receive, you may not be able to decide why a sender speaks softly, grimaces, grabs your hand, raises eyebrows, or interjects an "uh" every few words. Indeed, the sender may not know why.

Analyze yourself, the sender, and the environment carefully. Try to understand how physical, psychological, and environmental factors affect your nonverbal receiving.

Identify Channel

Because the qualities of channels vary, make a conscious effort to isolate the channel that is being used for the messages you choose to receive.

For example, suppose you become so preoccupied with a person's good looks that you overlook the intellectual and human content of other nonverbal and verbal messages. In that situation, you have let a narrow channel choice do both you and the sender a disservice.

Control Interference

Nonverbal reception does not always require the intellectual power necessary for verbal reception. However, the potential for interference looms up for five senses instead of two.

For instance, suppose a sender chooses a facial channel for transmitting an image of happiness, but has a face frozen into an expression of sadness. Obviously, then, interference to the desired transfer exists.

If a message of strength is entrusted to vocal cues that emanate from a singularly weak voice, the channel choice has erected a roadblock in the path of success.

Interference exists when a person stands in your line of vision as you attempt to observe a speaker's gestures. It emerges when the sounds of a low-flying airplane cover the sighs of a colleague who is discontented.

Potential barriers to effective nonverbal communication appear when verbal and nonverbal messages contradict one another.

The overriding interference to nonverbal reception, however, resides with the receiver's failure to recognize the value of nonverbal messages. For whatever reasons, many people function as communicative cripples. They do so because they do not develop the appropriate awareness and appreciation of the wealth of information available through nonverbal channels.

Select, Observe, and Decode Messages

As is true for both reading and listening, the test of nonverbal reception lies with the ability to assign meanings to received messages. Dictionaries of nonverbal symbols do not exist, and most nonverbal behaviors possess no common or accepted meanings. As a culminating problem for the decoder, many nonverbal messages come from unwitting senders.

To improve your ability to decode nonverbal messages, study formal research findings about possible meanings for the various nonverbal types. More important, develop your own personal research and awareness.

Use Feedback

Nonverbal feedback sometimes tells more about a person's emotional state than he or she might communicate with words. Nonverbal channels, however, cannot handle feedback of abstract or technical data.

Evaluate

Evaluate the progress of nonverbal communication toward meeting both your and the sender's purposes. Adjust accordingly.

TECHNIQUES FOR RECEIVING NONVERBAL MESSAGES

Complete this study of nonverbal reception by considering some suggestions for improving your appreciation of nonverbal messages. Consider how best to:

1. Select proper nonverbal receiving mode
2. Concentrate and think
3. Be an active nonverbal receiver
4. Improve symbol/meaning manipulation
5. Control physical and psychological setting
6. Receive for retention
7. Preview
8. Review
9. Practice

Select Proper Nonverbal Receiving Mode

Nonverbal messages involve less abstraction than verbal ones. Therefore, the selection of a receiving mode involves different emphasis than for reading and listening. You select reading and listening modes primarily on the basis of desired levels of comprehension and retention. While you need to attend to comprehension and retention as you select the nonverbal receiving mode, you also must consider what sensory combinations are available because of the very nature of nonverbal receiving.

As one example, cast yourself into the role of an executive of a large corporation. Because morale in your section has been low, you determine to learn the reasons in order to try to solve whatever problems exist. You think carefully about how best to gather the information.

First, you consider distributing a multiple-choice questionnaire. You realize, however, that you might not be able to write questions that will get to the heart of the concerns. In addition, you know that a potential wealth of information you might receive from nonverbal messages will be lost through such an instrument.

Next, you consider an open-end questionnaire. You decide that some employees might volunteer some useful information. However, you also realize that many would be hesitant to commit feelings to writing for fear the permanent record would be used against them. Moreover, you once again must lose revealing nonverbal data that simply could not accompany a document. You continue to consider alternatives.

Ultimately, you decide that you will use three channels: (1) a combined multiple-choice, open-end questionnaire, (2) some small group discussions, and (3) one-to-one interviews with any who desire to participate. Adding the face-to-face oral verbal and nonverbal dimensions to the written verbal ones greatly improves the chances for a successful determination.

Concentrate and Think

As a receiver, develop the ability to concentrate upon nonverbal components of communication transactions. Make yourself aware that they exist. Consciously and continually think about them and develop meanings for them.

Be an Active Nonverbal Receiver

As a nonverbal receiver, take a responsible part for the nonverbal aspects of exchanges. Because senders often create nonverbal messages from a subconscious state, your work as a nonverbal receiver becomes even more difficult than for many verbal messages.

Improve Symbol/Meaning Manipulation

Overcome some of the difficulties of extracting meanings from nonverbal messages by asking questions about them. You can pose the questions through either verbal or nonverbal channels.

Ask such verbal questions as: "Are you angry?" "I notice that you've been holding your head; are you feeling ill?" "Are you as happy as your laughter makes you sound?" "Do you dislike the way I'm doing this?"

By doing so, you will elicit a response and learn something from the response. You might receive confirmation, contradiction, or a mixed reaction to your original interpretation.

Such questions also will bring the sender's subjective state to a level of consciousness. By your perception-checking process, then, you help others to become more aware of how they communicate without using words. You also lead them to think about whether their nonverbal messages reflect their feelings correctly.

Take one precaution as you increase the testing of your interpretation of others' nonverbal messages, though: Do not become so strident that you make people self-conscious about any rather inhibited clues to their identity. When you feel that the probability is high that you have interpreted nonverbal cues correctly, use subtle, nonverbal checks. Reserve the overt, verbal checks for situations serious enough to warrant them, and for the occasions when you are unsure about your ability to decode properly.

You may be thinking that the ability to interpret some nonverbal messages requires psychiatric or, at the least, psychological training. Indeed, instinctive non-verbal cues form one of the major communication categories available to psychiatrists or psychologists. Their skills are perhaps the epitome of nonverbal receiving. However, you can develop your ability to perform as a competent nonverbal receiver without extensive study in psychiatry—if you will read, think, and become human-centered.

Another hurdle to decoding involves the restrictions on the numbers of abstractions that can be communicated nonverbally. Again, take a practical approach. Accept that you certainly cannot explain Bayesian theory without using words. However, also accept that you can do a better job of explaining it if you accompany the words with every possible nonverbal means you can use.

Though the nonverbal alone cannot carry abstract messages, avoid dismissing the importance of nonverbal contributions to their communication. A very abstract message occurs when someone turns heel and walks away from you in the midst of a discussion.

Control Physical and Psychological Setting

Visual and aural nonverbal receiving happens under the same general types of circumstances as verbal receiving.

Because nonverbal reception may involve touching, develop an appropriate mental and physical sensitivity to it. If you accept touching as a beneficial nonverbal contributor, create circumstances in which it can take place. Receive a handshake warmly and with a firm, but not crushing response. Lean toward a person if you believe he or she wants to communicate through a touch to the shoulder.

Though not a popular topic, human odor probably does communicate something of a person's being. Though both emitted and received at an instinctual level, humans' odors may contribute a small part to the overall interpretation of messages.

Receive for Retention

The same devices used to improve retention of information gained from reading and listening also apply to the improvement of nonverbal retention.

For example, say you want to remember the nonverbal shapes of the graphs of the cumulative frequency polygons (Chapter 16). To do so, you might liken them to forward- and backward-bending lazy-S curves, or to halves of bell-shaped curves.

Preview

The preview technique does not apply as fully to nonverbal receiving as to verbal. However, many nonverbal situations do call for careful preliminary thinking. Consider a few examples. If you plan to attend a dance performance, you will improve your reception by learning ahead of time about the performers and the program. Suppose you plan to attend a workshop which you know will involve a large number of media presentations. Try to learn the types and titles and read summaries of them if possible. For an upcoming briefing, try to picture the kinds of charts, graphs, and nonverbal human exchanges that may accompany it.

Review

During and after completion of a nonverbal reception, review what you have just experienced. The review process will aid comprehension and retention, will help you learn from the transaction, and will help you to set the stage for the next reception.

Practice

A summary recommendation for improving nonverbal reception calls for you to practice. Repetition of correct procedures for nonverbal receiving contributes significantly to improved performance. First, you likely will improve your performance as a nonverbal receiver as you practice your performance as a nonverbal sender, and vice versa. Good senders are often good receivers. Therefore, practice in both nonverbal capacities to aid your receiving.

Early in your practice, try to lengthen the time of your exposure to nonverbal messages. To a point, the accuracy of decoding increases as the time of exposure increases. As you become more proficient, try to make your interpretation in shorter and shorter periods of time.

As you practice, learn to distinguish between nonverbal cues that have accepted meanings and those that do not. For example, many facial expressions are learned and carry with them common meanings.

As you practice, learn to recognize and deal with messages with double meanings. Avoid falling prey to the commonly held belief that the nonverbal always represents the truth when it conflicts with the verbal.

Practice in some deliberately contrived formal learning situations. Examples include role-playing and other interactions before a group, with feedback from the observing group and the other participants. Also use media presentations including videotapes of you and others interacting.

Practice nonverbal receiving in the real-life arena. Solicit feedback primarily through the kind of perception-checking that does not arouse defensiveness in the sender.

The keys to practiced efficiency as a nonverbal receiver, then, are several. They include a positive attitude toward nonverbal receiving, knowledge of the process, a great deal of successful personal experience, and the resolve to make yourself into a superior nonverbal receiver.

SUMMARY

Nonverbal communication is wordless, yet accompanies all verbal communication. Nonverbal communication can exist without verbal communication, however. In fact, you communicated nonverbally as a baby long before you uttered your first word.

You engage in nonverbal communication when you listen to instrumental music, taste an apple, hold hands with a child, look at an oil painting, and smell the aroma of a spring day. Unfortunately, nonverbal communication often has gone virtually unnoticed by the academic and business sectors. However, the serious student should not ignore the nonverbal realm; it is an integral part of communicating.

Nonverbal communication constitutes the majority of communication. It involves symbols emanating from the human and nonhuman worlds. Nonverbal communication, which often occurs at a subconscious level, conveys emotions and attitudes, not complex information.

One classification of types of nonverbal communication is organized around *immediacy*, *power*, and *responsiveness* behaviors.

The *face*, *eyes*, and *voice* create nonverbal messages. *Paralanguage* includes vocal *qualifiers*, *segregates*, *differentiators*, and *qualities*.

Human *movement* also contributes to nonverbal transactions. Five categories describe such movement: (1) *emblems*, (2) *illustrators*, (3) *regulators*, (4) *adaptors*, and (5) *postures* and *gestures*.

Touch is another way in which humans send and receive nonverbal messages.

Appearance affects nonverbal transactions. Relevant features include body features and type, hair and skin color, cleanliness, physical handicaps, clothing, the attractiveness of the person, and accessories.

The strong need for *personal space* and *territory* plays an important role in nonverbal communication.

Time and timing affect communication.

The nonverbal environment in which you operate includes people, things, and nature.

Communication guidelines for nonverbal receiving are:

1. Define purposes, participants, and environment.
2. Identify nonverbal channel.
3. Control interference.
4. Select, observe, and decode messages in light of purposes, participants, environment, channel, and interference.
5. Use feedback.
6. Evaluate.

Techniques for effectively receiving within the nonverbal guidelines are:

1. Select proper nonverbal receiving mode.
2. Concentrate and think.
3. Be an active nonverbal receiver.
4. Improve symbol/meaning manipulation.
5. Control physical and psychological setting.
6. Receive for retention.

7. Preview.
8. Review.
9. Practice.

Practice

1. Describe what type of person each of the following is. What is the person's mood? Is he or she "saying" something? What?

JOHN   ELIZABETH   RODNEY   NORA

2. Read the following sentence aloud several times to express alternately happiness, anger, fear, discomfort, boredom, and condescension.

   The general carriage and demeanor of a person report something of the status and power of that person.

   What was your tone of voice and facial expression for each mood?

3. Watch for and record the nonverbal actions of a professor in one of your other classes. Pay particular attention to facial expressions, body movements and gestures, and appearance as described in this chapter. Does the professor's nonverbal behavior support or contradict her or his verbal actions? Explain. (Do not identify the professor in your record.)

4. In your opinion, what forms of dress and types of grooming habits make a person look strong and serious? Weak and frivolous? You may want to discuss this in a four- or five-person group.

5. Height, race, sex, physical handicaps, and a great deal of a person's physical appearance cannot be changed. Make a list of at least five ways you can overcome any prejudices you have against people who are tall or short, of another race, of the other sex, physically handicapped, or not particularly good-looking.

6. What is communicated by each of these nonverbal states?
   a. A business executive with dirty hair
   b. Loud music in a medical doctor's office
   c. A professor with her arms folded across her stomach
   d. A colleague with perspiration on his brow
   e. An open book on an unoccupied desk
   f. An overflowing trash can in an otherwise clean office
   g. A sigh
   h. A soft, comfortable visitor's chair outside the manager's office
   i. A crowded, noisy, hot room
   j. High-heeled shoes and a short, sheer dress
   k. An unbuttoned shirt and tight slacks
   l. Strong cologne or after-shave

     m. Dyed hair

     n. A person who smells of onions

     o. A person whose face is within inches of your face

     p. A person who interrupts your sentences

7. Meet in groups. Choose one person to read the paragraph provided. The speaker should try to support nonverbally the intent of the paragraph (a welcoming speech). Evaluate her or his performance. What nonverbal acts supported or contradicted the speaker's message?

> Welcome to the Snelton Automobile Plant. As you tour the main assembly line, feel free to ask questions or make comments. We are particularly interested in your criticisms. Thanks for coming. We have looked forward to your visit for weeks. Enjoy!

8. What nonverbal aspects of your person or your behavior do you wish to change? How can you go about changing them? Will the changes allow you to communicate more honestly and effectively?

9. Videotape or at least audiotape yourself. Listen to, view, and evaluate the nonverbal messages you send. Invite others to participate.

10. What nonverbal states and behaviors do you find distracting or downright maddening? For instance, some people do not like to have others yawn in their faces. Why do you find each of the states and behaviors distracting? What do they communicate to you? Do you sometimes exhibit these states and behaviors?

11. Meet with your group. You and each other group member give a short talk on what you would wear to a job interview with a conservative accounting firm. Center your evaluation of each group member's performance around these questions:

     a. Did the speaker use vocal segregates during her or his speech? If so, what were they?

     b. What did the speaker's vocal qualifiers communicate?

     c. What, if any, vocal differentiators did the speaker use?

     d. What was the general quality of the speaker's voice (pitch, volume, rate, resonance, rhythm, inflection, and enunciation)?

12. Six potential clients will be visiting your data processing firm in August. You have been chosen to give a sales presentation to the visitors. Your manager wants the presentation to last about an hour, with a thirty-minute discussion period to follow the presentation. You also are in charge of all of the arrangements for the meeting. What can you do before and during the meeting to overcome these nonverbal communication problems?

     a. Your office building is not air-conditioned. All of your offices are very hot in August, particularly in the afternoon.

     b. One of your company's conference rooms holds 200 people. The other conference room holds fifteen people, but is next to a noisy print shop.

     c. You want to wear a conservative suit, but you fear that you will get very hot in it.

     d. When you speak in front of a group of people, you wave your arms a great deal and frown frequently, both out of nervousness.

     e. All of your potential clients are much older than you.

     f. You fear that an hour-long presentation could bore the audience.

13. You are one of 20 management analysts in the program management department of the Aztec Corporation. You have noticed that a number of your colleagues are sending sloppy letters and reports to your clients. The letters and reports are written in pencil or pen on notebook or scrap paper, are stuffed in dirty or wrinkled envelopes, and are mailed late. Your department's manager does not understand the problem, but said that he would not mind if you would write a memorandum addressing the nonverbal message problem. Write a memorandum that covers the most important aspects of making choices of stationery, envelope, printing, format, and time. Try to convince your colleagues that inappropriate nonverbal accompaniments detract from the written message. Remember that your boss and your colleagues do not recognize that a problem exists.

14. You are the manager of the Finance Department of a major corporation. You know that your employees regard you as closed-minded, pretentious, and frightening. Every time you talk to one of your employees, he or she seems very nervous and eager to end the conversation. You realize that you cannot be an effective manager if most of your employees fear you, so you decide that you can begin to change your image by changing the furniture in your office.

Your office seems cold and forbidding, and you want to give your employees a chance to relax when they visit you.

Draw a plan for changing your office. Use the space provided or a separate piece of paper. Assume that you have plenty of money to buy new furnishings. Explain the reasoning behind the changes that you make.

After you have drawn up a plan, list several other nonverbal changes that you could make that might contribute to your new image. For example, you could plan to use a mirror to practice making kind and open facial expressions.

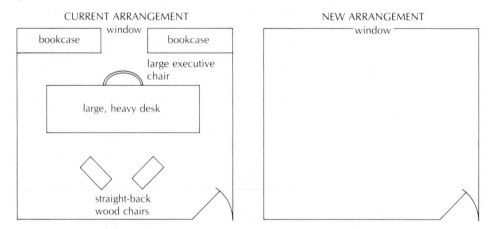

CURRENT ARRANGEMENT

NEW ARRANGEMENT

15. Study the following illustrated scene. Write a brief statement in response to each of these questions:

a. What is the relative status of each character?
b. What is the emotional state of the person seated behind the desk?
c. What is the emotional state of the person standing in front of the desk?
d. What nonverbal components in the scene led to the impressions stated in a–c?

You may want to meet with your group to discuss your written statements, the feelings associated with both roles, and how to overcome the nonverbal problems evident in the scene.

16. Hints for good time management include:
   a. Use a good reminder system.
   b. Increase reading and writing skills.
   c. Make routine decisions the first time you encounter the problems requiring them.
   d. Make monthly, weekly, and daily plans; put them in written form.
   e. Use the most efficient channel for each communication transaction.
   f. Announce meetings in advance.
   g. Cut the time spent on social conversation.
   h. Deliberately neglect low-priority problems; they may solve themselves.
   i. Have someone else take telephone calls, open mail, etc., and arrange the messages in order of importance for you.

   Think of two or three additional hints. Write a one- or two-page memorandum to your employees about time management. (Supply any information you need.) In the memorandum include expanded and illustrated versions for at least five of the hints listed here or suggested by you.

17. Use your dictionary and thesaurus to create meanings for these words. Use the words when you think, write, and speak so that you feel comfortable using them.

a. Acuity	h. Metaphor
b. Bastion	i. Poignant
c. Cliché	j. Punctual
d. Condescend	k. Ramification
e. Contradict	l. Status
f. Dominant	m. Stereotype
g. Intensionality	n. Triad

18. Take and score Self-Test 10 over the excerpt about time.

Self-Test 10
Excerpt about Time

A. (30 points each). For each multiple-choice question, select the most accurate answer.

1. Which one of these statements is true?
   a. Time plays only an indirect role in communication.
   b. Stereotypes about durations of time associated with given activities support the concept of flexible working hours.
   c. Americans generally consider being early for a party a faux pas.
   d. A person's status has nothing to do with how he or she may use time.
   e. People usually become restless when a committee meeting exceeds ten minutes.

2. Which one of these statements is *not* true?
   a. Time-management seminars reinforce the importance of time as a nonverbal communication factor.
   b. The precision of a plane schedule is evidence of the time-bound nature of Americans.

Self-Test 10 — (continued)
c. Both professors and students have expectations about the timing of classes.
d. Attitudes about "wasting" time have no impact on communication.
e. To be late for an appointment with a president probably is more serious than to be late for an appointment with a supervisor.

B. Inference (40 points). For the multiple-choice question, select the most accurate answer.

Which one of these statements is *not* true?
a. Seasonal changes have an effect on nonverbal communication.
b. The concept of "timing" can be just as important for a speaker as for a comedian.
c. Age is actually a function of time, and thus overlaps with other factors in communication.
d. Einstein's theory of relativity held the key that unlocked the secrets of nonverbal communication.
e. Attitudes about the coffee break have a nonverbal impact upon transactions.

Solution to Self-Test 10
Excerpt about Time

A. Recall (30 points each)
1. c
2. d

B. Inference (40 points)
d

19. Take and score Self-Test 11 over Chapter 3.

Self-Test 11
Chapter 3

A. Recall (20 points each). For each multiple-choice question, select the most accurate answer.
1. Which of the following is a true statement?
   a. According to authoritative estimates, nonverbal elements may carry 65, 80, or even 93 percent of the social meaning in interpersonal exchanges.
   b. The power metaphor is that humans approach the things they like and avoid the things they dislike.
   c. Responsiveness (adaptation) generally relates to size.
   d. The Withholder is inhibited, but uses a great deal of facial movement.
   e. Subordinates do not keep their eyes on dominant people.
2. Humidity can affect communication performance. Which of the following also affect(s) communication?
   a. Layout and location of a room
   b. Presence of other people
   c. Lighting
   d. Color of walls
   e. a–d
3. Physical appearance and dress:
   a. Do not affect communication events
   b. Have nothing to do with nonverbal communication
   c. Completely define the person
   d. Can communicate a great deal about people
   e. Not a–d

4. Which one of these statements is *not* true?
   a. The vocal segregates ("uh," "er," etc.) can interfere with communication.
   b. Emblems are nonverbal symbols that have relatively fixed interpretations.
   c. An ectomorph is anxious; a mesomorph, assertive; and an endomorph, complacent.
   d. People generally enjoy invading the territories of others.
   e. Human masses do not always have a negative impact on communication.

B. Inference (20 points). For the multiple-choice question, select the most accurate answer.

Nonverbal communication:
a. Cannot exist without verbal communication
b. Is virtually beyond the communicator's control
c. Does not lend itself to research
d. Lacks some sophistication, but contributes significantly to transactions—especially oral ones
e. Has received deserved attention from academicians

Solution to Self-Test 11
Chapter 3

A. Recall (20 points each)   **B.** Inference (20 points)
  1. a   **3.** d   d
  2. e   **4.** d

Part b

UNDERSTANDING
AND APPLYING
THEORY AND
GUIDELINES

4

The Process of Communication

Through Chapters 1–3 you have established patterns for improving communication receiving. Before considering the sending acts, turn to some theoretical aspects of the study of communication.

A DEFINITION OF HUMAN COMMUNICATION

To extend your understanding of the human communication process, start with a definition:

Human communication may be defined as the spiraling process of the transaction of meanings through symbolic action involving all elements associated with sending and receiving written, oral, and nonverbal messages.

Spiraling Process

The idea of a spiraling process emphasizes the dynamic nature of communication. Communication involves much more than sending (Figure 4–1) or even sending and receiving (Figure 4–2). It includes the looping effect created by feedback (a return or response) from the receiver to the sender (Figure 4–3).

Even a loop, however, implies that the feedback returns to the beginning point and simply reactivates the process in the original plane. The single-plane concept creates the image of a mere re-enactment of the original sequence.

As suggested by Dance, a more realistic picture of the process becomes apparent through the imagery of a helical spiral.[1] Figure 4–4 illustrates that imagery.

---

[1]Frank E. X. Dance, "Toward a Theory of Human Communication," in *Human Communication Theory: Original Essays,* ed. Frank E. X. Dance (New York: Holt, Rinehart and Winston, Inc., 1967), p. 296.

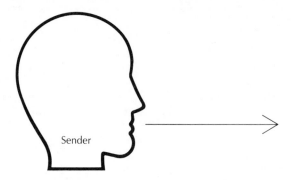

Figure 4–1   A very poor concept of the communication process

In Figure 4–4 the sender initiates the message and grows from the process and from other communication during any time lapse involved. The spiral continues as

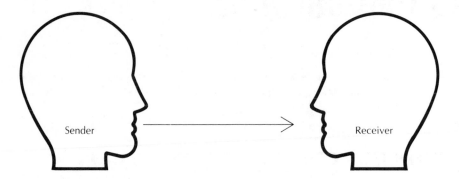

Figure 4–2   A poor concept of the communication process

the receiver also grows from the received message, from the act of initiating feedback, and from time-lapse communication. The feedback then contributes to the sender's growth, and the spiral continues.

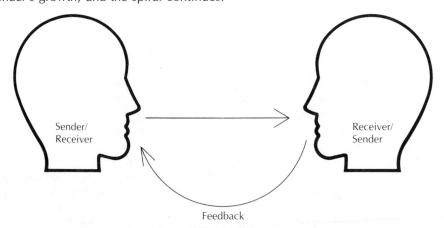

Figure 4–3   A better concept of the communication process

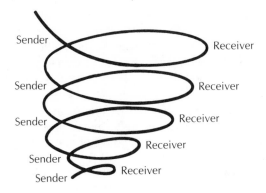

Figure 4–4   A much better concept of the communication process

SOURCE (Spiral Only): Frank E. X. Dance, "Toward a Theory of Human Communication," in *Human Communication Theory: Original Essays*, p. 296.

The figure illustrates a graceful symmetry. However, human reality dictates that grace and symmetry rarely characterize communication.

Senders and receivers do not always start at the same level or grow at the same rate. Abilities to develop messages vary. Interference has an impact. Time passes. Meanings assigned to symbols deviate. Other factors distort the spiral.

To reflect communication properly, therefore, spirals should balloon at times and virtually lie flat or deflate at others. They should always move with a hitching, asymmetrical awkwardness (Figure 4–5).

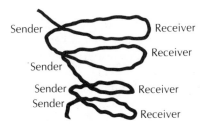

Figure 4–5   Illustration of a realistic communication process spiral

The theory of the spiral can be applied at whatever level the communication occurs. Therefore, a review of major communication levels, their spirals, and their relationships becomes appropriate here.

Levels of communication

 Traditionally, theorists have proposed three major human communication levels: *intrapersonal* (communication within oneself), *interpersonal* (communication between two or among a few people), and *mass* (communication between a complex organization and many people through electronic or print media). Some theorists reduce the number of levels to just two: interpersonal and mass.

Though either the two- or three-level approach has the advantage of a small number of classes, neither satisfactorily differentiates among the principal forms of communication. A defensible classification scheme could involve dozens of forms.

Five levels encompass the range reasonably well, however, and yet establish a manageable number: *intrapersonal, interpersonal, medio, person-to-group,* and *mass.*

As you read and think about the levels, keep in mind that the classification does not designate independent, mutually exclusive layers of communication behavior, but only represents a convenient means for analysis.

Intrapersonal communication   When you engage in a communication transaction within yourself, you communicate intrapersonally. You use neurophysiological activity to initiate, receive, and process messages through your own complete internal communication system. As you do so, you create communication spirals in which you yourself play both sending and receiving roles (Figures 4–4 and 4–5).

When you think, you talk to yourself. When you deliberate about a previous emotional interaction with someone else, an idea you have generated, some material you have just read, or a decision you must make, you are operating at the intrapersonal level.

Intrapersonal communication is vital to human growth. You use it to know yourself. You use it to develop your self-concept, self-determination, and self-motivation.

Self-communication provides the vehicle for dealing with the nonhuman environment. Intrapersonal communication also is critical as the foundation for the interpersonal, medio, person-to-group, and mass levels of communication. Your ability to communicate with others depends greatly upon your ability to communicate with yourself.

Interpersonal communication   You engage in interpersonal communication when you and one other or a few others send and receive messages face to face. The interpersonal level requires also that you know each other, are homogeneous, and are together privately in a relatively small space. Thus, conversations, dialogues, small-group discussions, committee meetings, and other similar interactions exemplify interpersonal communication.

The communication process for the interpersonal level is difficult to illustrate graphically because at least three spirals are at play. Figure 4–6 represents you and just one other person in a symmetrical interpersonal interchange. Your intrapersonal process is the spiral with the dotted line. The other person's spiral is a dashed line. The interactive spiral for the two of you appears as a solid line.

The placement of the interactive spiral shows that the whole (the interaction) is different from the sum of its parts (the two intrapersonal spirals). The growing interactive spiral overlaps with larger and larger segments of the participants' own growing spirals.

The illustration shows you and the other person moving closer together as the communication progresses. You do so because the chances of successful communication improve with each growth stage. The more your intrapersonal processes

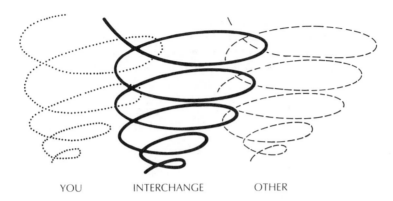

YOU   INTERCHANGE   OTHER

Figure 4–6 Interpersonal communication (solid line) between you (dotted line) and one other person (dashed line) as each of you communicates intrapersonally

overlap each other—the more each of you shares with the other—the better the interpersonal process will be.

Think of the complexities involved with the addition of more people to the transaction. Each person possesses a unique intrapersonal spiral. Each possible set of transacting participants introduces still another spiral. Finally, the interaction of all of the spirals creates one overriding spiral representing the whole transaction.

Medio communication Medio[2] communication occurs when two or a few people use some intermediate means for carrying their messages. Because the people are not present in the same space, they cannot communicate face to face.

Medio communication often involves a mechanical or electrical device that is used to transmit or receive messages. Examples of such devices include the telephone, closed-circuit television, mobile radio, radar, teletype, the home movie camera and projector, and monitoring equipment such as a communications satellite.

In addition, all of the written transactions involving only two or a few people use an intermediate device. They use such intermediaries as letters, reports, notes, forms, and interoffice memoranda. The communication spirals for the medio level resemble those for the interpersonal level. However, the intervention of a potentially distorting medium complicates the spiral. For example, you lose a great deal of the power provided by the nonverbal exchanges possible in face-to-face communication.

Suppose you as a business executive exchange a number of letters with an executive in another firm. In the process each of you operates out of your own personal arena—your own intrapersonal spiral.

Using your interpersonal skills and arts, you attempt to mesh your spirals through the medio process. However, you find the meshing difficult to accomplish

---

[2]The word "medio" is used, but in a more restricted sense, by Reed H. Blake and Edwin O. Haroldsen in *A Taxonomy of Concepts in Communication*, Humanistic Studies in the Communication Arts, ed. George N. Gordon (New York: Communication Arts Books, Hastings House, Publishers, 1975).

because you cannot see or hear the other executive and because of the time delay between messages. As a result, the composite communication spiral does not grow as rapidly as it would at the interpersonal level.

Figure 4–7 portrays how the barrier erected by an intervening medium reduces the quality of the communication.

(904 words including 45 words in footnote, but not including words from figures.)

(test on page 11)

BARRIER ERECTED BY
MEDIO CHANNEL

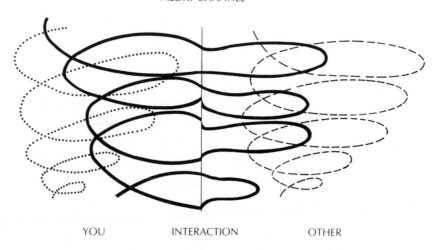

YOU   INTERACTION   OTHER

Figure 4–7   Medio communication (solid line) showing your intrapersonal spiral (dotted line) and the other person's intrapersonal spiral (dashed line) and the distortion created by the barrier erected by using an intermediate device.

Person-to-group communication   The person-to-group level involves one speaker and a live audience. The speaker usually faces the audience, and the audience members generally represent a relatively homogeneous group.

When the person-to-group situation is small and private, it often contains some of the characteristics of interpersonal communication. However, when the person-to-group situation involves large public groups, it loses the benefits provided by interpersonal exchanges.

The traditional speaker-and-audience setting may involve some technical instruments. They include microphones, projectors, tape players, and television sets. However, these instruments usually supplement the speech, rather than interfere with it. Therefore, they do not convert the circumstance into either a medio or mass one. If a microphone or other equipment does not function properly, though, it can destroy or abbreviate the communication.

As with the interpersonal and the medio levels, the person-to-group level represents a compound of the other levels. The composite person-to-group spiral becomes more and more complicated as the numbers in the audience increase.

Mass communication   Mass communication is traditionally limited to messages sent to large, public, heterogeneous, anonymous, distant audiences. Like medio communication, it depends upon some intermediate instrument of transfer. The instrument can be electronic (for example, radio, television, tape, film) or print (for example, newspaper, magazine, book, pamphlet, brochure, direct-mail campaign).

Of all of the characteristics of the mass channels, the restricted opportunity for interactive feedback becomes the most serious barrier to effective communication.

Relationships among the levels

The interrelationships among the levels reinforce the admission that this five-level description is an imperfect attempt to describe human communication. As an illustration of the imperfection, consider these everyday scenes and the questions they raise:

1. In an in-service training session comprised of five participants and a leader sitting around a table in a small room, the leader does 80 percent of the talking. Is the level interpersonal or person-to-group?

2. An evangelist speaks to 10,000 people in a stadium. The presentation is neither broadcast nor recorded. Is the level person-to-group or mass?

3. A manufacturer of dry-cleaning equipment sends copies of a sales letter to the 30 dry-cleaning firms listed in the telephone directory's yellow pages. Is the level medio or mass?

4. A speaker speaks to an audience of 75 people for 30 minutes and then conducts a 30-minute question-and-answer session. Is the level person-to-group or interpersonal?

5. An educational television station broadcasts a film on the derivation of the equation for the normal curve. Is the level medio or mass?

6. You sit in a library in the midst of other people and read from Woolf's *Orlando*. Is the level interpersonal or mass?

7. An individual writes a monograph on raising worms for profit, has it printed at the local print shop, and advertises it for sale in a few specialized publications. Is the level medio or mass?

Learning as a summary communication spiral

For any one human, learning and communication spirals virtually coincide. Using your own life as an example, consider how you have interacted with yourself and with your human and physical environments from the moment of conception.

The instant that you began to be introspective and stored anything gained through communication, you began to learn. The continuous nature of such activity defines your personal learning/communication spiral—a spiral that cannot be duplicated in anyone else.

Though quite simplistic, a strong case can be made for equating learning and communicating. Whatever the arguments in opposition to such a case, your learning cannot help but be enhanced by improvement in your communication arts and skills. Just as obviously, your communication cannot help but be enhanced by improvement in your learning arts and skills.

Transaction

A second important element of the definition of communication is the concept of a transaction between the participants.

Transactional communication calls on you to determine as much as you can about yourself and the other participant in the transaction. It also calls on you to use feedback fully in a two-way exchange.

Transaction and the intrapersonal level

Particular difficulty arises in trying to apply the idea of a transaction to the human's relationship with the nonhuman world. Although each of the five levels of communication includes at least one human participant, the intrapersonal level also forms the basis for the relationships of the human to the nonhuman environment.

In terms of transaction, then, can you think of water and flowers and colors and buildings as receivers as well as senders? Can you ascribe an interpretative, ideational power to such things? Can you conceive of such nonhuman elements as feeding back after interpreting a message from you? Probably not. Yet, the poet, the artist, and the musician regularly speak of communicating with nature.

Fabun actually identifies human-to-nonhuman connections as transactions:

> It is sometimes useful to think of human communications as "transactions." In the sense we mean here, a transaction involves the interaction of the observer and what . . . [the observer] observes. This can take place between ourselves and the world-outside-our-skin. Or it can take place between two or more human beings.[3]

Without belaboring the issue of whether humans transact with or merely receive from nonhumans, you probably can agree that some human-to-nonhuman connection does exist. You transact *with* yourself *about* what you actively receive from the nonhuman realm. Thus, those intrapersonal transactions about that realm become a dynamic part of your being.

Whether dealing with immediate receptions from humans or nonhumans, with internal self-generated ideas, or with previous receptions stored in the mind, the intrapersonal process involves a transaction.

Transaction and the interhuman levels

Transaction also occurs at the interpersonal, medio, person-to-group, and mass levels. However, the further removed the interhuman communication situation is from the interpersonal level, the less ideal the circumstances are for transaction. The loss of face-to-face and immediate-feedback characteristics dictates that failing.

The technique of transactional analysis (TA) developed by Eric Berne[4] and Thomas Harris[5] applies well to transactions at the interpersonal level. TA suggests that every being has only three transactional states—the Parent, the Adult, and the Child. TA techniques require that the participants in a transaction identify and adjust to their own states, the states of others, and the effects of the combinations of states. TA depends primarily on nonverbal cues to identify the states of others.

---

[3]COMMUNICATIONS: THE TRANSFER OF MEANING by Don Fabun, p. 32. Copyright© 1968 by Kaiser Aluminum & Chemical Corporation. Reprinted by permission of Glencoe Publishing Co., Inc.

[4]Eric Berne, *Games People Play* (New York: Random House, Inc., Grove Press, 1964).

[5]Thomas A. Harris, *I'm OK—You're OK* (Harper & Row, Publishers, Inc., Avon Books, 1969).

Even with the seeming one-directionalism of some multihuman communication, however, good communicators still attempt to understand the bases from which all participants operate. Such understanding is a determining characteristic of transactional communication at any level.

Meanings

If human communication includes a transaction, then, just what is transacted? Though many things seem to be, the ultimate transaction involves the meanings people assign to those things.

Support for the concept of meaning as the focal point of transaction can be found not only in the title of Fabun's book *Communications: The Transfer of Meaning,* but also in his conclusion that ". . . it is the transfer of meaning that is the goal of interhuman communications."[6]

Verderber puts such emphasis on meaning that he writes: "By definition then, *communication is the process of stimulating meaning.*"[7]

If communication involves transactions of meanings, what are "meanings"? Like any other word, "meaning" has no meaning—nor does the abstraction for which it stands. Meaning cannot exist in an external thing—whether the thing is the original thing or a symbolic thing (word, gesture, etc.) standing for the original thing.

To develop an acceptable definition for the word "meaning," consider the theory of symbolic interactionism. First, think about meanings that have already been formed. If meanings "exist," where do they exist? What are they? How are they formed? Why are they formed?

With rejection of the view that meanings exist in things themselves, the conclusion must be that they exist in the persons who created the meanings for the things. However, concluding that "meanings are in people, not in things," to paraphrase a cliché, does not tell where within the human the meanings exist. Even revising the phrase to ". . . in the minds of people" does not specifically answer the question "Where?" However, the mind remains such an enigma—even to those who spend their lives studying it—that the answer to the question will have to remain, "In the mind."

To deal with what meanings are, think of how they are created. They are created by people who continuously interpret the things that make up their individual worlds. The result, then, is that meanings are unique interpretations of the things in those worlds. They are unique because each person's world is different from every other. They are unique also because each person interprets even the things common to many worlds somewhat differently than anyone else.

An additional feature of meanings lies in their dynamic nature. Meanings live in the mind as tightly wound, quivering helical spirals. They are ready to spring into action for any interpretative processes the possessor initiates.

Once engaged in such processes, however, the spirals change. Therefore, any one version of an existent meaning can be of split-second duration.

Pause to examine your meaning for a thing (or the word "thing"). Possibly your interpretation is something like that of Blumer who treats "thing" and "object" as

---

[6]Fabun, *Communications: The Transfer of Meaning,* p. 26.

[7]Rudolph F. Verderber, *Communicate!* (Belmont, Calif.: Wadsworth Publishing Company, Inc., 1975), p. 4.

equivalent terms: A thing or an object ". . . is anything . . . that is pointed to or referred to," including the physical, the social, and the abstract.[8] If meanings are created for things or objects, then, you can think of such examples as: (1) physical— river, dog, train; (2) social—husband, classmate, senator; and (3) abstract— principles, morality, freedom.

While classification into one of the three categories may not always be obvious or important, the summary concept is. That concept is, to use Blumer's words, that ". . . things include everything that the human being may note in [her or] his world."[9]

With some partial concept of what meanings are, consider now how they become what they are. Already established is that they form through the interpretative process at the intrapersonal communication level. However, the significant element that gives rise to meanings is the process of interaction between and among people.

The final question related to the definition of meanings becomes "Why are meanings formed?" The answer brings the definition full circle: Meanings are formed for use in the interpretative process as the basis for action toward things. Meanings are *formed through* the interpretative process so that they may be *used in* the interpretative process.

As a summary description, then, Blumer defines meanings as unique, dynamic interpretations of things as derived from social interaction with one's associates. They are handled in, and modified through, an interpretative process used in dealing with things as the basis for living.[10]

Symbolic Action

Although the ultimate concern in communication lies with transactions of meanings, the communicator must add another "operator"—symbols. Humans cannot simply transfer meanings directly from one mind to another, nor can they think without symbols.

According to Pauly, symbols and the human action associated with them should be the focus of communication analysis:

> A good definition of communication ought to explain the common features of all symbolmaking activity. Perhaps a better way to look at communication is as symbolic action, as a process in which people create, transform, maintain, and celebrate a particular symbolic version of reality.[11]

As used in this book, the concept of symbolic action encompasses both verbal symbols (written and spoken words) *and* nonverbal (wordless) symbols.

A good communicator, then, develops the art of symbolic action. He or she inventories, evaluates, finds, creates, and even learns new ways to create symbols.

---

[8]Herbert Blumer, "Symbolic Interaction: An Approach to Human Communication," in *Approaches to Human Communication*, ed. Richard W. Budd and Brent D. Ruben (Rochelle Park, N.J.: Spartan Books, Hayden Book Company, Inc., 1972), p. 408.

[9]Ibid., p. 401.

[10]Ibid.

[11]John Pauly, "The Case for a New Model of Business Communication," *Journal of Business Communication* 14 (Summer 1977): 16.

All Elements Associated with Sending and Receiving

The fifth part of the definition stresses that communication involves all elements associated with two major acts, sending and receiving.

In a global sense, sending involves the application of the six communication guidelines developed in this book. The focus of the application is upon selecting, encoding, and transmitting messages. Encoding involves assigning symbols to meanings.

The total act of receiving also calls for the application of the guidelines. For this act, major emphasis falls upon selecting, receiving, and decoding messages. Decoding involves assigning meanings to symbols.

Both of the acts involve a great deal of mental activity. The key to that activity is the interpretative processing associated with encoding and decoding.

Written, Oral, and Nonverbal Messages

The last definitional component emphasizes the span of concern: the full range represented by verbal and nonverbal symbols.

In addition, the final word "message" has special meaning for the definition. Like meanings, messages develop through interpretative processing in the mind—whether the mind operates as sender or receiver.

As a sender, you mentally select the set of meanings—the set of mental symbols—to be sent. To make the transfer, however, you convert the internal message symbols into the best possible set of external message symbols. As a purposive sender, you want the receiver to change the set of external message symbols into the intended set of internal message symbols and meanings.

Such things as letters, notes, speeches, and a clenched fist waving in your face are only external messages; they only *represent* the true messages—the internal ones.

A MODEL OF THE COMMUNICATION PROCESS

Using the foundation formed by the definition, move now to a graphic model of the human communication process. Figure 4–8 illustrates the model applied to the first tier of a two-person transaction.

Observe that the model has two major units internal to the human—the sender/receiver and the receiver/sender. It has two major units external to the human—the external messages and the channel. It has one unit at once internal and external to the human—interference.

Sender/Receiver As Sender

For any given communication in which you participate as the sender/receiver, you initiate the spiral. You act first as a sender and second as a receiver of feedback.

As a sender, you act intrapersonally through the interaction of three mental operators and one mental/physical operator. The mental operators are the source/

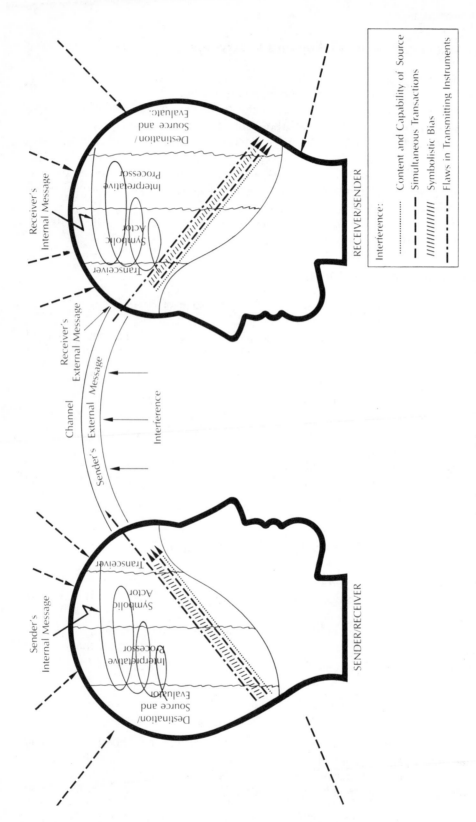

Figure 4–8 The first tier of the two-person communication model

destination and evaluator, the interpretative processor, and the symbolic actor. The mental/physical operator is the transceiver.

Source/destination and evaluator as source

The first component of the sender/receiver unit is your source/destination and evaluator. Your source serves as the fountainhead for sending action. Your destination performs as the controller and storage place for the results of receiving action. Your evaluator acts to determine how well objectives have been met. As a sender, you first engage the source.

Your source serves as the storehouse and supplier of everything that exists in your mind. It also acts as the planner, organizer, activator, motivator, and controller of the sending process. Finally, your source serves as an interactor with the other sending agents—particularly the interpretative processor.

Review this summary of the content and activities of the source:

The source stores and supplies meanings for such elements as:

1. Knowledge
2. Values and beliefs
3. Socialization
4. Emotions
5. Acculturation
6. Attitudes
7. Symbols
8. Communication methods

The source acts and interacts to:

1. Plan, organize, activate, motivate, and control the sending process
2. Use, revise, and create meanings for the stored components
3. Create the internal message unique to the purposes, receiver, channel, and interference

Interpretative processor as sender

The interpretative processor spins the intrapersonal activities forward. It also serves as the churning interpreter for both the source and the next unit, the symbolic actor.

The interpretative processor uses existing meanings from the source in conjunction with the special circumstances of the active communication. It acts as the melting pot for the creation of the new meanings necessary for the particular transaction.

The result of the churning and melting is a new concoction. The concoction is the internal symbol set (the internal message).

Through interaction with your symbolic actor, your interpretative processor helps to translate the internal symbol set into the external symbol set. It interprets by using, revising, or creating meanings for elements from the source. It also interprets meanings for the newly born internal messages and for the chosen external symbols.

In summary, the sending interpretative processor acts and interacts to:

1. Use, revise, and create meanings for the stored components
2. Create the internal message unique to the purposes, receiver, channel, and interference
3. Translate the internal message (symbol set) into the external message (symbol set)

Symbolic actor as sender

The symbolic actor (encoder) has the primary responsiblity for taking an internal set of message symbols and turning it into an external set of message symbols. It interacts with the source, the interpretative processor, and the transceiver. The spotlight falls upon taking something intrapersonal and making it into something that can become external.

A large stock of symbols alone will not assure effective symbolic action. The successful communicator must also possess the ability to convert the symbols into external messages that convey desired meanings and meet certain rules.

For verbal communication—whether written or oral—the messages involve words cast into phrases, sentences, and paragraphs. The applicable rules apply to such elements as grammar, spelling, sentence structure, punctuation, and style.

Slightly different rules exist for written verbal and oral verbal messages. Depending upon the situation, of course, the rules for oral messages are often less strict than for written ones.

To summarize, the sending symbolic actor acts and interacts to:

1. Create the internal message unique to the purposes, receiver, channel, and interference
2. Translate the internal message (symbol set) into the external message (symbol set)
3. Impel the external message (symbol set) from the human out into the channel

Transceiver as transmitter

Basically, the transmitting action of the sender/receiver involves interaction between the symbolic actor and the transceiver. The final version of the external symbol set is represented by the message ready for its journey through space and time to the receiver/sender. The transceiver functions to thrust the external message into the selected channel.

Transmission includes all of the external symbolmaking activities the physical being accomplishes. Your voice sends both verbal and nonverbal messages. Your fingers manipulate pens, pencils, typewriters, musical instruments, paint brushes, styluses, and other such instruments. Your body appears, touches, moves, postures, and even emits odors. Finally, if the possibility of extrasensory messages exists, you transmit them in some manner, perhaps through light and heat auras.

This book does not deal with how the hands and fingers transmit written, printed, painted, and musical symbols. Whether you do the work yourself or select others to do it, however, you are responsible for the quality of the transmitters that send your messages.

In summary, then, the sending transceiver acts and interacts to:

1. Translate the internal message (symbol set) into the external message (symbol set)
2. Impel the external message (symbol set) from the human out into the channel

Interference with Sender/Receiver As Sender

 Interference with the sender occurs in many different ways. However, the ways can be fit into four categories. They are (1) content and capability of the source, (2) simultaneous transactions, (3) symbolistic bias, and (4) flaws in transmitting instruments.

Content and capability of source

The quality of the content of your source can create bottlenecks within the sending process. For example, suppose you have stored such incorrect information about a subject that you encode inaccurate messages. In another case, interference may arise because your value system conflicts with that of the receiver.

Other factors related to the source can also create interference. These factors include (1) ability to gain and store knowledge, (2) accessibility to rich experience, (3) quantity of information, (4) organization, (5) retrieval ability, (6) evaluation skills, and (7) performance as the controller of the sending communication process.

Not only is your mind the source for your positive communication qualities, but it is also the source for your negative ones. As your source functions, it should identify its own potential for interference and attempt to prevent or control it.

Simultaneous transactions

Another kind of interference can arise when you participate in several communication transactions at the same time. Simultaneous transactions have a distinctive impact upon the interpretative processor.

As evidence of one such type of interference, the nonhuman world is forever sending messages to you. The messages sometimes support a given transaction, but often they interfere with it. For instance, say you are trying to develop an internal message. In that situation, a cold office or a jackhammer operating outside the window can severely damage the quality of your work.

Another conflict can occur if the source itself repeatedly breaks concentration by sending unrelated messages into the stream of consciousness. For example, suppose you are attempting to process a particularly difficult concept for summary in a report, and your source keeps interjecting thoughts about a party you will attend that evening.

A third type of simultaneous-interaction interference exists when other humans interact with you even as you attempt to concentrate on another transaction. As an example, say you are writing a memorandum. If other people pass your desk, talk to each other loudly, or talk to you, they may interfere with the quality of the memorandum.

Symbolistic bias

Because you have a uniquely biased set of symbols and meanings, your biases can interfere with your symbolic actor's message. You know what your symbols mean to you. However, they may not hold the same meanings for the receiver.

Consider a concrete example: Suppose you grew up in a region in which "slab" is a slang term for "highway." If you use "slab" in a message to someone not from that region, your symbolistic bias is introducing interference. The potential for such interference is compounded as you move from concrete to abstract symbols.

Flaws in transmitting instruments

Whether a transmitting agent is a part of you or outside of you, it can interfere with a transaction.

Some of the human-based transmitting barriers include a shaky voice, laryngitis, averted eyes, inappropriate dress, poor grooming, trembling hands, a weak handshake, being overweight, and poor typewriting skills.

Some examples of external interference include dirty type bars, faded typewriter ribbons, smudged erasures, burned-out bulbs in show windows, microphone noise, a power failure, and a broken pencil lead.

(539 words)
(test on page 113)

Observe in Figure 4–8 how the internal interference factors bombard the activities of the sending process.

Sender's Messages

For all but intrapersonal communication, a sender's message is actually comprised of at least two versions: the sender's internal message and the sender's external message.

For interhuman communication, your sender's internal-message-creation process begins with your source. Then it spirals through your interpretative processor and symbolic actor to your transmitter. Your symbolic actor and transmitter then interact to convert your internal message into an external one. All the stages finally merge to produce an external, physical, enchanneled message.

No such thing as *the* message, or even *a* message, exists for any communication level. Therefore, development of the concept must be accomplished in terms of "messages," not "message."

Even one tier of an intrapersonal spiral contains at least two messages. The messages are your personal sender's internal message and your personal receiver's internal message. The numbers of messages increase rapidly as additional spiral tiers appear.

As other internal messages, external messages, people, and tiers are added to form the interhuman levels, the numbers of messages increase significantly.

Observe in Figure 4–8 the internal message spiral in the sender/receiver.

Channel

For a sender's external message to reach the receiver, something must bear it through time and space. That "something" is typically identified as the channel. In this book the channel is treated as the physical form in which the message occurs.

Channels fall into three major categories: written verbal, oral verbal, and nonverbal. Within each of the three categories many specific channels exist.

Written verbal channels include notes, memoranda, letters, telegrams, reports, newspapers, magazines, books, and other similar forms. Oral verbal channels are telephones, televisions, radios, platform speeches, interviews, conferences, conversations, and other such media.

Nonverbal messages are enchanneled through virtually all sensory avenues— touch, visible things, sounds, aromas, and flavors. They supplement or take the place of written verbal and oral verbal messages.

Proper selection requires knowledge about the relative merits, costs, capacity, and availability of the various channels.

Interference with Sender's External Message

As the selected channel carries the sender's external message, extraneous elements from external sources can assail it. The elements may have little impact or they may distort or obliterate it.

As the external-message stage oral and unwritten nonverbal messages probably are more susceptible to interference than are written ones. For example, distractive whispers, audience hostility, a howling microphone, a pillar—all can block or change the oral and nonverbal messages transmitted by a speaker.

However, interference can occur with enchanneled written messages as well. The time lapse between transmission and receipt of messages, postal delays, and mutilation of letters by postal equipment are examples.

Receiver's Messages

The receiver deals with at least two messages—the receiver's external message and the receiver's internal message. The receiver's external message differs from the sender's external message to the extent that interference has changed it. At the point of impact with the receiver/sender's transceiver, the sender's external message becomes the receiver's external message.

Receiver/Sender As Receiver

When the receiver's external message reaches the transceiver of the receiver/sender unit, the internal operators engage in rapid, interactive sequence. In order, the operators are the receiver, the symbolic actor, the interpretative processor, and the destination/source and evaluator. Again, interference has an impact upon the process.

With minor shifts in emphasis and function, the operational sequence simply reverses that of the sending process.

Transceiver as receiver

When you act as a receiver, the first element activated is the receiving part of your transceiver—the mental/physical instruments. In addition, all reception activities involve sophisticated mental activities to a greater extent than they involve simple physical ones.

In summary, the receiving transceiver acts and interacts to:

1. Bring the external message (symbol set) from the channel into the human
2. Translate the external message (symbol set) into the internal message (symbol set)

Symbolic actor as receiver

Expanded reception acts such as listening, reading, and nonverbal observing merge with the symbolic-action (decoding) process. First, you receive external symbols, mechanically and symbolically. Then, your symbolic actor immediately begins to convert them into the internal symbols making up the internal message.

Ultimately, the test of the interhuman-communication sequence lies in decoding. It involves translation of external symbols sent from one mind into internal symbols that can create desired meanings within another mind.

To summarize, the receiving symbolic actor acts and interacts to:

1. Bring the external message (symbol set) from the channel into the human
2. Translate the external message (symbol set) into the internal message (symbol set)
3. Create the internal message unique to the purposes, sender, channel, and interference

Interpretative processor as receiver

The receiver's interpretative processor operates from the symbolic actor in the direction of the destination. It works with the symbolic actor to take the internal message symbols and form them into the internal message.

Just as important, however, it interacts with the destination to assign internal meaning to the internal message.

The receiver's interpretative processor, like the sender's, serves as the two-directional interpreter. It interprets the external symbol meanings in conjunction with the symbolic actor, and interprets the internal symbol meanings in conjunction with the destination.

In summary, the receiving interpretative processor acts and interacts to:

1. Translate the external message (symbol set) into the internal message (symbol set)
2. Create the internal message unique to purposes, sender, channel, and interference
3. Use, revise, and create meanings for the internal message

Destination/source and evaluator as destination

Your destination interacts with all components, but particularly with the interpretative processor. Together they establish the internal message and decide on meanings for it. As part of the activity, the destination receives and stores those dynamic meanings.

In the process of its action and interaction, your destination introduces your unique, personal being into the communication. It does so because the existing content of your destination determines the meanings you assign to internal messages.

Your destination forms the final segment for the receiving phase. However, it still serves as the planner, organizer, activator, motivator, and controller of the entire receiving process.

Your destination also acts and interacts to apply the six communication guidelines used in this book. In summary, then:

The destination acts and interacts to:

1. Create the internal message unique to the purposes, sender, channel, and interference
2. Use, revise, and create meanings for the internal message
3. Plan, organize, activate, motivate, and control the receiving process

The destination receives and stores meanings for such elements as:

1. Knowledge
2. Values and beliefs
3. Socialization
4. Emotions
5. Acculturation
6. Attitudes
7. Symbols
8. Communication methods

Destination/source and evaluator as evaluator

Your final receiving step involves assessing how well the message meets your purposes. In the process of doing so, you may also determine whether it meets the sender's purposes.

You send the results of your analysis, along with your feelings about the sender and the communication, to the destination/source for storage.

The evaluation also plants the seed from which feedback will spring. In outline form, then, the receiving evaluator acts and interacts to:

1. Evaluate to determine if the receiver's purposes have been met
2. Evaluate to determine if the sender's purposes have been met
3. Decide on the type of feedback needed

Interference with Receiver/Sender As Receiver

The interference for the receiver is virtually identical to that for the sender: Thus, simply recall or review Figure 4–8 and the discussion introduced in conjunction with the sender/receiver (pages 100-102). Also observe the receiver's internal message spiral in Figure 4–8.

Feedback

Once meanings lodge in the destination of the receiver, the receiver/sender initiates feedback. Feedback begins by activating the source portion of the destination/source and evaluator.

Receiver/sender as sender, and attendant interference

When the receiver initiates sending, the process simply recycles. Figure 4–9 shows the redirected interactive spiral (internal message) for the source, interpretative processor, symbolic actor, and transceiver.

Messages, channel, and attendant interference

Both the sender's internal and external messages form the thread carried through the receiver/sender's process. The channel carries the external message through time and space to the sender/receiver as the receiver. As interference operates upon the sender's external message, it becomes the receiver's external message.

Figure 4–10 shows the sender's internal message, the channel, the sender's external message, the external interference, the receiver's external message, and the external interference.

The original receiver's enchanneled feedback curves upward in order to engage the upward-shifted sender/receiver as receiver. The receiving sender/receiver has shifted upward because of intrapersonal growth from initiating the original communication and from other communication during the time lapse between messages.

Sender/receiver as receiver, and attendant interference

Upon reception by the transceiver, the receiver's internal message begins to develop. Interaction of the transceiver, symbolic actor, interpretative processor, and destination complete that development.

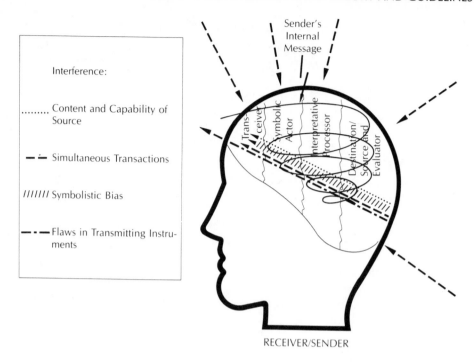

Figure 4–9   The destination/source and evaluator, interpretative processor, symbolic actor, transceiver, internal message, and interference of the receiver/sender as sender in the second tier of the two-person communication model

Source/destination and evaluator as evaluator

The evaluator spirals to recall preset purposes, to interpret feedback, and to judge how well the transaction has met the original purposes. That judgment, then, may become an initiator to the source if more interaction is needed. Interference again besets the receiving action in the same manner as described in previous paragraphs.

Figure 4–11 shows how the sender/receiver as the receiver becomes part of the model.

Third and Successive Tiers of the Model

Once the second tier is added, the communication spiral can grow indefinitely—just as long as sender and receiver choose to create feedback to the other.

Figure 4–12 illustrates several tiers in a simplified form of the growing model. In addition, a continuous, spiraling line overlays the units of the process. The over-riding spiral reintroduces and reinforces the concept of the whole and sets the roles of the parts in that whole into perspective.

Visualize the intrapersonal spirals and components for each tier. In addition, picture an intrapersonal spiral growing from bottom to top for each person.

As you review the model, recall several important conclusions: No communication sequence takes place in absolute isolation from others—whether they have gone before or occur simultaneously with it. The sender and receiver operate

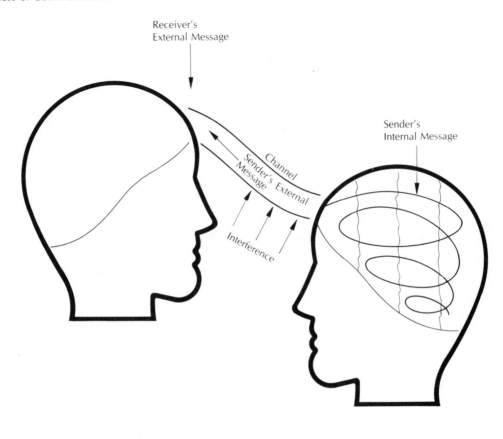

Figure 4–10   The sender's internal message, the channel, the external messages, and the channel interference of the second tier of the two-person communication model

from singular but dynamic mental bases created by lifetimes of communication. These bases pulse even as the given communication proceeds. Good intrapersonal and interhuman transactions stimulate growth and thus lift the spiral upward. However, interference slows growth, and checks the spiral temporarily. The figure, therefore, represents the symmetrical spiral of theory, not the clumsy one of reality.

Not only does the illustration portray unattainable perfection, but it does so for the simplest of interhuman constructs—only two persons. Therefore, think of how infinitely complex the model becomes as more and more people's spirals are added to it.

Finally, a model can belie the incomprehensibly rapid speed at which many transactions take place. Think of a motion picture instead of a still frame.

A DEFINITION OF BUSINESS COMMUNICATION

Business communication is simply a special case of human communication. Therefore, the universal definition, model, and principles apply directly to it.

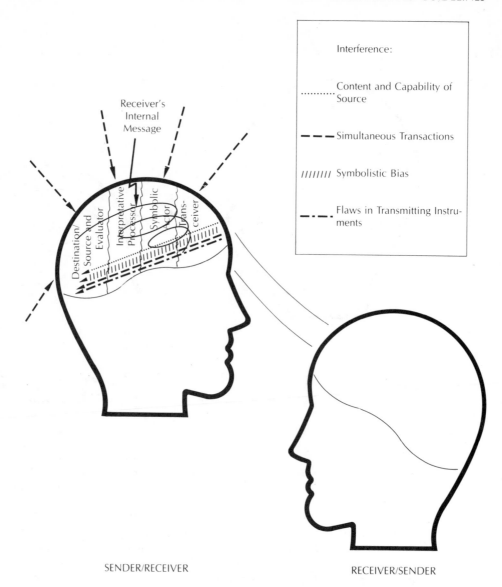

Figure 4–11   The transceiver, symbolic actor, interpretative processor, source/destination and evaluator, internal message, and interference of the sender/receiver as receiver of the second tier of the two-person communication model

To convert the definition of human communication into a definition of business communication, then, start with a definition of business:

Businesses are organizations of paid people working together to produce and market goods and services for profit.

From the definitions of human communication and business flows naturally a definition of business communication:

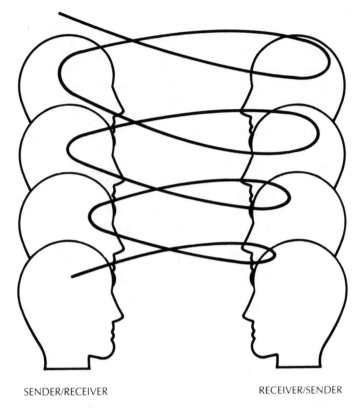

SENDER/RECEIVER   RECEIVER/SENDER

Figure 4–12 Multiple tiers in a simplified form of the two-person communication model

Business communication may be defined as the spiraling process of the transaction of meanings through symbolic action involving all elements associated with sending and receiving written, oral, and nonverbal messages internal and external to organizations of paid people working together to produce and market goods and services for profit.

The combined definition reinforces the major processes associated with human communication and with business. Most important, it reinforces the concept that at the hub of the business operation are people—people communicating within themselves and with one another.

Like the definition for human communication, the model for the process can be moved intact to apply to business communication.

Because the individual forms the basic unit for business, the intrapersonal spiral is ever present. Even as communication moves to the interpersonal, medio, person-to-group, and mass levels, human transactions still remain at the core of the process.

Most of the examples in this book present common business situations. However, because business communication is a special case of human communication, the arts and skills you develop from studying the examples will apply to the other arenas of your life.

SUMMARY

Human communication may be defined as the spiraling process of the transaction of meanings through symbolic action involving all elements associated with sending and receiving written, oral, and nonverbal messages.

Communication is a *spiraling process* that takes place at five levels: *intrapersonal, interpersonal, medio, person-to-group,* and *mass.*

Communication involves *transactions.* The transactional aspects of communication require that you determine as much as you can about the other in the transaction, and frame the message or feedback accordingly.

The definition of human communication also includes *meanings.* Meanings are not in words themselves, but are in the people who use them. Meanings change constantly and rarely are exactly the same for any two people. The sender and the receiver should attempt to find common meanings.

Symbolic action is also a part of the definition of communication. Humans transact meanings through the intermediary of *symbols,* verbal and nonverbal. As a good communicator, you should continually evaluate, maintain, search for, and create symbols and their meanings.

A graphic model can portray the human communication process, and illustrate the concept of the helical spiral.

In the model, the sender/receiver initiates the communication spiral. Within the mind of that person the *source/destination and evaluator* stores and supplies meanings and controls the process. The sending *interpretative processor* uses, revises, and creates meanings for the stored components. The *symbolic actor* takes an internal set of message symbols and turns it into an external set of message symbols. Finally, the *transceiver* acts as a mental/physical transmitter of the external message.

Interference within the sender can occur in a number of ways. The content and capability of your source may be inadequate for your purposes in this message. Simultaneous communication transactions can greatly interfere with your forming of your message. Symbolistic bias can cause your unique set of symbols to be misunderstood. Flaws in transmitting instruments can keep your message from emerging clearly.

A sender's message involves two versions: the internal message and the external message.

The sender's message must "travel" through a *channel,* the physical form in which the message occurs. Here again interference with the sender's external message can exist in many forms (noise, an uninterested audience, a hot room).

The receiver has to work with both the external and internal messages. The receiver's external message is the sender's external message, although it is more than likely distorted somewhat by interference.

The components of the receiving process are essentially the same as those of the sending process, only operating in reverse order: to receive, decode, and give meaning to the input received. Interference within the receiver can be very similar to interference within the sender.

Then when the original receiver sends, the result is *feedback,* the receiver's response to the sender's act. Interference can occur here as well. As sender/receiver and receiver/sender thus exchange roles, a multitiered model emerges. The model includes intrapersonal spirals and an overriding spiral superimposed on them.

Combining the definition for human communication and a definition for business, a definition for business communication becomes:

The spiraling process of the transaction of meanings through symbolic action involving all elements associated with sending and receiving written, oral, and nonverbal messages internal and external to organizations of paid people working together to produce and market goods and services for profit.

Practice

1. You are a business communication consultant. Write a short letter to your new client explaining the importance of good communication. Include in your letter a definition of human communication.

2. Three students are needed to complete this exercise. Each student reads a part (Ms. Jones, the manager; Mr. Higgins, the secretary; and Ms. Phillips, the job applicant). After you have read "A Play," discuss the questions listed at its end.

A PLAY

(Ms. Jones and Mr. Higgins are speaking on the intercom.)

Ms. Jones: Has Ms. Phillips arrived yet?

Mr. Higgins: No, she's ten minutes overdue. Would you like me to call her?

Ms. Jones: Let's wait another five minutes.

(Ms. Phillips enters Mr. Higgins' office.)

Mr. Higgins: May I help you?

Ms. Phillips: Yes. I'm Sara Phillips. I have an interview with Ms. Jones. I'm sorry I'm late.

Mr. Higgins: No problem. Ms. Jones' office is to my right. Knock and walk in.

Ms. Phillips: Thank you.

(Ms. Phillips knocks, then immediately walks into Ms. Jones's office.)

Ms. Jones: You startled me. Are you Sara Phillips?

Ms. Phillips: Yes. I'm sorry I'm a bit late. My car . . . .

(Ms. Jones interrupts.)

Ms. Jones: No need to explain. Have a seat.

END

a. Explain how "A Play" illustrates the spiraling communication process.

b. Were the people operating at a medio level? If not, at what level or levels were they operating? Explain.

c. Did the fact that Ms. Phillips arrived late affect the situation? Does her late arrival constitute a form of communication? Explain.

d. Is it possible that Mr. Higgins wanted Ms. Phillips to pause after she knocked on Ms. Jones' door, but that Ms. Phillips thought that he wanted her to knock and walk in immediately? Can words and phrases hold different meanings for different people? Explain.

3. Meet with your group to discuss the five levels of communication (intrapersonal, interpersonal, medio, person to group, and mass). Work together to develop three examples of communication at each level. Also discuss some of the problems that could exist in communicating at each level. Have one member of the group present the examples and conclusions to the class.

4. Determine which level of communication each of these situations represents. Remember that some situations do not fall into any one of the five categories.
   a. You shield your face from the sun.
   b. You speak to the League of Women Voters.
   c. You ponder your future.
   d. You talk to your professor.
   e. You write to your colleague in New York.
   f. You listen to a television program.
   g. You publish a newspaper.
   h. You read a section of a book to a class.
   i. You ask a friend to tell your manager that you will be late for work; your friend does as you ask.
   j. You write a letter that will be duplicated and sent to 200 people.
   k. You solve a present-value problem.

5. You work for the Joan Melton Corporation. You have been asked to conduct an in-house training program on human communication. You have been told that the program should run two hours a day for five days. Your boss wants a one- or two-page outline of the program tomorrow morning. Write the outline.

6. You teach a business communication course in a local high school. You are familiar with the definition of human communication set forth in this book. Rewrite the definition so that it can be understood easily by your fifteen-year-old students. Also develop at least one example that clearly illustrates each part of the definition.

7. [*Your professor will time this exercise.*] Write a few paragraphs on the importance of understanding the human communication process. Include several of the relevant aspects of communication theory.

8. List several channels you could use to make it known that you are running for mayor. Note the types of interference that could distort your message. What channel(s) would best serve your purposes?

9. Two students are needed to complete this exercise. One student should communicate the following to the other student without the use of the voice or paper.

   I am not feeling well. As soon as this class is over, I am going to go to see the doctor.

   Was the message too complex to be transmitted nonverbally? Discuss.

10. You own the Rugs for You Carpet Warehouse. You want to prepare a flyer announcing your first annual shag carpet sale. You will distribute the flyer to people in a working-class neighborhood. What should you consider before composing the flyer? What sorts of symbols could be misinterpreted? After you have explored the potential problems, prepare the flyer. Do you think your flyer will communicate what you intend it to communicate? Why?

11. Form groups to discuss the model of the communication process. Use the model to analyze this situation:

    Sara Mason decides that she needs to contact her client, John Dorn, because he seems to want daily progress reports. She uses her telephone to call John. After Sara says "Hello," static interrupts their conversation. John then says: "Bad connection, isn't it?"

    Answer these questions for both the sender (Sara Mason) and receiver (John Dorn):
    a. What part did the source/destination and evaluator play?
    b. How did the interpretative processor function?
    c. What was the symbolic actor's involvement?
    d. What functions did the transceiver perform?
    e. What types of interference occurred in the communication sequence?
    f. What, if anything, constituted feedback?
    Have one member present your group's analysis to the members of another group.

12. Read the section on dictation in Chapter 15 (pages 522-23). Then write a rough draft of a memorandum to your colleagues at the Norris Systems Management Corporation explaining the possible applications of the model of the communication process. Meet with your group. Every group member then dictate your memorandum to some other group member. Evaluate each member's dictating style.

13. You are a loan officer for a bank. You notice that the letters your superiors and colleagues send customers are full of typographical and grammatical errors, strange jargon, and arithmetic errors. The letters are written on hot orange stationery. Write a memorandum to your superiors and colleagues explaining that these practices constitute interference and should be avoided. Remember that the memorandum should not offend your superiors or co-workers.

14. Outline the definition of business communication. Meet with your group. You and each other group member dictate a complete version of the definition from your outline into an imaginary dictating machine. (For some hints about dictating, see pages 522-23.) Evaluate each other's performances by answering these questions:
    a. Was the dictator prepared?
    b. Did the dictator speak clearly?
    c. Did the dictator speak at an appropriate speed?
    d. Was the dictator able to dictate a coherent message from the outline?
    e. Did the dictator hesitate or correct herself or himself repeatedly?
    f. Did the dictator use correct grammar and idiom?
    g. Did the dictator provide enough instructions to allow a typist to transcribe with relative ease?

15. Consult your dictionary and thesaurus to create meanings for these words. Use the words when you think, write, and speak so that you feel comfortable using them.

a. Acculturation	g. Fundamental	m. Introspection
b. Compel	h. Hypothetical	n. Neurophysiological
c. Composite	i. Imagery	o. Obliterate
d. Contemporary	j. Impel	p. Sublimate
e. Dilemma	k. Inherent	q. Successive
f. Extraneous	l. Integral	r. Tack

16. Take and score this comprehension test over the timed section titled "Interference with Sender/Receiver as Sender" in this chapter.

Self-Test 12
Excerpt about Interference
with Sender/Receiver as Sender

A. Recall (25 points each). For each multiple-choice question, select the most accurate answer.

1. Which of the following may constitute interference?
   a. A less-than-perfect recall capability
   b. A conversation that you overhear while you are working
   c. Symbolistic bias
   d. Flaws or malfunctions in transmitting instruments
   e. a–d

2. Symbolistic bias refers to:
   a. The meanings you and only you hold for your set of symbols
   b. Simultaneous-interaction interference
   c. A letter full of misspellings and typographical errors
   d. The inability to speak a foreign language
   e. The inability to pronounce some words

Self-Test 12 — (continued)

3. Which of the following is *not* a flaw or malfunction in a transmitting instrument?
   a. Hoarseness
   b. A personal bias
   c. Loud clothing
   d. Flimsy paper
   e. A crushing handshake

B. Inference (25 points). Determine whether the statement is true or false.
   If people work with one another for a long period of time, they share identical meanings for most words and phrases.

Solution to Self-Test 12
Excerpt about Interference
with Sender/Receiver as Sender

A. Recall (25 points each)   B. Inference (25 points)
   1. e   3. b   False
   2. a

17. Complete and score this comprehension test over Chapter 4.

Self-Test 13
Chapter 4

A. Recall (9 points each). For each multiple-choice question, select the most accurate answer.

1. Intrapersonal communication:
   a. Takes place between or among two or a few people
   b. Takes place between a complex organization and many people
   c. Takes place within oneself
   d. Is primarily nonverbal
   e. Takes place between two people who know one another relatively well

2. Medio communication:
   a. Takes place between two people speaking face to face
   b. Involves some intermediate means for carrying the messages
   c. Excludes the use of letters, reports, or memoranda
   d. Is communication through television and newspapers
   e. Takes place within oneself

3. Human communication may be defined as:
   a. The two-way exchange of ideas between people
   b. Sending messages and receiving feedback
   c. A spiraling process
   d. The perfect exchange of information
   e. A one-way process

4. All human communication:
   a. Involves a simple process
   b. Involves the transaction of meanings through symbolic action
   c. Is verbal
   d. Involves inanimate objects
   e. Is static

5. Which of these is not a part of the first tier of the two-person communication model?
   a. Debugger/translator
   b. Source/destination and evaluator
   c. Interpretative processor
   d. Symbolic actor
   e. Transceiver

6. The channel is best defined as:
   a. Air waves
   b. Sound waves
   c. The form in which the message occurs
   d. A letter or television broadcast
   e. A messenger service

7. When the receiver's external message reaches the receiver/sender unit, what element is activated first?
   a. Source/destination and evaluator
   b. Symbolic actor
   c. Interpretative processor
   d. Transceiver
   e. Debugger/translator

8. Business is defined in this chapter as:
   a. A name given to an organization of paid people working together to produce and market goods or services for profit
   b. A name given to an organization of paid people or volunteers who produce goods and/or services for profit or charity
   c. A name given to an organization of people who provide services and manufacture products
   d. A name given to any group of people who work together
   e. A name given to any organization that provides goods and services for a 10 percent profit

B. Inference (14 points each). Indicate whether these statements are true or false.

1. The model of the communication process set forth in this book is an attempt to look at and understand some rather arbitrarily labeled parts of the communication process.

2. The sending act is the most important part of the communication process.

Solution to Self-Test 13
Chapter 4

A. Recall (9 points each)

1. c	5. a
2. b	6. c
3. c	7. d
4. b	8. a

B. Inference (14 points each)

1. True
2. False

Guidelines for Effective Communication: Purposes, Participants, Environment, and Channels

5

You have already read guidelines for reading, listening, and nonverbal observing. At this point review the guidelines stated in a form that will apply to any type of communication:

1. Define your purposes, the other participant's purposes, yourself, the other participant, and the environment.
2. Identify the channel.
3. Control the interference internal and external to you and the other participant.
4. Select, encode, decode, and transceive the messages in light of the purposes, the participants, the environment, the channel, and the interference.
5. Use feedback to and from the other participant.
6. Evaluate at each stage.

The bulk of *Business Communication Dynamics* deals with encoding, decoding, and transceiving (Guideline 4). Therefore, use this chapter and the next to expand the major elements of the other five guidelines. Review the first two guidelines in this one.

PURPOSES

To set the stage for a consideration of purposes,[1] review these summary statements:

1. Business communication is purposive communication—with profit as the ultimate goal.
2. Purpose and profit carry with them ethical responsibilities.

---

[1]Although distinctions can be made among the words "goals," "purposes," "objectives," and "missions," they are used interchangeably in *Business Communication Dynamics*.

3. Purposes can be
    a. Immediate or ultimate
    b. Short term, intermediate term, or long term
    c. Primary or secondary
    d. Conscious or subconscious
    e. Intrapersonal or interhuman
    f. Singular or multiple
    g. Sender based or receiver based
    h. Consistent or inconsistent with those of the other participant
    i. Stated or unstated
    j. Directly or indirectly related to a problem
4. The basic goal for a sender is to bring about some desired action by the receiver.
5. The basic goal of the receiver is to act in a way that will satisfy some need or want.
6. Whether sending or receiving, define your own purposes as well as those of the other participant.

Profit

Profit is the ultimate goal of business in a free-enterprise system. Therefore, no matter how far removed a given business-communication transaction may be from profit, it should fit into a larger plan pointing toward that goal.

Purposive activities form such an important part of business that many firms practice management by objectives (MBO). The key to that practice lies in the ability to communicate. Thus, management by objectives involves communication by objectives.

Ethics

Any time purposes and profits enter into an arena, the communicator must accept the responsibilities associated with achieving them. Concepts like persuading, manipulating, maneuvering, shaping behavior, and even creating demand strongly imply a need for ethical accountability.

To illustrate the difficulty of making ethical decisions, consider these situations:

1. A product has been shown to be detrimental to the health of those who use it. The sale of the product is legal, however, and the industry employs thousands of workers. Would you feel right about writing sales letters to persuade people to buy the product? Would you be able to help produce the product if you did not work directly in sales?

2. Your firm has filed a strong affirmative action plan, and you personally agree with its provisions. As the personnel officer, you must fill a particular position and have identified a well-qualified minority woman for it. However, the supervisor for whom she would work has made the work situation for minorities and women unbearable in the past. This attitude has hurt not only the employees, but the productivity of the department. Will you decide to hire or to reject her? Whatever your decision, how will you communicate the circumstances surrounding the decision to her?

3. Inwardly, you agree with a customer that the adjustment your firm has made is unfair to the customer. Do you smile and affirm the company's decision as appropriate, or do you support the customer?

4. You know that safety standards are not being met in your work place and that workers are being endangered. You also know that management balks at the standards, not only because of the expense involved in meeting them, but because of the inconvenience they sometimes cause the workers. Do you communicate with the Occupational Safety and Health Administration (OSHA) or remain silent?

5. You know that an elderly man in a department you manage is not producing well. In addition, he may actually be jeopardizing other workers because of slowed responses. He has attained such a high wage level because of long years of service that two young workers could be hired for about the wages necessary to pay him. You know that he could retire with a comfortable retirement benefit. What will be your decision and how will you communicate it?

No "right" answers exist for any of the questions posed or for virtually any others like them that could be contrived. However, with profit as a goal, purposive business communicators have to develop answers for just such questions.

Variety

Purposes appear in a variety of forms. Consider these examples:

1. While profit is the ultimate purpose, collecting a past-due account may be an immediate one.

2. You may set the receipt of an order as a short-term objective, increased sales as an intermediate objective, and profitability as a long-term objective.

3. You may establish as a primary objective the completion of a report by the time your superior needs it for negotiations. At the same time you may set as a secondary objective winning the approval of your superior for the quality of your work.

4. When you set targets for production, you consciously establish objectives. At the same time, you likely have subconscious objectives related to profit, satisfying a boss, and keeping your job.

5. If you set yourself a time limit for completing five letters you must write, the goal is intrapersonal. However, if you make your objective the acceptance of your bid for a contract, the goal is interhuman.

6. Once you recognize that a delinquent customer is not going to pay of her or his own volition, your objective of collection becomes overriding. Prior to that point, however, multiple objectives of collection, maintenance of goodwill, and even possible resale are operative.

7. The objective of receiving applications from qualified people is based in the writer of a notice about a job opening. However, the objective of learning about jobs by reading notices lies in the receiver.

8. When a salesperson tries to persuade you to buy a product at a price higher than you want to pay, your purposes conflict. When you want the product and the price is the lowest you have found, your purposes correspond.

9. When a firm practices MBO, the participants state the objectives. However, firms without MBO may never formally state their goals.

10. If you set as the goal of your letter the purchase of a lawn mower by a customer, you have established a direct goal. However, if you send a catalogue to a customer, you have an indirect goal of receiving an undefined order.

Sending

Theoreticians suggest several approaches to communication purposes. Three such approaches indicate that people communicate to: (1) stimulate, or elicit response; (2) inform, entertain, or persuade; or (3) bring about action and interaction.

The first approach carries with it Skinnerian imagery of humans acting as automatons. The second approach places the emphasis on the sender, to the exclusion of the receiver. The third approach, however, features goals tied to actions of a receiver and interactions between a sender and a receiver.

Because of its focus, this third approach forms the basis for this book. It suggests that you think of purposes in terms of desired actions and interactions.

Actions and interactions

A purposive sender, then, raises questions about the receiver and the desired action: What do I want the receiver to do? What do I want her to believe? What do I want him to say? How do I want her to behave? What do I want the receiver to become as a result of the message I send? Unless you adopt this purposive orientation, messages may miss their targets. You may unwisely be emphasizing the act of sending (writing, speaking, drawing, etc.) instead of bringing about the desired outcomes.

For example, if you write a letter asking for some information, think that your purpose is not to inquire, but rather to receive the information you desire. The mission of an advertisement is not to sell, but to prompt people to place orders.

Statements of purpose

Some reminders may help you establish good statements of purpose. They include:

1. Prestate the objectives.
2. Make the statements clear and concise.
3. Include the who, what, when, where, how, and why.
4. Establish criteria for evaluation.
5. Frame the objectives and evaluative criteria in action/interaction (behavioral) terms.

Prestatement   Always try to prestate your objectives. Presetting helps you to plan and prepare well—to organize your thinking.

Clarity and conciseness   State objectives precisely and concisely. Even if an objective is yours alone, pretend to develop it for someone else's use. In that way, you will use the clearest of terms.

Who, what, when, where, how, why   Good purposes relate to the who, what, when, where, how, and particularly to the why of communication. Thus, they include some treatment of the participants, the environment, message content, message channel, and message timing. However, the primary concern lies with the reasons for—and results desired from—the communicative action.

Criteria   To set the stage for evaluation, establish criteria for measuring how well a transaction met your purposes. Each objective may have one or many such criteria.
Examples of objectives and accompanying criteria include:

1. Objective: To increase the number of orders received this quarter over last quarter.
   Criteria: a. Receive at least 300 orders by April 30.
   b. Receive at least 600 orders by May 31.
   c. Receive at least 900 orders by June 30.

2. Objective: To hire a qualified employee by November 7
   Criteria: a. By October 17 identify at least four applicants who meet other requirements and who score 78 or higher on the entrance examination.
   b. By October 22 interview those applicants.
   c. By October 24 make an offer to one of them; call for response by October 29.
   d. By November 3 make subsequent offer(s) if necessary.
   e. By November 7 receive acceptance from qualified applicant.

3. Objective: To increase the proportion of contract awards.
   Criterion: Be awarded at least 40 percent of the bids submitted next month.

The section on evaluation contains more information on criteria. However, at this point understand that criteria provide an objective basis for determining the level of success of an activity. Also understand that the statement of purpose may include the criteria written into it.

Action/interaction   Make statements in terms of actions and interactions. To do so, first establish some behavioral categories under which goals can be pursued: first, the *cognitive* (knowledge and intellect); second, the *emotional* (interests, attitudes, values, and beliefs); and finally, the *nonverbal.*
As you develop objectives, think of outcomes measured in all three classes. One of the major benefits of doing so lies in the reminder that people exist not just on intellectual planes, but at the emotional and nonverbal levels as well.
Here are some examples of phrases that state purposes in forms suggesting action by the receiver:

1. To return the card
2. To buy the clock
3. To place an order
4. To send the list
5. To answer the question
6. To sign the agreement
7. To read and return comments on the five-year plan
8. To audit and deliver a report on the financial records
9. To applaud
10. To laugh
11. To make an offer in writing
12. To make a payment
13. To complete and return the questionnaire

Example of sending objectives

Consider an expanded example that illustrates action goals. It also illustrates several of the other elements of a good objective as well.

Suppose that you head a production department at a large corporation. For two days Line A has produced so many defective products that the process has been statistically out of control. After the usual adjustments fail to reduce the proportion of defectives, you think about how you will proceed to attack the problem.

Temporarily, you ignore such intermediate- and long-term objectives as profit, production levels, your image, and even correction of the cause of the excessive defectives. Instead, you concentrate on the immediate problem—definition of the cause.

You decide to have a meeting of key staff people this afternoon. You establish your objective for the meeting:

> To have the group identify and record every possible valid hypothesis that might explain the production of a significantly high number of defectives on Line A for the past two days.

The objective falls primarily in the cognitive realm. However, no objective can fall purely into any one realm. Therefore, emotional and nonverbal elements undoubtedly will enter into even this simple situation.

For example, suppose that the Line A supervisor feels defensive about the problem. He might fall back into a value system that is generally antagonistic toward men with long hair. He might then suggest the hypothesis that Allen Tooms and George Chek are doing sloppy work—based subconsciously on nothing other than the fact that their hair is long.

As another example, a statistical quality-control engineer in the meeting may believe that the excess of defectives occurs because of improper hand-and-arm motions. She might actually demonstrate those motions and sketch them on a piece of paper (nonverbal acts) to illustrate her hypothesis.

Your original objective is prestated in relatively clear and concise terms. It includes, explicitly or implicitly, the who, what, when, where, how, and why related to the immediate problem. It also includes an observable action as the end result—the list of hypotheses.

The list that evolves can also serve as a criterion for evaluating the success of the meeting. However, can you evaluate whether the group identifies "every possible hypothesis"? Can you know that the hypotheses are "valid"?

Tying this goal to more evaluatable criteria would be quite difficult, however. For example, would you logically want the group to generate "at least five hypotheses"? As far as the validity is concerned, the statement implies that you trust the group to judge whether the hypotheses are valid or invalid before recording them.

Receiving

Though the initiative in communication comes from the sender, the receiver also acts out of purpose—whether ill or well defined. To establish well-defined receiving purposes, try to apply the five suggestions introduced early in the preceding section.

Though applying them now may be less profitable than it is in sending situations, the effort can improve receiving.

Prestate your purposes whenever possible. When you cannot develop them before the transaction, do so as early as you can during the transaction.

As a receiver, your statements of purpose probably will be more often mental than written. Nevertheless, they can be clear and concise. The who, what, when, where, how, and why need to be there. In addition, your objectives should be couched in evaluatable terms with criteria for that evaluation.

You receive in order to acquire, comprehend, use, and act upon messages initiated by the sender. As a receiver you choose to act and interact basically to satisfy your own needs and wants.

To apply the principles of purposive receiving, consider again the circumstances created by the department head's calling a meeting of the staff to develop hypotheses about the quality-control problem. This time, however, cast yourself in the role of the supervisor of Line B.

Imagine that you have received a telephone call setting up the meeting for this afternoon. Also assume that the communiqué includes the purpose for the meeting—to develop every possible valid hypothesis to explain the excessive defectives on Line A.

When you first receive the notice of the meeting, you begin to receive with purpose. You quickly identify the sender and the sender's purpose. You instantly decide that you should accept and act upon the message. After all, you are an employee with responsibilities to meet. Thus, your immediate action is to put the time on your calendar and fix it firmly in mind so that you will attend the meeting.

Some receivers of such a message would stop there. However, as an active receiver, you think more about purposes.

Concerns about profit, production objectives, and your image flash through your mind. However, you concentrate on the more immediate objectives of your upcoming participation.

Your most immediate objective will be to contribute as many valid hypotheses as you can. First, you think of every possible reason for the overproduction of defectives on Line A. You analyze them, reject those that do not appear to be valid, and jot down those that you believe are.

Next, you picture yourself offering your hypotheses to the others at the meeting. You decide what they might think or say about the quality of your suggestions. You then revise or develop arguments in support of your suggestions.

You also think about what the others might suggest, and develop your strategy for supporting or discounting their ideas.

You think about the personalities involved and how you might best interact with them in order to persuade them of the validity of your hypotheses. You continue to think about every potential interaction until you can develop a brief set of written notes to help you in the meeting.

At the meeting then, you follow your strategy. However, you adapt your purposes and actions to any situation that you did not anticipate as you pictured the scene.

Even though adaptability is necessary, practice this active-receiver preparation for any similar communication. You will be surprised at how clearly you can learn to foresee future interchanges. You also will be pleased at how much your performance as a communicator improves as a result.

In hypothetical and real situations, your improved communication may help you satisfy many needs and wants; you may achieve such important goals as promotion, respect, and self-satisfaction.

Both Participants' Purposes

Whether sending or receiving, consider not only your own purposes, but those of the other. When your purposes coincide, the transaction runs smoother than when they differ.

When they do differ, determine the extent of that difference. As a sender try to adjust your messages to meet some of the receiver's purposes. In that way, your chances for accomplishing the desired interaction increase.

PARTICIPANTS AND ENVIRONMENT

One of the most important stages of the communication process involves the careful definition of yourself, the other participant, and the environment of the transaction.

Self-definition depends primarily upon intrapersonal processing. Definitions of the other and the environment depend upon both intrapersonal and interhuman processing. However, all three definitions depend upon an understanding of a broad base of human and environmental factors. As you evaluate many of those factors, emphasize them from the viewpoint of a sender or receiver trying to define the other participant.

The focus for this other-centered approach is adaptation. As a sender, you try to encode messages to fit the receiver's world. As a receiver, you try to decode messages in light of the sender's world.

To identify yourself, the other participant, and the environment, again consider the who and whom, what, when, where, how, and why of the situation.

Who and Whom

To know yourself and the other participant—the who and whom—you need to understand the full complement of human factors. The factors are generally comprised of the psychological (both cognitive and emotional), the social, the cultural, and the physical.

General factors

For the four general categories, consider some examples of the types of things you need to know:

1. Personality type
   a. Extroverted or introverted
   b. Relaxed or high strung
   c. Aggressive or passive
   d. Friendly or unfriendly (affilia-tive or nonaffiliative)
   e. Open minded or closed minded
   f. Logical or emotional
   g. Meticulous or careless

2. Values, beliefs, attitudes, morals, prejudices, stereotypes, preconceptions
3. Motives, desires, needs, wants, goals
    a. Food, shelter, clothing
    b. Good health
    c. Security from injury or harm
    d. Comfort
    e. Acceptance, liking, belonging, love, respect, admiration
    f. Creativity and contributiveness
    g. Action and interaction
    h. Service
    i. Self-satisfaction
4. Self-image
5. Psychological reference groups
6. Moods, fears, hopes
7. Interests, likes, dislikes
8. Aptitudes
9. Intelligence
10. Knowledge, arts, skills
11. Perceptual abilities
12. Store of symbols
13. Communication arts and skills
14. General cultural customs, standards, norms
    a. Nationality, race, ethnicity
    b. Religion
    c. Age
    d. Sex
    e. Politics
    f. Economic level
    g. Geographics (including rural versus urban)
    h. Occupation
15. Specific social affiliations
    a. Family
    b. Friends
    c. Neighborhood
    d. School
    e. Church
    f. Work
    g. Organizations (professional, civic, political, social)
16. Physical characteristics
    a. Age
    b. Body type, height, weight
    c. Facial features, hair, appearance
    d. Motor abilities
    e. Handicaps

You can never understand all of these things about anybody—not even yourself. However, if you can establish a profile for some of the key factors, you may understand better than you would by ignoring them.

To illustrate in just one category, culture, could you not correctly expect some differences in these pairings of people?

American and Russian
Black and White
German-settlement American and Native American
Catholic and Orthodox Jew
Sixty-year-old and 20-year-old
Man and woman
Communist and capitalist
Born millionaire and born pauper
Born Georgian and born Californian
Kansas Citian and San Franciscan
Office worker and truck driver

Similar pairings exist for all of the categories. People are what they are because of the unique combinations of personal, cultural, social, and physical factors that define their lives.

From the treatment of the factors about which you want knowledge, turn to some observable data for garnering that knowledge.

Demographic factors

You have a better chance of knowing the other if you have some demographic data. Such data include:

1. Name	8. Income and spending
2. Address	9. Reference groups
3. Age	10. Interests
4. Sex	11. Nationality, race, and ethnicity
5. Marital and family status	12. Physical characteristics
6. Education and intelligence	13. Dress and appearance
7. Occupation	14. Religion

Name   If you cannot see the other person, the name may become a valuable substitute. Even for the face-to-face level, the name can add information to that which you observe.

The name alone often identifies the other as a female or a male. If it does, then you can begin to make some assumptions about the personality traits that go with initiation into the female and male subcultures. If it does not (Gale, Dale, for example), you will have to depend upon other avenues for determining the person's sex.

The name used by a woman can reflect a great deal about her personality. It can reveal whether she has been absorbed by the culture or has revised her values to reflect something different.

For example, if a woman gives her name as "Mrs. Joe Bloke," you can feel fairly certain that she is still in the original cultural mode—with most of the values associated with it.

If she gives her name as "Mrs. Mary Bloke," she has changed to the extent that she uses her first name. Such a change reflects a slightly revised set of norms.

Say she drops the "Mrs." and becomes "Mary Bloke" (even though she and Joe are married). The change would lead you to another assessment of her attitudes.

If she and Joe are married, but she calls herself "Mary Doe" (retaining her original surname), you would make still a different evaluation of her system of beliefs.

Similar examples could be drawn for the uses of "Miss" and "Ms."

Another way that names can be clues to identity exists when the name is clearly nationalistic, ethnic, or racial. For example, if you need to write a letter to Jay H. Runningbear, you can be fairly sure that some of the receiver's personality traits relate to his being of Native American extraction.

However, because of the cultural tradition of the married woman's taking her husband's name, you could not be sure about the heritage of someone named Della Runningbear. She could be of Native American extraction herself—or simply married to a Native American.

Even if a name is relatively clearly tied to a racial or ethnic group, you cannot make sweeping generalizations about the culture of the person. For example, Jay H. Runningbear probably would be a different person if he grew up on a reservation in Arizona than if he grew up as a member of a middle-income family in Chicago.

Similarly, a "-sky," an "-eone," a "-moto," a "-stein," a "-burg," or a "Mc-," may be so far removed from the ethnic origins that they "tell" you no more than a "Smith" or a "Jones" does.

Another naming custom that provides a potential clue to a man's makeup can be found in names like Henry Hall, Jr., and George Adams, III. *Perhaps* you can conclude that that person's acculturation has come from a strong, patriarchal tradition.

Another aspect of names that may provide information about their possessors includes the assignment of "girls' names" to boys, and the assignment of "boys' names" to girls. Such assignments may have an effect on personality development.

Because of the nature of the culture, giving a boy a girl's name is considered to be much worse than giving a girl a boy's name. Thus, you can be sure that the "boy named Sue" in the Johnny Cash song of the 1970's did have some personality features that would have been nonexistent in a boy named Ted.

Similarly, names like Candy, Precious, and Chastity surely put a permanent cultural stamp on the women who carry them.

Become aware of any stereotypes you may have about names. Even as you take account of what they might reveal about a person, avoid any tendencies that might keep you from taking a Dolly as seriously as a Ruth, a Donnie as seriously as a Frank, or a Joan as seriously as a Jack.

Address   The address can provide some data about a person. It can indicate geographic location and the predominant culture and social structure associated with that location. It also can indicate whether the location is urban, suburban, or rural. Try even to determine whether the person lives in a private home, an apartment, or a dormitory.

Age   The age of a person can be a major definer of psychological, cultural, social, and physical characteristics. Holding all else constant, knowledge about age can identify broad value sets as well as any other single feature.

In a videotaped program, Massey reinforces a commonly held view about the establishment of values: Human behavior is a function of sets of values programmed basically by the age of 10 and firmly established by the age of 20.[2]

Massey suggests that two basic cultural groups exist in the United States. These key words describe the traditional group and the "rejection" group:

Traditional Group	Rejection Group
Programmed during the 1920's, 1930's, and 1940's	Programmed during the 1960's
World War I	Space program
Flapper era	Civil rights
Depression	Kennedy's assassination
World War II	Vietnam War
The Establishment	Rebellious heroes
Group/team oriented	Computers
Spectators	Individualistic
Cling to "social order"	Participators
Want women and minorities "in their place"	Want equality based on ability to perform
	Sensually oriented

[2]Morris E. Massey, "What You Are, Is Where You Were When," videotape (Boulder, Col.: University of Colorado, 1978).

Traditional Group	Rejection Group
Puritanical	Question and want to be
Accept institutional leaders	involved in decision making
Like stability and routine	Experiment
Emphasize the value of money	Enjoy informal life and work
Want the traditional nuclear	Practice self-expression
family	Take money for granted
Problem oriented, systematic,	Practice alternative family styles
analytical	Enjoy involvement in
"Tunnel vision"	"causes"[3]

Massey also suggests that people who were programmed in the 1950's form an in-between group. Their childhood involved a period of affluence, permissiveness, television, and an overindulgence of youth.[4]

He also believes that the group programmed in the 1970's form the synthesis group—a culture group whose characteristics are just emerging. Even though the synthesis group members' qualities are yet to be determined, they, too, will make the ritual passages through the years until they become the "establishment."[5]

Although Massey's case for age as the major determinant of people's cultural, psychological, and social value systems is strong, even it cannot be used alone. Though values tend to be fixed by age 20, they can be changed by what Massey calls a significant emotional event.[6]

Establishing an approximate age for another can be difficult for other than face-to-face communication. However, some of the other demographic factors may help.

For example, people within similar age ranges tend to have homes or apartments in similar areas. Occupational levels loosely parallel age spans. To a point, educational attainment can give hints about age.

Sex Sex can be an important determinant of one's acculturation and socialization. For instance, the traditional female and male likely believe that he is the strong, dominant, wage-earning sex, and she is the weak, passive, homemaking sex. In contrast, the "rejection" female and male are likely to dismiss the previously described roles.

Many women are moving away from the sex markers provided by courtesy titles—and even toward the use of initials instead of names. Therefore, identification of the sex of someone by name alone becomes more difficult. For example, if you receive a letter signed "Jan Bales" or "B. G. Shoop," you cannot automatically assume the writer is a man.

Marital and family status If you can learn what a person's life style is, you can make some estimates about her or his total value system. Marital and family status gives good clues to life style.

---

[3]Ibid.

[4]Ibid.

[5]Ibid.

[6]Ibid.

The traditional view often is that a family includes a working husband, a stay-at-home wife, and children at home. However, statistics show that only 15.9 percent of American households match the traditional view, with several larger proportions represented by households with different compositions.

Table 2 shows that the business communicator can no longer assume that all people live in or accept the traditional life style.

TABLE 2   PROPORTIONS OF HOUSEHOLDS IN THE UNITED STATES BY HUMAN COMPOSITION, 1977

Composition of Household	Percent of Households
Married couples, no children or no children at home	30.5
Single persons	20.6
Wage-earning father, wage-earning mother, one or more children at home	18.5
Wage-earning father, full-time-homemaking mother, one or more children at home	15.9
Single-parent mother, one or more children at home	6.2
Female or male head of household, relatives other than spouse or children	5.3
Unrelated persons living together	2.5
Single-parent father, one or more children at home	.6
Total	100.1*

SOURCE: "Who is the *Real* Family?," Ms., August 1978, p. 43, summarizing data from the *Statistical Abstract of the United States,* 1977.

*Total does not equal 100 because of rounding.

Education and intelligence   Another demographic factor that contributes to your assessment of the other is education/intelligence.

If you communicate at the interpersonal or telephone level, you can make some judgment about the intellectual and educational level of the other individual.

Even in the written medio level, you can make some assessment if the other person has written something without the help or intervention of anyone else. For example, if you receive a handwritten letter from someone, you would be safe to judge that it is a reasonably fair reflection of that person's literacy.

Occupation *may* provide some indirect clues to education and intelligence.

More direct clues appear in the form of years of schooling. In addition, the names of educational institutions may indicate the quality and the type of education received. A graduate of The University of California at Berkeley likely would have a different kind of education and value system than a graduate of Oral Roberts University in Tulsa, Oklahoma.

Occupation   Just knowing a person's occupation can aid a great deal in understanding that person. Try to learn job titles, names of firms, and locations of firms, as well as broad occupational groups.

For many business communication situations, you can find the job title, firm, and location easily. By so doing, you have some clues to that person's identity.

In many other business interactions, however, you do not have access to occupational information. For instance, if you receive a letter from an irate customer, it likely does not include such information.

Income and spending   Knowledge of the level of income may help you define a person.

Estimates about income can be gained indirectly through knowledge of occupation, residence address, type of clothes worn, type of car owned, and other such factors. Usually, little can be learned directly, however.

Spending patterns also reveal something of the person's nature. Someone who owns one suit and tithes 10 percent to a church probably has different values than one who owns 30 suits and gives nothing to a church.

Reference groups   Knowledge of the groups with which a person affiliates reveals substantial information. Try to learn about family, friends, neighborhood, charities, schools, church, and place of work. Then try to add information about active participation in clubs, societies, associations, organizations, political parties, and social movements.

One's beliefs can be quite visible through the reference groups chosen. For example, you would judge the values of one who works actively with the American Civil Liberties Union to be different from the values of one who works actively with the John Birch Society.

Interests   The way a person spends leisure time helps in the definition. Thus, try to learn about interests, recreational activities, entertainment choices, media preferences, television-viewing and radio-listening habits, and hobbies.

As for some of the other demographic factors, the category related to interests may be difficult to define.

Nationality, race, and ethnicity   If nationality, race, or ethnicity is not readily apparent, it probably has had minimal impact upon the value-structure development of that person. Indeed, experience shows that for the bulk of Americans of European extraction, the distinctions based upon ethnicity become less and less definable with each passing decade.

On the other hand, even with the movements toward integration of minorities into the mainstream, a resurgence of cultural identification and pride has emerged. Native Americans, Blacks, and Mexican Americans actively call attention to their differentiating characteristics.

Physical characteristics   Physical characteristics and associated nonverbal cues communicate a great deal about an individual's self-concept and value system. A few examples include body type (endomorph, mesomorph, and ectomorph), height, weight, attractiveness, and hair length.

Physical handicaps represent particularly important physical characteristics that affect definitions of people. If you or someone with whom you communicate has any kind of traditionally defined handicap, it will enter into the communication in one way or another.

Even if both the nonhandicapped person and the handicapped person have reduced the effect of the handicap, it still exists in the personality traits of both. Acknowledgment of the reality of the handicap—by both parties—seems to be the best approach to preventing its intrusion into the desired conduct of the communication.

Dress and appearance   When you can see the person with whom you communicate, you may identify that person by observing dress and general appearance.

Clothing style, quality, variety, costliness, cleanliness, and state of repair all communicate something about the wearer's view of her or his place in the world. In addition, the general state of grooming conveys something of the person to another.

Religion   Though religion often relates directly to other demographic factors, it can form a distinct external exhibit of some internal beliefs and values. For the predominant religious groups in America—Protestant, Catholic, and Jewish—the broad differences are well known. However, if you find that someone with whom you are communicating "belongs" to one of the three, you still have a great deal more to learn.

Wide ranges exist within each group. A particularly large number of denominations fall within the Protestant class of Christians.

To continue the example, once you know a person to be, say, of Jewish faith, you still need to know the branch of Judaism, the geographic location, and even the name of the synagogue attended.

Use of demographic data

As you interpret demographic data, avoid stereotyping people according to any one or a few general classes. Human beings vary widely even within a single class.

For example, even though age can be an important identifying factor, many people in a given age bracket do not fit the mold of that bracket.

Therefore, even as you identify as many factors as you can, recognize that infinite numbers of combinations and variations occur to establish people as they are.

What

To understand the participants and the environment, also understand the situation. Consider three sets of factors that help in that assessment: circumstance, style, and topic.

Circumstance

The circumstances in which you attempt to communicate with another greatly affect both you and the other. Is the communication internal (upward, downward, lateral), external, formal, or informal? Each type of transaction makes its own demands.

At what communication level are you operating? Recognizing that you are communicating at the interpersonal level, or the medio level, or the person-to-group level, or the mass level affects your performance.

The same sort of differentiation in circumstances counts for the channels within each of the levels and, in broader terms, for the oral, written, and nonverbal types. For example, a speech delivered before a small dinner gathering will be different from the same speech delivered before an auditorium full of people. Everyone is markedly different when the setting is a golf game rather than a legal hearing.

Still another circumstantial feature arises because of the interference associated with the situation. For instance, a listener who has to stand because the seats are all taken is generally not the same as he or she would be if seated comfortably.

Some other factors associated with the occasion include:

Temperature	Status of everyone involved
Lighting	Political situation
Room size	Extent of participation
Arrangement of seating and equipment in a room	Distance between participants
	Voice qualities
Number of others involved	Visual qualities

Many other circumstantial factors exist. However, these brief examples should serve as reminders that the setting contributes a great deal to the identification of the participants.

Style

Style, the manner in which a thing is done, involves many elements. Though style overlaps with several of the other factors in analysis, it adds its own distinct flavor.

Linguistic accents in oral exchanges are stylistic features that often affect people. For example, a Bostonian accent may create a reaction in Texas equal to that which a Texan's creates in Boston.

Similarly, the *form* of expression (idiom) colors a transaction. Suppose that you use idiom familiar in Appalachia, but strange to someone from New Jersey; that hearer will be distracted by your style—your use of "strange" expressions.

The level of drama greatly affects a situation. People do not react to highly dramatic situations as they do to subdued ones.

Types of humor also play a part in style. People not only use varying styles of humor, they react differently to different kinds of jokes.

Another stylistic feature is the choice of brevity as opposed to full detail in a presentation. Style can also be reflected through the use of a direct approach rather than an indirect one.

Another element of style is the choice of discriminatory or nondiscriminatory communication modes. Symbols can discriminate on the basis of sex, race, ethnicity, age, religion, handicap, or other characteristic. Many people react negatively to the discriminatory styles, whereas others, regrettably, practically try to insist you join them in name-calling and slurs.

The qualities of credibility and charisma override many other aspects of style. Both the presence and the absence of these qualities can affect the definition of participants significantly.

Just as you are a different person in each and every setting, so is every other person. Everyone in essence becomes a *part* of each communication setting—and thus serves as a contributing factor to *what* the other person becomes in that unique situation.

Topic

The topic of the communication also has great potential impact upon the definition of the participants.

For example, if your topic for a given transaction is to grant credit to someone, you may safely assume that the person will be positive about you and your company. On the other hand, if your topic is to deny credit to that same person, you must expect her or him to be rather negative.

Knowing the interest level of the topic can also help you understand the participants. As an example, say that your assigned topic for a speech to a group of line workers involves company growth patterns over the past ten years. You analyze the audience and decide that the members just are not interested in cold statistics, profit-and-loss statements, auditor's reports, and cost ratios.

You then decide that the workers would be interested in a presentation tracing the impact of company growth patterns on the typical worker. You decide to show for the typical worker how wages and benefits have increased through the years.

Thus, by analyzing the receivers in this situation, you decided to change your approach in order to make the topic more interesting. Such adaptability represents the essence of good communication.

Your analysis should also include concern for the factor of relevancy. Determine whether the topic deals with needs, wants, knowledge, and other such human-based qualities. Try to tie the subject to the other's world indirectly even if you cannot do so directly.

When

The time dimension can affect communication in important ways. Examples of the facets of time requiring consideration include:

1. The time of day, the week, the month, or the year
2. The position in a business cycle (prosperity, recession, depression, recovery)
3. The length of a transaction
4. The timing relative to other events
5. The punctuality of the participants
6. The time expectations and customs of the participants
7. The position within each participant's personal time clock

A complete analysis of participants and environment, then, includes identification of and adaptation to all these factors.

Where

The location of a communication transaction also affects its success. Consider all the factors associated with such circumstances as:

Location	Furnishings	Interior temperature,
Space	Density	and ventilation
Territory	Crowding	Weather
Distance	Seating arrangements	Climate
Structure	Aesthetics	Geography

SENDER/RECEIVER ANALYSIS FORM

1. MY NAME _____ DATE OF ANALYSIS _____

2. SUBJECT AND/OR TYPE OF COMMUNICATION _____
   _____

3. CHANNEL _____

4. I AM ACTING AS _____ _____
                     Sender   Receiver

5. IN CAPACITY OF _____
                        (Superior, Subordinate, Peer, Seller, Buyer, etc.)

6. OCCASION OF COMMUNICATION _____

7. WHO AM I AS I ACT IN THIS CAPACITY? _____
   _____
   _____
   _____
   _____

   (List relevant characteristics such as age, sex, occupation, education, knowledge of
   subject, emotional state, race, reference groups, culture, religion, interest in subject, aptitudes, communication abilities, etc.)

8. NAME(S) OF OTHER PERSON(S) _____
   _____

9. ACTING AS _____ _____
                  Sender   Receiver

10. IN CAPACITY(IES) OF _____
    _____
    (Superior, Subordinate, Peer, Seller, Buyer, etc.)

Figure 5–1   Sender/receiver analysis form

How and Why

The how of a transaction relates primarily to the levels of communication and the channel. Therefore, coverage of this topic belongs to the next section on identification of the channel.

When you seek to establish the reasons for communicating, you are dealing with purposes, a topic already covered fully.

11. WHO IS/ARE OTHER(S) ACTING IN THIS CAPACITY? _____

_____

_____

(List relevant characteristics such as those listed with No. 7)

12. WHEN MESSAGE SENT/TO BE SENT? _____

13. WHEN MESSAGE RECEIVED/TO BE RECEIVED? _____

14. FROM WHERE MESSAGE SENT? _____

15. TO WHERE MESSAGE SENT? _____

16. MY PURPOSE(S) _____

_____

_____

_____

_____

(Include the desired actions and interactions)

17. PURPOSE(S) OF OTHER(S) _____

_____

_____

_____

_____

18. ACTION OR INTERACTION RESULTING FROM ANALYSIS _____

_____

_____

_____

_____

(What I did or will do as a result of the analysis)

Figure 5–1 (continued)

Sender/Receiver Analysis Form

A sender/receiver analysis form can be used to summarize the relevant factors in defining the purposes, participants, and environment of a transaction. Figure 5–1 illustrates such a form. As you review it, observe how it forces the user to make the decisions necessary for successful communication.

CHANNELS

Whether acting in the role of sender or receiver, try to understand the features of the various available channels for messages. As a sender, convert your knowledge into the choice of the best channel for the particular communication you are initiating. As a receiver, assess the implications of the channel choice made by another, as well as the strengths and limitations of the channel itself.

Business Communication Dynamics treats channels from both general and specific standpoints. General types include the oral/nonverbal, the written/nonverbal, the nonverbal, and the oral/written/nonverbal. Specific types represent the many vehicles available in each of the general categories. For example, specific channels include such vehicles as the memorandum, the speech, the group discussion, the advertisement, and the photograph.

Hierarchy for Channel Effectiveness

Review a hierarchy for interhuman channel effectiveness. It contains ranks from 1 through 4 in order from richest to poorest:

Rank 1. Two-way, face-to-face channels (interpersonal)
Rank 2. Two-way, not-face-to-face channels (some medio)
Rank 3. One-way, face-to-face channels (person-to-group)
Rank 4. One-way, not-face-to-face channels (mass and some medio)

Rank 1: Two-way, face-to-face channels

Rank 1 includes the specific channels associated with the interpersonal level, basically a combination of oral and nonverbal dialogue.

Because such channels involve only two or a few people in a face-to-face context, communication effectiveness is heightened over the other ranks for several reasons. Other-identification is fuller. More nonverbal symbols enter into the interaction. Feedback is more plentiful and immediate. The players can more rapidly switch in and out of sender and receiver roles. In addition, the associated nonverbal exchanges can involve the fullest range possible—visual, aural, tactile, and even olfactory symbols.

Use Rank 1 communication for conversations about confidential and sensitive issues, for simple exchanges, and for the personal "touch." Also use it for assuring understanding, for speedy interchanges, for relaxed, free-flowing or brainstorming discussion, and for meeting psychological and social needs.

Basic face-to-face oral/nonverbal communication can be strengthened by the addition of written or oral/nonverbal supplements. For example, the use of written materials can improve a discussion of a complex subject. The use of audiovisual presentations such as tapes and films also can strengthen it.

Some examples of the Rank 1 channels are:

Conversation	Interviewing
Dialogue	Briefing
Discussion	Brainstorming
Meeting	Problem-solving
Rumor, gossip, grapevine	Negotiation

Rank 2: Two-way, not face-to-face channels

The second choice for channels should come from the two-way, not-face-to-face, oral/nonverbal realm. Elements of the medio communication level fit into this rank.

As an example, if time, cost, or other considerations prohibit a face-to-face transaction with someone, make the telephone your next channel choice. Though you do not interact in the presence of one another, you do have many of the advantages of the interpersonal level.

Though reduced in effectiveness, the Rank 2 channels allow you to retain important aspects of other-identification, nonverbal symbols, feedback, and rapid role reversal for sender and receiver.

For the telephone—when compared to Rank 1 conversations—the major loss of effectiveness stems from the lack of visual, tactile, and olfactory symbols. The burden rests upon the aural interchange.

By using the conference call, the telephone can be extended to include several people in a discussion. The coming of the picturephone will return some of the visual potential of the interpersonal exchange to the Rank 2 position.

Another Rank 2 channel is found in certain versions of closed-circuit television (CCTV). Two forms of CCTV qualify for Rank 2 status: sound camera projections in two directions and projections in only one direction, with the "talkback" telephone hookup feeding in the other direction. Both interactions gain the advantages inherent in two-way communication.

Two-way radio represents another Rank 2 channel. Ham frequencies, privately licensed FM frequencies, CB frequencies, and even walkie-talkies offer varying levels of efficiency for two-way transactions. The portability of the transceiving instruments provides unusual capabilities for contact between people in auto-mobiles, trucks, boats, ships, trains, and aircraft—or between one person at a fixed station and another on any of the mobile carriers. When tied to standard telephone services or to repeaters—including satellites—the somewhat limited-distance capac-ity for some radio setups can be extended indefinitely.

Paging and signaling systems (including beepers) can also extend the link made possible by two-way-radio and telephone-line networks.

Additional two-way potential exists through the telegraph and other two-way electronic media. However, because they do not involve the oral/nonverbal levels, such exchanges retain only the rapid feedback and role-reversal benefits of the two-way process.

As is true for Rank 1 communication, reinforcement through the written/non-verbal level can improve the use of Rank 2. For example, suppose that decentralized staff need to reach an important decision. The coordinator can distribute a written report by courier to arrive at least one day ahead of a scheduled conference call to resolve the matter.

Examples of channels at the Rank 2 level are:

Two-person telephone conversation
Conference-call telephone conversation
Intercommunication system
Closed-circuit television
Two-way radio (ham, citizens band, private FM, walkie-talkie)
Two-way radio in conjunction with standard telephone service
Typewriter-to-typewriter exchange

Computer-to-computer exchange
Facsimile exchange
Two-way telegraphy
Conveyor system (belts, pull wires and clips, pneumatic tubes)

Rank 3: One-way, face-to-face channels

Roughly paralleling the person-to-group level, Rank 3 channels offer a third choice for efficiency. Because the channels involve oral/nonverbal combinations, they capitalize on some of the features of the interpersonal level.

However, rapid role-reversal is not a part of the speaker-to-group situation. In addition, Rank 3 channels restrict other-identification and audience response.

In addition, audiences tend to follow person-to-group protocol. Therefore, the nonverbal symbols that do emanate from them may not reflect genuine feelings.

One-directionalism proves to be the most limiting feature of Rank 3. With only nonverbal feedback on a fixed-sender, fixed-receiver basis, the opportunities for full transaction of meanings become severely restricted. Even if accompanied by written or audiovisual instruments, the one-way nature of the speaker-with-listeners situation remains inefficient compared to Ranks 1 and 2.

Some of the channels falling into the Rank 3 category are:

Report	Briefing
Speech	Instructions
Lecture	

Rank 4: One-way, not face-to-face channels

The poorest channels fall at the Rank 4 level. They not only are one-way, they do not even have the benefits accruing to the face-to-face characteristics of Rank 3.

Some medio types fall into this category. In addition, all of the mass communication channels belong to Rank 4.

Rank 4 channels operate with minimal identification of the other participant, limited and relatively slow feedback, and slow (if any) role-exchange for sender and receiver.

As an example of the weaknesses of Rank 4, consider an exchange of only two regular-mail letters between correspondents in Dallas and Albany. Even if the original receiver-turned-sender responds on the day of receipt of the letter, and even if the postal service functions well, the exchange takes a minimum of five *days*.

For the majority of business-letter exchanges, the transactions could be completed by telephone in five *minutes*.

Feedback from mass communication channels often becomes virtually impossible. For such media as radio, television, newspaper, magazine, and book, feedback usually occurs only indirectly, at best.

The key to the reduced effectiveness of Rank 4 lies in its one-directionalism devoid of any of the redeeming characteristics provided by a face-to-face channel. Thus, even with the visual and aural verbal and nonverbal features available to television, it still works in only one direction.

Then when the aural is lost in media such as the newspaper, the stimulation to the senses is reduced even more. Though the nonverbal capacity still exists, it is relegated to such things as one-way photographs, sketches, setups, and designs.

With the letter, the potential for nonverbal accompaniment becomes even less.

Rank 4 functions at the exclusively nonverbal level through such channels as paintings, sculpture, music, and magazine advertisements that include no words. Again, the transaction of meanings can be quite difficult; the one-way, nonfeedback nature of the communication makes it so.

Though Rank 4 channels are the least desirable, some advantages do exist. Written communication extends the time and space in which both the sender and receiver can ponder the character and content of the transaction. Both the sender and receiver can store and retrieve written communication, which can be permanent, objective, and often prestigious. The readability, precision, and portability of written communication also stand as advantages.

Written communication lends itself to such things as standardization and mass distribution. It also lends itself to the use of extensive detail and exactness in recording research findings, statistical and accounting data, and other complex material.

A written account of Rank 1, 2, or 3 transactions can serve as a supplement to and permanent record of them. The supplement can provide verification when necessary.

Other Rank 4 channels, including movies, records, announcements over a loudspeaker, magazines, and art exhibits can communicate in a manner distinct from the other ranks.

Some of the channels available at the Rank 4 level are:

Directive	Letter
Report	Memorandum
Research proposal	Note
Computer	Telecopy
Teletype	Print-out
Policy or rule handbook	Company newsletter, newspaper,
One-directional closed-	or magazine
circuit television	Piped-in music
Announcements over	Tape recording
loudspeaker	Movie
Television	Record
Book	Radio
Journal	Magazine
Radar	Newspaper
Novel	Facsimile reproduction
Poem	Painting
Sculpture	Photograph
Courier/messenger	Telephone message service
service	Postal-mail service
Electronic mail service	Automatic telephone message
Display	recording

(1461 words)
(test on page 149)

Defining Channels

Every factor discussed in the sections on defining purposes, people, environment, and the hierarchy applies to defining channels. However, review these summary categories for certain key factors: (1) availability, (2) feedback potential, (3) custom, (4) impact, (5) difficulty of message, (6) storage and retrieval, (7) number of receivers, (8) time, (9) distance, (10) cost/return, and (11) other factors.

Availability

Sheer availability of channels forms an obvious decision criterion for the sender. Thus, practicality requires that you establish a mental catalog of channels available to you. If you believe that certain channels should be added at your firm, determine that they will be. As you become convinced of the importance of using the most effective ranks frequently, you will want to add available channels to Ranks 1 and 2, particularly. You will even go to the extent of urging that travel funds be made available so that Rank 1 channels can be utilized even when you are some distance from your receivers.

Feedback potential

Always use a channel with the best potential for feedback. The higher the channel falls in the effectiveness hierarchy, the better the chance for optimal feedback.

Even if you find that decision factors force you into a poor channel, establish the best possible feedback mechanism. For example, if you must use the letter as a channel for a sales message to a customer, include a stamped return envelope to facilitate a response. In similar fashion, if you place an advertisement in a local newspaper, include a coupon for an item so that turned-in coupons will provide evidence of feedback from the advertisement.

Custom

Custom also carries weight in a channel decision. If tradition calls for written invitations to a reception, you would be unwise to use the richer telephone call. On the other hand, do not blindly follow custom. Often the realized gains from employing a new channel could offset any momentary losses associated with not honoring tradition. For instance, suppose that you have always conversed by telephone with an important supplier. Though the first reaction to a personal visit by you might be one of surprise, the potential for improved relations could be worth breaking out of the traces.

Impact

Some styles of channels carry more weight than others. The relative importance of the various channels, then, becomes another criterion for channel analysis.

Marshall McLuhan feels so strongly about this subject that he proposed that the medium (the channel) is the message. Such a theory suggests that the channel absorbs the message. The channel becomes the package, and the impact upon the receiver comes from the package.

Therefore, if you package your meanings in a Rank 1 channel, the receiver actually will assign them different meanings than if you package them in a lower-ranked channel.

Difficulty of message

Another criterion for channel definition is the complexity of the material contained in the message. Certain channels simply do not have the capacity to carry difficult messages. For example, a Rank 1 channel alone cannot carry the extensive data needed for an annual report to stockholders.

You do not want to overload a channel. Neither do you want to waste the capacity of a channel.

The error of underloading a channel becomes particularly serious when a rich channel could handle the material that you have committed to a poor one simply because of a bad choice on your part. Why write a letter to someone when a telephone call or personal visit could handle the subject matter—and provide a richer interchange in the process?

Storage and retrieval

Another feature of channel definition lies in its potential for storage and eventual retrieval. Clearly, the written channels from Rank 4 have the highest rating here.

Those messages that need to be retained for future reference cannot be entrusted to human minds alone. Minds continually reinterpret, bury, and lose material. Minds disagree with one another. Minds become inaccessible. Minds die.

With the concept of storage and retrieval comes the recognition that the computer is an essential part of the communication system. It uses symbols and even interacts with humans and other computers. In addition, it provides incredibly extensive storage and retrieval capacity for certain kinds of information.

Number of receivers

Another factor influencing channel choice is the number of receivers. By definition, if more than a few people constitute the intended receiver group, the interpersonal and medio levels cannot be engaged.

Time

Time emerges as a factor in channel choice when a speedy transaction is required or desired. No one-way channel would serve if you needed to contact people within a few minutes.

Time itself can become an element of a channel. For example, a night letter is a different channel than a telegram—simply because of the time of day each is sent. (Though a telegraph company sends both types of messages, the night letter costs less. In addition, because the night letter is sent at night to arrive the next day, it does not carry as much psychological weight as a telegram.)

The timing of a message also carries meaning in and of itself. If your telephone rings at 2 A.M., this medium becomes a different channel than it is when it rings at 2 P.M.

The day of the week and the seasons of the year also contribute to channel definition. For example, sales messages in the winter months add different tones than those present for the same channel during the summer months.

Distance

The distance between sender and receiver has an impact upon channel usage. If you are 500 miles from the location of your receiver, you cannot casually walk over for a Rank 1 interchange.

Ranks 2 and 4 offer the obvious channels for distant participants. However, distance alone should not dictate their choice. Make the decision on the basis of an analysis of all relevant factors, particularly the cost/return and subject matter. In some circumstances you well may need to spend the travel money necessary to make an interpersonal contact possible.

Cost/return

An important criterion for selecting channels involves costs and return on investment.

To illustrate, people tend to think that letters cost much less than telephone calls. In reality, if you assign all labor, material, service, postal, and overhead expenses to the production of a letter and to the production of a telephone call, the letter often costs more. For a five-minute call from Oklahoma City to New York City during business hours, the cost would be about $3 (including the wages of the participants and the overhead). Depending upon the wages of the people involved, estimates of the cost to produce and mail a single letter ranges from $2 to $7, with an average of about $5. Thus, for the illustration, a telephone exchange at $3 is less than even the minimum cost of a two-letter exchange at $4.

Such a comparison becomes particularly apt when you have access to a Wide Area Telephone Service (WATS) line. For one fixed fee, you may make as many long-distance telephone calls as you wish. As the number of calls increases, the average cost for a call reduces. In addition, toll-free numbers allow people to make long-distance calls to a firm at no expense to them.

The cost of a national television commercial can seem prohibitive on the surface. However, the cost for each person reached can be relatively small when compared to a mass mailing of letters.

Similar comparisons of costs could be made for channels within different ranks. However, the most expensive of the channels—the transfer of human beings so that they can communicate at the Rank 1 level—deserves expanded treatment.

As suggested, the richness of a Rank 1 transaction may be worth the investment in transporting people to accomplish it. If the subject calls for face-to-face communication for effectiveness, investment in an exchange of letters—or even telephone calls—can be a virtual waste.

As an example, Holland, Stead, and Leibrock concluded from their research related to channel cost/benefit considerations:

> 1) Managers employing relatively inexperienced technical personnel should be prepared to supply plenty of interpersonal internal consulting help for them. . . .
> 2) Managers should be careful not to preclude the use of richer forms of information transfer during periods of uncertainty. Unfortunately, many organizations tend to *reduce* information budgets (restraining long-distance calls, trips, etc.) during periods of uncertainty since such periods may coincide with increased economic constraints. . . .
> 3) Employees who must spend a great deal of their time working with highly uncertain problems should probably not be geographically isolated. Such employees should be located in work space where the richer channels of communication are more easily usable (e.g., accessibility to the phone and to face-to-face contact with other organization members). . . .

4) Managers should attempt to develop and maintain a "warm" organization climate that encourages rather than hinders interpersonal communication.[7]

Other factors

Though the listing of channel considerations could continue indefinitely, four more of a rather distinct nature will complete this coverage.

First, the differentiation between intended and unintended receivers relates to channel definition. An unintended receiver can actually become a channel. If you send a message to an identified person and an unintended receiver intercepts it, that unintended receiver becomes a secondary channel for carrying the message to others.

In an interesting twist, you can pretend to send a message to an identified receiver when you *want* another to monitor it. In the process you deliberately use an indirect receiver as a channel.

Gossip, rumor, hearsay, and the grapevine take the shape of maverick channels. However, they exist, and thus require wise use. Many of your messages can move through this informal network much more rapidly than through more formal channels.

The third unusual channel choice takes the form of the deliberate use of interference as a channel. A classic example involves knocking at the door of a house or telephoning during meal-preparation time—or some other busy time. The theory is that the pressure of meal preparation will cause the receiver to buy a product or sign up for something simply to get rid of the caller and get back to work. Such deliberate use of interference channels, however, can have negative outcomes. Antagonistic feelings may arise from encroachment upon one's privacy and busy times.

Another channel decision relates to using certain human characteristics as channels. As an example, some senders deliberately use handicapped persons for door-to-door selling. The handicap itself becomes a channel in those instances.

Undoubtedly, such a channel has led to many sales. However, others undoubtedly have led to lost sales because of the perception that such channels are improper choices.

Other similar, but less dramatic channels include standing instead of sitting, speaking softly instead of loudly, and playing golf or having a drink during an exchange.

SUMMARY

Six guidelines that enhance any type of communication are:

1. Define purposes, participants, and environment.
2. Identify channel.

---

[7]Winford E. Holland, Bette Ann Stead, and Robert C. Leibrock, "Information Channel/Source Selection as a Correlate of Technical Uncertainty in a Research and Development Organization," *IEEE Transactions on Engineering Management* EM–23 (November 1976): 166-167.

3. Control interference.
4. Select, encode, decode, and transceive messages in light of purposes, participants, environment, channel, and interference.
5. Use feedback.
6. Evaluate.

Chapter 5 reviews Guidelines 1 and 2.

Business communication is *purposive communication*. Purpose and profit carry with them *ethical responsibilities*. Purposes can be complex, but the basic goal for a sender is *to bring some desired action* by the receiver. The basic goal for a receiver is to act in a way that will satisfy some need or want. Whether sending or receiving, define both participants' purposes.

As a sender, (1) prestate the objectives; (2) make the statements clear and concise; (3) include the who, what, when, where, how, and why; (4) establish criteria for evaluation; and (5) frame the objectives and criteria in action/interaction (behavioral) terms.

As an active receiver, be just as diligent as the sender in applying the preceding five suggestions.

To identify yourself, the other participant, and the environment, again *define the who and whom, what, when, where, how, and why* of the situation.

For all human beings involved, understand the psychological, social, cultural, and physical ramifications. The most available evidence about those elements include these *demographic factors:*

Name	Income and spending
Address	Reference groups
Age	Interests
Sex	Nationality, race, and ethnicity
Marital and family status	Physical characteristics
Education and intelligence	Dress and appearance
Occupation	Religion

To define the what of a communication situation, consider (1) *circumstances,* (2) *style,* and (3) *topic.* They all have a bearing on the transaction.

The *time,* the *location,* and the *channel* for communication also greatly affect the exchange. The why of a communication situation speaks, again, of the purposes.

To choose and use channels wisely, understand the *hierarchy for channel effectiveness,* in order from *richest* to *poorest:*

Rank 1. Two-way, face-to-face channels (interpersonal)
Rank 2. Two-way, not-face-to-face channels (some medio)
Rank 3. One-way, face-to-face channels (person-to-group)
Rank 4. One-way, not-face-to-face channels (mass and some medio)

Also, when choosing channels, consider their (1) availability, (2) feedback potential, (3) custom, (4) impact, (5) difficulty of message, (6) storage and retrieval needs, (7) number of receivers, (8) time, (9) distance, (10) cost/return implications, and (11) other relevant factors.

Practice

1. You must present a paper in your marketing class. The paper is worth half of your grade. Though you would like an "A" in the course, you need only a "C" to get your degree. What are your purposes? What are the professor's purposes? Explain.

2. You bought a miniature electric train. After you operated it for an hour, it ceased to work. You are angry. You put the train in its box and walk to the store where you bought it. You fear that the store will not take it back because it was a sale item. You wish to be firm and communicate that you want your money back or you want a train that works. You also want to relate that the salesperson who sold you the train misled you about its capabilities. In brief, clear terms, what are your objectives? What will your first statement be?

3. What does the word "cool" mean to you? What might it mean to a rock star? a ghetto inhabitant? a scientist? a socialite? a grave digger? a chef?

4. You have just met Jack Livingtree. You will be sharing an office with him at the accounting firm for which you work. You want to know him well enough to communicate effectively. What questions would you ask him in order to understand who he is and what his views are? Does his name give you any information?

5. You were just transferred to your company's Los Angeles division. You will meet your new manager, Joan Alexander, tomorrow, at which time you will discuss your new assignment with her. All you know about Alexander is that she earned her B.A. and M.B.A. at Harvard, that she grew up in New York City, that she turned 32 this month, and that she has been with the company for eight years. Answer these questions in writing:
   a. What are your purposes? What do you suppose are Alexander's purposes?
   b. Who is Alexander? Do you know enough about her to plan for tomorrow's meeting? If not, what additional information do you need? Where or how will you get it?
   c. What is the environment in which Alexander operates? What is the environment of tomorrow's meeting?

6. After you have answered the questions in No. 5, meet with your group. Read and discuss your plans for the meeting . Also skim and briefly discuss the concept of role-playing described on page 513. Now choose a group member to play the role of Ms. Alexander and another to act as the employee. Act out the meeting. Evaluate the exchange. Did the student who played the part of the employee act in accordance with her or his expressed purposes and assessment of the participants and the environment? Discuss.

7. You are the supervisor of a group of salespeople who sell a line of children's books directly to grocery stores. You aren't satisfied with the performance of your salespeople and suspect that they do little or no planning before they meet with their potential customers. Write a memorandum that clearly explains the importance of defining purposes, the participants, and the environment. Include some practical suggestions on how to gather, analyze, and use the information.

8. Use the sender/receiver analysis form on page 134 for a communication event in which you will participate in the next week. After the event has taken place, evaluate the usefulness of the form. Did you feel better prepared to communicate after using it? Were you able to communicate more directly and competently?

9. You want a face-to-face meeting with your accountant to discuss his failure to keep your tax records in order. He insists that you put your complaints in writing and mail them to him. What do you do? Assume he avoids meeting with you. Write a letter that clearly states your complaints and demands. Will your letter be as effective as a face-to-face conversation might have been? Why?

10. You are the owner and manager of a research firm. Your employees are specialists in a number of fields and work alone on small projects. What can you do to overcome the communication problems that arise when employees work in virtual isolation? Identify the problems and solutions.

11. Choose the specific channel or channels that you feel would be most appropriate for these communication situations. Explain your choices.
    a. Your manager sends a memorandum asking you what amount you would like your raise to be.
    b. You need to get in touch with your London office to relay some very important, detailed financial information.
    c. You need to let your 150 employees know that a major company reorganization will begin next week.
    d. You need to decide whether or not to apply for a promotion.
    e. You are the chief marketer for a large oil company. You know what your company's public image is deteriorating rapidly because consumers are upset over the fact that your company is making unusually high profits. You wish to improve that image by letting the consuming public know that you are using those profits to develop solar energy systems.
    f. You are dissatisfied with the man with whom you share an office. He talks all of the time and smokes several packs of cigarettes a day. You are allergic to cigarette smoke. You know that Ms. Andrews, your supervisor, is the person who makes office assignments.

12. Decide which of the four ranks in the hierarchy for channel effectiveness would be appropriate for each of these situations. Once you have chosen Rank 1, 2, 3, or 4, select a specific channel within it.
    a. You need to communicate with a customer whom you know to be illiterate.
    b. You need to convey important information to 72 centrally located employees immediately.
    c. You need to communicate with a customer who reacts negatively to sexist language. Your personal style still includes such sexist terms as the "-man" words and "he," "his," and "him" as "neutral" references, though you are trying to eliminate them. You could choose a Rank 4 written channel so that you could edit to remove the offending language. However, you prefer a richer channel. What could you do?
    d. You have to lay off an employee.
    e. You receive a telephone call from a supplier. The supplier spends ten minutes reciting stock numbers, quantities of back-ordered items, prices, terms, and other such numerical data, evidently expecting you to capture all of it. The supplier makes no mention of supplementing the call with a written document. What might you do to change the channel choice?
    f. You want to contact a client in an office in Atlanta. It is 4:30 on a Friday afternoon in Chicago.

13. Meet with your group. Discuss the following situations. All you know about each of these potential clients is what you read here. As a life insurance salesperson, how would you approach each person? Why?
    a. Elaine "Lou-Lou" Werner, the owner of a garden supply store, dresses in rather loud colors. She likes big cars, and works long hours. She dislikes long meetings.
    b. Willard Fasteau just retired from his job. He had worked as a welder for 40 years. He lives alone, wears dressy clothes, has never been married, and flies an American flag in front of his small house. You heard that he is nice once you get to know him.
    c. Sharon Torres is a teller at a bank. She is married and has four children. She is a member of the League of Women Voters, and she dresses very conservatively. A "No Peddlers" sign is nailed to the door of her house.

    d. Mike Frank is a graduate student in sociology at the local university. He shares on old house with three other students. You have seen him playing softball with neighborhood children. He is a chain smoker, and he usually wears jeans and Hawaiian shirts. Have one of your group members present one of your answers to the class.

14. You quite likely will work with a number of "others" who will not share your view of the world. Most of these people will be tolerant of you, but some of your co-workers will be preachers—they will try to convert you to their way of thinking. Because you do not want to fight with these people, you must think of ways to keep the peace and yet get your work done. List some tactful techniques that you might use.

15. What can you do to overcome the problems associated with the channels used in these situations?

    a. You just completed a short report you wrote for your Washington, D.C., office. You cannot mail the report because it is due in Washington today; thus, you must transmit its contents by phone.

    b. Though you believe that complex financial information should be transmitted in written form, you boss wants you to make an oral presentation of this year's sales figures to your company's managers at the annual sales meeting. Your boss does not want you to use visual aids or written handouts.

    c. Because the company for which you want to work cannot afford to fly you to North Dakota for an interview, you must conduct the entire interview process by mail and telephone.

16. Meet with your group. Discuss how you would handle each of these communication problems.

    a. Bill dominates the conversation at almost every staff meeting. When asked to allow someone else to speak, Bill usually says: "I'll be through in a minute." He is rarely through in a minute.

    b. Sally, your department's computer expert, is very shy. When you ask her important computer-related questions, she doesn't give you much information. She expresses herself beautifully on paper, but sometimes you need your questions answered immediately.

    c. Clark, your boss, usually interrupts you when you speak. You often have something very important to say.

17. Do you believe that the profit motive significantly distinguishes business organizations from not-for-profit organizations? Why? If you believe that the profit motive does make a substantial difference, what effect does it have on communication in business organizations?

18. You are the editor of publications for the Jenks Lumber Company. Your boss asks you to write a one-page statement of purposes for the company for distribution to all employees. Include these points:

    a. The Jenks Lumber Company puts "customers first, employees second, and profits last."

    b. The company wants hard work from its employees in order to provide its customers with a quality product.

    c. The company wants to retain its small-company image while taking every opportunity to grow.

    d. The company discourages union organizing.

19. You have worked at the Fancy Company for two years. You have yet to receive a raise, though your performance ratings have always been high. You make an appointment with Mr. Biggs, the company president, to discuss a raise. What are your purposes? What would you think Mr. Biggs' purposes will be? How can an understanding of Mr. Biggs' purposes beforehand help you prepare your case?

20. You are a debt collector for the Anne Johnson and Daughters Department Store. You must call three people today to give them notice that they have a week to make their overdue payments. If they do not make the payments within a week, your company will have to take legal action. You are a good communicator and are aware of the importance of the environment of the other. You know the following about the debtors:

a. John is a carpenter who always makes late payments. He hates to talk on the telephone.

b. Elizabeth was just fired from her job. You do not know why. You do know that she is the sole support of her two children and that she is in dire financial straits.

c. Bob is a Wall Street executive who has never been behind on a payment before. The last time you called (when the bill was 60 days overdue) he referred you to his accountant, who said that she would put the payment in the mail the next day.

How would you handle each call?

21. Knowing who and what you are is important in order to communicate effectively. Write a short paper assessing your strengths, weaknesses, and personal values. Here are some questions you might answer in writing the assessment. (You may add to or subtract from the lists for each of the questions.)

a. How would you rank these in order of importance to you? (You may add to or subtract from the list.)

☐ Love	☐ Recognition
☐ Achievement	☐ Family
☐ Affiliation/Friendship	☐ Recreation
☐ Wealth	☐ Health
☐ Hobbies	☐ Power
☐ Religion	☐ Career

b. What do you believe concerning these issues or subjects?
  ☐ Separation of church and state
  ☐ The death penalty
  ☐ Human rights
  ☐ Regulation by the government
  ☐ Conservation
  ☐ Nuclear power
  ☐ Civil rights
  ☐ Women's movement
  ☐ Management styles (authoritarian or nonauthoritarian)
  ☐ Gun control
  ☐ Labor unions
  ☐ Living together before marriage
  ☐ Euthanasia
  ☐ Abortion
  ☐ Corporate Responsibility
  ☐ Mass transportation

c. Which of these are your strengths? weaknesses?
  ☐ Are you intelligent?
  ☐ Are you skilled?
  ☐ Are you kind?
  ☐ Are you hard-working?
  ☐ Do you like your personality?
  ☐ Are you graceful?
  ☐ Do you speak well?
  ☐ Do you write well?
  ☐ Do you listen well?
  ☐ Are you sensitive to other people's feelings?

□ Are you usually happy?
□ Do you get along well with others?
□ Do you eat the right foods?
□ Do you exercise regularly?
□ Are you tolerant?

22. Use your dictionary and thesaurus to create meanings for these words. Use the words when you think, write, and speak so that you feel comfortable using them.

a. Antagonistic	**i.** Hypothesis
b. Cessation	**j.** Ideational
c. Cognitive	**k.** Inevitable
d. Context	**l.** Interact
e. Exclusive	**m.** Predominant
f. Extensive	**n.** Tactile
g. Facilitate	**o.** Treatise
h. Hierarchy	**p.** Verbatim

23. Take and score Self-Test 14 over the excerpt about the hierarchy for communication channel effectiveness.

Self-Test 14
Excerpt about Hierarchy for Channel Effectiveness

A. Recall (25 points each). For each multiple-choice question, select the most accurate answer.

1. Which of these *cannot* qualify as a Rank 2 (two-way, not-face-to-face) channel?
   a. Two-way radio
   b. Typewriter-to-typewriter exchange
   c. Lecture to an employee group
   d. Intercommunication system
   e. Conference-call telephone conversation

2. If you often slip and use racist expressions, which specific communication channel would be best for you to use until you have rid your language of that problem?
   a. Phone
   b. Careful letter
   c. Face-to-face conversation
   d. Quick memorandum
   e. CCTV with "talkback" features

3. Which one of these statements is true?
   a. The briefing falls at the Rank 1 (two-way, face-to-face) level of communication.
   b. Mass communication channels fall at the Rank 3 (one-way, face-to-face) level.
   c. The major advantages of the written channels at the Rank 4 (one-way, not face-to-face) level are their abilities to form a permanent, precise record of complex information.
   d. The good communicator avoids using more than one channel at a time.
   e. A primary disadvantage of the Rank 2 (two-way, not face-to-face) channels is that oral feedback is lost.

B. Inference (25 points). Indicate whether this statement is true or false.

Regardless of the reason for initiating a communication exchange, a face-to-face conversation is always the best channel choice.

Solution to Self-Test 14
Excerpt about Hierarchy for Channel Effectiveness

A. Recall (25 points each)   **B.** Inference (25 points)

  1. c   **3.** c   False
  2. b

24. Take and score Self-Test 15 over Chapter 5.

Self-Test 15
Chapter 5

A. Recall (10 points each). For each multiple-choice question, select the most accurate answer.

   1. Which of these statements is *not* true?
       a. Business communication is purposive communication—with profit as the ultimate goal.
       b. Purposes can be immediate or ultimate, conscious or subconscious.
       c. The specific goal of purposive communication is to bring about some desired action or interaction.
       d. Communication purposes are independent of the environment for which they are defined.
       e. The source/destination and evaluator functions as the generator of purposes.

   2. When you consider human factors, consider:
       a. Educational background
       b. Ability to hear, see, and speak
       c. State of mind
       d. Rank in the company
       e. a–d

   3. When analyzing the other participant in the communication process, pay the greatest attention to the _____ question.
       a. Who or whom
       b. What
       c. Where
       d. When
       e. How
       f. Why

   4. Time is a critical factor in characterizing the other participant. Here time refers to:
       a. Business cycles
       b. The other's personal time clock
       c. The time of the day
       d. Not a–c
       e. a–c

   5. Which one of these statements is *not* true?
       a. Criteria supply objective bases for determining the level of success of an activity.
       b. The receiver can preset objectives.
       c. Reference groups for a person include the groups with which he or she affiliates.
       d. The largest percentage of households have a wage-earning father, full-time homemaking mother, and one or more children at home.

      e. Style is the manner in which things are done—and includes such things as linguistic accents, levels of drama, and humor.

  6. Which one of these statements is true?

      a. Letters are usually less expensive than telephone calls.

      b. Custom has nothing to do with channel choice.

      c. Sometimes a firm is wise to invest in transportation in order to bring people into face-to-face transactions.

      d. The potential for feedback is an unimportant factor in choosing channels.

      e. The company newsletter falls at the Rank 3 (one-way, face-to-face) level of effectiveness.

  7. You will more than likely act ethically if you

      a. Always pursue a course of action that allows your company to make the greatest profits

      b. Remain loyal to your superiors at all times

      c. Pursue the course of action that is good for people and your company

      d. Always do your work exactly as you are told

      e. Never question the decisions of others

B. Inference (15 points each). Indicate whether these statements are true or false.

  1. An easily determinable morally sound course of action exists for every business situation.

  2. You cannot assess purposes, the participants, and the environment if you do not know beforehand that the communication event will occur.

Solution to Self-Test 15

Chapter 5

A. Recall (10 points each)

  1. d   **5.** d

  2. e   **6.** c

  3. a   **7.** c

  4. e

B. Inference (15 points each)

  1. False

  2. False

6

Guidelines for Effective Communication: Interference, Feedback, and Evaluation

To complete the coverage of the guidelines, review the roles of interference, feedback, and evaluation in the communication process.

INTERFERENCE

The communication model and the applied guidelines in previous chapters deal with the important concept of interference. As you recall, it involves senders and receivers, emanates from humans and nonhumans, and occurs at all stages of the process.

However interference occurs, try to anticipate, prevent, and eliminate it. If you cannot do so, at least weigh its impact upon your transactions.

To expand the coverage, consider the importance of understanding and controlling three important bases of interference: (1) the communication process itself, (2) human beings, and (3) the environment.

Communication Process

The application of the communication guidelines provides one of the best ways to control interference. Therefore, even as you review the one specific guideline on controlling interference, review how all of the guidelines relate to it.

Purposes

Barriers may arise simply because you and the other participant define purposes poorly—or do not define them at all. Similarly, they may arise if you determine only your own purposes, but not those of the other participant.

Interference also often occurs when the objectives of sender and receiver conflict—or even differ significantly.

For instance, suppose that you receive a promotion to department head. You know that a man in your department had also filed for the position—and resents that you were selected. One of your purposes for communicating with him is to assure him that you are competent and fair. In contrast, one of his receiving purposes is to catch you making mistakes. Both of you want to do your work well. However, the undercurrent of clashing purposes can swamp every attempt one makes to deal with the other.

In another example, suppose that you are listening to a woman as she tries to convince you to accept a research proposal you have rejected once. If your only purpose for receiving is to learn her arguments so that you can counter them, she likely will not realize her purposes.

Participants

Your role varies at least somewhat with each transaction in which you participate. Thus, if you do not freshly analyze yourself each time, interference may arise.

You may speak too slowly or too rapidly for the circumstances. You may be so preoccupied that you do not listen well. You may offend by saying, "I tried to 'Jew' him down on the price" instead of "I haggled over the price." Poor spelling in your letter of application may cost you a job for which you qualify.

View yourself as the major potential barrier to any communication in which you participate. Not only will that view lead you to know, develop, and adjust, but it will remove another serious communication obstacle. That obstacle is the tendency to make the other person in the transaction responsible for any communication failure or success.

Another important reason for understanding and developing yourself lies in the contribution such acts make to your understanding of other people. The more you understand your own private world, the more likely you will be able to pierce into the worlds of others.

If you do not try to understand and adapt to other participants in a transaction, interference likely will occur. Without empathy the transaction certainly will fall short of its potential. You may not speak loudly enough to suit your listener. You may attribute to a writer a motive that does not exist. You may decide that an actual supporter of your project opposes it, just because of the probing style of dialogue he employs. You may tell ethnic jokes in the presence of one offended by them. You may miss the chance to grow through the exposure to other ideas and values. You may fall prey to the classical interference: hearing only what you want to hear.

Environment

Both human and nonhuman elements of the environment may interfere with communication. Therefore, as you identify those elements, you improve your chances of controlling them.

Channel

Wise use of channels offsets a great deal of interference. Therefore, good control of the communication process requires good control of channels.

Understand the strengths and weaknesses of the various channels. Recall and apply the hierarchy for channel effectiveness. As a sender, choose a channel as close to the Rank 1 (two-way, face-to-face) channels as you can.

As both sender and receiver, recognize the interference potential inherent in whatever channel is used. Be alert to it so that you can overcome it.

Interference

One of the major types of interference is the failure to deal with interference. Thus, to control communication, apply the guideline that calls for you to recognize and overcome potential and actual interference.

You may have to apply the guidelines fleetingly. In addition, even though you try, you may not be able to do much to overcome the interference.

Even in those circumstances in which you cannot eliminate interference, however, grow by recognizing it for what it is. Remember what the interference did to weaken a transaction, and try to prevent any repetition of that failure.

Encoding/decoding

Poor encoding and decoding form substantial barriers to effective communication. To surmount the barriers, select and interpret messages and symbols in light of your knowledge about yourself, the other participant, the channel, and the interference.

Feedback

One of the best ways to prevent and overcome damaging interference is to use feedback extensively and continually. As a sender, select the richest possible channels and solicit feedback. As a receiver, feed back as quickly and completely as possible.

With intensive and aware feedback, even barriers that emerge unexpectedly during a transaction can be controlled.

Evaluation

Evaluation, too, helps to remove the negative impact of communication barriers. Stage-by-stage and terminal evaluation allow you to correct for interference immediately. It also contributes to your knowledge of interference and how to eliminate it.

Human Beings

The greatest barriers to communication reside within the people who perform the acts. The barriers arise within both minds and physical beings.

As you reviewed in Chapter 4, human-based interference falls into four major categories:

1. Content and capability of source
2. Simultaneous transactions
3. Symbolistic bias
4. Flaws in transmitting instruments

You may want to review pages 100-102 to aid in the recall of their descriptions.

At this point, though, expand your knowledge about one of them—symbolistic bias. To understand and overcome symbolistic bias, understand the concepts of general semantics, perceptions and meanings, and some specific devices for dealing with symbolistic bias.

General semantics

General semantics is the branch of linguistics dealing with the relations between symbols and meanings. It often is treated as a theory of communication in and of itself. Korzybski is the acknowledged founder of the modern discipline.[1]

The basic semantic obstacle exists because of the one-word, one-meaning misconception. In truth, however, meanings vary within people. Moreover, just as soon as certain words begin to take on relatively common meanings for many people, their meanings shift, or troublesome new words are added.

Even as symbols and meanings make communication possible, they also act as major obstacles to it. The word "run" has about ninety "meanings" listed in the dictionary. The word "blue" can mean a color or a mood. The term "labor union" holds one set of meanings for its members and another for business managers.

Furthermore, symbols carry both rational and emotional overtones. Thus, a safe symbol for some people can draw out negative meanings for others.

To begin to overcome the semantic barrier, recall and apply the definition and model of communication developed in Chapter 4: Meanings exist within the minds of people, not within the symbols themselves. The symbols merely represent those meanings.

Perceptions and meanings

Perception is the ability to convert the sensations received through the five senses into internal meanings. The senses themselves serves as filters—that is, as potential barriers.

The major filters, however, exist within the mind. The mind assigns meanings to what the senses receive. As a sender, understand that symbol choice should take into account potential perceptual differences. As a receiver, understand that received symbols often differ significantly from the transmitted ones because of the filter of your perceptions. In both roles, understand that you perceive from a different base of experience than any other person on earth.

To extend your grasp of perceptions and meanings, review the four types of meanings suggested by Berlo: (1) denotative, (2) structural, (3) contextual, and (4) connotative.[2]

Denotative meanings   Denotative meanings are those widely accepted, uniform meanings for physical-world objects to which humans can actually point. Examples include "desk," "dirt," "hours," "walk," and "run." Dictionaries do not include denotative meanings. They cannot point to physical objects; instead, dictionaries use words to describe words.

Even though denotation can lead to a base level of shared meanings, it has a serious limitation created by the frequent unavailability of physical objects. Illustrations and pictures can, however, substitute for the objects themselves. Say you use just the simple word "shoe" without pointing to the actual shoe or a photograph or drawing of it. You have not created a denotative meaning. The "shoe" could be one of a variety of human shoes—men's, women's, high-heeled, low-heeled, canvas,

[1]Alfred Korzybski, *Science and Sanity: An Introduction to Non-Aristotelian Systems and General Semantics* (Lancaster, Pa.: Science Press Printing Co., 1933).

[2]David K. Berlo, *The Process of Communication: An Introduction to Theory and Practice* (New York: Holt, Rinehart and Winston, 1960), p. 190.

leather, hiking, jogging, tennis, . . . It could also be a horseshoe, a brake shoe, or the shoe of a tire.

The desired meanings for denotative symbols cannot be taken for granted in general communication. Even for denotative symbols, the meanings still exist within the minds of the people who create them.

Structural meanings   Berlo's second type of meaning is based on structure—grammar, syntax, the sequencing of symbols into sentences.

To illustrate meanings gained through structural expectations, consider this sentence: "Several chairpersons selected many of the committee members on the basis of friendship rather than the members' qualifications." You expect the word that follows the word "several" to be plural, and "chairpersons" is. The verb "selected" denotes a certain action in the past. You now anticipate that the action is moving from "several chairpersons" to some object. The object is "many of the committee members"—another plural form. The word "many" itself predicts a plural word to follow. The sequencing of the phrase "on the basis of" leads to the expectation of an object. The object is "friendship." The words "rather than" introduce a rejected object—"the members' qualifications." Included in the final phrase, the word "members'" meets the structural convention of showing plural possession.

Redundancy is also an important structural feature of the examples. The words "several" and "chairpersons" reinforce the concept of more than one sender. The words "many," "members," and "members'" repeat the plural nature of the receivers.

The importance of structure to meaning also appears in the sheer order of words in the illustrative sentence. Think of the significant revision of meaning that would occur just by trading the phrases "several committee chairpersons" and "many of the committee members." Also, think about the dramatic revision of meaning created by converting the final segment to read ". . . on the basis of the members' qualifications rather than friendship."

Consider this sentence as a final example: "That machine operator said the supervisor is a thief." As punctuated, the meaning is substantially different than when the same words become: "That machine operator," said the supervisor, "is a thief."

Contextual meanings   Berlo's next perceptual/meanings class—context—borrows from the denotative and structural classes.

To illustrate, consider a paragraph developed for this book, but in the style used by Berlo.[3] The paragraph contains familiar denotative words and customary sentence structure, but it also contains some contrived denotative "words" for which you need to try to supply meanings. Even as you read the paragraph, analyze how you came to supply familiar words for the artificial ones.

A large number of outalucks have the druc. Some of them have even been confined to the infirmary with it. Because many of the outalucks' professors have the druc too—coughing and sneezing all over the place—the professors will let the outalucks make up their final sockos as the beginning of the next term. At least three professors are already so gloop that graduate bools will administer their sockos. Most of the professors will also accept term duples late.

---

[3]Ibid., p. 207.

To illustrate more realistically, recall the multiple meanings of the word "shoe." Then consider how the establishment of a context focuses the meaning:

George took off his shoes and put on his slippers.
The blacksmith fit the shoes perfectly to the horse's hooves.
The automobile's brakes failed because of faulty brake shoes.
The blowout was caused by damage to the shoe of the tire.
The woman came to the shop to have a new shoe put on her cane.

Connotative meanings   Connotative meanings make up the final type described by Berlo. Connotative meanings arise from the person's being. That being is defined primarily by private, vaguely sensed, but dynamic abstractions of social experience.

For example, the words "liberal" and "conservative" are symbols for abstract meanings within a person. The meanings exist as a result of previous encounters with the words and the socially based concepts associated with them.

Any given symbol can play all roles—denotative, structural, contextual, and connotative. As an example, pretend that at 12:30 P.M. a colleague states to you: "My boss is out to lunch." The word "boss" has structural meaning as a noun serving as the subject of the sentence. It is denotative in the sense that it refers to someone higher on the organizational chart than your colleague. The limited contextual meaning would be that the person labeled "boss" is in a restaurant somewhere eating the noon meal (also a denotative meaning).

Suppose the colleague made the statement at 6 P.M. with this inflection: "My boss is 'out to lunch.'" The meanings would be entirely different. Without the benefit of preceding or subsequent sentences, contextual meaning is incomplete. The connotative meanings that emerge about the word "boss" could differ between you and your colleague. They would depend upon the personal "boss" experiences and perceptions of each.

When you select or observe symbols, think of the wide range of potential meanings for them. The more abstract a symbol is, the more likely that your meaning will not be the same as that held by the other person.

To illustrate, examine the concept of a symbolic intensity scale by viewing Figure 6–1. Because each individual's scale is unique, you may disagree with the placement of some of the symbols. However, the key to the concept lies in the progressive nature of symbolic intensity, not in any attempt to show artificial, discrete points along a line.

The review of symbolic intensity is not meant to suggest that you should discard highly abstract symbols. However, it does suggest that you use denotative and low-abstraction connotative symbols when you can. It also suggests that when you use high-abstraction connotative symbols, you use them carefully.

For example, if, as a sender, you want to write about people whom you call "liberals," you would do well to write something like:

I define a liberal as one who publicly favors a national health plan, a guaranteed annual income, . . . Thus, I consider L. B. Rawl to be a liberal. With these definitions in mind, then, I propose that liberals are . . . .

Suppose you pick up an article about "conservatives" that does not include a definition or referent for what the writer thinks a "conservative" is. In that case, you participate even more actively than usual in the communication process. You look at

| | Symbolic (Interpertative) Intensity | |
No Symbolic (Inter-pretative) Intensity	Low (Denotative)	High (Connotative)
1. Heat when it causes perspiration	1. Concrete words and sentences such as "Andrea was skating on the sidewalk in front of her home"	1. Highly abstract words and sentences such as "A revolutionary thinker epitomizes all that is cerebral"
2. Food in the mouth when it causes salivation		
3. Pollen in the air when it causes sneezing	2. Numbers and simple operation codes such as +, −, ×, ÷	2. A counter offer in a collective bargaining process
4. A knife when it cuts the skin and causes bleeding	3. The unannounced appearance of your boss	3. The seizure of a nation's ship by another nation
5. A ball coming toward you when it causes rapid eye blink	4. A loud, unexpected explosion	4. A chart for trivariate regression analysis
6. A slammed door when it causes a person to jump		

Additional Low (Denotative) column items:
2. An abstract painting
3. Advanced mathematical codes such as ∫
4. Someone banging on your door and crying "Help!"

Figure 6–1 Symbolic (interpretative) intensity scale with examples

the author's name, recall previous statements by that author, and decide whether that writer is a "liberal" or a "conservative," if you can. You then use the denotative, structural, and contextual meanings you derive from the article itself to put the author's and your own meanings of "conservative" into perspective.

If the communication about "conservatives" initiated by another is at the interpersonal level, use feedback to determine the sender's referent for the word. For example, you could interject questions like these: "How do you define a 'conserva-tive'?" "Do you consider a 'conservative' to be one who . . . .?" "Would you name a couple of well-known people whom you consider to be 'conservatives'?"

Overcoming symbolistic barriers

To review a summary of major symbolistic barriers—and means for overcoming them—consider ten guidelines developed by Schneider, Donaghy, and Newman from the literature of general semantics[4]:

1. *Check the accuracy of symbols by going directly to the reality whenever possible.* . . . Remember, symbols are merely pointers or representations of reality, not the reality itself.

2. *It is not enough to be positive of the denotative meaning of a word or symbol. What may be of more importance and influential is what the denotative and/or contextual meaning of the symbol represents to the user.* . . . Words and symbols may serve many purposes, but it is only when the sender and the receiver are in total agreement on what the meaning is that we have true and agreed-upon communication.

3. *Maintain an awareness of whether you are transmitting and/or receiving the facts or the generalizations, and whether your judgments and conclusions are based on the reality of hard, objective facts.* Facts and inferences may sound very much alike, but they definitely are based on different types of information.

4. *Learn to mentally attach the word "etc." to anything you say, hear, write, or see (i.e., "fact, etc.")* . . . . The word "etc." reminds one that we selectively and unconsciously abstract from reality.

5. *Develop the habit of mentally dating your information (i.e., "fact, 1945").* . . . Dating information reminds one that reality in truth may have changed as the calendar time passed.

6. *Develop an awareness of the importance of mentally indexing information, that is, numbering the items (i.e., "fact 1—fact 2—fact 3").* Indexing prevents us from confusing one piece of information with another simply because they may have common characteristics.

7. *Check to determine if a given situation involves an either/or, polarized contradiction or contrary parameters, where middle-ground possibilities should be included.*

---

[4]Schneider, Donaghy, and Newman list as sources: Samuel J. Bois, *Explorations in Awareness* (New York: Harper & Brothers, 1957), Stuart Chase, *The Power of Words* (New York: Harcourt, Brace and Co., 1954), Wendell Johnson, *Your Most Enchanted Listener* (New York: Harper & Brothers, 1956), S. I. Hayakawa, *Language in Thought and Action*, 2d ed. (New York: Harcourt, Brace & World, Inc., 1964), Kenneth S. Keyes, *How to Develop Your Thinking Ability* (New York: McGraw-Hill Book Company, 1950), Irving Lee, *Language Habits in Human Affairs* (New York: Harper & Brothers, 1941), and Harry L. Weinberg, *Levels of Knowing and Existence* (New York: Harper & Row, Publishers, Inc., 1959).

8. *Use the verb "to be" correctly.* The word "is" can be used not only as an auxiliary word, but also as a directive ("Business is business"), as a level-of-abstraction confuser ("Mr. Miller is a Jew"), and as a thought freezer ("This is the best company of its kind"). The latter two uses (projection and identity) obviously cause the most problems.

9. *Be careful of situations where affective symbols are being used in place of informative ones.* . . . they are sometimes called purr and snarl words. They are bad not in and of themselves, but only when used in place of information.

10. *As a rule, size up the total situation (analyze it, get more data, and look for alternatives) before you react as a communicator.* . . . Give yourself time to analyze all aspects of input or transmission before you commit yourself.[5]

Go to the reality   Symbolistic barriers often arise when communicators function from a map of a territory rather than from the territory itself. One example is an executive dealing with employees based on memories of his treatment as an employee (the map), rather than the nature of the employees themselves (the territory).

A similar example occurs in a classroom: A professor instructs her classes from her internal map of how she was instructed; she uses the lecture method exclusively. The lecture was necessary in times when books could not be mass produced, but is rarely appropriate for the contemporary learning territory.

Blindness to a territory can also occur when a communicator unknowingly defines a problem in narrow symbols from a map that shrouds the scope of the problem. So-called men's and women's products illustrate this concept. For example, until recently most men would not even consider coloring their graying hair simply because rinses and dyes were labeled and advertised exclusively for women. However, when a manufacturer distributed its "formula" for men, sales boomed. Similar shrouding occurs in association with deodorants, shampoos, bath soaps, and other consumer items.

As another example of a restricted definition of a problem, suppose you must solve a serious paper-flow bottleneck. You observe that it occurs in an area with two new employees. You speak harshly to the new employees and threaten their jobs. Later you find that the source of the problem was in the equipment, not in the performance of the new employees.

To solve the problem of dealing with narrow and internal symbols, move into the broad and external world of reality. Extend beyond yourself to observe the territory, not recollections and impressions that constitute your internal maps of it.

Determine connotative or contextual meanings   One type of interference occurs when communicators confuse the denotative and connotative meanings of symbols. In such situations communicators often respond to meanings within themselves as if they were responding to the things themselves.

To illustrate, suppose that you motion toward a building and tell a friend in the car with you, "That's my old high school." You actually denote a physical structure as you use the words "high school." However, the words also recall meanings

---

[5]Arnold E. Schneider, William C. Donaghy, and Pamela Jane Newman, *Organizational Communication* (New York: McGraw-Hill Book Company, 1975), p. 19.

within you and your friend. Your emotions about "high school" may be pleasant ones, but your friend's may not. To the extent that either of you treats the feelings as if they were the building, interference arises.

Similarly, suppose that as a manager, you say to an employee, "I hear you've been making some rather dramatic suggestions about the work of the department. Come to my office tomorrow at 2 P.M. to discuss the matter." Your meanings associated with the word "meeting" reflect your desire to discuss the ideas of an obviously bright employee. However, the employee may be worried that she has overstepped her bounds in making suggestions. She may even supply for the word "meeting" a meaning of reprimand.

To overcome the problem of confusing denotative and connotative meanings, look beyond the denotative meanings to the possible connotative meanings symbols may carry for the other participant. Choose and interpret the symbols in light of both sets of meanings.

A related barrier arises when the meanings of even rather straightforward denotative words miss each other in the transaction between communicators. Such interference may occur when people use the same words, but have different meanings for them. It can also occur if they use different words, but intend the same meanings from them.

An example of using the same symbols with different meanings actually happened in an office. The supervisor left a note asking a clerk to take a handwritten list of names written in natural order (first name followed by surname), put the names in reverse order, alphabetize them, and type a new list after doing so. When the supervisor returned, she found that the typed list contained the names still in natural order, but arranged alphabetically by surname with the Z's at the top of the page and the A's at the bottom.

To overcome such barriers to communication, ask questions, restate the messages, and observe the contexts of the messages.

Distinguish between facts and generalizations   Risks occur when a communicator makes a generalization and treats it as if it were an actual fact. For example, say you see a colleague come from the office of a supervisor who opposes a currently debated project you support. You infer that your colleague has been in the office because he also opposes the project. Without asking him you act upon the fact of the exit from the supervisor's office by telling others that he is a member of the opposition and to be avoided. You take the risk that if your generalization is wrong, you have alienated a potential supporter.

To overcome the confusion of facts and generalizations, always distinguish between the two. Habitually ask yourself: "Is this statement I've just made or heard limited to facts or is it generalization beyond those facts?"

Attach "etc." to all messages   A major obstacle to the exchange of meanings lies with the assumption that a message contains everything about the subject. The problems of arrogance, prejudice, closed-mindedness, and intolerance of others' views can result.

Such closed-mindedness occurs if you judge a department store as cold and impersonal because the only clerk you have encountered there is cold and impersonal. If you work in finance and succumb to such arrogance, you view finance as the most important of the firm's functions and mentally place other areas in subordination to it.

One solution to the problem is simply to understand that no one can ever know everything about a subject. Be suspicious of yourself any time you feel too certain about a topic; such a moment can be most dangerous. Search for more on the very topic you think you have conquered.

The final correction for the false assumption of having a total grasp of any subject is always to attach the concept of "etc." to messages. By doing so, you recognize that no one can communicate the final word on any topic. By always considering the "etc.," you also consciously establish a proper humility in the face of the enormity of human knowledge.

Date information Miscommunication often occurs simply because people draw conclusions and assume that they are correct for the past, the present, and the future. For example, parents often view their children at some immature state—even after they are mature and successful. Some superiors tend always to see a male employee as the gangly kid delivering the mail. When a woman has earned and received executive status, many people continue to view her as a secretary.

Fixed views of people obviously are dangerous, because humans continually change. Equally risky are fixed evaluations of such factors as physical surroundings, economic conditions, business practices, and even "the times." Just because a certain advertising strategy worked for five years does not mean that it will continue to work.

Solutions to the problem of the fixed conclusion lie in an awareness of change and in dating information. As you view any person, place, or thing, do not assume any constancy. For instance, do *not* assume:

Woman, 1982 = Woman, 1970

Recession, 1980 = Recession, 1967

Workers, 1981 = Workers, 1948

Consumer Behavior, 1981 = Consumer Behavior, 1982

Index information When communicators do not differentiate between similarities and differences, they increase the chances for semantic interference. For example, say that because you are a manager, you are stereotyped by workers as unapproachable, cold, uncaring, mechanistic, and concerned only about productivity. The stereotype is an obstacle to their recognition of you as a unique person who happens to be cast into a management role.

In like manner, if you are a worker, management may characterize you as lazy, uneducated, unprofessional, interested only in pay and benefits, and uncaring about the firm.

The great danger in such generalizations lies in the unconsciousness of the labeling process. Many people create virtual caricatures about whole classes of people and things and accept the caricatures without challenge or differentiation.

The key to correcting the interference resulting from the lack of differentiation is to index information. For example, always differentiate among:

Union Member 1	Union Member 2	Union Member 3
Man 1	Man 2	Man 3
Black 1	Black 2	Black 3

Catholic 1	Catholic 2	Catholic 3
Democrat 1	Democrat 2	Democrat 3
Feminist 1	Feminist 2	Feminist 3
Corporation 1	Corporation 2	Corporation 3
Southerner 1	Southerner 2	Southerner 3
Charity 1	Charity 2	Charity 3
Politician 1	Politician 2	Politician 3

Look for middle ground   Communicators often tend to take extreme stances. They operate as if all situations can be cast at the poles, with no intermediate values between them.

Some circumstances do exist as clear either/or dichotomies. For example, you either mailed your federal tax return by April 15 or you did not. A relay just off of the production line is either defective or not according to the criteria the company employs.

Most communication transactions, however, explore a range of alternatives about the subject at hand. If participants always ignore such ranges and act as if only two contradictory classes exist, interference is bound to occur.

As an example, consider how people tend to think of the use of marijuana as either good or bad. They do not accept that its use creates a range of outcomes: Marijuana serves well as a medicinal agent in some controlled circumstances. It provides degrees of relaxation and pleasure in others. For some people it can be temporarily debilitating. For others it can create permanent physical and mental damage.

In similar fashion, consider how communicators often treat such topics as these as polarities:

Nuclear power	Affirmative action programs
Politicians	Doctors
Governments	Oil companies
Occupational Safety and Health Administration	Environmental Protection Agency

Polarities include such dichotomies as good/bad, moral/immoral, ethical/unethical, legal/illegal, intelligent/stupid, brave/cowardly, honest/dishonest, sane/insane, and competent/incompetent.

To overcome the tendency toward dichotomies, determine the degree on a reasonable scale for seemingly polarized situations. The most clear-cut degrees are numerical. Instead of saying, "She earns a good salary," say, "She earns more than $20,000 a year." Instead of referring to a man as "large," say, "He is over six feet tall and weighs at least 250 pounds."

For those circumstances that do not yield to quantification, use other symbols from the intermediate values on the scale. One way is to introduce qualitative words that imply some degree of measurement. To illustrate, consider some qualitative expressions that show differences along the stupid/smart scale. (Dozens more could be added to the list.)

astute	empty-headed	intelligent	senseless
average	excellent	keen	shallow
brainy	good	moronic	sharp
bright	half-witted	muddle-headed	shrewd

brilliant	idiotic	normal	slow
dense	ignorant	obtuse	thick
dopey	illiterate	ordinary	thinking
dull	imbecilic	quick	unenlightened
dumb	inane	scatterbrained	unwitting
eggheaded	intellectual	scholarly	witless

Also consider how these words act as qualifiers that imply quantification:

almost	many	often	some
considerably	moderately	overwhelmingly	sometimes
fairly	most	rarely	usually
few	mostly	reasonably	very
generally	nearly	slightly	virtually

Use "to be" correctly   Related to other semantic barriers, the misuse of the "to be" verbs can lead to serious interference in the transaction of meanings. Avoid the restrictiveness of statements that project stereotyped attributes and that imply an absolute equation between the elements joined with a "to be" verb.

Consider how a statement like "She is a Socialist" projects an undifferentiated image associated with socialism. Also think about how "Albert is the best possible candidate for the position" implies an undisputable identity between "Albert" and "best possible candidate."

To overcome the barriers erected by misuse of the "to be" verbs, avoid using them to project arrogant, final-word images of permanent truth. Insert qualifiers such as "likely," "probably," "may," "seems," and "in my opinion." Acknowledge that very little in life deserves the finality of "is."

Question affective symbols used in place of informative ones   The use of affective (emotional) symbols instead of informative ones introduces another category of semantic barriers. For example, name calling subverts the meanings of messages by arousing negative feelings—particularly when the receiver bears the brunt of the choice of symbols. Though not pleasant to acknowledge, these and other words about people's physical makeups do exist to destroy communication transactions in which they occur:

Shrimp	Shorty	Shortstuff	Fatso
Beanpole	Weasel	Scarface	Harelip
One-arm	Squeaky	Gimp	Snaggletooth
Weakling	Goon	Sleepy	Crip
Poky	Wimp	Hag	Witch
Dogface	Pig	Porky	Four-eyes

Possibly just as devastating to communication are the names that come with organizational and social relationships:

Union scab	Women's libber	Divorceé	Redneck
Pinko	Union sympathizer	Radical	Male chauvinist pig
John Bircher	Welfare mother	Jock	Aggie
Rube	Hillbilly	Womanizer	Tramp
Pollack	Swinger	Honkey	White
Loose woman	Uncle Tom	Fag	Dumb blonde
Nigger	Banker	Bum	Drunk

The association that goes with the label blocks out any consideration for the person as a many-faceted being. The sketchy map is held so close to the mind that it overshadows the territory it purports to represent.

Consider how presidents, ambassadors, senators, civil rights leaders, and other officials for movements are ultimately assassinated for the names they carry. Then consider how people less at the forefront of activities keep their lives, but are punished insidiously for the labels that have attached to them.

To correct the misuse of affective symbols, always be aware of the paired nature of symbols—their denotative and connotative functions.

Use euphemisms (positive substitutes) for symbols that may create negative meanings. The use of "decline" and "trough" for "recession" and "depression" represents such an approach.

Dysphemisms (negative variations for symbols) also exist. Therefore, replace dysphemisms with neutral expressions or euphemisms.

As an example, if a person calls someone else a "wild-eyed radical," do not accept that label without analysis of your own. React to the person, not the label. The person remains the same whether labeled "wild-eyed radical" (dysphemism), "strong leader for a good cause" (euphemism), or "someone who believes firmly in a cause that others label extreme" (neutral).

The concept of the self-fulfilling prophecy also forms an important reason for moving from negative to positive affective symbols. The replacement of dysphemisms by euphemisms often results in the self-fulfilling prophecy of success instead of failure.

Think before reacting   Many obstacles to effective communication arise simply because people react without thinking. If such reactions come as sheer reflexes, they are generally harmless and can even be beneficial. In any case, they cannot be avoided. Figure 6–1 includes some examples of responses that involve little or no symbolic interpretation.

Other automatic reponses—those that are learned—also serve humans well. For example, you would not want to have to think carefully about each of the motions involved in such acts as walking, eating, driving, dialing a telephone, cleaning the house, mowing the lawn, typewriting, and stroking the keys on the calculator.

Many other types of nonthinking responses can be seriously damaging, however. For instance, suppose someone says something to you that you do not believe. If you respond with "You're a liar," you have erected an enormously high hurdle for two communicators to try to surmount.

Sometimes you must make quick judgments. However, you usually can spare at least a few seconds of thinking time. You may save not only the communication, but the very lives affected by that communication. Consider the classic case of the discovery of a fire in a crowded room. The unthinking reactions of those in it have caused the deaths of hundreds who could have lived.

Suppose you tell your supervisor that her established machine setup for a factory floor may be dangerous. She reacts immediately to your comment by yelling at you, with others overhearing, that she makes those decisions and you are not to criticize them any more.

Even if her particular setup does not cause any immediate damage, you and the others who overheard will be hesitant to make any suggestions that smack of criticism to her—no matter how justified the suggestions may be. Of course, if her machine setup does lead to injury, her undelayed reaction has been a direct cause of an even more serious outcome.

The basic correction for *all* of the types of miscommunication is to think before responding.

Environment

Interference also arises from many environmental sources. Areas include (1) external transceivers, (2) number of links in the chain, (3) organizational structure, and (4) other external factors.

External transceivers

You often relegate to others such acts as handwriting, typewriting, setting type, drawing, photographing, speaking, listening, reading, and taping. When you do, you still remain responsible for controlling such external processes.

Learn about good form and composition. Evaluate what has been transmitted or received for you by someone else. Try to select reliable people and equipment to accomplish what you want accomplished.

Number of links in the chain

Another of the major barriers to effective communication lies in the number of links in the chain between the sender and the ultimate receiver.

You may have played the game "Gossip" (or "Telephone"). In it, you recall, one person whispers a message (preferably a written one) in the ear of another. The whispered "chaining" continues until the message moves from one to another through all people in the circle. The last person to receive the message states it aloud, and the originator orally compares the final received message with the original message. The final message usually bears little resemblance to the original.

While the destruction of a message can be fun at a party, it becomes serious for purposive communication endeavors. Thus, try to reduce the number of intermediate links. With each added station, the chances of a message accomplishing its purpose diminish significantly.

Organizational structure

Another environmental factor, organizational structure, also has an impact on communication.

Interference may arise from the relative status and power of the participants, the exercise of traditional roles, and incompatible needs and expectations. It may arise because of centralization or decentralization. It may originate in contradictory management policies, or too many levels of management, or the clash between line and staff operations. It may be caused by the specialized nature of functions or even the special languages of those functions. It may have its source in formal, informal, or grapevine transactions.

Closed doors at any of the levels of management inevitably interfere with the communication flow. The closed-door approach is particularly guilty of blocking upward communication.

Sometimes, even if subordinates feel no fear of superiors with a genuine open-door policy, they still may encounter an upward barrier. That barrier occurs in the sheer overload of information the superiors must handle.

Obstacles also may arise in extra-organizational communication. Obviously, the more "publics" with which a business must deal, the faster interference can compound.

Other external factors

Recall how external factors can bombard the enchanneled message. Loud noises, distracting visual images, faulty television pictures, smeared ink, a blank page in a newspaper, underexposure of film, type too small to read, "cross-talk" on the telephone—all can create "noise" in ongoing communication.

The channel itself can be a barrier. In the process of defining the very ranks of communication effectiveness, the ranks of interference become apparent.

Also part of external interference are all of the nonverbal environmental factors described in Chapter 3.

FEEDBACK

Feedback from the original receiver to the original sender simply reverses the original roles. Therefore, virtually everything that improves communication improves feedback.

In this section, then, consider the characteristics and applications of feedback as a particular stage in the communication process.

Characteristics

Review the characteristics of feedback in two parts, the general and the organizational.

General

The basic necessities for creating good feedback include people who accept themselves and others, who can establish some shared objectives, and who show that they are willing to communicate together. Feedback involves actions by the original receiver. The actions may or may not be those desired by a purposive sender. However, because meanings of received messages reside in the receiver, feedback provides the only avenue through which a sender can evaluate the success of a transaction.

Feedback takes many forms: It can be a question calling for more information or for clarification or it can be the answer to a question. It can be a paraphrase of the sender's message. It can be a puzzled expression, a nod of acceptance, silence, or applause. Feedback can take the form of a completed questionnaire or a progress report from a subordinate to a superior. One can feed back through an exam paper or a bank statement and canceled checks. One can respond by passing the salt as requested. Feedback, in short, can be anything that results from the receipt of a message.

Feedback can be interspersed throughout a transaction or delayed until all of the sender's message is received.

The continual nature of the feedback provided through face-to-face encounters enables the participants to evaluate and revise messages during the transaction. The capacity for such change makes the interaction potentially more effective.

Even with poorer channels, however, feedback can be useful. For example, in an exchange of business letters, each letter gives the receiver the opportunity to make necessary adjustments before writing again.

Not only does feedback benefit individual transactions, but it also adds to the cumulative growth of the user. Therefore, try to analyze and evaluate all of the feedback you send and receive, and apply what you learn through the process. You may even benefit from the mistakes.[6]

Organizational

Feedback is an important factor within the business organization and also between that organization and bodies external to it. Such feedback is effective when it is substantive and positive.

Substantive Relationships between workers and superiors seem to improve when feedback is substantive. Substantive feedback is frequent, specific, timely, consistent, and sufficient. Such feedback about performance can improve attitudes, motivation, and the quality of the performance itself.

A free flow of good organizational feedback also often leads to confident and pleasant interactions among the employees themselves. Such feedback seems to be particularly necessary for employees low in self-esteem and self-confidence.

Many causes of an insufficient flow of good organizational feedback exist. One is the restriction of communication to formal, upward-flow channels. A mere declaration of a so-called open-door policy at the upper-management level usually does not overcome the restriction.

Similarly, the sanctioned communication system too often prohibits employees from generating and receiving upward, downward, and lateral feedback freely. In those organizations informal systems, notably the grapevine, flourish. They provide the informal, rich avenues necessary for human transactions.

Another reason for poor feedback is a negative climate. Such a climate causes people to feel fearful, manipulated, threatened, judged, and unappreciated. In such environments people usually do not provide verbal feedback other than the basic amount required for the job.

Even if a climate is neutral, employees tend to tell superiors what they want to hear. They hesitate to be vehicles of negative feedback. Therefore, management needs to establish an effective communication network whereby all employees can meet among themselves and with managers on a regular, open basis.

---

[6]The original use of the word "feedback" was for technical systems, particularly computer systems. Errors or deviations fed back to the control center so that it could correct them. Because communication is a closed-loop system, then, the output produces an effect on the input, just as for technical systems. Feedback provides a control that is accomplished by reinserting the results of previous performances into the communication process.

Positive   Positive feedback refers to the manner in which the feedback is made. It does not imply that the answer is always "Yes" or that praise is always appropriate. Obviously, people must deny requests and people make errors.

Positive feedback does not attack the person. It is constructive and objective. It deals with specific acts in a direct, supportive way. Positive feedback softens criticism—or bad news of any kind—by wedging it between sincere expressions of good news.

Pretend that you are supervising a training session for an office-machine operation. You demonstrate the pattern and then have each employee move through it. When an employee does not do well, you supply feedback.

Contrast the impact of these two types of feedback:

- "There's no way you're ever going to learn this operation. Here, let me demonstrate one more time."
- "Hey, you're doing OK. Let me stand here behind you and take your arm through the pattern a few times. You'll get it."

Both feedback messages acknowledge that the trainee is not completing the operation properly. However, the trainee usually would react better to the positive feedback.

Similarly, a study of positive and negative claim-granting and claim-denying letters shows:

1. The receivers will react most favorably to a message containing a combination of good news (granting the claim) and positive treatment. They will react most unfavorably to a message containing bad news (refusing the claim) and negative treatment.

2. The receivers will react more favorably to a message containing bad news but positive treatment than to a message containing good news but negative treatment. In other words, the negative treatment of a message may cancel any favorable feedback which good news might elicit from the receiver.[7]

These results reinforce the importance of positive feedback regardless of the channel used.

(567 words)
(test on page 185)

Sending

The original sender should plan how to stimulate feedback even as he or she formulates the original message. In addition, the original sender has special responsibilities associated with the reception of feedback.

Stimulating feedback

As a purposive sender, you need good feedback to form the basis for evaluation and growth. Even as a nonpurposive sender, you want to remain open to constructive feedback from others. Consider how to stimulate feedback at each of the five levels of communication.

---

[7]Adnan Almaney, "The Effect of Message Treatment on Feedback in Business Communication," *Journal of Business Communication* 9 (Spring 1972): 22.

Intrapersonal level   Because you act as both sender and receiver when you function intrapersonally, you feed back to yourself. Even at this level, though, you need to close all loops—to field all of your own messages.

Interpersonal level   As an interpersonal sender, you have the best of all opportunities to receive immediate and complete feedback. However, even at this level, you can improve feedback if you deliberately seek it.

As you converse, ask questions that check perception through feedback: "Which one of my suggestions do you like best?" "What do you think?" "What do you like or dislike about my solution?" "Have you ever had a similar experience?"

Another perceptual-checking device for group discussion calls for the leader to stop the discussion when two succeeding statements conflict. The leader asks the second person to restate her or his comment so that it shows understanding of the preceding person's statement.

Do not dominate a conversation. Use nonverbal cues to invite the other to feed back at comfortable intervals. Display a sincere interest in listening to the other.

In training discussions, announce any end-of-meeting tests at the beginning. In this way, you can assure that people will be organizing feedback thoughts as they proceed.

Tear down personal barriers to feedback. Develop and exhibit a nondefensive attitude. Be receptive to both good and bad news. Mentally meet people on their own ground. Use nonverbal invitations for the other to respond. Avoid formality. Be warm and open.

Use feedforward—learning about the receiver—in order to know how best to stimulate feedback. If you know about the other, you can picture what feedback you might expect in addition to what you want.

Create a climate that acknowledges the value system, attitudes, and customs of the other. At least avoid an atmosphere that flies in the face of the strong feelings the other holds.

For example, if you want to obtain some information from a man known to oppose smoking and drinking, you would not take him to a bar. Even if you yourself do enjoy a bar, you are not practicing hypocrisy by taking this man somewhere else. You simply show sensitivity to another from whom you want feedback.

Reverse the attitudes described in the example: *You* oppose drinking—and have never been in a bar in your life. You find that a woman from whom you want some information likes to have discussions in a bar over a drink. Does that mean you should meet in a bar? No. However, you might want to meet in a restaurant that serves drinks so that your guest may have one if she desires.

The examples about meeting in a bar deal with obvious circumstances. However, try to use the same sensitivity in less obvious circumstances.

If you want feedback about you as a person, or about your performance as a communicator, ask for it or demonstrate nonverbally that you welcome it. Most people hesitate to feed back about personal matters—particularly if the content of the feedback is not complimentary.

As a manager, do not ignore rumors and the grapevine. In fact, tap into them to take advantage of the feedback they provide. By seeking out the news that travels the grapevine, you increase your opportunities to learn about morale, attitudes toward policies, solutions to problems, reactions to decisions, and the feelings of the employees.

Of course, if you solicit information from the grapevine, you take some risk that you will receive incorrect feedback. The choice of the contact person is critical, for your information is only as good as that person's perceptions. Learn who the leaders and communicators are and get information to them and solicit it from them.

Another way to stimulate feedback from workers to management is to develop upward, interpersonal flows of information. Establish a regular pattern of meetings between supervisors and their subordinates at all levels of the operation. From them, important information will rise to the top.

In addition, establish a genuine open-door policy at the upper level of management. Such a policy should allow an employee to skip levels when time and circumstances do not allow the person to go through channels.

Organizations also can stimulate interpersonal feedback by interviewing all departing employees. In addition, companies can establish grievance procedures that include face-to-face conversations at each step.

To stimulate interpersonal exchanges and feedback in another way, establish the appropriate physical arrangements. Provide a centralized lounge and snack area. Put open doorways between associated offices and other work areas. Move people who need to gather feedback close to each other. For decentralized situations, periodically transport people to settings where they can be with others for interpersonal transactions.

Medio level   Stimulating feedback at the medio level involves some of the same kinds of activities as are involved at the interpersonal level. However, because a medium intervenes between the participants, the process takes on some special features.

When you talk by telephone, your voice must provide the nonverbal cues for turn-taking. Tone, volume, pitch, inflection, speed, pauses, and other such elements can invite or resist feedback. Questions such as "Do you understand?" and "Would you repeat that?" also solicit immediate feedback. When the need exists, less direct questions can test understanding.

If you send a letter to which the receiver is not strictly *obliged* to respond, include a postage-paid, addressed envelope or return card to promote returns. You may even send a check-off or short-answer form if appropriate. You may want to use self-carboned, tear-off reply forms. They allow both you and the receiver to retain copies of the messages.

As a managing organizational communicator, you may stimulate feedback through the medio level in several ways. You may conduct attitude surveys by distributing written questionnaires. Though the days of the suggestion box are about gone, you may obtain the same kind of feedback through more modern means. You may set up a special telephone number which an employee can dial and then leave a recorded message—an idea, a complaint, a compliment. You may even include with that dialing set a recorded message from an officer of the firm.

You may include return forms in the company newsletter or magazine asking for news items, suggestions, or specific information. You may even offer prizes for the best suggestions received for a given period of time.

You may call for supervisors to prepare detailed records on employee tardiness, absenteeism, productivity, unusually competent performance, innovative ideas, and other such written feedback.

Person-to-group level   In addition to creating a positive communication climate, other devices exist for stimulating feedback from your audience. Use what you know about them to draw them into your presentation. For example, if you know of some incident common to the group, weave that incident into your speech. If you have the chance, move among the group prior to your speech. Learn some names—particularly of well-liked people. During your speech interject some questions directly to those people for simple one- or two-word answers. Oftentimes, you will make the question a humorous one.

Another device is to ask a question or two that calls for a show of hands by the members of the audience. Raise your hand as you call for them to do so. The feedback gives you information and also allows the audience to participate actively in the ongoing process.

Include some statements that call for laughter, groans, applause, or other nonverbal participation. You can gauge how well the speech is going by the participation you stimulate in this way.

If a speech is long, have people stand for a minute about halfway through it. If the group is small, have each person introduce herself or himself at the beginning.

If possible, follow the speech by a question-and-answer segment. Because you return somewhat to the rich interpersonal level, you increase feedback significantly by the use of this device.

Mass level   Useful, valid feedback can be difficult to obtain from mass audiences. However, some techniques can help to overcome the problems.

One technique involves treating any data collection as a controlled scientific experiment. For instance, use probability sampling and statistical testing of results.

Sound techniques include surveys, readership studies, polls, and television-viewing rating systems. These techniques usually use an experimental design.

Other techniques for stimulating feedback include coded cents-off coupons, refund offers, contests, and "giveaway" drawings. Postage-paid return envelopes and cards, including "blow-out" cards in magazines and newspapers, can aid feedback. So can questionnaires placed with menus in restaurants. Phone-in radio and television shows sometimes provide valuable feedback.

Marketing researchers often use product-testing panels. The members of the panel usually provide feedback by completing and mailing questionnaires or diaries about the products they test.

Sometimes a free mass publication is distributed by placing stacks in busy areas. To gain feedback, watch people as they pass the stacks. Determine the proportion who take copies. See whether they begin to read immediately. Approach some of them and ask what they think. Observe whether they throw copies of the publication into trash cans or leave them on chairs or tables in the area. Listen to conversations to determine whether people discuss anything that they read in your publication.

Receiving feedback

Apply all of the principles for effective communication receiving to feedback receiving. However, use some special techniques for improving the reception.

Be alert to even momentary feedback. Nonverbal feedback can be elusive if you do not consciously receive it.

Particularly overcome defensiveness within yourself. Be open to receive even negative feedback. If a problem exists, admit it and isolate it. Find the causes. If they resulted from the actions of you or others, deal with the circumstances without attacking the worth of anybody—including yourself.

Interpret feedback accurately. Though often difficult to do, always strive to find the core of truth in feedback messages. For example, suppose you have sought feedback by asking the question "Do you understand?" Carefully analyze any answer you receive, particularly the answer "Yes." Though that answer may be accurate (the person does understand), it could also be inaccurate. If it is inaccurate, the person may think he or she understands, but does not understand. On the other hand, the person may know that he or she does not understand, but out of embarrassment does not admit it.

As a manager, be aware of the feedback available in such personnel activities as tardiness, absenteeism, productivity, insubordination, innovativeness, turnover rates, and unusual or disruptive behavior. With an acute ability, you will even be able to spot personnel problems related to such difficulties as alcoholism, drug abuse, neuroses, psychoses, or personal-life trauma.

Consider some examples of feedback adjustment during ongoing exchanges. If in an interpersonal transaction, you observe a receiver showing nonverbally that he or she wants to speak, give up your turn. By contrast, notice a distant look, and bring the receiver back when you observe one.

When feedback indicates that people do not understand, recode the message to bring about clarification. When someone tells you that he or she is distracted by the "uh's" in your speech pattern, concentrate upon removing them.

Receiving

The suggestions related to improving feedback as a sender also apply to improving feedback as a receiver. However, consider some recommendations specifically pertinent to your feedback role as the initial receiver in a transaction.

Receiving messages about desired feedback

Sensitivity again defines the good receiver's approach to learning the senders' desires about feedback. As an original receiver, try to determine what original senders want in the way of feedback. On the other hand, if you decide that the senders are not asking for feedback, try to find whether they are receptive to unsolicited feedback.

For the situations in which you want to give uninvited feedback to senders, consider asking them whether they want it. For example, if you think a colleague should improve the use of the telephone, ask, "Would you like for me to share some hints I learned about telephone techniques?"

Feeding back

Feed back as soon as you can in light of the circumstances. Immediate feedback is much more contributive than delayed feedback—for both sender and receiver.

Use as many channels as good feedback requires. Use the richest possible channels, and both verbal and nonverbal expressions. Even if the original message you received was couched in negative form, respond positively. Describe, interpret, and clarify. Feed back in a mature, accepting fashion. Avoid defensiveness. Make your feedback appropriate, straightforward, specific, and factual to the extent possible. If your feedback is a judgment call, assess actions, not personalities.

If you cannot decide what a sender wants by way of feedback, first feed back by asking questions, or by rephrasing the received message as a perception check. If the answers clarify the situation, you may then begin to formulate the originally desired type of feedback.

Be particularly sensitive as you generate unsolicited feedback about the other's behavior or personality. As suggested, first be sure that the other is ready to receive such information. Make it constructive. Make it relate to something the other can change. When well done, such information can be most valuable.

EVALUATION

You will improve your communication significantly by evaluating every transaction in which you participate. Test not only at the end of an exchange, but continually during it.

Through evaluation you will learn how well you achieve your specific goals. You also will learn which communication procedures seem to work and which do not. You then can apply your cumulative learning to succeeding interchanges in order to improve them.

Evaluation involves making many distinctions. Review just a few of them:

1. Purposive or nonpurposive communication
2. Personal-development or performance objectives
3. Single or multiple objectives
4. Criteria- or noncriteria-based objectives
5. Long- or short-term objectives
6. Formal or informal communication or evaluation
7. Simple or complex communication or evaluation
8. Intermediate or terminal evaluation
9. Written verbal, oral verbal, or nonverbal communication
10. Rich or weak channel
11. Single or multiple channel
12. Sender or receiver communication or evaluation
13. Internal or external evaluation
14. Quantitative or qualitative evaluation
15. Individual or group evaluation
16. Form- or nonform-based evaluation
17. Feedback- or nonfeedback-associated evaluation
18. Intrapersonal, interpersonal, medio, person-to-group, or mass level communication
19. Objective or subjective evaluation
20. Cost- or noncost-based effectiveness

With such an array of factors associated with communication assessment, the necessarily abbreviated coverage in this chapter requires a delimited scope. Therefore, review the subject in only two broad categories: (1) general evaluation and (2) organizational evaluation.

General

For the best evaluation:

1. Establish purposes which include the who, what, when, where, how, and why.
2. Establish objective criteria—quantitative, if possible—to match the purposes; include levels for various degrees of success.
3. Use feedback as the basis for evaluation.
4. Use written objective tests tied to the criteria; establish evaluation forms for repeated activities.
5. Adjust purposes and criteria if intermediate assessments indicate that the revision would improve the communication.
6. Analyze using methods appropriate to the objectives and criteria.

Review the suggestions in three parts: (1) purposes, criteria, and analysis, (2) feedback, and (3) forms.

Purposes, criteria, and analysis

To paraphrase an old saying, how can you know if or when you reach your communication goals if you do not select your goals before you begin the communication? Therefore, as discussed in Chapter 5, communication evaluation proceeds most efficiently when you establish explicit purposes and objective criteria against which you can measure their attainment. With well-developed purposes and criteria, the evaluation stage is a much-simplified test of communication results.

Objective criteria   Efficient goal- and criteria-setting procedures for communication closely parallel the initial steps of the scientific research process: Identify the problem. Set as the purpose of the research the solution of the problem. Establish hypotheses to be tested to determine whether you have successfully accomplished that solution.

The problem/purpose component of research dovetails perfectly into the problem/purpose of communication. The hypothesis is the research counterpart of the test criterion for communication purposes. Therefore, the more scientific you can make your approach, the more readily you will be able to perform the communication evaluation.

At best, any evaluation you make will include your judgments of the worth of that communication measured against your own value system. Therefore, make the criteria and the assessment as objective as possible.

One of the best ways to set and test objective criteria is to use quantitative instead of qualitative data. By translating qualitative components into quantitative ones, you also introduce the potential for statistical testing of results.

Suppose that you have just developed a new series of three form collection letters for your firm. You would like to know if your messages actually will improve the collection of past-due accounts. Begin your analysis of the evaluation function by considering objectives.

In qualitative terms, your objective for the communication (the collection series) could be:

To establish a better collection record

Consider the flaws in the statement. First, a situation perfectly suited to quantification appears in qualitative terms. The statement includes no criteria for evaluation. It does not include the who, what, when, where, why, and how. It does not indicate a definition for "better."

An improved statement could be:

To establish a much better collection record during 1982 using the new collection series than was established during 1981 using the old collection series. The criterion is the total dollar value of collections for 1982 compared to that for 1981.

The statement does not include some of the flaws in the original statement. In addition, the use of the total dollar values of collections introduces some quantification. However, the statement is still basically a weak qualitative objective that cannot be tested in its present form.

Even if collections are higher in 1982, how many dollars constitute "much better?" How much, if any, of the increase can be attributed to the new series rather than to increases in credit sales, inflation, cycle, trend, or some other factors? Collections may actually have increased in spite of the new series, not because of it.

Though suggestions for the correction of the weakness of the qualitative approach could be extensive, just a few will make the point here.

First, the objective and evaluation should be based on precise, measurable criteria. Such criteria could compare the new and old series on the basis of the proportions of those who make payment within two weeks after each of the three letters. They also could involve summary proportions at the end of the series.

To overcome the possible biases associated with comparing data from 1982 with those from 1981, conduct a controlled research project.

First, use a probability sampling process to divide the collection series accounts into two groups. Send the old series to the people in one of the samples, and the new series to the people in the other sample.

Test the proportions of returns after each of the three letters and the summary proportions at the end of the series. When you do, you test only the relative qualities of the messages, not factors associated with different time periods—factors such as seasonality, trend, cycle, irregular components, and inflation.

You could add another quantitative element to the evaluation. You could test to determine whether the mean dollar amounts of payments differ significantly between the two samples. You could conduct the tests in the same four stages as the proportions tests—testing after each letter and finding summary means at the end of the series.

If you plan to conduct all eight tests, you would establish eight objectives:

1. To obtain a significantly higher proportion of returns from those receiving the first letter of the new series (N_1) than from those receiving the first letter of the old series (O_1)
2. To obtain a significantly higher proportion of returns those receiving N_2 than from those receiving O_2
3. To obtain a significantly higher porportion of returns from those receiving N_3 than from those receiving O_3
4. To obtain a significantly higher proportion of total returns from those receiving N than from those receiving O
5. To receive a significantly larger mean dollar amount of payments ($\bar{X}_1$) from those receiving N_1 than from those receiving O_1

6. To receive a significantly larger $\bar{X}_2$ from those receiving N_2 than from those receiving O_2
7. To receive a significantly larger $\bar{X}_3$ from those receiving N_3 than from those receiving O_3
8. To receive a significantly larger $\bar{X}$ total from those receiving N than from those receiving O

Once you collect the data, you will analyze it. To analyze the first four objectives, you would use one-tail tests of significance for two sample proportions. For the latter four objectives, you would use one-tail tests of significance for two sample means.[8]

As another example of the importance of objectivity, cast yourself in the role of a furniture-store manager. You are in a heated discussion with a long-term customer. The customer is irate over damage done to a one-of-a-kind sofa during delivery from your store.

Your immediate objectives for the exchange are to repair or replace the sofa in the shortest possible time and maintain the customer's goodwill. Your long-term objective is to have the customer purchase additional furniture from you.

You feel yourself becoming defensive at the customer's personal attacks and unreasonableness. Thus, you know that you cannot possibly accomplish your objectives unless you can change the transaction. Thus, you decide to remove the communication and its feedback-inspired evaluation from the subjective to the objective state.

You continue to nod and "uh-huh" to the customer's ranting, most of the content of which you shut out of your mind. However, even as you retain surface contact, you reach for paper and pencil and begin to draft a statement with these options to:

1. Repair the damage
2. Immediately order another sofa similar to the original
3. Replace the sofa with a higher-priced one from the floor
4. Refund the purchase price and pick up the sofa

In addition, you write that whatever the customer's decision, you will give the customer a voucher for $100 off of any subsequent purchase of $500 or more.

When the document is complete, you show it to the customer as you explain its provisions. You ask the customer to choose an option from the list or to suggest another.

With the removal of parts of the communication from the subjective arena to the objective, the likelihood of reaching your goals increases.

The voucher will serve as objective evidence of the intent to retain goodwill. It will also serve as a criterion for judging whether the customer will return to your store. If the customer does come back and use it, you will have met your goal of keeping the customer—at least for one more purchase.

---

[8]This example of evaluation overlaps with communication research—a topic considered briefly in Chapter 14. Extensive coverage of research methods and quantitative analytical tools are the subjects of other types of books. However, the evaluation stage of the communication process often requires that the communicator consult such books.

Subjective criteria The preceding case illustrates that a skillful communicator may introduce some objectivity even into an interpersonal exchange. However, the greater weight of the evaluation in that exchange still remains at the subjective level.

The lack of external criteria is not unusual. Therefore, the wise communicator develops confidence in subjective methods—particularly for assessing personal communication effectiveness. Such confidence depends greatly upon communicative experience and maturation.

To practice communication self-evaluation, try to assess your performance in every transaction in which you participate. When external feedback comes, compare it with your own independently evolved evaluation. If the two assessments differ, decide which is more likely to be the correct one—yours or the other person's. Adjust subsequent communication in light of the decision.

Independent intrapersonal competence becomes more and more necessary as business advancements come. An unwritten rule seems to suggest that the higher you rise within a company, the less others feed back about your performance—be that performance good or bad. Therefore, the high-level person must become proficient in self-evaluation.

One of the major psychological obstacles to such self-sufficiency often arises from the very academic system in which people learn to become business practitioners. Students usually are systematically conditioned to depend upon others' evaluations. They expect others to judge them—and to reward them and punish them on the bases of the judgments.

In startling contrast, employees find a large part of that external evaluation/reward/punishment system to be missing. Employees often perform in a milieu in which they must evaluate their own performances and assign their own "grades." Trauma often results from the withdrawal of that external-reward support system.

For instance, suppose you are just out of college and working at your first professional job. As one of your first assignments, you work very hard to write a particularly difficult report. You submit it to the authorizing person. You wait. You receive no response. No one says, "Good job," or commends you in any way. No one puts an "A" on your "paper." Unless you have developed the power to know within yourself that your work is good, to reward yourself for it, and to be satisfied with such a self-generated reward, you will suffer from the absence of the interhuman feedback.

In short, continue to strive to establish external action objectives as bases for communication evaluation. However, also develop your intrapersonal forces fully. Such forces can then supplement the external when you successfully activate the external, and replace the external when they must.

Feedback

Feedback and evaluation are inseparable, for feedback provides the major portion of the data upon which evaluation is based. Feedback closes the loop between the sender and receiver.

As an example, assume that you have set for a direct-mail sales campaign an objective of obtaining at least $150,000 in mail orders. To gain measurable feedback, you include order forms and envelopes identified with this one campaign. In that way, your feedback—the returned orders—can be evaluated against your preset objectives and criteria.

Feedback for more complicated transactions becomes more difficult to isolate and evaluate. For example, suppose you conducted the sales campaign through television advertising to stimulate sales at retail outlets. Evaluating the success of the campaign in terms of the $150,000 objective becomes more cumbersome. A very real difficulty will be to separate the sales that would have been made without the television advertising from the sales made because of it.

Feedback forms an integral part of both ongoing and terminal evaluation—particularly for the richer ranks of communication.

For example, suppose you chair an important committee. You set as a goal of an interpersonal exchange that your colleague will agree to come onto the committee as secretary. Early during the discussion of your suggestion, you read your colleague's nonverbal and verbal feedback to mean that he does not like being a secretary—that you will not attain your goal. Therefore, you revise your goal to call for him simply to join the committee without serving as secretary.

The example shows how continual evaluation through feedback can contribute significantly to the improvement of communication.

Forms

When possible, use preprinted forms as the basis for evaluation. Through their use, you make the evaluation external and relatively unbiased.

Use forms to evaluate both the content and the process of a transaction. Also use them to evaluate your personal performance.

Forms apply particularly well at the interhuman levels. However, try some objective instruments for evaluating even your intrapersonal processing. They can sharpen the thinking and learning that take place at that level.

Though you may use evaluative forms designed by others, you probably will want to develop your own. Appendix B includes samples of forms for evaluating some of the elements of the group discussion.

Organizational

The communication audit represents a contemporary evaluative process for organizations. Similar to accounting audits, communication audits usually involve inside or outside consultants who diagnose the current status of the communication in them.

Organizations operate through the flow of messages among interdependent people both within and without the organization. Therefore, measurement of the effectiveness of that flow is critical to meeting the objectives of the organization. The objectives include profit, productivity, social responsibility, employee morale, flexibility, and long-term goals.

The audit usually assesses the effectiveness of the elements of the communication process; sources of information; channels; quantity of information; timing, correctness, and usefulness of messages; formal/informal and internal/external networks; and results of transactions, particularly in conjunction with employee morale.

Communication auditors use questionnaires, interviews, and content analysis of written messages. They also use reports of critical incidents, communication diaries, and other analytical and collection techniques.

They appraise information flow, personnel perceptions and attitudes, and message quality.

With the results of the audit, managers can move to improve many facets of organizational life, including control, leadership styles, communication methods, and training. They include morale, job enrichment activities, job satisfaction, feedback systems, counseling, interpersonal relationships, and human development programs. They also include motivation, participation, employee retention, employee commitment, employee communication, and perceptions and attainment of organizational goals.

Evaluation and control go hand in hand. A manager can use communication evaluation as a basis for establishing a healthy communication climate—one free of adversarial relationships. With that accomplished, much of the remainder of the package of managerial reponsibilities falls readily into place.

SUMMARY

Chapter 6 covers Guidelines 3, 5, and 6—*interference, feedback,* and *evaluation.*

Interference can be based in senders or receivers, human or nonhuman factors, and can occur in all stages of the communication process.

However interference occurs, try to anticipate, prevent, and eliminate it. To do so, apply the six guidelines carefully: Understand and control the purposes, yourself, the other participant, the environment, the channel, the interference, the encoding and decoding, the feedback, and the evaluation.

Humans form the greatest barriers to communication. *Symbolistic bias* is one of the most critical of the human interference factors. To overcome it, understand and apply the concepts of *general semantics, perception and meanings,* and ten *guidelines derived from them.*

The principal semantic obstacle exists because of the *one-word, one-meaning misconception.* One aid to controlling perceptions and meanings is to understand four types of meanings: (1) *denotative,* (2) *structural,* (3) *contextual,* and (4) *connotative.*

Schneider, Donaghy, and Newman summarize ten guidelines for overcoming semantic interference:

1. *Go to the reality.*
2. *Determine connotative or contextual meanings.*
3. *Distinguish between facts and generalizations.*
4. *Attach "etc." to all messages.*
5. *Date information.*
6. *Index information.*
7. *Look for middle ground.*
8. *Use "to be" correctly.*
9. *Question affective symbols used in place of informative ones.*
10. *Think before reacting.*

The *environment* also serves as a source of interference. Such interference exists in *external transceivers,* the *number of links in the chain, organizational structure,* and *other external factors.*

As the sender or receiver, use and stimulate feedback at all five levels of communication. Use such devices as *perceptual-checking questions, the grapevine, surveys, direct questions to members of an audience, alertness, nondefensiveness, and sensitivity.* Organizational feedback should be *substantive* and *positive.*

Consistent evaluation improves communication. Evaluation assesses many factors, including purposiveness, number of purposes or channels, level of difficulty, level of formality, and degree of objectivity.

For the best evaluation, (1) *establish purposes* to include the who, what, when, where, how, and why; (2) *set objective criteria*—in quantitative form, if possible; (3) *use feedback* as the primary basis for the evaluation, (4) *use written or form evaluations,* (5) *adjust purposes and criteria* as necessary, and (6) *use appropriate analytical methods.* Even as you attempt to establish objective criteria, however, develop *subjective evaluative techniques* fully.

The *communication audit* is becoming an important tool for evaluating the effectiveness of organizational communication.

Practice

1. Describe the differences among the denotative, structural, contextual, and connotative meanings of the word "servant."
2. John, your best friend, tells you that your office mate is a "crazy alcoholic." Though you do not know her well, she seems to be kind and competent. But the statement that John made about her sticks in your mind. Is it possible that John is wrong? Could John intend the words "crazy alcoholic" to be a compliment? If the description is somehow true, does her "alcoholism" affect her work or her relationship with you? What should you do?
3. The top manager of the company for which you work has heard that you are taking a business communication course. He sends you a note asking you to write a one- or two-page essay on interference and how to overcome it. He asks you to give the essay to your immediate supervisor who will in turn give it to him. What is important to consider before you write the essay? Can you identify potential sources of interference in carrying out this task? Write the essay. Would you have worded it diferently had your colleague asked for it? Your teacher? Your mother?
4. You will meet separately with each of your ten employees to discuss their work over the last six-month period. What types of internal and external interference could be a part of each meeting? How will the interference affect the quality of each meeting?
5. Some people believe that even the absence of outside noise and activity can constitute interference. Do you agree? Why?
6. Your friend believes that people agree on the meanings of most words because the dictionary defines them. You realize that your friend is somewhat misguided. You know that even if every person in the world had access to and used the same dictionary, each person would interpret the dictionary's descriptions differently. Explain the cliché that "meanings are in people, not in things" to your friend.
7. Your friend always calls adult women "girls." Every time he uses the word "girls," you think of female children. In fact, one time he told you that your girl was welcome at the manager's banquet, so you brought your eight-year-old daughter. She was the only child at the banquet. Your friend had meant for you to bring your secretary, a forty-year-old woman. How would you tactfully clear up the confusion surrounding the word "girl"?

8. Meet with your group. Discuss and determine the types of interference associated with these communication situations and channels. What can you do to lessen the impact of the interference? Be specific.

   a. You call your San Diego office to talk with a colleague you have never met.

   b. You dictate a letter to your division manager (your superior). Your secretary types the letter.

   c. You speak to someone you suspect of saying negative things about you to your boss.

   d. You speak to a group of businesspeople from Canada.

   e. You write a memorandum that will be distributed to all of your employees.

9. Meet with your group. Develop examples of each of Schneider, Donaghy, and Newman's guidelines for overcoming semantic barriers. Choose one group member to read the examples to the class.

10. [*Your professor will time this exercise.*] You have just been hired as manager of the 25-person marketing department of the Chicago Consulting Group (CCG). During your first week at CCG you discover that your subordinates do not want to work for you because they have heard that your degree is in finance, not marketing, and that you have a reputation as an unfeeling slave driver of only moderate intelligence. When you talk to your employees, they give terse answers to your questions and are unwilling to discuss their ideas with you. Most of your subordinates are well-educated relatively young men and women who have been with CCG for several years. You hear that at least ten of them had applied for your job. Most resent the fact that CCG did not promote from within. Consequently, you realize that a number of serious communication problems exist. Draft a two-, three-, or four-page plan for a meeting you will ask your employees to attend. At the meeting you wish to begin to relieve the tension in your department. Your plan should essentially address the six guidelines for communication.

11. You have been chosen to give a presentation on your department's plan for increasing the Big Chocolate candy bar's market share. You will give the presentation to 57 of your company's professional employees, none of whom are familiar with your department's work. You are forced to give the presentation in your company's rather small conference room. You will have no microphone. What types of interference will you likely face? How can you minimize the damage?

12. Meet with your group. You and each other group member read one of these communication situations. Identify and discuss the feedback in each situation. Discuss what you think the feedback means and how you can use it.

   a. YOU: Mr. Simmons, could I talk to you? I need to discuss a problem I'm having with the issue paper you asked me to do.

   MR. SIMMONS: I'm rather busy, you know. I wish you had made an appointment. Oh well, come on in. I can give you a minute or two, I guess.

   b. YOU: Ms. Franklin, what did you think of the report?

   MS. FRANKLIN: Well, it was certainly long! You are a prolific writer.

   c. YOU: Mr. Albert, I am interested in applying for a management associate position. I just finished my B.B.A. in management and feel that I'm not using my talents in the typing pool.

   MR. ALBERT: Yes, please sit down. There are several openings in the program management department. Which one are you interested in?

   d. You sent a letter to Ms. Jones, a prospective client. In your letter you wrote that you would like to meet with her in the near future. Ms. Jones calls and leaves a message with your secretary that she is busy this month but may be able to meet with you next month.

   e. You have just given your annual state-of-the-company address to your 200 employees. You ask if anyone has a question. No one responds. A few people are yawning. Some are frowning. Most are staring past you.

13. Meet with your group. Discuss this chapter's treatment of the importance of evaluating both during and after a communication exchange. You and each other group member evaluate the discussion by completing the evaluation forms in Appendix B.

14. Develop your own evaluation form for use in appraising your communication transactions. Include questions that are of particular interest to you.

15. For each of these vaguely worded purposes, write at least one strong, objective criterion. Create any additional information you may need.
    a. To improve my relationship with the employees
    b. To decrease expense-account expenditures for the sales staff
    c. To reduce the absentee rate
    d. To interest the employees in the evening seminars your firm sponsors
    e. To improve morale
    f. To reduce waste of office supplies
    g. To choose the correct person for promotion
    h. To solve the problem of petty thievery by employees
    i. To cut shoplifting

16. For the following situation, identify the actual interference, identify the feedback and explain how you would use it, and describe how you would evaluate at each stage.

    Mary Harris, a good friend of yours, wrote you a letter asking you to think about opening a financial management firm with her in New York City. You call her and ask her if you would be equal partners in the firm. She says that you would have to contribute $50,000 to the firm if you want partner status. You ask when she needs the money. "Soon," she says. "When exactly?," you ask. "In a month or two," she replies. She then says she needs to go to a meeting, so she will talk to you later.

17. You have been asked to give a short, serious talk at the beginning of your company's Thanksgiving banquet. All religions as well as agnosticism and atheism are represented in your company. Write the short talk.

18. Two of your friends argue a great deal. Both take strong, extreme stands on opposite sides of almost every issue. Neither will admit that any other's stand exists, though you know better. List at least one other position that could be taken on each of your friends' issues.
    a. John believes that unions are the answer to all of labor's problems. Susan believes that unions cannot solve any of labor's problems.
    b. John believes that all workers would be very productive if managers would get out of their way. Susan believes that managers must closely supervise workers because workers will not work on their own.
    c. John believes that people should be hired only on the basis of their experience. Susan believes that people should be hired only on the basis of their education.
    d. John believes that the office coffee-making chores should be shared by clerical, professional, and managerial personnel alike. Susan believes that the secretaries should always make the coffee.
    e. John believes that people cannot exercise any control over communication interference. Susan believes that people can overcome all communication interference.

19. Use your dictionary and thesaurus to develop meanings for these words. Use the words when you think, write, and speak so that you will feel comfortable using them.

    a. Affective   f. Differentiation
    b. Chauvinist   g. Diminish
    c. Compatible   h. Dysphemism
    d. Constraint   i. Enigma
    e. Criterion, criteria   j. Euphemism

k.	Feminist	**q.**	Resolve
l.	Milieu	**r.**	Restrict
m.	Perspective	**s.**	Self-fulfilling prophecy
n.	Procedural	**t.**	Subtle
o.	Quietude	**u.**	Supplement
p.	Reinforce	**v.**	Transceive

20. Take and score Self-Test 16 over the excerpt on organizational feedback.

Self-Test 16
Excerpt about Organizational Feedback

A. Recall (25 points each). For each multiple-choice question, select the most accurate answer.

  1. Substantive feedback refers to:
  a. Written feedback
  b. Oral feedback from an important person in the organization
  c. Frequent, specific, timely, consistent, and sufficient feedback
  d. Feedback for which you ask
  e. a and d

  2. Positive feedback refers to:
  a. Saying only good things about a person's work
  b. Constructive and objective feedback
  c. Feedback an employee gives to a manager
  d. Feedback that does not include any criticism
  e. c and d

  3. Which one of these statements is true?
  a. A simple declaration of an open-door policy at the upper-management level usually overcomes bottlenecks in upward flows of feedback.
  b. People who feel fearful and manipulated are usually eager to initiate upward feedback.
  c. Even in a neutral climate employees tend to tell superiors what they want to hear.
  d. Research shows that receivers always overlook negative treatment if the content brings good news.
  e. A free flow of good organizational feedback is more necessary for employees high in self-esteem than for employees low in self-esteem.

B. Inference (25 points). Indicate whether this statement is an example of positive feedback.

"Ellen, I really appreciate the fact that you are getting all of your reports in on time. If you have a few minutes, I'd like to give you a few pointers on how to make your evaluation sections even stronger."

Solution to Self-Test 16
Excerpt about Organizational Feedback

A. Recall (25 points each)   **B.** Inference (25 points)
  1. c   **3.** c   Yes, it is positive.
  2. b

---

21. Take and score Self-Test 17 over Chapter 6.

Self-Test 17
Chapter 6

A. Recall (12 points each). For each multiple-choice question, select the most accurate answer.

1. What is the major potential barrier to any communication exchange in which you participate?
   a. You
   b. Noise
   c. Your health
   d. Cultural differences
   e. Purposes

2. Which one of these is *not* a semantic barrier?
   a. Treating the map as if it is the territory
   b. Operating at the poles—the extremes
   c. Treating symbols as having only denotative meanings
   d. Attaching "etc." to everything you send or receive
   e. Using affective dysphemisms

3. In order to control external interference:
   a. Learn what constitutes good form and composition.
   b. Learn to evaluate what has been transmitted or received for you.
   c. Learn to select appropriate people and equipment to accomplish what you want accomplished.
   d. Listen carefully and ask for clarification.
   e. a–d

4. Which of these does *not* describe positive feedback?
   a. Does not attack a person
   b. Deals with specific acts in a direct and supportive way
   c. Can occur even when the message does not bring good news
   d. Always occurs when the response is "Yes"
   e. Respects human dignity

5. Connotative meanings are defined as:
   a. Meanings on which most people agree
   b. Meanings that are personal, private, and not shared
   c. Meanings that the dictionary lists for words
   d. Meanings shared by people of similar cultures
   e. Meanings that cannot be expressed or understood by anyone

6. A communication audit:
   a. Is similar to an accounting audit
   b. Represents a contemporary evaluative process for organizations
   c. Often involves outside consultants
   d. Involves measuring the effectiveness of critical communication flows
   e. a–d

B. Inference (14 points each). Indicate whether these statements are true or false.

1. The good communicator needs to strike a reasonable balance between quantitative and qualitative evaluation of communication effectiveness.

2. Interference is anything that somehow alters intended messages or makes them less than correct in the first place.

Solution to Self-Test 17
Chapter 6

A. Recall (12 points each)

    1. a   **4.** d

    2. d   **5.** b

    3. e   **6.** e

B. Inference (14 points)

    1. True

    2. True

Part c

SENDING

7

Writing

In Chapters 1–3 you reviewed applications for the receiving acts. Now that you have completed the coverage of theory and principles in Chapter 4–6, return to applications—this time to the sending acts. Begin in this chapter with some basic principles of writing.

First, review some of the major characteristics of the written channels. They:

1. Belong to the medio and mass levels of communication, thus to Ranks 2 and 4 of the effectiveness hierarchy
2. Serve as excellent supplements and reinforcements for the intrapersonal, interpersonal, and person-to-group levels
3. Often require better communication abilities than the oral channels because of the relatively permanent nature of the messages
4. Provide the permanency, accuracy, and storage capacity necessary for complex, technical, and legal information
5. Prevent or cover some of the kinds of emotionality that can occur in oral transactions
6. Add formality to messages
7. Allow for some kinds of distant and time-consuming transactions not possible through the oral channels
8. Meet traditional requirements for certain kinds of messages; for example, invitations to formal events

Even as you acknowledge the importance of observing tradition in some realms, avoid observing it everywhere. Always choose the richest channel possible under the circumstances. Particularly avoid blind acceptance of the written channels simply because "it's always been done that way."

Compared to some of the other kinds of writing, much of business writing often is rather formal, traditional, dull, technical, and jargon-ridden. However, business writing need not always be so. It can be lively, natural, fresh, and understandable.

One of the best ways to learn to write is to read. Therefore, Chapters 8–14, 17, and 18 include many examples of letters, reports, memoranda, forms, and other messages. Most of them appear in the formats actually used in business.

This book cannot possibly cover the full spectrum of the business writing field. However, it does contain principles enough to help you write most of the messages you will encounter as a general business communicator.

The writing process involves application of the guidelines, one of which covers the actual selecting, encoding, and transmitting of written messages. That process covers these logical steps:

1. Selecting
2. Drafting
3. Revising
4. Transmitting

APPLYING THE GUIDELINES FOR WRITING

The six communication guidelines for writing become:

1. Define your purposes, the reader's purposes, yourself, the reader, and the environment.
2. Select the writing channel.
3. Control the interference internal and external to you and the reader.
4. Write and transmit the messages in light of the purposes, the participants, the environment, the channel, and the interference.
5. Use feedback from and to the reader.
6. Evaluate at each stage.

Defining the purposes, the reader, and the environment for the written channels can be difficult. In spite of the difficulty—or perhaps because of it—you need to concentrate on this guideline.

Once you move into the written/nonverbal category of channels, your next step is to choose from the many channels available there. Think about the advantages and disadvantages of each: relative costs, speed of transmission, vulnerability to interference, nonverbal elements, stimulation of feedback, and adaptability to custom.

Evaluate potential interference associated with written channels. The major source of it is reduced feedback. Once you begin a transmission, continue to anticipate and control actual interference as it develops.

The bulk of this chapter presents methods for encoding written business messages. Therefore, the summary suggestion here is: As you write, keep in mind the reader, the environment, the features of the channel, the purposes, and the potential and actual interference.

As a writer, you cannot see your reader. However, still try to stimulate feedback, be aware of it when it does occur, and use it to improve and evaluate the specific transaction on which it comments. Also use feedback to improve future transactions.

Evaluation depends upon the purposes, the criteria identified with them, and the quality of the feedback received. Thus, evaluation for written channels can be hard to accomplish. However, it remains just as important as for other channels.

SELECTING

The message-selection process begins at the instant of your awareness of the need for a message. It continues to grow as you work through the preliminaries and through the writing itself. The purpose-setting stage is particularly important, for it identifies and delimits the topic to be covered in the proposed message.

The selection of messages eventually takes place in your mind, of course. However, at first you may not have all of the information you need stored there. Therefore, you often have to search outside of your mind to obtain it.

You may collect such information in many ways, several of which are described in Chapter 13. Such methods involve primary data (data you collect yourself) and secondary data (data others have collected). They involve written, oral, and nonverbal processes.

DRAFTING

Once you have collected the information and have begun to select the internal messages, move into the drafting stage.

Several approaches exist for converting internal messages into drafts of external ones. All of the effective approaches involve both writing and organizing. However, the two definitive but opposite approaches simply reverse the order of these two acts. Therefore, first consider the best order for writing and organizing. Then consider some suggestions for the acts themselves.

Order of Writing and Organizing

Many writers recommend organizing first and writing second. Many others recommend writing first and organizing second. Others recommend a combined approach.

Organizing and writing

The writers who recommend organizing first and writing second urge that they save time and effort by doing so. They suggest that pre-organizing prevents you from:

1. Omitting important elements and including unnecessary ones
2. Placing parts in illogical order
3. Including parts in one section that belong in another
4. Spending too much time on unimportant parts and too little on important ones
5. Including too much or too little information

Pre-organization always involves choosing a developmental pattern and establishing an outline. If you pre-organize, you may want to do so even before you collect information at the selecting stage.

The key feature of the organize-then-write technique is that you do not allow yourself to write until you complete the organization. When you begin writing, you develop the sentences and paragraphs to fit your plan.

Writing and organizing

The writers who recommend the just-write method urge that choosing it saves time and effort as compared to the other approach. They suggest that you just write. Forget developmental patterns, outlines, spelling, logic, grammar, transitions, punctuation, factual accuracy, format, tone, and anything else that will slow your progress. Just spill the thoughts as quickly as they come to you. Unload them before they escape.

One problem with the idea-dumping method is that you think at about 400 w.a.m. and write longhand at about 25 w.a.m. Therefore, if you use the approach, do whatever you can to overcome some of that gap.

Use shorthand or the typewriter if you have those skills. Abbreviate words. Write single key words or sentence fragments. Cross through words rather than erase them—if you take the time to do even that much. Keep a pad and pencil at hand at all times so that you can capture random outpourings. Use a tape recorder for random thoughts, for the intitial emptying for a draft, and for revising a draft. (Recall that you can speak at 125 w.a.m. or more, while you can write at only 25 w.a.m.)

If you are one of the many people who fear or dislike writing, the just-write method may help you overcome those feelings. When you accept that you do not have to write perfectly, you may no longer sit and stare at a blank sheet of paper. You may no longer write one or two words and then crumple the paper and throw it in the wastebasket. You may no longer avoid the process by sharpening nine pencils, collecting more data, or deciding to put the writing off till tomorrow.

Sometimes when you sit down to write, your thoughts simply will not turn to the subject. In such cases, begin writing anyway. Write anything—any words, phrases, or off-the-topic thoughts you may have. Miraculously, the words quickly turn to those needed for the topic for which you began the session.

With the just-write method, force yourself to complete the entire draft before you begin to organize. Organizing, then, becomes part of the revising stage.

Combining approaches

Perhaps the best methods for writing lie in a combination of the two polar approaches just described. A combined process can involve the best elements of both.

A combined method might include these steps:

1. Use the just-write technique to spill key words on paper.
2. Quickly organize the key words into a rough preliminary outline for a chosen developmental pattern. Still do not worry about correctness of form.
3. Use the just-write technique to unload thoughts about each part of the outline. Add other parts or reorganize as desired.
4. Quickly revise the outline if necessary. Leave it rough.
5. Use the just-write technique to write the entire draft of the message.
6. Complete the organization during the revising stage.

Organizing

Whether accomplished before or after writing, organizing involves the two major elements introduced in the preceding section: developmental patterns and outlines.

Developmental patterns

The pattern of development you choose for the parts of a message has an impact upon both the logical and the psychological elements of its evolution. Consider seven such patterns:

1. Inductive
2. Deductive
3. Chronological
4. Spatial
5. Analytical
6. Comparative
7. Ranked

Inductive   The inductive (indirect) pattern moves the message from the specific to the general, from the parts to the whole. It moves it from the sample to the universe and from the factual bits to a general conclusion or principle built from them.

The inductive pattern is useful for delivering unpleasant messages. Used in those situations, induction establishes an indirect process that softens the blow of bad news somewhat. It also often appears in reports of research.

For example, if you write a letter to refuse a request for credit, you would cite such factors as poor credit record and insufficient income before you make the refusal.

Deductive   The deductive (direct) plan reverses the inductive. It develops from the general to the specific or from the whole to the parts. It develops from the universe to the sample or from the conclusion or principle to the factual bits that properly fall under it.

The deductive plan works well for messages that include routine or pleasant information. For instance, a message of invitation usually begins with the invitation. Then it supplies the details.

Chronological   If a message features the order of events as the key dimension, then it uses the chronological pattern.

Suppose that you file an automobile-accident claim with an insurance company. Sometime during the process you will provide a narrative of events in the step-by-step sequence of their occurrence.

Chronological descriptions can also tell how to perform production-line operations, how to assemble a tricycle, or how to break down a substance for chemical analysis.

Spatial   Some messages logically unfold through a spatial pattern. For example, if you write a report about your firm's international operations, you could develop it by geographical areas.

Another spatial pattern covers the topic from top to bottom or from bottom to top. For instance, business analyses often proceed in organization chart fashion— from the president down, or from the line supervisor up.

Other spatial patterns encompass the topic from left to right, from right to left, from inside to outside, from outside to inside, from near to far, and from far to near. Topics natural to such organization include communication patterns for (1) lateral flows, (2) internal-to-external and external-to-internal processing, and (3) movements from a central office to decentralized offices, and from decentralized offices back to a central one.

Analytical   The word "analyze" means to separate the whole into its constituent elements for careful scrutiny. Therefore, an analytical pattern proves to be logical for many kinds of messages. For instance, when you write a résumé, you usually break it down into descriptive parts such as education, experience, personal data, and references.

Many business reports also separate wholes into component elements. One example is a report breaking the subject into the functions of finance, marketing, and production.

Comparative   The organization of a message often involves a comparative pattern. To illustrate, a report could compare:

1. Qualities of a decentralized and centralized organizational structure
2. Advantages and disadvantages of three proposed locations for your new plant
3. Views of both laborers and managers on a given issue
4. Alternative solutions to a problem

Ranked   You may arrange the components of a message in the ranked pattern—either ascending or descending. The ascending style overlaps the inductive, and the descending style overlaps the deductive.

Some examples of ranked development include:

1. Describing the qualities ascribed to a good managerial style
2. Ranking job factors in order of importance
3. Asking questions in order of importance
4. Arranging budget requests in order of importance

Outlines

As a skeleton display of the parts of the message, an outline can include topics or short sentences.

The topic outline includes phrases or sentence fragments that identify the subjects of the parts. The sentence outline includes complete sentences—sentences that may eventually serve as the topic sentences for the paragraphs of the message itself.

For simple writing—most letters, memoranda, notes, and forms—the topic outline serves well. However, for more involved messages, try writing the topic outline first and then converting it into a sentence outline.

To develop outlines, establish the parts and select a format.

Parts   First, establish an appropriate number of major parts for a message. The appropriate number depends basically upon the nature of the subject matter. However, it also depends upon other factors, including the length of the message.

A 600-page book may properly include 20 major parts (chapters). On the other hand, a five-page report with 20 major parts probably is incorrectly designed.

As you identify the major parts, carry in mind the basic concepts of a three-part message (beginning, middle, ending). However, establish major parts of relatively equal importance as they relate logically to the subject, not as they relate to the three-part plan. As an obvious example, you would not label the major parts as "Opening," "Body," and "Ending." First, such an outline communicates nothing about the subject matter itself. Second, it lumps the bulk of the subject matter into one section—the body.

To divide the subject into logical major parts of relatively equal importance, first look at the whole.

For instance, if your subject for the letter channel is a request for a major credit card for a high line of credit, you would hardly choose your political party as a major factor. Your party membership does not logically belong to the subject.

Even factors that meet the test of logic may not meet the test of equivalency. For the credit-request letter outline, you might place your credit-payment record as a major division, but would not include your checking-account balance of $132.50 at that same level. If you deal with your checking account at all, you would place it in subordination to a major division dealing with assets.

In addition to selecting major parts relatively equal in importance and logically derived from the subject, make them collectively exhaustive and mutually exclusive.

To illustrate collective exhaustion, assume your purpose is to compare the forms of business organization in the United States. If you use partnerships and corporations as the two major divisions, you have not exhausted the whole. Without sole proprietorships, the coverage is incomplete.

To illustrate mutual exclusion, assume that you are analyzing the personnel function. If you try to establish training and development as two of the major categories, you are creating overlapping classes. Training and development are not mutually exclusive.

Also consider the sheer volume of words necessary for each major part. If you find too much disparity in the volumes for the parts, you may try to adjust the outline to make the volumes more nearly equal.

For example, suppose your topic is a summary of management thought. When you list the major contributors, you find little to write about three of them. Therefore, you might lump them into one category called "Other Contributors."

As you write heads for the major parts, make the word patterns parallel. Choices include:

1. All complete sentences
2. All verbs and verb phrases
3. All nouns or noun phrases
4. All adjectives
5. All questions
6. All declarative statements

Consider these samples of pairings of incorrect and correct parallel structures:

	INCORRECT	CORRECT
1.	The Manager Plans	Planning
	Organize	Organizing
	Directing	Directing
	Controlling Function	Controlling

2. Wholesale	Wholesale
Retailers	Retail
3. Collecting Data	Collection
Organization of Data	Organization
Analyze Data	Analysis
Interpreting	Interpretation

After you select the major parts (at least two), place them in the order dictated by the selected developmental pattern. Next establish the first level of subparts. Then continue the subdivisions until you have exhausted the subordinated components of the subject matter.

Use essentially the same principles for subdivisions that you use for the major divisions:

(1) Establish an appropriate number of subdivisions. Once you reach this level, apply the general rule that you should have at least two and no more than ten subdivisions for each category. The best range probably is three to six.

(2) Establish logical subdivision topics of relatively equal importance.

(3) Make the subdivisions collectively exhaustive and mutually exclusive of the part they represent.

(4) Make the word patterns parallel within each level. Though you should use parallel structure within each level, you may vary it among levels. For example, you may select noun phrases for the major parts, adjectives for one group of subparts, and complete sentences for another.

(5) Place the subparts in logical order according to the developmental pattern.

Formats   The classical format for outlines identifies the major divisions as capital roman numerals with periods aligned. More contemporary arrangements identify them with arabic numbers.

I.	1.0	1
II.	2.0	2
III.	3.0	3
IV.	4.0	4
V.	5.0	5
VI.	6.0	6

The expanded formats appear as Figure 7–1.

The more contemporary styles do not require the indention that the traditional format does. However, the traditional design is still used widely.

For your own drafting purposes, choose any of the types shown—or one of your own design. However, if you intend for others to see the outline, use a correct, formal style.

Examples   Observe how the topics of the outline for this chapter also form the headings for it:

VII. Writing

    A. Guidelines for writing

    B. Selecting

I.			**1.0**	**1**
	A.		**1.1**	**1a**
		1.	**1.11**	**1a1**
		a.	**1.111**	**1a1a**
		(1)	**1.1111**	**1a1a1**
		(a)	**1.11111**	**1a1a1a**
		(b)	**1.11112**	**1a1a1b**
		(2)	**1.1112**	**1a1a2**
		b.	**1.112**	**1a1b·**
		2.	**1.12**	**1a2**
	B.		**1.2**	**1b**
II.			**2.0**	**2**
	A.		**2.1**	**2a**
	B.		**2.2**	**2b**
	C.		**2.3**	**2c**

Figure 7—1   Outline formats

   C. Drafting
      1. Order of writing and organizing
         a. Organizing and writing
         b. Writing and organizing
         c. Combining approaches

      2. Organizing
         a. Developmental patterns
            (1) Inductive
            (2) Deductive
            (3) Chronological
            (4) Spatial
            (5) Analytical
            (6) Comparative
            (7) Ranked

         b. Outlines
            (1) Parts
            (2) Formats
            (3) Examples

Examples of conversions of a few of the preceding topics into sentence-outline form include:

   VII. Writing is a sending act that involves applying the guidelines and selecting, drafting, revising, and transmitting the message.

      A. The six writing guidelines parallel those for the other communication acts.

      B. Selecting messages involves choosing and collecting information and molding it for transmission to another.

Writing

As suggested, even if you organize first, you may find that the just-write tactic aids in drafting the message. However, whether you use the just-write approach or some other, you eventually must add structure to the message.

One good way to establish structure is to develop the body first, the opening second, and the ending third. The suggestion applies particularly well to long messages.

The body of a message may be one paragraph or hundreds of paragraphs. Whatever its length, it contains the substance—the meat—of the message.

The opening part of a message occupies less space than the body. However, it plays an important role. It often gains the reader's attention, establishes the background, makes a transition, and introduces the material to follow.

The ending section of a message also occupies less space than the body. Like the opening, it serves important purposes. It often summarizes the message, spotlights the conclusion, provides a light touch, adds courtesy, and calls for acceptance and action.

As you structure each of the three sections, begin with the topic sentences.

Topic sentences

Whether it falls at the beginning, the middle, or the end, the topic sentence is the focal point of the paragraph. It communicates the fundamental message. It is the heart—the main idea.

When you start organizing a part, first establish all of the topic sentences for it. Then review them for logic and content. However, do not revise them for structural detail at this point. Instead, move to the paragraphs.

Paragraphs

A paragraph contains one or more sentences. It contains a topic sentence and any other sentences necessary to develop the topic introduced in it.

Like any unit of writing, a paragraph probably contains a beginning, a body, and an end. The beginning often makes a transition from the preceding material. It may do so as it gains the reader's attention and even flashes a forecast of the topic. The body of a paragraph often features the topic and the development of the topic and subtopics. Though the topic sentence may appear anywhere in the paragraph, it should appear soon after any transitional opening that may be used. Therefore, whatever the developmental plan for the entire message, use the deductive plan for most of the paragraphs within it. You may use an ending word, phrase, or sentence to complete a paragraph. It may give a result, a conclusion, a summary, or even an emphatic reinforcement of the key topic of the paragraph.

Of the three paragraph elements, the body is the only critical one. The second in importance probably is the opening. It creates a flow and coherence for the message. The paragraph conclusion is the most dispensable. Particularly for short paragraphs, a concluding statement may be nothing more than redundancy. In practice, the transitional opening for a new paragraph often serves also as the conclusion for the preceding one. However, even if you do not always write a concluding sentence, try to include in the last sentence a word or a phrase that at least implies some climax or finality to the paragraph.

Consider ten sentences as a practical upper limit for the number in a paragraph. If you need more than ten to develop the topic, you probably need to subdivide the topic and treat each of the subdivisions in a separate paragraph.

(562 words)
(test on page 222)

Once you have drafted all of the paragraphs of a message, move to the revision.

REVISING

No one is a good writer—only a good rewriter. Therefore, though you begin to apply writing principles as you develop the draft, you still need to review it for revision.

Preview some suggestions for revising. They relate to: (1) content, (2) mechanics, (3) word choice, (4) tone, and (5) integrity.

Content

Three components define your concern with content: completeness, accuracy, and definition of terms.

Completeness

The good message contains everything necessary to create a desired meaning within the receiver.

Think of how the purpose of a message would be defeated by carelessly omitting such information as the:

1. Date of the announced event
2. Time of the event
3. Place of the event
4. Address to which an ordered or requested item is to be sent
5. Exact name, description, or catalog number of the item being ordered
6. Color or size of the item being ordered

Accuracy

You may destroy a message with inaccuracies in the information you do include.

You can easily think of examples of what may—or may not—happen as a result of errors in statements of dates, times, places, addresses, descriptions, colors, sizes, and other similar bits of information.

When your message includes figures, proofread it particularly carefully. Writing invoice numbers, stock numbers, dollar amounts, totals, and other numbers is a particularly error-prone task.

Definition of terms

Suppose that you are writing a message about some research you did dealing with "small farms." If you do not define what you mean by "small farms," your message is incomplete. To complete that aspect of it, you could simply include a statement that you defined small farms as those of less than 20 acres.

Think of the problems that might arise from these references to undefined terms:

- In a questionnaire:
  What is the size of the company you work for?
  _____ Large
  _____ Medium
  _____ Small
- In a credit-application form:
  List your assets:

  List your liabilities:

- In a research report to a receiver not versed in statistical methods:
  The F test showed that the null hypothesis ($\mu_1 = \mu_2 = \mu_3$) should be rejected

Mechanics

As you revise messages, look to the mechanics—the rules for language and structure. Many readers are so appalled by errors in mechanics that they dismiss the writer as unworthy of their attention.

Review this coverage of mechanics in seven parts: (1) grammar, (2) punctuation, (3) spelling, (4) word usage, (5) sentence structure, (6) format, and (7) other mechanics.

Grammar

Grammar rules the structure and forms of words and guides their arrangement and interrelationships in phrases and sentences. The structures covered here include subject-verb agreement, noun-pronoun agreement, and subjective and objective pronoun cases. Appendix C develops these topics substantially.

Punctuation

Punctuation is another essential element of the literate written piece. The marks of punctuation serve to identify, separate, clarify, interrupt, emphasize, and terminate series of words. Without them a page of words would be an unintelligible blur. They help to provide the rhythm for the written word that is supplied by pauses, tone of voice, etc. for the spoken word.

Appendix C provides a brief review of the use of periods, exclamation points, question marks, commas, colons, semicolons, dashes, quotation marks, hyphens, parentheses, italics, underlines, and apostrophes.

Spelling

The accomplished writer spells words correctly. Probably second only to grammatical errors, misspellings cause untold anguish for the educated reader.

Appendix C includes some suggestions for becoming a better speller. It also includes suggestions for proper pronunciation of troublesome words.

Word usage

The concern for proper word usage relates both to spelling and grammar. However, certain kinds of words lead to such common problems that Appendix C features them. Examples include *accept/except, personal/personnel, affect/effect, counsel/council,* among others.

Sentence structure

Appendix C also covers some bothersome facets of sentence structure. The following types of misplaced modifiers illustrate the need to review the topic:

- The woman sitting at the desk with the gray hair is the supervisor of this section.
- Rotting in the vegetable bin, he threw the potatoes away.
- The chefs discussed how to make a salad with their assistants.

Format

As you revise messages, correct errors in format. Whether you choose a letter, a memorandum, a formal report, or some other channel, observe a format appropriate to it. For example, letters are traditionally single spaced, while many reports are double spaced. Letters often include salutations; memoranda do not.

Acceptable forms for letters appear in Chapters 8–11. Chapter 12 illustrates correct formats for memoranda, notes, forms, and some other written channels. Chapters 13 and 14 deal with proper styles for written reports. In addition, Appendix C includes some suggestions about footnotes and bibliographies—elements of formal reports.

Other mechanics

Appendix C also includes suggestions related to correctly handling such items as numbers, possessives, syllabication, capitalization, abbreviations, and contractions.

Word Choice

The words in the English language number about one million. Yet even that number is quite small compared to the almost infinite numbers of meanings that people carry in their minds.

On the other hand, the number of words that people actually use and understand is quite small compared to the one million. Estimates suggest that many people live their entire lives using no more than one or two thousand words. Therefore, choose words that the reader is likely to understand.

Consider five categories dealing with word choice: (1) clearness, (2) appropriateness, (3) concreteness, (4) colorfulness, and (5) freshness.

Clearness

Select words and patterns of words that make your meaning clear. One basic rule for clarity is to use the shortest possible words. Place the short words in short sentences. Then place the short sentences in short paragraphs.

Arrange paragraphs so that the topic sentence appears first or just after any transitional words used. Follow the topic sentence with just enough words to develop the idea. If you use a concluding statement in the paragraph, keep it brief.

Brevity and good paragraph order cannot assure clarity, however. Long words do not necessarily muddy a passage; neither do short words necessarily clarify it.

To illustrate, contrast the clarity of some short and longer words. The words in the first column contain one or two syllables. The words in the second column mean about the same thing as those in the first column. Most of the words in the second column contain three or more syllables—long words according to the readability formulas described in a subsequent section. Decide which word in each pair you would choose for the average reader.

jounce	agitate
arch	cunning
abash	embarrass
abate	diminish
abet	encourage
bane	nuisance
cant	insincerity
cede	surrender
cogent	persuasive
rife	plentiful
surfeit	sufficiency
ken	knowledge
scion	descendant
tyro	beginner
obtund	paralyze

Clarity mainly requires selecting words that come closest to conveying the precise denotative and connotative meanings that you want the receiver to create. Though many words do have roughly equivalent synonyms, many others do not. If the best word is not likely to be familiar to the reader, at least in the context in which it appears, either recast the sentence or define the word right then and there.

A dictionary definition itself sometimes contains usable substitutes for a word. It also usually lists some synonyms for it.

Because the basic purpose of a thesaurus is to give synonyms, it proves to be a particularly good source for alternatives to long or obscure words.

As you try new words, take care to satisfy idiomatic requirements—to join words in customary patterns. For example, assume you decide to use the word "rife." Though it is an adjective and means "abundant," you would not properly write "The report has a rife number of errors." Instead, you would write, "The report is rife with errors." Correct idiom requires the insertion of "with" after "rife."

Appropriateness

Appropriate level of formality forms a second criterion for word selection. These groups of words illustrate the range of formality available for some expressions:

gut feeling	hunch	premonition
all set	ready	prepared
chow down	eat	dine
bellyache		complain
	won't	will not
give the once-over	run over	examine cursorily
big shot		celebrity
dough		money
place	home	abode
copycat		imitator

The choice from among any such set of words depends upon several factors—particularly the receiver's preferences, the occasion, and the channel. You likely would not issue an invitation to a formal ball that dubbed the affair a "bash." In contrast, you probably would not invite a few friends to your home for a "festivity."

The decision about whether to use contractions can be a difficult one. Generally, if you question their appropriateness in a given message, do not use them.

Though contractions add a conversational tone, they are informal—and may detract from the impact of a message. Thus, you probably would not use them in formal reports and other messages to top management.

On the other hand, if you write a persuasive sales message to be sent to the general public, you well may choose to use contractions.

Concreteness

Choose concrete words whenever you can. Concrete words refer to things that can be perceived by the five senses. Thus, they not only help make a message clear, they also hold the reader's interest better than abstract words.

Words like "desk," "tape recorder," and "paper clip" make direct, concrete references to physical objects. Even words like "inch," "gravity," "twelve," "80 percent," and "parallel" are concrete. They have denotative meanings basically derived from the physical world.

Qualitative words for comparison, however, are not concrete words. For instance, problems of interpretation often arise for words such as "greatly," "highly," "soon," "fair," "good," "excellent," "superior," "slowly," "far," and "near." Therefore, use concrete (even quantitative) words instead of qualitative ones when appropriate.

Consider some examples of the use or the deliberate avoidance of concrete words:

- You place an order. To avoid the hazy "as soon as possible," you write "Please ship the materials to arrive no later than May 12."
- You hedge on an unknown fact by the overt use of qualitative comparison: "I understand that the problem actually started long ago." (How long ago is "long ago"?)
- You are disappointed that only 132 attended the reception for the Citizen of the Year last week. Therefore, you avoid any concrete references by writing in a news release, "A large number of people attended to pay their respects to Archer."

You cannot avoid abstract words, nor would you want to do so. They form an important part of advanced human communication. However, because abstract words do not vividly attach to the physical world, try to elaborate upon them with concrete illustrations.

For instance, assume you are a supervisor completing an evaluation form for a new employee. You write: "She does not seem to be adjusting to her job." However, because "adjusting" is an abstraction, you add these sentences:

> She has averaged three or four serious posting errors a week. Even though two others joined the firm at the same time she did, she consistently produces the smallest number of daily postings in her section. Most significantly, however, all but one of the other clerks have complained at least twice each that she is rude and uncooperative. I have also found her to act that way. Once when I was trying to help her with a complicated posting, she said, "Get off my back, you jerk."

Briefly think how you might clarify each of the following abstractions with concrete words: "insecure," "thoughtless," "scientific method," "disheartening," "nuisance," "maneuver," "honest," "lazy," "pretentious," and "righteous."

Colorfulness

Use colorful words when you can. They keep attention better than drab ones. These pairs of words may illustrate the difference:

investigate	snoop
exaggeration	caricature
informer	turncoat
receive	pocket
tempt	cajole
tease	vex
thin	bony
bad	wicked
worry	fret
hate	loathe

Verbs   The preceding list contains several verbs. However, verbs play such an important role in imparting colorfulness to your writing that they receive additional attention.

First, review some examples of how a change in the verb and accompanying sentence structure adds vibrancy to the expression:

1. The children ate their supper.   The children devoured their supper.
2. Her skills developed rapidly.   Her skills ripened rapidly.
3. The crowd passes by.   The crowd streams past.
4. She felt for the keys in her purse.   She groped for the keys in her purse.
5. He left his past behind.   He abandoned his past.
6. Planning is a significant part of the   Planning contribues significantly to
   managerial process.   the managerial process.
7. It is said that managers. . . .   Managers report that. . . .
8. There are too many members on the   The committee has far too many
   committee.   members.
9. They think that sales will increase.   They expect sales to increase.

Observe that numbers 6, 7, and 8 include "to be" verbs in the less vivid constructions. Therefore, avoid overuse of the "to be" verbs:

am	shall be	has been	shall have been
is	will be	have been	could have been
are	may be	had been	should have been
was	etc.		etc.

Because the "to be" verbs perform indispensable grammatical functions, virtually any message contains some of them sprinkled throughout. However, just as soon as the "to be" verbs start to predominate, they destroy the vitality of a message. Conversely, if all sentences contain sparkling verbs, even they begin to lose their impact.

Expletives   Numbers 7 and 8 also show the weakness of the use of "it" and "there" as expletives. When words serve only as place holders, they waste space, muddy meaning, and dull the prose, Not only do expletives use the lifeless "to be" verbs, they also show a haziness of reference. The words, "It is said," hedge on the answer to the question, "Who says?"

Consider some more examples eliminating expletives from the style:

It has been written that	Jones wrote that . . . .
There are many examples of	Examples abound to explain . . . .
There is no significant difference between	No significant difference exists between . . . .
It is clear that	Clearly
It is too bad that	Unfortunately
It is a foregone conclusion that	Obviously

The only situation for which expletives prove useful involves negative information. Like the passive voice reviewed in a subsequent section, expletives subordinate the negative. Contrast these two sentences:

You should have said . . . .
It is better to say . . . .

Even in this circumstance—as indeed in most others—the writer may still avoid the expletive by adopting a third choice: "You might have said . . . ."

Freshness

Form your messages with fresh words. Hackneyed, trite, jargon-ridden phrasing tends to arouse negative feelings within receivers.

To keep your writing fresh, avoid the types of clichés shown in the left-hand column of terms that follow. Try to replace them with the kinds of fresh, usually briefer words shown in the right-hand column:

along the lines of	like
as a case in point	as an example
as compared to	compared to
as of this date	now
as soon as possible	by April 4
due to	because
effectuate	effect

finalize (prioritize, routinize, positionize, etc.)	finish (Replace contrived "ize" words with others)
First and foremost, be sure to	Be sure to . . . .
for the purposes of	for
for the reason that (on the grounds that)	because
impact on	affect
in accordance with	by
in case of	if
in terms of	in
in the nature of	like
Last, but not least, the	Last, the . . . .
on the basis of	by
orientate	orient
Please find enclosed	Here is
. . . said as follows:	. . . said:
satisfaction reaction (and other double nouns)	satisfaction (Remove one of the nouns or rephrase)
To make a long story short, Mary said	Mary said . . . .
viable	alive, living
with the result that	so that
with reference to	about

Tone

As you revise messages, check them for tone. Check for (1) courtesy, (2) positive style, (3) "you" attitude, (4) active voice, and (5) nondiscriminatory symbols.

Courtesy

Common courtesy strengthens messages. Here are some examples of the kinds of words that help greatly to convert blunt messages into courteous ones:

Please	I look forward to
Thank you	If you can
Thanks	You are invited
May I	Dear Mr.
You are welcome	Dear Ms.
Would you	Ladies and Gentlemen
If you like	Best wishes
I should appreciate	Greetings

Positive style

The courtesies alone cannot overcome a negative style. Therefore, check to be sure that your writing on the whole reflects positive style.

Review these pairings of negative and positive expressions:

You sent your order too late for us to fill it by the time you requested.	We shipped your order yesterday—the day we received it. However, because an order takes at least five days to reach Framingham, it will be two or three days later than you requested.
You obviously did not follow the instructions	The instructions suggest that you . . . .
You should have known that the warranty does not provide for	Though the warranty does provide for . . ., it does not include . . . .
We are sorry, but we no longer carry the sweater you ordered in tan.	Though the sweater you ordered is no longer available in tan, we can give it to you in the attractive beige shown in the enclosed brochure.
Because you sent the wrong . . ., we cannot	As soon as you send . . ., we shall be able to . . . .

The buffer opening, positive sandwich, and inductive style also are important devices for softening negative content.

Buffer opening Assume you must write a letter to turn down a policyholder's claim. Avoid beginning with such words as: "We cannot pay your claim." Instead, use a buffer opening something like this:

> We were happy to examine the claim you submitted. In fact, you have been such a good customer that we exhausted every avenue to try to pay it for you.

Positive sandwich To change a buffer opening into a positive sandwich, simply wedge the bad news between a buffer opening and a buffer closing.

For the preceding example, you could use a buffer opening, explain positively that you cannot pay the claim, and give the reasons. Then you could close with something like: "Do not ever hestiate to submit a claim. We shall do everything within the provisions of your policy to grant it."

Inductive pattern The inductive developmental pattern can also pad the impact of bad news. For the claim denial, you could begin with:

> Thank you for your letter of June 12 in which you described the claim resulting from cigarette-burn damage to your carpet. On the day that we received it, we began our investigation. First, we checked . . . .

You would then build to a conclusion—the denial of the claim. However, you could follow that conclusion with a buffer sentence or two to combine the inductive method with a positive sandwich.

"You" attitude

The communication approach that concentrates upon the other may be called the "you" attitude. When you focus upon the reader's needs and point of view, the "you" attitude is genuine and pervades the entire message.

One device is to avoid the overuse of "I" and "we." Particularly in brief messages such as letters, notes, forms, and memoranda, remove most of the "I" and the "we" references. Replace them with "you"—either written or implied. When you do use "I" and "we," try not to open paragraphs with them.

You may sometimes use the "I" or "we" attitude simply to avoid a passive writing style. However, test every inclination to write "I" and "we" to be sure you have no other alternatives.

Review these examples of ways to avoid the "I" attitude, introduce the "you" attitude, and yet retain a reasonably active writing style:

Would you like to . . . .
Thank you for the . . . . (still retains the implied subject "I")
You may want . . . .
Have you ever . . .?
You will be happy to know that you now have credit at . . . .
You are invited . . . .
You did outstanding work on the project.

Active voice

Another feature of good tone appears in the use of the active voice instead of the passive. In the active voice, the subject creates the action. In the passive, the subject receives the action. Thus, the active provides more vigor and animation than does the passive voice. It also often removes the colorless "to be" verbs from the construction. Observe the difference in the liveliness and directness of these paired expressions:

PASSIVE	ACTIVE
The file cabinet was inspected by Elizabeth.	Elizabeth inspected the file cabinet.
More insurance should be carried by you.	You should carry more insurance.
Many such pieces of equipment are owned by us.	We own many such pieces of equipment.
Many decisions must be made by auditing department personnel every day.	Auditing department personnel must make many decisions every day.

Notice that you may write active-voice sentences even while avoiding the first-person pronouns ("I," "we," "my," "our," etc.) However, the task can be more difficult with the impersonal style (writing without first- and second-person pronouns) than with the personal style (writing with first- and second-person pronouns). With the personal style, the pronouns provide a wider range of possible subjects.

You sometimes may deliberately use the passive voice as a means for improving the tone of a negative message. Contrast these two sentences:

Complete your report by Friday.
Your report should be completed by Friday.

Though the difference between the two sentences is not dramatic, the second one does not contain the demanding tone of the first. The writer likely will complete the report by Friday in both cases. However, the second statement may make her or him feel better about doing it.

Nondiscriminatory symbols

Good tone calls for the use of nondiscriminatory symbols.

Discriminatory symbols are those that stereotype individuals on the basis of some characteristic common to or imputed to a class of humans. Some of these characteristics are race, ethnicity, age, sex, handicap, and religion.

The most pervasive communication discrimination attaches to the characteristic of sex. The language can be unfair to both sexes, but is particularly unfair to females. Therefore, to avoid sexist language, remove all references that treat the male as the norm and that cast people into sex-based roles.

Because of the extensiveness of sexism in the language, Appendix D includes guidelines for nonsexist communication. However, a few examples appear here, along with some for the other kinds of discrimination. Observe how the revised expression removes the discriminatory reference without hurting the idiom at all:

Each manager should be sure that his	All managers should be sure that their . . . .
Suppose an executive told his secretary that she should	Suppose an executive told a secretary to . . . .
In all the history of mankind	In all the history of humankind . . . .
The firemen, policemen, and garbagemen	The firefighters, police officers, and garbage collectors . . . .
As drunk as an Indian	Drunk
Welfare recipients do not support this legislation, because it would take away their gravy train.	Some welfare recipients do not support this legislation, because they say it would remove some deserving people from the rolls.
I tried to Jew the salesman down on the price.	I haggled with the salesperson over the price.
Did you hear the joke about the Pollack who	Did you hear the joke about the man/woman/person who . . . .
Neither black nor white	Neither bad nor good
Old fogy	Fogy
Golden years	Older years
Senior citizens	Older people/persons
Plain Jane	Ordinary in appearance
John has difficulty walking because of a gimpy leg.	John has difficulty walking because of his injured leg.
At the meeting she came across like a cross-eyed fool.	At the meeting she came across as a frenzied person.
Fish eaters	Catholics

Nondiscriminatory symbols are important because they support human dignity. However, they are also important because discriminatory language has legal implications. People have begun to file suits on the basis of discrimination in such messages as job descriptions and job titles.

Integrity

The final stage of the revision process involves viewing the entire message to assure that it has integrity. Integrity involves: (1) unity and coherence, (2) pace, (3) consistency, (4) conciseness, and (5) readability.

Unity and coherence

Tie the message into one unified whole. To do so, be sure that the parts belong—and belong in the sequence in which you present them. Check for all of the logical elements already described in the section on organization.

Also revise to assure that the message flows from one part to another to provide the intended coherent message. To assure coherence, use good transition, and remove awkward constructions.

Provide transition Transitional devices connect the parts—whether they be phrases, sentences, paragraphs, or sections.

These devices contribute to transition:

1. Prepare the reader for what will follow. Example: *"Although you may know that . . . ."*
2. Use transitional words such as:

but	still	next
even so	yet	moreover
like	and	finally
unlike	however	rather
thus	likewise	subsequently
therefore	otherwise	on the other hand
hence	for example	similarly
consequently	again	in spite of
conversely	then	despite
as a result	also	at the same time
to illustrate	afterwards	in contrast
accordingly	furthermore	on the contrary
so	first (second, third, ...)	in summary
besides	in addition	nevertheless

3. Use pronoun references to a word or phrase in the preceding sentence. Example: "Avoid the 'to be' verbs. Compared to many other verbs, *they* have no spirit."
4. Use the same word or phrase to introduce successive sentences. Example: *"Select words* that make your meaning clear. *Select words* that make your message concise."
5. Use numerical sequences of items: Example: "Use three steps to accomplish the task. *First,* . . . *Second,* . . . *Third,* . . ."
6. Use the same word in successive sentences. Example: "Avoid *using* 'this,' 'these' and other adjectives as nouns. *Such use* represents not only inaccurate gramma-

tical structure, but a weak, indefinite writing style as well. Also avoid *using* nouns as adjectives, as in 'this type person.' Nouns are nouns, not modifiers of other nouns."
7. Use the first and last sentences of paragraphs to carry the meaning forward. Example:

> ". . . *Transitional devices* contribute a great deal to coherence.
> *One such transitional device* includes . . . ."

Remove awkwardness   Another way to assure unity and coherence is to restructure awkward sentences. All of the rules for good writing apply to such restructuring.
   Consider an example of revision to remove awkwardness:

Though 15 people from our department (accounting) attended the workshop, 12 of them, including Jerry Bale, had no background for the topic of the workshop ("Advanced Sampling Techniques for the Auditor") offered by the CPA Association of Des Moines last week.	Last week 15 people from our accounting department attended the workshop on Advanced Sampling Techniques for the Auditor. The CPA Association of Des Moines conducted it. Of the 15 who attended, Jerry Bale and 11 others did not have the background for it.

Pace

Appropriate pace also contributes to the integrity of a message through emphasis, subordination, and variety.

Emphasis   You may emphasize ideas through several means.
1. Place an important idea in context with other important ideas.
2. Position the key idea at the beginning or the end of the structural unit—sentence, paragraph, section, or longer unit. Both positions emphasize the content.
3. Choose the developmental pattern on the basis of desired emphasis. The deductive and declining-rank styles emphasize ideas particularly well.
4. Allot space on the basis of the importance of ideas.
5. Repeat key ideas.
6. Place the vital idea in an independent clause, with the subordinate clauses and phrases supporting it.
7. Use sentences that build to a climax.
8. Use transitional words and phrases that feature the most important idea.
9. Use attention-getting words.
10. Choose words that present the idea in the most vivid and active forms.
11. Preview and summarize key ideas.
12. Use, but do not overuse, mechanical devices: underlines, exclamation points, frames built with lines or space, indented formats, blocked formats, all capitals, dashes, different style of type, different colors, special arrangements of letters, and variations in headings.

Subordination   To subordinate ideas, simply reverse the suggestions for emphasizing ideas. For instance, place a negative idea in the body of a message—not as the beginning or ending.

Variety   To give your message a pleasant pace, vary the structures of it. Mix the four basic sentence types in order to provide the desired variety:

Standard sentences place the subject first and the verb second. They may also include modifiers, direct objects, indirect objects, complements, expletives, and passive structures. Examples include:

- Lynn sang well.
- The purchasing manager ordered the materials.
- Elva bought her mother a calculator.
- Harold is a blonde.
- There are more than enough application blanks.
- The book was returned by Fran.

The *parallel sentence* emphasizes coordinate parts. The featured words, phrases, and clauses often appear in a series. Consider these illustrations:

- To communicate well is to live well.
- Courtesy, positiveness, activity—these qualities contribute significantly to good tone.

Like the parallel sentence, the *balanced sentence* spotlights coordinate elements. However, the special feature of the balanced sentence lies in its contrast of the coordinate ideas. The appropriate conjunction becomes "but" instead of "and." These sentences illustrate balance:

- People should use nondiscriminatory language—not because they fear lawsuits, but because they respect human dignity.
- The true test of the manager is not the ability to issue orders, but the ability to order issues.

The *periodic sentence* uses a series of words, phrases, or clauses to build to a climax. Review these examples:

- To understand others, to understand the interaction between you and others, understand yourself.
- Through intrapersonal transactions, through interpersonal transactions, through medio transactions, through person-to-group transactions, through mass transactions, you become a whole communicator.

Avoid overusing any one of the four types of sentence structures. Instead, introduce variety by alternating them.

Consistency

Consistency contributes to good pace in messages. The major aspect of consistency is parallel structure. Review that concept here by observing the improvement evident in the second message of each pair:

- He likes swimming, to jog, and tennis.

  He likes to swim, to jog, and to play tennis.

- The men's group and the ladies' group met for a planning session.

  The men's group and the women's group met for a planning session.

Conciseness

Examine the message to determine whether you can eliminate words without breaking structural rules or introducing choppiness.

One particular target is a series of redundant or unneeded words. Observe how the second sentence in each pair uses fewer words to convey the same meaning as the first:

- The delayed shipment seriously obstructed, blocked, and impeded our progress on the project.

  The delayed shipment seriously impeded progress on the project.

- Each of the persons made a significant, substantial, important contribution from her or his own functional specialty.

  Each person contributed substantially from a functional specialty.

Readability

All of the preceding suggestions point toward readable copy. However, consider a special concept related to calculations of message density—the concept of readability.

Since the early 1920's researchers have developed more than 50 readability formulas. Two of the most-used rating systems are the Flesch Reading Ease score and the Gunning Fog Index. Both formulas yield results expressed at grade levels of reading difficulty. For application of the Flesch formula, see *The Art of Readable Writing*[1] and "A New Readability Yardstick."[2]

Calculation of the Gunning Fog Index follows these steps paraphrased from *The Techniques of Clear Writing:*

1. Randomly choose several samples of about one hundred words each. Count the number of words. Count the number of sentences. Find the average sentence length by dividing the number of words by the number of sentences.
2. Count the number of hard words (words of three or more syllables). Do not count proper names. Do not count words formed by combining short, easy words (bookkeeping, grandmother). Do not count verb forms that become three syllables because of the addition of "-ed" or "-es." Divide the number of hard words by the total number of words and multiply by 100. This number is the percent of hard words in the passage.
3. To obtain the Fog Index, add the average sentence length and the percent of hard words. Multiply the result by 0.4.[3]

Apply the Gunning Fog Index to this passage about the use of readability formulas:

> Formulas are for *rating,* not for *writing.* Since the variables in the formula were selected only as indices of difficulty . . . changing them does not necessarily cause the difficulty of the writing to change accordingly. What you frequently get when you make such changes is an artificially altered readability score, one that is not reflected in increased comprehension by the reader. The changes needed in rewriting are more subtle and complex than a formula can suggest. . . .

---

[1]Rudolf Flesch, *The Art of Readable Writing,* 25th anniv. ed. (New York: Harper & Row Publishers, Inc., 1974), pp. 247-250.

[2]Rudolf Flesh, "A New Readability Yardstick," *Journal of Applied Psychology* 32 (June 1948): 225.

[3]Robert Gunning, *The Techniques of Clear Writing,* rev. ed. (New York: McGraw-Hill Book Company, 1968), p. 38. The Gunning Fog Index (SM) is the property of Gunning-Mueller Clear Writing Institute, and is used with permission.

Once your material has been rewritten (without regard to the formula), *then* apply the formula again. If the material now appears to be appropriate, fine. If not, rewrite again and apply the formula again.

If this business of checking readability, rewriting, checking again, then rewriting again, seems time-consuming or difficult—it is, at first. After some experience, however, you usually get a feel for the appropriate level for a given body of readers, and the process gets much faster and easier. Readers are likely to be turned off by writing that seems unnecessarily difficult. Your extra time will not only save *time* for them, perhaps even thousands of hours; it will also encourage them to read more of what you have written. And that is what readable writing is all about.[4]

Because the passage is short, base the readability calculation on all of it. Counting and calculating yield these data:

Number of words	= 206	Number of hard words	= 35
Number of sentences	= 13	Percent of hard words	= 17
Average sentence length	= 16	Gunning Fog Index	= 13

Thus, the Gunning Fog Index suggests that the material is appropriate for 13th-grade (college-level) readers.

Gunning places a "danger line" for reading difficulty between the 12th and 13th grades. He labels the 10th grade and lower as the "easy-reading range." Thus, he leaves the 11th and 12th grades in a range of moderate difficulty.[5]

To analyze the difficulty of reading material from another viewpoint, consider Lipman and Joyner's summary of approximate proportions of adults who can read at the various grade levels[6]:

School Grade Level	Approximate Percent of Adults Who Can Read at this Level
5th	93%
6th	90%
7th	88%
8–9th	76%
9th	52%
College	24%
College Graduates	6%

As a warning about application of the summary, Lipman and Joyner write: "Like all charts, this is an approximation. It is intended as a guide to readability rather than . . . [estimates] yielding scientific accuracy."[7]

To reinforce the requirement for cautious interpretation of readability concepts, return for a moment to the *content* of the excerpt from Klare's *A Manual for Readable Writing*. The point made there is to take a realistic view of the application of readabil-

---

[4]George R. Klare, *A Manual for Readable Writing* (Glen Burnie, Md.: REM Company, 1975), p. 48.

[5]Gunning, *The Techniques of Clear Writing*, p. 40.

[6]Michel Lipman and Russell Joyner, *How to Write Clearly* (San Francisco: International Society for General Semantics, 1979), p. 8.

[7]Ibid.

ity formulas. They are mechanical means for *estimating* readability levels—not a final, scientific authority on what is readable and what is not.

Occasionally check the readability level of your writing. If it falls much above the ninth or tenth grade, you may want to examine your style.

TRANSMITTING

Once you have selected, drafted, and revised a message, you are ready to transmit it. For written messages the transmission stage includes putting the revised draft into final form, making necessary copies, and delivering them to the receivers.

Review some of the transceiving equipment, services, and systems now in use.

Dictation Equipment

Dictation equipment allows you to dictate messages into a recorder for conversion into printed form. Desk-top and portable dictation machines use microphones attached to the recorders. Centralized systems use standard telephones connected to a central recorder.

The two basic centralized systems use private wire systems and private branch exchange (PBX). The private systems do not connect with telephone-company equipment. The PBX systems do.

Standard and Electric Typewriters

Certainly the typewriter contributes significantly to the encoding and transmitting process. Modern typewriters allow the typist to type faster than ever before. Additional features include rapid correction of errors and the quick change of styles of type.

Automatic Typewriters

By attaching a recorder to the Selectric typewriter, IBM introduced the era of the automatic typewriter. The attachment makes possible the storage, correction, revision, recall, and reproduction of information at rapid rates. Now various makes and models allow operators to insert selected cards containing prerecorded information to produce custom-ordered, errorless messages at rapid speeds.

Duplicating Equipment

Several kinds of machines for producing copies of messages (reprography) contribute substantially to the work of the communicator.

Photocopying equipment is a particular boon to the communication process. For one copy or hundreds, copiers can do the work formerly left to carbon paper, spirit duplicators, mimeograph machines, offset press, and printers. Some copiers make copies at the rate of about eighty a minute. Xerox, A. B. Dick, IBM, Royal, Savin, Remington, and Pitney Bowes are among those that make plain paper copiers.

The offset press and printers still serve important duplicating functions. Modern phototypesetting processes have reduced considerably the time necessary to produce good copy.

Printing is particularly good for mass messages and for some medio messages, because it reduces the demand for space by about 40 percent. The savings in paper and distribution costs can be significant.

Mail and Messenger Services

The United States Postal Service is the largest mail service in the country. Details of some of its services appear in Chapter 8. Private concerns also provide personal message-delivery service. The United Parcel Service (UPS) specializes in delivering packages. Courier services such as Purolator and Federal Express make one-day deliveries between cities served by major airports.

Electronic Mail Service

Through the use of private lines, telephone lines, Western Union (TWX, Telex, and Mailgrams), laser beams, facsimile equipment, computer-to-computer hookups, and typewriter-to-typewriter hookups, communicators now transmit messages electronically. The encoder inserts a message at one end of the connection, and it appears in readable form at the other.

Electronic mail service requires special equipment. However, because of the speed of transmission, more and more businesses take advantage of it.

Word Processing

Word processing is a relatively new integrated approach to the transmitting act. McCabe and Popham suggest:

> Broadly defined, word processing is the automatic production of typed documents or the automation of secretarial work.[8] The systems approach deals with office procedures, personnel, and equipment as an organized whole, rather than with each part separately.[9]

Word processing promises to do for words what electronic data processing does for numbers. Someone still has to create (encode) the unit messages. However, once internal to the word-processing equipment, they may be retrieved and even combined to produce individually typewritten messages at a rapid rate of speed.

The key components of a word processing system are the dictation and transcription equipment and the automatic typewriters.

For a single letter, the dictator usually outlines the letter and dictates it in final form into the recorder—a much more rapid process than handwriting. The word processor uses the appropriate transcribing equipment to listen to the recording and type the final copy.

---

[8]*Dartnell's Glossary of Word Processing Terms* (Chicago: The Dartnell Corporation, 1975), p. 47.

[9]Helen M. McCabe and Estelle L. Popham, *Word Processing: A Systems Approach to the Office* (New York: Harcourt Brace Jovanovich, Inc., 1977), pp. 1–2.

The transcription process usually involves a rough draft on the automatic typewriter, which stores the draft message even as the processor types it. The processor then proofreads the draft and corrects errors on the stored draft. Then he or she sets the equipment to type the corrected message automatically.

The potential contribution of the word-processing concept is staggering. McCabe and Popham write:

> Most experts agree that automated office systems are not far off and that word processing is the most likely means for bringing them about. Case studies indicate that a start is already being made to combine word processing and data processing. These efforts—together with new advances in telecommunications and records management—may produce the long-awaited total management information system . . . .[10]

SUMMARY

The written channels of communication belong to the medio and mass levels of communication. Written communication makes possible the *permanency, accuracy,* and *storage capacity* necessary for many kinds of information—particularly the complex and technical information of many business interactions.

The guidelines for writing are:

1. Define purposes, participants, and environment.
2. Select writing channel.
3. Control interference.
4. Write and transmit messages in light of purposes, participants, environment, channel, and interference.
5. Use feedback.
6. Evaluate.

The encoding and transmitting steps include (1) *selecting,* (2) *drafting,* (3) *revising,* and (4) *transmitting.*

In the selection process, begin selecting messages to form the final message. Sometimes you must collect additional information.

At the drafting stage, use the order of *organizing and then writing,* or use *writing and then organizing,* or use the best features of both processes. The *just-write process* has you spill ideas on paper.

To organize, first choose a *developmental pattern* and develop an outline. Then organize the body, the opening, and the ending, in that order, by selecting *topic sentences* and structuring paragraphs.

Some of the developmental patterns are the *inductive, deductive, chronological, spatial, analytical, comparative,* and *ranked.*

During the revising phase, check and correct for content, mechanics, word choice, tone, and integrity.

Introduce *completeness, accuracy,* and *definitions* of terms into the content. Establish *good mechanics* by polishing grammar, punctuation, spelling, word usage, sentence structure, format, and other mechanics.

---

[10]Ibid, p. 9.

Assure good word choice through *clearness, appropriateness, concreteness, colorfulness,* and *freshness.* To introduce colorfulness, select vibrant verbs and avoid "it" and "there" as *expletives.*

Courtesy, a *positive style,* the *"you"* attitude, the *active voice,* and *nondiscriminatory symbols* create a good *tone.* The *buffer opening, positive sandwich,* and *inductive developmental pattern* aid in establishing a positive style.

To revise for *integrity,* seek *unity* and *coherence, pace, consistency, conciseness,* and *readability.* For unity and coherence, provide *transitions* and remove awkwardness. For good pace, establish proper *emphasis, subordination,* and *variety.* Accomplish *variety* by using mixtures of standard sentences, parallel sentences, and periodic sentences.

The concept of readability concerns the measurement of message density. The *Gunning Fog Index* is one well-known readability formula. Its application results in indexes expressed in school-grade levels of reading difficulty. Most writing should fall no higher than the 9th- or 10th-grade level.

The transmission of messages may involve dictating equipment, typewriters, duplicating equipment, postal and messenger services, and electronic mailing services. It also may involve word processing—an integrated approach to transmission.

Practice

1. You are the personnel manager for a corporation based in Kansas City. Your new hiring procedures have been approved by all of the appropriate people. You must now commit the procedures to paper and distribute them to all of the people involved in the hiring process. Answer these questions:
   a. What are your purposes for printing and distributing the procedures? What are the readers' purposes for reading? Who are you in this situation? Who are the readers? What is the environment?
   b. What writing channel is appropriate for these procedures?
   c. What are the types of potential and actual interference involved in this communication situation? How will you control the interference?
   d. How will you print and distribute the procedures in light of the purposes, the participants, the environment, the channel, and the interference?
   e. How will you use feedback from and to the readers of your procedures?
   f. How will you evaluate at each stage of the communication process?
   You need not write the actual procedures.
2. Meet with your group. Determine and discuss the special problems associated with written messages. What can you as good communicators do to overcome some of the problems? Have a member of your group read your group's conclusions and suggestions to the rest of the class.
3. [*Your professor will time this exercise.*] You are the Director of Employee Communications at an automobile assembly plant. You are asked to write a memorandum that will be distributed to 300 of your employees. In the memorandum you must let the employees know that:
   a. They will be laid off for six weeks.
   b. They are free to look for other jobs.
   c. The automobile industry is currently depressed, hence the decision to lay off employees.

d. These particular employees are being laid off because they are the most recently hired.

e. All questions and comments concerning the layoff should be directed to the employee communications office; no other department will accept questions or comments.

f. The employees' last paychecks will be mailed to them; they are not to come to the plant to get them.

Write the memorandum. Remember to try to soften the impact of the bad news. You may wish to discuss the difficulty of this task with your group after you have completed the memorandum. One question you might discuss: Would another channel have been more appropriate in this communication situation? Why?

4. Visit the showroom of an office-machines dealer who specializes in word-processing equipment. Learn the characteristics and capacities of four or five different types of equipment. Write a one- or two-page summary of your findings.

5. Write a one- or two-paragraph body of a letter or memorandum for each of these situations.

a. Jessie Jones is six weeks late on his house payment. He has never been late before. Your company owns the house.

b. Your company is forced to charge more than was originally agreed upon for the office furniture it is building for Wiggins, Higgins, and Smart, a law firm.

c. The daughter of one of your company's welders has just received a scholarship to study at the Harvard Business School. You know that the welder, Sara Smith, is quite proud of her daughter. Write one paragraph for a letter to Sara Smith and a different paragraph for her daughter, Elizabeth Smith.

d. You are ordering six boxes of parchment bond (item 606) and two book cabinets (item 409B) from the Fairlington Office Supply Co. You want the paper in white and the cabinets in oak. You want the paper to be sent within two weeks or not at all. You are in no hurry for the book cabinets.

e. You wish to set up an interview with Robert James, the accounting manager at the firm for which you would like to work. You earned a B.B.A. in accounting, were an honor graduate, plan to take your C.P.A. examinations next month, and worked as an accounting intern for two summers. You would be willing to relocate if necessary.

f. You are interested in purchasing the services of the Oklahoma Consulting Group (OCG). You want the OCG to do a communication audit at your firm. You want to know if OCG has experience in communication auditing, how much an audit will cost, and when the audit could be conducted.

g. You ordered a copy of *Even Timid People Can Manage a Big Business* from the R. I. Poff Publishing Co. You placed your order six months ago and the check you sent with the order was cashed five months ago. You want your book as soon as possible. If you cannot have the book, you want your money back.

6. You have noticed that your employees' written messages are difficult to read and often do not contain the appropriate information. Several of your employees stated that they are aware of the problem, but really do not know how to approach their writing projects. You assured them that you would give them some assistance in the form of a paper that describes the four steps of writing (selecting, drafting, revising, and transmitting). You promised that your paper would contain practical advice on accomplishing each of the steps. Write the three- or four-page paper.

7. Write one or two paragraphs that illustrate each of the seven developmental plans: (1) inductive, (2) deductive, (3) chronological, (4) spatial, (5) analytical, (6) comparative, and (7) ranked.

8. You must write James Sea a letter denying his request for an interview with your company's Transportation Department. Sea wants to work in the department, but no openings exist. He has indicated that he is also interested in a position in the Office Services Department, where you do have an opening. Although he is overqualified for that, you do want to let him know about it. Develop a topic outline for the letter to James Sea.

9. Develop a sentence outline from the topic outline you prepared in Question 8.
10. Using the sentence outline you developed for Question 9, write the letter to James Sea.
11. You have just been asked to write a memorandum that deals with the relative merits of brainstorming. You know that one of the best ways to begin the writing process is to immediately write down every remotely relevant thought that you have on the subject about which you must write. Now take a piece of paper and write down everything that comes into your mind about the subject of brainstorming. You need not put the material into memorandum form.
12. Write end-of-message time-and-place paragraphs for these situations:
    a. You want a job applicant to send you his résumé by September 6. You need the résumé by then because your boss will leave for a two-month vacation on September 7, and she makes all the hiring decisions.
    b. You want an overdue payment to be sent to you by December 1. The overdue amount is $39.43.
    c. You need to know by October 1 whether the receiver will be able to speak at the October 15 conference in Muncie, Indiana.
    d. You want the receiver to meet you at the Carel, Montana, office on either March 6 or March 13. You need to know by March 1 which date is acceptable.
    e. You want 40 reams of 20-pound bond to be sent to you by January 30. If the paper will not reach you by then, you do not want it at all.
13. Find a two- or three-page piece of your own writing, perhaps the paper you wrote for Question 6. Use the Gunning Formula to determine the readability index for your work.
14. Use your dictionary and thesaurus to create meanings for these words. Use the words when you think, write, and speak so that you feel comfortable using them.

a. Albeit	f. Integrity
b. Chronological	g. Mediate
c. Diligent	h. Realistic
d. Discourse	i. Systematic
e. Hierarchal, hierarchic, hierarchical	j. Tendency

15. Take and score Self-Test 18 over the excerpt about writing the draft.

Self-Test 18
Excerpt about Writing the Draft

A. Recall (33 points each). For each multiple-choice question, select the most accurate answer.

1. Unless the message is relatively short, which part should you write first?
   a. Opening
   b. Body
   c. Ending
   d. Address
   e. Summary

2. What is the practical upper limit for the number of sentences in a paragraph?
   a. Fifteen
   b. Ten
   c. Five
   d. No limit exists
   e. Six or seven

B. Inference (34 points). Indicate whether this statement is true or false.

   Once you have written the body of a message, the opening and ending are easier to write.

Solution to Self-Test 18
Excerpt about Writing the Draft

A. Recall (33 points each)   **B.** Inference (34 points)
    1. b   **2.** b   True

16. Take and score Self-Test 19 over Chapter 7.

Self-Test 19
Chapter 7

A. Recall (25 points each). For each multiple-choice question, select the most accurate answer.
    1. Analytical development is most clearly found in:
        a. A message that unfolds through space rather than time
        b. Comparative messages
        c. Sequential patterns in a message
        d. Chronological ordering of a message
        e. Messages that first describe the wholes and then the parts that make up the wholes
    2. An important purpose of the opening of a message is to:
        a. Gain the receiver's attention
        b. Present the major argument
        c. Summarize the message
        d. Establish who the writer is
        e. Describe the main points of the message
    3. Which set of words does not represent the correct parallel structure?
        a. Plan, organize, direct, and control
        b. Collecting, analyzing, and interpretation
        c. Explaining, describing, and understanding
        d. Who, what, when, and where
        e. Select, organize, draft, revise, and transmit

B. Inference (25 points). Indicate whether this statement is true or false.

The concept of readability is not pertinent to oral messages.

Solution to Self-Test 19
Chapter 7

A. Recall (25 points each)   **B.** Inference (25 points)
    1. e   **3.** b   False
    2. a

8

Writing Letters

Letters apply general principles of writing to a specific process. This chapter covers the guidelines for writing letters, with particular emphasis upon formats.

GUIDELINES FOR WRITING LETTERS

Adjust the guidelines for writing to become the guidelines for writing letters:

1. Define your purposes for writing the letter, the reader's purposes for reading the letter, yourself, the reader, and the environment.
2. Identify the letter channel.
3. Control the interference internal and external to you and the reader.
4. Write and transmit the letter in light of the purposes, the participants, the environment, the channel, and the interference.
5. Use feedback from and to the reader of the letter.
6. Evaluate at each stage.

Define Purposes, Participants, and Environment

When writing a letter, define the purposes, participants, and environment carefully.

Your purposes

To establish your purposes, first decide exactly what you want the receiver to do as a result of your letter. Do you want her or him to pay a bill? order some merchandise? send some merchandise? establish a credit account? settle a claim? send more information? think your company is a good one?

Review the possible purposes listed in the preceding paragraph. Observe that most of them need to be tied to a time line. Letter-writing purposes often relate to short-, intermediate-, or long-term goals, or some combination of them. Therefore, clarify the timing you envision in association with the purposes you establish.

A single letter may have more than one purpose—whether in one time frame or in multiple time frames. For example, the objective to have a reader "think your company is a good one" could be coupled with any other purpose. Similarly, "order some merchandise" often appears in conjunction with others such as "establish a credit account." Therefore, try to include all possibilities as you clarify the purpose(s) for a letter.

Think about evaluation as you identify purposes. A purpose such as having a customer pay a bill by a given date proves to be simple to evaluate. The person either does or does not respond by the stated date. However, without careful planning during the initial stages of sending a message, evaluation of less concrete goals can be difficult.

When you set as objectives such intangibles as creating goodwill, try to combine them with other objectives that call for tangible responses.

Suppose one purpose of a letter is to transmit a refund check for faulty merchandise and another is to keep the customer's goodwill. You could combine them with still a third purpose—a reorder objective—by including a sales brochure and an order blank. If the customer reorders, goodwill probably still exists.

Even tangible/intangible pairings cannot always make a desired response measurable. However, even nonresponse *can* be a satisfying response—the old no-news-is-good-news approach to setting goals.

The reader

Learning about the purposes, characteristics, and setting of even one intended receiver of a letter can be a difficult task. When several people form the target, the assignment may appear impossible. Yet, with care and practice, the task can be reasonably well contained.

For an identified person, the firm usually has some defining data on file. Messages from that person provide additional information. Well-founded and tested generalizations about "classes" of people also contribute to the assessment. The nature of the problem and purpose provides clues as well.

The overriding determinant of success in perceiving the intended receiver, however, lies in human sensitivity. Your ability to create empathy for the other person can add a dimension to an assessment never provided by mechanical or scientific activities alone.

To repeat, when masses of people are the intended receivers, their description becomes quite complex. One traditional rule suggests identifying the lowest level—the lowest educational, reading, or decoding-ability level, in particular. However, avoid sending a common message to a group that is too heterogeneous in nature. The danger is that you might be reaching the base group, but "talking down" to the more capable people—and alienating them in the process. Try dividing a heterogeneous group into several smaller, homogeneous groups and encoding a different message for each smaller group.

Identify Letter Channel

The letter is an important tool of business. For example, research conducted by Mintzberg shows that managers use, in order of time devoted to each, the telephone, meetings, tours, and the mail.[1]

As a written medio-level channel, the letter has the advantages of allowing you to: (1) keep a permanent record of your messages, (2) edit and perfect troublesome messages, (3) handle detail, (4) deal with complex information, and (5) disseminate mass messages at relatively low cost.

The letter has the disadvantages of limiting or preventing (1) rapid feedback, (2) nonverbal exchanges, and (3) the warmth of oral transactions.

Certain characteristics set the business letter apart from other communication channels. Some characteristics relate to writing in general and some to writing letters in particular. Such characteristics receive treatment in subsequent chapters.

You will review the routine features and formats of letters and envelopes in this chapter. However, because the coverage constitutes such a large portion of the chapter, it is delayed until completion of the guidelines.

Control Interference

Do your best to anticipate and overcome any interference that may arise from the purposes, the environment, and the channel. However, the success of transactions depends primarily upon overcoming interference within you and the readers. It depends upon your ability to understand receivers well enough to develop messages to meet their needs and abilities.

The external interference sources most likely to affect the enchanneled letter involve time and space. For example, if a letter transmitting a refund check is delayed in delivery, goodwill may be lost.

Although electronic transmission of a letter can occur in a few seconds, it requires special equipment for sending and receiving. Therefore, its use cannot overcome the time problems for ordinary transmission of letters. In addition, even electronic equipment can function improperly and introduce interference.

If a letter contains errors, smudges, faint print, or improper format, negative impressions often arise. Such impressions can interfere significantly with the transaction.

Write and Transmit

If you complete preparatory activities well, the task of writing the letter is already well on its way to accomplishment. As discussed in Chapter 7, you picture the receiver and begin your task, eventually carrying through all these stages:

1. Select the messages, collecting additional information if necessary.

---

[1]Henry Mintzberg, *The Nature of Managerial Work* (New York: Harper & Row, Publishers, Inc., 1973), pp. 190–191.

2. Draft the letter.
   a. Just write.
   b. Organize.
      (1) Choose developmental pattern.
      (2) Outline.
      (3) Structure sentences and paragraphs.
3. Revise to meet all characteristics of good letters.
4. Transmit.
   a. Type in good form.
   b. Mail or transmit electronically.

Transmit a letter in such a fashion that it will be least vulnerable to attack from the external interference identified at the planning stages. Consider timing, distance, security, cost, and the legal aspects of the situation. On the basis of your analysis, choose a messenger service, a mail service, or an electronic mail service.

If you choose the conventional mail, be aware of the range of choices available to you. The United States Postal Service offers many different services. A summary of them appears as Figure 8–1.

---

1. **Express Mail.** Articles received by 5:00 P.M. delivered by 3:00 P.M. the next day. For any mailable article up to 70 lbs. High rates.
2. **First Class.** Letters, post cards, presort rates, business reply mail. Two- to three-day service for higher rates.
3. **Second Class.** Newspapers and periodicals with second-class mail privileges.
4. **Third Class.** Circulars, books, catalogs, and other printed matter; merchandise, etc. weighing less than 16 ounces. Low rates. Bulk rate available.
5. **Priority Mail** (heavy pieces). Equivalent of first class service for pieces weighing over 12 ounces up to 70 lbs.
6. **Fourth Class** (Parcel Post). Parcels weighing up to 70 lbs. Slower service and lower rates than priority mail and express mail.
7. **Special Handling.** Careful handling. For third and fourth class only. Additional fee.
8. **Special Delivery.** Personal delivery by letter carrier. Cannot be left in mail box. For all classes. Additional fee.
9. **COD** (Cash on Delivery). Receiver pays for goods and COD fee upon receipt.
10. **Certified Mail.** Provides proof of mailing and delivery. For first class only. Additional fee.
11. **Return Receipt.** Shows to whom and when delivered. For insured certified and registered mail. Additional fee.
12. **Insurance.** For coverage against loss or damage. Additional fee according to liability up to $400.
13. **Registry.** For maximum protection and security. For first class only. Additional fee according to value.

Figure 8–1   Selected services of the United States Postal Service.

Source: U.S. Postal Service, *Domestic Postage Rates, Fees, and Information,* Notice 59 (June 1979).

Use Feedback

Feedback as the result of a letter can use any channel. However, it usually takes the form of another letter—or, occasionally, a telephone call. The destination/source encodes a message that perhaps fulfills the desired action, or exhibits misunderstanding, or asks for clarification or for more data.

Whatever form the feedback takes, and whatever precipitated it, use it efficiently as the basis for evaluating and correcting the original message. Feedback is a vital tool for removing the clouds of interference, for consummating purposes, and for solving the basic problem or need.

When the original letter provides an action-response avenue, the receiver does not always respond within the time allotted. You may then want to initiate another message (perhaps a telephone call) that attempts to stimulate feedback. If, after an appropriate number of attempts, no feedback results, then you must move on to the final evaluation stage.

Evaluate

If you plan and complete a letter transaction well, you already have built-in evaluative criteria. You need only apply them.

For example, if your immediate objective is for a customer to place an order by the 15th, your evaluation is simple. However, as previously suggested, not all evaluation is that simple. Therefore, develop action criteria for as many of your objectives as you can.

LETTER CHANNEL

Return now to the formats and parts of letters and envelopes. Many elements of the discussion actually represent nonverbal sending (Chapter 16). However, they relate so closely to the verbal elements of letters that they fit here just as well. Consider letter formats, letter components, and envelopes.

Letter Formats

The company for which you work almost always specifies the format for letters. However, review four of the major styles and the parts composing them.

The basic formats are the block, modified block with blocked paragraphs, modified block with indented paragraphs, and simplified. In addition, the format of the continuation page has special characteristics.

Block

In the block style, every part of the letter begins at the left margin. Figure 8–2 shows that format—as well as displaying many of the traditional letter components. The individual components themselves receive treatment in a subsequent section.

EEE
VANS
LECTRIC
QUIPMENT

February 20, 198X

CONFIDENTIAL

Ms. Sara Bray, Director of
   Customer Relations
AC Electric
21 B Road S.W.
Red Oak, Iowa 51566

Dear Ms. Bray:

_____
_____
_____

_____
_____
_____

_____
_____
_____

Cordially yours,

J. C. Evans

President

JCEvans:rs

cc: V. G. Allen

92 X Street
Penn, PA 15675
Call *Toll Free:* 800-444-4444

Figure 8–2   Block; closed punctuation; classification notation; copy notation

Modified block with blocked paragraphs

Figure 8–3 illustrates that with the exception of the date line and signature block, every line of the modified-block, blocked-paragraph letter begins at the left margin. The components for the modified-block form remain the same as for the traditional block format.

Modified block with indented paragraphs

The modified-block, indented-paragraph format simply indents the paragraphs of the basic modified-block plan. Figure 8–4 shows the style.

SEEKERS, INC.

7834 Firefighter's Lane/Shiloh, Virginia 22549
(666) 666-6666

Board of Directors   19 April 198X

A. A. Ashe
President
Ashe Corp.

                    Onlycoping, Inc.
                    One 58 Street
B. B. Barnes   Niantic, IL 62551
President
Barnes Company   Attention: Claims Agent

                    Ladies and Gentlemen

C. C. Carney   CLAIM—INVOICE NO. 79243
Vice President
Oak Tree, Inc.   _____
                    _____
                    _____
                    _____

D. D. Dalley   _____
Director   _____
Public Relations   _____
Freebie Co.   _____

                    _____
E. E. Ellis   _____
General Manager   _____
Cellar Corp.
                                        Sincerely yours

                                        SEEKERS, INC.

F. F. Frates   *J. J. Jeffers*
President
Future Shock   Ms. J. J. Jeffers
                                        Assistant to the President

                    rp

                    bc: A. A. Alton

                    _____
                    _____

We search the globe for rare and exotic gifts

Figure 8–3   Modified block with blocked paragraphs; open punctuation; attention line; subject line; typewritten company name; blind copy notation (appears only on copy); postscript

Simplified

The simplified format follows the block setup for the letter. In addition, it eliminates the salutation and the complimentary close, while including a subject line as a

HAPPEE CORPORATION

222 High Street
Guthrie, Oklahoma 73044
(405) 111-1111

Office of the Manager   20 January 198X

Sales Manager
Cane, Inc.
Hilo, HI 96720

Dear Sales Manager:

_____

_____
_____

_____
_____
_____

_____
_____
_____
_____

                              Sincerely,

                              Alice Jenkins
                                      dlp

                              Alice Jenkins, Manager
                              Production and Distribution

AJ/dlp

Enclosures: Sales brochure
            Order form

copies: Sharon Carr
        David Furr
        Carl Hull

Figure 8–4   Modified block with indented paragraphs; closed punctuation; enclosure
notation; copy notation

standard part. Thus, the simplified form discards some of the older letter components, and becomes the most nontraditional of the formats considered. Figure 8–5
illustrates the simplified form.

Continuation

When a letter is too long to be contained on one page, a continuation page is
necessary. Do not use letterhead stationery for that page. Instead, use plain paper of

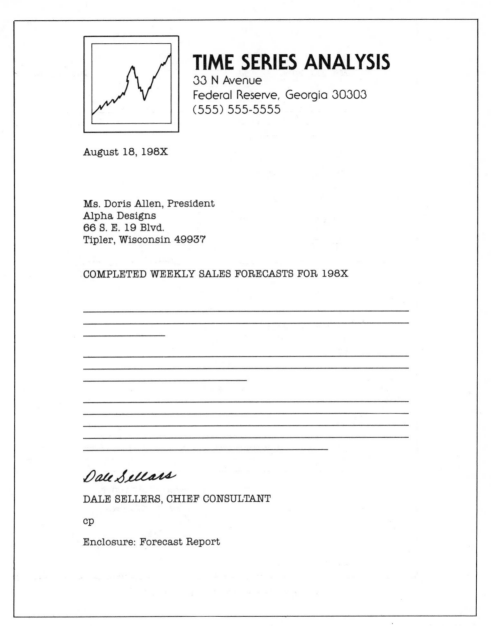

Figure 8–5   Simplified; enclosure notation

the same quality as the letterhead, and typewrite the heading. Use the same margin settings as those for the first page. Place the first line of the heading about one inch from the top of the page. Leave two blank lines after the heading.

The heading includes the name of the receiver, the date, and the page number. A continuation page should contain at least one paragraph of the body of the letter— followed by the closing parts. Figure 8–6 illustrates two acceptable continuation-page formats.

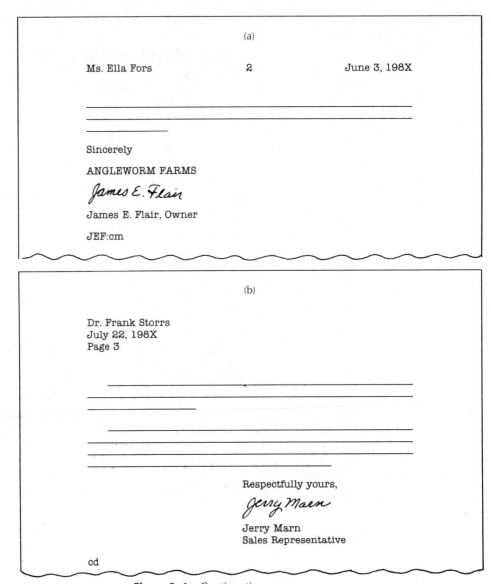

Figure 8–6 Continuation pages

Letter Components

A letter can include as many as 15 components: (1) stationery and letterhead/return address, (2) date line, (3) special designations, (4) inside address, (5) attention line, (6) salutation, (7) subject line, (8) body, (9) complimentary close, (10) company name, (11) signature block, (12) reference initials, (13) enclosure notation, (14) copy notation, and (15) postscript.

The standard parts of the business letter are the stationery and letterhead, date line, inside address, salutation, body, complimentary close, signature block, and reference initials. The remaining seven parts can be used as needed or desired. Of course, the simplified format omits the salutation and complimentary close and adds the subject line as a fixed part.

Stationery and letterhead/return address

Stationery and the letterhead/return address contribute significantly to a message. The wording and design of the letterhead/return address contribute both verbally and nonverbally. The stationery contributes nonverbally.

Design   Companies usually engage specialists to design letterheads and envelopes.

The good letterhead should include at least the firm name, telephone number, and address. It may include a few-word explanation of what the firm does if the design is a simple, straightforward one. Figures 8–2, 8–4, and 8–5 illustrate.

Additional information often creates a jumbled, distracting appearance that defeats the letterhead's communicative purpose—that of pleasant identification. For example, Figure 8–3 shows printed stationery that may contain too much information.

Letterhead designers use color, embossing, standard or unusual styles of type, and a variety of sizes and arrangements of type. Through them, they try to make the letterhead communicate the desired image.

When you use paper without a printed letterhead, include a return address. Place it at the top in a position that fits the format chosen. Include only the mailing address, not your name.

In the block and simplified formats, the return address begins at the left margin. In the modified-block formats, the return address either begins at horizontal center or ends at the right margin. For all formats, the return address starts about one and three-fourths inches from the top of the page. Figure 8–7 illustrates the proper placement of return addresses for plain paper.

Stationery   The quality, weight, texture, fabric content, size, and color of paper also have an important impact on the communication.

For letterheads, envelopes, and plain sheets, use a quality bond. Most offices use a 20-pound watermarked paper with some fabric content. Some use 16-pound paper without the watermark or fabric content.

Always insert the paper so that the typewriting appears on the felt side of it. For watermarked paper, the felt side is the side that allows the watermark to appear in the correct reading position. For paper without a watermark, the wrapper usually includes a notation showing which is the felt side. However, you can always identify the felt side by using a magnifying glass to select the side with the smooth, felt-like appearance. (The other side—the screen or wire side—has a rough, granular appearance.)

The most common size for letterhead stationery is 8½ inches wide by 11 inches long, with the letterhead placed across the top of the width of the page. However, sometimes the page is treated as 11 inches wide by 8½ inches long, with the letterhead at the top of the width (Figure 8–8). Occasionally, the letterhead appears at the bottom of the sheet, whichever dimension is considered the width.

The other sizes for stationery include the 7½- by 10½-inch, 7½- by 11-inch, and 5½- by 8½-inch sheets. Information usually appears at the top, but may appear at the bottom of such sheets.

```
                                    (a)
                            Block and Simplified


            1111 18th Street
            Souder, MO 65751
            March 15, 198X



            Dr. Jan Cory
            14 Dover Street, N.W.
            Woodstock, VA 22664
```

```
                                    (b)
                            Modified Block


                               1111 18th Street
                               Souder, MO 65751
                               March 15, 198X


            Dear Jan,
```

Figure 8–7   Typewritten return address for (a) block and simplified formats in a formal
letter and (b) modified-block formats in a personal letter

The most common color for stationery is white. However, some designers use color, particularly if the products or services of the firm warrant the added nonverbal flair.

Avoid the erasable papers. Generally, they smudge and smear easily and have a slick finish that makes marking upon them difficult.

Always use the same quality and weight of paper for second and successive pages of a letter that you use for the first page. Never use a letterhead as a second sheet.

You may use lightweight paper for carbon copies. You may even use onionskin for file copies.

If you distribute carbon copies to receivers, be sure that the print is sharp and dark. Make corrections on the carbon copies as well as on the original copies.

Be sure that ribbons, inks, type bars, and other such materials and equipment make clean, sharp impressions. Carbon ribbons generally do a better job than reusable ribbons. Unless cleaned regularly, the type bars will imprint filled-in letters and numbers—particularly o's, e's, p's, q's, b's, 4's, 6's, 8's, and 9's.

Date line

All four basic designs include the date line as part of the format. Place it at least two lines below the letterhead. Start it at the left margin in the block and simplified styles

(Figures 8–2 and 8–5). For the modified-block styles, start the date line at horizontal center, or end it at the right margin (Figures 8–3 and 8–4).

Firms often adjust or revise these customary placements to enhance visual appearance. For example, notice how the date line complements "Office of the Manager" in Figure 8–4. Observe in Figure 8–3 how moving both the date line and the signature block to end with the right margin would improve artistic perspective.

Place the date line for a plain-paper return address one line below the city and state. Examples in Figure 8–7 show the arrangement.

Business organizations still seem to prefer the "May 14, 198X" style for dates. However, the military "14 May 198X" format is gaining acceptance (Figure 8–3). The "5/14/8X" style is unacceptable. Spell out the month, omit such endings as "-nd" for the day, and include all digits in the year designation.

Special designations

You occasionally may address letters that will be sent by something other than first-class mail. You may also want to identify a letter as personal, confidential, or to be held for arrival. In such cases, the special designation should be placed two or three lines above the first line of the inside address. Capitalize and/or underline the letters to set the designation apart from the address itself: Priority Mail, AIR MAIL, SPECIAL DELIVERY, Confidential, PERSONAL, Hold for Arrival. Figure 8–2 illustrates the placement.

Inside address

The inside address includes the name and address of the person and/or organization to which the letter is directed.

Standard formats   For the standard formats, the inside address appears at the left margin several lines below the date line or two or three lines below a special designation when the letter includes one. Figures 8–2, 8–3, 8–4, 8–5, and 8–7a include examples.

Nonstandard formats   For two nonstandard forms—the official letter style and the personal business letter—the inside address is placed at the left margin two or three lines *below* the last line of the signature block.

Figure 8–8 illustrates the setup for the official letter, and Figure 8–9 illustrates it for the personal business letter.

Both official and personal business-letter formats usually take the modified-block format with indented paragraphs. The official style is formal, and the personal business style is relatively informal.

You may omit the inside address in a personal letter on plain paper. Figure 8–7a includes the inside address; Figure 8–7b does not.

Order of elements   A general rule for the order of the elements of an address is to put them in order logically from the last destination on the top line through the first destination on the bottom line. An easy way to remember the order is to picture postal workers following steps from the bottom line up to the top line. Some variations of this rule are beginning to appear.

THE SERIOUS CORPORATION

Management
Consulting

785 Nirvana Drive / Panacea, Florida 32346

(333) 333-3333

June 3, 198X

My dear Mr. Collins:

Yours very respectfully,

Sharon Phelps

Sharon Phelps
Consultant

Mr. Ernest Collins
Executive Secretary
Evermore, Inc.
88 Frontier Place
Oxford, Indiana 47971

sp:cm

Figure 8–8   Official letter format; closed punctuation; letterhead placed on 11-inch width of paper

STRUGGLING GROCERY WHOLESALERS

740 Freedom Boulevard   Woodville, Alabama 35776

July 22, 198X

Dear Terry,

_____
_____
_____

_____
_____
_____
_____

_____
_____
_____

_____

                              Cordially,

                              Jim

                              James L. Friar

Ms. Terry McLendon
14 Oak Circle, Apt. 132
Pine Bluffs, WY 82082

Figure 8–9   Personal business letter; closed punctuation

Courtesy titles   When the last destination (the first line of the address) is a person, try to begin that line with an appropriate title. Here are some of the most common ones:

Mr.	Sergeant
Ms.	President
Miss	Professor
Mrs.	Senator
Dr.	Representative
Dean	The Reverend
Commander	The Honorable

Notice both the abbreviated and the spelled-out titles. They show conventional usage.

The traditional courtesy titles for women, "Mrs." and "Miss," introduce discriminatory language into the inside address. When "Ms." is accepted universally to replace both "Mrs." and "Miss," the problem will be solved. In the meantime, though, a good way to deal with the problem is to use "Miss" and "Mrs." only for women who indicate a preference for them. For all other women, use "Ms."

Position title   A position title often follows the name of a person being addressed. Depending upon its length, it may be placed on the line with the person's name, placed on a separate line, or divided between two lines. Figures 8–2, 8–5, and 8–8 illustrate the technique.

If you do not know the name of the person occupying a certain position in another company, you may address the letter to the appropriate title. Figure 8–4 shows this approach.

Organization name   An organization name usually follows the name of the person or a position title—or can stand alone as the first line of the address. Write the name of the organization exactly as firm representatives write it. If the company name includes such abbreviations and symbols as &, Inc., Co., and Corp., copy them exactly. Likewise, if Company is spelled in full, do not abbreviate it.

Street address   A street address normally comes after the name of the person or organization. Present such addresses concisely.

For a street number, you may omit the number endings such as "-st." You may, however, spell out a one-word number for clarity—especially "one" (Figure 8–3). If a designation such as N.W. belongs after a street number, you may or may not separate it from the street number or name by a comma (Figures 8–2 and 8–7). If a street address represents an apartment house, include the apartment number: 875 Linus Avenue, Apt. 403 (Figure 8–9).

Abbreviations such as Apt. for Apartment, Blvd. for Boulevard, S.W. for Southwest, and state abbreviations such as TX for Texas and IL for Illinois are acceptable. Some people are offended by the cluttered look created by the excessive use of abbreviations. Thus, a middle-ground view might be to use state abbreviations and abbreviations for nontitle words of two or more syllables, but to spell out other words. A list of the two-letter state abbreviations appears as Figure 8–10.

Each address must include the appropriate zip code. It follows the state name—always on the same line and one or two spaces after it. Though the examples in this book illustrate the five-digit zip codes in use at the time of its writing, the United States Postal Service plans to introduce nine-digit codes in 1981.

Attention line

The attention line is not actually a part of the inside address. However, it does represent a destination and does come immediately after the inside address.

The purpose of the attention line is to indicate that though the letter is addressed to an organization, it should be routed to the person or position title designation in the attention line.

Though the use of the attention line may be declining, it still remains as a proper part of the letter.

Alabama	AL	Montana	MT
Alaska	AK	Nebraska	NE
Arizona	AZ	Nevada	NV
Arkansas	AR	New Hampshire	NH
California	CA	New Jersey	NJ
Canal Zone	CZ	New Mexico	NM
Colorado	CO	New York	NY
Connecticut	CT	North Carolina	NC
Delaware	DE	North Dakota	ND
District of Columbia	DC	Ohio	OH
Florida	FL	Oklahoma	OK
Georgia	GA	Oregon	OR
Guam	GU	Pennsylvania	PA
Hawaii	HI	Puerto Rico	PR
Idaho	ID	Rhode Island	RI
Illinois	IL	South Carolina	SC
Indiana	IN	South Dakota	SD
Iowa	IA	Tennessee	TN
Kansas	KS	Texas	TX
Kentucky	KY	Utah	UT
Louisiana	LA	Vermont	VT
Maine	ME	Virginia	VA
Maryland	MD	Virgin Islands	VI
Massachusetts	MA	Washington	WA
Michigan	MI	West Virginia	WV
Minnesota	MN	Wisconsin	WI
Mississippi	MS	Wyoming	WY
Missouri	MO		

Figure 8–10   Two-letter abbreviations for states

If you elect to use an attention line, position it two lines below the inside address and two lines above the salutation. Start it at the left margin, or indent it if you indent paragraphs, or center it. Underscore it if you wish. Figure 8–3 includes an attention line.

Salutation

A salutation usually follows the inside address (or attention line, if included). It begins at the left margin, two lines below the last line of the address. As established, the simplified letter form omits the salutation.

The salutation is the greeting to the receiver. For a person or a title, it usually takes the "Dear . . ." form and may be followed by a colon or comma (closed style) or no punctuation at all (open style). The colon is required for all business letters except the personal business letter, in which the comma may be used (Figure 8–9). The comma is appropriate for the salutation of a personal letter on plain paper (Figure 8–7).

Designated person   Figures 8–2, 8–4, 8–7, 8–8, and 8–9 include salutations directed to designated people or titles. Observe that for the informal, personal style, the first name of the person may be used (Figures 8–7 and 8–9). Observe also that moderately formal salutations include "Dear" followed by the correct courtesy title and the surname (Figure 8–2) or by a position title (Figure 8–4). Figure 8–8 shows a formal salutation: "My dear" followed by a title and surname. Avoid the most stilted of all salutations: "Dear Sir," "Dear Madam," "My dear Sir," and "My dear Madam."

Company   When the letter is addressed to a company, with or without an attention line, the salutation traditionally has been "Gentlemen." However, because the word is sexist, the up-to-date form is "Ladies and Gentlemen"—a familiar form of address already used in oral communication. (See Figure 8–3.) *Never* use "Dear Sirs," "Dear Mesdames," or "Dear Ladies and Gentlemen."

Appendix D includes other suggestions for correcting the discriminatory language of the old forms.

Formality   Here is a summary of types of salutations—listed in descending order of formality:

Sir/Madam
My dear Sir/My dear Madam
Dear Sir/Dear Madam
Gentlemen (for a firm comprised only of men)/Mesdames or Ladies (for a firm comprised only of women)
Ladies and Gentlemen (for a firm comprised of men and women, or of unknown composition)
My dear Mr. Jones/My dear Ms. Jones
Dear Mr. Jones/Dear Ms. Jones
Dear Director
Would you like to be part of an important survey?
My dear Mary/My dear Fred
Dear Mary/Dear Fred
Mary/Fred
Hello
Hello, Mary/Hello, Fred
Hi, how are you?
Hi, Mary/Hi, Fred

When an informal phrase such as "Would you like to be part of an important survey?" takes the place of a salutation, it combines elements of the salutation and the subject line. The phrase acts as a greeting, but also often introduces the topic of the letter.

Subject line

The subject line provides a preview of what the letter covers. It is a standard part of the simplified format and may be used with other styles.

For a letter with both a subject line and a salutation, place the subject line two lines below the salutation at the left margin, or two lines above the salutation at the left margin, or centered on the salutation line. Typewrite it with solid capitals, with keyword capitals, and/or with underlines.

The subject line in the simplified format goes three lines below the last line of the inside address and three lines above the first line of the body of the letter. It begins at the left margin and is typewritten in solid capitals.

Figures 8–3 and 8–5 include subject lines. Neither includes the words "Subject," "About," "In re," or "Re." You may still see such words preceding the subject statement, but their use is declining.

Body

The encoded message forms the body of the letter. Therefore, apply the writing guidelines already discussed to its composition.

The chosen letter format dictates whether to indent the paragraphs. The first line of the body begins two lines below the salutation or subject line for all but the simplified style. For the simplified style it begins three lines below the subject line.

With the exception of certain novelty letters, all business letters are single spaced, with double spacing between paragraphs.

Carefully choose the margin settings and vertical placement of the body and other parts to create an attractive, picture-framed layout. Decisions depend primarily upon the length of the letter, but also upon the letterhead design. Control vertical placement through variation in the number of spaces between the date line and the first line of the inside address. Control horizontal placement through the margin settings.

Complimentary close

The complimentary close is the leave-taking phrase that parallels the greeting phrase formed by the salutation. Therefore, its formality should correspond with that set by the salutation. From the most formal to the least formal, some of the conventional complimentary closes are:

Very respectfully yours	Yours cordially
Yours very respectfully	Cordially yours
Respectfully submitted	Cordially
Respectfully yours	
Respectfully	Yours faithfully
	Faithfully yours
Very truly yours	Faithfully
Yours very truly	
Yours truly	
Very sincerely yours	
Yours very sincerely	
Yours sincerely	
Sincerely yours	
Sincerely	

Though not so conventional, some examples of additional informal complimentary closes are:

Yours for good television viewing
Best wishes
Good luck
See you at market
Till the convention
Goodby
Farewell

You may use the less conventional complimentary closes for informal or personal business letters—and for your personal letters as well. However, avoid being contrived or "cutesy." Also consider your receiver's tastes.

Place the complimentary close two lines below the last line of the body. Start it at the left margin or at the center of the page, depending upon the style of the chosen format. Capitalize only the first word. Follow the complimentary close with a comma (closed punctuation) or include no punctuation mark (open punctuation). Match the punctuation style of the salutation.

(211 words)
(test on page 254)

Except for Figure 8–5, all the samples shown so far include complimentary closes. Figure 8–5 shows the simplified format; by definition, that format does not.

Company name

Some organizations include the typewritten name of the company after the complimentary close—particularly in a two-page letter.

The original purpose for including the company name with the signature was to assign legal responsibility to the company for the employee's message. However, court decisions have now established that responsibility even when the typewritten company name does not appear.

When included, the company name appears in solid capitals two lines below the complimentary close. Figures 8–3 and 8–6a show the placement.

Signature block

The signature block consists of the signature and typewritten name of the signer and/or the signer's position title.

Penwrite your signature personally. If circumstances ever dictate that another must sign for you, that person should place her or his initials after the signature (Figure 8–4).

For the traditional style, place your signature in the space between the complimentary close and the typewritten name or title, or between the company name and the typewritten name or title.

For the simplified style, sign between the last line of the body and the typewritten name (Figure 8–5).

Your signature may be different from your typewritten name—depending upon the level of formality of the letter. For example, for a letter to a receiver you know well, you may sign only your first name even though your full name appears in the typewritten line (Figure 8–9).

The typewritten name and/or position title of the encoder belong four lines below the complimentary close or company name in the traditional letter. Typically, five or more blank lines fall between the last line in the body and the typewritten name in the simplified letter (Figure 8–5).

If you are a woman, you need to decide how you will sign and typewrite your name. The contemporary style calls for you to omit the courtesy title just as men do (Figure 8–4). However, if you use initials or have a name that is common to both men and women (for example, Gale, Dale, Chris, Jan, Marion, Dana, Leslie, Lynn, Jerry, Terry), you may want to include "Ms." with your name on the typewritten name line (Figure 8–3). Otherwise, you might find yourself addressed as "Mr." on return correspondence from those who do not know you are a woman.

Consider the dilemma of Doris Allen as she prepares to respond to the letter from Dale Sellers (Figure 8–5). She will not know whether to use "Mr." or "Ms." However, because of the historical assumption that the writer is a man unless proven otherwise, she probably will choose "Mr."

A custom still observed by some people calls for women to include "Miss" or "Mrs." on the typewritten name line. Therefore, you will still receive letters following that custom. When you respond to such a woman, respect her wishes by using the implicitly requested marital-status courtesy title on your return letter.

If you are a man, you should not include "Mr." on the typewritten name line. However, as conventions change, you may want to begin doing so if you have a sex-neutral name (Gale, Dale, etc.).

Reference initials

Reference initials appear in most business letters. They appear at the left margin two lines below the last line of the signature block.

The usual practice is to include only the stenographer's initials (Figures 8–3, 8–5, and 8–6b). However, the dictator's initials can precede the stenographer's initials (Figures 8–4 and 8–6a).

In addition, if the writer's typewritten name does not appear in the signature block, her or his name should appear with the stenographer's initials. Figure 8–2 illustrates that setup.

Enclosure notation

If you insert anything other than the letter into the envelope, you should show an enclosure notation on the letter. The enclosure notation begins at the left margin two lines below the reference initials. It includes the word or abbreviation "Enclosure(s)," "Encl(s).," or "enc(s).," followed by a colon and either the number of enclosures or a list of the enclosure items. Figure 8–4 includes an enclosure notation.

Copy notation

The copy notation lets the receiver know who, other than the addressee receives a copy of the letter. The notation "cc" stands for "carbon copy(ies)," but is still used even when the copy is made by another process (Figure 8–2). The word "copy(ies)" or the phrase "copy(ies) to" may be used instead of "cc" (Figure 8–4). The notation "xc" for "xerox copy" is beginning to gain acceptance.

The notation "bc" stands for "blind copy" and appears only on the copy, not on the original letter. Use it when you do not want the receiver to know that you have sent a copy to someone else. Figure 8–3 includes a blind copy notation as it would appear only on the copy. The original would simply show a blank space for that line.

The copy notation begins at the left margin. It falls two lines below the enclosure notation, or below the reference initials if no enclosure notation appears.

Postscript

The postscript—typewritten or handwritten, preferably without "P.S."—is the last part of a letter. It falls at least two lines below the preceding letter component. It should contain no more than a few sentences. Depending on the format, it may be indented or started at the left margin.

Avoid using the postscript—particularly if it includes an obvious afterthought. Preplan your letters so that a postscript is unnecessary.

If your plan suggests that a postscript can reinforce some point already made in the body, though, go ahead and use it.

Figure 8–3 shows a postscript following a blind copy notation.

Envelopes

The type, weight, and color of paper in envelopes should match those of the letterhead stationery. Type sharp, clean impressions on them, using good equipment.

The imprinted return address on an envelope usually appears in the upper left-hand corner of the front of the envelope. Occasionally, it appears on the flap of the back. The design should match that of the letterhead reasonably well, but should include little more than the firm name and address. Excessive use of drawings and slogans detracts from the desired impression.

For plain envelopes, type the return address in the upper left-hand corner. Unlike the typewritten return address on a letter, the return address on an envelope does include the sender's name (Figure 8–11b). Begin the return address on the second or third line from the top edge and in the third or fourth space from the left edge.

The most-used size for business envelopes is the No. 10 (9½ by 4⅛ inches). However, writers use the smaller No. 6¾ (6½ by 3⅝ inches) quite frequently. Unusual kinds of mailings may require different sizes and shapes. However, be sure that the dimensions of such envelopes meet postal requirements.

With the exception of the placement of the attention lines and special designations, addresses on envelopes should parallel inside addresses. For best use of electronic mail sorters, however, the United States Postal Service offers these guidelines:

1. Block and single space all lines of the address.
2. Put the city, state, and zip code on the bottom line, with the street address on the line just above it.
3. Include the number of an apartment, room, suite, or other unit immediately after the street address on the same line—never above, below, or in front of the street address.
4. Place the address well within a scanning field that meets these specifications:
   a. A margin of at least 1 inch on the left
   b. A margin of at least ⅝ inch on the bottom
   c. No print to the right of or below the address[2]

A good way to be sure to place the address horizontally within the electronic scanning area is to start the address several spaces to the left of the center of the envelope and end it to leave a margin of at least 1¼ inches. To place the address vertically within the scanning area, start it about 2½ inches from the top of a No. 10 envelope and about 2 inches from the top of No. 6¾ envelope. Such placement not only meets postal requirements, but also creates a visually attractive balance.

---

[2]U.S. Postal Service, *Mailroom Addressing for Automation*, Customer Services Dept. Notice 23–C (October 1977).

Though not required for electronic scanning, the Postal Service recommends these additional features for addresses:

1. Two-letter abbreviations for states
2. All capital letters for all words in the address
3. The omission of punctuation[3]

Figure 8–11 shows several acceptable styles for envelope addresses, including these features:

1. Envelope b shows the receiver's address in capital letters.
2. Envelope c includes an attention line. The attention line also may appear on the third line below the last line of the return address.
3. Envelopes b and d show special notations properly placed at the left.
4. Envelopes a, c, and d have imprinted return addresses.
5. The imprinted company name and address on envelope d leaves space for insertion of a person's name.
6. Envelope b has a typewritten return address. Observe that the typewritten return address includes the writer's name as well as the address.

```
Action                              (a)
 Advertisers
  30 N.E. Front Bay
   Dexter, ME  04930




                  Mr. Blair Coates, Chairperson
                  United Fund Drive
                  77  55 Street
                  Craftsbury Common, VT  05827
```

```
Joan Bard                           (b)
One Trail's End
Vildo, TN  38072

SPECIAL DELIVERY


                  MS. CLAIRE DALE
                  SALES AGENT
                  FORESEE DISTRIBUTORS
                  44 WEST 42 STREET
                  NEW YORK NY  10036
```

Figure 8–11   Envelope formats

---

[3]Ibid.

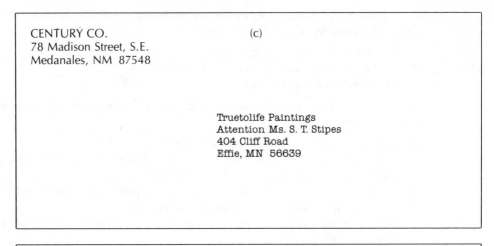

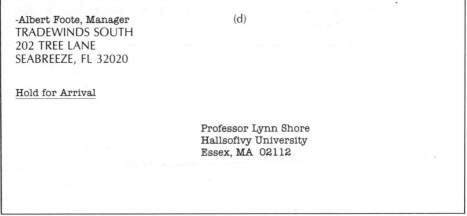

Figure 8–11   (continued)

Figure 8–12 illustrates how to fold and insert 8½- by 11-inch pages into a No. 10 envelope, and 5½- by 8½-inch pages into a No. 6¾ envelope. Figure 8–13 shows the same procedures for inserting 8½- by 11-inch pages into a No. 6¾ envelope.

To use a window envelope, type the receiver's name and address in the appropriate position on the letter. Then fold the letter accordion-style so that the address shows through the window. Stationery suppliers and office manuals usually provide instructions for placement and folding.

SUMMARY

To write letters, again apply the six communication guidelines—adapted to letter writing:

1. Define purposes, participants, and environment.
2. Identify letter channel.
3. Control interference.

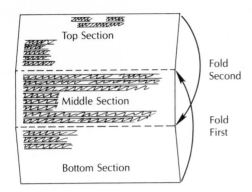

Step 1.   Fold bottom section (one-twelfth inch less than one-third of the page) up over middle section. Fold top section down so that it overlaps the bottom and middle sections by one-fourth inch. (Try to make creases straight.)

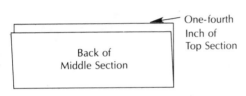

Step 2.   Turn the letter so that its top section is farthest from you. The one-fourth-inch section of the top of the page should be visible.

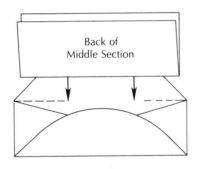

Step 3.   Insert the letter as indicated.

Figure 8–12   Procedure for folding and inserting 8½- by 11-inch pages into a No. 10 envelope, and 5½- by 8½-inch pages into a No. 6¾ envelope

4. Write and transmit letter in light of purposes, participants, environment, channel, and interference.
5. Use feedback.
6. Evaluate.

As you define the participants and the environment, also decide exactly what you want the receiver to do as a result of your letter—the *action objective* of the exchange.

Your use of the written medio-level channel allows you to: (1) keep a *permanent record* of your messages, (2) *edit* and perfect troublesome messages, (3) handle *detail*, (4) deal with *complex information*, and (5) *disseminate mass messages* at a relatively *low cost*.

The types of interference that most likely will affect your letter involve humans, time, and space.

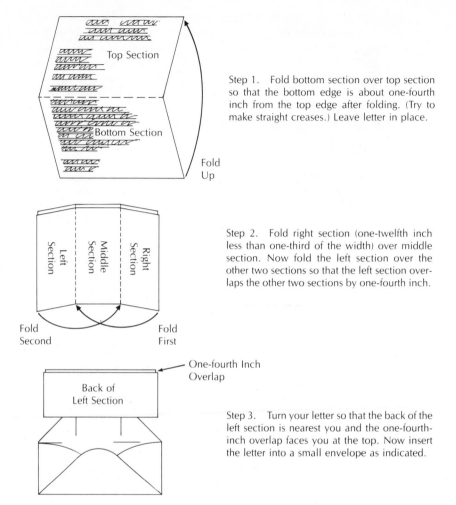

Step 1.   Fold bottom section over top section so that the bottom edge is about one-fourth inch from the top edge after folding. (Try to make straight creases.) Leave letter in place.

Step 2.   Fold right section (one-twelfth inch less than one-third of the width) over middle section. Now fold the left section over the other two sections so that the left section overlaps the other two sections by one-fourth inch.

Step 3.   Turn your letter so that the back of the left section is nearest you and the one-fourth-inch overlap faces you at the top. Now insert the letter into a small envelope as indicated.

Figure 8–13   Procedure for folding and inserting 8½- by 11-inch pages into a No. 6¾ envelope

Make the process of selecting, drafting, revising, and transmitting your letters a highly conscious process.

Feedback that comes as a result of your letter usually takes the form of another letter or a telephone call. Utilize it to correct the problems created by interference, to complete your purposes, and to solve basic problems or needs. Also remember to evaluate the communication at each stage of the process.

Standard letter formats include the *block, modified block with blocked paragraphs, modified block with indented paragraphs,* and *simplified.* The continuation page also has a defined format.

A letter can include as many as 15 parts: (1) stationery and letterhead/return address, (2) date line, (3) special designations, (4) inside address, (5) attention line, (6) salutation, (7) subject line, (8) body, (9) complimentary close, (10) company name, (11) signature block, (12) reference initials, (13) enclosure notation (14) copy notation, (15) postscript. The standard parts of the business letter are the stationery and letterhead/return address, date line, inside address, salutation, body, complimentary close, signature block, and reference initials. The simplified format does not include a salutation and complimentary close, and the subject line is a fixed part.

Addresses on envelopes should parallel the inside addresses. Do not include the attention line and the special designations in the same position, however. Observe postal regulations when addressing envelopes. Also use correct methods for folding letters for insertion into envelopes.

Practice

1. When you define your purposes, you decide exactly what you want the receiver to do as a result of your letter. In other words, you need to ask yourself if you want the receiver to buy a car, sell a car, order a car, order party balloons, give you information regarding job openings, think your company is socially responsible, or what. Determine and write what your purposes are (again, what you want the receiver to do as a result of your letter) in each of the following situations:

   a. You are interested in working for Smith, French, and Bernstein, Inc., an accounting firm. You read that Ellen Smith, one of the name partners in the firm, will visit your city to give a speech to the local chapter of the National Organization for Women. Smith, who is known to be willing to interview soon-to-be-graduated business students, will be in town for two days. You will write a letter to her.

   b. You just completed the five-year management plan for your client's department store chain. Your client, David Trudeau, lives 600 miles away; so you are forced to mail the plan. It is the last piece of work you agreed to do for him. In other words, the management plan is the final contract deliverable for Trudeau's firm. You would like Trudeau to give your company more business. You realize, too, that he must send you written confirmation that you have now met the terms of the contract. You will write a cover letter to accompany the plan.

   c. You interviewed Rachel Jaivin for a financial analyst position in your department. You were quite impressed with her and would like to hire her. You know that a number of other firms have given her rather attractive job offers. During the interview, Jaivin stated that she thinks your company's benefits package is excellent. You will write a letter to her.

   d. You have been asked to write a letter that will be sent to all of the owners of the Jet III sports car, an automobile that your company, U.S. Motors, builds and sells. You have found that the brakes in the Jet III are defective and could prove quite dangerous. As far as you know, no government agency knows of the problem—not yet. U.S. Motors will replace the defective parts free of charge if the owner brings the car to any U.S. Motors garage. You cannot write a personal letter to each of the 3,400 owners; thus your letter must carry a rather general salutation. You will write the letter.

2. Write the letter for the situation and the purposes established in question 1a. Use your imagination to supply additional information. Use the block format.

3. Write the letter for the situation and the purposes established in question 1b. Use your imagination to supply additional information. Use the modified-block, blocked-paragraph format.

4. Write the letter for the situation and the purposes established in question 1c. Use your imagination to supply additional information. Use the modified-block, indented-paragraph format.

5. Write the letter for the situation and the purposes established in question 1d. Use your imagination to supply additional information. Use the simplified format.

6. Collect five business letters and the envelopes in which they came. Evaluate and write one or two paragraphs about each. Cover at least these points:

    a. Stationery and letterhead
       (1) Does the letterhead establish the who, what, and where?
       (2) Is the letterhead streamlined or cluttered?
       (3) Is the paper of good quality? attractive color? appropriate size?
       (4) Do the design and paper of the envelope match those of the letterhead?
    b. Layout
       (1) Is the body framed well?
       (2) Is the letter crowded on the page?
       (3) Does the letter present an attractive appearance?
    c. Components and format
       (1) Does the letter include all of the standard parts?
       (2) Does it include any of the less standard parts?
       (3) Which of the basic formats does it take?
       (4) Does it include any unusual parts or features?
       (5) Is the print clean and sharp?
    d. Envelope address
       (1) Does the address fall in the scanning field for electronic sorting?
       (2) Does the address meet the other guidelines suggested by the United States Postal Service?
    e. Overall impression

7. Obtain from the local post office the most recent publications about mail services, rates, addressing envelopes to meet the requirements of electronic scanning, etc. Write a one- or two-page summary of the types of information that will be useful in a business office.

8. Decide what paper, envelope, and format choices you would use in each of these situations. Explain the reasoning behind your choices.
    a. You are sending a copy of your company's annual report to a potential employee. You will attach a cover letter to the report.
    b. You just had an interview with a potential employer. You are writing a follow-up letter. You currently work at another accounting firm and could use its letterhead.
    c. An old friend just took you to lunch. You enjoyed the meal and wish to write a thank-you letter.
    d. You just finished writing an important report. It will be sent to your company's most valuable client. The report is 323 pages long, contains a number of tables and graphs, and will be used extensively by the client. Your client is very conservative. (In addition to making paper and format choices, you must make important cover, binding, and printing choices in this situation.)
    e. You just completed drafting your résumé. You want it to receive attention, yet you do not want it to look too strange.

9. You decide that you should write a letter announcing that Adam Faber has joined your firm, Naturally Tasty Foods, Inc., as the District IV sales manager. District IV covers Washington, Oregon, Idaho, and Utah. Faber worked as a sales representative for Sunny and Good Products, Inc., before joining your firm. Faber earned his B.B.A. at Irving College, Irving, Iowa, and enjoys playing softball and basketball with his daughters, Elaine and Ann Faber-Kaufman. Faber's wife, Esther Kaufman, is a professor of biology at the University of Longworth. Use either the block or modified-block-with-indented-paragraph format. Your firm's address is 600 North Sixth Avenue, Longworth, Oregon 97444. You will address the letter to all of your present and potential District IV customers (grocery stores, health food stores, and discount stores).

10. Because you sometimes cannot recall the differences among the letter formats (block, etc.), you decide that you want to prepare a short reference manual that includes examples and descriptions of each. You want to keep the manual at your desk for your use. Prepare the manual in the form that will prove most helpful to you.

11. Write a letter to Karen MacDonald of MacDonald and Tung Real Estate, Inc. In the letter, explain why you would like to work for MacDonald and Tung. Also include what abilities

you feel you can offer the firm. After you have written the letter, meet with your group. You and each other group member review the letters written by each of you. Choose a letter and have its author read it to the class. If possible, have a transparency made of the letter so that it can be displayed as well as read.

12. A business letter can include as many as 15 parts. Write a letter that includes all 15 parts. After you have typed the letter, label each of the 15 parts. Make and label a sample envelope for the letter (you can draw it on a regular sheet of paper). You may wish to attach the letter and the sample envelope sheet to the reference manual you prepared in question 10.

13. [*Your professor will time this exercise.*] Use your imagination to write a simple letter. Write the letter using a block format, closed punctuation, and copy notation. Design your own letterhead. Your work will not be graded on the beauty of your design, however.

14. Correct these salutations:
   a. Dear Mrs. Franklin (Franklin has never used the "Mrs." courtesy title.)
   b. Dear Ms. Brown (Brown always uses "Miss.")
   c. Gentlemen (The firm has both women and men in it.)
   d. My dear Sir (Your letter is not extremely formal.)
   e. Dear Mrs. Graham (You know that Graham is a woman, but do not know which courtesy title she prefers.)
   f. Dear _____ Levenson (You do not know the sex of the person you are writing.)
   g. Dear Housewife (You know that some homemakers are male.)

15. Correct these complimentary closes:
   a. You're a great interviewer, Rosie (in a letter to the accountant who interviewed you yesterday)
   b. Very respectfully yours (in a handwritten thank-you note to a close friend and business associate)
   c. Seriously (in a letter to a prospective client)
   d. Keep up the good work (in a letter to your company's president)
   e. God bless you (in a letter to a new client)
   f. Be good (in a form letter that will be sent to your company's customers)

16. What do you think each of these signatures communicates?

   a. *Mary Smith*

   b. *[signature]*

   c. *John E. Sinnell*

   d. *Carol S. White*

   e. *Debbi Sue Jones* ☺

   f. *J. P. "Bruiser" Walters !*

   g. *Lane Ellington Stokes*

   h. *Jimmy Joe Barnes*

Which signature do you like best? Why? How will you sign *your* formal letters?

17. Use your dictionary and thesaurus to create meanings for these words. Use the words when you think, write, and speak so that you feel comfortable using them.

a. Complementary	**f.** Homogeneous
b. Complimentary	**g.** Resultant
c. Conversational	**h.** Stationary
d. Designate	**i.** Stationery
e. Heterogeneous	**j.** Straightforward

18. Take and score Self-Test 20 over the excerpt about the complimentary close.

Self-Test 20
Excerpt about the Complimentary Close

A. Recall (33 points each). For each multiple-choice question, select the most accurate answer.

1. The complimentary close is best described as:
a. A signature with a few kind words directly beneath it
b. The postscript
c. An enclosure notation
d. The leave-taking phrase that parallels the salutation as a greeting phrase
e. The company name, address, and phone number

2. You should use the less conventional complimentary closes for:
a. Informal or personal letters
b. Most business letters
c. All good news letters
d. a–d

B. Inference (34 points). Indicate whether this statement is true or false.

The more formal the complimentary close you use, the more serious your receiver will think that you are, regardless of the content of your message.

Solution to Self-Test 20
Excerpt About the Complimentary Close

A. Recall (33 points each)   **B.** Inference (34 points)

 1. d   **2.** a   False

---

19. Take and score Self-Test 21 over Chapter 8.

Self-Test 21
Chapter 8

A. Recall (25 points each). For each multiple-choice question, select the most accurate answer.

1. When you use paper without a printed letterhead, you should:
a. Put your address under your signature
b. Not put a return address in the letter because you will write it on the envelope
c. Include a return address at the top of the letter in a position that fits the format chosen
d. Include your name and mailing address at the top of the letter
e. Put your return address in the body of the letter

2. A general rule for the order of the elements of an address is to arrange them:
a. With the company name on the top line and the person's name on the second line

     b. With the attention line at the top and the address on the second line

     c. With the last destination on the top line through the first destination on the bottom line

     d. With the first destination on the top line through the last destination on the bottom line

     e. In the order that fits the tone of the letter

3. Which of these statements is *not* true?

     a. When the company name is included after the complimentary close, it appears in solid capitals two lines below the complimentary close.

     b. If possible, you should penwrite your signature personally.

     c. Your signature may be different from your typewritten name—depending upon the level of formality of the letter.

     d. If you insert anything other than the letter into the envelope, you should show an enclosure notation on the letter.

     e. The postscript can be about as short or as long as is necessary, though 20 sentences should be the upper limit.

B. Inference (25 points). Indicate whether this statement is true or false.

A handwritten business letter usually carries a great deal more weight than a typewritten one.

Solution to Self-Test 21
Chapter 8

A. Recall (25 points each)

  1. c   **3.** e

  2. c

B. Inference (25 points)

False

9

Writing Neutral and Good-News Messages

Consider letters in three broad categories: (1) neutral and good-news messages, (2) bad-news messages, and (3) persuasive messages. This chapter covers the first type. Chapters 10 and 11 deal with the other two.

WRITING NEUTRAL MESSAGES

Neutral letters compose a significant portion of the day-to-day written interchanges of business. As the word "neutral" suggests, such letters carry messages that fall somewhere between good news and bad news. However, elements of both good and bad news spill over into many neutral letters. Therefore, the routine nature of the letters does more to define them than does any other characteristic.

The routineness of neutral letters makes them relatively easy to develop. The style usually includes these features:

1. Deductive or descending-rank pattern of development
2. Straightforwardness coupled with simple courtesy
3. Conciseness
4. Completeness
5. Clearness
6. Action closing (dated when appropriate)
7. Provision of clear feedback channel

Three general types constitute the coverage of neutral letters: (1) direct-response solicitors, (2) indirect-response solicitors, and (3) responses.

Direct-Response Solicitors

A direct-response solicitor overtly asks the receiver to supply something or do something in direct response to the message. Consider three kinds of direct-response solicitors: (1) order letters, (2) inquiry letters, and (3) request letters.

Order letters

You may use letters to place orders for materials or services for purchase, lease, or rent.

When you order materials, include columnar setups of appropriate data: catalog numbers (if available), names and descriptions of items (including colors, sizes, qualities, and model numbers, if necessary), quantities, unit prices, price extensions (total item prices), and weights. In addition, include shipping instructions, descriptions of how you are paying or will pay, names and addresses of receivers, and desired dates of delivery.

Material items ordered for purchase include the full range of consumer and industrial goods. Material items ordered for lease or rent include films, tapes, and equipment.

When you order services, try to be just as specific and detailed as when you order goods. However, you often will order services through word descriptions rather than catalog descriptions. In addition, you will not always know prices when you place orders for services.

Services you might order by letter include subscriptions; food catering; building inspection; repairs; hotel reservations; paid speakers, media presenters, and entertainers; and transportation reservations and tickets.

For ordering, you also may use, instead of letters, the telephone, order blanks, requisition forms, and purchase-order forms.

Figure 9–1 illustrates a simple order for a subscription to a magazine. Figure 9–2 is an example of a more involved order letter. As you review them, think of yourself as the writer. Imagine how you applied the six writing guidelines as you prepared for writing and then completed the letters.

Observe how both Figures 9–1 and 9–2 illustrate the deductive plan. They begin with the most important message first and then supply the details that support it.

Inquiry letters

As the writer of a letter of inquiry, you seek the answers to questions. Business inquiry letters usually fall into four classes: (1) products and services, (2) employment, (3) credit, and (4) operations and procedures.

Products and services   In an inquiry about a product or service, ask specific questions in a courteous framework. Figure 9–3 is a letter of inquiry about copy service.

Employment   A potential employer of an applicant for a job often writes to a former employer to inquire about the applicant's qualities, attitudes, and performance. The former employer may or may not be listed as a reference on the applicant's data sheet. The potential employer also often writes to character references listed by an applicant.

SEEYA CO.

2020 75 Street
Acra, NY 12405
(000) 000-0000

February 3, 198X

International Geographic
16th and M Streets N.W.
Washington, D. C. 20036

Ladies and Gentlemen:

Please enter a one-year subscription to International
Geographic for:

> Ms. Dell Rankin
> Office Manager
> Seeya Co.
> 2020 75 Street
> Acra, NY 12405

Please begin delivery as soon as possible, bill Seeya Co., and send
the bill to Ms. Rankin. I understand that the subscription rate is
$12 for 12 issues.

Sincerely,

Y. R. Self

Y. R. Self
Clerk-Typist

Copy to: Ms. Rankin

Figure 9–1   Order for subscription service

Be specific in your questions about a prospective employee. To illustrate, which of these queries would better elicit the response you want?

- What kind of employee was Mr. Milam when he was with your firm?
- Would you please briefly evaluate Mr. Milam's abilities as an employee with your firm, including your assessment of his: (1) job performance, (2) written and oral communication arts and skills, (3) logical and original thinking, (4) perseverance and dependability, (5) cooperativeness, (6) self-image, (7) appearance, and (8) absenteeism?

Most respondents prefer the second type. They can answer specific questions rather than having to write general statements or trying to guess what kind of information the inquirer wants.

MODULAR
MANUFACTURING

707 S. W. Avenue
Mulga, AL 35118
(700) 221-2111

January 21, 198X

Resa Suppliers
6092 Super Street
Picacho, AZ 85241

ORDER FOR $2,736.33 WORTH OF EQUIPMENT

Please ship these items as listed in your January sales brochure:

Qty.	Name of Item	Cat. No.	Lbs.	Price	Total Price
1	Drill press with ½-HP motor	7-1139A	235	$ 489.48	$ 489.48
2	¾-HP drill	6-2222C	9	74.92	149.84
2	½-HP automatic scroll saw	9-4123A	9	84.39	168.78
1	Metal-turning lathe and cabinet	7-2491A	500	2,148.60	2,148.60
			753		$2,956.70

Less 10% Preferred Customer discount   295.67

$2,661.03

Plus Shipping Charges @ $.10 a lb.   75.30

$2,736.33

Please ship the equipment, freight prepaid, to arrive no later than February 28. Please bill us at the established 2/20, n/60 terms.

Y. R. Self

Y. R. Self
Shop Supervisor

YRS:jt

Figure 9–2   Order for merchandise

1984 Elton Drive, Apt. 208
Blanchard, Oklahoma 73010
January 14, 198X

Copiesoquik, Inc.
23 South Broadway
Moore, OK 73060

Gentlepeople:

Would you please answer these questions about your copy service:

1. What do you charge for running 300 copies of 1 original? 3 copies each of 100 originals? 1500 copies of 1 original? 3 copies each of 500 originals?

2. What reprography process do you use?

3. What weight of paper do you use?

4. Do you collate? If so, what do you charge?

5. Do you bind sets of copies? If so, what do you charge?

6. How much time would you need for each of the runs described in No. 1?

7. What are your business hours?

Please reply by January 22. I need to make my choice of copy service by January 25 so that I may complete my work by February 1.

Sincerely yours,

Y. R. Self

Y. R. Self

Figure 9–3 Inquiry about a service

Forms often take the place of letters about applicants for jobs.

When inquiring about people, you must deal with the issues associated with confidentiality. Court rulings and legislation have opened many personnel files to the subjects of these files. Therefore, no one can ever assure another of absolute confidentiality.

As a writer, though, go ahead and tell the receiver that you are acting in a professional capacity and will keep all information confidential. In such circumstances, the likelihood of legal action against the writer is significantly reduced.

ALLTHEANGLES, INC.

21918 44 Street, N.W.
Dover, DE 19901

April 19, 198X

Elsburg Corporation
3221 Daniel Avenue
Nixon, NJ 08818

Attention: Mr. Watergate

Ladies and Gentlemen:

Katherine Jones-Bush has applied to us for a position as a computer programmer. She has listed you as a former employer. Acting in your professional capacity, would you please answer a few confidential questions about Ms. Jones-Bush's tenure with you:

1. How long did she work for you as a computer programmer?

2. Relative to all computer programmers who have worked for you, in which of these classes would you place her performance? Upper 5%, upper 10%, upper 25%, upper 50%, lower 50%, lower 25%, lower 10%, lower 5%.

3. Under what circumstances did she leave your employ?

4. How did she get along with her co-workers?

5. How did she get along with her supervisors and managers?

6. How was her attendance?

7. Would you hire her again as a computer programmer? Why?

We shall appreciate your responses to these questions—and any other information that might help us in our decision.

Sincerely yours,

J. R. Self

Y. R. Self
Director of Personnel

jt

Figure 9–4 Inquiry about employment

Because of even the slight chance of legal action, however, many respondents to inquiries about people avoid making any negative statements. Therefore, you need to question the validity and value of any such responses that you receive.

Figure 9–4 is an example of a letter of inquiry about a former employee.

ANGELO'S DEPARTMENT STORES, INC.

Omaha Branch/1700 East Drive/Omaha, NE 68102/(504) 777-7777

December 19, 198X

Credit Manager
Pratt & Pratt Sales
9823 West Boulevard
Lincoln, NE 68503

Dear Credit Manager:

CREDIT RECORD OF MYRON DALTON

Myron Dalton, 17 West Circle, Omaha 68104, is an applicant for a credit line of $1,000 with Angelo's. He has listed your firm as a credit reference, stating that he has had an account with you for the past eight years.

Please help in the evaluation of Mr. Dalton's application by responding to some questions. Space is provided after each so that you may answer directly on this letter if you like.

1. Has Mr. Dalton had credit with you for the stated eight years?   If not, for how long?

2. Have you placed a credit limit on the Dalton account?   If so, how much?

3. How many purchases has he charged to his account in the years he has been with you?

4. What is the largest amount he has ever owed you?

5. How many times has he been late with a payment?   If he has been late, what is the average number of days he has been late?

6. How much does he owe you now?

7. If he owes you now, is any of the amount past due?   If any is past due, how much?   For how long?

8. If you were Angelo's, would you grant credit to Mr. Dalton?   If so, for a $1,000 line?

Your answers will be kept confidential. We hope that we may have the opportunity to help you in a similar way sometime.

Yours sincerely,

Y. R. Self

Y. R. Self
Credit and Collections

YRS:mjj

Figure 9–5 Inquiry about credit

Credit   Many credit letters involve simple inquiries about the payment records and credit ratings of applicants for credit with your company.

The same kinds of precautions about confidentiality apply to credit transactions as apply to employment transactions.

Credit investigators use forms and telephone queries as much as letters.

As an illustration of routine credit inquiries, suppose that you work in the credit department of a large retail store. You receive an inquiry from Myron Dalton about how to establish credit at your store. You send Dalton a credit-application blank.

Once you receive Dalton's completed application blank, you call or write the appropriate agencies. Such agencies might include his bank, the credit references he listed on the application, the appropriate credit bureau, and, if he is in business, such reporting organizations as Dun & Bradstreet.

Because the inquiries to all of the agencies would be quite similar, review one letter as representative of all of them (Figure 9–5). It is a letter sent to one of the references named by Dalton.

Operations and procedures   Inquiries often seek information about organizational operations and procedures. Case 1 illustrates the evolution of one such inquiry.

Case Study 1

Inquiry Letter

You want to open a motorcycle dealership in Bend, Oregon. You know that dealerships already exist there for David Harleyson, Zukisu, Yemehee, Absconda, Cudati, and Tonnor motorcycles. Therefore, you decide that the dealerships for Saki-kawa, WMB Umphtri, and Dohaka seem to be your best business possibilities. You set out to gain the information that will help you know whether you will want to and be able to acquire the dealerships. In addition, you want to know how to proceed in applying for the dealership if you make that decision.

You apply the guidelines and make these decisions:

1. Purposes, participants, and environment
   a. My objectives
      (1) Long term: To acquire the one or more dealerships that will lead to maximum profit
      (2) Intermediate term: To analyze information about the Sakikawa, WMB Umphtri, and Dohaka dealerships in order to determine what combination seems to be available and potentially most profitable
      (3) Short term: To receive from the three distributors the information necessary to begin the analysis
   b. Distributors' objectives
      (1) Long term: To grant significant numbers of dealerships to high sales achievers
      (2) Intermediate term: To analyze the data provided by applicants for a dealership to find whether they appear to be potential high sales achievers
      (3) Short term: To provide the necessary information to potential applicants
   c. Receivers
      (1) Sakikawa Motorcycles
         1818 Kihei
         Honolulu, HI 96802

        (2) WMB Umphtri, Ltd.
            One Alsap Boulevard
            Bellingham, WA 98225

        (3) Dohaka Distributors
            P.O. Box 222, South Branch
            Long Beach, CA 90803

    d. Environment not a major factor
2. Channel
    a. Dismiss interpersonal at this stage because of expense and uncertainty
    b. Dismiss telephone because too much information needed
    c. Choose letter because it will provide a consistent basis for obtaining information from three different distributors
3. Interference
    a. Interference possible if I do not produce complete list of information needed
    b. Do not anticipate any serious external interference
4. Writing
    a. Select list of information needed from each distributor
        (1) Initial and continuing costs for dealership?
        (2) Capital requirements for me?
        . . . .
        (22) What information dealer needs to process application?
    b. Draft
        (1) Use just-write method
        (2) Organize
            (a) Select inductive pattern
            (b) Outline
    c. Revise
    d. Transmit
        (1) Choose simplified style
        (2) Typewrite same message for each of three distributors, with only distributor name changed (Figure 9–6)
        (3) Mail first class
5. Feedback plan
    a. Use feedback responses from three distributors to complete analysis set out in objectives
    b. Feed back to distributors if more information or clarification is needed
    c. Feed back completed application to distributors if decision warrants
6. Evaluate
    a. My objectives met
        (1) Short term: When complete replies to inquiries received
        (2) Intermediate term: When analysis of information yields the most profitable dealership combination
        (3) Long term: When profitable dealership(s) acquired
    b. Distributors' objectives met
        (1) Short term: When replies to inquiries completed
        (2) Intermediate term: When analysis of applications completed
        (3) Long term: When dealerships granted to high sales achievers

Figure 9–6 illustrates the final result of Case 1.

2323 Sisters Lane
Bend, Oregon 97701
January 7, 198X

Dohaka Distributors
P.O. Box 222, South Branch
Long Beach, CA 90803

INQUIRY ABOUT DEALERSHIP

At age 14 I rode my first motorcycle. Fifteen years later I am still an
enthusiast. For 11 of the past 12 years I have been fortunate enough to
combine my enthusiasm for the sport with my jobs. I have worked for three
different motorcycle dealers during that time—with the work involving just
about everything associated with motorcycles. I have held jobs in mechanics,
sales, parts, shop supervision, and office management—all quite successfully.

A year ago I moved to Bend and presently work as a salesperson for an
automobile agency. However, I want to return to motorcycles. With my
savings, the backing of a relative, and the establishment of a good line of
credit with a local bank, I will be able to set up my own motorcycle sales
and service shop here in Bend within the next year. Therefore, I am now
looking into the possibilities for dealerships.

Bend does not have a Dohaka dealer. As nearly as I can determine, it never
has had one. I like the Dohaka and am beginning my analysis of the
potential for a Dohaka dealership now. To help make the analysis, would you
please answer these questions:

1. Do you require dealers to pay any initiation or continuation fees for a
   Dohaka dealership?

2. How much capital do you suggest I need in order to become a Dohaka
   dealer?

3. If I become a Dohaka dealer, do you grant me an exclusive Dohaka
   dealership for a given area? If so, how do you define the area?

4. If I carry the Dohaka, may I also carry other makes of motorcycles?

5. Do you offer discounts for volume purchases? If so, please explain.

6. What is your retail sales markup and pricing policy? Do you establish
   minimum or maximum retail prices for your dealers? Do you advertise
   suggested retail prices? Do you control or limit in any way the dealer's
   markup and sales policies?

7. What credit arrangements do you make with your dealers?

Figure 9–6   Inquiry about operations and procedures

Dohaka Distributors   2   January 7, 198X

8. Do you use a consignment system? If so, what provisions do you have for consignment?

9. Do you set sales quotas? If so, please describe your policy.

10. Do you have any Dohaka dealers within a 100-mile radius of Bend?

11. What sort of shipment and delivery schedules would be possible for Bend?

12. Do you provide service schools for Dohaka mechanics? If so, where are they located? What are the costs to the dealer?

13. Does Bend meet your population density requirements?

14. Would you help me make a market analysis of the Bend area?

15. Do you provide customer mailings and showroom displays?

16. Do you pay or help pay for local radio and television spots and newspaper ads?

17. Have you completed a readership analysis in the Bend area for magazines and newspapers carrying your ads? If you have, what did you find? If you have not, would you?

18. What is the Dohaka warranty? How do you handle the costs of warranty service? Would I perform the service and you pay me? Would I return the cycle or parts for you to repair? Do you use a combination of the two service approaches?

19. What Dohaka models are now available? Will you have any new models coming out in the next six months?

20. What is Dohaka's share of the motorcycle market in the United States? Could you send me a copy of the latest annual report of Dohaka, Inc.?

21. How do I apply for a Dohaka dealership?

22. What types of information will I need to supply when I make application for a dealership?

23. Can you think of anything else I should know about Dohaka dealership arrangements?

Please supply this information soon. I am making my analysis now and must make dealership decisions by April.

Y. R. Self

Y. R. Self

Figure 9–6   (continued)

Request letters

The simple request closely parallels the inquiry and order. However, unlike either, the writer asks for more than information—usually for free goods or services.

If a request moves beyond the simple and routine, it can become a persuasive message. For example, if you invite someone from the local telephone office to make a speech or media presentation about the company, you need not use persuasion. Such personnel are eager to take their messages to the public. However, if you ask a busy and popular speaker to speak at the monthly meeting of your organization, you might need to use some of the persuasive techniques described in Chapter 11.

Similarly, if you make a routine request for credit—a request that you know will be granted—you need not write a persuasive message. If you ask for a line of credit higher than you have ever had, if you have some flaws in your credit record, or if you have no credit record, you should develop a persuasive message.

A letter of request can also include some good news or bad news. As an example, assume you receive one of a limited number of invitations to attend a reception for a visiting dignitary. The invitation qualifies as a request for your presence, but also as an honor to you for being selected.

Consider the neutral request letter in five classes: those seeking (1) materials, (2) financial transactions, (3) services, (4) corrections, and (5) attendance.

Materials   Many letters request material items. Such requests may be for gifts or loans of the materials: They might be (1) blanks or forms for applying for a job, for credit, for insurance, for a permit, or for a license; (2) free catalogs, brochures, pamphlets, and other publications; (3) items of merchandise from businesses for use as door prizes or giveaways for conferences and conventions; or (4) samples of products.

Requests for material loans may ask for (1) books and other publications; (2) tapes, films, and other audiovisual presentations—either to use outright or to preview with the possibility of subsequent purchase; or (3) equipment or products to use in demonstrations or exhibitions at workshops, conferences, and conventions.

The letter in Figure 9–7 illustrates a request for material items. Does it satisfy the six writing guidelines? Why? Does it border on the persuasive? Why?

Financial transactions   Letters of request often involve financial transactions. Consider some examples:

1. A letter to members of an organization asking them to pay their annual dues. Such a request amounts to nothing more than a dues statement accompanied by a persuasive nudge.
2. Statements and bills for goods and services. Such requests are so simple that they often appear as forms instead of letters. Only when a payment becomes past due should you move from the routine to the persuasive.
3. A routine letter to the members of an organization asking for their regular annual contributions to a fund or foundation. Such messages often take the form of a pledge or contribution card instead of a letter.
4. A letter to ask for a refund on a product tried on a money-back offer. Appropriate proofs of purchase accompany it.
5. A letter asking for credit that will be granted automatically.

YOURTOWN CHAMBER OF COMMERCE

2222 Business Boulevard
Yourtown, Youessaye 00000

June 22, 198X

Mr./Ms. xxxxxx xx xxxxxxxxx
Yourstore Sales
xxxx xxxx xxxxxxxxxx
Yourtown, Youessaye 00000

Dear Mr./Ms. xxxxxxxxxx:

The annual Yourtown Chamber of Commerce Teacher Recognition Day luncheon will be on September 18 this year. The Chamber again will provide the meal, the awards, and the door prizes for this always-fun occasion.

Would you participate by contributing a door prize or two: any piece of merchandise, a gift certificate for merchandise or services, money, or even a gag gift or white elephant. The teachers enjoy and appreciate all of them. Last year Yourtown merchants donated 22 prizes. With your help we can increase the number to at least 30 this year.

As Chamber members distribute your prizes at the luncheon, your firm's name will be called over the loud speaker. In addition, your gifts will have attached to them cards showing that you donated them.

In July we will telephone you to find out when we may pick up your items. For right now, though, would you please complete and mail the enclosed card to show that you plan to participate?

Let's make this Teacher Recognition Day a clear expression of our joint appreciation for the teachers of Yourtown.

Sincerely yours,

Y. R. Self

Y. R. Self, Chairperson
Teacher Recognition Day
Door Prize Committee

lol

Enclosure: Return card

Figure 9–7   Request for door-prize donations

6. A letter to a credit union or insurance company requesting a routine loan of money.

An illustration of a letter of request related to financial transactions appears as Figure 9–8. It is a bill for payment for a service—a consulting fee.

ENTRAL
COMMUNICATION
CONSULTANTS

1771 Alfalfa Trail
Independence, MO 64001
(010) 010-0101

February 9, 198X

Ms. Catherine Dors
Communication Specialist
Elko Whosesalers, Inc.
Two Allendale Drive
Independence, MO 64004

Dear Ms. Dors:

Brada Allen and Sol Degiusti told me how much they enjoyed
working with all of you at Elko. They are particularly pleased
that you feel that both the in-service sessions and the
communication audit were productive contributions to the
progress of Elko.

As agreed when the consultation began, the basic fee for the
services of the team is $200 an hour. For the 15 hours spent
with you, then, the basic fee is $3,000. The cost of the special
supplies and materials is $389.43 (itemized on the attached
sheet). Therefore, the total due Central Communication
Consultants is $3,389.43.

Thank you for the opportunity to work with you. If you decide
you would like the additional sessions you mentioned, we shall
be glad to talk with you about them.

Sincerely,

Y. R. Self

Y. R. Self, Director
Corporate Relations

YRS:stu

Encl.

Figure 9–8   Request for consultation fee

Services   A routine letter often includes a request for services for which a traditional
fee is not charged. Through such a letter, you may ask someone to: (1) write a report
or criticize a report written by another; (2) speak, perform, make an audiovisual
presentation, or conduct a workshop; (3) serve on a committee; (4) work at your
organization's booth at a convention; (5) expedite some process; (6) adjust an insurance claim; or (7) transfer funds from one account to another at your savings and
loan association or bank.

LEARNALOT UNIVERSITY

1818 Undergraduate Drive
University, NV 89507
(500) 505-0505

College of Business
Office of the Dean

February 22, 198X

Ms. Vera Styles, President
Styles Manufacturing
754 Assembly Road
University, NV 89507

Dear Ms. Styles:

Will you and a guest please join us for the annual Business Week banquet? It will be held in the Great Hall of the Student Center at 7:00 p.m., Friday, April 17.

As in the past, we should like for you and your guest to sit at the head table. You will be introduced as a representative of Styles Manufacturing and as a member of the Advisory Board for the College of Business.

You are also invited to the reception for our speaker, Senator Herbert Brightfull. It begins at 6:15 p.m. in the Desert Room.

Please complete and mail the enclosed card to let us know of your plans. Once we hear from you, we will send you your complimentary tickets.

We look forward to seeing you on April 17.

Sincerely yours,

Y. R. Self

Y. R. Self, Ph.D.
Dean

O. Whatta Leader

O. Whatta Leader, Chair
Business Week Student Committee

op

Enclosure: Reply card

Figure 9–10 Request for attendance

Behind all of these announcements lies your desire that the receiver take some action. You may wish customers to frequent a new, moved, or expanded business. You may wish your receivers to attend or send someone to attend a learning session. You would like your readers to feel or express congratulations, respect, or goodwill. Perhaps you even desire the receivers to vote for you.

I. R. ESS TAX SERVICES

12 Honor Heights/Swanlake, ID 83281/(707) 707-0707

January 3, 198X

Mr. Bill Chronister
Ms. Jane Delgado
1314 Dodge Blvd., Apt. 302
Swanlake, ID 83281

Dear Mr. Chronister and Ms. Delgado:

The offices of I. R. Ess Tax Services have been moved to 12
Honor Heights—next door to Singleton's Sporting Goods in the
new Honor Heights Mall in southeast Swanlake.

We have been pleased to prepare your tax returns for you in the
past and look forward to preparing them again this year.

Yours sincerely,

Y. R. Self

Y. R. Self
Tax Consultant

lol

Tax time is here. Remember, the new address of I. R. Ess Tax
Services is 12 Honor Heights.

Figure 9–11   Announcement of new location

You may never directly observe the desired action resulting from an indirect-response solicitation. Even if a number of people come to your new store, attend your lecture, or vote for you in an election, you rarely will know exactly who did. Even if you knew that, you usually do not know whether they did so because of the announcement. Therefore, the evaluation often becomes just as indirect as the name of the class of messages conveys.

A sample announcement appears as Figure 9–11. It is an individually type-written letter produced and distributed by a firm engaged in tax services.

Notices

Notices are similar to announcements. They provide information without really inviting direct responses. However, the term "notice" is used here to indicate that the information is more formal and legal than that transmitted in an announcement.

Many government and private contracts and programs require notices for certain events. For example, corporations, credit unions, and electric cooperatives must notify their stockholders and members of impending annual meetings and elections. Ostensibly, such notices include invitations to attend. In practice, however, the receivers usually do not attend. Therefore, proxy statements often accompany the notices, with the request that the receivers sign and return them.

Notices also often go to employees to apprise them of changes in policies. Some of these policies relate to changes in insurance, retirement, stock options, tax shelter programs, worker's compensation, and unemployment compensation. Others relate to credit unions, Social Security benefits, taxes, vacations, holidays, educational support, and other such programs. The changes themselves may be good news, bad news, or neutral news. However, the form of the message is routine, by definition.

Another kind of notice applies when a mass error necessitates mass correction. For example, if the catalog you mailed to 1,500 customers last week includes an incorrect price list or mailing address for orders, you will have to mail out 1,500 correction notices.

Figure 9–12 shows a notice to employees about a revision of their retirement program. The notice is a form letter sent to each employee's home address. Direct responses will come only from those who have questions about how the provisions apply to them or about their accounts.

Invitations

Many invitations qualify as indirect-response solicitors. They differ from the direct requests for attendance described earlier for any of three major reasons: (1) They go to a large mailing list chosen without a great deal of selectivity. (2) A large proportion of the receivers do not attend the event. (3) The writer cannot expect to observe individual responses to the message—only general ones.

Indirect-response invitations ask people to attend the same kinds of events that direct-response invitations do. Observe these kinds of differences, however:

• *Direct-response solicitor*: You send invitations with R.S.V.P. notations to thirty carefully selected people asking them to the opening of your law offices and to the reception associated with it.

Indirect-response solicitor: In addition to an ad in the newspaper, you send invitations without R.S.V.P. notations to a mailing list of 5,000 people asking them to the grand opening of your new northside Floor-Mart discount store. You offer free soft drinks and popcorn to those who attend.

• *Direct-response solicitor*: You mail letters to 12 people inviting them to attend the private swearing-in ceremony for a federal judge, to be held in the judge's chambers in the Federal Building. You include a sentence asking the receivers to let you know ahead of time whether they will be able to attend.

Indirect-response solicitor: You place a notice in the local newspapers and also mail letters to every organization in the community inviting all organization members to attend the swearing-in ceremony of the mayor. The ceremony is to be held in a local stadium.

Figure 9–13 is an example of an indirect-response invitation. It also involves some persuasion.

Waystein Pianos
22 IVORY AVENUE
EIGHTY EIGHT, KY 42130
(333) 333-3333

June 18, 198X

Dear Employee:

NOTICE OF MODIFICATION IN RETIREMENT PLAN FOR WAYSTEIN EMPLOYEES EMPLOYER I.D. NO. 22-2222222; PLAN I.D. NO. 002

Upon approval by the Board of Directors, and subject to approval by the Internal Revenue Service, effective July 1, 198X, the Waystein Pianos Retirement Plan will be changed in this way: Waystein Pianos will credit to retirement accounts the prior service of all regular full-time employees who have had breaks in service, provided they meet either of these conditions:

1. Fulfillment of vesting requirements (8 years of continuous employment and attainment of age 30) before the break in service

2. Length of the break in service does not equal or exceed the length of continuous employment before the break

If you have had a break in service with Waystein, check the enclosed statement to determine how the change affects you. If the statement is not enclosed or if you believe it contains an error, contact Larry Tooner in our Eighty Eight office. If you should like to call, his extension number is 333.

Respectfully,

WAYSTEIN PIANOS

Y. R. Self

Y. R. Self, Chairperson
Retirement Plan Administration
    Committee

yy

Encl. for affected employees:
    Statement of effect of change

Figure 9–12   Notice of change in retirement plan

Unsolicited transmittals

Letters often serve primarily to transmit something to the receiver. When the writer initiates the transmittal, it usually qualifies as an indirect-response solicitor.

If you voluntarily send a catalog and a letter of explanation to one person or a mailing list of persons, the letter is an unsolicited transmittal. The example would be equally apt if the article sent were a product sample, schedule of events, convention

GOINGGON AUCTIONS INC. 666-666-6666

34 Nodd Street
Galveston, TX 77550

June 19, 198X

Ms. Pat Harmon
200 Bay Drive
Baytown, TX 77520

Dear Ms. Harmon:

As one who appreciates fine estate auctions, you will be pleased
to know that Goinggon again will bring you the opportunity to
participate in one. At auction will be:

The Wells Estate
Seven Northeast River Road
Galveston, Texas
Saturday, September 25, 198X
12:00 noon
Inspection from 1:00 to 7:00 p.m.
September 24
and
9:00–11:45 a.m.
September 25

Please review the auction notice included with this letter. You
will see that the ten-room home, outbuildings, and two acres are
offered in addition to unusually elegant furnishings.

If you want a basis for comparison, the Wells Estate parallels
closely the quality of the Dominguez estate of southeast
Houston. As you recall, Goinggon conducted the auction of that
fine estate last March.

Please plan to be a part of this exceptional event.

Sincerely,

Y. R. Self

Y. R. Self, Director
Public Information

top

Enclosure

Figure 9–13   Request for attendance

program, telephone directory, questionnaire, special publication, manuscript of a
book, or a report.

Because the primary purpose of a transmittal letter (cover letter, covering letter)
is to accompany something else of more importance than the letter itself, it qualifies
as a routine type. However, it may include tinges of persuasion.

Think about how some of the listed types of transmittals lead only to indirect responses:

1. Your transmittal of a catalog may eventually lead to an order of some kind, but you often will have difficulty tying the order to the transmittal letter itself.

2. If you send a cover letter with a sample of a product, the combination may provide the stimulus for the customer to buy the product. However, unless you accompany the sample and letter with a coupon keyed to the mailing, you may never know about such a purchase. Even with such a coupon, you may never know. Many people do not use coupons even when they do make the desired purchases.

3. When you transmit a schedule of events, you have little likelihood of knowing who attends because you sent it.

4. You have a better chance of observing responses to a convention mailing. Those who attend usually register, and you can match the mailing and registration lists.

5. Unless returned questionnaires contain the respondents' names or some invisible means of identification (a legally questionable practice), you will not be able to know exactly which receivers cooperated. However, you can calculate proportions of return.

6. Assume you transmit unsolicited copies of a speech delivered by your company president, a policy statement, the proceedings of a convention or conference, or an article. You likely will never hear from the recipient or be able to observe any response.

When writing a letter of transmittal, avoid using hackneyed opening phrases. Particularly avoid such phrases as "Enclosed please find," "Enclosed herewith," "Attached hereto," and "Attached you will find." Even avoid "Enclosed is" and "Attached is" when you can.

Some acceptable parallels to the correct "Here is" approach are:

1. "As suggested by Lee Engle, I am sending you this copy of . . . ."
2. "You may want to read the enclosed copy of . . . ."
3. "Please accept the attached copy of . . . with our compliments."
4. "This brochure may help you to improve . . . ."
5. "Take a look at the . . . included in this envelope."
6. "We are pleased to send you this trial-size bar of Sunup Soap."
7. "Because of the importance of knowing how you feel about current topics, I am asking you to complete the questionnaire enclosed with this letter."
8. "Please consider for publication this article entitled . . . ."

A sample unsolicited transmittal letter appears as Figure 9–14.

Responses

The routine letter forms a good channel for responses to both direct- and indirect-response solicitors. Review five classes: (1) acknowledgments, (2) solicited transmittals, (3) approvals, (4) information and explanation, and (5) instructions and directions.

Letters of response should feed back messages appropriate to the initiating communication.

synergy pharmaceuticals, inc.

2098 Aspurn Drive
Mineral Springs, Arkansas 71851
(602) 026-2060

August 2, 198X

Dr. James Lo
Suite 900
Pasteur Complex
Radium, CO 80472

Dear Dr. Lo:

Here is your copy of the 198X annual report of Synergy
Pharmaceuticals, Inc.

As a stockholder of Synergy, you will be particularly pleased to
read page 16. It presents a summary of the major indicators of
a corporation's financial position—all of which show marked
stability and growth for Synergy.

If you have comments or questions about the report, please
contact us.

Respectfully yours,

Y. R. Self

Y. R. Self, Director
Owner Relations

ss

Enc.: 198X Annual Report

Figure 9–14 Unsolicited transmittal of annual report

For instance, if a representative of Dohaka Distributors replies to your letter asking for information about a Dohaka dealership (Figure 9–6), he or she should answer all questions in a straightforward and precise manner. Unless the writer is effusive in a persuasive attempt to make you a dealer, or sharply turns down your request, the letter fits naturally into the neutral category.

Acknowledgments

Sometimes the major purpose of a letter is to confirm that you have received something from someone. At other times, it is to communicate that you or someone else will complete some action, but must delay that completion. At still other times, it is to communicate routinely that you cannot complete some action. All of these circumstances lead to messages of acknowledgment—messages that serve in much the same way as written receipts for payments of money.

Written acknowledgments usually relate to direct- rather than indirect-response solicitors. They sometimes acknowledge a transaction initiated through an oral channel.

An acknowledgment always provides an excellent avenue for feedback during the time lapse between communication actions. You know how uncertain you feel when you send a watch or a calculator to a factory for repair service and hear nothing for six weeks. Recall that feeling when you are in a position to allay someone else's frustration. A simple acknowledgment or confirmation message often is sufficient to do so.

Consider acknowledgment letters in four categories—those noting receipt of (1) orders, (2) inquiries, (3) requests, and (4) messages in oral channels.

Orders   You may acknowledge orders for both goods and services at different times and in different ways. You may acknowledge:

1. Receiving an order—particularly if it is the first from a potentially good customer
2. An unusually large order from a regular customer
3. The same order twice—once to the one who placed it to be delivered to another, and once to the one who will receive it (A gift subscription to a magazine would lead to such a dual acknowledgment)
4. An order as you fill it
5. An order for which you must delay action
6. An order which you partially fill, with the remainder to follow soon
7. An order as you fill part of it, but offer to substitute, back order, or cancel the order for the other unavailable items or services
8. The receipt of goods or services which you ordered
9. Hotel and transportation reservations

Acknowledgments related to delays or substitutes for ordered items or services can represent bad news for the receiver. However, if the delays are short and the offered substitutes relatively equivalent to the original, you may write the messages in a routine style.

Figure 9–15 illustrates a letter acknowledging an order. It also reports the necessity of delaying part of the order and offers a substitute.

Inquiries   Occasionally, you will receive an inquiry of such moment that you should acknowledge it immediately, rather than wait until you respond to it fully.

As an illustration, suppose that you are the president of a corporation and the governor has written a personal letter to ask you for your opinions on several current topics. Even if you will be able to respond within the week, you should promptly acknowledge the governor's message and say when you will respond.

You also need to acknowledge the receipt of messages when you must ask for additional information or delay your response beyond reasonable expectation.

A related circumstance arises when a letter of inquiry comes into your office while you are away for an extended period. If you have empowered someone to check your mail during such a period, he or she should send an acknowledgment explaining to the inquirer that your response will necessarily be delayed.

Tiaf · Yoytota · Wolksvagen · Leop · Nodah · Snudat · Pacri

IMPORT CAR-TALOG SALES, INC.

1802 South Grand Prix   Telephone: 333-333-3334
Durants Neck, NC 27930   Toll Free: 800-333-3333
Replacement Parts · Accessories · Supplies · Custom Parts

September 3, 198X

Ms. Eleanor Parkins
4298 15 Street
Seabrook, NH 03874

Dear Ms. Parkins

Thank you for your order for parts and accessories for your
1980 Tiaf Sedan. As you can see by the enclosed invoice, today
we shipped six of the seven items you ordered. You should
receive them in about six to ten days.

We are temporarily out of the 86 TF 20622CR Star Mag Wheel at
$78.90. Our supplier promises that we will have a shipment by
September 22. Therefore, we could send the four you ordered to
arrive no later than the first week in October.

As another alternative, we can ship immediately four 89 TF
21622CR Super Star Mag Wheels at $80.90. The Super Star is
identical to the Star except that it has a triple-chrome-plated
center cap instead of a single-plated one.

Just call our toll free number (800-333-3333) and tell me your
decision. If I should be out when you call, Dee Stone will take
your message.

                                        Sincerely yours

                                        Y. R. Self

                                        Y. R. Self, Supervisor
                                        Shipping Department

rr

Enclosure: Invoice

Figure 9–15 Acknowledgment of order with statement of necessity
to delay or substitute for part of order

   The letter in Figure 9–16 acknowledges receipt of a letter from Gary Wheaton,
a friend and a manager for Ohsogood Corporation. Gary has asked about your firm's
policies related to employee absenteeism. Evaluate how well you think the letter
deals with Gary's inquiry.

hanginthere, inc.   (222) 222-2222

18 Cos Cobb Place
Hazardville, CT 06036   October 20, 198X

Dear Gary,

You're right—it has been far too long since we've had a chance
to talk. Let's try to remedy that unfortunate situation soon.

Gary, we're having the same kinds of problems with our
absenteeism policy that you describe for Ohsogood. However, I
do want to collect my thoughts on the issue and put them on
paper for you. Perhaps through an exchange of ideas, we can
come up with some solutions.

Right now, though, we're just beginning contract negotiations
with the local, and I'm able to eke out only 30 minutes or so a
day to answer mail. Although the negotiations are particularly
sensitive this year, we should be able to finish them by the end
of the month. The first part of November, then, I'll get something off to you.

In the meantime, I'm going to keep some of your comments in
mind as we deal with the topic of absenteeism during the
negotiations. I'm sure I'll also gain new information to add to
the dialogue you've initiated.

When do you think you may be up this direction again? I really
have no plans to be in the Lost Springs area any time soon. So,
if we cannot come up with a way to get together before then,
let's make a point to go out for dinner one evening while we're
attending the national conference in Seattle in April. We just
must keep at least that once-a-year face-to-face contact going.

                              Best wishes,

                              Y. R. Self

                              Y. R. Self

Mr. Gary Wheaton
Marketing Manager
Ohsogood Corporation
2980 East Main Street
Lost Springs, KS 66859

Figure 9–16   Acknowledgment of inquiry

Requests   Acknowledgments of requests parallel closely those of orders for goods
and services. The basic difference is that orders involve money, and requests usually
do not.

Here are some examples that clarify the need for request acknowledgments:

1. You receive a request from a high school teacher for 50 copies of your
company's brochure *Careers in Insurance*. You have only 10 copies available, but

have ordered more from a print shop. You acknowledge the request, send the 10 copies, and promise the other 40 within two weeks.

2. You receive a letter asking you to be the leader for a local library discussion group for four weeks in September. You write that you cannot because you will be out of town during two of the scheduled meetings. You add that you would, however, be glad to lead the October or November discussions.

3. You receive a letter accompanying a digital clock. The writer explains that the clock is not operating correctly and that it is still under warranty. You check, and it is. You write to explain that you will repair the clock free of charge, but that it will take at least six weeks.

4. You receive an invitation to attend the annual Chamber of Commerce dinner as the guest of the Chamber. You write to thank the Chamber and to accept the invitation.

5. You receive a copy of a manuscript with a cover letter asking you to review it. You send a letter explaining that you will send it to an appropriate editor, but that the process could take up to three months.

6. You receive a mailed application for a job. You write to acknowledge receipt and state whether it will be processed or filed until a job opening occurs.

7. You chair a company committee that performs its functions well. You write each member to acknowledge that performance.

8. You write the speaker for your civic club's annual dinner to acknowledge her fine presentation. The letter also serves as a transmittal if an honorarium is enclosed.

Analyze Figure 9–17. It illustrates the combination of an acknowledgment and a request for more information.

Messages in oral channels   You may want to use the written form to confirm a telephone conversation, an interpersonal agreement, something said by a speaker, or a message through any of the other countless oral channels available at all communication levels.

Consider these examples: (1) confirming a telephone request for an appointment, (2) confirming an appointment made as you talked in a hall, and (3) writing to a speaker you heard last week to ask whether you understood his proposed theory correctly.

Figure 9–18 illustrates a letter acknowledging an interpersonal agreement to lend some films.

Solicited transmittals

As established in the section on unsolicited transmittals, a transmittal letter may accompany anything sent to the receiver. The illustrations in that section cast you into the role of volunteering the transmittal for some initial purposes of your own.

The illustrations in this section place you in the position of responding to the request of another. You still have purposes behind your transmittal, but the instigating purposes lie with the original sender.

To convert an unsolicited transmittal into a solicited one, just add an opening that acknowledges the sender's request for the transmittal.

For example, suppose that a new stockholder has written to ask for a copy of your latest annual report. The opening sentence of the transmittal letter in Figure

ALLSUBURBIA
INSURANCE COMPANY
Rising Sun, Maryland 21911   (112) 211-2111

January 2, 198X

Ms. Judy Coyne-Temple
1818 South Security, Apt. 19A
Sundell, MI 49888

Dear Ms. Coyne-Temple:

Your request for a $1,000 loan on your insurance policy
certainly will be honored. You qualify fully for it.

Before we can make the loan, however, we need a completed
agreement for repayment. Therefore, would you please review
the enclosed agreement, have your signature notarized, and
return the form in the envelope.

Your check will be mailed within one day of receipt of the
completed agreement form.

Sincerely yours,

Y. R. Self

Y. R. Self, Supervisor
Loan Department

sop

Enc.: Loan Agreement

Figure 9–17   Acknowledgment of request for loan with request
to supply more information

9–14 would then become "Here is the copy of the annual report of Synergy Pharmaceuticals, Inc., that you requested." The remainder could remain as originally
written.

The remittance letter is one type of solicited transmittal. It accompanies a
check, a money order, or some other form of payment for goods or services furnished
by another. It is a simple, straight-to-the-point letter, as illustrated in Figure 9–19.

Consider how these situations also represent solicited transmittal messages:

1. A letter in a package that fills an order. It basically says, "Thanks for your order;
   here it is."
2. A report about an assigned research project accompanied by a letter. The core of

SILVERAY ELECTRONICS
1800 Spacecraft Landing
Airway Heights, WA 99001
(200) 000-0000

July 31, 198X

Mr. Chris Jenks, Director
Human Resource Development
Galaxie Manufacturing
One North Aether Way
Airway Heights, WA 99001

Dear Chris

Thanks for the lunch and the pleasant and productive conversation. I always enjoy these chances to combine "shop talk" with some moments of relaxation.

Thanks also for offering to lend me your two films on human relations. As we decided, I will be in your office at 3:15 p.m. on Friday, August 7, to pick them up. I will show them to Silveray employees during the week of August 10 and return them to you at 8:30 a.m. on Monday, August 17.

Let's meet for lunch again soon. Perhaps we can schedule a good time for both of us when I see you next Friday.

Cordially

Y.R.Self

Y. R. Self
Training Specialist

Figure 9–18   Acknowledgment of exchange in oral channel

the message is, "As you suggested in our meeting of August 3, I am submitting a report of . . . ."
3. A copy of a convention program to a friend. You introduce the letter with "Here is a copy of the program you wanted."
4. An enclosure in answer to a request, beginning: "Thank you for the opportunity to provide you this . . . ." Such a transmittal is particularly appropriate when the writer's request lent itself to your following the transmittal with a routine sales message.

   You have already reviewed one solicited transmittal letter—the remittance presented as Figure 9–19. Another transmittal letter appears as Figure 9–20. It is the type of transmittal that allows you to make a sales pitch in conjunction with it.

FLAVORBURST CANDIES
One Gumdrop Drive/Sugar House, Utah 84106
(777) 777-7777

November 18, 198X

Checkers Sugar Co.
18 Peanuts Avenue
Sweetwater, TX 79556

Ladies and Gentlemen:

The enclosed check for $1,403.85 is payment for the sugar you
shipped on November 12.

According to your Invoice No. 3492 (a copy enclosed), the total
bill was $1,432.50. However, because we are paying within ten
days we subtracted the 2 percent discount ($28.65) from the
total.

Sincerely yours,

Y. R. Self

Y. R. Self

Enclosures: Check
            Copy of invoice

Figure 9–19   Solicited transmittal of a remittance

Approvals

Though the word "approval" carries a good-news tone, many approval letters are
quite routine. They involve:

Issuing a credit card to someone who had no doubt about receiving it

Approving the repair of merchandise under warranty

Accepting an invitation to a banquet

Agreeing to speak to a club meeting

Correcting a mistake in filling an order

Replacing a faulty piece of new merchandise

Correcting an error in a remittance

Adjusting a covered insurance claim

Be gracious in approving requests—even those that call attention to some error
by you or involve a questionable claim. For example, consider how you would feel if
a company sent you this message:

HOMESPA
FITNESS
EQUIPMENT

2228 Jogging Lane
Sparta, TN 38583
(603) 111-1111

April 3, 198X

Ms. Mary Thon
300 S Street N. W.
Lewis Run, PA 16738

Dear Ms. Thon:

Thank you for your interest in the new line of Homespa Fitness Equipment. The enclosed catalog includes pictures, descriptions, warranty provisions, and prices for the complete line.

You probably will be particularly interested in the Homespa Walkajog—one of the first gym-quality treadmills affordable for the home. Full information about it appears on page 19 of the catalog. I have encircled the description for you.

The Homespa dealer nearest you is in Pittsburgh (as marked on page 26 of the catalog). However, you may also order direct from the distribution center here in Sparta. We promise to ship your orders within two days of receipt. The catalog includes order blanks and instructions for completing them (pages 22-25).

As one obviously committed to physical and mental fitness, you will appreciate the excellence of Homespa equipment. Therefore, if you order within two weeks, you will receive a 10 percent discount for any order totaling $350 or more. Pages 20–21 include a credit application form and information about payment alternatives.

Just write or call if I can assist you in your decision to become a Homespa Fitness Equipment owner.

To your health,

Y. R. Self

Y. R. Self, Head
Sales Department

gs

Enclosure

Figure 9–20   Solicited transmittal of catalog, including sales "pitch"

Dear Ms. Ellis:

Your toaster was received. We just cannot believe that the malfunction could be our fault. However, we are going ahead and repairing it *this time*. In the future, remember that your warranties with A. Pliance, Inc., do not cover any misuse by you.

Sincerely,

Next, think about how you would feel with this slightly improved tone for the same message:

Dear Ms. Ellis:

We received your toaster yesterday and examined it immediately. Although we have some question about the cause of the malfunction, we will repair it because it is still under warranty.

Sincerely,

Finally, consider this greatly improved tone:

Dear Ms. Ellis:

Thank you for the chance to put your fine A. Pliance toaster back into good working order. You should receive it in like-new shape by August 10.

Sincerely,

Figure 9–21 includes an example of a simple letter of approval.

Information and explanation

This section concentrates on information/explanation responses to the messages initiated by others. However, the rules for writing them remain essentially the same as those for initiating them.

When you write the letter of recommendation for Katherine Jones-Bush, the job applicant (Figure 9–4), that letter will explain and inform.

For the classification used here, consider information and explanation letters to be those in which clear-cut facts, data, news, and interpretations form the bulk of the messages.

Some examples of types of information/explanation letters of response include:

1. The response to Gary's request for your company's policies on absenteeism (Figure 9–16)
2. The information sought concerning Myron Dalton's credit record with Pratt & Pratt Sales (Figure 9–5)
3. Answers to the questions asked of Copiesoquik, Inc. (Figure 9–3)
4. An explanation to a university student to explain your ideas about the importance of communication in business
5. Explanation of the specific qualities of your new Handee-Dandee potato slicer
6. Information about your attic-insulation service in a letter to a potential customer who has written to ask about it
7. A letter of introduction for a manager moving to another branch

To write good response letters of information/explanation, make the full measure of requested data the aim of your message.

Figure 9–22 is a sample information/explanation response letter.

Instructions and directions

Closely akin to the information/explanation message is the message that instructs or directs. Whichever the category, the encoding rules remain essentially the same.

The instructions/directions letter often logically follows the chronological developmental plan. It also depends upon concrete words and illustrations for clear expression.

motorsaplenty, inc.

February 9, 198X

Mr. Michael Storie
789 Fourth Street, West
Volborg, MT 59351

Dear Mr. Storie:

You are right. The motor you returned to us overheats badly. We shipped a carefully tested replacement today, and you should receive it by Monday of next week.

Because you had the bother and expense of returning a brand-new piece of equipment, I am enclosing a check for $15. It should at least cover your freight cost.

Please check with us again the next time you need quality equipment. I can assure you that the experience will be better next time.

Sincerely yours,

Y.R. Self

Y. R. Self
Customer Relations

att

25 Deece Avenue
Electric Mills, MS 39329

Figure 9–21   Approval of a claim

Examples of the types of messages containing instructions or directions are:

1. A step-by-step description of how to assemble or dismantle anything from a toy train to a giant refinery engine
2. A travel route
3. How to get a job
4. Procedure for using a computer terminal
5. A computer program for the solution of a specified problem
6. The channels an employee should use in order to talk directly with the president
7. The required sequences for ordering materials both within and without the firm

SEARCH, INC.
1718 15 Street
Donnybrook, ND 58734

Research
Consultants
555-555-5555

March 19, 198X

Ms. Ada Cannon Wyndham
North Campus Hall, Room 108
Scholarshippia College
Jiggs, NV 89827

Dear Ms. Wyndham:

Your letter asking about the meaning and methods of research shows admirable perception and interest in a vital topic. I am glad to respond to such an eager quest for knowledge:

Research is a dynamic search for the answers to questions, for the solutions to problems.

Research may be undertaken for the express purpose of satisfying curiosity or contributing to the body of human knowledge. This kind of research is basic research. Research may be undertaken for the express purpose of removing some roadblock in the path toward some goal. This kind of research is applied research. Many findings from basic research eventually make their way into application. Most of business research is applied research.

Research primarily uses the scientific method. However, as for any human endeavor, it also employs art and sheer operational mechanics even as the scientific method unfolds:

1. Recognize and define the problem and the purposes of the research.
2. Review the literature.
3. State the hypothesis(es).
4. Design the investigation.
5. Write the proposal for the research.
6. Collect the data.
7. Organize the data.
8. Analyze the data.
9. Interpret the data.
10. Draw conclusions.
11. Develop recommendations.
12. Write the final report and disseminate.
13. Follow up.

Figure 9–22 Information/explanation response

Ms. Ada Cannon Wyndham   2   March 19, 198X

Empirical research may be classified in several ways. Though neither mutually exclusive nor collectively exhaustive, one such classification includes:

1. Qualitative description
2. Quantitative description
3. Classification
4. Estimation
5. Comparison
6. Relationships
7. Cause-and-effect relationships
8. Mapping and modeling
9. One-time decision-making under uncertainty
10. Time series analysis

Research involves logical reasoning. It involves quantitative and qualitative data. It involves flashes of creativity and the basest of tedium. Most of all it involves an inquiring mind ever seeking to pierce the unknown.

Place these few words and outlines into perspective: They represent only the barest beginnings and the sketchiest of a skeleton of my views about the totality of action that defines the research process. Each point alone deserves many pages for full development. However, perhaps this brief essay will whet your appetite for searching out your own meanings for research. Best wishes as you do so.

Sincerely yours,

Y. R. Self

Y. R. Self, Chief
Corporate Research Division

sm

Figure 9–22   (continued)

The letter in Figure 9–23 should give you an idea of how you might develop a letter of instructions/directions. It responds to a request from a regional manager asking how to draw a good sample from the records of 2,083 employees. The purpose of drawing the sample is to estimate the proportion of employees who have more than two years of college without having to look at all of the records.

WRITING GOOD-NEWS MESSAGES

A suggestion threaded throughout the preceding sections on neutral letters is that the line of distinction between neutral and good-news letters is a fine one. Therefore, this coverage of good-news letters is not elaborate.

Consider how these messages slip ever so slightly from the neutral to the good-news category:

1. You make an announcement, but an announcement congratulating the receiver for being named the recipient of an unusual honor.
2. You issue an invitation to attend some function, an invitation to such an exclusive event that only a few selected people ever receive one.
3. You write an acknowledgment of someone's outstanding performance in some capacity.
4. You write an acknowledgment of a public announcement of an award bestowed upon the receiver.
5. You write a letter of credit approval, but an approval that is not usual or expected for the circumstances of the application.
6. You write a letter of approval for the adjustment of a claim for an adjustment not under warranty and not really expected.
7. You write a notice that the recipient has passed the C.P.A. or bar examination.
8. You write an announcement that your firm will give every employee a substantial Christmas bonus this year.
9. You write a request that the recipient join your firm in a higher-level, higher-paying position than she ever thought possible.
10. You write a response to a request, saying that you will fly in to speak to a group—and will not even have to charge because you can combine the speaking engagement with a business trip.
11. You write a response to a writer telling him that you have accepted his manuscript for publication.
12. You write an unexpected approval of a loan request.

The deductive and descending-rank developmental patterns are most appropriate to the good-news letter. Put the good news first. Report dramatically, but not falsely. Give the little additional information that is needed, and conclude. The pleasantness of the news itself removes from you the burden of a difficult encoding process.

(343 words)
(test on page 300)

Three brief messages illustrate the minor features that distinguish a good-news letter from a neutral letter.

ASSEMBLINE PRODUCERS, INC.

1189 18 Street
Warwick, RI 02886
(666) 666-6666

September 17, 198X

Mr. Herbert Gatlin, Manager
Galivants Ferry Plant
3099 Sycamore Drive
Galivants Ferry, SC 29544

Herb:

Your research sounds interesting and productive, and, of course, I'll be glad to help.

Divide the sampling process into two parts: (1) Determine the sample size. (2) Select the employees to be included in the sample.

1. To determine the desired sample size, use this formula:

$$n = \frac{pq}{\left(\dfrac{e}{z}\right)^2 + \dfrac{pq}{N}}$$

Where: n = sample size; p = proportion you estimate have more than two years of college, or .5 if you have no estimate; q = 1 − p; e = allowable error (one-half of desired confidence interval); N = universe size; z = standard normal deviate

To illustrate, you will obtain a sample size of 406 if you use these values in the formula: p = .7; q = .3; e = .04 (meaning that you are willing to work with an interval of .08 from lower to upper limit—or to have an error of ± .04); N = 2,083 (the total number of employees); z = 1.96 for a confidence level of .95.

If you keep everything the same except e, which you change to .03, the sample size will be 626. If you use p = .5, q = .5, and e = .03, but keep everything else as listed, n will equal 706.

2. To select the employees to be included in the sample, use the systematic sampling process:

    a.   Randomly choose one of the file drawers containing the personnel folders. Say you choose drawer No. 4.
    b.   Open drawer No. 4 and randomly choose a folder. That folder will be the first in your sample. Pull it, but hold your place in the drawer.

Figure 9–23   Instructions/directions response

Mr. Herbert Gatlin   2   September 17, 198X

   c.   From the position of that first folder, move back through the
        remainder of drawer No. 4, pulling every kth folder, where k =
        N/n. For example, if you decide to use the calculated sample size of
        706, k = 2,083/706 = 3. Therefore, you would pull every 3rd folder
        (skip 2 after each folder you pull). If you have 1 or 2 folders left at
        the back of drawer No. 4, carry the count over to drawer No. 5.
   d.   Beginning as the carryover from drawer No. 4 dictates, pull every
        3rd folder from drawer No. 5. Again carry over the count from the
        back of drawer No. 5 to drawer No. 6.
   e.   Continue the process until you exhaust the last drawer containing
        folders, say drawer No. 20.
   f.   Carrying over any extra folders from drawer No. 20, return to
        drawer No. 1, and pull every 3rd folder.
   g.   Continue the process through drawer Nos. 2 and 3 and through the
        first part of drawer No. 4 not previously covered. You will end
        within 1 or 2 folders of the first folder you pulled.

Because the value of k is a rounded figure, you will not come out with
exactly 706 folders. However, examine all that you have pulled to obtain the
information you want.

If you should have any questions about either of the procedures, write or
call. Also, if I can help you develop your confidence interval estimate of the
proportion who have more than two years of college, I'll be glad to do that
also.

                              Cordially yours,

                              Y. R. Self

                              Y. R. Self
                              Statistician

bll

Figure 9–23   (continued)

arroyo industries, inc.
19 Isla Verde
Descalabrado, PR 00757
(888) 888-8888

December 9, 198X

Ms. Nikita Waukomis, Director
South Dakota Foundation for
  the Native American Arts
2098 East Cheyenne Trail
Brandon, SD 57005

Dear Ms. Waukomis:

Please consider the enclosed check for $10,000 the contribution
of Arroyo Industries, Inc., to the fine work of the South Dakota
Foundation for the Native American Arts.

Each year the Arroyo Board of Directors carefully chooses the
five considered most deserving from the requests for contributions received that year. Each of the five then receives a
check for $10,000.

Arroyo Industries, Inc., wishes you continued success as you
preserve and perpetuate the rich contributions made by Native
American artists.

Sincerely yours,

Y. R. Self

Y. R. Self, Chair
Board of Directors

ll

Enclosure

Figure 9–24   Good-news response to request for contribution

Figure 9–24 is your favorable response to a request for a contribution. It also
serves as a transmittal, but not a routine one.

In the letter presented as Figure 9–25, you grant credit to Ronald Clemons
although his record would not be viewed by every credit manager as warranting it.
Because Clemons had some question that he would be approved, he obviously will
view the message as good news.

The message in Figure 9–26 may seem to be nothing more than a simple
acknowledgment. Yet, if you are a respected business and civic leader whom she has
never met, Kay Cantwell undoubtedly will feel pleasure upon reading your message.

PASSPORTACARD CREDIT CENTER
One Foundation Circle/Charleston, WV 25301
(918) 918-9189

March 19, 198X

Mr. Ronald Clemons
22 West Hardship Road
Prosperity, WV 25909

Dear Mr. Clemons:

In the belief that the strength of your credit record this past
year offsets your record for the two years preceding it, we
approve your request for a full $300 line of credit with
PASSPORTACARD.

Your temporary card and an explanatory brochure are enclosed.
Your laminated card should arrive within two weeks. Note that
as standard procedure your card will expire one year from now,
but is renewable as a virtual formality if your record warrants
it.

Use your PASSPORTACARD well. It can be your passport to
financial strength.

Sincerely,

Y. R. Self

Y. R. Self, Manager
New Customer Service

iou

Encs.: Temporary card
        Brochure

Figure 9–25 Good-news approval of request for credit

SUMMARY

Neutral letters constitute a good number of the daily written exchanges of business. Neutral letters carry messages that fall somewhere between good news and bad news, though some of the elements of both are often contained in neutral letters. Neutral letters feature the *deductive* and *descending-rank patterns, straight-forwardness, conciseness, completeness, clearness, action closings*, and *provision of clear feedback. Direct-response solicitors, indirect-response solicitors*, and *responses* are the three types of neutral letters.

Direct-response-solicitor letters involve someone overtly asking another person to supply or do something in direct response to the message. Direct-response solicitors include *order letters, letters of inquiry*, and *request letters*.

N. R. GEE CONSERVATION
2112 Anaktruvuk Passage
Anchorage, AK 99506

January 6, 198X

Ms. Kay Cantwell
Madre Club
19 Chefornak Drive
Anchorage, AK 99502

Dear Ms. Cantwell:

Congratulations on being named the recipient of the prestigious
S. T. Kenai Award of Conservation Excellence. Your
accomplishments show clearly that you deserve the honor.

I wish you well in your work and look forward to meeting you
at the annual presentation ceremony on the 18th.

Respectfully yours,

Y. R. Self

Y. R. Self
Chief Consultant

hs

Figure 9–26 Good-news acknowledgment of accomplishment of another

Order letters send for materials or services for purchase, lease, or rent. Letters of inquiry ask for answers to questions. In business, the inquiries are generally about products and services, employment, credit, and operations and procedures.

The request letter is similar to the inquiry and order letters. However, in contrast to the order letter, the request letter often asks for goods and services free of charge. In contrast to the inquiry letter, the request letter usually asks for more than just information. Neutral request letters fall into five classes: those dealing with (1) materials, (2) financial transactions, (3) services, (4) corrections, and (5) attendance.

The category of indirect-response solicitors is comprised of *announcements, notices, invitations,* and *unsolicited transmittals*. Announcements provide information for the receiver. Notices also provide information, but without really inviting a direct response.

Indirect-response-soliciting invitations are those messages distributed to a large number of people who neither expect to attend the event nor respond individually to the letter. An invitation to attend a stockholders' meeting is an example.

When you voluntarily send a catalog and a letter of explanation to one person or a mailing list of persons, the letter is an unsolicited *transmittal*. The primary purpose of the transmittal letter is to transmit something of more importance than the letter itself.

You will often use the routine letter as the channel for responses to both direct- and indirect-response solicitors. *Neutral response letters* include *acknowledgments, solicited transmittals, approvals, information and explanation*, and *instructions and directions*.

Acknowledgments confirm the receipt of orders, inquiries, requests, and oral messages.

Solicited transmittals respond to the request of another person. A letter that accompanies an order is a solicited transmittal.

Examples of approval letters include issuing credit cards, correcting mistakes in filling orders, replacing defective merchandise, adjusting insurance claims, and agreeing to give presentations.

Some letters respond to requests for information and explanation. Similar response letters are those that instruct or direct at the request of senders.

As the name suggests, the *good-news letter* brings welcome news. Unlike the neutral letter, the good-news message is one that brings rather special tidings. The neutral letter might announce a meeting, but the good-news letter would invite the receiver to a gathering that is a high honor to attend.

Write good-news letters in much the same way that you write neutral letters. However, make a special effort to emphasize the significance of the good news at the outset of the former.

Practice

1. You are interested in hiring Don Santiago, a consultant, to conduct several writing workshops for your firm. You want to know what he charges for his services and how he conducts his workshops before you decide whether to hire him. Write the letter, supplying whatever additional information you need.

2. You need to buy some accounting reference books for your office. You want two hardbound copies of *International Accounting*, one soft-bound copy of the fifth edition of *Managerial Accounting Practices in Europe* (without appendixes), four copies (either soft- or hard-bound) of the *Financial Accounting Reference Manual*, and, if it costs less than $75, one copy of *Depreciation Methods for Natural Resources* (soft-bound). You also want the microfiche edition of *Who's Who in Accounting*. Write the letter, supplying whatever additional information you need.

3. The mayor of your city, Christine Falk, is running for reelection. You would like her to participate in your business club's candidates' forum. Because she is campaigning, you know that she would be glad to participate in the forum. Write the letter, supplying whatever additional information you need.

4. You wish to hire the John Westfall Janitorial Service to clean your office building Wednesday and Sunday evenings. You know that Westfall charges $50 per janitor per six-hour work period. This figure includes all supplies and supervisors' salaries. You feel that you need five janitors on a regular basis, and one additional janitor the second Sunday of each month for special cleaning jobs. You want to hire the service for a six-month trial period. If you like the janitors' work, you will hire the service on a year-to-year contract. Write the letter, supplying whatever additional information you need.

5. Meet with your group. Discuss these messages and determine what, if anything, is wrong with them. Add information and correct them if necessary.

IDLE COMPANY
60 Able Avenue
Orville 66660

Prestige Business Card Co.
Mrs. Ann Elizabeth Fry
1616 Filbert Way
Silo, Wisconsin

My dear Miss Fry,

We heard you sell cards. We would like to buy some. We want
sets of cards for three of our employees. Here are there names:
John Ray, Deborah Leitz, and Mr. W.C. Lord. How much do they
cost? I don't want to pay over $30. Could you send paper too?

Thanks so much

Don Spelling

BANK OF THE FIR TREES
1111116 Fir Tree Plaza
Jennifer, Idaho 16160
Monday, August 19

Dear Sirs;

I really appreicate your help. I've heard really nice things
about all of you.
A lady by the name of Augusta Aardvark applied for a teller
position at my bank. She said she used to work for you.
Would you please tell me everything you know about her?

Susan Telephone
Bank President

P.S. Your a big help!

---

6. Every year you write a letter to your employees (to be sent to their homes) asking them to donate canned goods to your company's Drive for Needy Families. You want only nonperishable canned goods, canned meats in particular. As usual, you want the employees to put the food in the special bins located by the soft-drink machines on each floor. The drive will run from September 6 through October 1. Write the letter. (You can make up the necessary names, addresses, and so forth.)

7. [*Your professor will time this exercise.*] You hired a temporary secretary through Human-power Temporaries, Inc. You were told that the cost would be $180 for five days. You paid in advance. The secretary, Tom, did not show up for the last of the five days of work. Write a letter requesting a refund for the day Tom (you do not know his last name) did not work.

8. Use your imagination to write an invitation soliciting an individual response. Meet with your group. You and each other group member read your letter aloud. Choose one of the letters and have its author read it to the rest of the class.

9. Sonya Rich orders 400 of your company's best table lamps. This is her first order. You know that Rich owns large hotels in at least 16 major cities. You cannot ship the lamps

until the middle of next month. Write the letter of response, supplying whatever additional information you need.

10. Harry Field ordered 60 staplers and 10 pen and pencil sets from your company. You are out of the pen and pencil sets, but do have them on order. You expect them to arrive in two months. Write the letter of response, supplying whatever additional information you need.

11. You are the director of corporate relations for a major grocery store chain. A newspaper reporter, Nancy Von Hoff, writes you a letter asking you a number of questions, most of which deal with your company's rather unconventional pricing practices. You will be out of town on business for a week, but will answer Von Hoff's questions when you return. You decide that you should at least acknowledge the reporter's inquiry before you leave town. Write the letter, supplying whatever additional information you need.

12. You receive a call from Sam Ching, a broker with a major San Francisco investment firm. Ching says that he may be interested in hiring you, and that he will mail you a company brochure. You decide that you want to write a letter to thank him for his call. You also want to express interest in the job. Write the letter, supplying whatever additional information you need.

13. You just had dinner with an important potential client, Helen Sky. She asked you to send her a copy of your annual report. You discover that you have no reports on hand, but that several hundred copies will be printed by the end of next week. Write the letter, supplying whatever additional information you need.

14. Some communication specialists believe that most neutral letters can be made into good-news letters if written properly. What do you think?

15. [*This is an exercise in dictation.*] You have decided to hire Larry Nagy as a public relations assistant for your firm. His starting pay will be $1,200 a month, and you want him to begin work in your Lafayette office at 8 A.M. on Monday, June 1, 198X. Outline the letter that you will send to Mr. Nagy. Make up the names and addresses, and add information as you wish. Now meet with your group. You and each other group member dictate your letters. Evaluate each person's performance immediately after he or she has spoken.

16. Rewrite each of these neutral or good-news sentences.
    a. The order will get there in a week or two.
    b. We've decided to let you have the Ellen F. Bear Scholarship.
    c. Letterhead stationery is what we want in white or off-white item number 609LS.
    d. Send the books we ordered immediately.
    e. Because you want it so much, I'll grant you an interview.
    f. Your payment is three days overdue. For that reason, we will not allow you to use your charge card anymore.

17. Use your dictionary and thesaurus to create meanings for these words. Use the words when you think, write, and speak so that you feel comfortable using them.

a. Allay	g. Incur
b. Amenity	h. Libel
c. Appraise	i. Neutral
d. Apprise	j. Ostensibly
e. Convey	k. Proxy
f. Illustrative	l. Query

18. Take and score Self-Test 22 over the excerpt about writing good-news letters.

Self-Test 22
Excerpt About Writing Good-News Letters

A. Recall (33 points each). For each multiple-choice question, select the most accurate answer.

1. Which of these would *not* be classified as a good-news letter?
    a. A letter announcing that the Maria Stokes Foundation will again award a scholarship to a promising business student
    b. A letter announcing that you have won the Maria Stokes Foundation scholarship
    c. A letter inviting the "social elite" to a fund-raising event
    d. A letter approving credit for someone who under most circumstances would not receive credit
    e. A letter requesting that you join the staff of the First Bank as a vice president, a position few people your age are offered
2. When you write a good-news letter, you should:
    a. Build up to the good news
    b. Ask that the receiver call you so that you can give the good news over the telephone, a more personal channel
    c. Put the good news first
    d. Put the good news after the introductory paragraphs
    e. Downplay the good news

B. Inference (34 points). Indicate whether this statement is true or false.

If you are not sure that the letter you are writing should be a good-news letter, try to decide whether your receiver will consider your message to be good news.

Solution to Self-Test 22
Excerpt About Writing Good News Letters

A. Recall (33 points each)   B. Inference (34 points)
   1. a   True
   2. c

19. Take and score Self–Test 23 over Chapter 9.

Self-Test 23
Chapter 9

A. Recall (25 points each). For each multiple-choice question, select the most accurate answer.
   1. Neutral letters:
      a. Carry messages that will have no effect on the receiver
      b. Are really bad-news letters that have been softened
      c. Are letters that you write when you have no definite feelings on an issue
      d. Are rarely written in the business world
      e. Carry messages that fall somewhere between good and bad news
   2. Which of these statements is *not* true?
      a. Direct-response solicitors are letters that involve someone overtly asking another to supply or do something in direct response to the message.
      b. When you write a letter to order services, you should be just as specific and detailed as you are when you order goods.
      c. When you include the "R.S.V.P." or "Please reply" line in an invitation, be sure to provide within the message itself a phone number or an address to which the reader can reply.
      d. When writing an inquiry letter regarding a prospective employee, ask only general questions such as: "Was Ms. Nassed a good employee?"

Self-Test 23 — (continued)

   e. In contrast to an order letter, the request letter often asks for goods and services free of charge.

3. In which of these situations would an indirect-response solicitor *not* be appropriate?

   a. You wish to invite your 3,500 stockholders to the annual stockholders' meeting.

   b. You wish to announce that your bank has opened a new branch.

   c. You wish to invite several potential clients to a presentation you are giving just for them.

   d. You wish to send a letter with the brochure you will send to the people on your mailing list.

   e. You wish to write a letter that corrects a mistake in your company's widely distributed catalog.

B. Inference (25 points). Indicate whether this statement is true or false.

You should write a letter of acknowledgment only when you have been specifically asked to do so.

Solution to Self-Test 23
Chapter 9

A. Recall (25 points each)   **B.** Inference (25 points)

   1. e   **3.** c   False

   2. d

10

Writing Bad-News Messages

From neutral and good-news messages, turn to some others that require more finesse—bad-news messages. Because of people's reaction to bad news, the guidelines and principles covered in earlier chapters become even more critical than they are for some of the simpler types of writing.

As suggested in Chapter 9, neutral messages can carry routine bad news. Thus, the topics of some bad-news exchanges allow a relatively direct approach. Figures 9–15 and 9–16 contain examples.

The distinction between a routine bad-news message and a full-fledged bad-news message is not always clear-cut. However, consider a bad-news situation to exist when:

1. Content of the message may lead to an irreparable loss of the goodwill of the recipient.
2. The news probably will disturb the recipient.
3. The message cannot be converted into a neutral letter by adding a substantive good-news alternative to the bad news.
4. The news clearly runs counter to the interests of the recipient.
5. The situation is serious enough to warrant the investment of time and money necessary to develop a bad-news message.

PRINCIPLES FOR WRITING ABOUT BAD NEWS

When a situation requires that you deliver bad news, do so with particular care. To emphasize the kind of care needed, recall some appropriate suggestions from Chapter 7:

1. Select the inductive, ascending-rank, or chronological pattern of development.
2. Adopt a positive writing style.

3. Use a buffer opening.
4. Create a positive sandwich.
5. Choose words carefully.
6. Establish the "you" attitude.

Developmental Patterns

Choose an indirect developmental pattern for the body of the message. The indirect patterns include the inductive, ascending-rank, and chronological plans. All three plans begin with details and build to the conclusion—the bad news.

Avoid the directness inherent in the deductive and descending-rank plans. Because they would begin with the bad news and then supply the details, they would almost certainly introduce a psychologically defeating overtone.

Contrast the inductive and deductive sequence for the body of a bad-news message:

Deductive	Inductive
1. Bad news	1. Details
2. Details	2. Bad news

Positive Style

A positive writing style can overcome a great deal of the inherent negativity of a bad-news message. Positiveness arises from empathy and reaches expression through actions and words that convey that empathy.

If bad news involves an unfavorable reply to a message initiated by another, try to reply just as promptly as you would if you were delivering good news. Sometimes, such promptness can communicate as much as the verbal symbols do. It expresses an understanding attitude toward the receiver's needs.

No matter how much in the right you may be, maintain self-control and courtesy. Avoid demeaning or blaming the other. Avoid abruptness, condescension, and harshness of tone.

Convey a sense of rationality as you avoid hackneyed, false apologetic phrases such as:

We humbly regret that . . . .
Please forgive the necessity to . . . .
We beg your forgiveness for . . . .
We are so sorry that . . . .
We offer our humblest apologies for having to . . . .

This suggestion does not mean that messages should never include words such as "sorry," "regret," and "apologize." However, it does mean that the words belong within sincere apologies for situations actually involving the correction of errors. Such situations do not lead to bad-news messages. In fact, apologies and corrections of errors usually are characterized as good or neutral news.

As you plan messages, develop strategies that will subordinate the negative aspects. Try to live up to the classical image of the optimist: Write about a half-full glass rather than a half-empty one whenever possible. Emphasize what you can and will do, not what you cannot and will not do. However, try to do so without contrivance.

The half-full glass may involve a substitute at a discount. It may involve sending another speaker in your place. It may offer a compromise on a claim that should be denied outright. It may suggest an alternative supplier.

Explain the bad news itself briefly and clearly. Subordinate it to the positive sections.

Always keep in mind the duality of your goal—to solve the specific problem *and* to keep the goodwill of the receiver. Appeal to her or his sense of fairness as you attempt to accomplish both parts of the goal.

Buffer Opening

Improve upon the indirect developmental pattern by opening bad-news messages with a buffer.

Deliver a sincere compliment or agree with the other about something; comment on a topic that is warm, positive, or perhaps just neutral. In all cases, though, relate the buffer to the message in the body of the letter.

Avoid flashy attention-getting devices. Instead, use the buffer to establish a controlled approach to the topic. Contrast these openings:

We are sorry, but we cannot	Thank you for writing about . . . .
You should know that we cannot	Your concern about . . . is commendable.
We cannot understand why you would think	We appreciate your interest in . . . .
Your request for . . . is totally out of line.	Your request for . . . caused me to do some thinking.

Positive Sandwich

Also add a buffer to the end of a message to create a positive sandwich. Encase the substance of a bad-news message within buffers. Doing so will reduce the intensity of the transaction.

The positive sandwich adds two stages to the basic sequence of the inductive pattern. It becomes:

1. Buffer
2. Details (including any positive option you may offer)
3. Bad news
4. Buffer

Use a neutral, but pleasant, closing buffer for a bad-news message. Avoid the apologetic clichés here, too. Make the closing statement either relate to the situation, or avoid it entirely. In either case, concentrate upon goodwill at this point in the message. Soften the impact of the negative message by wedging it between two positive messages.

Word Choice

For bad-news situations, choose each word carefully. Wise choices can make the difference between a successful and an unsuccessful transaction.

Previous paragraphs include suggestions about good word choice. However, another one relates to the sentence structure itself.

For the delivery of the actual bad news, frequently use the complex sentence—the sentence with an independent and a dependent clause. Place the bad news in the dependent clause in order to subordinate it. Consider these examples:

- Though no opening presently exists in a position that matches your fine qualifications, I have placed your application in a top-priority position.
- Although it does not include the $2,500 credit line you requested, your credit card with a $1,500 credit line is enclosed.
- Even though I cannot speak to your group this month, I can speak in September or October.

Contrast the positive tone of the preceding indirect statements with the negative tone of these direct ones:

- Our policies do not allow us to . . . .
- To grant your request would be against company policy.
- If we adjusted your unwarranted claim, we would have to do the same thing for others.
- I personally would like to make the adjustment, but I am just one small cog in a giant wheel.
- We received your request; however, we will not be able to grant it.

Notice particularly the negative effect of using "but" and "however." Such words virtually announce that bad news is coming.

"You" Attitude

The concept of the "you" attitude pervades the preceding paragraphs. However, focus upon it in isolation momentarily.

The "you"-centered approach springs from knowing and trying to meet the needs of the receiver. As that knowledge grows, the ability to "get outside of" oneself contributes significantly to defusing bad-news messages.

Though a genuine "you" attitude usually shines through a message, words also particularly cultivate it. Thus, avoid overusing "I" and "we," and do use the stated or implied "you."

TYPES OF BAD-NEWS MESSAGES

You may have to write letters to convey many types of negative messages. However, consider only four major categories here: (1) refusals, (2) claims and adjustments, (3) unfavorable recommendations, and (4) unsolicited news of a negative nature.

CHARGERRIFIC, INC.

619 East Valley Street
Wilson, Connecticut 33219

November 9, 198X   Telex No. 17-4444

Mr. Samuel Wayne
849 Oakbrook, Apartment 16C
Wilson, Connecticut 06095

Dear Mr. Wayne:

Thank you for taking the time to look into the services offered
here at Chargerrific. In addition to issuing charge cards,
Chargerrific offers an array of merchandise at discount prices
to both its charge customers and its cash customers.

While we cannot give you a charge card at this time because you
do not meet our requirement of a $10,000 annual salary, we are
adding your name to our mailing list. Now you will receive our
discount merchandise catalogues. You will also receive a $5 gift
certificate with your first Chargerrific catalogue.

Welcome to Chargerrific as a new customer. Should you wish to
reapply for a Chargerrific Card in the future, we will gladly
consider your application.

Yours sincerely,

Ellen Fernandez

Ellen Fernandez
Credit Manager

aa

Figure 10–1   Rejection of request for credit

Refusals

In Chapter 9 you learned that you can say "Yes" or not say "No" relatively easily.
However, when you must say "No," you may have more difficulty. Consider four
broad types of refusal messages: (1) credit, loan, and insurance; (2) claim and
adjustment; (3) order; and (4) general request and inquiry.

Credit, loan, and insurance

You cannot always grant credit, a loan, or insurance to someone who applies for it.
When you must refuse, try to understand the receiver's disappointment, and write
accordingly.

FIRST VALLEY BANK
One Hildegard Plaza
Hildegard, New Jersey 22374
(555) 343-3192

December 15, 198X

Ms. Lee Fong
5006 Knox Road
Hildegard, New Jersey 22374

Dear Ms. Fong:

Thank you for visiting First Valley Bank last Thursday.

After careful analysis of your financial status, we find that you
qualify for VIProfessional Checking, a checking account for
on-the-go business and professional persons. VIProfessional
Checking offers free checks, no service charge, and $100
overdraft protection. Mr. Don Klein, our VIProfessional
assistant, will be glad to help you open your account.

Although we cannot grant you the $3,000 loan you requested
because you have not lived in Hildegard for two years, we will
be happy to consider your loan request when you have fulfilled
the residence requirement.

Please come in soon to open your VIProfessional checking
account.

Sincerely,

Ronald Wilshire

Ronald Wilshire
Loan Officer

bb

Figure 10–2   Refusal of request for loan

Avoid using form rejections. If the volume of work requires forms, develop
several versions. In this way, you may at least fit the refusal somewhat specifically to
the particular case.

In either an individually written or a form rejection, try to give the real reason
for the rejection. At least avoid a blanket statement. It leaves the receiver without a
basis for correcting the situation so that the next similar request may be honored.

Figure 10–1 provides an illustration of a letter rejecting a request for credit.
Analyze it to determine how well you think it exemplifies the suggestions made in
the preceding section.

Carson Insurance Company
P.O. BOX 52   TAYLOR, MISSISSIPPI 59993

December 1, 198X

Dear Applicant:

Thank you for contacting Carson Insurance Company for help
with your insurance needs. Carson offers a number of low-cost
health insurance plans to people who have no history of major
illness.

Because of your medical history, we are referring you to our
subsidiary, Golden Times Insurance. Golden Times insures
people with a history of major illness. Golden Times charges
only slightly higher rates than Carson and offers the same
excellent service. A Golden Times brochure and application
blank are enclosed.

We appreciate your contacting us, and we know that the people
at Golden Times Insurance look forward to hearing from you.

Sincerely,

Ann Faulkner

Ann Faulkner
Insurance Assistant

AF:cc

Enclosures

Figure 10–3   Rejection of request for insurance

Figure 10–2 is an example of a letter refusing to lend money to an applicant.
Though it takes a traditional form, it does identify the specific reasons for the denial.

Figure 10–3 illustrates a form rejection of an application for insurance.
Examine it for how well you would receive the news it bears.

Claim and adjustment

Sometimes letters deny writers' requests for claims and adjustments. They may deny
a request outright, or they may offer an alternative that brings the messages back into
the not-such-bad-news realm.

A letter may carry the news to a claimant that a warranty has expired. It may
also report that without proof of date of purchase or warranty registration, an item
cannot be repaired or replaced.

A message may notify a claimant that he or she did not meet the terms of an agreement or warranty. One of the most difficult of such situations involves the decision that someone misused or damaged a product, thus negating the provisions of a warranty.

Messages sometimes shift the responsibility of a problem to a third party. Some of the parties include the shipper, the retailer, the wholesaler, and the producer.

Sometimes, a message may tell a customer that he or she took an unjust discount on a payment. This event borders on the routine.

A letter may report that the firm cannot match a request exactly, but will be able to assume some responsibility or offer some mutually satisfactory solution. It may offer to repair an out-of-warranty item at cost or even less. It may offer a replacement for an irreparably damaged item at producer's or wholesaler's cost.

For all of your responses to requests for claims and adjustments, keep the treatment as unbiased as possible. Create a response specific to the circumstances. Do not bury the bad news so well that you mislead the receiver into thinking that you will do something that you will not do. Search for a way to offer some good news that will overshadow the bad—even to the extent of offering an alternative you would not legally or ethically have to offer.

Adopt a natural, helpful approach to bad-news messages. If you maintain such an approach, you will not create the feeling within the claimant that he or she is being given the "runaround."

For example, if you must transfer the claim to another for satisfaction, facilitate the transfer. One way to do so is to make the transfer yourself rather than telling the reader to do so. As an illustration, contrast these two treatments of the same request:

The matter is out of our hands. You will have to write to	Although we cannot correct the situation here, I have sent a copy of your letter to . . . . I asked for a quick and fair consideration of your request. A copy of my letter is enclosed.

Notice how the contrast between the two messages again makes the point that "less" is not always better. Avoid the curtness that can result from a summary dismissal of a problem. That problem is a very large one to the recipient of your message.

Also related to the importance of specificity and clarity is the reminder to avoid the form message for nonroutine claims and adjustments. Possibly nothing creates more frustration and anger in a receiver than to read words obviously not quite applicable to her or his case. With frustration and anger comes the loss of any hope for retaining goodwill.

You no doubt can call up negative feelings toward an organization which has treated your claim in an offhand manner. When you deal with people making a claim or calling for adjustment, relive your own feelings when you were the claimant in an exchange. Such situations call for a solid understanding and real sympathy.

Certainly, cost effectiveness sometimes dictates that you cannot offer any relief to the requestor—even to the extent that you may lose a customer. However, you can reduce that risk significantly through the investment of some time and thoughtfulness. Try to deal directly with the situation, instead of throwing it into a generic class with dozens of others. Use the facts of the specific case to appeal to logic, reason, and fair play. As a result, even the most frustrated of claimants may eventually say, "I don't like the results, but I can see why the decision must be this one."

A classical tale well summarizes the improper consideration of a claimant: A dissatisfied customer writes to a large company to make a complaint. He or she receives a nonspecific, but courteous response. Inadvertently still attached to the response is a hand-written note telling a word processor to "use paragraphs A, D, and J to answer this grouch."

You may find the grind of dealing with complainers difficult at times— especially when they often do make unfair attacks, charges, and claims. However, retreat into your knowledge of human relations, put yourself in the other's place, and adapt your thinking accordingly. If you do so, your success rate for gaining the desired acceptance of the company's action will increase significantly.

No list of "cookbook" methods or "recipes" can do nearly as much to aid you in developing bad-news messages as can the resolve to project yourself into the shoes of the receiver.

(896 words)
(test on page 325)

Figure 10–4 contains an example of the refusal of a claim. How do you think you would react if you received it?

Order

Many bad-news messages about orders refuse requests for credit. Others report that an item is out of stock or has never been carried. Still others report increases in prices, call for more information before completing the order, or indicate a delay.

If handled well, several of the listed situations fall more into the routine or even good-news categories than into the bad-news category.

Credit   Refusing to fill an order because the person does not qualify for a credit sale calls for great care. You want to make the sale, receive subsequent orders, and receive payment. Therefore, try to offer the potential customer some compromise. At least suggest the means by which he or she may qualify for credit. Such means might include the number or volume of prepaid orders that would lead to credit-customer status.

Out-of-stock items   Imagine that you do not have an ordered item in stock, but can offer a slightly higher-priced item for the same price. The receiver might well accept the potential bad news as good news. In such situations the seller invests a little money rather than running the risk of losing a satisfied customer.

If you do not carry an ordered item or anything like it, you must decide whether you should simply tell the ordering customer that fact, or suggest an alternative source.

If you suggest an alternative source, you divert some business away from your firm. However, if you do not, you may create ill will in the ordering person.

One intermediate method of dealing with such a situation is to suggest that the person may want to check the yellow pages in order to find a source for the goods.

ASKO BUSINESS MACHINES, INC.
446 East Broadway
Lawrence, Massachusetts 64198
(555) 212-9419

April 21, 198X

Mr. Albert VanDunn
Cranston Dormitory, Box 16
Minville University
Minville, Massachusetts 64190

Dear Mr. VanDunn:

Thank you for purchasing your Business Manager II typewriter
at Asko Business Machines and for your letter of April 16. We
take particular pleasure in serving students.

Asko provides a ninety-day warranty on all of the office
machines it sells. Berryhill Corporation, the manufacturer of
your Business Manager II, provides a five-year limited warranty
on its typewriters. Because you purchased your typewriter from
us over a year ago, you can take it to any Berryhill Repair
Center for service. We have enclosed a list of Berryhill Repair
Centers—one center is located in nearby Baileyville.

We are now carrying the Heavy-Duty Speedtype typewriter, a
perfect machine for students who must do a lot of heavy typing
work. We can offer you the Heavy-Duty Speedtype at a 15
percent student discount.

We would be happy to give you a complete demonstration at our
Lawrence store. Please come in soon—no appointment is
necessary.

Sincerely,

John Dade

John Dade
Manager

dd

Enclosure

Figure 10–4 Refusal of claim

Price increase   Suppose someone uses an outdated price list or catalog and sends
too little money. Simple courtesy and frankness can move the response to such a
message into the routine class. If the price increase is not substantial, you may simply
go ahead and ship the order and include the message about the increase as part of a
transmittal.

Added information   Similarly, if you need more information before you can ship an order, write a prompt, nonblaming, but straightforward message asking for it. In effect, then, you often shift the message into the routine classification, rather than the negative one.

Delay   When you must delay shipment or offer a substitute, try to convert the situation into a neutral one. However, sometimes you cannot supply a higher-priced substitute for the same price as the original item. Sometimes you do not even have a satisfactory substitute and simply must delay the shipment for a period of time. Of course, the longer the proposed delay, the more distressing it will be to the person placing the order.

Again picture the receiver and weigh which would be the greater loss for your company—the customer or some outright investment of funds. You may even reach the conclusion that you will contact another supplier and have someone there fill the order for your customer. You would, of course, contact your customer to explain what you have done. In addition, you would explain why you have done it, and assure her or him that you will try not to allow the circumstances to arise again. Your reader might be disarmed enough by your interest in her or his welfare to remain your customer.

Figure 10–5 illustrates a bad-news message associated with an order. Read it from the viewpoint of the person who placed the order. Do you think you would feel that you have been treated fairly? Would you remain a customer?

General request and inquiry

As you recall from Chapter 9, requests and inquiries relate to many topics other than credit, loans, claims, adjustments, and orders. Therefore, you often may have to write refusals for requests other than these just listed.

Invitation   Sometimes you may need to decline an invitation to attend an event, and that fact amounts to bad news for the person inviting you. When you know that it will have a negative effect, do not treat your response routinely. Encode it as carefully as you would any bad-news message. Give your reasons sensitively, but as honestly as diplomacy allows.

Speaking date   If you must refuse to be the speaker for a group, develop your message just as conscientiously as you would if you were denying credit to a requestor. In essence, you are turning down a request from each member of the potential audience.

As you do when you decline an invitation to an event, encode the turndown of a speaking engagement in a sensitive, but forthright manner. Try to suggest an alternative date for yourself, in addition to the name of another speaker for the event. Express sincere appreciation for the respect accorded you by their request.

Loan   When you cannot give or lend materials requested by someone, consider the impact on the requestor. Explain why you cannot make the loan, and try to offer an alternative.

Service   Likewise, if you cannot perform a requested service, courteously describe the reasons you must decline. Try to offer another reasonable avenue through which the requestor may obtain the service.

INTERNATIONAL
TELEVISION
CORPORATION   43 Oak Road, Mason, New York 32907

June 14, 198X

Ms. Irene Lawson
ZEX Property Management, Inc.
1515 Arbor Boulevard
Rilling, Arkansas 96411

Dear Ms. Lawson:

Your order for 100 dust screens for your ITC Color XI units was
received today. We are pleased to know that the television sets have served
you well, so well that you wish to keep them in your motels for several more
years. Our ITC Color XI sets are built to last a lifetime.

Because of the pressures of inflation, the International Television
Corporation no longer produces most of its television accessories, including
the dust screens you ordered. Of course, ITC still manufactures a complete
line of quality television repair parts, all of which will be available to you at
a discount for the life of your ITC television sets. Our new parts catalogue is
enclosed.

We feel sure that a number of custom plastics shops would be glad to fill
your large order for dust screens. We called one shop in your area, Katz
Plastics in Flame, Arkansas. The shop's owner, Joanne Katz, stated that she
could produce 100 dust screens in about four weeks. She was unable to give
us a price at the time, but assured us that her prices are competitive.

Please let us know if we can place the order for you at Katz Plastics or
another shop. We would be most happy to handle all of the details. Please
send us your request in the enclosed postpaid envelope.

Sincerely,

Mary Santino

Mary Santino
Service Representative

ms/ee

Enclosures

Figure 10–5   Rejection of order because of inability to fill

For example, suppose your firm owns a film that someone would like to borrow to show to an organization. If you cannot lend it, you might suggest that the requestor rent it at low cost from a university media center that you know owns a print of the film.

Inquiry   Suppose you receive an inquiry about a situation that you cannot handle. Whether the inquiry comes from someone of little or great importance, answer promptly and state clearly the reasons for not being able to answer the questions. If possible, suggest another channel through which the inquirer may obtain the desired answers.

Handle with care any other kinds of general requests and inquiries that you must refuse in one way or another. Understand and anticipate the writer's disappointment when you must say "No" to something he or she wants. Write your message of response with the image of the disappointed receiver in mind.

Review Figure 10–6 as an example of a refusal of a request. Observe how the letter includes an alternative course of action for the original writer.

Chapter 9 includes other kinds of request and inquiry letters that may lead to bad-news responses.

Claims and Adjustments

As established, refusals of requests for claims or adjustments often are difficult to write. So, in fact, are the messages making the original claim or requesting the adjustment. Indeed, the claim or adjustment message is itself a bad-news message to the businessperson who is the recipient.

As illustrated in Chapter 9, many claim and adjustment letters are routine. Figure 9–9 exemplifies that routineness.

On the other hand, messages sometimes relate to claims or adjustments when the amount of money involved is large, or someone's rights are in question, or a cloud hangs over the situation. Approach such transactions with the same delicacy as you do any other bad-news circumstance.

Analyze how you expect the news to affect the receiver. Establish your purposes in terms of the action you desire from the receiver. Use all of the strategy, tact, courtesy, logic, and psychology you can bring to bear.

Of course, such a claim or adjustment letter not only carries bad news to the receiver, but often requires the use of some persuasive processes by you. Therefore, when you read Chapter 11 on persuasive messages, think of how the processes apply to the claim and adjustment situations.

Also review Figure 10–7 to observe how the writer tried to maintain a sensitive balance between communicating bad news and trying to persuade the receiver to take the desired action.

Unfavorable Recommendations

Letters about applicants for jobs sometimes include unfavorable information. Most writers tend to select only the positive qualities of the applicants. However, they sometimes feel ethically bound to describe some negative ones.

BARSTOW AND KEEDY MANUFACTURING, INC.
391 Henderson Avenue
Ivell, Wisconsin 39421
(555) 624-2462

March 1, 198X

Mr. Jerome Faxlin
Korsika Chamber of Commerce
P.O. Box 899
Korsika, Wisconsin 39426

Dear Mr. Faxlin:

The Industry Speaks to Korsika workshop series you are planning sounds most interesting. Your idea to include both managers and workers on each panel is brilliant! Workers' views of industry conditions are so often overlooked.

Every year I make a number of trips to our office in Atlanta, Georgia, and I am scheduled to attend two very important meetings there during the week of your workshops. Luckily, Elizabeth McPhree, Barstow and Keedy's top marketing specialist, is free to serve as a panelist on Monday, June 6, or Tuesday, June 7. As you may know, she is a well-known speaker. She also is the co-author of Beyond Selling: Marketing Strategies for Executives, a textbook used in many graduate schools of management. Ms. McPhree shares my enthusiasm about your fine program.

I am honored that you asked me to participate in your workshop series, because I am confident that the series will be a smashing success. Please let us know if you would like Ms. McPhree to serve as a panelist. We would be glad to answer any of your questions.

Again, thank you for giving me the opportunity to be a part of the Industry Speaks to Korsika workshop series. I hope that I can participate in one of your future programs.

Sincerely,

Marvin Rosen

Marvin Rosen
Marketing Manager

ff

Figure 10–6   Refusal of request to participate in workshop

R C J SECURITY ALARM, INC.
6298 Perman Street
Jenray, Alabama 38974
(555) 629-9268

June 3, 198X

Ms. Beatrice Albert
Gravely Security Suppliers, Inc.
Route 2, Box 84R
Dorlin, Minnesota 22215

Dear Ms. Albert:

Thank you for responding so promptly to our last order for 40
Deluxe Protection II alarm systems. All of the units arrived last
week, and we have already installed several of them in area
businesses and homes.

Last year we ordered nine Economy Protection I alarm systems
from you. We installed one in our own home and the rest in
homes in our neighborhood. Recently, burglars robbed three of
our neighbors, all of whom have Economy Protection I systems.
Unfortunately, not one of the systems functioned during the
burglaries. We checked our own system and found that it does
not function either.

Because we are extremely concerned, we spent many hours
inspecting the Economy Protection I alarm systems, but we
were unable to locate the problem. However, because we
installed over a thousand other alarm systems in the last five
years and we received no reports of malfunctions, we must
conclude that our installation method is not the problem. Thus,
we fear that the Economy Protection I alarm systems themselves are at fault.

Because we and our neighbors are eager to protect our homes,
please send nine Deluxe Protection I systems as soon as
possible to replace the faulty Economy Protection I systems. We
will then install the replacement systems at no charge to our

Figure 10–7   Claim

In such cases, the bad news is negative toward the applicant rather than toward
the receiver of the letter itself. However, even the receiver often may find such news
disagreeable. He or she may be disappointed about a candidate thought to be a
strong applicant for the position.

The applicant may at one time or another see a letter of recommendation, even
if the requestor assures confidentiality of the exchange. Therefore, recall the
discussion in Chapter 9 on confidentiality.

Ms. Beatrice Albert   2   June 3, 198X

somewhat distressed customers. Of course, we know that you
will provide the new alarm systems at no cost to us, and we
would be glad to send back the faulty systems if you will cover
the postage charges. We realize that you would like to have a
chance to inspect one of the faulty systems so that you can
avoid problems with the Economy Protection I systems you
produce in the future.

Again, we have had no trouble with the other alarm systems
you have sent to us. We expect to be your customer for years to
come because you provide us with such excellent service.

Sincerely,

Lucinda Miller

Lucinda Miller
Co-Owner

gg

Figure 10–7 (continued)

Both for your own protection and that of the applicant, then, be absolutely sure
of the foundation for your negative comments before you write them. When you do
write them, make them factual. Introduce well-documented statistics to describe a
poor attendance record or poor productivity. Cite brief examples of clashes with
other employees or customers, and state the frequency with which they occurred.
Also cite brief examples of insubordination or uncooperativeness—again reporting
the frequency of occurrence.

LOGAN NILO SAVINGS & LOAN
One Streil Plaza
Harbor Pond, Maine 62419

July 21, 198X

Mr. Jackson Riley
C & R Savings and Loan
946 Stewart Road
Perry, Missouri 41986

Dear Mr. Riley:

It is a pleasure to help you evaluate Mr. Dan Smith's suitability for a
position at C & R Savings and Loan. I both trained and supervised Mr. Smith
during the time that he worked at Logan Nilo.

Mr. Smith worked as an assistant loan officer at Logan Nilo for three years.
We hired him immediately after he was graduated from Harbor Pond
Community College with a two-year degree in accounting. He was very eager
to learn about the savings and loan business, and several customers told me
that he was one of our most courteous employees. Mr. Smith did a fine job of
working with his customers.

Mr. Smith missed 32 days of work in 1977, 41 days in 1978, and 36 days in
1979. Most of his absences were because of illness, and each absence lasted
one or two days. On ten occasions Mr. Smith failed to call us to say that he
would be unable to come to work.

Mr. Smith also made frequent errors in processing loan applications.
Though he seemed to try to avoid mistakes, little of his work was free of
errors. In fact, I began reviewing all of Mr. Smith's work in order to correct
his errors. He was quite willing to discuss his mistakes so that he could
learn to overcome them.

Because of the attendance and the work problems I just mentioned, we
asked Mr. Smith to leave Logan Nilo on November 16, 1979. We were
somewhat reluctant to ask him to leave because he had developed rapport
with his customers. He was also eager to learn, loyal to me and his
co-workers, and honest. Mr. Smith had a wonderful sense of humor, and was
a very positive influence on office morale. I do believe that he has the ability
to become a good loan officer if he can cultivate good health and learn to
concentrate on his work.

Hopefully, the information I provided will be of some help to you. Please call
or write me if you have further questions.

Sincerely,

Ellen Warrick

Ellen Warrick
Loan Manager

EW:hh

Figure 10–8   Unfavorable recommendation

Do not just report vague references to high absenteeism or low productivity. Do not just write, "S/he does not get along well with others," or "S/he shows no respect for her/his superiors."

Just as for any bad-news message, wedge the negative aspects between some good ones. Assure the reader that the judgments are yours from the context of your observance. Do not leave the impression that you are the all-knowing judge and that the weaknesses you describe are true for the person in every context and for all time.

Read the letter in Figure 10–8 to determine whether you think it communicates some bad news relatively well. How would you react if you received it? Because so many writers of recommendation letters say only glowing things about a job applicant, would you decide that this applicant must be poor, indeed?

Unsolicited News of a Negative Nature

Now and again you will have to initiate a bad-news message. You may have to:

1. Write policy holders to notify them of an increase in premiums or a decrease in coverage
2. Write to other types of customers to inform them of rate or price increases or decreases in service
3. Remove a customer from the approved credit list
4. Notify employees that you will have to lower wages or cut benefits
5. Notify an employee that he or she will be laid off
6. Tell your clients that a company in which they invested is defunct

You can no doubt think of many other examples of the kind of bad news initiated in unsolicited messages. However, they all have one thing in common—the need to compose the messages with sensitivity toward the feelings of the other.

Even though you are not refusing a direct request, you nonetheless deal with the psychology pertinent to unfavorable responses to requests. In fact, an unsolicited message that contains bad news may be more devastating to the receiver than a solicited message containing bad news. After all, a requestor knows that a message is forthcoming and thus that the news contained in it may be bad. The recipient of the bad news in an unsolicited message often has no warning.

To write the unsolicited message carrying bad news, then, apply all of the general and special guidelines and principles particularly carefully. Protect the receiver as much as you can, but do not hedge about the truth.

Consider the message in Figure 10–9 as an illustration of the unsolicited message of bad news. Put yourself in the place of the receiver, and evaluate the success of the letter in accomplishing its obvious objective.

SUMMARY

Take great care in writing messages that carry negative news. The best developmental styles for them are the inductive, ascending-rank, and chronological plans. The weakest styles are the deductive and descending-rank plans.

CARLETON ELECTRIC COMPANY
P.O. Box 145, Carleton, Indiana 14987

August 1, 198X

Dear Customer:

During the past two years, the Carleton Electric Company has experienced rapidly increasing labor and equipment costs. We at Carleton tried to make a number of internal changes so that you, our valued customer, would not have to shoulder the burden.

As you know, we were successful: Your rates did not increase for two full years. While you were paying more and more for other products and services, you did not pay one penny more for electricity supplied by the Carleton Electric Company.

After conducting a thorough review of our operations, we find that we can no longer absorb all of our still-increasing costs. We have, however, found a way to hold the required rate increase to only 5.5 percent. And 5.5 percent is much less than the 15 percent annual inflation rate. The typical consumer will pay only $2 a month more for service.

The new rates will take effect on August 1, and you can count on no additional rate increases for at least one year after that. We have again succeeded in shouldering a great deal of the inflation burden ourselves.

Please call or write if you have any questions or comments concerning the rate change. Your views are very important to us.

You can continue to rely on us to fight inflation for you.

Sincerely,

Emory L. Thaxer

Emory L. Thaxer
Customer Relations Manager

rr

Figure 10–9   Unsolicited letter containing bad news

These are the four major categories of bad-news messages: (1) refusal, (2) claim and adjustment, (3) unfavorable recommendation, and (4) unsolicited news of a negative nature.

Refusal messages deny credit, refuse requests for claims and adjustments, refuse to fill an order, or deny a general request or inquiry. If possible, offer some sort of positive alternative in refusal messages.

Claim and adjustment messages are messages that make the claim or request the adjustment. Try to maintain a sensitive balance between communicating the bad news and trying to persuade the receiver to take the desired action.

Unfavorable recommendation letters are among those that are the most difficult to write. Always be sure of the foundation of negative comments before writing them. Make your comments statements of facts, and do not make vague references to unsatisfactory performance. Also try to include the strengths of the employee. Few people are all bad or all good.

You may have to initiate bad-news messages at times. Such *unsolicited messages* may inform customers that they can no longer use their credit cards, or they may notify employees that their wages and benefits will be cut. Again, offset bad news with a positive alternative or some good news.

Practice

1. This is an unsatisfactory bad-news letter. Correct it and explain the reasoning behind your changes. Concentrate on the content, not the format of the letter.

FIRST BIG BANK
1432 East Creswell Avenue
Leona, Oregon 16154

August 1, 198X

Mr. I. I. Warren
1069 Elm Street
Wixler, Oregon 16165

Dear Mr. Warren:

We cannot give you the $2,000 loan you requested because you have a less-than-satisfactory credit record. We also do not like to give loans to elementary school teachers because they do not make a good salary and they are unemployed in the summer.

We will allow you to keep your checking account at our bank, though.

Sincerely,

F. I. Mouth

F. I. Mouth
Loan Officer

---

2. This is an unsatisfactory bad-news letter. Correct it and explain the reasoning behind your changes. Concentrate on the content, not the format of the letter.

EXCELO COMPANY
17 MOX ROAD
WINSOME, NEVADA 66663

March 18, 198X

Ramona Sleeve
Arbo Furniture, Inc.
115 North Booth Street
Wales, Vermont 88883

Dear Ms. Sleeve:

The six file cabinets we ordered from you are unsatisfactory.
They arrived all dented and scratched, and none of the drawers
works correctly. We have used them for only one year.

Pick them up immediately and send a refund.

Sincerely,

T.O.O.Late

T. O. O. Late
Facilities Manager

---

3. This is an unsatisfactory bad-news letter. Correct it and explain the reasoning behind your changes. Concentrate on the content, not the format of the letter.

DAVIS AND LEVENSON CONSULTING GROUP
99 East Oak Lane
Edmonds, Arkansas 33364
(555) 666–1390

April 1, 198X

Ms. Elizabeth Geil
Geil Systems Management, Inc.
130 Allen Avenue
Edmonds, Arkansas 33364

Dear Ms. Geil:

I am pleased to respond to your request for an evaluation of
Frank Smith's performance at Davis and Levenson. Unfortunately, Smith was one of our worst employees. He was late
sometimes and I heard that he did not work very hard. It was
said that he had a bad attitude. He may have some troubles at
home. I just cannot bring myself to recommend him for a job.

I hope that I have been of assistance.

Sincerely,

N.V.Nice

N. V. Nice
Personnel Director

---

4. This is an unsatisfactory bad-news letter. Correct it and explain the reasoning behind your changes. Concentrate on the content, not the format of the letter.

GRAHAM CABLE TELEVISION, INC.
1149 North Road
Charlestown, California 41963
(555) 439–6629

November 9, 198X

Dear Cable Customer:

We are raising your monthly residential cable fee by $10.50. You now should pay Graham Cable Television, Inc., $22.50 every month. We are forced to raise the residential rate because we are losing money on all of you residential customers. You ask us to make too many service calls.

Make your payments on time, please.

Sincerely,

N. O. Tact

N. O. Tact
Payments Clerk

---

5. Meet with your group. Discuss and correct these poorly worded sentences that were written for bad-news messages. Have one of your group members read the improved sentences to the rest of the class.
   a. You always make your payments late, so we are lowering your credit limit to $100.
   b. Your request came much too late for us to do anything about it.
   c. You are a bad insurance risk, thus we must refuse your request for the Golden Sixties coverage.
   d. Your salespeople lied to me.
   e. We won't fill your order until you make a big payment.
   f. However, you can apply for a loan when you start making a good salary.
   g. She was not a decent employee.
   h. Please forgive us for what we had to do, and we hope you will use cash to buy things from us from now on.
   i. Now don't be too mad at us.
   j. We have bad news for you.
   k. Now don't get upset, but you are in grave danger of losing your house.
   l. Why do you always make late payments?
6. You did not choose to hire the receiver of your letter for the production manager position for which he interviewed. Write a letter informing him of your decision. Supply any needed information.
7. You cannot fill the receiver's order because she has not paid for her last order. You also want her to pay what she owes. Write the letter, supplying any needed information.
8. You must refuse an advertisement because it does not meet your magazine's standards. You feel that the advertisement is both sexist and racist. Write the letter, supplying any needed information.
9. You will not grant a requested interview because you do not approve of the general

policies and content of the publication the interviewer represents. Write the letter, supplying any needed information.

10. Write a letter in response to T. O. O. Late's message in Number 2. Supply additional information as needed.

11. P. R. Risk has written to you to ask for credit at your clothing store. You investigate and learn that P. R. Risk:

    Is new in town
    Has no credit record elsewhere
    Has a job that pays $10,000 a year
    Rents an apartment
    Has debts of $2,000
    Is a single parent of one two-year-old child
    Has a high-school eduction
    Is 23 years of age

    On the basis of the information, you decide you cannot extend the credit. Write the letter of refusal. Give some reasons, and offer some suggestion about how Risk might become eligible.

12. You must tell your 250 employees that economic conditions are forcing you to close your plant for an indefinite period beginning October 1 (one month from now). You have begun to make some contacts that may allow you to start production again the first of the year, but nothing is firm at this point. You do plan to bring in an employment-counseling team the last week of this month. The team will be available to help the employees conduct job searches. Write a general letter to the employees, supplying additional information as needed.

13. Respond to the order letter in Figure 9–2 (page 260) with the news that you will not be able to ship the metal-turning lathe and cabinet until March 15. The only lathe you can ship to arrive by February 28 lists at $500 more. However, it has added features enough to warrant the added expense. Your supervisor says that you can cut 10 percent off of that $500—in addition to giving the person the Preferred Customer discount.

14. Use your dictionary and thesaurus to create meanings for these words. Use the words when you think, write, and speak so that you feel comfortable using them.

a. Buffer		**h.** Hackneyed	
b. Commendable		**i.** Insincere	
c. Contrivance		**j.** Irreparable	
d. Empathy		**k.** Pervade	
e. Duality		**l.** Rapport	
f. Finesse		**m.** Subservient	
g. Gracious		**n.** Tact	

15. Take and score Self-Test 24 over the excerpt about claim and adjustment.

Self-Test 24
Excerpt About Claim and Adjustment

A. Recall (33 points each). For each multiple-choice question, select the most appropriate answer.

1. Which of these is *not* a good way to soften a letter that denies the writer's request for a claim or adjustment?

   a. Offer an alternative.

   b. If possible, shift the responsibility to a third party (only if it is the third party's responsibility).

   c. Offer a compromise.

   d. Try to prove that the writer was completely at fault.

   e. Offer to send a replacement.

Self-Test 24 — (continued)

2. Which of these statements concerning denying claim and adjustment requests is *not* correct?
   a. Do not bury the bad news so well that you mislead the receiver into thinking that you will do something that you do not plan to do.
   b. Try to be honest so that the receiver does not feel that he is or she is being given the "runaround."
   c. Try to use a form letter for nonroutine claims and adjustments.
   d. Try to retain the receiver's goodwill.
   e. Avoid being curt.

B. Inference (34 points). For the multiple-choice question, select the most accurate answer.

   Which of the following does not constitute a courteous denial of a claim or request for adjustment?
   a. Although we cannot repair your watch, we have enclosed a list of excellent discount repair services.
   b. We know that doing without your radio has been an inconvenience, but because your warranty has run out, we cannot repair or replace it. Because you are a valued customer, we will send you an extremely helpful "do-it-yourself" repair kit.
   c. We find no record of your April 12 payment. Because it is possible that we have overlooked it, please send a copy of your cancelled check to us in the enclosed postpaid envelope.
   d. Because your insurance does not cover dental work, we cannot send you a check at this time. For only an additional $6.50 a month, however, we can cover *all* of your dental bills.
   e. All of our products are covered by a 90-day warranty. You have owned your toaster for over a year and should know that we are no longer responsible for any problems. You must bear the repair expense.

Solution to Self-Test 24
Excerpt About Claim and Adjustment

A. Recall (33 points each)   B. Inference (34 points)
   1. d   **2.** c   e

16. Take and score Self-Test 25 over Chapter 10.

Self-Test 25
Chapter 10

A. Recall (25 points each). For each multiple-choice question, select the most accurate answer.

   1. The best developmental patterns for bad-news messages are:
      a. Inductive, ascending-rank, and chronological
      b. Deductive, inductive, and spatial
      c. Chronological, analytical, and direct
      d. Inductive, chronological, and descending-rank
      e. Deductive, indirect, and analytical

2. When you write an unfavorable recommendation, try to:
   a. Be vague about the employee's drawbacks.
   b. List as many of the employees' weaknesses as possible.
   c. Be specific about the employee's weaknesses and try also to bring out her or his strengths.
   d. Convince the receiver not to hire the employee.
   e. Make the employee look better than he or she is so that you can get rid of her or him.

3. Which of these is *not* appropriate for bad-news messages?
   a. Sentences containing both an independent and a dependent clause (complex sentence)
   b. A blanket form that covers the rejection of all claims
   c. Buffer opening
   d. Positive sandwich
   e. Empathy

B. Inference (25 points). For the multiple-choice question, select the most accurate answer.

Which of these statements is true?
   a. Bad-news messages employ significantly different techniques and principles than neutral and good-news letters.
   b. A person who has sent an article to a factory for repair assumes that no news is good news.
   c. When someone makes unfair demands, your responsibility for making a positive response remains the same as for less-demanding people.
   d. Frankness has no place in bad-news messages.
   e. The best way to establish a "you" attitude is to use the word "you" several times during the message.

Solution to Self-Test 25
Chapter 10

A. Recall (25 points each)   B. Inference (25 points)

   1. a   3. b   c
   2. c

11

Writing
Persuasive Messages

In many ways every message you prepare is a persuasive message. Whatever other objectives may be involved, you usually at least want to persuade the receiver of your abilities and personal qualities.

GENERAL CONCEPTS

For this coverage, though, consider persuasive messages to be those developed to try to get people to take some action beyond the routine or to accept a different idea or belief. The action/acceptance may involve the receiver's expending large amounts of energy, time, or money for potentially great rewards. It may involve only slight expenditures, but ask the reader to act or accept without apparent benefits. Some actions or acceptances even require the receiver to expend energy, time, or money that may lead not to profits, but to risks or painful results.

Action/Acceptance

Consider how persuasive messages try to get someone to:

Purchase goods or services	Do some kind of favor
Adopt a plan for an operational change	Donate to a foundation
	Pay a bill
Appear before a group	Hire you
Accept a proposed research project	Change her or his mind about an
Attend some function	issue

Though this book uses the traditional word "persuasive," the actual spotlight is upon the desired action/acceptance, not upon the persuasion itself.

Needs of Receiver

The successful persuasive message somehow establishes benefits to the receiver. The identified benefits must be strong enough to overcome inertia or outright resistance. Thus, the focus of activity falls into the realm of defining purposes and understanding the receiver.

Ethics

Persuasion involves using knowledge about a receiver in order to obtain goals. Therefore, the topic of ethics must again enter into the discussion.

Some people equate persuasion with manipulation, and thus with unethical activity. They do so particularly when the activity leads to profit.

Persuasive techniques are used by virtually everyone in every walk of life. Children try to convince other children to do what they want. So do politicians, elected government officials, and attorneys. So do teachers, researchers, ministers, newspaper editors, writers, and representatives of not-for-profit organizations.

A great many processes may be used by unethical people. However, the use of certain techniques by unethical people does not make the techniques themselves unethical. Ethics reside in people's motives, not in the processes they employ.

Do raise questions about business and persuasion, though. Do you think that advertising creates demand? If you do, do you think creation of "artificial" demand is unethical? Do you think the use of subliminal suggestion in selling is ethical?

Do you favor government action restraining advertising? Should the government prohibit or restrict advertisements for sales of "junk" foods? refined sugar? saccharin? tobacco? alcoholic beverages and other drugs? personal products? pornographic literature? adult book stores? X-rated movies? massage parlors? legal services? medical and dental services? eyeglasses? Does government action itself represent unethical interference into business and into the professional and private lives of people?

As you raise such questions about the Madison-Avenue approach to persuasion, ask the same questions about the use of persuasion in other arenas:

1. Should charismatic speakers be allowed to persuade people to accept certain beliefs?
2. Should not-for-profit organizations be permitted to approach people to contribute to any and all causes?
3. Should active groups be allowed to demonstrate for or against such things as war, nuclear power, and ecology?
4. Should investigative reporters be allowed to write persuasive pieces—particularly if they do not reveal their sources?
5. Should laws be passed to prohibit the activities of organizations that espouse beliefs counter to those that prevail in a nation? (Should the Nazi Party, the Communist Party, and the Ku Klux Klan be allowed to continue to use persuasion to bring members into their folds?)
6. Should consumer advocates be allowed to persuade legislators to enact protective laws?

Consider these questions to be deliberate reminders about the hopelessness of trying to restrict the use of persuasive techniques to the "right" groups or "proper" topics. The problem is that the definitions of "right" and "proper" vary from person to person and from group to group. No amount of legislation will change that fact.

For business communication, then, consider ethics as you create persuasive messages, and use rational, critical approaches as you receive them.

PRINCIPLES

To develop some principles for persuasive messages, recall the communication guidelines and the writing suggestions in Chapter 7. The concerns with purposes, participants, environment, channel, interference, messages, feedback, and evaluation relate extraordinarily well to persuasion. Many of the examples in previous chapters involve persuasion to a significant extent.

At this point, though, begin to expand the discussion by reviewing three of the components: purposes, receiver, and message.

Purposes

For any situation involving persuasive techniques, establish the objectives precisely. In addition, carefully establish the criteria for evaluating success in attaining them.

Also try to understand the receiver's purposes as completely as possible. Understanding them involves understanding the receiver.

Receiver

To understand receivers, look into human wants, needs, and motivations. Once you understand why people behave as they do, you stand a better chance of matching appeals to motives within them. People usually choose to do what will help them attain *their* goals, not yours.

For example, no debtor really *wants* to pay a past-due bill. However, a straightforward statement of plans for legal action may make its own appeal. Though most debtors do not want to pay, neither do they want to be engaged in illegal acts or even receive social disapproval.

To help in selecting appropriate persuasive approaches, recall the general human needs and motivations covered in previous chapters—Chapters 2, 4, and 5 in particular. Recognize that values, beliefs, attitudes, and life styles change through time. Appeals that worked 30, 20, or even 10 years ago will not necessarily work today.

The review of types of persuasive messages in subsequent sections features some of the relevant human motivators. It also helps to match appeals to those human factors.

Message

At the writing stage of developing a persuasive message, once again select, draft, revise, and transmit messages carefully. Select messages and appeals to match the motives identified during the preliminary stages. Draft messages using whatever method works best for you. Revise and transmit messages to meet the standards established for the chosen channel.

Whatever method you use to draft messages, organization eventually takes place. For persuasive messages, the developmental plan and basic parts of the message become particularly important.

Developmental plans

Persuasive messages lend themselves to inductive, ascending-rank, chronological, deductive, and descending-rank plans for development.

If a persuasive message also includes some bad news, you generally will choose one of the three indirect methods—inductive, ascending-rank, and chronological. Many collection letters fall into this pattern.

Sales and job-application messages, however, fall quite naturally into the direct patterns—the deductive and descending-rank plans.

Parts

The basic persuasive outline recognizes that every message has at least three major parts—a beginning, a middle, and an end. For persuasive messages, however, the plan usually involves four parts. One plan places the persuasive message into the AIDA pattern—attention, interest, desire, and action. A similar plan uses AICA—attention, interest, conviction, and action. A third variation involves the APCA formula—attention, perception, comprehension, action/acceptance.

Whether you use one of these outlines or an entirely different one, the concepts associated with those parts are important. Consider them in a form that combines the three outlines—the expanded APCA formula:

1. Attention
2. Perception/Interest
3. Comprehension/Conviction/Desire
4. Action/Acceptance

Attention   The opening of any message should gain the receiver's attention and introduce the topic. However, persuasive messages—particularly sales messages—virtually demand attention-getting openings. Unless the opening captures the reader's attention, he or she may never read past it to the body and the stimulus to action—unless the reading is required. Even for required reading, attention-getting devices greatly increase interest and concentration.

The best way to gain attention is to encode some detail that shows relevance to the reader's life or that whets the reader's appetite for more information. If you can sweep the reader into the message by appealing to human needs, you have a chance to hold her or him for the remainder of the message.

Consider several attention-getting devices:

1. Use *attractive nonverbal symbols*: paper, color, letterhead, format, layout, graphs, pictures, drawings, size and kind of type, a dash of handwriting, clean type, even margins, short messages.
2. Open with a *natural conversational lead-in* in addition to or instead of a salutation: "Yes, I agree that . . . ." "You're so right—we should . . . ." "Hi, Dick; how's it going?" "Hello. My name is Y. R. Self. As a representative of Spittinimage Portraits, Inc., I enjoy telling . . . ."
3. Tie your message to a *current topic*: "The gasoline shortage affects all of us."

4. Use a *striking subject line*: "Money Market Certificates: Exciting Alternatives to Traditional Savings Accounts"
5. Raise a *question*: "Have you ever wished you could have your own personalized stationery?"
6. Insert *the receiver's name*: "Take a look at the enclosed brochure, Ms. Tate; you will like what you see."
7. Set a *scene*: "Transport yourself to a quiet beach . . . the sound of waves as they caress the shore . . . the stirring of a cool breeze through the palms . . ."
8. Use *action words*: "Strike a blow for financial security." "Reach out . . . ." "Control your own . . . ." "Take the plunge."
9. Make a *dramatic or unexpected statement*: "You may be one of the millions who have high blood pressure and do not know it."
10. Spotlight a *single, dramatic key word*: "Energy" "Growth" "Security" "Hunger" "Crime" "Profit."
11. Use *common courtesies*: "Thanks! I appreciate your thoughtfulness." "Please, for the sake of our children, read on."
12. Enclose something in *quotation marks*: " 'That's the best cake I've ever eaten.' So said Alma Goren of Rooneyville, West Virginia." " 'To err is human'—and are we ever human!"

Avoid artificiality—too much of the trite, too much hype, too many buzz words. On the other hand, rise above the drab and the colorless.

Some people do not consider the "Please" and "Thank you" approaches in the preceding list to be attention-getting devices at all. They suggest that through extensive usage, even they have become trite. Others still consider them quite useful and logical openings, particularly for low-key persuasive messages.

Choose attention-catching techniques to fit the circumstances of the transaction.

For example, when you write to persuade the receiver to be a speaker at a formal occasion, you usually do not begin with a flambuoyant attention-getting sentence. However, when you write to persuade someone to buy a product or service, you often do.

Likewise, when you write a first-stage collection letter, you ordinarily use the attention position for a buffer rather than for anything very striking. Yet, when you write a final-stage collection letter, you well may use a startling opening message to gain the reader's attention.

Perception/interest   The second stage of the evolving message attempts to assure that the reader perceives or becomes interested in the subject of the message. Though the attention phase introduces the subject, it usually is not sufficient to develop full perception or interest. The attention phase should hold readers long enough to move them into the perception/interest section—words designed to clarify the topic and engage the reader in it.

The perception/interest phase spins directly out of the attention phase. To illustrate, consider some words that could follow a few of the examples of attention-getting words in the preceding section:

1. Add some words to complete the first conversational lead-in in Number 2: "Yes, I agree that the date for our conference needs to be set now." The reader slips

quickly from attention into perception and, hopefully, interest. The perception/ interest is that the topic of this message is an important conference date.

2. From Number 3, observe how a second sentence expands an attention-getting reference into a perception/interest reference: "The gasoline shortage affects us all. But if you change to a Vechette, you'll average close to 40 miles a gallon." The reader would immediately switch from thoughts about the gasoline shortage in general to a consideration of a Vechette as a gasoline-saving automobile.

3. Even the example in Number 7 could be followed by words establishing clearer topics. As you review a few variants, think how critical the perception/interest stage is for moving the message forward: "Hawaii awaits you." "Visit the golden shores of Miami Beach." "How about following the annual conference of the Financial Analysts Association with a week end at Malibu?"

4. Consider how the addition of a few words brings perception/interest to the first attention-getter listed in Number 8: "Strike a blow for financial security. Purchase a life insurance policy from Drupential."

5. Add this sentence to Number 9: "For only $19.95 you can keep a regular check on this serious health problem by owning a Disys brand anneroid blood pressure monitor and stethoscope."

The keystone to a successful perception/interest phase, then, is the specification of the subject. It should be so well done that the attention gained in the opening leads to an interest that will continue into the heart of the message.

Comprehension/conviction/desire   The comprehension/conviction/desire segment spirals the reader beyond mere perception and interest into a personal grasp and understanding of the whole subject. Both the attention and perception/interest elements may take only one or two sentences. However, full development of the comprehension/conviction/desire phase usually requires several sentences, if not paragraphs or sections. Consider the attention stage to be the introduction, the comprehension/conviction/desire stage to be the body, and the perception/interest stage to bridge the two while playing a part in both.

The crux of the writing process, then, lies at the comprehension/conviction/ desire stage. Therefore, as suggested in Chapter 7, many writers develop the body before developing the other parts.

Action/acceptance   Use the final section of a persuasive message to call for action, or at least acceptance.

The action-setting paragraph(s) (usually just one) clearly define the desired actions. To do so, they identify all of the appropriate elements of the who, what, when, where, how, and why characteristics of the actions.

Examples of action closings include:

• Please ship the materials to arrive by June 9.
• The report should be on my desk by September 19.
• If you cannot attend the meeting on the 30th, please let me know by the 25th.
• Would you please send your reply by August 22. I need the information for a project due the end of the month.
• I shall appreciate your sending the brochure within the next week.
• Make your payment by October 19 if you want to avoid legal action.
• Order now. This special offer expires on April 1.

Even for persuasive messages, however, writers sometimes have to be satisfied with indirect-action or acceptance goals. Therefore, the final section of a message may not always be a call to some concrete action.

For instance, assume you write a letter trying to persuade 286 colleagues to vote for you for an office in your credit union. Though you can observe the collective results, you rarely will know exactly which ones voted for you or against you, or did not vote at all. Even less observable results would occur if you wrote to thousands of employees trying to persuade them to present a positive image of the company in their private lives.

Whichever the case—call to action or call to acceptance—wrap up the message so that the reader knows what the desired response is. Let her or him know what feedback you want, and write in a way that motivates the reader to give you that feedback.

Many varieties and levels of directness of action/acceptance words correspond with the types of messages involved. Yet, all messages should conclude with some clear answer to the question, "So what?"

These suggestions summarize the features of the action/acceptance portion of your message:

1. Tie the action/acceptance to your own and the reader's purposes.
2. End the message with the clearest possible call to action/acceptance.
3. Motivate the reader to complete the desired action/acceptance.
4. Make the action/acceptance as easy as possible by including stamped envelopes, giving telephone numbers and addresses, and offering to do something in return.

TYPES OF PERSUASIVE MESSAGES

The principles for effective content in persuasive messages obviously overlap with those for other types. Many messages in the persuasive-request category fit the neutral classification relatively well. Collection messages include both persuasion and bad news. Even good-news messages sometimes involve some persuasion.

Though this chapter features messages in the format of letters, the same types of persuasive messages also may take the form of memoranda, forms, reports, and oral presentations.

Four broad classes define the scope of persuasive messages: (1) persuasive requests, (2) collection messages, (3) sales messages, and (4) employment messages. Chapters 17 and 18 cover employment messages, so the first three categories form the substance of the remainder of this chapter.

Persuasive Requests

The category of persuasive requests includes an assortment of the miscellaneous persuasive messages that do not fit neatly into the sales, collection, or employment classes. They deal with any request that moves beyond the routine. They also involve message development that meets a characteristic presented earlier—the power to overcome apathy or resistance in the receiver.

Examples

These examples of desired actions illustrate the need for persuasive messages:

Contribute to a charity	Grant a personal leave
Share sensitive information	Complete a questionnaire
Collect complex information	Authorize research
Lend money	Grant a promotion
Grant an interview	Grant a raise
Lend expensive equipment	Break a lease
Grant a nonroutine claim or adjustment	Grant special privileges
Give permission to use private facilities for a meeting	Endorse a political candidate
	Accept a speaking engagement that does not pay an honorarium
Attend an event as a dignitary	Give permission to buy a special piece of equipment
Approve a transfer to another department	Agree to take an organizational office
Rezone property from residential to business	Grant exclusive franchise
Approve membership to an exclusive organization	Change dates for an audit
	Give an extension of time for payment of a past-due loan

Decide for each particular case whether to use a routine or persuasive approach. Base the decisions on the usual determining factors—the purposes, the personality of the receiver, and the circumstances.

Organization

Generally choose the inductive order combined with the APCA design for persuasive requests. Because the receiver may not have a natural inclination to respond favorably, build the case from the specific facts to the general conclusion—your request.

Open with some mild attention-getting reference to the topic. Then use the perception/interest segment as your transition from the introduction to the comprehension/conviction/desire part. In the body, develop the inductive reasoning fully, and culminate it with a clear, positive statement of the desired action/acceptance.

Try to ease the impact of the request by following it with a courteous closing statement.

Occasionally, you may use the deductive order for a persuasive request. Using that order you deliberately start with the request and then follow it with the arguments in support of the request.

Throughout the entire process, whether inductive or deductive, name or imply the potential rewards of the desired action to the receiver. Appeal to as many of the basic needs and wants of the receiver as you can.

Carefully identify anything that may interfere with your request, and try to prevent its occurrence. As you know, the greatest source of interference lies within the minds of you and the receiver. Therefore, cast yourself into the receiver's role and try to anticipate any negative reactions to what you propose. Then write so as to eliminate or subordinate all points that might lead to objections. Also emphasize points that will be likely to lead to feelings positive enough to overshadow any negative ones.

FULL LIFE, INC.
a nonprofit corporation

32 Lee Road
Marion, Iowa 22659
(555) 621-1213

October 11, 198X

Dear Marion Businessperson:

Over 2,000 people will turn 65 in the Marion, Iowa, area this year. They will join the 62,000 Marion residents who are already members of the 65-and-older generation. They, like Marion's other older people, will likely find that they have more free time, less money, and more medical problems than they had in their younger years.

Marion has one activity center for older persons. It holds only 50 people. Marion has no housing for low-income older people. Nor does our city operate a medical clinic for older people who need medical care at a low cost. In fact, Marion, Iowa, has all but ignored its older people.

We at Full Life, Inc., want to end the neglect of our older friends. And we most definitely need your help.

Full Life, Inc., a nonprofit corporation devoted to helping Marion's older citizens, is asking you and other Marion businesspersons to make donations of $25, $50, $100, or whatever amount you can afford to support Full Life's first major project—the building of the much-needed Full Life Center in the downtown area. The $2 million center will hold 500 people, and it will house a swimming pool, a cafeteria, a small gymnasium, and a number of meeting and game rooms. If enough money is donated, a medical clinic will also be a part of the Center. The Center will provide a number of the services so lacking in our city.

Over 100 Full Life volunteers have already collected $200,000 of our $2 million goal. These volunteers donate both their time and their money to this good cause. They want to give some-

Figure 11–1 Request for contribution

As an overriding thread through your thinking—and through the message itself—anticipate that the receiver will grant the request. Such an attitude often proves to create a self-fulfilling prophecy of success.

Figure 11–1 includes a letter written persuasively. Analyze the development. Is it inductive or deductive? Do you think it would overcome apathy or resistance in the

Marion Businessperson   2   October 11, 198X

thing to the 64,000 Marion residents who are their parents,
neighbors, and friends. Again, we need your help too so that we
can reach our $2 million goal by January 31.

Enclosed is a brochure that explains the Full Life Center project.
Also enclosed are a donation card and postpaid envelope for
your contribution. Note that if you donate $100 or more, you
will be named a Friend of the Center, and your name will appear
on the Friends of the Center plaque that will mark the Center's
entrance. Remember that your donation is tax-deductible.

We are all growing older. Your donation will not only help your
older neighbor, but it will be an investment for your future as
well.

Please return the enclosed donation card and your contribution
by November 15, 198X. Feel free to call me at 621-1213 if you
have any questions.

Sincerely,

Jane Woshki

Jane Woshki
Chairperson, Center Fund Drive

hh

Enclosures

Figure 11–1 (continued)

receiver? If you were the receiver, would you be likely to respond as the writer
wants?

Another persuasive request appears as Figure 11–2. Analyze it as you did
Figure 11–1.

Figure 11–3 illustrates a persuasive invitation to a prospective speaker.
Observe the deductive developmental pattern.

LANE YOUNG BUSINESS OWNERS
P.O. Box 4962
Lane, Nebraska 48621

April 9, 198X

Mr. Albert Larent
First Presbyterian Church
2954 North River Road
Lane, Nebraska 48621

Dear Mr. Larent:

Each summer my organization, the Lane Young Business Owners, holds a series of workshops for low-income high school students who have expressed an interest in business. The series usually lasts for two days—Friday and Saturday—and lunch is provided to the participants on both days.

In the past, we have held the two-day series in the Lane Chamber of Commerce meeting room. The meeting room, though, holds only 50 people, and we expect at least 90 students to participate in the workshops this summer. Thus, we would like to reserve your large First Presbyterian Church meeting hall for this year's workshop series.

We will need your meeting hall—as well as the downstairs bathrooms—from 8 a.m. to 5 p.m. on both Friday and Saturday, July 10 and 11. A local restaurant will provide box lunches on both days, and we will do the clean-up work at the end of each day.

Three Lane Young Business Owners members will be assigned to keep an eye on the students to make sure that no one takes or damages any property during the program. The Lane Chamber of Commerce will verify that no problems have occurred during past workshops. All of the workshops have been a great success in every way.

We would be most grateful if you allow us to use your meeting hall so we can continue to give needy students this valuable experience.

Please let me know by May 1, 198X, whether you can grant my request to use your meeting hall from 8 a.m. until 5 p.m. on Friday and Saturday, July 10 and 11. You can call me at 911-6241 (home) or 411-6444 (work).

Sincerely,

Maxwell Fish

Maxwell Fish
President

ii

Figure 11–2 Request for use of facilities

Big Ninth Accounting Service

Airport Road and Ayers—Madison, WI 53701 · (006) 060-6060

September 1, 198X

Mr. John Childs, C.P.A.
Partner, Debit Accounting Co.
19 North Solstice Avenue
Milwaukee, WI 53207

Dear Mr. Childs:

Will you please be the speaker for the October 19 meeting of the Madison
C.P.A. Association? When I was the guest of Esther Murray at the meeting of
your Association last March, I had the good fortune to hear you speak. Right
then I vowed to try to bring that same good fortune to the other Madison
Association members.

The dinner meeting begins at 7:30 p.m. in the Crystal Room of the Wilburton
Hotel. Preceding it is a hospitality hour starting at 6:30 p.m. in the adjoin-
ing Applewood Room.

Your presentation would begin at about 8:00 and end at about 8:30, with
another 10 minutes for questions if you like. A business meeting follows the
speaker. Therefore, though you would be welcome to stay, you could leave
immediately after your presentation in order to return to Milwaukee by a
reasonable hour.

Please speak on any subject that you choose. Your presentation "There's No
Accounting for Inflation" would be excellent.

The Association will, of course, provide your dinner and hospitality-hour
refreshments. In addition, Esther will be pleased to drive you over from
Madison, or the Association will provide $35 to cover your expenses if you
prefer to provide your own transportation.

I hope you will accept this invitation, and also look forward to learning the
subject of your speech. If you decide you would like Esther to drive you, let
me know, and I will ask her to contact you to make the arrangements. Could
you let me know by September 20 whether you will be able to come?

Sincerely yours,

Y. R. Self

Y. R. Self, C.P.A.
198X Programs
Madison C.P.A. Association

st

Figure 11–3   Request for speaker

Collection Messages

Messages designed to collect past-due accounts run the gamut from the routine to the demanding or threatening. The persuasive messages fall at an intermediate stage between the two extremes.

Because this chapter concentrates upon the application of communication principles to persuasion, emphasis is upon the intermediate stage. However, because of the nature of the collection process, it also covers the routine and demanding stages of the collection sequence.

Importance of collection

The basic reason for collecting money is obviously to make a profit, or just to survive in business. However, some of the details associated with the importance of proper collection procedures deserve some review.

In addition to the serious losses sustained when a debtor never pays, a firm loses money even when payments arrive late. Of course, the later they arrive, the greater the loss. The reasons include:

1. The reduction of cash flow often necessitates borrowing at high interest rates.
2. The collection procedures themselves require heavy expenditures for the personnel and materials necessary to complete them.
3. Repossessions of durable goods are costly.
4. Improper collection procedures often cause greater losses than would be sustained with good collection procedures.
5. Debtors often reduce the number of purchases or even cease to be customers, particularly if the firm uses poor collection procedures.
6. Offended debtors often turn other customers or potential customers against a firm.

Thus, the key to managing delinquent accounts lies in understanding that the action has two goals: collecting the money as soon as possible and retaining the goodwill of the customer. Good collection procedures, then, depend heavily upon good communication and the good psychology associated with it.

Communication for collection

As for any form of persuasion, knowledge about the receiver is critical for the collection process. Why do debtors not pay their bills? With correct answers to this question, you have a better chance of developing successful collection messages. Trying to see it from her/his point of view, consider some of the possible answers:

1. Am careless or forgetful.
2. Do not have enough money this month, but will have enough next month.
3. Have been out of town.
4. Am ill.
5. Have moved and mail has not been forwarded correctly.
6. Creditor made error in billing.
7. Dissatisfied with product or service and want an adjustment in the amount owed; if product, plan to return.
8. Other members of family incurred charges without my knowledge.
9. Lost my job after incurring the debt.

HILLEY GIFTS, INC.
4213 Avery Street · Mill, Ohio 62198

August 15, 198X

Mr. David Bonrell   R E M I N D E R
130 West Sixth Street, Apt. 3
Allen, Wyoming 86619

Dear Mr. Bonrell:

JUST A REMINDER—that all Hilley Gifts, Inc., payments are due
within 30 days of the date that you receive your bill. We have
not yet received your July 15 payment for $60.

Please take the time to send us a check for $60 in the enclosed
postpaid envelope. Then you will have the satisfaction of
knowing that your account is paid through July.

You are one of our most valued customers.

Sincerely,

Donna Raren

Donna Raren
Credit Manager

jj

Enclosure   Account No. 55151

Figure 11–4   First first-stage collection message

10. Owe too many creditors; overextended; may have to get counseling and/or take bankruptcy.
11. Am just unwilling to pay.

Once you understand the reasons for nonpayment, you can encode the message(s) to try to meet the receiver's specific wants and needs. During the middle, nonroutine, stage, offer a positive way out of the dilemma—partial payments, counseling, etc.

Combine written messages with the richer and often-more-productive level provided by telephone messages.

Even during the later stages, avoid threats of force. Suggest the possibility of legal action only when you intend to use it.

Treat collection messages as combinations of bad news and persuasion.

Basically use the positive sandwich and inductive format through the intermediate stage of persuasion. During the initial and ending stages, however, use a more direct approach. At the early stage, even use some originality—perhaps some

HILLEY GIFTS, INC.
4213 Avery Street · Mill, Ohio 62198

September 15, 198X

Mr. David Bonrell   S E C O N D   N O T I C E
130 West Sixth Street, Apt. 3
Allen, Wyoming 86619

Dear Mr. Bonrell:

WE ALL FORGET TO DO THINGS SOMETIMES!

HAVE YOU FORGOTTEN TO SEND US
YOUR LAST TWO PAYMENTS?

Perhaps both your July 15 and August 15 Hilley Gifts payments
have just slipped your mind.

Please send the $120 in overdue payments to us promptly in the
postpaid envelope enclosed for your convenience.

Don't forget to send your payment today!

Sincerely,

Donna Raren

Donna Raren
Credit Manager

jj

Enclosure   Account No. 55151

Figure 11–5   Second first-stage collection message

humor in conjunction with the direct attention-getting opening. During the final stage, however, your directness must take the form of a sharp demand for immediate payment.

At whatever stage, include the amount owed in every message. Tie the amount to due date(s). When the business is large, include the account number in every message. For the masses of collections that disallow custom-made messages, use form messages—often established to be transmitted as a timed series. When well done, even they reflect an understanding of people.

Develop several series to fit the distinct features of the circumstances surrounding the need to collect. With or without automatic equipment, leave places to insert amount due, due date, and account numbers on each message.

When a large firm uses form messages—even if typewritten individually in a word-processing center—management often engages professional writers to develop

HILLEY GIFTS, INC.
4213 Avery Street · Mill, Ohio 62198

September 30, 198X

Mr. David Bonrell   C A N   W E   H E L P?
130 West Sixth Street, Apt. 3
Allen, Wyoming 86619

Dear Mr. Bonrell:

We are puzzled. You usually make your payments promptly, yet
you are two payments behind now. In fact, you will be three
payments behind if we do not receive a check from you in 15
days. We are concerned because you are one of our best
customers.

Perhaps you have merely forgotten. Or you have been out of
town. Or you are just having a little trouble paying your bills
right now. But whatever the reason, we need to know so that we
can help.

Please send us your check for $120 to cover your overdue July
15 and August 15 payments. The enclosed postpaid envelope is
for your convenience. Or, if something prevents you from
making a prompt payment, let us know by writing us today.

We expect to hear from you before October 10, 198X.

Sincerely,

Donna Raren

Donna Raren
Credit Manager

jj

Enclosure   Account No. 55151

Figure 11–6 Third first-stage collection message

them. However, review the concept of the series so that you may understand the
principles and psychology involved.

Collection series

As already implied, a series of collection messages goes through three major stages.

First stage This includes routine contacts with the debtor. The first message often is
no more than a duplicate of the original statement with words like "Second Statement," "Second Notice," or "Reminder" stamped across it. See Figure 11–4 for an
example.

HILLEY GIFTS, INC.
4213 Avery Street · Mill, Ohio 62198

October 10, 198X

Mr. David Bonrell
130 West Sixth Street, Apt. 3
Allen, Wyoming 86619

Dear Mr. Bonrell:

You are proud of your good credit rating, aren't you? It allows
you to enjoy all manner of goods and services. We want you to
continue to enjoy the privileges that a good credit rating affords
you.

Because you do want to protect your excellent credit rating, we
at Hilley Gifts are confident that you will promptly pay the
$180 you owe us. We have sent you several reminders and are
very concerned that you have not made your last three
payments—July 15, August 15, and September 15.

Protect your good credit rating by mailing your payment today!

Sincerely,

Donna Raren

Donna Raren
Credit Manager

jj   Account No. 55151

Figure 11–7   First intermediate-stage collection message

A second message in this early stage may move to a repetition of the statement,
but with a clearer reminder. The reminder may use words like "Third Notice: Please
Pay Promptly," "Second Reminder," or even a humorous "Did you Forget?" The
humorous approach might accompany a sketch of a person scratching his or her
head, or a finger with a string tied around it. Figure 11–5 illustrates a reminder.

If one or two simple reminders fail, and you know that the customer usually
pays on time, you might want to send a message of inquiry about why the customer
has not paid. Stress the need for payment, but give the customer a chance to explain
the circumstances leading to the unusual delay. Continue to give the receiver the
benefit of the doubt. Analyze Figure 11–6 as an example of an inquiry letter still in
the first collection stage.

Intermediate stage   If an inquiry fails to gain a response, move into the second stage

HILLEY GIFTS, INC.
4213 Avery Street · Mill, Ohio 62198

October 20, 198X

Mr. David Bonrell
130 West Sixth Street, Apt. 3
Allen, Wyoming 86619

Dear Mr. Bonrell:

A string of overdue bills can do great damage to a good credit
rating. Most people who have worked hard to earn their good
credit ratings do not want to do anything to hurt them.

We doubt that you want to endanger your credit rating, Mr.
Bonrell. Unless we receive the $180 you owe us for your last
three payments, however, we will be forced to begin a review of
your account. The review process does involve a critical
reevaluation of your credit standing.

Send $180 for your July, August, and September payments today
so that we do not have to begin the review. Remember that your
credit rating is one of your most valuable assets.

Sincerely,

Donna Raren

Donna Raren
Credit Manager

jj   Account No. 55151

Figure 11–8   Second intermediate-stage collection message

of the collection process. The intermediate stage changes the emphasis from the
rather routine into the persuasive.

Along with the shift to the persuasive comes a shift in developmental style.
Though routine messages usually take the deductive style, persuasive messages
usually take the indirect or cause-and-effect pattern.

Once you move to persuasion, also move to a more careful development of the
facts in the perception/interest and comprehension/conviction/desire segments of the
message. Pay particular attention to the potential benefits of payment for the
receiver. Basically appeal to the sense of fair play, to pride, and to social approval.

Build the pressure upon the receiver at a steady pace through two or three
well-timed messages. However, even as you increase the pressure, maintain the
positive, correctly buffered approach to the content. Leave the receiver with alterna-

HILLEY GIFTS, INC.

4213 Avery Street · Mill, Ohio 62198

November 1, 198X

Mr. David Bonrell
130 West Sixth Street, Apt. 3
Allen, Wyoming 86619

Dear Mr. Bonrell:

When we are forced to review one of our customer's charge accounts, we must also review that customer's credit standing. We will be forced to begin a review of your account at Hilley Gifts, Inc., if we do not receive the $240 you owe us by November 15. You are now four months behind on your payments, and you have given us no reason for the delay.

Five reminders have been mailed to you concerning the four payments that will be overdue on November 15:

July 15—	$	60
August 15—	$	60
September 15—	$	60
October 15—	$	60
TOTAL	$240	

You can avoid a review of your account by sending a check for $240 now!

Sincerely,

Donna Raren

Donna Raren
Credit Manager

jj   Account No. 55151

Figure 11–9   Third intermediate-stage collection message

tives that allow her or him to recover from the transaction with dignity intact. However, end each persuasive message with the call to action—with the call for payment.

Figures 11–7, 11–8, and 11–9 serve as examples of the intermediate, persuasive stage of a collection series. They also illustrate the progressively heavier stress on the need for action, if the receiver wishes to preserve a good name.

Demand stage   Once you complete the intermediate stage, shift into the final stage. It moves from persuasion into demand.

HILLEY GIFTS, INC.
4213 Avery Street · Mill, Ohio 62198

November 15, 198X

Mr. David Bonrell
130 West Sixth Street, Apt. 3
Allen, Wyoming 86619

Dear Mr. Bonrell:

You did not respond to our last request for payment; therefore,
we have begun a review of your account. One result is that we
will not allow you to make any more charges on your Hilley
charge card. And as you know, your credit rating is also in
grave danger.

You are seriously behind in your payments—four months, in
fact. Unless you send the $240 you owe us or make other
arrangements by December 1, we will be forced to take even
more drastic collection action.

Time is running out. Send your payment today.

Sincerely,

Donna Raren

Donna Raren
Credit Manager

jj   Account No. 55151

Figure 11–10   First demand-stage collection message

In the demand stage, revert to a direct, deductive style. Set a date by which you
must receive payment, or, occasionally, a response that includes a partial payment
and a clear, believable plan for completing payment. When you reach the demand
stage, be ready to go through with any actions you state you will take.

Review Figures 11–10 and 11–11. They are examples of the demand stage of
the process.

If the debtor does not meet the final demand, turn the debt over to the legal
department or firm. Then notify the debtor courteously, but directly, that you have
done so. Figure 11–12 includes such a post-collection-series message.

HILLEY GIFTS, INC.
4213 Avery Street · Mill, Ohio 62198

December 1, 198X

Mr. David Bonrell   F I N A L   N O T I C E
130 West Sixth Street, Apt. 3
Allen, Wyoming 86619

Dear Mr. Bonrell:

We have completed the review of your account. On December 15, you will be five months—$300—behind on your payments, and you have responded to none of our letters. We have no choice but to make this your last chance to send your payment or to call us to discuss other arrangements.

If we have not heard from you by December 15, we will refer your overdue account to our attorneys. Please send your $300 payment now so both of us can avoid the legal collection process.

Sincerely,

Donna Raren

Donna Raren
Credit Manager

jj   Account No. 55151

Figure 11–11   Final demand-stage collection message

Whether you use individually developed messages or form messages, still think of the collection process as including the three stages just cited. Also observe careful timing and sequencing for both types of messages. The concept of a periodic pattern transmitting the various kinds of messages is crucial to the creation of an unfolding, increasingly persuasive sequence.

Even with the careful pacing and formality of a chain of collection messages, however, try to maintain some flexibility. With provision of flexibility, a collection process may be applied to the unique characteristics of each special situation. In certain circumstances, you might skip the first or intermediate stages entirely. In others you may also want to vary the timing from the prescribed time schedule for the typical sequence.

HILLEY GIFTS, INC.
4213 Avery Street · Mill, Ohio 62198

December 23, 198X

Mr. David Bonrell
130 West Sixth Street, Apt. 3
Allen, Wyoming 86619

Dear Mr. Bonrell:

We have referred your account to our law firm, Williams, Fong &
Micci, P.C., for legal action. The firm will now handle all facets
of the collection process concerning your Hilley Gifts, Inc.,
charge account. An attorney will call you within the next two
weeks.

Call Williams, Fong & Micci, P.C., at (555) 614–9987 if you have
any questions. The firm's address is 1319 Elm Street, Mill, Ohio
62198.

Sincerely,

Donna Raren

Donna Raren
Credit Manager

jj   Account No. 55151

Figure 11–12   Post-collection-series message

Sales Messages

Like collection messages, mass sales messages usually are written by professional
writers, not by the regular personnel of a business office. However, you can learn a
great deal about persuasion and communication just by reviewing a few of the
principles associated with sales communication.

Characteristics

Sales messages may take many forms, including letters, memoranda, leaflets, flyers,
newspaper and magazine advertisements, catalogs, outdoor advertisements, and
television and radio commercials. Though the concentration here is upon the letter,
many of the concepts apply to the other channels as well.

Originality   Sales messages allow for more originality and creativity in design and
development than do any other types of business messages. As the writer, you may
use unlimited imagination in designing them.

Use virtually any developmental style. Include or omit salutations in letters. Write formally or informally. Use both rational and emotional appeals. Use dramatic or subtle techniques. Include or offer free gifts. Enclose coins, stick-on stamps, return cards or envelopes marked "Yes" and "No," product samples, and other such objects related to the topic. Include lavish photographs, pictures, charts, sketches, tables, tapes, small records, and even scratch-patches that give off the fragrance found in a soap, cologne, or shaving lotion.

Analysis   Learn about the prospective buyer. Learn about the product or service you want the buyer to buy.

Use the procedures described in Chapter 5 to define the prospective buyer. The general items from the list of demographic factors contribute particularly well to developing messages for distribution to the masses. Motivational research (briefly discussed in Chapter 14) may also help in the definition. However, a marketing research department or outside agency usually conducts such research.

To learn about the product or service, meet with the designers and producers.

Appeal   Once you understand the qualities of the product/service and the prospect, you can match the two. Select one or two major features and build an appeal around them. Avoid broadcasting so many features that the receiver does not accept any of them.

Build the entire appeal around the desired action—the purchase of the goods or services. Make the purchase both attractive and easy. Enclose return envelopes, order blanks, and simple, complete instructions.

Use the APCA pattern to its fullest. Review or recall the attention-getting devices discussed earlier in this chapter. Be sure that the attention section is related to the basic appeal and that the other sections unfold naturally from that initial statement. Spotlight the acceptance/action section properly. Call for the purchase as you recall the basic rational or emotional appeal and the benefit of the purchase to the buyer.

Just as the major appeals for collection letters are based on pride, a sense of fair play, and social approval, the major appeals for sales letters have their foundation in the multitude of human needs and wants, both rational and emotional. The Direct Mail Advertising Association suggests that people spend money in order to:

Save money	Conserve possessions
Make money	Have safety in buying
Save time	Avoid criticism
Avoid effort	Protect family
Provide comfort	Be in style
Assure cleanliness	Have beautiful possessions
Have enjoyment	Satisfy appetite
Gratify curiosity	Emulate others
Bring good health	Be individualistic
Escape physical pain	Protect reputation
Receive praise	Take advantage of opportunities
Be popular	Avoid trouble
Attract the opposite sex	

Many other motivations fit the list. In addition, variations and combinations create innumerable others.

F.R.M. Sutical Corp.

783 Capsule Road
Iron Springs, AZ 86330

Dear Consumer:

Enclosed is the free sample of VIMVIG VITAMINS you asked for.

As you will discover, VIMVIG is a special vitamin compound. VIMVIG consistently leaves you with more energy and without as many colds.

VIMVIG is available in most grocery, drug, and discount stores in bottles of 50, 100, or 200 capsules.

Thank you for responding to our free sample offer. We feel sure you will like VIMVIG so well that you will want to purchase VIMVIG when the sample is gone.

Good health,

Carroll Jeeves

Carroll Jeeves

F.R.M.S.80

D7418–6/5/80

Figure 11–13 Sales message as an enclosure

Variety The major reason for developing sales messages is to make direct sales. However, other, less-direct objectives also exist. Consider some examples:

1. To create general demand for a service or product rather than to make specific sales
2. To build sales for dealers, thus indirectly building the producer's or wholesaler's sales
3. To prepare prospects for a salesperson's call
4. To contact former customers
5. To solicit inquiries
6. To respond to inquiries
7. To announce new or remodeled products or services
8. To announce the results of tests on your products and services
9. To establish goodwill—goodwill that may ultimately lead to sales

Types

Four major types of written sales messages are enclosures, personal messages, one-time mass mailings, and sales series.

LIFE SUPPLIERS, INC.
436 East Broadway
El Toro, California 79241

May 15, 198X

Dear Runner:

Your body does great things for you. It lets you run. It keeps you warm. And it allows you to enjoy your full life. In short,

YOUR BODY DOES EVERYTHING FOR YOU!

(But have you done anything for your body lately?)

Because you run hard and lead an active life, your body needs more than a regular vitamin. Much more. So you can do something for your body by giving it a Runner's Tab, a multiple vitamin developed just for you, the hard-working runner. Because Runner's Tab is the result of ten years of research, it is the most complete vitamin tablet for runners on the market today. You need take only one Runner's Tab a day, and your running body will have all of the vitamin support it needs.

To order your three-months' supply of Runner's Tab, just complete the enclosed card and mail it with your check or money order in the postpaid envelope. A three-months' supply of Runner's Tab will be priced at $11.95 only through June 15, after which the price will be $14.95. Hurry so that you can take advantage of this special offer.

Your body does great things for you. Do something great for your body with Runner's Tab. Order now!

Sincerely,

Raymond Merrill

Raymond Merrill
Health Director

RM/cc

Enclosure

Figure 11–14   Letter selling mail-order product

Enclosures   As suggested in Chapter 9, transmittal messages often include a sales pitch. They often accompany filled orders, coupons, product samples, refunds, and responses to other messages.

Figure 11–13 illustrates a simple sales enclosure.

Personal messages   Selling often becomes part of individually created messages. As developed in Chapter 9, inquiries about products and services provide perfect

ERRAND RUNNERS, INC.
9560 Oregon Avenue, Lanewell, Oregon 96411
(555) 322-1121

Dear Businessperson:

You have a challenging job. And you make very good money.
You are moving up fast, almost faster than you ever dreamed.
You have all of this, but you rarely have

                            TIME.

After work you must go to the bank, buy the groceries,
pay the phone bill, pick up the children, take the dog to the
veterinarian, and do a thousand other small jobs. You have a
few errands to run practically every evening. Why does a
well-paid businessperson like you spend so much time running
errands?

          WE WILL RUN YOUR ERRANDS FOR YOU.

Think about it. Your free time is valuable because you have
so little of it. You work hard so that you can better the quality
of your life. But is your life better when you have no time to live
it?

     WE WILL RUN YOUR ERRANDS FOR YOU FOR LESS THAN
             HALF OF WHAT IT COSTS YOU NOW.

We know that you are not paid by the hour, but if you were
to estimate your hourly wage, you would find that we can do
your small jobs for less than half of what you make in an hour.
Wouldn't it be great to pay such a low price for

                       MORE TIME?

Time to read. Time to run and swim and ride your bicycle.
Time to be with your spouse and children. Time to attend
lectures and concerts and plays. Time to watch the sun dip
below the mountains.

Figure 11–15 Message selling a local service

opportunities for sales responses. Similarly, acknowledgments of orders prior to
shipping offer a chance to try to persuade the purchaser to buy something else.

Observe how the Homespa Fitness letter in Figure 9–20 (page 287) is as much
a personal sales message as it is a response to an inquiry.

(2)

WE WILL GIVE YOU THAT TIME FOR JUST $4 AN HOUR, OR
JUST $16 FOR FIVE HOURS A WEEK.

We run all of your errands. All you do is take a few minutes
a week to fill out one of the short errand forms we provide. Mail
the form to us, and then we do the rest. And if you think of
something else that you'd like us to do for you, just give us a
call. We add the errand to your week's list.

The enclosed brochure explains all of the details of our
service. The most important aspect of our service, though, is
that you'll get back part of your

PRECIOUS FREE TIME.

You can get more time now. Just call us at 322–1121 and
we'll start running your errands today! And if you wish, I'll be
glad to meet with you to answer your questions.

Remember, if you call us now, you can watch the sun set
tonight.

Sincerely,

Helen Wayland

Helen Wayland
Manager

HW/rv

Enclosures

Figure 11–15   (continued)

One-time mass mailings   Firms often prepare a sales message, duplicate it, and
distribute it to a mailing list—one time. Figures 11–14, 11–15, 11–16, and 11–17
illustrate such sales letters. They exemplify a variety of sound sales techniques.
Analyze them for construction and content.

CAREFUL CAR WASH
317 Harrison Way
Lakeview, Arizona 81941

March 25, 198X

(There's an offer in this letter that you can't pass up.)

Dear Neighbor:

Careful Car Wash wants to get acquainted with you, our neighbor. We could think of no better way to get to know you than to offer to clean your car—inside and outside—for a special price!

YOUR CAR WILL RECEIVE

A WASH,

A WAX,

A SHINE, AND

AN INSIDE VACUUM

FOR JUST $2.50—EXACTLY HALF THE REGULAR $5 PRICE.

This special offer is YOURS because we want to get to know YOU. We also want you to know what a fine job Careful Car Wash does on YOUR car. No automatic car wash could compete with the thorough job our people do at Careful. Just come on in and see for yourself!

Bring this letter in between 9 and 7 Monday through Saturday to have your car receive the BEST cleaning, shining, and vacuuming it has ever had—all for just $2.50! Hurry, though, because this extra special offer ends on April 15!

We're looking forward to getting to know you.

Sincerely,

Lisa Johnson

Lisa Johnson
Owner

Figure 11–16 Letter advertising "get acquainted" offer

Laurel Boutique

25 North Park Street   Vine, New Mexico 33219

August 1, 198X

Dear Preferred Customer:

SALE

SALE

SALE

SALE

SALE

SALE

SALE

Most other stores have sales, and they all seem to be alike. But when we allow only our Preferred Charge Card customers to buy anything in our store at a 25 percent discount, it is an event.

We are holding our very special event for you on Friday, August 17, from 10 to 5. And only you, our Preferred Charge Card customer, can buy elegant dresses, silky scarves, and anything in the boutique for a mere 75 percent of the regular price.

Most sales last for weeks. Our event lasts only one day.

Be there.

Sincerely,

Priscilla Poteau

Priscilla Poteau
Owner

Figure 11–17 Letter advertising a special sale

[To the student: Skip over the figures that serve as examples when taking the following Timed Exercise. You can return to them later.]

Sales series Direct-mail selling as a mass-media approach often involves unsolicited sales letters in a series. Three types of series define such an approach: (1) the continual (sometimes called "continuous") series, (2) the wear-out series, and (3) the campaign series.

PARCHMENT-LIKE, PERSONALIZED STATIONERY FOR JUST $4.95?

YOU'VE GOT TO BE KIDDING?

But at Elegant Economy Stationery, we never KID. We just make beautiful, heavy-bond, personalized stationery at a price most everyone can afford. For only $4.95, you can receive 50 personalized letter sheets, 50 plain sheets, and 50 personalized envelopes.

AND AGAIN, WE'RE NOT KIDDING. JUST LOOK:

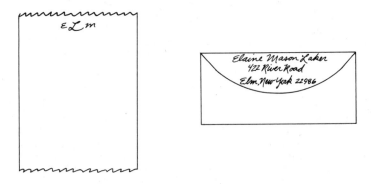

The price is low because our letter sheets and envelopes come in only one size and one color. We also use only one print style, color, and size. The sheets are 8″ x 11″, and both the parchment-like sheets and envelopes come in an elegant Golden White color.

Your initials and name are printed in Night Bark, a deep, bold brown. Your name and full address go on all of your 50 envelopes; and your initials—with your last initial in the middle—go on 50 of your letter sheets.

WHY NOT WRITE YOUR LETTERS ON ELEGANT STATIONERY?
ORDER NOW!?

Name and address as you want them to appear on your envelopes
_____ (Name)
_____ (Street)
_____ (City, State, Zip)
Mailing address
_____ (Name)
_____ (Street)
_____ (City, State, Zip)

Please allow six weeks for delivery.

Initials as you want them to appear on your letter paper

_____
  First   Last   Middle

Send a $4.95 check or money order to:
    Elegant Economy Stationery
    P. O. Box 69
    Ware, New Jersey 60492

Figure 11–18 Continual-series enclosure

Through a *continual* series, sellers send pieces at relatively regular intervals for an indefinite length of time. The messages often accompany other pieces such as statements, catalogs, price lists, and first- and even second-stage collection messages. Such enclosures serve to resell existing customers—an important concept in selling.

Because you include continual-series pieces with other messages, the expenses are much less than for series mailed independently. Therefore, the continual series usually costs less than any other type.

Figure 11–18 includes an example of a continual-series enclosure. Inspect it to determine whether it might appeal to you as the receiver.

With the *wear-out* series, begin with a mailing list of prospective purchasers. Then create and mail a sales message that stands on its own. It may include a letter that carries the bulk of the message, along with some accompanying verbal and nonverbal messages.

After a period of time, check the returns from the first mailing. Then mark off the names of those who responded to the first mailing. However, you may leave the original purchasers' names on the list if you think a second mailing might bring additional sales.

Then send a second mailing to the revised list. The messages may be new and self-contained, or they may be the same as those included in the first mailing.

Following the second mailing, revise the list again, and send another mailing. Continue the process until you no longer receive enough returns to make continuing the process worthwhile—until you "wear out" the list.

Because it involves a series of independent mailings, the wear-out system costs more than the continual system. However, it costs less than the campaign series discussed next.

Figures 11–19 and 11–20 illustrate two letters from a wear-out series. Observe how each message is self-contained, yet related to the other.

The *campaign* sales series involves the careful development of several coordinated mailings—all of which are sent in sequence to every person on the mailing list. Because everyone receives every piece, the series itself may build through the APCA plan. The first letter may emphasize the attention phase; the second, the perception/interest; the third, the comprehension/conviction/desire. However, each message features the action phase—calling for an order. Indeed, each message contains all the elements. The only difference is that each successive message shifts the emphasis to a new component.

As suggested, the campaign series costs more than either the continual or wear-out series. Thus, its use is limited to sales of the kinds of expensive items that warrant large expenditures.

(478 words)
(test on page 370)

Figures 11–21, 11–22, and 11–23 show the combined effect of a series of letters in a sales campaign. Observe how the messages complement one another as they build through the persuasion.

Dawson Lucci Dance Company

2319 West Ninth Avenue
El Paso, Kansas 23999
(555) 236-1984

July 1, 198X

Dear Friend:

Larry Blieve of the <u>Kansas Weekly</u> called the Dawson Lucci Dance Company "Brilliant!," and Meredith Morris of the <u>El Paso Courier</u> wrote: "The Dawson Lucci Dance Company shines brighter than any star in the sky."

We want to give you a special, before-the-box-office-opens opportunity to become a subscriber to the full season of the dance company that practically always receives rave reviews, El Paso's own Dawson Lucci Dance Company. The Dawson Lucci Dance Company will give you many evenings of exciting performances if you subscribe.

The company is composed of 25 dancers, all of whom studied under some of the greatest teachers in New York and Europe. And the Dawson Lucci Dance Company does not limit itself to one dance form: It performs ballet, jazz, and modern dance with equal ease.

This year's Dawson Lucci season includes six concerts, all of which will be held at the beautiful El Paso Performing Arts Center. You can see all six concerts for just $25—that's six concerts for the price of five.

Last season all but one of the Dawson Lucci Dance Company's performances were sold out. You can be sure to see all of this season's concerts from your reserved seat if you become a season subscriber now. Just fill out the enclosed subscription card and mail it with your check or money order today. And hurry! Only a limited number of season subscriptions are available.

Don't risk missing even one of the "Brilliant!" Dawson Lucci Dance Company performances.

Sincerely,

Allen Santini

Allen Santini
Manager

AS/ln

Enclosures

Figure 11–19   First wear-out series letter

Dawson Lucci Dance Company

2319 West Ninth Avenue
El Paso, Kansas 23999
(555) 236-1984

August 17, 198X

Dear Friend:

The Dawson Lucci Dance Company just got back from its summer road tour. The dancers went to New York, Montreal, and London. And everywhere they went, they received high praise.

Mary Frankel of the <u>New York Guard</u> wrote: "No other regional dance company could match last night's performance of the Dawson Lucci troupe." "Absolutely fantastic!" were the words Harold Jarms, a <u>Montreal World</u> critic, used to describe the Dawson Lucci Dance Company. And Maureen O'Dean of the <u>London Week in Review</u> called Dawson Lucci ". . . the best American dance company I have seen in years."

The Dawson Lucci Dance Company's home is also your home: El Paso, Kansas. And you can see all of the company's El Paso performances from your reserved seat if you subscribe now.

The 25 dancers of the Dawson Lucci Dance Company will perform all six of this season's concerts at the elegant El Paso Performing Arts Center. The company will perform jazz, ballet, and modern dance, and each performance is something to remember.

You can see all six concerts for just $25—that's six concerts for the price of five. To become a season subscriber, just fill out the enclosed subscription card and mail it with your check or money order today. We regret that we cannot give you a third chance to subscribe after this second one. Our mailing costs are high and the season subscriptions are going fast. So this is essentially your last chance to subscribe.

The critics in New York, Montreal, and London seemed to agree that a performance of the Dawson Lucci Dance Company should not be missed. If you subscribe now, you won't miss a single one.

Sincerely,

Allen Santini

Allen Santini
Manager

AS/ln

Enclosures

Don't delay! Complete the enclosed subscription card and mail it with your check or money order for $25 TODAY.

Figure 11–20   Second and final wear-out series letter

DECK CARPENTERS, INC.

2211 Sunnyvale Road, Sherman, Washington 42226
(555) 916-6116

March 1, 198X

Dear Home Owner:

In a few weeks beautiful weather will move into the Sherman area for
its usual seven-month stay. The sun will shine nearly every day. And you
will want to spend more and more of each wonderful day outdoors in the
midst of the sun and the grass and the flowers.

Deck Carpenters make your outdoor life more comfortable and more
beautiful. We build wood patios and decks that make any yard into a
summertime paradise. And why use expensive gasoline to get away from it
all when you can escape to your own lovely back yard?

We would be very happy to visit your home to discuss your deck and
patio needs and to give you a free estimate. Or, if you want us to begin work
now, just give us a call and we'll begin construction on your deck or patio
within a week. You can choose one of many designs (we've enclosed our
brochure which includes some of our most popular designs) or work with
one of our associates to design your own personalized deck or patio.

You can call us at 916–6116. Or drop by our office at 2211 Sunnyvale
Road. We'd love to talk to you.

You can have your own deck or patio before summer starts if you call
Deck Carpenters today.

Yours sincerely,

Mary Jane Francis

Mary Jane Francis
Owner

MJF/rp

Enclosure: Brochure

Figure 11–21   First campaign series letter

DECK CARPENTERS, INC.
2211 Sunnyvale Road, Sherman, Washington 42226
(555) 916-6116

April 1, 198X

Dear Home Owner:

All decks and patios built by Deck Carpenters, Inc., are beautifully designed, perfectly built, and fully guaranteed for ten years.

All Deck Carpenters architects are certified building designers, and our carpenters are the finest craftspeople in the area. They never cut corners because they take great pride in their work. And the materials we use are the best available: We refuse to use anything but quality woods and hardware.

Your deck could cover your entire back yard, and you could put a hot tub or swimming pool right in the middle of it. Or you could enjoy your summer on a split-level patio, a patio that includes interesting steps and beautiful built-in planters. The brochure we enclose includes over fifty of our original designs.

No matter what we build for you, though, you'll know that you are sitting on the finest piece of work available. We build solid, functional, beautiful decks and patios, decks and patios that will last through decades of summers.

There's still time to have your deck built before the beginning of summer. Just call us at 916–6116 or visit our office at 2211 Sunnyvale Road for a free consultation.

You'll be proud of the quality work we'll do for you.

Call now!

Sincerely,

Mary Jane Francis

Mary Jane Francis
Owner

MJF/rp

Enclosure: Brochure

Figure 11–22   Second campaign series letter

DECK CARPENTERS, INC.
2211 Sunnyvale Road, Sherman, Washington 42226
(555) 916-6116

May 1, 198X

Dear Friend:

You may think that we at Deck Carpenters would have to charge high
prices for our quality work and our quality materials. Actually, our rates are
competitive with the rates charged by other patio and deck builders in this
area, and we know our wood and construction techniques are superior.

Just to prove our point, we enclosed our price list. And because we want
you to know that our prices are more than reasonable, we included the
prices of two of our competitors.

REMEMBER: We always use the highest quality materials that are on
the market. In addition, we take the time to include the "little extras" that
make our decks and patios very strong as well as very beautiful.

Summer is almost upon us. You still have time to enjoy most of the
sunny season from your Deck Carpenters deck or patio. If you call now, we
can start building your fully guaranteed backyard paradise within ten days.
And just to make things a little easier, we've enclosed a $50 gift certificate
to apply to any deck or patio we build for you. Hurry, though, because the
$50 gift certificate is good only through May 25.

Please call us at 916–6116 for a free home consultation—or come by our
office at 2211 Sunnyvale Road.

Make your yard into a paradise. Use your $50 gift certificate on a
beautiful, solid, reasonably priced Deck Carpenters patio or deck today!

Sincerely,

Mary Jane Francis

Mary Jane Francis
Owner

MJF/rp

Enclosures: Price list
            Gift certificate
            Brochure

Figure 11–23   Final campaign series letter

SUMMARY

Persuasive messages are those developed to attempt to get people to take some action beyond the routine or to accept a different idea or belief. They try to persuade people to pay a bill, buy goods and services, or convert to a belief.

Concentrate on the desired *action/acceptance*, not the persuasion itself, when you write a persuasive message. To develop the message, carefully use the guidelines for communication. Pay particular attention to the purposes, the receiver's needs, ethics, and the content of the message.

Persuasive messages fit into *inductive, ascending-rank, chronological, deductive*, and *descending-rank* plans for development. However, use the inductive plan when the persuasive message also contains bad news.

The parts of a persuasive message should be fitted into the *APCA pattern (attention, perception/interest, comprehension/conviction/desire, action/acceptance).*

Four broad classes of persuasive messages exist: (1) persuasive requests, (2) collection messages, (3) sales messages, and (4) employment messages (covered in Chapters 17 and 18).

Persuasive requests are nonroutine requests. A persuasive request asks a person to complete a questionnaire, endorse a candidate, or grant a promotion. Because the receiver may not have a natural inclination to respond favorably, build the case through the inductive plan—from the specific facts to the general conclusion, the request.

Collection messages are designed to collect past-due accounts in timely fashion in order to make profits. The goal of writing a collection message is to collect the money and to retain the goodwill of the customer.

Understand why people do not pay their debts. Tie that understanding to a *three-stage series*. The first stage includes one or more routine reminders written in the deductive style. The intermediate stage includes two or three persuasive messages written in the inductive style. The final stage involves one or more deductive-style demands for payment. The final message of the demand stage usually notifies the debtor that the debt is in the hands of the legal department.

Sales messages take many forms, including letters, memoranda, leaflets, flyers, newspaper and magazine advertisements, and television and radio commercials. Sales messages require *originality*, perceptive *analysis* of receiver and product/service, *appeals* to human needs, and a clear understanding of *purposes*.

Four major types of sales messages are *enclosures, personal messages, one-time mass mailings*, and *sales series*. Types of series include the continual, the wear-out, and the campaign. The *continual series* involves inserts with periodic mailings. The *wear-out series* involves mailings of self-contained messages to the same mailing list, reduced at each stage by removing the names of those who have made purchases. The *campaign series* involves several coordinated mailings sent in sequence to every person on the mailing list.

Practice

1. You are the collection manager for the Berry and Flom Department Store. Every month you must close the accounts of thirty or forty people because they have not made payments in the preceding six months. Because you cannot write a personal letter to every customer, you prepare a form letter that will be sent to the customers whose accounts must be closed. In the form letter, you inform them that their accounts are being closed and that a collection agency has been hired to collect the debt. Write the form letter.

2. These are poor persuasive messages. Correct each message and explain the reasoning behind your changes. Concentrate on the content, not the format, of each message.

a.

DIMCO, INC.
Staple Plaza, Suite 900
Winner, Montana 46218
(555) 336–9412

January 29, 198X

Dear Customer:

Now that you have had a chance to use your new Dimco Typewriter, we know that you really want a Dimco Copier.

The Dimco Copier works just as well as the Dimco Typewriter.

We will be expecting your order.

Sincerely,

N. T. Bright

N. T. Bright
Salesperson

---

b. This is a flyer.

FRISCO'S DRY CLEANERS

BRING YOUR DIRTY, SMELLY CLOTHES TO US !!!

> COUPON
> 25% OFF
> COUPON

---

c.

AMERICAN CHARITIES, INC.
1700 East Park Street, Suite 1200
Monroe, Florida 76660
(555) 343–3157

October 9, 198X

Mr. Milton Vance
84 Macon Street
Palm Springs, Georgia 84611

Dear Mr. Vance:

We know that you are a relatively wealthy man and a proud American. We want your donation so that we can help poor children all over the world.

We are a reputable organization, so send at least $100.

If you do not give, your conscience will hurt you.

Please! Please! Please!

Sincerely,

S. L. Zee

S. L. Zee
President

---

d.

LAMONT, INC.
602 Vella Street
Thorne, Arizona 99962
(555) 462–9914

February 16, 198X

Ms. Ellen Stake
3960 Benton Road
Thorne, Arizona 99962

Dear Ms. Stake:

Why in the world are you a month late on your Lamont Charge payment? You have never done this to us before!

Please send the payment right now so that we do not have to ask you again.

We value our customers.

Sincerely,

O. V. React

O. V. React
Collection Clerk

---

e.

QUANTITY PURSES, INC.
P.O. Box 19B
Dover, Idaho 41163

Dear Housewife:

We know that you are having trouble making ends meet. We also know that you like to look good when you leave the house. So, you need our LUXURY PLASTIC PURSE! It's cheap, yet it looks expensive. Just look:

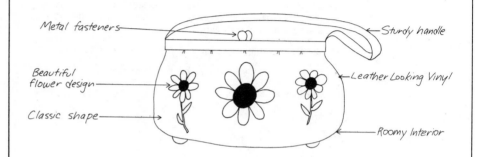

Metal fasteners • Sturdy handle • Beautiful flower design • Leather Looking Vinyl • Classic shape • Roomy Interior

Even <u>you</u> can afford this magnificent purse. It's only $9.95 plus postage and handling.

You do want to look decent when you leave the house, don't you?

Order now!

Sincerely,

I. N. Sulting
Consumer Sales

QUANTITY PURSES, Inc., P. O. Box 19B, Dover, Idaho 41163

I want _____ LUXURY PLASTIC PURSES at $9.95 plus $1.50 for postage and handling. I want my purse in ___ white ___ pink ___ red ___ green. I have enclosed a check for $_____.

Name _____ Address _____
Allow nine weeks for delivery.

3. Prepare a four-letter wear-out series for a new monthly magazine, *Kever Life*. You publish the magazine and hope to reach prospective subscribers in the Kever, Oregon area. The magazine includes local news; short stories, essays, and poetry written by local writers;

quizzes and crossword puzzles; a special children's section; numerous full-color photographs; a calendar of local cultural events; and book, movie, and theatre reviews. A one-year subscription to *Kever Life* is $10, a two-year subscription is $18, and a three-year subscription is $25. The first 250 subscribers will receive two extra months of *Kever Life* free. The first issue will be mailed in early April. You want subscribers to enclose their checks with their orders and send them to:

> KEVER LIFE
> Route 6, Box 492
> Kever, Oregon 88814

4. [*This is both a timed exercise and a dictation exercise.*] Barry Bones, your best customer, called to complain that one of your salespeople just insulted him. Because of the insult, Mr. Bones told you that his grocery store chain will not carry your company's line of canned vegetables—Tasty Veggies—any longer. You do not want to lose Mr. Bones as a customer. You cannot get in touch with the salesperson in question, so you decide to write Mr. Bones a letter of apology. You also want to try to persuade Mr. Bones not to drop your Tasty Veggies line. You want to get the letter in the mail as soon as possible. Outline the letter. Make up the necessary names and addresses. Now dictate the letter (from your outline) to another student. Then have that student dictate her or his letter to you. You and the other student evaluate both your letters and your dictating skills.

5. Because most of your colleagues at the Extremely Big Corporation do not understand the "you" attitude, write a memorandum persuading them of its importance. Include at least one example of a "you"-attitude persuasive letter.

6. Write sentences that tactfully express each of these messages. The sentences that you write will constitute the main part of persuasive letters. You want:
   a. The receiver of your letter to speak to a group of your employees. The speaker usually charges for her speeches, but you have no money to pay her.
   b. Your boss to promote you to the position of chief economist.
   c. The receiver to grant you an exclusive interview.
   d. The receiver to complete an enclosed questionnaire.

7. Write one reminder, two persuasive, and two demand letters for the collection of $432.80 from Darlene Tenmire. Supply any information you need.

8. Write a letter to convince your boss to let you buy an expensive piece of equipment for your work. Make up the facts or cite information about an actual piece of equipment.

9. You are an accountant employed by the Simmons-Norman Corporation. You are performing an audit of the company's books and discover that the company is giving sizable bribes to foreign diplomats who are helping the company establish offices overseas. You then overhear that your company is planning to try to justify a rate increase by pointing to higher labor costs. You know that the bribery expenses are much higher than the increase in labor costs. What will you do? What should you consider before making a decision? Would your response be different if the amounts of the bribes were so small that the company's customers weren't affected? Write a brief paper answering these questions and trying to persuade the reader to accept the validity of your answers.

10. Write a humorous reminder to be sent to your customers who miss their payments by a few days. Supply whatever information you need.

11. Collect five or more actual sales letters. Analyze each. Identify the developmental plan, the treatment of the APCA pattern, the writing style, and any other relevant factors. Evaluate the quality of the message. Pay particular attention to the attention-getting and action/acceptance sections.

12. Write a simple enclosure sales message to accompany refunds you make when customers send you three boxtops. Supply needed information.

13. Use your dictionary and thesaurus to create meanings for these words. Use the words when you think, write, and speak so that you feel comfortable using them.

a. Compose		**i.** Emanate	
b. Comprehension		**j.** Espouse	
c. Comprise		**k.** Ethics	
d. Concept		**l.** Exploit	
e. Constitute		**m.** Motivation	
f. Continual		**n.** Persuasion	
g. Continuous		**o.** Relevant	
h. Crux		**p.** Subliminal	

14. Take and score Self-Test 26 over the excerpt about the sales series.

Self-Test 26
Excerpt about Sales Series

A. Recall (25 points each). For each multiple-choice question, select the most accurate answer.

1. The continual series involves:
  a. Solicited messages
  b. Smaller expenditures than the wear-out series
  c. A special, one-time mailing
  d. Mailing lists purchased especially for the series
  e. Inserts for the demand stage of the collection series

2. The campaign series involves:
  a. The careful development of several coordinated mailings—all of which are sent in sequence to every person on the mailing list
  b. Expenses less than the wear-out series
  c. Inexpensive products or services
  d. Several independent messages
  e. Messages that include only one of the APCA elements

3. The wear-out series involves:
  a. The most expensive products
  b. At least three independent mailing lists
  c. Letters that cannot stand alone
  d. Never sending a second letter to a person who has made a purchase
  e. Continuing the mailings until the point of diminishing returns

B. Inference (25 points). Indicate whether this statement is true or false.
Sales series letters fall at the medio level of communication.

Solution to Self-Test 26
Excerpt about Sales Series

A. Recall (25 points each)

   1. b   **3.** e

   2. a

B. Inference (25 points)

False

---

15. Take and score Self-Test 27 over Chapter 11.

Self-Test 27
Chapter 11

A. Recall (12 points each). For each multiple-choice question, select the most accurate answer.

1. Which one of these statements is true?
   a. The goal of every persuasive message is an action observable through the five senses.
   b. Persuasive techniques are ethical when used by an evangelist, but unethical when used by business.
   c. Persuasive messages should use only the deductive developmental pattern.
   d. The appeal in a sales message should match the receiver to the product or service.
   e. The larger the number of appeals in a sales letter, the better.

2. Which one of the statements is *not* true?
   a. The attention phase need not relate to the topic at all.
   b. "Please" and "Thank you" are not always considered to be attention-getting devices.
   c. The perception/interest stage ties the attention stage to the body.
   d. The comprehension/conviction/desire phase probably should be written first.
   e. Job-application messages are persuasive messages.

3. Which one of these statements is true?
   a. Persuasive messages fall into the routine category.
   b. The best rule for all collection messages is to assume the worst about the debtor.
   c. Some messages include both persuasion and bad news.
   d. The collection series need not keep repeating the amount owed.
   e. The only objective of collection letters is to collect the money—eventually.

4. Which of these statements concerning sales messages is *not* correct?
   a. Sales messages allow a great deal of originality and creativity in design and development.
   b. You should build your appeal around the qualities of the product or service, the qualities of the prospective buyer, and the desired action.
   c. Avoid overwhelming the prospective buyer with too much information.
   d. The major purpose of sales messages is to let consumers know that a product or service exists.
   e. Be sure that the attention section is related to the basic appeal.

5. Business ethics concerns:
   a. Mores, values, and honesty
   b. Specific ways to act in all situations
   c. Hiding misdeeds
   d. Only the people in the public relations department
   e. Learning to emphasize the positive

B. Inference (40 points). Indicate whether this statement is true or false.

   You need not conduct motivational research if your product or service is not complicated.

Solution to Self-Test 27
Chapter 11

A. Recall (12 points each)   **B.** Inference (40 points)

   1. d   **4.** d   False

   2. a   **5.** a

   3. c

12

Writing Memoranda, Notes, Forms, and Other Messages

Now that you have studied the letter, turn to some other kinds of business channels. Consider the memorandum, the note, the form, and certain other business-message vehicles.

Many of these business channels remain internal to the organization. Therefore, they often are more routine and informal than the letter transmitted to someone outside of the firm. Memoranda and some forms fall into this class.

Even the types that do carry messages to someone external often involve routine transactions. Several of the forms fall into this category.

Some of the other channels presented here may be rather formal and technical; for example, job descriptions, job specifications, policy statements, and policy manuals. At least three channels—newsletter, news magazine, and press release—actually fall into a category calling for a journalistic style of writing.

WRITING MEMORANDA AND NOTES

The memorandum and note are brief versions of the letter. You will most often use them for exchanging messages within the organization. Rarely will you adopt either format for extracompany transactions.

Memoranda

The function of the memorandum (memo) belongs so exclusively to intracompany transactions that it is often called the interoffice memorandum.

The firm usually provides stationery printed to contain the form of heading chosen specifically for the company's own use. As the writer, you may also supply your own memo heading on plain paper or letterhead stationery. Some of the formats appear in Figure 12–1.

Stationery

The preprinted stationery for the memorandum is often smaller in size than that for the letter. Two common sizes are the half sheet (8½ by 5½ inches) and the quarter sheet (4¼ by 5½ inches). The paper usually is 16-pound weight—without fabric content.

(a)

February 12, 198X

To: Members of the Committee on Personnel Policies
       (Bates, Estes, Farmer, Kyle, Perry)

From: Y. R. Self *yRS*

Subject: Meeting of February 18, 198X

(b)

Interoffice Memo   **Cagey, Inc.**

TO: Sara Brains   **DATE:**   12/17/198X

FROM: Y. R. Self *yRS*   **FILE NO.**   410129

(c)

WILEY CO.   **MEMORANDUM**

MEMO TO: Einbert Alstein

FROM: Y. R. *yRS*

DATE: October 9, 198X

SUBJECT: Relativity of the proposed theory

Figure 12–1 Forms for headings of memoranda

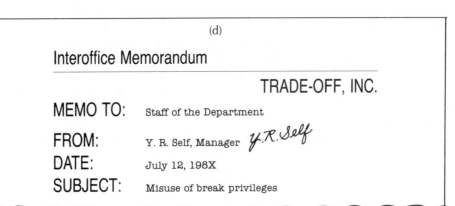

Figure 12–1 (continued)

Self-carboned packs of stationery are available for memoranda just as for letters and forms. Some packs include three sheets and a format that allows the response to be placed on the same sheet as the original message.

One such pack has you write your message on the top half of the first sheet, tear off and retain a carbon copy, and send the original and one copy to the receiver. The receiver then writes her or his response on the bottom half of the original, returns it to you, and keeps the copy (which now contains both messages).

Of course, the approach can be accomplished by using a standard sheet of paper for the original message, making a photocopy, using the bottom part of the original for the response, and making another photocopy. However, for economy and conservation of materials and energy, eliminate copies whenever you can.

Format

Though the memorandum is usually typewritten, it differs from the letter in several ways.

First, it often does not include a courtesy title for the addressee. Of course, if you use a courtesy title when you speak to the person, include it in the memorandum.

The memorandum does not include an inside address, a salutation, a complimentary close, or a standard signature block. As a sender, you generally place your initials or signature beside your typewritten name placed after "From." Omit official titles after your name unless the receiver does not know your position. The committee members in Figure 12–1a know that you are the chairperson; therefore, you do not include that title.

The deductive style fits the memorandum well. The statements often appear in a numbered sequence. Use single spacing within paragraphs, and double spacing between. Use a double or triple space after the last line of the heading.

The nature of the memorandum permits the use of concise, straightforward language. Though you maintain the "you" attitude, positive tone, and courtesy, you still may use some shortcuts as compared to messages for people outside of your firm.

Spotlight the references to your objectives in the subject line and the first and other paragraphs. Add only enough developmental information to reinforce these objectives.

Though you may write a memorandum about virtually any business topic, here are a few examples:

1. Announcement of a meeting and an agenda for it
2. Change in a policy affecting employees
3. Notification of an upcoming event—an audit, a visit by a dignitary, a fire drill, or the conversion of a process
4. Inquiry about the performance of an employee
5. Request for materials, equipment, or a service
6. Description of a procedure
7. Thank-you message for a job completed well
8. Acknowledgment of receipt of something
9. Suggestion for improvement of an internal procedure
10. Question about progress on an assigned task
11. Summary of some activity
12. Transmittal of a report
13. Request for permission to be away from the office

Figure 12–2 illustrates a simple memorandum.

Notes

Notes are even more informal than memoranda. They often carry handwritten messages about routine topics.

Though some companies provide preprinted note-form stationery, you often will use a personalized type or just a plain piece of paper. Sixteen-pound note paper usually comes in relatively small sizes: 4 by 5 inches, 4¼ by 5½ inches, 4 by 7 inches, 5 by 8 inches, and 5½ by 8½ inches. Review some of the styles for note paper shown in Figure 12–3.

Generally, the suggestions for the formats of memoranda also apply to notes. However, notes usually do not carry technical information or mass amounts of it. In addition, writers rarely retain copies of notes. Many times they do not even expect a response.

Consider these casual situations for which the personal, handwritten note is correct.

1. Congratulating a friend on being selected president of the local chapter of a professional organization
2. Telling an assistant what to do

MEMORANDUM   AFTERTASTE SODA, INC.

TO: Members of Retirement Dinner Committee
             (Baird, Farris, Hale, Jardin, Lacy, Rust)

FROM: Y. R. Self *YRS*

DATE: March 2, 198X

SUBJECT: Meeting of March 9, 198X

The Retirement Dinner Committee will meet at 2 p.m. on
Thursday, March 9, in Conference Room B. The purpose for the
meeting is to make these decisions:

1. Date

2. Site

3. Menu

4. Program

    a. Speaker

    b. Tributes

    c. Entertainment

    d. Emcee

5. Retirees' names

6. Gifts

7. Establishment of subcommittees

8. Date of next meeting

Please do some preliminary thinking about these topics before
next Thursday. We will plan to adjourn at about 3:30.

Figure 12–2 Interoffice memorandum setting date and agenda for meeting

3. Jotting down a telephone message for someone else
4. Suggesting a luncheon date
5. Inviting a colleague to join a discussion group
6. Responding to a letter or memorandum by handwriting a note across the bottom
   of it

   Figure 12–4 includes two examples of notes.

DESIGNING AND USING FORMS

As suggested in Chapter 9, many routine business messages may be reduced to
forms. They may save a great deal of time and money.

(a)

FROM THE DESK OF Y. R. Self
TO: Tracy   DATE: 1/22/8X

(b)

FROM THE DESK OF: _____
TO: _____
DATE: _____
SUBJECT: _____

(c)

CHRIS FRAZIER

(d)

MEMO from   Y. R. Self

_____

To _____ Date _____ Time _____

Figure 12–3   Forms for headings of handwritten notes

Creating Forms

Carefully develop forms that you will use repetitively. Though the form destroys any appearance of a personal or custom message, it can communicate quite satisfactorily.

Consider some suggestions for creating good forms.

1. Leave plenty of space for each answer.
2. Arrange the elements in logical groupings and in logical order.
3. Include complete and clear instructions.
4. Give the form a title.
5. Exhaust all elements associated with the topic.

(a)

FROM THE DESK OF
Y. R. SELF

1-28-8X

George —

Thanks for the invitation to the computer demonstration on Monday. I'll be there.

Y.R.

(b)

Strummin Guitars, Inc.

FROM THE DESK OF: *Y.R.*
TO: *Jane*
DATE: *17 June 8X*

Here is the copy of the report you wanted. Let me know what you think!

Figure 12–4 Acknowledgment and transmittal notes

6. Leave space for providing additional information not specifically requested, or suggest that the writer may attach additional pages.
7. Word the items at the lowest readability level anticipated in the audience.
8. Condense the form in as little space as possible without sacrificing completion space or creating a crowded appearance.
9. Use a size of type large enough that people can read the form.
10. Write clear questions and lead-in statements for all items.
11. If you distribute forms to people who do not request them, make return easy and desirable by enclosing postpaid return envelopes and providing incentives such as money, products, and gifts.

12. If you promise anonymity, do not try to identify the respondent by using some hidden or secret identification on forms or envelopes. Such secret codes are unethical and are even being tested in the courts for legality.
13. When appropriate, assure confidentiality.
14. If the person completing a form must return it by mail, be sure to include the mailing address on both the cover letter and form.
15. Regularly revise forms to keep them up to date.

As suggested by some of the items listed, some forms remain inside an organization, and others go outside of it. Forms fall at both the medio and mass levels. Consider some examples of the types of forms used in both instances:

Application for credit	Invoice
Inquiry about credit rating	Attendance report
Application for job	Tracer for lost shipment
Recommendation/appraisal/reference for applicant for job	Notice of expiration/renewal of certificates of deposit, magazine subscriptions, etc.
Application for insurance	
Application for loan	Membership card
Notice for dues or fees	Check-off form for explaining what kind of additional information is needed
Statement or bill	
Request for contributions or pledges	
Authorization to release information	Confirmation of reservation for hotel, transportation, etc.
Notification of gift subscription to a magazine	
	Tax form
Coupon for requesting refund on purchase of product	Quality control chart
	Routing slip

These forms represent but a few of those used in business and organizational work. Each area has its own needs for channels to facilitate communication and record-keeping. Figures 12–5 through 12–13 include examples of some of the others.

Using Forms

Just as the communication guidelines and principles apply to designing forms, they apply to completing them.

General suggestions

Consider these general suggestions for completing forms:

1. Read instructions carefully, skimming the entire form before beginning.
2. Follow instructions precisely; particularly be sure to use script, printing, or typewriting as specified.
3. Before beginning to write, determine whether the information goes above or below the line.
4. For many forms, put something in each blank, even if you just place a dash, a zero, "none," or "NA" ("not applicable," "not available") in it.

EXCELEBRATE, INC. ORDER FORM

(Please Typewrite or Print)

NAME Ms. Jo Creighton

MAILING ADDRESS 1718 Spruce Ave., Apt. 203

CITY Ray   STATE AR   ZIP 85244

TELEPHONE NUMBER (777) 777-7777

Page No.	Catalog Number	Name of Item	Color No.	Size	Price Each		Qty.	Total Price		Shpg. Wt. Lbs.	Oz.
48	4-8291	Watch	—		69	99	1	69	99		4
73	28-C389	35gal. Trash Can	—		24	79	2	49	58	22	26
2	1-3076-B	zip-lined Trench Coat	6-B (tan)		74	99	1	74	99	3	8

Totals	194	56	25	38

Check Type of Payment:

☑ Check or Money Order Enclosed

☐ National Express

☐ Supercharge

☐ Savi

☐ Excelebrate

			Changed Wt. (P. 38)
Tax (SEE P. 39)	9	73	
Shipping (SEE P. 38)	9	42	27	6
Amount Owed on Previous Order	0	00	
Total Amount	213	71	

Account or Card number:

Signature _____

Exp. Date: _____ Mo.: _____ Year: _____

Mail to:

Excelebrate, Inc.
4099 Darrell Way
Cecil, AL 36013

Figure 12–5 Completed retail order form

Send me more information about:

- [ ] Life insurance
- [✓] Health insurance
- [✓] Home insurance
  - [ ] Homeowner
  - [✓] Renter
  - [ ] Condominium Owner
  - [ ] Mobile Home Owner/Renter
- [✓] Auto insurance
- [ ] Business insurance
- [ ] Small Employers Group Insurance
- [ ] ROC Motor Club

ROC INSURANCE
One Queen's Drive
Amorita, OK 73719

Name _C. L. Korda_

Address _14 South Central_

City _Lynn_

State _AR_   Zip _72440_

Phone _333-333-3333_

I understand that no sales representative will come to my home without my permission. I also understand that I am under no obligation.

2009

Figure 12–6   Completed form requesting information

MESSAGE

For _Mr. Roland_

Date _2/19/8X_   Time _9:27 a.m._

M _G 7 Manning_

From _Surety Corp._

Phone No. _444-4444_

Message _Wants to set up an appointment to go over the Surety account with you. She will be in her office today, but not tomorrow_

by _it_

✓	Telephoned
	Returned your call
	Came to see you
	Will call again
✓	Wants to see you
✓	Wants you to phone

Figure 12–7   Completed form for message

PURPLE EX
PURPLE ARMOR
of Renfrew

1818 West 7
P.O. Box 4343
Renfrew, PA 17053

⌐Fred R. Quicksilver⌐
P.O. Box 893
⌊Leroy, O.H. 44251⌋

Date: __5/31/8X__

Group Number: _____

Process Number: __79845__

Processor: __jt__

Thank you for your recent request for membership in PURPLE EX/PURPLE ARMOR of Renfrew. We shall be glad to proceed with the processing as soon as we receive the information identified in this listing:

☐ Please take the _____ enclosed form(s) for medical examination to a physician who will give the listed person(s) physical examination(s) and complete the form(s). Please complete the examination(s) and have the physician return the form(s) in the enclosed envelope within three weeks of the date of this letter.

☑ Please sign the __3__ enclosed form(s) authorizing the release of medical information. Then send each form to the physician listed on it. Send each form soon so that the physician may return it to arrive in this office within three weeks of the date of this letter. The form itself includes a notation asking the physician to return it within two weeks of receipt.

☑ Please answer the following question(s) directly on this letter and return it in the enclosed envelope within two weeks of the date of this letter.

1. *Though you are applying only for yourself, what is your wife's name?*
   _____

2. *Does your wife have any group insurance?* _____ *If so, with what company?* _____ *what group number?* _____

Sincerely yours,

Processing Department

2.33 (7–81)

Figure 12–8 Completed form requesting additional medical information

Overextended Corp.

CREDIT ACCOUNT APPLICATION

(Subject to Credit Approval by Overextended Corp.)

(Please Print)

Account to be in the name of: Mr. ☐   Ms. ☒   Other:

First Name _Mary_   Middle Initial _R._   Last Name _Smith_   Age _35_

Street Address _32 Oak Creek Road_   City _Leaf Valley_   State _VA_   Zip _22226_

If applicant's spouse is authorized to buy on the account, print name here: _NA_

How long at present address _6 years_   Own ☒ Rent ☐   Board ☐ Other ☐   Monthly rent or mortgage payments _$340_

Previous address if less than 2 years at present address:

_NA_   How long _NA_

Home Phone _(703)528-5991_   Birth Date _9/25/45_   Number of Dependents _2_

Occupation _Accountant_   Employer _Warren, Perez, & Shakes_

Employer's Address _526 North Road, Leaf Valley, VA_   Business Phone _(703)528-9951_

How Long _7 years_   Salary $ _3,008_   Weekly ☐ Monthly ☒

Previous employer if less than 1 year with present employer:

_NA_   How long _NA_

Other Income $ _1,050_   . Weekly ☐ Monthly ☒   Sources _Part-time consulting_

Alimony, child support, or separate maintenance income need not be revealed if you do not want us to consider it in evaluating your application.

Bank Name	Bank Address	
Valley Bank	_43 Broadway, Leaf Valley, VA_	Savings ✓ Checking ✓ Loan ✓

Credit references (bank cards, nat'l credit cards, stores, finance companies, etc.)

Name _National Charge_   Address _P.O. Box 69, New York, NY_   Account No. _668-168-68_

Name _Kayco Gas Company_ Address _13 Smithton St., Knox, VA_ Account No. _446-19 KS_

Name and address of relative or personal reference other than spouse:

Catherine Smith, Ph.D., 39 W. Frank Rd., Rim, NJ 39964

Overextended Corp. is authorized to investigate my credit record and to verify my credit, employment, and income references:

Signature _Mary R. Smith_   Social Security Number _555-55-5555_ Date _6/1/8X_

Figure 12–9   Completed form for application for credit

| CATHY COMPANY | Requisition for Purchase 9184 |

Date ___6/1/80_____ Account No. ___39214CT_____

Requisitioned by ___Arnold Dietrich_____

Department ___Accounting_____

Required Delivery Date ___10/1/80 ·_____

Name of Vendor ___Daymar Furniture, Inc._____

Address of Vendor ___9864 Farrell Avenue_____

            Pixie, Wisconsin 98640_____

Terms offered by vendor ___2/10, n/30_____

Qty.	Catalog Number	Description	Unit Price	Total Price	Shpg. Wt.
6	84EB	Safety File Cabinet	129.95	779.70	240 lbs.
2	662F	Deluxe Walnut Desk	389.95	779.90	400 lbs.
			Total	1559.60	640 lbs.

Required Signatures:

Arnold Dietrich   6/1/80
Requisitioner   Date

Anna Mavis   6/1/81
Department Head   Date

Figure 12–10 Completed form requisitioning materials to be supplied from outside the organization

COUNT ME ....

    (Please Print)

    Name _Carol France_

    Address _19 Graydon Drive_

    City _Ben Lomand_   State _CA_   Zip _95005_

    Telephone No. _(666) 666-6666_

.... A SUPPORTER OF DROPIN UNIVERSITY

☑ I will join the
   DROPIN ASSOCIATION

    ☐ I am enclosing a check for
       my annual dues of $35.

    ☑ Charge my annual dues
       of $35 as shown.

☑ I will contribute to the
   DROPIN DEVELOPMENT FUND

    ☐ I am enclosing a check
       for $ _____.

    ☑ Charge my contribution
       of $ _50—_ as shown.

Charge _$85—_ to Savi ☑ or Supercharge ☐

Card No. _1111-111-111-1111_   Exp. Date _12-8 X_

Signature _Carol France_

    (Please sign whether sending a check or charging.)

Figure 12–11 Completed form for membership/contribution

I'll take you up on the FREE SAMPLE!

ACHESAWAY TABLETS
  Relief for arthritis, but no stomach upset

Do you presently use a medication for arthritis?

☒ Yes   Brand _Arthritabol_

☐ No

Name _Don Miller_

              (Please print clearly)

Address _3470 East Baynes Street_

City _Lorma_   State _CA_   Zip _44492_

One sample per family and household. Not available outside U.S. Void where prohibited, taxed, or otherwise regulated. Offer restricted to persons 18 years or older. Offer expires 9/30/8X.

Figure 12–12 Completed form requesting a free sample
(on mail-in card with address on other side)

TRAVIVI CAMERA REGISTRATION

Please return this form within two weeks of date or purchase.

☐ Mr.   ☐ Ms.   ☑ Other title: _Dr_

Name

R	u	t	h		H	o	l	d	e	n	–	S	a	y	r	e	s					

Address

1	9	9	1		E	a	s	t		1	0	7		S	t	r	e	e	t			

City **State** **Zip**

D	o	r	o	t	h	y								N	J		0	8	3	1	7

Serial Number: _TR–7543A_ ____ Date of Purchase: _7/11/8X_

Name of Store at
Which Puchased: _Y.G.&T._

Address of Store: _Trails Shopping Center_
Dorothy, N.J.   08317

Figure 12–13 Completed form registering a product under warranty
(on mail-in card with address on other side)

5. If typewriting, set machine so that the bottoms of the letters just clear the lines.
6. If the instructions do not indicate that you may add extra pages to the form, put your information in the space allowed.
7. If you may add pages, refer to them on the form, and arrange them logically.

If you decide not to provide information requested on the form, be sure that the omission serves your purposes. For example, you may be within your legal rights in omitting such things as your age, sex, race, income, and marital status. However, you may be risking the opportunity to obtain something you want badly by doing so. Make the decision whether a small compromise of principles and rights might be worth a potential gain.

If you decide not to supply information, you might choose to use "NA." It is a designation that may be interpreted to mean that the question itself is not applicable.

Figures 12–5 through 12–13 include examples of some properly completed forms. Others appear in subsequent chapters.

The examples of completed forms are relatively familiar and self-explanatory. However, two types—the purchase requisition and purchase order—receive added treatment here.

Purchase requisition and order

The requisition shown in Figure 12–10 is for the purchase of materials from a known outside supplier. The form also serves as a requisition for services.

The requisitioner sends the completed form to the purchasing department. The department often sends a purchase order to the supplier.

The purchase order is a form used by a firm for ordering materials or services from an external organization. It looks very much like the order forms supplied by sellers, but contains the printed name and address of the ordering firm and the typed-in name and address of the supplying firm. Businesses often use their own purchase-order forms instead of order blanks to provide consistency for all of their orders.

Organizations sometimes use the type of form shown in Figure 12–10 for ordering supplies and services from within the organization. For the internal process the requisition serves as the order; no additional processing takes place.

Some organizations also use a requisition form to direct a purchasing department to place an order with a supplier of the purchasing department's choice. If the form serves only that one purpose, it will not include the headings for vendor name and address or for unit price, total price, and shipping weight. It likely will provide extensive space in which the requisitioner may establish the specifications for the materials and services requisitioned.

By observing such a process, a purchasing department functions not only to place orders, but to find the best prices for the materials and services needed. Purchasing often requires suppliers to place bids for filling such orders.

WRITING OTHER BUSINESS MESSAGES

Though the messages carried by them overlap with the kinds carried by letters, memoranda, notes, forms, and reports, several other channels deserve some mention. Review (1) general informational and persuasive messages, (2) legal and organizational messages, (3) traditional news messages, (4) job descriptions and specifications, and (5) telegrams and cards.

General Informational and Persuasive Messages

Think of this class as containing five subparts: (1) extensive and complex messages, (2) brief and simple messages, (3) recruitment messages, (4) listing and outline messages, and (5) flow charts and organizational charts.

Extensive and complex messages

Some messages are rather involved, complex, technical, or extensive. Examples include catalogs; brochures, pamphlets, and booklets; policy statements; policy manuals and handbooks; other manuals and handbooks; and position papers. These suggestions apply generally to all of them:

1. Collect complete and accurate information.
2. Choose verbal and nonverbal symbols that convey the information in a manner understandable and acceptable to the readers—usually matched to the lowest readability level represented by the receivers.
3. Make the message as brief as possible, while retaining enough content and courtesy to accomplish the purposes.
4. Attend to the quality of the transmission—particularly to such elements as paper, binding, style of type, spacing, layout, color, spelling, grammar, punctuation, and mechanics.

5. Apply the suggestions specific to the general type of channel—be it informational or persuasive.
6. To accomplish your purpose, observe appropriate developmental patterns.

Catalogs   The catalog can contain no more than a few simple, mimeographed pages listing a few items offered for sale. It can, however, include more than a thousand printed, glossy pages of pictures, colors, and flashy words designed to describe and sell more than a hundred thousand items.

Brochures, pamphlets, and booklets   Brochures, pamphlets, and booklets usually go outside the firm. They generally attempt to inform and persuade.

Such messages often take the form of glossy, colorful, pictorial, professionally printed, and elaborately folded or bound messages on heavy stock. However, they also may appear as black-and-white, typewritten, photocopied reproductions on lightweight, stapled pages. Contents often include information about:

Programs offered by an insurance company
Investments and services available from a financial institution
Features of products
Recruitment information
Services provided by a travel agency
Annual data collected by industrial associations
Features and procedures associated with membership in an organization
Health subjects such as blood pressure, smoking, vitamins, and exercise
First-aid and safety subjects such as driving, fires, poisons, and heart attacks
National and international topics
Political, consumer, economic, cultural, social, or recreational topics

When writing such messages, again try to visualize the reader as he or she picks up the piece and reads it. Adapt the message to that image as much as money and time allow. You may be able to purchase some of the professionally developed literature-rack publications more inexpensively than you can produce them.

Policy statements   Statements of policy represent broad guides to the personnel of an organization as they act and interact to carry out the functional operations necessary to accomplish the established goals. Therefore, a good statement of policy comes only after people with the authority engage in extensive research and careful formulation based upon clear objectives. Once the appropriate people establish a policy, the actual writing must reflect the intent clearly, completely, and concisely.

Couch a policy statement in symbols understood by the readership. Too often written policies carry with them a legalistic jargon inappropriate for the level of the message.

Understand that the people who use policies must have some latitude in their interpretation. A policy should not and cannot cover every minute detail of a function or operation. In addition, the conditions upon which policies depend change frequently. Therefore, be prepared to examine, revise, formulate, write, and rewrite statements on a regular basis.

(532 words)
(test on page 420)

Figure 12–14 illustrates a simple statement of policy.

1.72. POLICY ON JOB POSTINGS

Effective April 1, 198X all job openings for Grade 6 and higher will be posted so that employees may bid on them. The jobs will remain posted for ten working days.

To bid for a job, the employee will obtain a form from any office or supervisor, complete it, and return it to the office of the manager of the department in which the opening occurs. The employee must submit the bid no later than 5:00 p.m. on the tenth day of the posting.

When the posting period closes, a management-appointed screening committee will interview all bidders. They will then select the top three and notify them that they have been chosen for a second interview. They will send letters to the remaining bidders explaining why they were not chosen to be in the top three.

The supervisor for the area in which the open job occurs will join the screening committee for the interviews with the top three bidders and for the decision. The supervisor and committee will notify the top bidder that he or she has been selected for the job. They will also send letters to the other two explaining why they were not chosen.

Figure 12–14   Statement of policy of job postings

Policy manuals and handbooks   A policy manual or handbook is nothing more than an exhaustive collection of statements of policy for a given organization. It sometimes takes the form of a looseleaf publication distributed to each affected employee. When policies change, management distributes new pages to replace the outdated ones.

Other manuals and handbooks   Manuals and handbooks often contain other information besides policies. Here are some examples:

Procedures	Repairs
Employee benefits	Welding codes
Worker functions	Safety codes
Supervisory functions	Materials specifications
Job specifications	Shop operations
Job descriptions	Parts for equipment
Employment	Information processing
Appraisal	Styles for letters, memoranda,
Government regulations	forms, reports, and other elements
Operating rules	of communication channels

Manuals need to be clear, complete, concise, accurate, and straightforward. Whether manuals stay within an organization or go outside of it, they have a utilitarian purpose.

Position papers Business people sometimes use the position paper to transmit a logically developed position on an issue. Though the message does not try to sell a material good or service, it does try to present and even sell the writer's views on a given topic. It may even be likened to one side of an oral debate.

Research the subject of a position paper thoroughly. Choose the arguments carefully. Understand the opponent's arguments, and build yours to refute them. Develop and revise the paper to reflect logical thinking and organization. Put the paper aside for several days, reread it, and rewrite it if necessary to move it toward a perfected state. Have some colleagues read and evaluate it. Revise it once again if you need to do so.

Brief and simple messages

Examples of brief and simple messages include flyers, circulars, leaflets, bulletins, handbills, and insertions with paychecks or statements.

These channels often involve direct, concise, plain, handwritten or typewritten messages duplicated by a mimeograph, spirit-duplication, or photocopy process. They usually fill only one or two pages and often involve no color or pictorial effects. However, such messages may also appear as expensive, elaborate productions.

Picture (1) the types of flyers put under the windshield wipers of parked cars, (2) sales circulars received in the mail, (3) leaflets distributed on street corners, (4) messages posted on bulletin boards, (5) handbills placed in public places to announce such activities as auctions and coin shows, and (6) the kinds of information contained on paycheck insertions.

Figure 12–15 includes a simple, brief message to illustrate one of the types just introduced. It is a photocopied message inserted in all envelopes containing the quarterly statements of activity in credit-union accounts.

Recruitment messages

Messages often attempt to recruit people to attend an educational institution, to apply for a position with a firm, or to join an organization (including the military). They all inform and persuade to action. They may take many of the forms just described—brochures, booklets, and even flyers, circulars, pamphlets and handbills.

Educational institutions You probably have received literature urging you to become a student in the institution you now attend, or in another. Someone undoubtedly wrote it to feature the attractive qualities of the school. Do you recall what the features were? Do you recall whether the message was an influencing factor in your decision?

Companies When you graduate, you likely will encounter some sophisticated recruitment literature. Such literature often includes a professional piece featuring both narrative and pictorial presentations about the firm that distributes it.

Companies preparing recruitment messages often distribute them in conjunction with campus interviews scheduled by the placement office. The messages customarily follow a title including words something like "Your Accounting Career with Teap, Wickmar, Ellmitch & Co."

Organizations Solicitation of membership in an organization may come from the international, national, regional, or local level. It may come from large and wealthy

As required for your protection, the Sensible Corporation Employees Credit Union is undergoing its annual audit by a Certified Public Accounting firm. One part of the audit involves a direct check with members to determine whether the records reflect correct transactions and balances.

If the transactions and balances on the enclosed statement are correct, PLEASE DO NOT REPLY. If, however, you find an error, please complete the reverse side of this notice and mail it directly to:

> HOUSE WATERPRICE & CO.
> Certified Public Accountants
> Suite 1200
> 8 Park Drive
> Security, MD 21235

DO NOT CONTACT ANY EMPLOYEE OR OFFICER OF THE CREDIT UNION. ONLY CONTACT HOUSE WATERPRICE & CO.

(front)

If you find errors in your statement, list them here:

Name As It
Appears on Statement _____

Signature _____ Date _____

Account Number _____

(back)

Figure 12–15   Audit verification inserted with statement of
account of company credit union

organizations or from small and poor ones. Therefore, the types of messages range from the elaborate brochure to the one-page, mimeographed flyer. Figure 12–16 includes a familiar type.

Listing and outline messages

Several informational channels fall into a category that might be called listing and outline channels. Examples include procedures, guidelines, criteria, instructions and directions, and programs.

JOIN AND PARTICIPATE IN THE
ACTIVITIES OF THE

MARKETING
SOCIETY

Fall Organizational Meeting
September 11, 198X

—Dues only $5 a semester

—Meetings at 7:30 p.m. in
Auditorium B on the second
Thursday of each month—
August through May

—Informal, productive meetings

—Committee work optional

—New officers each semester

—Speakers from business and
industry

—Job fair in the spring—at
least 30 interviewers

—Fall dinner and dance

—Spring picnic

—Tours

—Scholarship opportunities

Join at the Membership Tables Located at the
East and West Ends of the First-Floor Halls Sept. 8-12
or
Join at Any Meeting
or
Pick up a Membership Card
in the Dean's Office

Figure 12–16   Flyer recruiting students to join organization

Each of the types involves a series of brief statements arranged in logical order to form the specific message. Though the statements often include an introductory paragraph or two, the crux of the message lies in the listed items.

Procedures A procedural statement lists a step-by-step sequence for performing some operation. Some organizations or departments within them devote entire manuals to the procedures associated with various activities. Picture how statements are useful and necessary for people who take part in these procedures:

Processing a requisition and a purchase order
Filing a grievance
Filing an insurance claim
Using an expense account
Applying for insurance
Requesting an audience with top management
Participating in word-processing activities
Reporting an accident
Auditing
Filing for political office
Taking an opinion poll
Lodging a complaint
Taking early retirement
Installing and starting heavy equipment
Traveling at company expense
Taking inventory
Performing factory operations
Establishing a tax-sheltered account
Applying for unemployment compensation
Conducting an interview
Hiring
Appraising
Firing
Conducting an election

Figure 12–17 illustrates a statement of grievance procedures for a nonunion organization. Assume that the statement appears in a manual for employees.

Guidelines Guidelines are statements that establish principles or standards by which to determine a course of action, make judgments, or establish a policy. The communication guidelines featured in this book provide one example of an approach to guidelines for action.

Criteria Criteria form another category of written lists involving relatively discrete, but related parts. The concept of criteria arose in conjunction with the techniques of communication evaluation in Chapter 6.

As established in that discussion, a criterion is a rule, a standard, or a test used as the basis for a judgment. The criterion relates to a carefully defined objective or purpose. In addition, the more objective—and even quantified—the criteria, the easier the evaluation.

The concept of criteria fits any evaluative situation. Consider these examples of circumstances in which criteria are appropriate:

Admitting students to a college
Assigning grades or ratings in educational settings
Judging applicants for jobs
Deciding whether to fire employees
Selecting items for a sample
Assessing behavior
Testing items from an assembly line
Choosing committee or team members

GRIEVANCE PROCEDURE

The grievance process involves the person filing the grievance, the Grievance Committee, the affected officers, and any other persons affected by the process or the final decision. The grievance procedure takes this sequence:

1. The aggrieved person first exhausts all established channels for solving the problem, following the chain from the immediate superior through the division manager. If the grievance is with a superior in that chain, the person should still discuss the matter in the order dictated.

2. If the exhaustion of the established channels does not satisfy the person, s/he reviews the definition of a grievance (page 17 of this manual) to determine whether the particular case fits it.

3. If the person decides that the case fits the definition, s/he obtains a grievance form from the Personnel office and completes it. S/he attaches any additional pages or materials thought necessary to present the grievance and supporting evidence.

4. The person submits the completed form and accompanying materials to the Chairperson of the Grievance Committee (defined on page 18).

5. The Grievance Committee meets within five days of receipt of the grievance and as many times thereafter as necessary to complete the work. (See page 18 for a description of Committee procedures.)

6. The Committee reaches a decision, writes a report, and sends copies to the aggrieved person, to the vice president for the division in which that person works, and to others if deemed appropriate. (See page 18.)

7. The vice president reviews the report, completes whatever additional investigation s/he needs, and reaches a decision. S/he communicates the decision to the aggrieved person and to any other persons affected by it.

8. If the decision requires some action, the affected persons then participate in that action.

Figure 12–17 Statement of a grievance procedure contained in a manual for employees

Appraising performance on the job	Voting on candidates
Determining merit raises	Rating alternative strategies
Determining promotions	Choosing from among several brands
Testing incoming material for use in production	Judging livestock
Deciding on grievance cases	Deciding on a case in a court of law
Deciding on claims	Determining success of a program
	Selecting members of a jury

Make criteria clear, complete, and concise. Though not every situation that needs to be evaluated lends itself to objective statements of criteria, move as much in that direction as you can. Evaluate these examples for their quality as criteria:

- The applicant must score at least 78 on the entrance examination.
- To be promoted, the employee must be well liked by the others in the department.
- The candidate must receive a mean rating of 7 or higher from at least three of the five judges.
- The customer must pick up the product and examine it for at least four seconds.
- The customer must have a pleasant expression.
- The program must meet the needs of the participants.
- The weld on the relay must have a strength of between 6 and 8 psi.

Instructions and directions   Instructional and directional statements are quite similar. They even overlap with the concept of procedures—except that procedures possibly involve more extensive processes.

Instructions or directions aid in completing examinations or forms, assembling bookshelves or picnic tables, driving a car, writing a proposal, or even flying an airplane.

Keep instructions and directions brief, clear, and complete. Whether the listing appears in numerical sequence or in narrative form, cast each sentence to carry its own distinct meaning. However, be sure that the sentences combine to form the desired whole message.

Programs   Programs show the logical ordering of events. Though the items may not form complete sentences, each still holds its own discrete message, even as all of the discrete parts add up to a coherent whole.

Establish attractive formats for programs.

Programs for artistic presentations, dinner meetings, conventions, and other such events often include sections other than the unfolding elements of the events. Such sections may be lists of committee members, donors, menus, or biographical sketches of participants.

Make all parts clear, concise, complete, and parallel. Treat the body much as an outline—an outline without numbers. Such an approach will help maintain logic in major and minor headings.

Flow charts and organizational charts

Though most charts fall primarily into the category of nonverbal communication—covered in Chapter 16—at least two special types involve more writing and logic than the actual mechanics of charting. The two are flow charts and organizational charts.

Flow charts   A flow chart actually places a series of operations or procedures into a logical sequence. It joins geometric shapes by arrows showing the direction of the flow. The shapes represent key stations such as positions, operations, or units.

Writers of computer programs use the flow-chart technique extensively. It provides a graphic way to assure that the program covers all necessary commands and operations in proper sequence.

Figure 12–18 shows a chart for the flow of a purchasing process involving the requisition, order, and payment for goods from a known vendor. You previously read about that process in the section on forms. Figure 12–19 is a flow chart showing how the federal government measures unemployment.

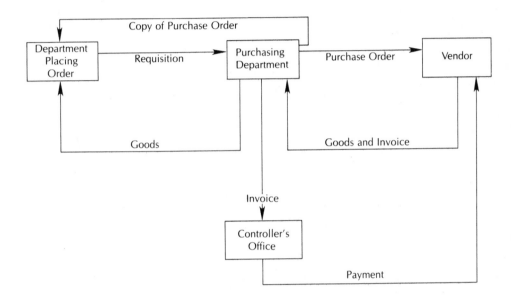

Figure 12–18   Flow chart showing purchasing process for goods from a known vendor

Organizational charts   The organizational chart shows the structure of work and authority for a firm. The traditional format (Figure 12–20) uses the vertical arrangement, with solid lines showing direct, "line" relationships and broken lines showing indirect, "staff" relationships.

The line elements participate directly in the activities that define the organization's thrust. They both supervise and are supervised. The staff elements provide services that aid the line elements in accomplishing their work. They do not supervise, but are supervised.

Most organizational charts fit the traditional design. However, innovators have introduced new designs to describe what they consider to be more realistic approaches to the authority and responsibility of people and organizations.

One type is the ladder organization. On the ladder are specialists who can move up and down and work with employees at all levels. Thus, they are not fixed at traditional levels on the chart.

Another structure involves a series of three-dimensional circles. They are arranged in concentric circles like a beehive.

CHART 1.

STATUS OF THE LABOR FORCE
(Figures shown are for second quarter
of 1977, seasonally adjusted)

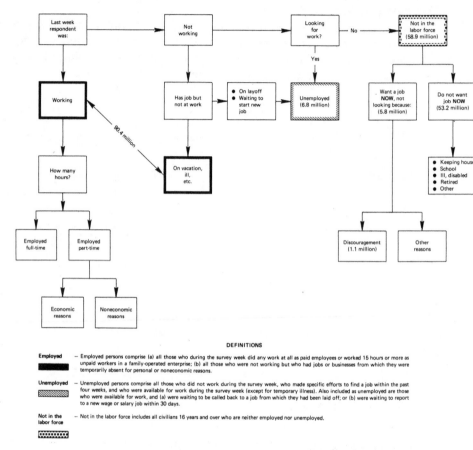

DEFINITIONS

Employed
— Employed persons comprise (a) all those who during the survey week did any work at all as paid employees or worked 15 hours or more as unpaid workers in a family-operated enterprise; (b) all those who were not working but who had jobs or businesses from which they were temporarily absent for personal or noneconomic reasons.

Unemployed
— Unemployed persons comprise all those who did not work during the survey week, who made specific efforts to find a job within the past four weeks, and who were available for work during the survey week (except for temporary illness). Also included as unemployed are those who were available for work, and (a) were waiting to be called back to a job from which they had been laid off; or (b) were waiting to report to a new wage or salary job within 30 days.

Not in the labor force
— Not in the labor force includes all civilians 16 years and over who are neither employed nor unemployed.

Figure 12–19 Flow chart showing measurement of unemployment

SOURCE: U.S., Department of Labor, Bureau of Labor Statistics, *How the Government Measures Unemployment,* BLS Rept. 505 (Washington, D. C.: Government Printing Office, 1977), p. 3.

   The project management structure is like a bunch of grapes. When the organization is concerned with many projects, each project becomes a grape. When the staff completes a project, that grape is removed from the cluster.

   The matrix organizational chart shows actions cutting across many levels and functions. The concept of teams of functional specialists fits this design well.

   The doughnut shape places management in the center, staff personnel just around the center, divisional officers in the next ring, and the remaining levels in rings extending to the outer circle of workers.

   Whatever the shape of the organizational design, the key is the need to attempt to portray the actual situation as well as possible. Some people even urge that no design be imposed because it squelches originality and creative interactions.

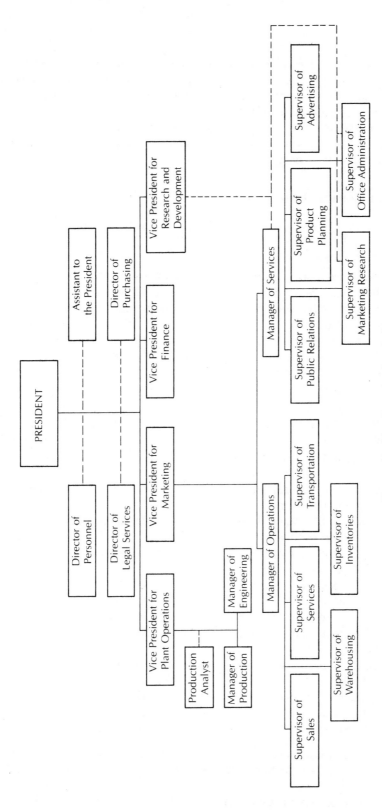

Figure 12–20 Organizational chart

399

As suggested in Figure 12–20, you may divide the parts of the whole according to function, or by titles associated with functions. You may also divide it by product, territory, process, or type of customer. The important factor is the segmentation into parts that will contribute to the functioning of the whole.

In practice the actual and organizational-chart structures usually differ. However, the chart does provide some guidance to the chain of interactions—both vertically and horizontally.

Legal and Organizational Messages

Some kinds of messages deal with legal and quasi-legal organizational situations.

Legal messages

Unless you are a lawyer, you will not be composing legal documents outright. You may, however, participate in developing the content of legal documents, or at least complete forms that contribute to the makeup of legal documents. In addition, you certainly will be bound by some legal documents and thus will need to learn to interpret them for your personal or business activities.

Picture just a few of the kinds of legal matters and messages with which business communicators deal:

Contract law
Agency law
Property law
Bankruptcy
Protection of confidentiality
Open files rulings
Collective bargaining and other union activities
Lawsuits from employees, customers, and suppliers
Lawsuits against others
Tax laws
Social Security payments and benefits
Retirement programs and funds
Workers' Compensation
Unemployment compensation
Laws of partnerships and corporations
Regulations of noncompetitive practices
International law

Extension of credit
Civil Rights Act of 1964
Equal Employment Opportunity Commission Requirements
Affirmative Action plans
Equal Pay Act
Environmental Protection Agency rules
Occupational Safety and Health Administration provisions
Government rules and regulations for reporting
Libel
Consumer protections
Insurance claims
Warranties
Receipts
Zoning laws
Proxy statements
Disability provisions
Sick-leave issues
Auditing

Though these examples overlap with one another and with other communication channels, they do hint at the pervasiveness of legal issues in the activities of business.

Use accepted legal forms and guidelines as models for any legal writing you do. Even if you add words to a preprinted legal form, use an approved completed model until you are sure you understand the importance of every word you use. Periodically reread the associated guidelines so that you know you communicate properly.

Many legal writers have converted to more natural language. Much of that change results from statutory requirements spearheaded by consumer groups. Whenever you have the opportunity, urge the conversion from "legalese" to a simpler, conversational idiom. So long as it meets the requirements of the law, a natural legal message is far superior to a legalistic one.

The legal instrument should be clear, complete, concise, and accurate. The omission of a date, the misspelling of a name, a typographical error on a land description, the transposition of some numbers, or the failure to put "None" or "NA" in a blank—each may be enough to allow a legal document to be challenged.

Figure 12–21 includes an excerpt from the kind of contract form used by many realtors. Notice that it still contains the legalistic style of language.

Organizational messages

Business communicators also use quasi-legal messages that govern the activities and meetings of the organizations in which they participate. Consider constitutions, bylaws, and operating codes; parliamentary procedures; motions and resolutions; agendas; and minutes of meetings.

Constitutions, bylaws, and operating codes   The development of organizational constitutions, bylaws, and operating codes is an extensive group process. It usually requires substantial thinking, brainstorming, and decision-making before and during the actual writing process.

When you write such documents, use common sense and a fresh approach. Again, cut out as much ponderous, legalistic language as you can. Write clearly. Use an outline and numbering system that makes references to the document easy. Be sure that the messages carry the appropriate legal intent. Be particularly careful to meet the laws related to the tax consequences for not-for-profit organizations. Be brief, but cover as many potential problem-creating situations as possible. Make provisions for both ratification and amendment of the documents.

As an example, Figure 12–22 shows an excerpt from the constitution of a faculty senate at an institution for higher learning.

Parliamentary procedures   Parliamentary procedures have a legal impact upon the meetings of organizations. Therefore, if you participate frequently in meetings governed by parliamentary procedures, become familiar with them.

Any organization may, of course, set all the rules governing it. However, many organizations establish some rules—through its constitution, bylaws, and operating code—and then supplement the specific rules with some standard set. Probably the best known of all such standard sets is *Robert's Rules of Order*.

Whatever your method of operating, use procedures to facilitate meetings—not as obstacles to impede them.

Motions and resolutions   Any formal meeting requires motions as part of the operating procedures. Resolutions also frequently result from such meetings.

Most motions are oral. However, many are written ahead of time to be sure they transmit intended messages properly.

PURCHASE CONTRACT FOR
REAL ESTATE

This is a legally binding contract; if not understood, seek competent legal advice.

_____   _____
City   State   Zip   Date

I, or we, hereby agree to purchase the following described real property, to-wit:

together with all the improvements thereon and the appurtenances, if any, thereunto belonging, including _____
of the mineral rights, and subject to existing zoning ordinances, restrictions and easements. Seller certifies that all mechanical, plumbing, and electrical installations, will be in proper working order at closing. Purchaser shall satisfy herself/himself in this regard prior to closing. Failure of Purchaser to notify Seller or Agent in writing of any defect prior to closing, shall constitute a waiver of claim for correction of such defect, if any. The seller agrees to deliver the property and the improvements thereon in their present conditions, ordinary wear and tear excepted.

I, or we, agree to pay for said real property the sum of

_____Dollars

($_____) payable as follows: The sum of $_____

which is hereby deposited with _____

Agent _____ receipt of which is hereby acknowledged, to

be applied on the purchase price, and the further sum of $_____, subject to adjustment at the time of closing, as follows:

The seller, within _____ days from date of acceptance, shall furnish an abstract of title to said real property to the _____

_____, extended to this date, showing merchantable title in the seller, according to the standards.

. . . .

Figure 12–21 Excerpt from a form contract for purchase of real estate

CONSTITUTION
FACULTY SENATE OF MATRICULATE COLLEGE

Revision of May, 198X

PREAMBLE

Recognizing the need to involve the faculty as the University progresses toward the solution of its problems and accomplishment of its goals, the faculty, administration, and the Board of Regents of Matriculate College establish the Matriculate College Faculty Association and its Senate. It shall be governed by the following articles:

ARTICLE I.   FACULTY ASSOCIATION AND FACULTY SENATE
The Faculty Association of Matriculate College is composed of all full-time teaching faculty members (including department and division chairpersons), all full-time professional administrators (as officially designated), and all full-time professional librarians (as officially designated). The Faculty Senate is the body elected to represent the Faculty Association.

ARTICLE II. PLAN OF REPRESENTATION

Section 1.   Each election unit (the professional library staff, the full-time advisors, and each school except the Graduate School) shall be represented in the Faculty Senate according to the formula N/W, in which N is the number of Faculty Association members in the unit and W is the total number of Faculty Association members divided by thirty-five (35)—the desired Senate size. However, no school shall have fewer than four (4) Senators. The quotient N/W shall be rounded to the next larger whole number if the remainder is one-half (½) or more. A committee of the Faculty Senate, with the approval of the Senate, shall be responsible for applying the formula and informing each unit of the number of Senators allotted to it.

Section 2.   The full-time professional administrators shall name from among them three (3) senators.

Section 3.   The Student Senate shall be invited to send one of its members to the Faculty Senate as a nonvoting representative of the student body.

. . . .

Figure 12–22   Excerpt from a constitution for a college faculty senate

---

MOTION

I move that we form a committee made up of five members,
with one member selected by nomination and secret-ballot
election in each of the five departments in the division. The
committee shall select its own chairperson. The committee shall
have the responsibility to develop a plan by which departmental
employees may participate significantly in the policy-making of
the company. The committee shall complete its work during
May so that this body may review the plan at its June meeting.

Figure 12–23   A motion complicated enough to be put in written form

Resolutions are motions; they simply take a rather prescribed form that requires a written presentation. The traditional form includes a preamble, a series of "Whereas" phrases, and a final phrase beginning with "Therefore, be it resolved."

Figure 12–23 shows a written motion. Figure 12–24 shows a traditional resolution. Because the historical style of the resolution is unlike a natural conversation, you may elect not to use that style. Therefore, Figure 12–24 also includes a more natural version of the traditional resolution.

Agendas   The agenda is the program for a meeting. Within limits, it follows an order prescribed by tradition and the standard operating rules for meetings. Figure 12–25 contains an example of an agenda.

Minutes   The minutes of meetings constitute the official record of the formal activities of that organization. Like the agenda, minutes follow relatively prescribed form and order.

Minutes should include at least every key element of the meeting: who, what, when, where, how, and why. Some organizations want the minutes to include a rather full statement of the discussion and debate in addition to the skeleton features of the meeting.

Accuracy is a cardinal requirement for good minutes. If necessary, use a tape recorder in addition to taking notes.

Figure 12–26 includes the outline and some excerpts from the minutes for a simple meeting. Observe how the outline follows the agenda, making it nearly impossible to omit any major component.

The style shown in Figure 12–26 is appropriate only for brief minutes. It wastes a great deal of space. For lengthy minutes, use a standard report style without the headings or with the headings placed above paragraphs instead of at the sides of them.

Traditional News Messages

Business writers sometimes use traditional journalistic channels. Newsletters, news magazines, and press releases represent three of the instances. If you write for such

TRADITIONAL RESOLUTION

On January 23, 198X, management reduced the Employees' Council from ten to three members. Therefore, the three-member Council has been functioning for nearly a year. The members doubt the efficiency of such a small group and offer this resolution for improvement:

WHEREAS   a three-member Employees' Council cannot fairly represent seven departments,

WHEREAS   a three-member Employees' Council cannot do the volume of work that a larger council can,

WHEREAS   the three-member Employees' Council in effect since January 23, 198X, has had little success in solving the management-employee-relations problems brought before it,

WHEREAS   the ten-member Employees' Council of 198X had a much better record, and

WHEREAS   a secret-ballot election of the employees showed the desire to increase the size,

THEREFORE, BE IT RESOLVED that the Employees' Council and 213 of the 283 employees represented by it call for a seven-member Employees' Council containing one elected representative from each of the seven departments.

CONTEMPORARY VERSION OF THE
SAME RESOLUTION

On January 23, 198X, management reduced the Employees' Council from ten to three members. Therefore, the three-member Council has been functioning for nearly a year. The members doubt the efficiency of such a small group and offer this resolution for improvement:

A three-member Employees' Council cannot fairly represent seven departments. A three-member Employees' Council cannot do the volume of work that a larger council can. The three-member Employees' Council in effect since January 23, 198X, has had little success in solving the management-employee-relations problems brought before it. The ten-member Employees' Council of 198X had a much better record. A secret-ballot election of the employees showed the desire to increase the size.

Therefore, the Employees' Council and 213 of the 283 employees represented by it call for a seven-member Employees' Council containing one elected representative from each of the seven departments.

Figure 12–24 Traditional and contemporary versions of the same resolution

```
                          AGENDA
                    MANAGEMENT SOCIETY
                   Tuesday, April 17, 198X
                         Room 222
                        Mercer Hall
                         7:30 p.m.

     1.  Call to order

     2.  Consideration of minutes for March 13, 198X

     3.  Treasurer's report

     4.  President's report

     5.  Vice President's report

     6.  Committee reports

         a.  Finance: Erma Irby

         b.  Service: Edra Gerald

         c.  Scholarship: S. J. Grace

         d.  Business Day: Edith John

         e.  Tour of Eastern Electric: M. C. Earl

         f.  Homecoming reception: Irene Carl

     7.  Unfinished business

     8.  New business

     9.  Adjournment
```

Figure 12–25   Agenda for meeting

channels, apply the guidelines and principles even as you take on some of the style of a journalist. Take particular care to establish the six "W's"—who, what, when, where, how, why—and to change the discriminatory styles often practiced by news writers. (See Appendix D.)

Newsletters and news magazines

Newsletters and news magazines for employees—house organs—include stories and news items much as do regular magazines and newspapers. Therefore, the writers and editors for such business publications often come from journalistic educational backgrounds.

Many business and organizational newsletters and news magazines take on the complexity and trappings of mass publications. However, others may be quite simple. Newsletters may even be put into typewritten form and duplicated on a mimeograph or photocopy machine in the office.

If you ever write such news pieces, take care to use conciseness, factual accuracy, attention-getting devices, mechanical correctness, and logical order.

MINUTES OF THE MANAGEMENT SOCIETY MEETING
April 17, 198X, Room 222, Mercer Hall
Scholar Lee University, Goin, TN

Members Present	Arst, Carl, Clemons, Crane, Dearborn, Dormar, Earl, J. Ellis, S. Ellis, Frank, Fulcher, Gerald, Grace, Hall, Harris, Henthorn, Hilldegard, Irby, John, Karne, Kitely, Lanier, Lipps, Mitchell, Moore, Myers, Quinn, Watkins
Members Absent	Adair, Bearden, Bundrick, Hair, Olvan, Parker
Call to Order	With a quorum present, President Hall called the regular monthly meeting to order.
Minutes of March 13	The minutes of the meeting of March 13, 198X, were approved as written.
Treasurer's Report	Secretary-Treasurer Lanier distributed a copy of the activity in the Management Society account since the beginning of the year (copy attached). The balance on April 12 was $287.15.
President's Report	President Hall reported on his meeting with the President's Council of the School of Business on April 8 and his participation in the regional Management Society conference in Memphis, March 17–19. He reported that . . . .
Vice President's Report	Vice President Quinn listed the programs for the remainder of the semester. They are: (1) . . . . She introduced two new members: Donya Ellis and Vern Lipps.
Committee Reports	Finance. Chairperson Irby listed five fund-raising projects: (1) . . . Irby moved that the committee report be accepted and that the projects be considered one at a time in order. Mitchell seconded. The motion carried. Irby moved and Moore seconded that project No. 1 be approved. Discussion followed. The motion failed. Irby moved . . . .
Unfinished Business	. . . .
New Business	. . . .
Adournment	The meeting was adjourned at 9:15 p.m.

Respectfully submitted

JR Lanier

J. R. Lanier
Secretary-Treasurer

Figure 12–26 Minutes of meeting

INCHESAWAY SALONS
1818 Steam Drive/Carrie, KY 41725
(777) 777-7777

April 3, 198X

AREA RELEASE FOR APRIL 5, 198X

INCHESAWAY PLANS NEW SALON

Construction will begin in May on a building for a new
Inchesaway Salon at 7 Runway Court. So reported Nora Fields,
District Manager for the corporation.

When completed in January, 198X, the building will bring
the number of salons in Carrie to four. The others are located at
the corner of Boecking and Slye, 14 Treadmill Circle, and in the
Fitzgerald Plaza.

The building will cost about $850,000 for 14,000 square feet
of space. It will house complete salon facilities as well as a suite
of administrative offices on the top floor of the split-level, cedar-
sided structure.

Fields said that Angle, Level, and Hammer Architects
designed the building. The contractor is Steele Construction Co.

Figure 12–27   Press release

Introduce simple headlines. If possible, use such nonverbal devices as pictures, color, and traditional layout and design.

Press releases

Representatives from news bureaus, public information offices, and public relations departments often distribute press releases (news releases) to the media. The releases go to newspapers, magazines, radio, television, and other mass channels.

A press release includes the desired date of the release, the date of the message, the name of the sender, and the source(s) of information. It sometimes indicates the area of the release—whether to immediate area, statewide, or national.

Answer the "W" questions. Introduce the message with a journalistic-style headline. Use the deductive organizational style typical of news writing.

Transmit the release to the appropriate media. Depending upon the nature of the news, you may use the mail, messenger service, telegram, telephone, or other channels for the distribution.

Figure 12–27 shows an example of a simple press release.

Job Descriptions and Specifications

Job analysis, job descriptions, and job specifications (job requirements) require substantial research and decision-making by people skilled in the process. Thus, at this point concentrate only on their formats and the proper writing style.

Job descriptions

As the name suggests, a job description describes the nature of a job—the duties and reponsibilities that define it.

Above all, make a job description complete and clear. Performance appraisals naturally flow from descriptions. Therefore, the job description helps the worker to know both the reponsibilities of the position and the criteria by which performance will be judged.

Figure 12–28 includes a typical design for a job description. It also includes enough information to illustrate the writing style.

Job specifications

Job specifications (job requirements) describe the qualifications required of the person who fills the job. Job specifications include education, experience, arts, and skills that the person should possess.

Again, the key features of the message are the clarity and completeness of the information. Figure 12–29 illustrates the job specifications for the word-processing supervisory position described in Figure 12–28.

Telegrams and Cards

Telegrams, postal cards, and other cards carry brief messages.

Telegrams

You likely will send a telegram by dictating a message over the telephone to the local telegraph office or a central toll-free number. Write it before placing the call. As an alternative, you may simply write the message at a telegraph office counter and submit it.

The personnel in the receiving telegraph office usually telephone the message to the recipient. The offices rarely use messengers to deliver telegrams anymore.

Operators transmit full-rate telegrams during the day. They guarantee the lower-rate overnight telegram to arrive by 2 P.M. the next day.

Another version of the telegram is the mailgram. With it, the local telegraph office transmits the message directly to one of the nearly three hundred post offices in the United States that participate in the service—a post office in the receiver's locale. The post office then delivers the mailgram as part of the regular mail. The mailgram usually arrives the next day.

Radiograms, cablegrams, and letter telegrams (lower-rate night telegrams) are special versions of the telegram for transmission overseas. Using radios and cables for transmission, these channels provide reasonably rapid service. The sender places the message with a local telegraph office or a toll-free telephone number.

JOB DESCRIPTION*

Job Title _____ Salary Grade _____

Job Number _____ Department _____

Effective Date _____

The Supervisor of Word Processing, under the supervision of the Manager of the Word Processing Center, performs supervisory duties including interviewing, selecting, and appraising the performance of personnel; planning, organizing, directing, and controlling the personnel and work of the department; and maintaining standards and confidentiality.

JOB DUTIES

Interviews applicants

Chooses personnel

Appraises performance of personnel

Trains personnel

Creates a positive climate for work

Develops annual budget

Defines work procedures and controls

Schedules and coordinates work flow

Maintains performance standards

Presides at regular staff meetings

Corrects problems arising between users and Center

Establishes and uses a reporting system for work measurement and standards

Protects confidentiality of information processed in the Center

_____

*This job description includes enough information to evaluate and differentiate it from other jobs. However, it is not written to be a complete description of the function and every duty and responsibility associated with it.

Figure 12–28 Job description

JOB SPECIFICATIONS

For Job no. B—82, Supervisor of Word Processing

Education

Four-year college degree or completion of two-year or business-college program supplemented by appropriate experience.

Experience

About six years of experience in related fields, with at least two years in word processing. Some supervisory experience. Some secretarial experience.

Special Arts

Ability to train and motivate employees.

Special Skills

Ability to perform word-processing activities and develop budgets.

Responsibility

Extensive responsibility for human interactions, establishing and maintaining standards, and solving problems.

Resourcefulness

Ability to make judgments related to personnel selection and appraisal, solving problems, and creation of a good work environment.

Supervision

As a supervisory position, requires complete range of administrative abilities.

Mental Ability

Medium to high intellectual ability.

Physical Ability

Minimal, except for skills for using word-processing equipment.

Contacts

Ability to maintain productive contacts with management, with users of the Center, and with employees.

General Abilities

Abilities to adapt to the pressures of a demanding and fast-paced activity.

Figure 12–29 Job specifications

Conciseness is the essential criterion for telegrams, mailgrams, radiograms, and cablegrams. Often even abbreviations and codes are employed in such transmissions. However, make the content clear, or the savings made possible by conserving words will turn into a loss.

Choose the telegram and the other versions when you want speed somewhere between that of the telephone and the postal service. Choose them when someone cannot be reached by telephone. Also choose them instead of the telephone when you want a written record of detailed or complex information.

Analyze the cost of the telegram and the other versions of it as you make your channel choice. Generally, for the same number of words, full-rate telegrams, radiograms, and cablegrams cost more than either telephone calls or first-class letters—with all calculations taking labor and materials costs into account. However, for mailgrams, overnight telegrams, and letter telegrams, the costs may become more competitive.

Figure 12–30 shows the abbreviated pattern of a message in a full-rate telegram. Observe the different elements of the form.

Cards

Virtually any message may be printed on card stock instead of paper stock. However, the major use of card stock is for mailings of nonconfidential messages that are not inserted into envelopes.

As suggested earlier, cards may be constructed to include a reply message on one side and the mailing address on the other. Such a card may be inserted into an envelope along with the original message requesting the return. It may also be attached to another card containing the original message. Figures 12–12 and 12–13 illustrate two such reply-card messages.

The United States Postal Service sells both single and double postpaid postal cards. Many of the examples of messages previously described could be put onto them. However, many senders print their own cards and pay the postage in addition to the cost of the printing. The sender may obtain a special presort rate or business-reply rate.

Choose the card channel when the message is brief, informal, and non-confidential. (Some fold-over, stapled card arrangements even allow for some confidentiality.)

Choose it when other circumstances warrant the choice. It saves money over the cost of a letter. Not only does the postage cost about 50 percent less than the letter, but the process of preparation costs less. The card includes the receiver's and the return address only once. Using it involves no expenditure of time for folding, inserting into an expensive envelope, and sealing.

Figure 12–31 contains the same information that could be put in letter form—at greater cost.

SUMMARY

The memorandum and note are brief versions of the letter. Employees use the memorandum, usually typewritten, mostly for intracompany transactions. Firms often provide printed 16-pound stationery for memoranda.

Telegram

western union

MSG. NO	NO. WDS. CL. OF SVC.	PD.—COLL.	CASH NO.	ACCOUNTING INFORMATION	DATE	FILING TIME		SENT TIME	
				Charge 666-666-6666		A.M. / P.M.		A.M. / P.M.	

Send the following message, subject to the terms on back hereof, which are hereby agreed to.

☐ OVERNIGHT TELEGRAM
UNLESS BOX ABOVE IS CHECKED THIS MESSAGE WILL BE SENT AS A TELEGRAM

CARE OF OR APT. NO.

TO Mr. Harold Diggs

ADDRESS & TELEPHONE NO. Miltonia Hotel, 908 Fors Drive   (999) 999-9999

CITY — STATE & ZIP CODE Dialville, TX 75761

Additional information on customer. Call me before contacting her.

Dana

SENDER'S TEL. NO. 666-666-6666   NAME & ADDRESS Hale's Sales, 2 Cliff Mall, Oshtemo, MI 49077

Figure 12-30 Completed telegram

413

```
┌─────────────────────────────────────────────────────────────────────┐
│                                                                       │
│        Plan to join us at the next meeting of your ASQC Chapter:      │
│                                                                       │
│        Dinner:                      Twill's Cafeteria                 │
│        6:30 p.m.                    18 Pilar Drive                     │
│                                     (Just go through the line)        │
│                                                                       │
│        Speaker:              J. T. Wyatt, QC Engineer, Eastern Electric│
│        7:15 p.m.             "Nonparametric Statistics—Sturdy Techniques"│
│                                                                       │
│        Business:             Plans for national convention            │
│        8:00 p.m.             Selection of scholarship recipient        │
│                              Awards to winners of membership drive     │
│                              Welcome to new members                    │
│                              Plans for fund-raising drive              │
│                                                                       │
└─────────────────────────────────────────────────────────────────────┘
```

Figure 12–31   Invitation to a meeting using a card

A *memorandum* can deal with virtually any business topic.

Notes are even more informal than memoranda. Notes usually involve handwritten messages on personalized or plain pieces of paper. They usually do not contain complex or extensive information.

Many routine business messages may be reduced to forms, which can save both time and money.

When creating a good *form,* leave plenty of space for each answer, arrange the elements in logical groupings and order, include complete and clear instructions, give the form a title, and do whatever else is necessary to assure that the form accomplishes its work. Requisition forms, purchase orders, credit forms, application forms, and questionnaires are examples of forms used both inside and outside the firm.

When completing forms, read and follow the instructions, determine whether the information goes above or below the line, typewrite the answers if necessary, and arrange additional pages logically.

Other types of business messages include: (1) general informational and persuasive messages, (2) legal and organizational messages, (3) traditional news messages, (4) job descriptions and specifications, and (5) telegrams and cards.

General informational and persuasive messages include extensive and complex messages, brief and simple messages, recruitment messages, listing and outline messages, and flow and organizational charts.

Extensive and complex messages use such channels as catalogs, brochures, policy statements, policy manuals, other manuals, and position papers. When writing a complex message, collect complete information, choose understandable verbal and nonverbal symbols, make the message as brief as is appropriate, attend to the quality of the transmission, apply the suggestions specific to the purpose and channel, and use an appropriate developmental pattern and outline.

Flyers, circulars, leaflets, and bulletins are examples of *brief and simple message channels.* These channels often involve direct, concise, plain (handwritten or typewritten) messages duplicated by a mimeograph, spirit-duplication, or photocopy process.

Recruitment messages take many forms such as brochures, booklets, and flyers. When you write recruitment literature, spotlight the benefits of your organization to your reader and use low-key persuasive techniques.

When you write listing and outline messages such as *procedures, guidelines, instructions, criteria,* and *programs,* make them clear, complete, and concise. Try to put the elements of each in a logical order.

Two special types of charts involve more writing and logic than the actual mechanics of charting. *Flow charts* place a series of operations and procedures into a logical sequence. *Organizational charts* show the structure of work and authority for a particular firm.

Legal and organizational messages include warranties, workers' compensation policies, affirmative action plans, and proxy statements. Obviously, the writer studies the legal aspects of each before writing such messages.

Quasi-legal organizational messages include constitutions, bylaws, and operating codes; parliamentary procedures; motions and resolutions; agendas; and minutes of meetings.

Business writers sometimes use traditional news channels such as *newsletters, news magazines,* and *press releases.* When writing these messages, use a journalistic style of writing. Use simple headlines and the nonverbal techniques associated with pictures, color, layout, and design.

A *job description* describes the nature of the job—the duties and reponsibilities that define it. A *job specification* describes the human qualifications required to complete the job.

You usually send *telegrams* by dictating prewritten messages by telephone. Use clear, concise, and abbreviated messages.

The *card channel* serves economically for such messages as announcements, notices, and invitations. Make the messages brief, informal, and nonconfidential.

Practice

1. You have decided to change your Program Management Department's rules on working hours. The current rule is that all of your employees must arrive at work no later than eight o'clock and cannot leave before five o'clock. Employees may take an hour for lunch. You now want to allow your employees to arrive between six o'clock and ten o'clock and leave after they have worked at least eight hours. If they wish, they may do without lunch, eat while working, take a long lunch period, or take one or several breaks, just as long as they work eight hours. You also want your employees to operate on an honor system: They need not check with you every time they take a break, go to the dentist, or decide to come to work earlier or later than usual. You do want them to let their secretaries know where they can be contacted, though, in case of an emergency. Write a memorandum describing your new rule.

2. Meet with your group. You and each other group member read one of these situations to the rest of the group. The group members who are not reading should write short notes appropriate to each situation. Evaluate the notes.

   a. The person with whom you share an office, Aaron Silkel, is ill today. You answer his phone, and the caller asks if Aaron is in. When you respond that he is ill, the caller asks you to tell Aaron that the Dixon plan will not be finished for six weeks and that the progress report should reflect the delay. The caller, Jane Bachrach, wants Aaron to contact her as soon as possible.

b. You go to Joan Dann's office to ask her to join you for lunch. She is not at her desk. You leave a note.

c. Matthew Timms asked you to review his integrated logistics support plan. You read it and thought it was quite good. You found only one mistake: He left out an important paragraph on reporting requirements on page 17. You write a note that you will attach to the plan.

d. You would like to discuss a work problem with your boss, Andrea Frame. When you call her, neither she nor her secretary is in. You would like to talk to her today if possible. You write a note that you will place on Frame's desk.

e. You want six of your colleagues to review your marketing plan for Naturally Sweet Bran Cereal. You want each of them to read for major content flaws only. You want the plan to go to Rick first, and then to Catherine, Willie, Margaret, Jason, and Sandra, in that order. You want each reader to write her or his comments in the margins of the plan itself.

3. Design a form for your use in checking the accuracy and completeness of memoranda you write. This is an example of part of such a form:

MEMORANDUM CHECKLIST

TODAY'S DATE _____ DATE MEMORANDUM SHOULD BE TYPED _____

DATE MEMORANDUM SHOULD BE DISTRIBUTED _____

SUBJECT OF MEMORANDUM _____

Use yes, no, or NN for not necessary

Have I checked:
1. Spelling _____
2. Grammar _____
3. Format _____
4. Accuracy of information _____
5. Clarity of message _____
6. Completeness of message _____
7. Conciseness of message _____

Have I included:
1. Date _____
2. File number _____
3. My name _____
4. Receiver's name _____
5. Subject _____
6. Meeting date _____
7. Meeting time _____
8. Meeting place _____

---

4. You have noticed that a great deal of the work in your department is routine; thus, the employees could do it more efficiently through the use of forms. You realize that most of the employees probably know better than you what forms they need, but do not know how to design or use them. Write a memorandum that describes how to develop and use forms.

5. Meet with your group. Develop a simple brochure (fold one sheet of plain paper and use all sides) that includes at least this information (you may add more information if necessary):

a. Company name, address, and phone number:

Diet-for-Life Service
9844 Del Mar Court, Suite 1100
Samson, Florida 99446
(555) 555-1213

b. Hours:

> Monday through Friday—10 A.M. to 6 P.M.
> Saturday—10 A.M. to 4 P.M.
> Closed Sunday

c. Products and services offered:

> Diet counseling
> Nutrition counseling
> Exercise counseling
> Physical inventories
> Health check-ups
> Special diet plans and books
> Medical library
> Personalized diet program

d. Personnel:

> Registered nurses
> Dieticians
> Trained diet counselors
> Exercise specialists

e. Motto:

> "You need never worry about losing weight again."

f. Description of program:

> No pills
> No strenuous exercise
> No starving
> Customer can see a counselor daily if he or she chooses

g. Special offers:

> First two counseling sessions are free.
> If a person does not lose at least fifteen pounds in the first three months of the program, he or she will receive a full refund from the Diet for Life Service.

After you have finished developing the brochure, have one of your group members (preferably someone who has not spoken in front of the class very often) display and describe your group's brochure to the rest of the class.

6. You are resonsible for putting together the program for your department's monthly meeting. Prepare the agenda from the following information:

a. Robert Lasser wants to give a 15-minute presentation on the proposal he is writing for the Onyx contract.

b. Jane Lee wants to invite department members to attend the computer simulation workshop she will conduct.

c. Albert Leung wants to discuss the results of his employee survey.

d. Rachel Stein, your department's manager, will give a special talk on the company's new management plan. She will also preside over the meeting.

e. David Sams, Alice Strong, Henry Arlington, Ann Bailey, and Jane Tucson each has a departmental problem he or she wishes to discuss.

f. All group leaders will give work progress reports.

g. Arnold Fitzbinder wants to ask department members for their suggestions concerning the company dance.

h. One coffee break should be scheduled.

i. Anna Greentree wants to ask department members to join her softball team.

7. [*Your professor will time this exercise.*] What, if anything, is wrong with this brief job description for a classified advertisement or bulletin-board posting? Make corrections and add information if necessary (use your imagination).

JOB DESCRIPTION

SECRETARY II   JANUARY 6, 198X

We need one girl to type, file, and answer

phones. She should be under 30 years of

age. She should have five years of

secretarial experience and take good

shorthand. She should do good work and

type fast to. She should have some college

background. She should work long hours and

on Saturday. She should be reliable. We

                                   willing
want references. She should be anxious to

write short letters. She should apply soon.

---

8. Correct this memorandum:

LEASETRUCK, INC.   MEMORANDUM

MEMO TO: Employees
    FROM: Don
    DATE: January 11, 1981
 SUBJECT: Meeting

We will start the meeting at 8 A.M. Please submit your topics ahead of time. Albert will provide the coffee. We need some doughnuts. Joan will give us her dept.'s progress report. Wayne will give his dept.'s problems before that. We'll have this dept. mgrs.' weekly staff meeting in the Lincoln Room. It's on the eighth floor. Lonnie will talk about his experiences at the Leasetruck Sales School in Lamone, Ohio. He was there for two months.

---

9. You want to order 36 light bulbs (item number 466B) at 50 cents each, 10 ladders (item number 1226C) at $40 each, and 8 pairs of scissors (item number 322S) at $8 each. The sales tax is 10 percent of the total order price. Shipping costs are included in the item price. You are submitting this order for your company, Very Huge Company, 6413 Elm Street, Townville, South Dakota 66116. Your company's telephone number is (555) 232–2323. You'll send a check with your order. Fill out the order form.

```
ALLYOUWANT SUPPLIES, INC.
ORDER FORM

(Please Print)

COMPANY NAME _____

YOUR NAME _____

COMPANY MAILING ADDRESS _____

CITY _____ STATE _____ ZIP _____

COMPANY TELEPHONE NUMBER _____
```

ITEM NUMBER	NAME OF ITEM	PRICE EACH	QUANTITY	TOTAL PRICE

Type of Payment	TOTAL	
CHECK ☐ MONEY ORDER ☐	SALES TAX	
Send to:	TOTAL AMOUNT	

ALLYOUWANT SUPPLIES, INC.
42 Industrial Boulevard
Dooley, South Dakota 66449

10. Obtain two or three simple blank forms (job application, credit application, insurance application, loan application, simple contract, questionnaire, insurance claim, etc.), and make a copy of each. Complete each copy, using hypothetical information if necessary. As you complete each, make a list of its strengths and weaknesses.
    a. For each form write a one-page summary of its strengths, weaknesses, and your overall evaluation of the form.
    b. Redesign the poorest of the blanks and type it in final form.
    c. Submit the one-page summaries, the redesigned form, and the three original blank forms to your professor.
11. Contact a telegraph office to determine rates and word allowances for the various services offered. Write a one-page summary of your findings.
12. Condense the message in Figure 9–26 (page 297) into ten or fewer words as if for a telegram.
13. Revise the information in Figure 12–16 (page 393) to fit onto a postal card in an attractive format. Instead of wasting an actual postal card, draw a rectangle the size of a postal card on a piece of paper.

14. Select a controversial business topic and write a two- or three-page position paper presenting your views on it.

15. You just learned that your company has been named the recipient of the prestigious annual Craig Foundation Award of Excellence in Human Relations. Supplying any needed information, write a one-page press release about the award.

16. You are the parliamentarian for a local professional organization. Though the organization does not need or want to observe every detail of parliamentary procedures it does want to observe the basic ones in order to facilitate order during meetings. Obtain a copy of *Robert's Rules of Order,* and examine it carefully. Write a one- or two-page outline of major points—an outline to which you can refer during meetings.

17. Use your dictionary and thesaurus to create meanings for these words. Use the words when you think, write, and speak so that you feel comfortable using them.

a. Compromise	**g.** Quasi-
b. Discreet	**h.** Routine
c. Discrete	**i.** Sarcasm
d. Generic	**j.** Specification
e. Precise	**k.** Trait
f. Prior	**l.** Trappings

18. Take and score Self-Test 28 over the excerpt about extensive and complex messages

Self-Test 28
Excerpt About Extensive and Complex Messages

A. Recall (33 points each). For each multiple-choice question, select the most accurate answer.

1. Which of these statements does *not* apply to writing extensive and complex messages:
   a. Collect complete and accurate information.
   b. Choose verbal and nonverbal symbols that convey the information in a manner understandable and acceptable to the reader.
   c. Because of the special nature of extensive and complex messages, do *not* try to make your message as brief as possible.
   d. Attend to the quality of the transmission.
   e. Apply the suggestions specific to the purposes or general type of channel—be it informational or persuasive.

2. Which of these statements is *not* true?
   a. Statements of policy represent broad guides to the personnel of an organization as they act and interact to carry out the functional operations necessary to accomplish the established goals.
   b. A good statement of policy comes only after careful research.
   c. Brochures, pamphlets, and booklets usually attempt to inform or persuade people outside the firm.
   d. Professionally developed literature-rack publications often cost less than locally developed ones.
   e. A policy statement usually should be written in memorandum form.

B. Inference (34 points). Indicate whether this statement is true or false.

Any brochure, pamphlet, or booklet that goes outside of the firm should be developed by an advertising agency or outside consultant.

Solution to Self-Test 28
Excerpt About Extensive and Complex Messages

A. Recall (33 points each)   **B.** Inference (34 points)

   1. c   **2.** e   False

19. Take and score Self-Test 29 over Chapter 12.

Self-Test 29
Chapter 12

A. Recall (25 points each). For each multiple-choice question, select the most accurate answer.

   1. A memorandum usually exhibits the _____ style of writing.
      a. Deductive
      b. Inductive
      c. Journalistic
      d. Chronological
      e. Comparative

   2. Develop and use forms for:
      a. Virtually every written business exchange
      b. Routine business messages
      c. Most external correspondence
      d. Most formal written messages
      e. Transmitting quantitative data only

   3. Which is *not* true regarding the minutes of a meeting?
      a. Minutes constitute the official record of the formal activities of the meeting participants.
      b. Minutes are the program for a meeting.
      c. Minutes should include every key element of the meeting.
      d. Minutes follow a relatively prescribed form and order.
      e. Accuracy is a cardinal requirement for good minutes.

B. Inference (25 points). Indicate whether this statement is true or false.

   Regardless of what you write, you should strive to be as concise as possible without allowing accuracy and completeness to suffer.

Solution to Self-Test 29
Chapter 12

A. Recall (25 points each)   **B.** Inference (25 points)

   1. a   **3.** b   True
   2. b

Writing Reports: Guidelines and Collecting Data

Reports form an important channel for the work of business. Consider them in two parts. This chapter covers basic concepts, the guidelines for writing reports, and the data-collection process. Chapter 14 covers the total research process and the types of reports.

CONCEPTS ABOUT REPORTS

For large organizations, reports form the primary supply line for information bound upward to decision-making personnel. Managers of small organizations also depend upon reports to supplement and reinforce the information they can collect more directly than managers of large ones.

In both large and small organizations, reports also provide vehicles for downward and lateral messages. Top managers may send reports down through the line participants on the organizational charts. Managers on the line often make reports to one another. In addition, both line and staff specialists often make reports to one another as well as to those on the line.

Whether large or small, organizations report to external entities—particularly to stockholders and to federal, state, and local governments. Furthermore, reports often flow inward to organizations from external entities such as consulting and auditing firms.

Characteristics

Reports may involve both the written/nonverbal and the oral/nonverbal channels. As established, the combined form takes on the advantages of both general channels. The written/nonverbal channels provide the capacity for information that is objective, permanent, complex, and voluminous. The form also accommodates long-distance transmission, review, deliberation, and distribution to large numbers of decentralized people. The oral/nonverbal channels provide the capacity for richness, for rapid turn-taking, for expanded feedback and evaluation, and for adjustment based on that feedback and evaluation.

Reports may be private or public, short or long, informal or formal. They may be informational or persuasive, routine or analytical, personal or impersonal, assigned or volunteered, regular (daily, weekly, monthly, quarterly, annually) or special.

Reports may involve inductive, deductive, or cause-and-effect reasoning. They may be based upon primary or secondary data. They may describe known situations or forecast or induce to unknown ones.

Reports may simply describe a problem, or they may describe a problem *and* a research procedure for trying to solve it. They may suggest a solution to a problem or provide the information by which another person may solve a problem.

Reports may result from introspection or scientific research.

Reports may deal with production, marketing, finance, or any other function or operation of the firm. They may relate to any management responsiblity—planning, organizing, directing, and controlling—but particularly they aid in controlling.

Reports may take the style of a completed, preprinted form, a letter, a memorandum, or a traditional manuscript. They may use any logical plan of development, but often appear either in the inductive, deductive, analytical, or comparative mode.

In the following pages you will consider, at least briefly, examples and descriptions of the major types of reports. You will, however, concentrate upon reports that possess these characteristics:

Private

Formal

Analytical or scientific

Impersonal

Assigned or special

Based on inductive or cause-and-effect reasoning

In the inductive, deductive, analytical, or comparative developmental order

Descriptive of a problem and a procedure for trying to solve it, or descriptive of a solution to a problem

In letter, memorandum, form, or manuscript format

Application

Many people claim that businesses prepare too many written reports. Small-business owners particularly decry the number of reports required by government.

Question the volume of reports produced by your unit or firm. Oftentimes, thousands of dollars may be saved simply by eliminating some reports that contribute virtually nothing to performance.

Even when all unnecessary reports have been cut from the process, however, you likely still will prepare many of them. A great deal of the evaluation of your performance will be based upon your ability to do so effectively—particularly as you rise in management.

GUIDELINES FOR WRITING REPORTS

The guidelines for developing reports become:

1. Define your purposes for writing the report, the reader's purposes for reading the report, yourself, the reader, and the environment.
2. Identify the report channel.
3. Control the interference internal and external to you and the reader.
4. Write and transmit the report in light of the purposes, the participants, the environment, the channel, and the interference.
5. Use feedback from and to the reader.
6. Evaluate at each stage.

Define Purposes, Participants, and Environment

When someone assigns a report, he or she also assigns the purposes. Therefore, set an objective of completing the report on time and in good form for satisfying the assigned purposes. Also, establish action criteria for evaluating the process.

Even many unsolicited reports still serve such standard functions that you may define your and the other's purposes quite easily.

For example, suppose you voluntarily develop a proposal or prospectus (a report defining a problem and suggesting a research process for its possible solution). First, you want the reader to understand and acknowledge the existence of the problem. Second, you want the reader to activate the proposed research process for its possible solution. Third, you want to receive the evaluation that you have performed well.

The reader of an unsolicited proposal probably wants to learn of genuine problems and to instigate the most likely and inexpensive activities to overcome them. He or she probably also wants to discover people talented at recognizing problems and describing methods for attacking them.

As illustrated, then, your purposes and those of a reader of a proposal often mesh well.

The reader of a report may be in or out of your company. If the intended reader occupies a position within your firm, he or she may be superior or subordinate to you, or on a level equal to yours. Whatever the relationship, however, define the reader, yourself, and the environment as completely as you can.

Most of your internal reports go to someone in a position superior to yours. (Think of the meanings associated with the words "I report to . . . .") Try, then, to understand not only the characteristics of communication from subordinate to superior, but the unique qualities that define the actual person occupying the superior position. If you do not correctly assess the style of a superior, you risk more than just a single unsuccessful communication.

Some superiors have such a style that they welcome a direct, open approach by subordinates. They seek and welcome opinions, recommendations, and follow-ups from them.

Many other superiors have personalities that require an indirect, extremely careful approach by subordinates. They neither ask for nor want opinions, recommendations, and follow-ups from them.

Identify Report Channel

Even when you have selected the written report as a channel, you still need to choose from among the kinds of reports available. Under one classification, they fall into the formats of the letter or memorandum, the form, and the manuscript. Coverage of these three basic formats follows this section on the guidelines.

Control Interference

The written report carries with it all of the potential for interference associated with any written medio channel. It lacks the richness provided by the oral channels. However, for routine reports, the loss of rapid turn-taking, immediate feedback, and ongoing evaluation does not erect any serious barrier to the kind of communication undertaken.

Even for the long, analytical, formal, and unsolicited reports, the advantages of the channel far outweigh the interference factors created by the written mode. Tradition and the needs and expectations that lead to written reports offset most of the negative features of them.

If you correctly assess and adapt to the psychological states of both you and your reader, you may eradicate even the pervasive "human" transactional barriers. The very nature of the topics, formats, and purposes of reports often imparts an objectivity that helps eradicate misunderstandings.

Write and Transmit

Much of the coverage in the preceding sections of this chapter deals with content even as it deals with the factors featured there. Other sources of information about selecting, writing, and transmitting the messages of a report fall in earlier chapters—Chapter 7, in particular.

Much of what you read in Chapter 7 applies more comprehensively to report writing than to many of the other kinds of business writing. You may be able to skip the formality of some of the encoding stages when you write a routine letter. However, you probably will not be able to skip them when you write a long, formal, analytical report.

Subsequent sections and Chapter 14 expand the coverage of this guideline.

Use Feedback

A report to another may or may not elicit direct, significant feedback. If the report is routine and you hear nothing, you may operate on the "no-news-is-good-news" assumption. However, when you submit a formal report, you may want to solicit feedback by including an appropriate statement in the message of transmittal.

Evaluate

Use whatever feedback you do receive from a report as the basis for evaluation. Generally, the evaluation will fall at the end of the process.

Use the criteria established at the beginning of the writing process to determine how well the transaction met both your and the other's purposes. Store the information gained as an aid to your next report-writing transaction.

FORMATS FOR REPORTS

Reports usually follow one of three basic formats: (1) letter or memorandum, (2) form, and (3) manuscript. Illustrations of the formats appear in Chapter 14.

Letter and Memorandum Reports

A letter report is a report coupled with the trappings of a letter. Likewise, a memorandum report includes paragraphs written under the heading of a memorandum.

Both types often exhibit some of the characteristics of the traditional manuscript. Some of those characteristics include objectivity, an analytical approach, inductive order, and specificity of details. They also include careful organization (even to the extent of using headings and subheadings), an impersonal tone, formality, nonverbal accompaniments such as graphs and tables, and multiple pages (usually two to five).

Use the letter report channel for transactions external to the organization and the memorandum format for those within it. As an example, outside auditors usually write a report to a firm they have audited in the form of a "management letter"—actually a report in the form of a letter. As another example, internal committees or task forces often write their reports to management in the format of a memorandum.

Form Reports

Another channel for reports begins with a form. Consider these examples of the kinds of information that may be added to preprinted forms:

Inventory	Sales
Production	Time and motion
Quality control	Consumer analysis
Attendance	Claim
Sick leave	Hiring
Annual leave	Firing
Accident	Wage and salary
Tax	Dock loadings and unloadings
Purchasing	Overtime

Credit	Lost time
Breakdown	Grievance
Traffic	Appraisal of property
Travel summary	Shipments
Proposal for research grant	Repairs

The form report often involves relatively mechanical completion. Still, the forms must capture the desired information in usable terms. Chapter 12 includes reminders for developing and completing forms.

Manuscript Reports

The traditional manuscript report includes narrative paragraphs with titles, headings, subheadings, footnotes or endnotes, tables, and illustrations. The report contains three major parts, with subdivisions under each:

1. Front matter
   a. Cover
   b. Title page
   c. Authorization letter or memorandum
   d. Acceptance letter or memorandum
   e. Transmittal letter or memorandum
   f. Table of contents
   g. List of illustrations
   h. List of tables
   i. Preface, foreword, or acknowledgments
   j. Abstract
2. Body
   a. Introduction
   b. Main body (usually consisting of several clearly defined divisions)
   c. Conclusions and/or recommendations
3. Back matter
   a. Endnotes (if used instead of footnotes)
   b. Appendix(ces)
   c. Bibliography

Appendices F and G illustrate most of the parts listed in the outline and described in the subsequent sections.

Front matter

Include at least a title page in the front matter of a formal business report. You may include some or all of the nine other components listed in the outline.

Cover A cover for a formal report protects the pages and gives a finished appearance. Put at least the title and the principal author's name on it. Some covers include all of the information that appears on the title page. If a title is too long to contain on a label, it can be shortened to fit.

Avoid the clamped clear plastic cover. It creates static electricity and does not allow the report to lie open well for reading and writing. In addition, the clamp often pops off, causing the reader the frustration of having to reorganize the pages of the report.

Title page   Even with a cover, include a title page in the report. Put on it the full title of the report, the name(s) of the author(s), the name(s) of the reader(s) to whom submitted, and the date. If appropriate, place the copyright date on the title page or the backside of it.

If you experiment with the placement of items on a title page, make your primary goal the establishment of an attractive page. Be sure to take into account the fact that the vertical visual center lies slightly higher than actual center.

Even when a report includes a title page, the title also appears on the first page of the body.

Authorization letter or memorandum   Include an authorization letter or memorandum when the authorizing person uses that channel to permit or assign the project leading to the report. The authorizer also often uses the message to state the problem and/or hypothesis and to establish the time and cost limitations for the activity.

You also may transmit the letter/memorandum of authorization as an independent message. Attach it to the front of the report, leave it loose inside the cover of the report, or simply include it in the envelope with the report.

Acceptance letter or memorandum   Through a letter or memorandum of acceptance, you respond to the authorization message by agreeing to the terms stated in it. Like the authorization, the acceptance may accompany the report rather than form a part of it.

Include a letter or memorandum of acceptance only as the response to a message of authorization. However, an authorization does not require an acceptance.

Transmittal letter or memorandum   Always use a letter or memorandum of transmittal with a report. Include it in the report in the order shown in the outline, or send it separate from the report.

The transmittal message includes a reference to an enclosure or an accompanying piece (the report itself). It also may include some low-key persuasive passages. Persuasion becomes particularly appropriate for unsolicited proposals. However, the quality of the report itself carries the best persuasion.

Table of contents   For a report that contains major divisions, put a table of contents in the front matter. The table refers by page number to the beginning points of such major divisions. It thus allows the reader to scan the contents and turn to the desired pages without having to skim all that precedes them.

Style manuals differ slightly on the preferred format for tables of contents.

List of illustrations   If a report has charts, graphs, maps, photographs, or other illustrations, include a list of illustrations in the front matter. Like the table of contents, the list of illustrations points the reader ahead toward the appropriate presentations.

Though styles vary, a graphic presentation usually carries the label "figure" in the body of the report, but "illustration" in the front matter. Chapter 16 contains examples.

Though the title of a figure in the body of a report includes a capital letter only for the first word and proper nouns, the front-matter list includes capital and small letters in the standard mixture.

List of tables   The inclusion of tables in the body of a report also calls for a list of tables in the front matter. For this list, simply copy the titles from the tables and show the pages upon which they appear.

Titles do not appear in the all-capitals style used in the body. Instead, the titles contain capitals and small letters.

Books containing either large or small numbers of illustrations and tables tied closely to the textual material need not include a list of illustrations or a list of tables.

Preface, foreword, or acknowledgments   You occasionally may want to include a preface, a foreword, or acknowledgments in the front matter. However, if you include a letter of transmittal as part of the front matter, you would do better to include the prefatory and acknowledgment information in it.

The preface and foreword serve as introductions to the material—messages that also may try to arouse interest in the report. The section on acknowledgments includes recognition of people or organizations who gave special help to the researcher/writer.

Abstract   The abstract (synopsis, summary, digest, précis) is a one- or two-page statement summarizing the problem, the procedures, the findings, and the conclusions. It comes just before the body of a report.

The abstract gives the reader a chance to preview the body of the report. It often provides her or him the opportunity to know whether to scan, skim, rapidly read, or carefully read the remainder.

Body

As suggested in the outline of the parts of a formal report, the body usually contains three major components: (1) introduction, (2) main body, and (3) conclusions and/or recommendations.

Introduction   The introduction may range from one paragraph to multiple paragraphs making up a complete section or chapter. For a full report, it should at least include *statements of the problem, purposes, scope, and limitations* of the topic.

The introduction also may include a *statement of authorization*. However, the statement fits better in a letter, memorandum, or even an abstract.

The introduction often includes a *background* discussion and/or a *review of related research or literature*. Academic research reports such as theses and dissertations virtually require the review of the literature.

As time allows and circumstances dictate, such a section also adds a great deal to business reports. Reading and reporting what others have found on the topic exhibits an attitude of respect for the contributions of others. It also may avoid repeating work already accomplished by others.

References to footnotes or endnotes accompany excerpts from the works of others.

Add to an introduction the statement of any *hypothesis(es)* formulated. Though not all problems involve a hypothesis, many do. When they do, include them near the statement of the problem and/or purposes.

A summary of the *significance of the topic* forms another relatively common part of the introduction. The main ideas of a statement of significance may just as well be placed in an authorization message—wherever located. However, a statement of the significance of and justification for the research needs to appear somewhere in the document.

A final report often includes a description of the process of *selecting the factors* for the work leading to that report. The description may become part of the background or occupy a separate section.

Another common component of the introduction is the description of the *methods* (procedures, design, methodology) used in the solution of the problem. If an extensive description of methods is important to the development of the report, move the section on methods to the main body and give it a heading of its own.

The section on methods usually deals with how the data were collected, organized, and analyzed. Sometimes it deals only with the collection phase, leaving the methods of organization and analysis for the sections that report the findings.

Definitions may form still another part of the introduction of the body of the report. Define any terms that are used in some special way.

Definitions may appear in a separate section titled something like "definitions of terms." They may also appear as simple sentences within the paragraphs devoted to the introduction.

Main body   The main body of a report first includes any of the previously described components too great to be a portion of the introduction. The section on *methods* is the most likely candidate for transfer to the main body.

The major component of the main body—and of the report itself—is the message about the results of the process leading to the report. The section reports the *findings* from the *collection, organization,* and *analysis* of the data.

In the main body, use words, tables, and illustrations to portray the data in organized form. Use the same vehicles to report the results of calculations or other analytical procedures. If you use statistical tests for analysis, report whether the results lead to a rejection or acceptance of the statistical hypothesis(es).

Also include in the main body the *interpretations* you put upon the analysis of the data. While the analysis should be scientific and objective, the interpretation (the meaning you assign to the analysis) allows you to introduce some judgment and creativity into the process.

Conclusions and recommendations   For the final part of the body, write the conclusions and sometimes the recommendations.

Though the word "conclusion" carries a certain finality with it, many researchers/reporters still use it to focus on the overall results of the study.

For example, the analysis may lead to a rejection of the hypothesis(es) and an interpretation of the meaning of that rejection. In that event, the conclusion would condense that result and interpretation into a few words tied to the original statement of the problem.

Reports sometimes include recommendations for a decision or an action to result from the study. You may include them because you have instructions to do so or because you know that the reader welcomes such recommendations.

Even if you do not include recommendations about how the reader might use the conclusions, you still may include recommendations of another kind. These recommendations suggest how a project might be continued, improved, or revised.

Back matter

Supplementary material often follows the body of a formal report.

Endnotes Such material may include endnotes keyed to the superior numbers in the text of the report. Endnotes take the place of footnotes. Thus, the rules for the form and content of endnotes are the same as for footnotes. Simply put the endnotes in a list numbered in sequence as they occur in the text.

Appendix C and Chapter 14 contain more information on footnotes and endnotes.

Appendix Sometimes you need to include some information that supports the body of the report, but does not quite belong in the body. In such circumstances, you may place the information in an appendix. Refer to the appendix in the text and then include it after the endnotes, if present.

A report may have more than one appendix. Although a single appendix does not require a title, multiple appendices do. Use Appendix A, Appendix B . . . or Appendix 1, Appendix 2 . . . .

Appendices may be tables or illustrations too detailed for presentation in the body. They may be copies of actual forms, documents, or questionnaires. They may be paragraphs of technical information, or cases too lengthy for the body. They may be guidelines or procedures associated with the investigative process or the subject matter. They may be complicated calculations not appropriate for the body.

The appendices at the end of this book illustrate the wide variety of types of material included in appendices.

Bibliography If you include excerpts and footnotes (endnotes), also include a bibliography listing all of the sources associated with them. Also include a bibliography if you want to refer to special or general publications related to the report.

Bibliographic entries differ from footnote or endnote entries. Use the same style manual for both the footnotes (endnotes) and the bibliography. Additional information about constructing a bibliography appears in Appendix C and in Chapter 14.

If a bibliography includes numerous items of a variety of types, you may divide it into sections. Such sections might be "books," "periodicals," and "interviews." If the listing does include anything other than published materials, the heading should be changed from "bibliography" or "selected bibliography" to "sources consulted."

Some manuals of style suggest that the bibliography may precede the appendices.

Mechanics

Use a style manual to obtain other necessary details for the pagination, spacing, headings, and other mechanics for a manuscript report. However, consider some general features here.

Paper Use 8½-by 11-inch, 20-pound, fabric-content bond paper. Type on the felt side of the paper. As you recall, the felt side is the side on which the watermark and fabric content appear in normal reading position.

Pagination The front matter typically includes lower-case roman numerals for pagination. The body and back matter include arabic numerals.

For the first page of a major section that begins a new page, either omit the number (but count it) or center it at the bottom of the page. For subsequent pages, place the number at the upper right margin or centered above the top line. Count the title page, but do not number it.

Spacing Most pages of a report have one-inch margins on all four sides after binding. However, the first page of a major section (the title page, the first page of the report, the first page of a new chapter, the table of contents, the list of illustrations, etc.) usually has a two-inch margin at the top.

Traditionally, typists have used double spacing and only one side of the paper for manuscript reports. However, to conserve paper, many writers have begun to use single spacing and both sides of the paper. Conservation becomes particularly important for situations requiring multiple copies.

Even with double spacing within the body of a report, appendices may involve single spacing. Likewise, footnotes usually appear in single-spaced form even when the body has double spacing.

Excerpts from the works of others may call for distinct spacing. Generally, if a direct quotation is three or fewer lines in length, place it within quotation marks and merge it into the narrative. However, once it occupies four or more lines, indent, block, and single space it. Eliminate the quotation marks from such blocked direct quotations.

Titles, headings, and subheadings The placement and structure of titles, headings, and subheadings contribute significantly to the readability of a report.

As one basic rule, just as for outlines, include at least two headings at each level introduced.

One hierarchy of levels is:

<u>First-Level, Centered Heading, Underlined</u>

Second-Level, Centered Heading,
Not Underlined

<u>Third-level, side heading
underlined, beginning at
left margin</u>

Fourth-level, side heading,
not underlined

<u>Fifth-level, heading run into paragraph and underlined.</u>

The particular style just shown involves capital and lower-case letters at the first and second levels, with only initial and proper-noun capitals at the other levels.

However, other styles use mixed capitals and small letters in the other levels as well. Some style manuals even allow all-capital headings in the body.

Other mechanics Many other mechanical elements have an impact upon the presentation of a report. For example, double-spaced reports require indented paragrahs, whereas single-spaced reports may include blocked paragraphs.

For guidance in all such mechanical elements, turn to a good manual of style.

COLLECTION OF DATA

Collection of information is a crucial part of the research process. Though Chapter 14 covers the research process, consider the collection phase here.

You may gather information through any of the channels, be they oral, written, or nonverbal. All of the suggestions for listening, reading, and observing apply. In addition, because you often must solicit data through sending action, all of the suggestions for good speaking, writing, and nonverbal sending apply as well.

Data may be primary (firsthand) or secondary (secondhand). Primary data usually are more difficult and expensive to obtain than secondary data.

Authors devote chapters and even entire books to data-collection processes. The present coverage includes only some general descriptions and suggestions for the oral, nonverbal, and written channels.

Oral

When you seek information through oral channels, plan the transaction ahead of time. If permitted, use a recorder for complex or extensive information. Take appropriate notes. Ask perception-checking questions when possible. Listen carefully.

For all the oral data-receiving situations, try to obtain supplemental written information if possible. For example, if you want a great deal of numerical data from an interviewee, you might just ask if you could have a copy of a report that contains it. If others in a group meeting or brainstorming session suggest relevant written information, ask them to provide copies for you.

As you select the desired information from all the information collected by oral methods, place each bit on a separate note card. On the card write the preliminary outline number (I–A, for example) and/or topic heading. In addition, write the source of the information, and whether it is a direct quotation, paraphrase, or summary if it is an excerpt from another's words. Also, prepare a bibliography card for the source.

Later, sort the note cards into stacks appropriate to the outline. Also alphabetize the bibliography cards to form the bibliography of the paper or report.

Interview

One example of an oral source for information is the interview of someone in a face-to-face exchange or by telephone.

If you have scheduled an interview, prepare an interview guide—an outline including some questions. Leave space for brief answers, or develop questions with multiple-choice questions and answers that you can check off in a simple fashion. If the interviewee agrees, use a tape recorder. Sometimes a personal interview is such that you cannot or should not use an interview guide, take notes, or use a recorder. In such cases you will need to carry a mental outline and questions, concentrate when you listen, and write down everything as soon as you are out of sight of the interviewee.

Person-to-group

For person-to-group presentations and meetings, the suggestions for listening made in Chapter 2 apply. Again, concentration is the key.

Dialogue and conversation

For a dialogue or simple conversation, you often do not take notes. As for some interviews, then, you must carry the material in your mind until you can place it on paper.

Brainstorming

A special kind of oral information-gathering transaction is called brainstorming. The brainstorming process requires a small group of interested and knowledgeable people. They sit around a table and do some creative, concentrated thinking out loud about an identified topic. The basic purpose of the meeting is to generate ideas through free expression, association, chaining, and interactive mental stimulation. They then reduce the ideas to a listing of the most usable for the circumstances.

A good way to begin a brainstorming session is to state the purpose of the meeting. Then someone states the first thing that comes to mind, and the others add whatever comes to their minds. Someone writes the associative chain of ideas on a chalkboard or poster for everyone to see. A tape recorder may capture it.

When no one has anything else to say, the group reduces the list by eliminating obvious duplications. Next, the group decides upon the major ideas and which of the other ideas fall under the major ones. Then, they eliminate the remaining duplications. Finally, the group makes decisions to form the final listing of organized ideas.

The first wave is the essential one. Set an atmosphere that assures participants that no idea should be withheld—and that if an idea is eliminated subsequently, the elimination does not disparage the contributor in any way.

The purposes for brainstorming can be as numerous as the types of problems that call for solution and the types of information needed to reach the solutions. A few examples of the myriad of purposes for brainstorming sessions include:

1. To develop the factors for analysis
2. To establish a specific research problem statement
3. To state the possible hypotheses for the research
4. To generate a list of marketing strategies
5. To produce suggestions for expanding a financial base
6. To discover new production methods

Nonverbal

To collect data through nonverbal means, use your senses as instruments of observation. A written observation form can aid the process a great deal.

For example, if you plan to stand in a supermarket for a long period of time and observe some defined aspect of consumer behavior, you will do well to have a preprinted observation form in hand. It will cause you to be consistent in recording each set of observations, and will also speed up the process.

Many nonverbal observations require the use of instruments of various kinds—instruments that measure, weigh, count, sense, or record in one way or another. When using instruments in a data-collection process, be sure that you and those you supervise know how to use them and record the results from them properly. Again, use an observationnaire for recording the observations.

As for oral and written data received, make up note cards for observations. Each card might summarize the observations for one item on the observationnaire. Make the usual outline identification on each card, and sort according to the identifications.

Written

Once you define the type of information needed, first try to find it in written secondary sources.

Standard publications

Standard types of publications often include the desired type of information. Examples include:

Dictionaries
Encyclopedias
Statistical Abstract of the United States
Monthly Labor Review
World Almanac and Book of Facts
Survey of Current Business
Federal Reserve Bulletin
Statistical Yearbook (United Nations)
Demograhic Year Book (United Nations)
Monthly Bulletin of Statistics (United Nations)
Business Week
Forbes
Information Please Almanac and Yearbook
Fortune
Sales Management
Textile World
Journal of Accounting
Journal of Business
Journal of Business Communication
Journal of Management Studies
Journal of Marketing
Journal of Marketing Research
Dissertation Abstracts
Congressional Record

Reference aids

If a standard type of publication does not yield the needed data, turn next to reference aids. Reference aids identify sources of information. They include organization by topics, authors, and other appropriate classifications. Examples of such aids include:

Business Periodicals Index
New York Times Index
Wall Street Journal Index
Accountants' Index
Sources of Business Information (Edwin T. Coman)
Applied Science and Technology Index
How to Use the Business Library (H. Webster Johnson)
Engineering Index
Business Information—How to Find and Use It (Marian Manley)
Social Science and Humanities Index
Monthly Catalog of United States Government Publications
Biological and Agricultural Index
Cumulative Book Index
Publishers' Weekly
Index Medicus
Chemical Abstracts
Dissertation Abstracts
Education Index
Readers' Guide to Periodical Literature
Vertical File Index
Bulletin of the Public Affairs Information Service

Search and retrieval systems

Two of the best-known systems for search and retrieval are *Datrix* (Direct Access to Reference Information) and *Eric* (Educational Research Information Center). Both systems use the computer to search for sources of information related to an identified topic. Both yield printouts of sources.

Unpublished sources

Unpublished sources primarily include the records of businesses and other organizations. Such computer systems as the *IBM Remac* disc memory facilitate the storage and retrieval of unpublished numerical information.

COLLECTION OF PRIMARY DATA
THROUGH OBSERVATION AND SURVEY

When secondary sources do not yield the desired data, you may need to use primary procedures to obtain them. This coverage of the primary collection process falls into three categories: (1) sampling procedures, (2) forms for recording direct observations, and (3) messages associated with surveys.

Sampling Procedures

A universe (population) contains every elementary unit possessing the characteristic to be observed. Elementary units may be people or things.

Sometimes the researcher observes every unit of a population. However, at other times he or she observes only a selected part of it—a sample.

When possible, select samples by a probability method. Probability sampling gives every item in the universe equal opportunity of being selected. The major probability types are the simple random sample, the systematic sample, the stratified sample, and the cluster sample. Appendix E includes descriptions of the four types—along with brief treatment of the concepts of adequacy (size) and representativeness.

Sometimes circumstances prevent the use of probability methods. In such nonprobability processes, select the samples to be as representative of the universes as possible. Use validation techniques to overcome the possible bias in nonprobability samples.

Forms for Recording Direct Observations

After identifying the items to be observed, a basic approach to collecting data involves direct observation through the five senses—particularly through the eyes and ears. You may count, measure, read, and observe the behavior and characteristics of people and things. You may listen, taste, smell, touch, and perform a myriad of other observational acts. Direct observation also often depends upon the ability to use simple or technical instruments and equipment.

Whichever type of direct observation you undertake, you should devise a form for recording the results. Such a form may be called an observationnaire. The good observationnaire includes or provides:

1. A title and/or some other designation such as a code number
2. Any special instructions for completion of the form
3. Spaces to record specific identifying information—such elements as the date, time, place, name of organization or person, and any special features associated with the observation
4. Space to identify the observer
5. Identification of all observations to be made along with sufficient space for recording them
6. A design that allows the observer to use check marks, X's, or circles—in short, to use a minimum number of words or numbers
7. A logical arrangement of the items
8. A design that allows the observer to add comments about unusual situations

Figure 13–1 illustrates an observationnaire. It has been designed for workers sent into the field to observe the characteristics of randomly selected parking lots at preselected times on preselected days. Evaluate the construction of the form. If the observer goes to five assigned parking lots on a given day, do you think the observationnaire would serve her or him well?

Messages Associated with Surveys

Observations of phenomena often occur in an indirect fashion. They still use the senses—again primarily those of seeing and hearing. However, the observations

CHARACTERISTICS OF COMMERCIAL PARKING LOTS AND GARAGES IN PARKWAY, MISSOURI, 198X
Researchers Unlimited Corp.
Box 793, Parkway, MO 64130

Observer: Arrive at 8:15 a.m. Show permit to operator on duty. Begin all occupancy observations exactly on time. Make other observations and take meals and breaks in the periods between occupancy observations. Show permit to new operators or supervisors as they come on duty.

Signature of observer _____ _____ _____

Date ___/___/8X Day of week: M ☐ Tu ☐ W ☐ Th ☐ F ☐ Sa ☐ Su ☐
        Mo. Day

Type of installation: Lot ☐ Garage ☐

Name and _____ _____
location
of garage _____ _____
or lot
          _____ _____

If garage, number of floors _____

Number of parking spaces _____ Parking spaces marked? Yes ☐ No ☐

Dimensions of parking spaces (in feet and inches)

Length _____ Width _____ Total square feet _____

Width of driving lanes (in feet and inches) _____
Number of parking spaces occupied:

    8:30 a.m. _____   6:30 p.m. _____

    10:30 a.m. _____   8:30 p.m. _____

    12:30 p.m. _____   10:30 p.m. _____

    2:30 p.m. _____   12:30 a.m. _____

    4:30 p.m. _____

Charges:

    Hourly _____   Weekly _____   Other _____

    Daily _____   Monthly _____

On the graph paper provided on the back of this sheet sketch the shape of the lot or of a typical parking floor of the garage. Show the nearest streets on all four sides, directions of one-way streets, the location of the toll booth, the entrances, the exits, and the dimensions of all sides (in feet and inches). You may turn the paper sideways if you wish, but mark clearly which direction is north.

Figure 13–1 Form for recording observations (observationnaire)

involve reading or hearing what other human beings write or say about the subject of the research.

The collection of data through indirect observation moves the research into the category of the survey. The surveying method uses three major vehicles: (1) personal interviews, (2) telephone interviews, and (3) mail questionnaires. All three involve the careful development of a plan, a set of instructions, and a set of questions designed to obtain the desired information.

Most of the time the instructions and questions take a written form—even if you ask them in person or over the telephone. Sometimes you memorize the instructions and questions for oral delivery. Occasionally, you preplan only the introduction to an oral interview—trusting the remainder of the interview to your ability to adapt to whatever course the interview takes.

Suggestions for the speaking acts associated with interviewing appear in Chapter 15 on oral transmissions and in Chapter 18 in conjunction with the search for employment. Therefore, review only the written instruments associated with surveys in this chapter.

Principles for survey instruments

The design of survey instruments calls for an inextricable blend of communication and research arts and skills. Thus, units on such design appear in the literature on both research and communication.

Researchers often differentiate among the basic survey instruments by using such words and phrases as "interview guide," "opinionnaire," and "questionnaire." However, for convenience, use "questionnaire" as the generic term.

Consider the principles for the construction of questionnaires in four broad categories: (1) general design, (2) types of questions, (3) qualities of good questions, and (4) types of construction to be avoided.

General design   To develop a questionnaire, consider these guidelines in addition to the guidelines for any communication:

1. Introduce yourself, the topic of the survey, and the purposes of the research and the questionnaire. However, do not disclose information that may be biasing. Assure confidentiality or anonymity when appropriate.

2. Include good instructions for completing the questionnaire. Questionnaires for interviews often include two sets of instructions—one to the interviewer and one to be given to the interviewee by the interviewer.

3. Use attention-getting, interest-holding, and persuasive devices in the introductory matter. Offer an incentive such as a material gift delivered with the questionnaire or promised upon its completion. Sometimes you even may offer a copy of the final report of the research.

4. Provide for ease of feedback; for mail questionnaires, include postpaid return envelopes.

5. For mail questionnaires, include dates of return and return addresses in the messages themselves. The receivers may misplace the return envelopes.

6. A separate letter or memorandum may accompany a questionnaire. It may include the introduction, topic/title/purposes, instructions, attention/perception/persuasive devices, date for return, and return address. If such a message is sent, repeat at least the topic/title, brief instructions, date of return, and return address on the questionnaire form itself.

7. Include filter and classification questions—questions that screen and identify the respondents according to the analytical factors of the research.

8. Include validating questions—questions that ask for the same information in different ways in order to check whether the respondent is answering truthfully.

9. Arrange the questions in logical order.

   a. Use a logical method of development.

   b. Gain and retain attention and interest within the questionnaire itself.

   c. Locate the most important questions where the respondents will most likely answer them. Locate them as early as possible, but only after proper order of development to that point.

   d. Arrange questions to take account of the impact one question may have on the next one.

   e. Include filter questions early. For example, if you plan to analyze the responses on a questionnaire only if the respondent owns two or more television sets, include early in the questionnaire a filter question about the number of sets owned.

   f. Include classification questions early. For example, suppose you need to know the person's sex, age, and income as the basis for analysis; put those questions early so that you will be sure to get the required answers.

   g. Separate validating questions.

   h. Place difficult questions somewhere in the middle—to avoid too early an encounter and also to avoid the fatigue that may set in near the end.

   i. Put similar types of questions together.

   j. Make smooth transitions from part to part and question to question.

10. Tend to the nonverbal aspects of the design—especially for questionnaires completed directly by the respondent.

   a. Leave plenty of space for responses.

   b. Do not crowd the material on the page.

   c. Use appropriate styles of type and printing.

   d. Attend to grammar, spelling, punctuation, and all other such factors.

   e. Use colors, format, and other features to attract the respondent.

11. Match the language level of the questionnaire to the abilities of the respondents.

12. Make the questions as easy to answer as possible for the information needed.

13. Keep the questionnaire reasonably short, even if you have to redefine your research.

14. Design the questionnaire for ease of tabulation and organization of the information to be collected.

15. Use parallel construction throughout.

16. Pretest and adjust the questionnaire as many times as necessary to perfect the instrument.

These general-design guidelines set the stage for a good collection effort. However, perfect the content of the questions as well.

Types of questions As you turn to a consideration of questions, think first about the available types. The basic types are: (1) open and (2) closed.

As the name indicates, the *open question* supplies no choice of answers. The respondent must supply all of the words that make the response to the question. In academic situations, the type is often called essay or short answer. These are two examples of open questions:

What are your views about the use of energy?
Describe the events of the accident.

Some of the positive qualities of the open question are:

1. It does not lead the respondent into a fixed set of responses.
2. It allows the respondent to express true feelings freely.
3. It causes the respondent to think deeply about the topic.
4. It gives the respondent a sense of participation and importance.
5. It often provides a good vehicle as an opening question with which to gain interest—particularly in interviews.

Some of the negative qualities of the open question are:

1. It may not yield the kind of information that can be organized for the desired analysis and interpretation.
2. Many people will not answer an open question because it requires too much thinking and time.
3. Clarity and specificity often are difficult to incorporate in the open question.
4. As the stages associated with open questioning in interviews unfold, the interviewer's biases may enter into the transaction.

On balance, avoid open questions unless they provide the only method to obtain the unstructured kind of information you need. The negative qualities far outweigh the positive ones.

Closed questions offer reponses from which the respondent chooses. The two major classes of closed questions are the dichotomous question and the multiple-choice question.

The dichotomous question offers only two possible responses. Certain kinds of questions lend themselves to this form. However, most questions of any consequence have more than two possible answers. Two examples of proper dichotomous questions are:

1. Did you vote in the presidential election of 198X?
   ☐ Yes
   ☐ No
2. How old are you?
   ☐ 29 years or less
   ☐ 30 years or more

The multiple-choice question simply extends the number of possible responses from two to a larger number. The number should represent enough responses to encompass the full range of possible responses in mutually exclusive form. The multiple-choice question often must include a final category that allows the respondent to add a response or responses that do not appear in the preset list. Such a category is often written "Other (please specify)." For such a response, be sure to include sufficient space for the respondent or the interviewer to write the alternative(s).

Multiple-choice questions may include responses that are discrete or that fall at discrete points along the semblance of a continuous scale. The continuous rating system is called a semantic-differential or Likert scale.

First, observe two questions written in a traditional multiple-choice style with discrete (discontinuous) options for responses. (The questions would appear in two different questionnaires.)

- What was your approximate income in 198X?
  - ☐ Under $10,000
  - ☐ $10,000 but under $20,000
  - ☐ 20,000 but under 30,000
  - ☐ 30,000 but under 40,000
  - ☐ 40,000 but under 50,000
  - ☐ 50,000 but under 60,000
  - ☐ 60,000 and over

- How was your meal?

☐	☐	☐	☐	☐
Superior	Excellent	Good	Fair	Poor

  Comments:

Observe that the second question combined an open question with a basic closed question. Such combinations often include the positive features of both types.

Consider two examples from a rating-scale design for the closed form of question. Again, the two questions would not necessarily appear in the same questionnaire.

- How would you rate your immediate supervisor's understanding of the human needs of those whom s/he supervises?

Has no understanding			Understands moderately well			Understands completely		
1	2	3	4	5	6	7	8	9

- Compared to other programs in the past, how would you rate this one?

Very poor					Same			Superior		
− 5	− 4	− 3	− 2	− 1	0	1	2	3	4	5

A slight variation on the basic construction of the multiple-choice questionnaire allows the respondent to select more than one answer in the checklist. Consider an example of such a question:

Which of these are reasons that you have not made a credit-card purchase at Freedom's Department Store in the past year? Check as many as you want, and please explain if you wish.

_____ a. Still shop at Freedom's, but pay cash
_____ b. Have moved from the area
_____ c. Have been out of town a great deal
_____ d. Prefer to shop elsewhere now
_____ e. Do not see your ads
_____ f. Had a problem with a clerk
_____ g. Had a problem with a bill
_____ h. Had a problem with delivery service
_____ i. Dislike your parking setup

_____ j. Road construction has been a deterrent
_____ k. Have not made many purchases anywhere, but will return to Freedom's when I do
_____ l. Other (please specify)

Comments and explanations:

The responses in the examples presented so far are sentence fragments. However, responses also may take the form of complete sentences.

The positive qualities of the closed-form question include:

1. Except for the open-end components such as "other (please specify)," the responses are easy to tabulate, organize, and analyze.
2. It is easy to answer.
3. If well written, it is usually clearer and more specific than an open question over the same topic.
4. For the general public the rate of response probably will be higher than for the open question.

The negative qualities of the closed-form question include:

1. It sometimes does not include all possible responses.
2. It does not provide much opportunity for freedom of expression.
3. It perhaps squelches the thinking process by forcing the respondent to choose from among preset responses. Even with the inclusion of the open-end choice, the respondent often chooses one of the listed ones simply to avoid having to think and write.
4. The possible range of responses is so wide for certain topics that they cannot be contained in a few itemized responses.

Qualities of good questions   Though several of the preceding discussions deal with the qualities of good questions, consider an extension and a summary here. Review these devices for developing good questions:

1. Make the questions clear and understandable; include only words with accepted meanings.
2. Use concrete words.
3. Write the questions in the most concise language possible.
4. Make the questions precise and accurate.
5. Draw the questions specifically to the topic.
6. Pose the question in the most positive and ethical terms possible.
7. Make the questions follow a natural chronology as you help the respondent answer difficult questions.
8. Assure mutual exclusion among responses on closed forms.
9. Establish collectively exhaustive responses on closed forms.
10. Use indirect questions for embarrassing or emotional topics.
11. Handle personal questions by establishing responses showing ranges for such information as income and age.
12. If you ask the respondent to choose and rank responses in order of importance, do not expect her/him to handle more than three or four such items.
13. When asking for opinions about the status of something, provide a basis for comparison.

14. Create questions that do not cause the respondent to have to think or recall too much. For example, if you want to know about a brand preference of a consumer, ask only about the most recent purchase—not all purchases within the last year.

15. If you want to know something that might be embarrassing for a respondent to admit, ask what the respondent believes others think about the subject.

16. Relate the questions to actual examples when possible; in personal interviews you may even let the respondent see, hear, or hold something about which you ask questions.

17. In personal interviews use certain kinds of open questions to gain psychological and motivational information from people. Examples of such questions include completion of sentences or stories; associations among words; and reactions to pictures, ink blots, abstract drawings, and objects.

18. Construct all responses to a question in parallel form—both structurally and psychologically.

19. Ask questions that do not threaten feelings of socially acceptable behavior. For example, provide a buffer statement such as "Many people have looked at pornographic magazines at one time or another out of curiosity about what they contain" before you ask, "Have you ever looked at a pornographic magazine?"

20. Include among multiple-choice responses "Don't know" and "No opinion" when appropriate.

21. Retain as courteous and nonprobing a tone as you can.

Types of construction to avoid   View the development of questions briefly from the other side of the coin—the kinds of questions not to write. Consider these suggestions for avoiding improper construction:

Do not write *leading questions*—questions that lead the respondent into a biased answer. Think of the leading nature of these questions:

- You do like comfort in a car, don't you?
- Do you prefer an in-ground swimming pool?
- Don't you think your supervisor is usually fair?
- Do you want the committee to work carefully to develop a good policy?

As an extension of the leading question, the *loaded question* includes words that would make anyone answering the "wrong" way feel foolish. The writer of such questions introduces a bias that indicates that he or she is not interested in research, but in supporting a predetermined position. Political questionnaires often are rife with such questions. Consider these examples of loaded questions:

- Do you believe that monopolistic, profit-hungry big business should be allowed to dictate what you may buy in the marketplace?
- Do you believe that gang-ridden unions should be allowed to seize control of the free-enterprise system?
- Could you ever be unAmerican enough to speak in support of some Communist organization?
- Are you in favor of continuing to reveal to the world how much of a weakling America can be?

Observe how both misleading and loaded questions attempt to convert into dichotomous questions the types of questions that should be posed otherwise. Not only should the biases be removed, but the questions should be put into open or multiple-choice form.

Avoid *biased questions and responses* of all kinds. Both the misleading and loaded questions introduce obvious bias and emotion into the transactions. However, the biases may also appear as leading or loaded words within the responses to multiple-choice questions. Review this illustration:

Now that you have read the new statement of policy, what do you think? (You may mark more than one.)

□ I accept it because it provides a control over those who misuse their privileges.

□ I accept it because I do my job and thus have nothing to fear from it.

□ I accept it because I realize that policies often must be written for the many in order to contain the few who would take advantage of a good situation.

□ I accept it because I trust my superiors to do what is best for the employees.

□ I accept it because I believe that managers have more information than the employees.

□ I accept it because I'm sure whatever management does is for the good of the organization.

□ I accept it because I know of no better place to work than here.

□ I don't accept it because it takes away some of the soft touches that I have had in the past.

The example is obviously overdrawn. In fact, if completed anonymously, some employees probably would check the last answer because they would be angered by the obvious bias. However, the example does make the point that the wording of answers may introduce as much bias as the questions themselves. It also illustrates the flaw introduced by not including a resonse of "Other," and the use of declarative sentences as multiple-choice responses.

Do not ask *multiple-topic questions*. Keep each question on one topic only. For instance, what would answers to these questions mean?

- Do you support gun-control legislation, anti-inflation measures, and national health insurance?
  □ Yes   □ No
- Do you like to watch comedy, western, and mystery shows on television?
  □ Yes   □ No

The multiple-topic question introduces an ambiguity that destroys the value of the responses. Unless the respondent is clever enough to move back to the multiple elements and write a "Yes" or a "No" above each one, the data are useless.

Avoid all *ambiguous questions*. Ambiguity is, of course, the opposite of clarity and specificity. If the reader or listener does not understand what you want or interprets the question differently than you intended, the answers cannot provide useful information. Even if a respondent does not understand a question, he or she likely will answer anyway, if for no other reason than to leave the impression of understanding.

Observe the ambiguity in these questions:

- Would you be interested in some expensive videotaping equipment?
  □ Yes   □ No
- What type of communication do you like best?

In analyzing the first question, did you wonder whether the word "interest" means "see," "know about the technical aspects of," or "own or lease"? If you decided that the question referred to ownership, did you then wonder whether "interested in some expensive videotaping equipment" relates to buying it or to receiving it as a prize or a gift? In the same vein, what did the word "expensive" mean to you?

For the second question—an open question—think of the wildly different kinds of answers that might be given:

Good	Telegram
Concrete	Courteous
Interpersonal	Formal
Written	Grammatically correct
Accurate	Dramatic
Concise	Television
Speedy	Nonverbal

The list could be continued indefinitely. As stated, the question is so ambiguous that the respondent would have no idea what the writer wants. If each respondent writes whatever answer comes to mind first, the writer will receive such diverse information that it will be useless.

Keep to a minimum the kind of question that causes the reader to *hop and skip* around in order to answer the questions. Sometimes a filter question will make such demands, but at least use no more than one such question in any questionnaire.

When you must use a question that causes the reader to hop forward, write clearly and try not to make the jump too great. If you route respondents in only two channels, try to arrange the two sets of responses side by side so that neither type has to skip at all. Consider this example of such an arrangement:

5 If your answer to question No. 4 is "Yes," please answer question Nos. 6-10. If your answer to question No. 4 is "No," please answer question Nos. 11-15. After completing either Nos. 6-10 or Nos. 11-15, please complete Nos. 16-22.

6 How many repairs did you . . . .?	11 What is your view of the . . . .?
a.	a.
b.	b.
c.	c.

Avoid questions that involve qualitative words with *unspecified meanings*. Consider the various meanings you could assign to the qualifiers in this sentence:

Do you often spend more money than you should for goods or services you do not really need?   □ Yes   □ No

How often is "often"? How much money is "more money than you should spend"? What goods and services are "goods and services you do not really need"?

Just as you do for criteria associated with purposes, make such questions quantitative when you possibly can. If you must keep the qualitative construct, at least convert it into a question of opinion based frankly upon the respondent's own definitions of terms already as specific as you can make them. For example, for the preceding question, you could ask:

Have you ever felt that you spent money for goods or services unnecessary to satisfy what you consider to be your basic needs?

Virtually all of the suggestions for good questionnaires in the preceding section could be cast into the reverse form to indicate the kinds of questions to avoid. Consider a few instances: Avoid questions that cause the respondent to do intensive thinking or recalling. Avoid personal questions and questions that arouse emotions; if included, use an indirect approach. Avoid questions that may cause the respondent to answer untruthfully because of the prestige or social acceptability associated with "correct" answers.

Types of Surveys

The three broad classes of surveys are: (1) personal interviews, (2) telephone interviews, and (3) mail questionnaires. Consider the features, strengths, and weaknesses of each type.

Personal interview

The personal interview occurs at the interpersonal level. The interviewer usually goes to the interviewees. For valid research, the interviewees must, of course, be chosen by some appropriate sampling method.

Strengths   Strengths of the personal interview include:

1. Because it functions at the interpersonal level, the potential for nonverbal messages, immediate feedback, evaluation, and adjustment is higher than for either the telephone interview or the mail questionnaire.
2. The proportion of response is significantly higher than for mail questionnaires. Therefore, the chances for a truly representative sample also are greater.
3. Through the interaction made possible by the face-to-face construct, the interviewer can explain instructions and answer questions. Thus he or she may create the possibility of more complete and accurate answers than from the mail questionnaire.
4. The interviewer can show products, charts, and other materials and objects that may help the respondent understand the message.
5. The potential for going into depth and detail on an issue is higher than for the other two types.

Weaknesses   The personal interview also has some weaknesses.

1. The personal interview is more expensive than the telephone interview or mail questionnaire. However, if the costs for each of the three are distributed over pieces of information obtained, the differential in costs reduces substantially.
2. Wide geograhic distribution of the people in the universe often makes the personal-interview survey difficult to accomplish.
3. Research often requires a "snapshot" instead of a "moving picture" of the observed variable. Such "snapshots" are difficult to obtain through personal interviews.
4. Many people consider interviews to be intrusions upon their privacy.
5. Many high office-holders simply do not grant personal interviews.
6. The qualities that provide the potential for interaction, feedback, and depth interviewing also provide the potential for the interviewer to act consciously or unconsciously to bias the results.

7. Locating, training, and retaining enough good interviewers may be difficult.
8. Some respondents will supply personal information in an anonymous mail questionnaire that they will not supply in a personal interview.
9. The time allotment for a personal interview often does not allow the interviewer to gain the kind of information that requires the respondent to search some records or do some deep thinking.
10. The interviewer often must make several calls before finding the selected interviewee at home, thus sometimes destroying the desired timing of the interview.

If for a given survey you can overcome the disadvantages of the personal interview, use it. The richness of the interpersonal level and the other cited advantages make it the strongest of the three types.

Telephone interview

The telephone interview is second to the personal interview in strength as a survey data-collection method. Though telephoning operates at the medio level, it still retains some of the qualities of the interpersonal level.

Strengths   First consider the strengths of the telephone interview:

1. Because the interviewer and interviewee are in oral contact, the potential for nonverbal messages, immediate feedback, evaluation, and adjustment is higher than for the mail questionnaire.
2. The proportion of response is significantly higher than for the mail questionnaires; therefore, the chances for a representative sample also are greater.
3. Through the interaction made possible by the speaking-and-listening construct, the interviewer may explain instructions and answer questions, thus creating the possibility of more complete and accurate answers than from the mail questionnaire.
4. The potential for going into depth and detail on an issue is higher than for the mail questionnaire.
5. The telephone directory provides a good basis for applying the systematic sampling technique.
6. The contacts may be made over even a wide geographic region in a much shorter time than that required for either the personal interview or the mail questionnaire.
7. Because of the speed with which telephone interviews may be made, virtual "snapshots" in time become possible.
8. Costs are significantly lower than in personal interviewing, and nearly as low as costs of the mail questionnaire.
9. Some people may consider a telephone inquiry to be less an intrusion upon privacy than a personal interview.
10. Some high office-holders may grant a telephone interview when they will not grant a personal one.
11. Some respondents may supply personal information in a telephone interview that they will not supply in a personal interview.
12. If one person selected by a probability process does not answer or does not wish to cooperate, the interviewer may easily and immediately choose a replacement by probability methods.

Weaknesses   Compared to the other types of survey, the telephone inquiry also has some weaknesses:

1. Populations cannot always be represented by the listed telephone subscribers in a directory on the date of its publication.
2. Compared to the personal interview, the telephone interview loses many of the advantages associated with the interpersonal level.
3. The interviewer cannot supply as many nonverbal cues as is possible with the personal interview.
4. The telephone interview cannot exceed about seven minutes; therefore, the potential for going into depth and detail on an issue is smaller than for the personal interview.
5. The telephone interview may be more expensive than the mail questionnaire.
6. Many people consider the telephone interview to be a more serious invasion of privacy than a mail questionnaire.
7. Many high office-holders do not grant telephone interviews.
8. The qualities that provide the potential for interaction, feedback, and depth interviewing also provide the potential for the interviewer to act consciously or unconsciously to bias the results.
9. Locating, training, and retaining capable interviewers may be difficult (but not as difficult as for the personal interview).
10. Some respondents will supply personal information in an anonymous mail questionnaire that they will not supply in a telephone interview.
11. The time allotment for a telephone interview does not allow the interviewer to gain the kind of information that requires the respondent to search some records or do some deep thinking.
12. The oral-only construct of the telephone interview allows only simpler questions to be asked.
13. Busy signals and "no-answers" often plague the interviewer.
14. Respondents generally feel freer to cut short a telephone interview than a personal one.

   If you can validate the telephone directory as representative of the universe you want to survey in some relatively simple way, select it. The telephone holds many of the important strengths of both the personal interview and the mail questionnaire. It keeps some of the richness of the interpersonal level while gaining the economic and speed advantages of the oral medio level. In most respects it surpasses the written medio level represented by the mail questionnaire.

Mail questionnaire

The mail questionnaire has the fewest strengths and the greatest number of weaknesses. Avoid it if you can possibly use one of the other two types.

Strengths   Strengths of the mail questionnaire include:

1. Depending upon the number of follow-ups and the difficulties associated with sampling and with instrument construction, the mail questionnaire usually runs lower in cost than any other survey method.
2. For a wide geographic distribution of the people in the universe, the mail questionnaire becomes more efficient than the personal interview.

3. Many people do not consider the mail questionnaire to be as great an invasion of privacy as personal and telephone interviews.
4. Because of the anonymity provided by the mail questionnaire, many people will answer it when they would not respond to an oral interview.
5. Some high office-holders will respond to a mail questionnaire when they will not give interviews.
6. The potential for the bias introduced by on-the-spot interviewers does not exist in the mail questionnaire.
7. Development and consummation of the mail-questionnaire survey do not require the numbers of qualified and trained people that the interview surveys do.
8. The mail questionnaire does not have the time restrictions that personal and telephone interviews do; therefore, the respondent has time to search some records or do some deep thinking.
9. The mail questionnaire may allow more depth and detail on an issue than a telephone inquiry—but only if the writer of the questionnaire can develop a written probe even approximating that possible through the oral exchange.
10. Compared to the telephone interview, the mail questionnaire offers more opportunity to ask complicated questions.

Weaknesses Weaknesses of the mail questionnaire include:

1. The opportunities for nonverbal messages, feedback, evaluation, and adjustment are limited severely.
2. The potential for response bias is the most serious of the three types; proportions of returns often fall as low as 20 percent.
3. When the response rate is low, and the questionnaires are anonymous, follow-ups and replacements are difficult.
4. Validation of a low-response sample as representative of the universe can be extremely difficult.
5. The mail questionnaire cannot satisfy the demands of the kinds of research that require "snapshots" of the factors under analysis.
6. Without the advantages of the oral transaction, the interviewer has no opportunity to explain the instructions or answer any questions; accuracy and completeness may suffer.
7. Identification of a probability sample from all people in a universe of mailing addresses can be quite difficult.
8. The mail survey takes a significant amount of time.
9. In general, to assure good return, the questionnaires cannot be so long that they require more than about twelve minutes to complete. Therefore, the questionnaire usually must ask for only limited information.
10. Generally, the nature of the mail questionnaire prohibits any true probes into the depth of a subject.
11. Though capable of handling material more complex than that possible for the telephone inquiry, the mail questionnaire still has limitations in that realm; many people simply will not bother with complex questionnaires.

The questionnaire may fit a universe of homogeneous, interested people. However, its weaknesses far outweigh its strengths.

(1,899 words)
(test on page 456)

SUMMARY

Reports form part of the supply line for information in both large and small organizations. Reports can be both written and oral, and all reports involve nonverbal communication.

Reports may be private or public, short or long, informal or formal, informational or persuasive, and routine or analytical. They may describe a problem, suggest a way to solve a problem, or offer a solution to a problem. Reports can be made in nearly any form for nearly any reason, but serve primarily for management control.

The guidelines for developing reports are:

1. Define purposes, participants, and the environment.
2. Identify report channel.
3. Control interference.
4. Write and transmit report in light of purposes, participants, environment, channel, and interference.
5. Use feedback.
6. Evaluate at each stage.

Reports usually take one of three basic formats: (1) letter or memorandum, (2) form, and (3) manuscript. The letter often travels from inside the firm to outside agencies or from the agencies into the firm. The memorandum format appears within the firm—usually flowing upward. Report-makers generally use the more formal manuscript format for comprehensive reports of analytical or research activities.

The traditional manuscript format includes three major parts: (1) front matter, (2) body, and (3) back matter. The three parts contain at least 16 possible subdivisions.

Collection of information is an important part of the research process. The oral channels for collection include interviews, person-to-group transactions, dialogues and conversations, and brainstorming. The nonverbal channels involve using the senses to observe nonword things. Written channels for secondary data include standard publications, reference aids, search and retrieval systems, and unpublished sources.

Collection of primary data involves observations and the survey. Both approaches may involve *sampling*.

Select sample by *probability methods* if possible. Establish samples to meet the criteria of *adequacy* and *representativeness*.

The collection of data through direct observation improves with the use of an *observationnaire*.

Principles for construction of survey questionnaires fall into four broad categories: (1) general design, (2) types of questions, (3) qualities of good questions, and (4) types of constructions to avoid.

Suggestions for general design deal with logic, appearance, and general content.

Two basic types of questions define the survey instrument: the open and the closed. The *open question* supplies no answers from which the respondent may choose. The *closed question* supplies answers. The closed question appears in dichotomous, multiple-choice, or rating scale form. The open question allows freer expression. The closed question is easier to collate and control.

Good questions require qualities that range from simple courtesy to avoiding embarrassment to the respondent.

Avoid *leading questions, loaded questions, biased questions* and responses, *multiple-topic questions, ambiguous questions, hop-and-skip questions,* and *unspecified-meanings questions.*

The three major survey methods are (1) *personal interviews,* (2) *telephone interviews,* and (3) *mail questionnaires.* All three involve the careful development of a plan, a set of instructions, and a set of questions designed to obtain the desired information. Each has its strengths and weaknesses. If all other considerations are equal, however, choose the interview.

Practice

1. Meet with your group. As a group, try to think of at least five business situations in which you would write a report. Define your purposes for writing the reports, the readers' purposes for reading the reports, the readers, and the environment of the readers. Then discuss the problems inherent in each situation. Have one of your group members present one of the situations and its associated problems to the class.

2. You interviewed 105 randomly selected clerical workers to learn how they viewed their jobs. You asked each clerical worker ten well-thought-out questions. Your most interesting finding was that 75 of the workers plan to quit their clerical jobs within two years because they find clerical work uninteresting and they do not feel that they are paid well. Of the 75 who plan to quit, 52 want to go to college to earn a four-year degree. Sixty-five of the people who plan to quit said that they would consider staying on at their company if they were given opportunities to train for entry-level professional positions. Of the 30 workers who do not plan to leave in the next two years, 23 said they plan to stay because they like the people with whom they work. You very much enjoyed working with the clerical personnel. Write an abstract that will introduce your report on the interviews with the clerical workers.

3. You have been asked by your employer to observe the activities at each of the pizza restaurants in your town. Your employer wants to know:
   a. The size of each restaurant
   b. The restaurant's parking arrangements
   c. The number of tables in the restaurants
   d. The maximum number of people the restaurant can hold
   e. The price and size of both the smallest and largest plain cheese pizzas
   f. The price and size of both the smallest and largest sausage pizzas
   g. The restaurant's hours
   h. The number of customers in the restaurant on the hour every hour on a Friday
   i. Whether the restaurant also serves submarine sandwiches
   Prepare a form for recording these observations. Include the more basic information (e.g., name of restaurant) as well.

4. You want to interview the 28 third-year computer-science students at a small university in your city, Mapleton, Arkansas. You want them to give you information regarding their career plans. You want to know:
   a. The field into which they plan to go
   b. The beginning salary they expect
   c. Whether they will seek work in Mapleton, outside of Mapleton but in Arkansas, or out of state

   d. Whether they plan to pursue a graduate degree, and if so, in what field

   e. The work title they would like to have in five years, in ten years, and in fifteen years

   f. The salary they would like to have in five years, in ten years, and in fifteen years

Design a survey instrument for your use during each interview. You can use either open or closed questions, whichever you feel would be more appropriate. Explain why you chose the one type of question over the other.

5. These are poorly constructed survey questions. Correct them.

   a. Did you attend former President Ford's lecture yesterday?

      ☐ Yes   ☐ I am a Democrat

      ☐ No   ☐ Maybe

   b. What is your age?

      ☐ Young   ☐ Old

      ☐ Middle   ☐ Quite ancient

   c. The employee completes her or his work on time

      ☐ Always   ☐ Never

   d. List everything that you like about politics. Be specific.

   e. Do you plan to stop taking advantage of the privileges your company gives you?

   f. How many bags of Pop-Pop Popcorn did you purchase in the last ten years?

   g. Do you advocate the removal of the beautiful trees that God gave us?

   h. Why don't you work hard?

   i. As a basketball player, how do you handle your loss of femininity?

   j. Do you support flexible office hours, better pay, employee lounges, and more vacation days?

      ☐ Yes   ☐ No

   k. Would you like better conditions here at Big Corporation?

      ☐ Yes   ☐ No

6. [*Your professor will time this exercise.*] You are the manager of the graphics department of a large corporation. You have been asked to keep a record of the attendance of each of your 15 workers for submission to your superior every month. Design an attendance report form. Include spaces for attendance, sick leave, and vacation leave for each worker.

7. Write a memorandum briefly defining the four basic methods for drawing probability samples (Appendix E). Give an example of the type of research for which each method would be appropriate.

8. Put each of these into footnote form:

   a. You quoted from Lamar T. Handley's *Managing Your Own Business,* a book that was printed in 1976 by the Wayside Publishing Company of Chapel Hill, North Carolina. Your quotation is from page 16 of the book. This is the first footnote in your paper.

   b. "Business Leaders Wake Up to Crime" is your source. The article was published in the April, 1980, issue of *Big Business,* a magazine. Your quotation was taken from pages 189 and 190 of the magazine. The article's authors are Sara Mason Winecoff and Maren Halvorsell. This is the fifth footnote in your paper.

   c. *The New Jersey Marketer's Guide* is the source for your eighth footnote. The guide was published in New Jersey by the New Jersey Association of Marketing Managers. You quoted from page 92 of the 1980 guide.

9. Meet with your group. Conduct a complete brainstorming session on any one or several of these topics. Write the findings, appoint a spokesperson, and report the findings to the class.

   a. The comparative characteristics and qualities of probability and nonprobability sampling. Also identify examples of both types.

   b. The advantages and disadvantages of the personal and impersonal writing styles.

     c. The definition and examples of plagiarism.

     d. The relative advantages and disadvantages of formality and informality in reporting style.

10. Meet with your group. Brainstorm to determine the content and design of a mail questionnaire to be sent to selected business people within the college community. The purpose of the questionnaire is to determine the views of businesspeople about the relative importance of business communication and other business courses or specialities to the smooth functioning of business. Before the brainstorming session, you may want to read a section on the topic in Chapter 15 (page 512) and/or consult some of the sources listed there. After the initial brainstorming session, assign group members to the tasks of drafting (1) a cover letter, (2) the heading and introduction on the questionnaire, and (3) the questions. Meet with the group again to compile the drafts and then develop the second draft. Present the drafts from the groups to the professor and/or class. From them, develop the final questionnaire. Retain it for use with an exercise in Chapter 14.

11. As a marketing research analyst, choose a commonly used household product (e.g., paper towels, detergent, bath soap, shampoo). Develop a telephone interview guide to determine such things as the preferred brand, the last brand purchased, and common and special uses for the product. Also plan to determine such information as the monthly quantity purchased, the number in the family, who in the family makes the purchases, etc. Also develop the introductory statements for the interview. Establish and test the introduction and the guide so that the entire interview takes no more than three minutes. Conduct the interview by telephone with each member of your group or with other acquaintances. Upon completion of the simulation, ask for their evaluation. Revise the guide to reflect the contribution of the evaluation.

12. Using Appendix E and/or other sources as a guide, make the sampling decisions and write the report for this case:

You will draw a sample from the 16,000 households in your city. You have no reason to believe that the telephone directory is a seriously biased representation of the population. The purpose of the survey is to estimate the mean weekly expenditure on gasoline and oil of all households in the city. You want the final interval to be no more than $2 from lower limit to upper limit at the .95 level of confidence. A similar study last year yielded a standard deviation of $4.

     a. Calculate the number of households to be included in the sample.

     b. Decide which type of sampling method you will use and exactly how to accomplish it.

     c. Write a detailed report of your decisions. Use the memorandum format, and address it to Althea R. Search, the specialist for whom you will do the research. Add additional information as needed.

13. Prepare an interview guide to be used to determine the facts and the attitudes of people in small business about the numbers and types of reports required by government agencies.

14. Use your dictionary and thesaurus to create meanings for these words. Use the words when you think, write, or speak so that you feel comfortable using them.

a. Charisma	**i.** Inextricable
b. Compendium	**j.** Negate
c. Consummation	**k.** Paraphrase
d. Dichotomous	**l.** Probability
e. Disarm	**m.** Statistics
f. Disparage	**n.** Valid
g. Encompass	**o.** Voluminous
h. Idiom	**p.** Voracious

15. Take and score Self–Test 30 over the excerpt about types of surveys.

Self-Test 30
Excerpt about Types of Surveys

A. Recall (33 points each). For each multiple-choice question, select the most accurate answer.

   1. Which of these statements regarding the personal interview is *not* true?
   a. The proportion of response is significantly higher than for mail questionnaires; therefore, the chances for a representative sample also are greater.
   b. Because it functions at the interpersonal level, the potential for nonverbal messages, immediate feedback, evaluation, and adjustment is higher than for either the telephone interview or the mail questionnaire.
   c. Because the interviewer is face to face with the interviewee, the potential for the interviewer to act consciously or unconsciously to bias the results is minimized.
   d. The potential for going into depth and detail on an issue is higher than for either the telephone interview or the mail questionnaire.
   e. The interviewer may show products, charts, and other materials and objects that may help the respondent understand the message.

   2. Which of these statements regarding the telephone interview is *not* true?
   a. It is generally better than the mail questionnaire.
   b. The interviewer may explain instructions and answer questions as the interview progresses.
   c. The contacts may be made over a wide geographic region in a much shorter time than that required for either the personal interview or the mail questionnaire.
   d. The costs are significantly lower than those for the personal interview.
   e. The samples taken from the telephone directory are always representative of the population as a whole.

B. Inference (34 points). Indicate whether this statement is true or false.

Because the mail questionnaire has so many weaknesses, one would do well not to use it at all.

Solution to Self-Test 30
Excerpt about Types of Surveys

A. Recall (33 points each).   **B.** Inference (34 points)

   1. c   **2.** e   False

16. Take and score Self–Test 31 over Chapter 13.

Self-Test 31
Chapter 13

A. Recall (25 points each). For each multiple-choice question, select the most accurate answer.

   1. When you design a survey instrument, do *not:*
   a. Use attention-getting, interest-holding, and persuasive devices in the introductory matter
   b. Include validating questions—questions that ask for the same information in different ways
   c. Arrange the questions in a logical order
   d. Design the instrument for ease of tabulation
   e. Include leading, loaded, biased, ambiguous, or multiple-topic questions

2. Which one of these statements is true?
   a. Most routine reports appear in the manuscript format.
   b. Every manuscript report should contain a preface, foreword, or acknowledgements.
   c. Each level of headings may include only one heading and accompanying section.
   d. Brainstorming is a form of depth interview; it requires that the group immediately challenge each idea put to the group.
   e. The wise researcher tries to find needed information from secondary sources before engaging in primary investigation.

3. Which one of these statements is *false?*
   a. Whenever possible, choose a nonprobability sample over a probability one.
   b. Whether conducted in person or by mail or telephone, a survey should involve preplanning and a preprinted form for completion.
   c. The observationnaire is a good instrument upon which to record direct observations.
   d. Filter and classification questions usually appear early in a survey document.
   e. The responses to a multiple-choice question should exhaust the possible answers.

B. Inference (25 points). Indicate whether this statement is true or false.

   The rating-scale design is particularly adaptable to ranges of qualitative responses to a question.

Solution to Self-Test 31
Chapter 13

A. Recall (25 points each)
   1. e   3. a
   2. e

B. Inference (25 points)
   True

Writing Reports: The Research Process and Types of Reports

Chapter 14 completes the discussion of report writing introduced in Chapter 13. It includes reviews of the research process and types of business reports.

THE RESEARCH PROCESS

Research is the search for solutions to problems. The problems may be puzzling questions or they may be obstacles in the path of the attainment of some goal. Basic research answers puzzling questions, and applied research overcomes obstacles. Thus, most business research falls in the category of applied research.

Persing summarizes what research is *not:*

1. Research is *not* writing—though writing is important to the process.
2. Research is *not* publishing—though publishing disseminates information gained from the process.
3. Research is *not* quantitative methods—though quantitative methods may contribute significantly to the process.
4. Research is *not* collecting information—though collecting information is a vital stage of the process.[1]

Thus, many people use the word "research" too narrowly. In terms of communication, the purpose of research is to solve problems, not to write reports or papers. In addition, not all reports and papers result from research. However, research is a process with communication acts inseparably woven into it, and communication is a process with research acts inseparably woven into it.

---

[1]Bobbye Sorrels Persing, "Search and Re-search for Solutions to Communication Problems," *Journal of Business Communication* 16 (Winter 1979): 19–23.

Because of the interwoven nature of research and communication, the good report writer understands and applies the steps of the research process. An assignment like "Write me a report about . . . ." involves much more than writing. Even a report not resulting from research requires professional application of at least the defining and collecting steps of the process.

While beginning report writers may not employ every research step in every assignment, their growth with a company often depends very much on developing the ability to do so. Rarely does management separate the assignment of research or major elements of it from the writing.

Even if management does assign the research to one person and the writing to another, the writer must understand the process well enough to write about it. Without experiencing that actual process or being able to experience it vicariously, a writer will be at an extreme disadvantage.

A report is not an end unto itself; it is the means to an end. It captures the results of research or some stage of the process. It summarizes a process suggesting a solution to a problem. It conveys information and/or possible solutions to a decision-maker, who then attempts to solve the problem.

Review the steps of the research process, types of empirical research, and two special applications of research—motivational research and communication research.

Steps of the Research Process

The research process involves science, art, technique, and decision-making applied to these basic steps:

1. Recognize and define the problem and the purposes of the research.
2. Review the literature.
3. State the hypothesis(es).
4. Design the investigation.
5. Write the proposal.
6. Collect the data.
7. Organize the data.
8. Analyze the data.
9. Interpret the results of the analysis.
10. Draw conclusions.
11. Develop recommendations.
12. Write and disseminate the final report.
13. Conduct a follow-up.

Though the steps receive elaboration in the section on the proposal (page 481), consider them here in brief.

Science, art, technique, and decision-making

Basically, research involves the scientific method. In fact, many researchers define steps 1, 3, 4, 6, 7, 8, 9, and 10 of the listing as the steps of the scientific method. However, research also involves art, technique, and the decision-making associated with the other three operations.

Science   The scientific method adds objectivity to the process of applying the research steps. It demands exact procedures, factual observations, experiments, and analysis.

Art   Art introduces human creativity into the research process. It may contribute significantly to the development of many of the stages.

Art contributes particularly to the thinking power necessary for identifying the possible factors associated with the problem, the posed hypothesis(es), and the design. It also contributes significantly to the stages of interpretation and recommendation.

Avoid completely subjective bias, however. Once creativity has contributed to opening doors for definitions, hypothesis(es), and design, the researcher must become the objective scientist. The scientist does not allow bias to affect the observations or analysis. He or she reengages art only at the stage of interpretation— or if circumstances require revising definitions or designs.

Technique   A great deal of the work in the research process involves nothing more than sheer technique—technical skills. Calculating an arithmetic mean, writing a computer program, using calipers to take measurements, constructing a grammatically correct sentence—all represent the application of technique.

The application of technical skills can be mechanical and even tedious. However, those skills play a critical role in the completion of research.

Decision-making   Decision-making overlays all of the scientific, artistic, and technical activities associated with research. The researcher must decide which factors to test and which to reject, which method of collection to employ, which analytical tools to use, which conclusions to draw, to name but a few choices.

One requirement for good decision-making is the ability to exercise it assertively. Some would-be researchers seem unable to make timely decisions— becoming virtually paralyzed in the face of the responsibility.

Such paralysis often relates to the impossibility of perfection in research models. However, the efficient decision-maker makes the decisions necessary to create the best possible circumstances, acknowledges the limitations, and proceeds to the next stage of the process.

Recognizing and defining the problem

One of the most demanding stages of the research process involves the recognition and definition of the problem. Techniques for doing so include brainstorming, reading, conversing, and observing.

The general problem is a broad question or obstacle in need of solution. As an example, a general problem for a firm might be a decline in productivity for the past three years.

The specific problem is the part of the larger problem to be solved by the research. Thus, the researcher carves the specific problem from the general problem.

To accomplish the carving, the researcher isolates a part of the whole—delimits the problem or establishes the scope of the problem. The boundaries of the isolated problem define it in terms of the appropriate W's—the who, what, when, and where, in particular.

For the general-problem example, then, a specific problem might become: Are monthly productivity rates for P. R. Blem, Inc., for 1975-1981 related to monthly turnover rates for the same period?

Reviewing the literature

The efficient researcher reads into the literature as an aid to identifying problems, perfecting the definition of a problem, or finding solutions to a defined problem or similar problems. Searching the literature also gives evidence of the researcher's attitudes of thoroughness and recognition of the work of others—two cardinal elements of the proper research posture.

Stating the hypothesis(es)

Application of the scientific method requires the statement of a hypothesis or hypotheses.

A hypothesis is a declarative statement to be tested through the analysis of collected data. It is not a question or a problem. On the basis of the analysis, the researcher accepts or rejects the prestated hypothesis.

A hypothesis for the productivity problem is: A significant correlation exists between monthly productivity rates and monthly turnover rates at P. R. Blem, Inc., for the period 1975-1981.

Designing the investigation

Research design requires decisions about how to collect, organize, and analyze data appropriate to the defined problem and hypothesis(es).

Decisions about collection involve precise definition of factors, location of information, methods of observation, and quantity of observation. They also may involve sampling methods and other topics.

Decisions about organization and analysis relate to preselection of the methods of analysis. Such decisions require a great deal of knowledge about both quantitative and qualitative approaches to examining information and reaching conclusions about it.

The quality of research depends substantially upon a good design. Thus, the wise researcher makes all of the design-stage decisions before even beginning to collect the data. Otherwise, the research may take an undesirable course—with wasted time, effort, and money as a result.

Writing the proposal

The proposal (prospectus) is a written report that includes at least the statement of the problem, a summary of the review of the literature, the hypothesis(es), and the design of the investigation.

The proposal often serves as the inherently persuasive request for permission, authorization, and/or monetary support for the research proposed in it. Therefore, it must be complete, competent, and precise in every detail.

Collecting the data

With a good design, the collecting stage becomes a formality. It simply completes the procedures about which decisions have already been made.

Collection may involve obtaining information from secondary sources. It may involve primary data gained from direct observation of actual or simulated events, or from indirect observation through surveys. It may involve any or all of the senses.

Chapter 13 includes an elaboration upon the collecting process.

Organizing the data

The design also indicates how to organize the data. Proper organization aligns the data effectively for the chosen analytical approach. It usually requires collation, tables, and graphs.

Analyzing the data

Once the researcher collects and organizes the data, the pre-selected analysis proceeds. Many analytical tools fall into the quantitative realm. Others use words instead of numbers.

Interpreting the results of the analysis

Interpretation adds art to the scientific methodology of the analysis. It supplies meaning for the results of the analysis. Basically, then, interpretation answers the question, "Now, what do the results of that analysis mean to me?"

Drawing conclusions

To draw conclusions is to focus the analysis and interpretation into a final summarized decision. The conclusion involves acceptance or rejection of the originally stated hypothesis. It also elaborates upon why the data, analysis, and interpretation led to that decision.

Developing recommendations

Many reports stop with the conclusions (results, findings, discussion) of the research, leaving the decision about action to others. This style occurs quite frequently in business situations: Staff researchers conduct the research, write reports of the research (making no recommendations), and leave the decision-making up to the line managers to whom they submit the reports.

Some managers use a different style. They charge researchers with the responsibility of developing recommendations. Such recommendations usually follow the conclusions and become modified action/acceptance components of the reports.

The recommendation is "toned down" because reports usually do not include the overt types of requests found in letters, notes, memoranda, and other forms. Instead, reports include brief and direct recommendations about the needs for additional research and/or the courses of action decision-makers might take. The recommendations tie clearly to the conclusions from which they sprang and may appear in ranked order.

Writing and disseminating the final report

Like the proposal, the final report includes the statement of the problem, the review of the literature, the hypothesis(es), and the design of the investigation. However, it also includes the collected data in organized form, a summary of the analysis, the interpretation, the conclusion, and recommendations (if appropriate). It may also include an abstract and other sections as well.

Even with recommendations, the final report of research usually remains more of an inherently persuasive message than an overtly persuasive one.

For business circumstances, reports of research usually go to a few selected, key managers—including the one who authorized the research in the first place. Thus, distribution remains rather fixed and private.

For some situations, however, the researcher distributes copies of research results rather widely—even to the extent of submitting them for publication. When published, results of course become widely disseminated.

Conducting a follow-up

Depending upon the instructions from and relationships with the authorizing manager, the researcher may or may not conduct a follow-up. When the researcher does engage in a follow-up, he or she may take any one or a combination of several courses of action:

1. Ask whether the manager needs additional information.
2. Ask which of several recommendations (if included) the manager will implement.
3. Try to persuade the manager to take a certain course of action or not to take another.
4. Offer additional recommendations.
5. Suggest additional research.
6. Ask the manager to evaluate the report.
7. Ask the manager to report on the success of the implementation of the recommendation(s) in the report.

Types of Research

Many classifications of types of research exist. One common system—based on the nature of the data—includes three classes:

Historical (searching for the meaning of history)
Survey (using observation to describe or analyze contemporary data)
Experimental (controlling the research to observe the effect of identified variables upon the outcome)

Historical and most descriptive survey methods are basically qualitative (verbal) in nature. However, the analytical survey, experimentation, and some descriptive survey methods are quantitative (numerical) in nature.

An expanded classification scheme provides some additional differentiations among the types of empirical research—research based on experience and observation. That classification includes:

1. Qualitative description
2. Quantitative description
3. Classification
4. Estimation
5. Comparison
6. Relationship
7. Cause-and-effect relationship
8. Mapping and modeling

9. Operations research
10. Time series and indexes[2]

Qualitative description

Qualitative description is description of observed phenomena with words. It can be one of the most difficult to accomplish. As an example, describing employee behavior with words alone requires advanced competencies.

Quantitative description

Quantitative description uses numbers to portray conditions as they exist. It includes observations quantified in such measures as raw numbers, totals, arrays, percentage distributions, arithmetic means, geometric means, harmonic means, medians, modes, average deviations, standard deviations, variances, quartile deviations, coefficients of variation, coefficients of correlation, regression equations, and indexes. Description with numbers stops short of inference.

The measures that involve formulas (beginning with the arithmetic mean in the preceding list) move into the realm of the analytical survey process.

Quantitative description often involves tabular and graphic presentations. Chapter 16 includes details on their development.

Classification

The development of mutually exclusive and collectively exhaustive systems of classification for qualitative data demands expertise. Such research is highly sophisticated and requires well-qualified researchers.

As an example, a neophyte researcher would have a difficult time developing a classification scheme for types of consumer behavior.

Estimation

Estimation of an unknown may involve qualitative inference—how a consumer will act, for example, or what the employee will say. However, the term "estimation" usually refers to quantitative analysis.

As a quantitative inferential technique, estimation involves observation of a characteristic of a sample and the use of that value as the basis for an estimate of the corresponding characteristic in the universe.

The characteristic of the sample is a point estimate, and a point estimate is subject to sampling error. Therefore, the researcher usually expands a point estimate into a confidence-interval estimate.

For instance, assume a researcher wants to know the proportion of workers who approve of a proposed change in a retirement policy. However, she must draw a sample instead of contacting all employees. She draws a representative sample, distributes a questionnaire to the chosen people, and calculates the proportion of the sample who approve of the policy. Finally, she calculates a factor to compensate for

---

[2]Adapted from a six-part classification by Julian L. Simon, *Basic Research Methods in Social Science: The Art of Empirical Investigation* (New York: Random House, 1969), pp. 52–72. Simon's classification does not include operations research or indexes and time series. It combines quantitative description and estimation into a single class. It combines relationships and cause-and-effect relationships into another single class.

sampling error, and adds that factor to and subtracts it from the sample proportion. Assume that the proportion in the sample is 42 percent and the factor is 8 percent. The confidence-interval estimate, then, is that between 34 and 50 percent of all employees approve of the policy.

Comparison

Comparison research may deal with qualitative or quantitative data. For both types it is an analytical method.

In research involving quantitative comparison (an inferential technique), the researcher wants to know whether chance or something other than chance explains the difference(s) among observed characteristics. The concept springs from the knowledge that no two things are identical—that a difference always exists. However, that difference may represent chance variation or genuine variation.

Quantitative comparison involves tests of significance based upon carefully defined models and probability distributions. The tests compare numerical values.

To illustrate, suppose that a marketing researcher wants to determine whether the mean monthly income of families in one area differs significantly from the mean monthly income in another area. The researcher takes a representative sample from each area and contacts each family in the samples to obtain the information. He then calculates the mean monthly income for each sample and tests to determine whether the means differ significantly.

Relationship

The determination of relationships between or among observed variables constitutes another important class of analytical research. Though researchers often analyze qualitative relationships, a codified body of analytical tools deals with quantitative relationships—with correlation and regression.

With the establishment of a high degree of relationship (correlation) between or among variables, one or more variables may predict another (regression analysis). With the uncertainty associated with business decisions, the concept of prediction is vital.

Though it involves analytical description, correlation also involves inference. By definition, regression analysis involves inference.

The association between entrance scores on tests and the sales made by salespersons illustrates the importance of predictability. If the test scores relate significantly to sales, management has an important criterion for hiring salespersons and for predicting sales.

Cause-and-effect relationship

Not all significant relationships indicate that cause and effect exist. Variables may relate to one another without the one causing the occurrence of the other. For example, tests of association show that the crime rate and the church-attendance rate relate significantly. However, that does not mean that the one causes the other.

Establishment of cause and effect requires the analysis and inference associated with an experimental design. An experimental design involves the establishment of absolute control over all untested factors so that only the tested factor varies.

For the example of the association between test scores and sales, the only way to be sure that good test scores *cause* good sales would be to remove or control every factor other than scores and sales from the analysis. The analyst would have to remove from the experiment or hold constant such elements as economic conditions, sizes of customers' needs for the product, and time factors. She would also have to remove or control such elements as sizes of sales territories, illnesses, educational levels, ages, and physical appearances.

This simple recitation of some of the factors that might affect sales illustrates the difficulty of establishing good experimental designs when people are the subjects. However, fortunately, to predict sales from test scores, the researcher need not establish cause and effect—if statistical testing shows that a significant correlation exists between the two factors.

Mapping and modeling

Mapping involves a complex qualitative and/or quantitative description of an existing system. Modeling may describe existing or planned systems.

Mapping and modeling processes present miniature replicas of the activities of the wholes of systems by using such vehicles as flow charts. They also may involve qualitative classification and comparison.

Mapping and modeling apply to such systems as flows of information, paper work, word processing, materials, and production.

Operations research

Operations research applies to one-time decision-making situations. It involves a special set of quantitative tools for analysis and inference. Queuing models, Monte Carlo simulation, and Bayesian models are three examples of methods.

Because operations research relates to decisions from designs that researchers cannot replicate, many researchers do not include it as a full-fledged type of research. However, because of its importance to business research, it appears in this list.

Time series and indexes

The construction of index numbers and the analysis of time series involve techniques of quantitative description, estimation, and relationships. Therefore, the classification scheme could fit them into other categories. However, index numbers and time series form such an important category for business research that this list includes them as a distinct analytical type.

Types of indexes include price indexes, quantity indexes, value indexes, and special-purpose indexes. For good representation of data (description) and for good prediction (inference) researchers usually use weighted aggregative models such as the Laspeyres and Paasche methods.

Time-series analysis may spring from several models. One of the most accepted is the multiplicative model involving trend, cycle, seasonal, and irregular components. Trend and cycle represent long-term movements, and seasonal and irregular represent short-term movements.

The most-used cyclical model includes a peak (prosperity), a decline (recession), a trough (depression), and an incline (recovery).

Researchers may develop models for predicting trend and seasonal variations relatively easily. However, they have more difficulty predicting cycle. By definition, the irregular component is unpredictable.

Special Applications

Two types of special applications of research apply well to this review of research and business communication: (1) motivational research and (2) communication research.

Motivational research

Motivational research is a type of research dealing with human behavior. It has as its goal the determination of why people act as they do.

One concept underlies all motivational research. It is the understanding that people generally cannot or will not reveal directly what their motives are. Thus, motivational research depends upon indirect methods.

Clover and Balsley suggest that many conditions exist to cause difficulties for the motivational researcher. In paraphrased form, these are the conditions they list:

1. Usually, no one reason exists for an action; instead, several reasons explain it.
2. Consequently, when respondents are asked to give "main reasons," they are faced with a difficult task because they must decide which one of several reasons to give. Several of the reasons may be of almost equal importance. Hence, respondents may not be able to decide which is most important. Ranking them accurately may be practically impossible.
3. For some actions, people will have irrational or subconscious reasons that they do not recognize themselves.
4. Some respondents will not give the real reasons "because the reasons are not socially acceptable, intellectually flattering, or are considered to be of a confidential nature."[3]

Because of the indirectness required, then, motivational research uses some special techniques—particularly for the collecting stage.

One such technique includes the use of carefully developed open-end questions or situations. Such items bring the attention to a broad topic, but allow the respondent to answer freely in response to it.

For instance, the researcher may begin a story and have the respondent finish it. She may begin a series of sentences and have the respondent finish them. She may simply list words and have the respondent write or say the first thing that comes to mind. She may show pictures, ink blots, and abstract sketches and ask the respondent to react to them.

The depth interview is another process available to the motivational researcher. It involves probing questions posed orally. Chapter 15 includes additional information on the depth interview.

Good motivational research requires personnel with the arts, skills, and experience necessary to conduct it. They must be able to develop and transmit the messages and to interpret the responses received. Thus, the field of motivational research requires special education and training.

Even for the nonspecialist, though, some knowledge about motivational research and the depth interviewing involved can lead to a clearer understanding of

---

[3]Reprinted with permission from BUSINESS RESEARCH METHODS , Second Edition, by Vernon T. Clover and Howard L. Balsley (Grid, Inc., Columbus, Ohio, 1978), pp. 113–114.

the importance of the field. In addition, even a nonspecialist can learn to assign meanings to the results of such research conducted by others.

Communication research

Like motivational research, communication research involves the same basic kinds of collection and analysis used in general research. However, it also involves some special variations.

Communication researchers deal with written, oral, and nonverbal communication. They deal with organizations, individuals, and messages. They use the laboratory to structure and study microcosms of organizations. They also move into the field and observe actual organizations at work. They use surveys and first-hand observations. They describe, classify, estimate, compare, and search for relationships. They use the experimental design to test for cause and effect.

Researchers into communication study interpersonal, medio, person-to-group, and mass levels of activities. They analyze channels and map and model actual and proposed systems. They study internal communication as it flows upward, downward, laterally, and along the grapevine. They analyze the flow of communication to and from external bodies. They conduct research into communication methods, abilities, policies, philosophies, barriers, and needs.

The techniques of comparison research apply particularly well to a technique called content analysis. Through content analysis the researcher analyzes the contents of the messages themselves in order to make inferences. The inferences are about the people who created the messages, the circumstances that surround them, and the topics with which they deal. The inferences about the communicators relate to attitudes, values, beliefs, abilities, and predispositions.

Through content analysis, researchers can compare such things as the proportions of space devoted in a newspaper to various kinds of business news. They can test to determine whether a given kind of complaint occurs more frequently in one office than in another. They can test whether personnel involved in a directive appraisal interview report less satisfaction in the process than do personnel in a nondirective situation.

Communication researchers also concentrate upon the readability of messages. As described in Chapter 7, readability formulas exist for this kind of analysis.

TYPES OF BUSINESS REPORTS

Business reports are a logical extension of the research process. Consider them in two major categories—abbreviated reports and comprehensive reports.

Comprehensive reports cover most or all of the steps of the research process. Abbreviated reports cover only a few of the steps—very often presenting only a simple problem and the collected, organized information.

Abbreviated Reports

Abbreviated reports usually do not include extensive analysis, conclusions, and recommendations. They do not show extensive application of the scientific method or the related development of a complex problem statement, hypothesis(es), or methods for solution of the problem. In reality, abbreviated reports often represent simple expositions of information collected on rather routine bases. Abbreviated reports may be inherently or overtly persuasive.

Though any one abbreviated report rarely matches a single set of characteristics, some characteristics do tend to identify it. Generally, the abbreviated report:

1. Represents the most common type of report; is often routine in nature
2. Does not qualify for long retention within the files of the firm
3. Is short—usually numbering no more than ten pages
4. Takes the format of a memorandum, letter, or form (usually one to five pages in length) or manuscript (usually six to ten pages in length)
5. Deletes or abbreviates some of the developmental passages present in comprehensive reports; for example, does not include an abstract, includes a briefer introduction, includes more enumerated or listed items than the comprehensive report
6. Reflects sometimes an informal, sometimes a formal style
7. Includes the personal writing style
8. Does not necessarily adhere to a rigid developmental plan of organization, but customarily uses the basic deductive plan
9. Is informational, and either inherently or overtly persuasive
10. Is assigned by management

Several other names are given to the abbreviated report. They include such designations as short report, memorandum report, letter report, form report, informal report, informational report.

Content, however, rather than length or some other criterion, sets apart this type of report. Four broad types of abbreviated reports classified by the scope of the content are: (1) operations; (2) management; (3) employee relations; and (4) customer, stockholder, government, and public relations.

[To the student: Skip over the Figures that serve as examples when taking the following Timed Exercise. You can return to them later.]

Operations

Reports about operations form the most common of all business reports and abbreviated reports, in particular. Because they report on ongoing operations, such messages cover the range of all the activities of a firm.

Operational reports deal on a regular basis with all of the line functions of the organization—production, marketing, and finance. In addition, they deal just as regularly with the support and staff operations.

Operational reports generally flow upward or laterally through the organization. They provide a steady supply of information about the normal activities that make up the work of the people in the firm. Much of this information creates a short-term historical record from which management controls current activities and makes decisions about future actions of the organization.

Reports on operations sometimes take a predominantly qualitative (narrative) form. However, they often contain more quantitative than qualitative information.

Because of their routine nature, operational reports usually fall into the periodic category: hourly, daily, weekly, monthly, quarterly, or annually.

Because of the mechanistic, repetitive communication prescribed for them, operational reports often involve the completion of forms, rather than original writing. Thus, though the collection and posting of the data may take a great deal of time and expertise, the actual reporting does not require high-level composition arts and skills.

The characteristics of operational reports vary somewhat among production, marketing, finance, and support and staff operations.

Production Some operational reports include summaries of information about the production arm of the organization. Such reports are so common that employees often refer to them as production reports.

The primary information contained in production reports summarizes the outputs of the production process. The report describes the numbers of each type or line of product or service produced in a given period of time. It often includes production figures for different shifts, for different production lines, and for different plants.

In addition to featuring outputs, production reports also frequently include other information. Examples include information about volume and sources of incoming materials, waste, quality-control data, inventories of both raw materials and finished products, storage and transfer of products, and the equipment used in production.

Marketing Marketing operational reports cover the complete marketing cycle—the four P's of the "marketing mix": product, price, promotion, and placement. Thus, they convey information about storing, transporting, financing, taking risks, researching, standardizing and grading, buying, and selling. They convey such information at both the wholesale and retail levels and for both goods and services.

Operational marketing reports include such information as:

Inventories	Pricing
Shipments	Promotional strategies
Packaging	Advertising
Labeling	Sales
Warranties	Consumers
Shifts in product lines	Simple research findings

Figure 14–1 is an example of an operational marketing report. It shows the completion of a preprinted form.

Finance Operational reports flow freely from the financial sector of the organization. They usually take the form of financial statements from the accounting arm of the operation. Managers use them for describing and controlling the financial activities of the firm.

Financial data form such reports as balance sheets, income statements, internal audits, flow-of-funds summaries, market reports, receivables, and payables.

Accurately summarizing the different facets of finance and accounting in an acceptable manner calls for reporting skills that exceed those described in this book. However, the arts and skills presented here still apply to the qualitative messages associated with quantitative financial reports.

Support and staff operations Support and staff operations require as much report-

```
                                                              Form S-3
                                                              9/80

                    LITTLETOWN DEPARTMENT STORE

                       MONTHLY SALES SUMMARY
```

Date <u>April 4, 1981</u>   Department <u>Large Appliances (62L)</u>

Name <u>Deborah S. Washington</u>   Title <u>Department Manager</u>

Report is for the month of March, 1981

1. List the month's sales (net of sales tax) in each of your department's
   product areas.

PRODUCT AREA	SALES (NET OF TAX)
Washers	$ 6,298.37
Dryers	2,136.46
Refrigerators	3,998.19
Dishwashers	2,590.13
Trash Compacters	390.90
Stoves/Ovens	4,996.28
TOTAL	$20,410.33

2. List the month's returns (net of sales tax) in each of your department's
   product areas.

PRODUCT AREA	SALES (NET OF TAX)
Washers	$ 0.00
Dryers	199.50
Refrigerators	0.00
Dishwashers	248.90
Trash Compacters	0.00
Stoves/Ovens	910.30
TOTAL	$1,358.70

Figure 14–1 Completed form report for sales

ing as do the line operations just described. Support and staff operations include
those represented by the personnel, research, purchasing, legal, computer, and
word-processing departments.

Staff members of a *personnel department* routinely report summaries on such
topics as absences, vacations, leaves, applications, retirements, voluntary and invol-
untary terminations, appraisals, affirmative-action activities, and organization development programs. Such reports often take a quantitative form. However, they
also often take a qualitative or combined form.

Figure 14–2 includes a report related to a personnel activity. It takes the form of
a memorandum.

3. List the circumstances of each of the returns involving $75 or more.

   a. $199.50 Clean II Dryer—Purchasers did not like the noise that it made.

   b. $248.90 Sparkling I Dishwasher—Did not fit in purchaser's kitchen.

   c. $410.30 Microwave Deluxe III Oven—Did not work at all. Sent back to manufacturer.

   d. $500 Littletown Special Range-Oven—Color did not match the color of purchaser's other appliances.

4. List any sales problems that you believe should be brought to the attention of the store manager.

   a. Have not yet received twelve Clean III Dryers ordered on September 6, 1980. Three customers wanted Clean III Dryers in March if had in stock. Customers would not wait for shipment to come in.

   b. Still do not have replacements for two salespersons who left in February, 1981.

   c. Large Appliances is doing great otherwise.

Figure 14–1 (continued)

The operational reports from a *research department* usually involve the routine activities rather than any significant findings from the research itself. The significant research findings also go to management, but they fall into the realm of abbreviated management reports or, more commonly, assume the shape of comprehensive research reports.

Employees of a *purchasing department* summarize departmental activities through regular reports to management. The reports include such information as the dollar amounts of requests and purchases, the names of requestors and suppliers, and the status of requisitions and purchase orders at given points in time.

Staff members of a *legal department* prepare routine summaries of their activi-

TO: Jason Jones, Training Director
FROM: Susan Armor, Assistant Training Director
SUBJECT: Speaker for October 10 Writing Workshop Luncheon
DATE: September 6, 1980

As you asked, I talked to several business communication professors at Dane University, Alco State University, and Dane County Community College. Here's what I found:

1. Nora Cambert, Ph.D., of Dane University would be willing to speak to the writing workshop participants at the luncheon. She has spoken at a number of writing workshops and seminars. She is the author of the popular Writing Straight: A Handbook for the Business Writer, and she is both personable and bright. Dr. Cambert would charge $250 to speak at the luncheon, and she needs to know our plans by September 15. Her topic would be: "Writing's Not Difficult if You're Drunk." She stated that the speech would be both informative and humorous.

2. Leonard James, M.A., of Alco State University is free to speak at the luncheon. He has made speeches on two other occasions, and he wrote "Words That Please," an article published in Today's Business Writer magazine. Mr. James, who is rather shy, would charge nothing to speak at the luncheon. He needs to know our plans by September 25, and he does not know on what subject he would speak.

3. Gordon Smith, Ed.D., of Alco State University will be out of town the week of the luncheon.

4. Ann Lee, Ed.D., of Dane County Community College would be glad to speak at the luncheon. She has spoken to over thirty groups, and she is the author of numerous communication articles, including "Writing Wizardry in the Business Office" for the Journal of Technical Communication. Dr. Lee, who was both kind and lucid, would charge $100 to speak at the luncheon. October 1 is the last day that she can accept our offer to speak. "Walking through Writing" would be the title of her speech, and she said that it would be an educational speech.

Figure 14–2   Memorandum report in a personnel department

ties on a periodic basis. Like purchasing-department personnel, those in legal attempt to develop a picture showing the changes during a given period as well as the status of events at the time of the report.

Similarly, designated employees of a *computer center* routinely describe the inputs and outputs of their operations for a stated period of time. They also summarize the status of work still internal to the system.

Jason Jones   2   September 6, 1980

5. Morris Davis, Ed.D., of Dane County Community College
   would like to speak at the luncheon. He has spoken to a
   number of local civic and business organizations, and he is
   the author of two basic business communication textbooks.
   Dr. Davis was friendly and interesting. He would charge
   $100 to speak at the luncheon, and he must know our plans
   by September 28. He does not yet know on what subject he
   would speak, though he indicated that he tries to make his
   talks both entertaining and educational.

My impression is that Dr. Cambert would make the most
engaging speech. But her $250 fee would put something of a
strain on our budget. My second choice is Dr. Davis. His $100
fee would not empty our training bank.

Figure 14–2   (continued)

The *word processing department* develops reports about such topics as numbers of messages produced, usage of equipment, need for equipment, repairs on
equipment, productivity, and quality of operators.

(860 words)
(test on page 499)

OFFICE MACHINES UNLIMITED

1818 Indention Boulevard   777 777-7777
Premium, KA 77777

April 8, 198X

Ms. Laura Bethel, Supervisor
Word Processing Center
Acketew Arial Insurance Co.
Premium, KA 77777

Dear Ms. Bethel:

As you requested, I asked each of the 25 typists in the typing
pool these questions:

1. What features do you like about the Barrier III Typespeeder?

2. What features do you not like about the Barrier III
   Typespeeder?

3. If you had to choose between the Barrier III Typespeeder and
   the Fox-Malcolm Typefaster, which typewriter would you
   choose?

Each of the 25 typists responded to all three questions. Here are
the results of the survey by question number.

1. These are the features the typists liked about the Barrier III
   Typespeeder:

FEATURE	NUMBER WHO MENTIONED
Rarely breaks down	22
Corrects easily	20
Ribbons easy to change	18
Light enough to move easily	12
Extra keys easy to reach	3
Relatively quiet	1

Figure 14–3   Letter report on informal survey for a word processing department

Figure 14–3 illustrates a letter report about some equipment in the word processing department.

Management

Managers use all kinds of incoming reports—including operational reports and comprehensive reports—as important bases for fulfilling their functions. However, consider here two types of abbreviated reports to management that do not fit neatly into

Ms. Laura Bethel   2   April 8, 198X

2. These are the features the typists did not like about the Barrier III Typespeeder:

FEATURE	NUMBER WHO MENTIONED
Too noisy	16
Paper slips out of place	15
Breaks down too often	3
Correction tape sticks to paper	1

3. These are the typewriter choices that the typists made:

TYPEWRITER	NUMBER WHO CHOSE
Barrier III Typespeeder	19
Fox-Malcolm Typefaster	6

I hope that this information will be of some help. Let me know if you have any questions.

Sincerely,

Arnold Lopez

Arnold Lopez
Manager

jj

Figure 14-3   (continued)

any of the other named categories. The progress/completion report and the justification report both aid the manager in planning, organizing, activating, and controlling the activities of the organization.

Progress/completion   When managers approve proposals for long-term activities, they usually require regular interim reports of progress toward completion of the activities. They may also require routine reports upon completion—reports that come to them even before the final comprehensive reports of the findings from the activities.

Progress and completion reports often appear on preprinted forms. However, they may also take the channel of brief letters or memoranda.

In either format, make the language straightforward, concise, and complete. Tie the report to the budget and schedule of time and work presented in the original proposal. Explain any deviations from the projected plans. Include in the progress report a section that summarizes any significant deviation from the original proposal.

Justification   The report of justification includes a request for approval of such things as a special purchase, a program, a service, a sale, a bid, or a procedural plan. The abbreviated justification report parallels closely the comprehensive proposal (covered in a subsequent section). Both include persuasion inherent in the facts and logic of the presentation. The basic differences, then, lie in the extent or complexity of the object of the request and in the overt persuasion sometimes included in a justification report.

Suppose the object of the request is relatively simple; for example, the purchase or sale of a piece of equipment or a minor change in a production procedure. The resulting report likely would fall into the justification category. It would involve some treatment of a problem, including some analysis. However, it would not do so to the extent that a research proposal does. Instead, it would feature supporting information located through a fact-finding collecting process.

Because the justification report qualifies as an abbreviated proposal, the suggestions for writing it parallel the suggestions for the proposal. However, the abbreviated report may move more to the direct, informal, personal, and compact style of presentation.

Figure 14–4 contains an example of a justification report in the form of a memorandum.

Employee relations

A large number of abbreviated reports are generated by management with the intent of improving relations with employees. Moreover, such reports often provide avenues for employees to communicate with management for the same purposes.

Many reports from management travel through channels already discussed. Such channels include policy statements, newsletters, and news magazines. Still other such messages that may serve double duty include copies of financial statements, progress reports, and annual reports.

In addition, management often prepares special reports drawing from information supplied through routine channels. Their purpose is to engage the support of employees for the activities of the firm.

Write reports for improving employee relations in language appropriate to the typical employee. Use positive devices to portray the organization in a good, but truthful light. Call attention to the benefits of being an employee. Spotlight the contributions of the organization to the community. Feature the role of the employee in creating a successful organization. Solicit active feedback from the employees. Respect the feedback by acknowledging it and acting upon it when possible.

Customer, stockholder, government, and public relations

Many abbreviated reports travel to external entities and serve different purposes, depending upon the nature of the intended receiver.

TO: Warren Fein, Manager, Systems Management Office

FROM: Allison Wakefield, Manager, Program Management
             Department

SUBJECT: Crowding Problem in Program Management
             Department

DATE: August 15, 1981

Problem

  As you know, the Program Management Department has
grown from ten analysts in August, 1979, to thirty analysts in
August, 1981. Last year, each of the ten analysts had a private
office. Now each analyst must share her or his office with two
other analysts, and three analysts are even forced to share their
desks.

  The offices are extremely crowded, deafeningly noisy, and
swelteringly hot. Of the twenty analysts with whom I spoke
about this situation, eighteen stated that they would consider
looking for other jobs if the crowding problem is not solved
before the end of this calendar year.

Alternative Solutions

  Three solutions seem practicable by December 31, 1981:

  1. If all of the walls were removed in the Program
Management Department, the 2,200 square feet of open floor
could accommodate thirty analysts' desks and ten secretaries'
desks in a sort of "bullpen" setting. The noise level would not
be reduced, but the crowding and heat problems would be
ameliorated. Though the analysts feel that this is the least
appealing solution, they do label it a giant step in the right
direction.

Figure 14–4   Memorandum report involving a persuasive justification

  For example, a company may prepare a *prospectus* for distribution to potential
purchasers of stocks. The prospectus summarizes the firm's statement of registration,
including information on the financial condition, earnings, lines of products, and the
qualifications and salaries of the officers of the firm. The purpose of the report is, of
course, to lead people to buy the stock.

  Each year many firms distribute *annual reports* of activities to stockholders,
employees, government officials, and even the general public. The writers empha-

Warren Fein   2   August 15, 1981

    2. If the neighboring Engineering Department were moved to another location, its ten offices could be used by the Program Management Department. This alternative would allow ten analysts to have private offices. The remaining ten offices would become two-person offices. The noise level would be reduced significantly, and the crowding and heat problems would be much improved. The analysts consider this a better solution than the "bullpen" alternative.

    3. By far the best alternative is to move the Program Mangement Department to the soon-to-be-completed suite of offices on the sixth floor. The Program Management Department could take over the twenty-eight offices in the west wing. Every analyst would have a private office, and the department could provide offices for up to seven new analysts. The analysts believe that this is the best solution.

Conclusion

    Of course the third solution would provide the greatest relief to the Program Management Department, but both the first and second solutions would yield some necessary comforts. Regardless of which alternative is chosen, time is of the essence. The help must come quickly so that the analysts in the Program Management Department do not become even more discouraged with the noise, the heat, and the crowding.

Figure 14–4 (continued)

size the financial aspects of the operation by including accounting reports such as balance sheets, income statements, and auditor's statements. Pictures, charts, color, and information about new products, wages, benefits, research, and other activities also engage the reader's attention.

Because the audience for the annual report is so diverse, select the readability level carefully. Write concisely, brightly, and engagingly. However, avoid converting the annual report from an honest portrayal into a persuasive, promotional piece.

Figure 14–5 shows sample pages from an annual report.

An *audit report* may go to external entities separate from an annual report. It often is a brief, simple, standardized statement that reports that an audit has been made of the financial records of the firm. However, the audit report may also occupy several pages and include some complex information unique to the situation.

Another type of abbreviated report that moves outside the firm is the *credit report*. The response to a letter requesting information about the credit record of someone often uses a preprinted form upon which the writer records the requested information. Accuracy and completeness, of course, form the major criteria for the good credit report.

Firms prepare many abbreviated *government reports*. Such reports often go to government agencies as completed forms. When the government requires information, it expects the requirement to be met in timely and correct fashion.

Comprehensive Reports

Though the words "comprehensive reports" do not describe the content, they do form a convenient label for certain reports. These are the kinds of reports that result from activities involving all or most of the steps of the research method.

Other names given to this type of report include long report, analytical report, formal report, research report, full report, and complete report.

In addition to including coverage of an activity that encompasses the important stages of the research method, the typical comprehensive report also possesses some other generally accepted characteristics. The comprehensive report:

1. Is not as common as the abbreviated report; is nonroutine in nature
2. Qualifies for long retention within the files of the firm
3. Is medium (six through ten pages) to long in length (more than ten pages)
4. Takes the format of a manuscript
5. Includes sections for each of the included research steps
6. Reflects a formal writing style
7. Includes the impersonal writing style
8. Uses relatively fixed inductive, analytical, or comparative developmental plan
9. Is informational and/or inherently persuasive (with overt persuasion carried by accompanying letter or memorandum of transmittal)
10. Is assigned by management or occasionally volunteered

The topic of a comprehensive report may relate to any problem in any facet of business.

Review two major types of comprehensive reports—the proposal for research and the final report of a comprehensive project.

Proposal for research

Through a proposal (prospectus), the researcher identifies a problem and describes the methods for attempting to solve it.

To make all the decisions reported in a proposal is to take the largest step

Patricia McCaskey and Edward Taylor, both of Tulsa, are two of the more than 2,300 employees who strive to provide customers with the most economical gas service possible.

EXPLORATION

ONG Exploration, Inc., participated in the drilling of 61 wells during the 1979 fiscal year, compared with 55 wells the year before. The success record in 1979 was 79 percent.

The Company farmed out or contributed acreage in support of an additional 62 wells drilled by other companies. This support gave ONG a "call" (first purchase rights) on a substantial part of the gas that is produced from these wells.

Drilling efforts were concentrated primarily in the western Oklahoma portion of the Anadarko Basin. Leaseholdings amounted to 126,763 acres of undeveloped leases and 80,536 acres of developed producing leases located primarily in Oklahoma.

OPERATING REVENUES

Consolidated operating revenues set a record again in the 1979 fiscal year and totaled $675,861,000, an increase of $42,045,000 over the previous year. Gas utility revenues in 1979 were $631,417,000, or 93 percent of operating revenues.

Revenues from utility gas sales to residential customers were $133,763,000,

or 22 percent of all utility gas sales; commercial sales, $71,411,000, or 11 percent; industrial sales, $317,082,000, or 51 percent; and wholesale sales, $100,459,000, or 16 percent. Operating revenues from gas sales increased because of the inclusion of substantially higher costs for gas in the field and a general rate increase effective January 27, 1978. Accounting for an increase in gas deliveries to residential customers was a heating season that was the third coldest in ONG's history — 2 percent colder than 1978 and 18 percent colder than normal. Deliveries to commercial customers were essentially the same as in 1978. Industrial gas sales increased due to greater deliveries to large-volume fertilizer plant customers.

The increases in revenues from gas sales to Oklahoma utility customers were partially offset by a decline of $34,188,000 in revenues from out-of-state sales. However, these sales, which supplemented ONG utility income for several years, were less important to overall profits due to the Oklahoma Corporation Commission decision in January, 1978, requiring the Company to give 90 percent of the gross profit from the sales to Oklahoma utility customers as credits on their gas bills.

Customers at fiscal year-end totaled 567,146, an increase of 14,883 over the previous year. The Company served 578,051 customers on February 28, 1979, an all-time record. Temporary summer disconnects reduced that figure to the year-end total.

Operating revenues from gas processing plant sales decreased essentially as the result of a decline in the volume of the products produced.

OPERATING EXPENSES

Operating expenses for the 1979 fiscal year totaled $626,223,000, or $48,042,000 more than in fiscal 1978. Gas purchase expense was $500,316,000, or $40,673,000 more than a year earlier primarily because of higher prices paid in the field. Operating expenses increased due to continuing inflationary increases resulting in higher costs of materials and supplies, payroll, and employee benefits. Payroll and employee benefits costs totaled $51,750,000 for the year, an increase of $7,209,000 over 1978.

Taxes totaled $36,991,000 for the year, a decrease of $4,388,000 compared with the previous year. Taxes on income decreased $10,452,000, due to decreased taxable net income, partially offset by decreased investment tax credit.

Other taxes, including ad valorem, gross production, and franchise taxes, increased during the year.

FINANCING

During the 1979 fiscal year the Company completed the sale of $35,000,000 in long-term notes.

The Company sold $20,000,000 of 20-year, 9¼ percent notes to eight insurance companies, receiving $10,000,000 in November, 1978, and $10,000,000 in February, 1979. Additionally, the Company placed $15,000,000 of 20-year, 9½ percent notes with five institutional investors and also received those funds in February, 1979.

The Company has guaranteed two bank loans made to Smart Drilling Company, a wholly owned subsidiary. The funds from a 7-year note for $3,200,000 at 9.95 percent were received in February, 1979, and funds from a 7-year note

Figure 14–5   Pages from an annual report

SOURCE: *Oklahoma Natural Gas Company 1979 Annual Report*, p. 17.

SEGMENT INFORMATION

(I) The following sets forth information for the years ended August 31, 1979 and 1978, relative to the Companies' operations in different industries (stated in thousands of dollars):

	Gas Utility		Oil and Gas Production and Processing		General Corporate and Other		Adjustments and Eliminations		Consolidated	
	1979	1978	1979	1978	1979	1978	1979	1978	1979	1978
Sales to unaffiliated customers	$631,417	$591,283	$33,453	$31,412	$10,991	$11,121	$ —	$ —	$675,861	$633,816
Intersegment sales	3,140	2,598	6,069	6,339	95	89	9,304	9,026	—	—
Total revenues	$634,557	$593,881	$39,522	$37,751	$11,086	$11,210	$9,304	$9,026	$675,861	$633,816
Operating profit	$ 53,300	$ 61,252	$14,018	$14,051	$ 1,946	$ 5,730	$ —	$ —	$ 69,264	$ 81,033
Income tax expense									19,626	25,398
Interest charges									17,135	14,519
Net income									$ 32,503	$ 41,116
Identifiable assets at end of year:										
Property, plant, and equipment (net)	$356,051	$330,449	$39,319	$33,741	$31,365	$24,498	$ —	$ —	$426,735	$388,688
Other	119,497	101,777	10,536	9,024	9,435	6,735	—	—	139,468	117,536
Total	$475,548	$432,226	$49,855	$42,765	$40,800	$31,233	$ —	$ —	$566,203	$506,224
Capital expenditures	$ 37,740	$ 34,690	$ 9,741	$ 6,063	$ 5,089	$ 670	$ —	$ —	$ 52,570	$ 41,423
Depreciation and depletion expense	$ 12,760	$ 11,187	$ 4,025	$ 4,699	$ 1,180	$ 759	$ —	$ —	$ 17,965	$ 16,645

The Company's business activities principally consist of two business segments: (1) Gas Utility and (2) Oil and Gas Production and Processing. Gas Utility includes operations related to the gathering, transmission, storage, and distribution of natural gas to wholesale and retail customers. These activities are subject to regulation by the Oklahoma Corporation Commission and the FERC. Oil and Gas Production and Processing includes oil and gas exploration, development and production activities, and gas processing plant operations.

Intersegment sales are accounted for on the same basis as sales to unaffiliated customers.

REPLACEMENT COST DATA — (UNAUDITED)

(J) The Securities and Exchange Commission requires major corporations to disclose selected replacement cost information concerning productive capacity and inventories together with related effects on depreciation and operating expenses. The accompanying consolidated financial statements reflect historical costs in accordance with generally accepted accounting principles and in accordance with requirements imposed by regulatory authorities. Because of the impact of inflation, the cost of replacing the productive capacity of the Companies would exceed the historical costs of such assets reported in the financial statements. Specific data regarding the required replacement cost estimates, basis of determination, and management's views concerning the data are contained in the Company's annual report to the Securities and Exchange Commission on Form 10-K.

ACQUISITION OF SUBSIDIARY

(K) Effective January 31, 1979, the Company exchanged 45,866 shares of its Common Stock for all of the outstanding capital stock of Smart Drilling Company (Smart). The Company's stock had a market value of $1,000,000, which exceeded the value of the underlying net assets of Smart by approximately $492,000. The excess of the purchase price over the acquired net assets was assigned to property and equipment and to intangible assets. This excess is being amortized over the lives of the assigned assets, such lives ranging from five to seven years. The acquisition was accounted for by the purchase method. If Smart had been acquired as of the beginning of the fiscal year, the resulting effect on the Company's operating revenues, net income, or earnings per share would not have been material.

Accountants' Report

The Board of Directors and Stockholders
Oklahoma Natural Gas Company:

We have examined the consolidated balance sheets of Oklahoma Natural Gas Company and subsidiaries as of August 31, 1979 and 1978 and the related consolidated statements of income, retained earnings and changes in financial position for the years then ended. Our examinations were made in accordance with generally accepted auditing standards, and accordingly included such tests of the accounting records and such other auditing procedures as we considered necessary in the circumstances.

In our opinion, the aforementioned consolidated financial statements present fairly the financial position of Oklahoma Natural Gas Company and subsidiaries at August 31, 1979 and 1978 and the results of their operations and the changes in their financial position for the years then ended, in conformity with generally accepted accounting principles applied on a consistent basis.

Peat, Marwick, Mitchell & Co.

Tulsa, Oklahoma
October 15, 1979

Figure 14–5   (continued)

toward accomplishing the research proposed within it. Therefore, whether required by management or not, always write a proposal.

Even if left in draft form, the proposal forces the codification of thinking. The process of committing thoughts to paper aids in the location of flaws and thus can lead to an improved research design. Try to make the proposal so clear and complete that another person could complete the proposed research.

Researchers sometimes develop and write proposals at the behest of others—even based upon problems, factors, and hypothesis(es) suggested or dictated by others. At other times they voluntarily create proposals to solve problems which they themselves identify.

Writers submit proposals to specified authoritative receivers. The objective is to have them activate the research proposed in them.

Receivers may be superiors within the firm, customers, a research foundation, or a government funding agency.

Researchers may seek outright grants of money from a foundation or government agency. However, whether seeking such grants, charging a fee to a customer, or committing a firm's internal resources to the research, the sponsor commits resources—resources for which the researcher is accountable.

Some external research agencies prescribe an outline, issue voluminous guidelines, or supply a form for completion of a proposal. However, occasionally, they may accept a simple proposal in abbreviated-report format, even as a letter or a memorandum.

A proposal may cite the need for activities other than research. It may propose a conference or a seminar. It may offer a bid for a contract. It may simply offer to do some work.

Written proposals for activities other than research often take on the trappings of communication instruments already covered. Examples include inquiries, requests, and persuasive messages in the forms of letters and memoranda. However, to the extent that the messages explaining proposed activities do not fit perfectly into such channels, they belong in the realm of the proposal.

Because the proposal is a clearly stated plan of action for solving some problem, its closest literary kinship remains with a proposed research project. Therefore, the illustrations here relate to research proposals. The illustrations, however, adapt to nonresearch proposals easily.

In addition to the components of the body, the proposal may include some of the front matter and back matter described in Chapter 13. A letter or memorandum of transmittal almost always accompanies it.

An outline of the components of the body of a proposal includes:

1. Title
2. Introduction/History/Background of the General Problem
3. Introduction/History/Background of the Specific Problem
4. Need/Contributions/Benefits/Significance
5. Statement of Specific Problem
6. Purposes/Objectives
7. Scope/Delimitation
8. Limitations
9. Assumptions
10. Hypothesis(es)

11. Related Literature/Related Research/Related Studies/Past Research
12. Definition of Terms
13. Design/Procedure(s)/Method(s)/Methodology
14. Plans for Reporting/Proposed Organization of the Final Report of the Research
15. Schedule of Time and Work
16. Budget/Estimated Cost
17. Facilities, Equipment, and Materials
18. Personnel and Training
19. Qualifications of Principal Investigator(s)

The outline includes a nearly exhaustive list of the various names and components that appear in the bodies of research proposals. Thus, while most proposals must contain certain of the key elements, rarely does a single proposal contain all of the components shown in the outline. Appendix F is an example of a research proposal illustrating many of the parts.

Title   Though the title appears as part of the front matter, it is also an integral part of the body. Because of the implicit persuasion bound up in a proposal, a complete, attention-getting, descriptive title is mandatory. It should include the who, what, when, and where, and often the how and why.

Introduction/history/background of the general problem   Begin the body of a proposal with a few sentences or paragraphs of introduction. The introduction should lead the reader to a section titled something like "History," "Background of the Problem," or "General Problem." Avoid using the title "Introduction" either prior to or following the initial paragraphs.

In the opening section, trace the development of the broad problem by using any of the logical development plans. The inductive, chronological, and ranked plans work particularly well.

The opening section may include some citations from reports on related research. It may include some tables and figures illustrating the nature of the problem. (Chapter 16 covers tabular and graphic construction.)

Depending upon the importance of the work and the length of the proposal, the general-problem background may occupy no more than a few paragraphs.

Introduction/history/background of the specific problem   Continue the introductory section by moving naturally from the background and description of the general problem into the background and description of the specific problem. Just continue the logic of the selected developmental plan and bring the spotlight to the specific parts extracted from the general whole.

Suppose that a general problem involves a steady decline in a firm's sales over the past five years.

The general introduction would trace that decline, probably using narrative, tables, and charts to do so. The next few paragraphs would identify the major factors that might be associated with that decline. Such factors might include advertising expenditures, number of salespersons, and the Gross National Product for the same five years.

A few sentences would then reject the factors that do not seem to correlate with the downward trend in sales and retain those that do. In this example, assume that the trend line for advertising expenditures fairly closely parallels the sagging sales trend line. Both decline, but with sales lagging about one quarter behind reduced advertising.

This developmental process moves from the general problem (the sales decline) through the background of the specific problem—the isolation of advertising as the immediate research factor.

Need/contributions/benefits/significance   Establish the need for the research. Show how attacking the specific problem may help solve the general problem. Cite the benefits that a solution will bring.

Place the description of the significance in the background section or in the section on the statement of the problem, or in a specially designated section.

Statement of specific problem   Precisely state the specific, immediate problem to be attacked by the proposed research. It becomes *the* research problem.

State the research problem in declarative, interrogative, or even fragmentary form. For instance, the statement of the problem for the example about advertising expenditures and sales could take any of these forms:

- The problem is to determine whether a significant degree of correlation exists between quarterly sales and quarterly advertising expenditures of the previous quarter.
- The problem is: Does a significant degree of correlation exist between quarterly sales and quarterly advertising expenditures of the previous quarter?
- Statement of the problem: To determine whether a significant degree of correlation exists between quarterly sales and quarterly advertising expenditures of the previous quarter.

The statement of the problem may include more information—the kind of information that answers all of the "W" questions. Alternately, such information may appear in a separate section on the scope or delimitation of the problem.

Some researchers use the word "purpose" as the equivalent of the words "specific problem" or "research problem" as used here. They would define *the* problem as declining sales—an obstacle in the path toward profitability. They would then report that "The purpose of the research is to determine whether a significant degree of correlation exists . . . ."

Purposes/objectives   Basically, the words "purposes" and "objectives" should relate to the why of the research. When a statement of purpose takes one direction in dealing with the reasons for the research, it belongs (and often appears) in the section on needs, contributions, benefits, or significance. The words in this approach become something like these: "The purpose of this research is to reverse the decline in sales so that profits will increase."

Still taking the tack of purposes as goals or objectives, this sentence makes the objective somewhat more immediate: "The purpose of the research is to determine whether a decline in advertising expenditures may lead to a decline in sales. If it does, then an increase in advertising expenditures may lead to an increase in sales, thus increasing profits."

As discussed in the preceding section, however, some researchers use the word "purpose" to refer to the specific or research problem. For these researchers, the problem is the obstacle, and the purpose is to reach some decisions in order to surmount that obstacle.

The very nature of semantics renders moot the issue over whether "problem" or "purpose" is "right."

Scope/delimitation Specify the boundaries or parameters of the investigation in time and space. Together, the statement of the problem and the statement of the scope or delimitation covers the who, what, when, and where. Narrow (delimit) the scope of the problem to identify any people who are involved (the who), the factors to be observed and analyzed (the what), the location of the people and/or factors (the where), and the time period involved (the when).

These descriptions show the scope or delimitation of the sales/advertising case:

The research will be limited to:

1. Zellink Corporation, 19 Cartridge Road, Pointblank, Texas 77364
2. Sales figures for the 20 quarters beginning with the first quarter of 1976 and ending with the fourth quarter of 1980
3. Advertising-expenditure figures for the 20 quarters beginning with the fourth quarter of 1975 and ending with the third quarter of 1980

The delimiting statements may follow the original statement of the problem, or they may be part of the statement itself. However, notice how long and cumbersome a single sentence can be:

The problem is to determine for Zellink Corporation, 19 Cartridge Road, Pointblank, Texas 77364, whether a significant degree of correlation exists between quarterly sales for the period 1976 through 1980 and quarterly advertising expenditures for the previous quarter (beginning with the fourth quarter of 1975 and ending with the third quarter of 1980).

Limitations Many researchers use the word "limitations" to mean the same thing as "scope" or "delimitation." However, others use the term to identify the factors that may restrict the research. Such factors include time, money, research assistance, available data, and difficulties in establishing representative samples.

To identify the potential limitations in the latter sense, first establish the perfect design for carrying out the research. Next, establish the practical design. Next, list everything omitted from the perfect plan in order to make it practical. That "gap" between the perfect and practical designs represents the limitations of the research.

For the illustration, then, some of the limitations to the research could be:

• Five years is a short period of time upon which to base the analysis.
• The five years do not represent a random sample.
• Most relationships cannot be limited to one independent variable. Variables in addition to advertising expenditures likely have an impact upon sales.
• Without random selection or validation that the data are the equivalent of a randomly selected sample, the design does not control the possible extraneous factors such as state of the economy and number of salespersons.
• Without establishing the randomness or validation, even a high degree of correlation cannot establish a cause-and-effect relationship between the variables.

Do not overemphasize the limitations. However, ethics require acknowledgment of their existence. In addition, listing them demonstrates an ability to recognize the possible shortcomings of a design.

Assumptions   Summarize as an assumption any underlying condition necessary to the research that is accepted as true without proof that it is true. For example, without a probability sample or prescribed techniques for establishing validity, the researcher may only assume that a sample represents a universe.

The assumptions parallel the limitations closely. For example, observe how to convert two of the statements of limitations in the preceding section into statements of assumptions:

Assumptions:
* Five years is a sufficiently long period of time upon which to base the analysis.
* The nonrandomly selected five-year period is the equivalent of a random sample

Because assumptions and limitations cover the same facets of the research, only from slightly different angles, both sections rarely appear in the same proposal.

Hypothesis(es)   State in declarative form the statements to be tested. For a well-defined specific problem, the hypothesis becomes a virtual repetition of the purpose in a slightly different form.

The research hypothesis for the continuing example would be:

A significant degree of correlation exists between quarterly sales and quarterly advertising expenditures for the previous quarter.

This hypothesis is written in the positive form. However, at the stage of the actual test, a quantitative hypothesis must be cast into the null form. For the example, the null form becomes:

No significant degree of correlation exists between quarterly sales and quarterly advertising expenditures for the previous quarter.

Though the research hypothesis may take either the positive or null form, the null form saves some confusion when the analysis involves a test of significance.

A hypothesis may repeat the delimiting information. For the example, then, the name of the company and the dates could appear in the hypothesis.

Avoid the concept of "proving" or "disproving" a hypothesis. The terms indicate too much finality. No research can prove or disprove a hypothesis once and for all.

Many pieces of research involve several hypotheses—one for each major set of factors being tested.

Though the scientific method prescribes otherwise, not all research deals with hypotheses. Qualitative and quantitative description do not. However, qualitative inference often does, and quantitative inference usually does.

Related literature/related research/related studies/past research   The thorough researcher reviews all available sources, first to determine whether others have conducted research that is like that proposed. Such a search of the literature sometimes removes the necessity for primary research entirely. It provides the desired information without the expenditures of time and money necessary to collect it.

Even more often the search into related studies saves steps in the research, or even changes the design of it. It may revise the choice of factors or unearth recommendations for improving the research. It certainly expands the base of knowledge about the subject.

Summarize some key pieces of related literature in a proposal. However, do not try to exhaust such reporting at that point. Simply indicate that the final report of the project will include a complete review.

Give full credit to sources of secondary information. When citing the material, use a clear lead so that the reader knows exactly where it begins. Examples include:

- According to Jones, ''. . . .''
- In contrast, Jones reports that . . . .
- The book *Just-Write Tactics* features a list of . . . .
- Included in the article ''Communications,'' the suggestion is that . . . .''
- Jones suggests:

_____

_____

_____

_____

Follow the lead with the excerpt. Excerpts take three forms—the direct quotation, the paraphrase, and the summary. The direct quotation includes the actual words of the writer. The paraphrase is a restatement of the words of another—with the substance intact. A summary is a statement that reduces material into a brief extraction of key points. Again, use a lead that gives credit to the source.

At the end of an excerpt place some sort of reference to a complete citation of the source. A common form of reference is the superior number in reference to a footnote or endnote. However, other systems exist.

Footnotes and endnotes follow prescribed formats. Style manuals describe them. Basically, a footnote contains the author's name in natural order; the name of the article or book; the name of the magazine or journal if an article; the city, publisher's name, and date; and the page numbers. Appendix C includes additional information and illustrations.

When a message contains excerpts and footnotes/endnotes, it also should include a bibliography. As described in Chapter 13, the bibliography is a collection of all of the cited sources in addition to others consulted but not cited. Appendices C and G include examples of bibliographic entries.

Avoid any tendency toward plagiarism in the use of the material of others. Even when you have summarized material in a distinctly different form, your citation should identify the author as the creator of the ideas.

Definition of terms   If any term has several possible interpretations, define it. Definitions sometimes appear in a rather lengthy alphabetized list. The list may form a section within the body of the proposal or in an appendix or glossary at the end of it. The list may include symbols and acronyms in addition to words.

Here are some examples of definitions. Some of them refer to the continuing illustration:

Dependent variable (Y): Quarterly sales
Group A: The control group; the employees taught in the traditional fashion
Group B: The treatment group; the employees taught by the new methods
Independent variable (Y): Quarterly advertising expenditures
Inner-city businesses: Those businesses with two or more full-time employees that are located within the area bounded by North 12th Street, South 14th Street, Ellis Avenue on the east, and Court Boulevard on the west

Definitions of only a few expressions may become part of the narrative or footnotes when first introduced.

To introduce acronyms for long, cumbersome, well-known, or oft-repeated names, first write the full term. Then follow it immediately with the acronym placed within parentheses. For example, to refer to the Government Accounting Office repeatedly within a report, simply introduce the acronym the first time the reference appears: ". . . Government Accounting Office (GAO) . . . ." Thereafter, simply use "GAO."

Avoid overusing acronyms, however. Writing sprinkled with them takes on a sloppy, cryptic appearance bothersome to many readers.

Design/procedure(s)/method(s)/methodology   To establish the design, report how to collect the information, how to organize it, and how to analyze it. Even look ahead to the interpretation, the conclusions, and perhaps the recommendations.

Report the size of any required samples. Report how to select the items in the sample. Report the details for making the observations. Design and report any forms (observationnaire, questionnaire, etc.) necessary for the observation.

Describe in detail the actual steps of the analysis. If the analysis is quantitative, name the exact models or tests to be used. Name the level of significance, the level of confidence, or any other such predetermined values necessary to the analysis.

The sales/advertising situation provides an example. Through the words "significant correlation," the problem itself indicates that the analytical tools fall in the realm of testing for relationships. However, the design stage includes a completion of the details:

The analytical tools are the coefficients of correlation, determination, and nondetermination and a test of significance of the coefficient of correlation at the .05 level of risk. In addition, the least-squares regression equation will be calculated, and selected confidence-interval estimates of sales will be established. The intervals will reflect a 95 percent level of confidence.

Cast the description of the proposed analysis in words understandable to the receiver. Elaborate upon the meanings of some of the terms for a reader unfamiliar with them. However, most people with the power to accept or reject a proposal usually understand basic statistical techniques and terminology.

End the section on procedures by stating that the interpretation and conclusion (results, findings, discussion) will follow the analysis. Many times the analysis, interpretation, conclusions, and recommendations blend into one common whole.

Plans for reporting/proposed organization of the final report of the research   The proposal often contains a section on plans for reporting the results of the research. The section usually includes the names of those to whom the report will go.

If someone has assigned the proposal, the final report will go to at least that person and perhaps to some others named by that person. Even for a volunteered proposal to someone internal or external to the firm, the names are known.

For a report of a research project submitted for publication, name the publication(s). Because the proposal (rewritten in the past tense) becomes an important part of the final report, adopt the publisher's format and style even for the proposal.

Sometimes the plans-for-reporting section contains a complete outline of the proposed final report. Such an outline not only helps the reader understand the proposal, but it leads her or him to have a high opinion of your ability. In addition, preparing the outline at this point reinforces thorough thinking about the entirety of the research.

Schedule of time and work   Time always is an important consideration for the business researcher. Losing time costs the firm or agency money from the standpoint of the investment in such support systems as personnel and facilities. In addition, it costs money from the standpoint of the losses associated with an unsolved problem. The timing of a research project also is important in terms of the concept of "moving pictures" versus "snapshots." For these reasons, then, the proposal often includes a schedule and the amount of work to be accomplished by each date.

Government agencies and research foundations often require schedules of time and work. They need to have proof of a carefully planned program of work.

Budget/estimated cost   Another important component of many proposals is the section describing the estimated expenses associated with the proposed project. Include the cost of salaries, services, supplies, materials, equipment, overhead, office space, laboratory space, fees, travel, personnel, training, and any other costs associated with the research. Itemize the requested funds in good budgetary form with as much detail as is appropriate to the project.

Funding agencies usually require the budgetary section.

Facilities, equipment, and materials   Not only does a proposal include the costs of special facilities, equipment, and material, but it often includes a description of the items themselves. For example, if the research requires a special wind tunnel, include the plans for building one, or a description of where to acquire one.

Personnel and training   The research often requires special personnel. The proposal includes a description of them—and of any training necessary to prepare them.

Qualifications of principal investigator(s)   Proposals often include summaries of the qualifications of the principal investigators. The summary may be a part of the front or back matter or may be included within the body.

Summarize the qualifications in the form of a traditional résumé (Chapter 17). However, stress the experiences relevant to the research rather than just the customary information. As an alternative, a specially designed abbreviated form may feature the relevant information.

Final report of research

The final report of a research project includes everything that a proposal does. In addition, and more important, it includes the results or findings from the research process originally defined in the proposal.

Basically, then, each of the elements included in the section on procedures in the proposal becomes a featured component of the final report. Use narrative, tabular, and charting methods to present the collected data and the analysis.

For the sales/advertising example used in the section on the proposal, a table and a scatter diagram would portray the advertising expenditures and sales figures, and words would describe the data in them.

For the analytical section, words and/or tables and charts would report the regression equation, the values of the coefficients of correlation, determination, and nondetermination, and the value of t for the test of significance of the coefficient of correlation.

The result of the analysis would be to accept or reject the null hypothesis. Because of the simplicity of this case, the acceptance or rejection would blend directly into the interpretation, conclusions, and recommendations. Assume that the research yielded the kind of data that led to these paragraphs listed under a heading like "Results":

> Compared to a tabular value of 2.101 for 18 degrees of freedom at the .05 level of risk, the calculated t value of 6.078 leads to a rejection of the null hypothesis. Therefore, quarterly sales and advertising expenditures one quarter earlier are significantly related.
>
> With a coefficient of correlation of .82 and a coefficient of determination of .67, 67 percent of the variability in sales is explained by variability in advertising expenditures. The coefficient of nondetermination of .33 shows that 33 percent of the variability in sales is unexplained by advertising expenditures.
>
> The conclusion is, then, that quarterly sales are significantly correlated with advertising expenditures for the preceding quarter.
>
> The recommendation for action is an immediate increase in advertising expenditures. However, the sample of quarters was not drawn on a probability basis and represents only a basically declining series. Thus, the design did not necessarily contain controls for extraneous effects and cannot be assumed to establish cause and effect between the variables. Therefore, an additional recommendation is that the data be analyzed at the end of each future quarter to determine whether the relationship remains significant through a period of increasing advertising expenditures.

Observe that the excerpt from the final report reflects the impersonal writing style.

Of all of the business messages, the research report is most likely to include all of the front matter, back matter, and body parts listed in Chapter 13 (page 428). A research report may be so extensive that it even includes chapters instead of sections with the customary headings.

An example of a final research report appears as Appendix G. It contains many of the components suggested for the most complete of the comprehensive reports. Observe how the research report simply expands the proposal into a report after the fact of the research.

SUMMARY

Chapter 14 completes the discussion of report writing by covering the research process and two major types of report.

Research is the search for solutions to problems. It involves science, art, technique, and decision-making applied to these basic steps: (1) recognize and define the problem and the purpose of the research, (2) review the literature, (3) state the hypothesis(es), (4) design the investigation, (5) write the proposal, (6) collect the data, (7) organize the data, (8) analyze the data, (9) interpret the results of the analysis, (10) draw conclusions, (11) develop recommendations, (12) write and disseminate the final report, and (13) conduct a follow-up.

Science involves objectivity, art involves creativity, technique involves applied skills, and decision-making involves making choices in the other three realms.

Define the general problem—the broad obstacle in the path toward the goals. Define the delimited specific problem to be attacked by the research. Establish the who, what, when, and where.

Review the literature to find equivalent or similar research, additional factors, and recommendations.

State the hypothesis(es) in positive or null form. A hypothesis is a declarative statement to be accepted or rejected as a result of the analysis.

The design of the investigation includes all of the procedures associated with collecting, organizing, and analyzing the data.

A proposal (prospectus) proposes the research. It includes the statement of the problem, a brief review of the literature, and the design of the investigation.

Collection, organization, and analysis proceed according to the design, with adjustment as needed.

Interpretation assigns meaning to the analysis. Conclusions (results, findings, discussion) summarize the analysis and interpretation and state whether the hypothesis is accepted or rejected.

Recommendations may follow conclusions. They may relate to future research or to actions to result from the completed research.

The final report summarizes the entire research process.

When the final report goes to an authorizer, the researcher may conduct a follow-up to offer additional information or to learn of the use of the research results.

Empirical research may be divided into ten types: (1) qualitative description, (2) quantitative description, (3) classification, (4) estimation, (5) comparison, (6) relationship, (7) cause-and-effect relationship, (8) mapping and modeling, (9) operations research, and (10) times series and indexes.

Qualitative description involves description with words. Quantitative description describes with numbers. Classification research divides qualitative universes into collectively exhaustive and mutually exclusive classes. Basically, estimation is a quantitative technique involving the creation of a *confidence-interval estimate* of a universe characteristic. *Quantitative comparison* involves tests of *significance*. The analysis of quantitative relationships involves degree of *association (correlation)* and *prediction (regression)*. Experimental designs—controlled circumstances—are necessary for establishing *cause and effect*. *Mapping* and *modeling* describe systems as wholes—often through *flow charts*. *Operations research* covers one-time decisions under uncertainty. *Time series* and *index numbers* describe and predict the movements of business series through time.

Motivational research tries to find why people act as they do. *Communication research* involves virtually all traditional models. *Content analysis* involves the observation and analysis of messages to learn about their creators and their environments.

Two major forms of reports are the comprehensive report and the abbreviated report.

The *abbreviated report* covers fewer of the research steps/parts than the comprehensive report. The abbreviated report concentrates upon the presentation of the collected and organized data. The four broad types of abbreviated reports are classified by the function of the content: (1) operations; (2) management; (3) employee relations; and (4) customer, stockholder, government, and public relations.

Abbreviated reports usually appear as forms, letters, and memoranda. They also take the manuscript form.

Comprehensive reports are those reports that result from activities involving most or all of the steps of the research method.

One type of comprehensive report is the proposal. The *proposal* identifies a problem and describes methods for solving it. The proposal may include about twenty parts, including a statement of the specific problem, the purposes and objectives, the hypotheses, and the design.

The final report of a research project includes everything that a proposal does. In addition, and more important, it includes the results or findings from the research process originally defined in the proposal.

Practice

1. You have noticed that most of your co-workers at the Worthington Corporation do not listen well. You suspect that they have never been taught how to listen. Because you would like to correct this problem, you want to hold three two-day listening workshops for all of the Worthington employees who would like to attend. Write a one- or two-page memorandum proposal for the workshops. The proposal will go to several of your Worthington superiors.

2. Your firm's manager of employee relations asked you to talk to all of the management analysts in your department to find out what they considered to be their major work problems. You did not prepare a questionnaire, but you did ask each of your colleagues to identify work-related problems. You interviewed all of your department's 15 analysts (yourself included). These are the problems that were mentioned, some of the points that the analysts made, and the number of analysts who identified each problem.

PROBLEM	NUMBER OF ANALYSTS WHO MENTIONED PROBLEM
a. Salaries too low ("Our salaries aren't keeping up with inflation.")	13
b. Lack of communication between management and employees ("Managers live in their own little world.")	11
c. Analysts not allowed to make own decisions ("When the managers deign to talk to us, they treat us like children.")	11
d. Vacation days too few ("We need more than two weeks a year away from this place if we are to be effective when we are here.")	10
e. Too few secretaries ("I end up doing my own typing half of the time.")	8
f. Analysts aren't allowed to determine own work hours ("I am old enough to know when I need to come to work or when I can come to work late.")	8
g. Offices too small ("My office mate and I bump into each other every time we move.")	6
h. Retirement plan not adequate ("Most companies match at least 25 percent of the employee's contribution.")	5
i. Company won't reimburse employees for tuition and books ("I'm spending a fortune for a degree that will be an asset to this company.")	3
j. Company doesn't give enough parties ("My last company gave a party every month.")	1

Write a letter report relating your work and your findings. Include at least one paragraph on conclusions, and use your imagination to add information if you wish. You will give your report to the Employee Relations Manager who asked you to do the work.

3. You are the staff researcher for a large organization. The marketing manager assigns you the responsibility of developing a proposal for research to determine whether the department can use a job-application factor as the predictor of sales performance. You do some thinking and reading and go through all of the preliminary steps. You define yourself, the marketing manager, and the environment within which you operate.
   a. Select one quantitative factor to use as a predictor (from such factors as age, examination score, years of education, and years of experience).
   b. Select the appropriate factor to be predicted (from such factors as average annual sales, average monthly sales, duration of the sales period under consideration).
   c. Establish the specific problem statement, scope and delimitations, hypothesis(es), and limitations/assumptions.

    d. Develop the design of the investigation.

       (1) Collection

       (2) Organization

       (3) Analysis (using the coefficients of correlation and determination, a test of signifi-
cance of the coefficient of correlation, and the regression equation)

    Write the draft of these sections of a proposal. Supply additional information as needed. The continuing example about advertising expenditures and sales (pages 485-492) involves similar research.

4. Meet with your group. Discuss the steps of the research process (page 460). Decide which of the steps might be omitted and still leave the basic research process intact. Select a spokesperson to summarize the discussion to the class.

5. As a communictions specialist at P. R. Duce, Inc., write an abbreviated report in memorandum form to persuade D. S. Instred, Marketing Specialist, of the need to apply a readability formula to outgoing messages. Include a description of the chosen formula and apply it to a passage of your choice. Supply any necessary information.

6. Obtain at least three office-equipment catalogs from different firms. Select a type of equipment common to all of them. Put yourself into the role of an employee who wants and needs the type of equipment. Write a justification report in manuscript form comparing the qualities of the various brands and ranking them in order of preference. Include only subtle persuasion for the brand you want. Provide and create whatever information you need.

7. [*This exercise is best for students who have some familiarity with statistics.*] As a staff researcher for the Expay Corporation, you have conducted assigned comparison research into the difference between the absentee rates for the East Plant and the West Plant. The assignment resulted from concern that the West Plant's absentee rate exceeded the East Plant's rate—to the detriment of production. Your null hypothesis was that no significant difference exists between the mean absentee rates for the two plants. To conduct the research, you rather arbitrarily chose to use monthly data for the past three years. You found the 36 monthly rates for each of the two plants and then found the mean rate for each. You then used a one-tail test of significance of the difference between two sample means at the .05 level of risk. Results of the quantitative analysis are:

$$\text{Mean rate for the West Plant} = .0647$$
$$\text{Mean rate for East Plant} = .0524$$
$$\text{Standard Error} = .0042$$

$$z = \frac{.0647 - .0524}{.0042} = \frac{.0123}{.0042} = 2.929$$

$$\begin{aligned}\text{Tabular value of } z \text{ at} \\ \text{.05 level of risk} \end{aligned} = 1.645$$

Because 2.929 is larger than 1.645, the null hypothesis was rejected. Therefore, a significant difference did exist between the two rates—the mean rate for the West Plant was significantly larger than the mean rate for the East Plant.

    Supplying additional information as needed, write a comprehensive report to include at least this information:

    Letter of transmittal

    Introduction and general problem

    Statement of specific problem, including scope and delimitations

    Limitations/assumptions

    Hypothesis

    Design

Collection and organization
Analysis
Conclusion
Interpretation
Recommendation

8. Meet with your group. Work as a task force of specialists employed at Meac Co. First, brainstorm to identify the factors that might explain a recent slump in sales for your company, Beef-Jerky Sales, Inc. Complete the brainstorming process by isolating the one or two factors most likely to explain it. Brainstorm again to establish all of the details of a research design for determining whether the factors are related to the slump. Brainstorm and supply all of the information needed to develop a complete research proposal. Divide the work, draft the parts of a proposal, meet to compile and refine the parts, and write the proposal. Use the manuscript form, the impersonal style, and the traditional parts.

9. For the case described in Exercise No. 12 in Chapter 13 (page 455), complete the research design and write a complete formal research proposal for the research.

10. For the case described in Exercise No. 10 in Chapter 13 (page 455), complete the research design, and write a formal proposal for the research.

11. Select a team from the class to choose the best research design from the proposals developed in Exercise No. 10—or to develop a proposal containing the best elements of the others. Divide the work and the expenses (if the institution cannot fund the project) among the class members. Complete the survey and the remainder of the proposed research.

12. Write the final report of the research completed in Exercise No. 11. Put it in the comprehensive, manuscript format for a final research report. Include all necessary parts.

13. Choose one of these topics or another suggested by your professor or through brainstorming with your group or class:

How business can reduce energy consumption
The content and features of annual reports
The content and features of prospectuses
The field in which you plan to work
A company for which you might want to work
The provisions and status of applications of the Equal Employment Opportunity Act
Organization development as a discipline
Retirement plans used by business
The current status of the national economy
Conflict of interest within business firms
Japan's productivity and the impact of the Deming approach to statistical analysis upon it

Develop an outline and a plan of attack upon the topic. Collect the information from secondary and/or primary sources. Develop a several-page manuscript report of the findings. Include in the report at least three excerpts from secondary sources (one of each of the three types), the footnotes associated with the excerpts, at least one table, and at least one graph. (See Chapter 16 for hints on tabular and graphic construction.) In addition, include headings and subheadings, a bibliography, and all other parts necessary to complete it.

14. For each of these problems, write at least one hypothesis testable by quantitative methods:

a. A manager claims that Department F is not operating as efficiently as Department G.
b. Management is concerned about the level of lost time this year compared with last year.
c. Customer returns of purchased goods seem to be running unusually high.

   d. Management needs to choose a supplier of production parts from three suppliers who have submitted identical low bids.
   e. A manager thinks that accidents are inversely related to years of experience.
15. For each of these situations, write at least one limitation or assumption:
   a. The researcher is using the telephone directory as the universe for research into levels of income.
   b. To find the public's opinion about a product, the researcher sets up a stand in a shopping mall and asks passers-by to test the product and complete a questionnaire.
   c. To develop an equation for predicting monthly sales for the next two years, the researcher arbitrarily chooses the past two years as a pattern.
   d. A researcher receives a 32 percent return from a mail survey.
   e. One of five field interviewers has a flamboyant style; the others do not.
16. Write a research definition for each of these terms:
   a. Small business
   b. Large manufacturer
   c. Student
   d. Smoker
   e. Manager
   f. Professional worker
17. Complete at least three personal interviews using the interview guide developed in Exercise No. 13 in Chapter 13 (page 455). Write a report summarizing the results of the interviews. If made into a class project, select the interviewees by some random process, divide them among the students, and compile the results before each student writes the report.
18. Decide which of the ten types of research (pages 464-467) each of these situations represents:
   a. You describe the flow of inputs and outputs for your production system.
   b. You have complete production reports for the past six months and find monthly averages for them by department.
   c. You use queuing theory to determine how many stations to have at a drive-in bank.
   d. You divide types of workers into six categories based upon their attitudes toward work.
   e. You stand near a counter in a shopping center and write brief sketches of the emotional states of the people who approach it and pass it by.
   f. You test to determine whether Brand A or Brand B has fewer defectives.
   g. You are developing an equation that will predict sales from the number of salespersons in the field.
   h. You are developing a set of indexes representing the weekly variations in retail sales.
   i. You set up a laboratory experiment to determine the impact of a certain additive upon the caustic powers of a compound.
   j. You want to know the proportion of people in the company's Southwest Region who plan to buy a new car next year. You cannot contact every person in the area, so you draw a sample, determine the proportion in the sample who plan to buy, and use that proportion as the basis for an approximation of the proportion in the region who plan to buy.
19. An employee in your department has been unusually irritable and inefficient for the past two weeks. His outbursts have affected the personnel and productivity of the entire department. Write a one-page report on the problem and how you might attack it.
20. Use your dictionary and thesaurus to create meanings for these words. Use the words when you think, write, and speak so that you feel comfortable using them.

a. Ambiguous	**d.** Culminate
b. Anonymous	**e.** Deign
c. Cryptic	**f.** Disseminate

           g. Flamboyant   **k.** Moot
           h. Inference   **l.** Overt
           i. Microcosm   **m.** Plagiarism
           j. Miniscule   **n.** Vicarious

21. Take and complete Self-Test 32 over the excerpt about operational reports.

Self-Test 32
Excerpt about Operational Reports

A. Recall (25 points each). For each multiple-choice question, select the most accurate answer.

  1. Which one of these statements is *false?*

    a. The primary information in production reports summarizes the inputs to the production process.

    b. Operational reports from the financial area of a firm usually take the form of financial statements such as the balance sheet.

    c. Computer-center personnel prepare routine operational reports of inputs and outputs.

    d. As a staff area, the word-processing center prepares operational reports on a regular basis.

    e. Operational reports often appear as completed forms.

  2. The operational report:

    a. Is a comprehensive report

    b. Usually flows downward in a firm

    c. Is probably the most common of the abbreviated reports

    d. Applies only to line operations

    e. Usually contains more qualitative than quantitative data

  3. Reports on operations:

    a. In a marketing department cover only promotion and pricing activities

    b. From a finance department often require more expertise than that summarized in a business communication textbook

    c. Usually require high-level composition skills for the narrative portions

    d. For a personnel department do not deal with such activities as hirings and firings

    e. From a department of research report the findings from research projects in comprehensive form

B. Inference (25 points). Indicate whether this statement is true or false.

Operational reports could be classified as management reports.

Solution to Self-Test 32
Excerpt about Operational Reports

A. Recall (25 points each)   **B.** Inference (25 points)

  1. a   **3.** b   True

  2. c

22. Take and complete Self-Test 33 over Chapter 14.

Self-Test 33
Chapter 14

A. Recall (16 points each). For each multiple-choice question, select the most accurate answer.

  1. A typical comprehensive report is *not:*
    a. Usually written in a personal reporting style
    b. From six to many pages long
    c. Usually assigned by management
    d. Written for nonroutine, special-purpose projects
    e. Written in an impersonal, formal reporting style

  2. Which one of these statements is true?
    a. Research is the same as quantitative analysis.
    b. The purpose of research is to identify problems for a report.
    c. Research methods depend solely on the scientific method.
    d. A hypothesis should be stated in declarative form.
    e. Empirical research is inferential research.

  3. Which one of these statements is true?
    a. Motivational research deals primarily with how people behave.
    b. The abbreviated report customarily uses the manuscript format.
    c. A justification report may include overt persuasion in addition to the persuasion inherent in the facts and logic of its presentation.
    d. A comprehensive report need not include any analysis.
    e. If a significant relationship exists between or among variables, one or more variables cause the occurrence of the other.

  4. Which one of these statements is true?
    a. Quantitative-comparison research involves regression analysis as a basic tool.
    b. All comprehensive research reports include recommendations for the action to result from the research.
    c. Communication research involving content analysis requires that the content of all personnel files be examined.
    d. A proposal may cover topics other than research projects.
    e. The review of the literature relates only to the data-collecting stage.

B. Inference (18 points each). Indicate whether each statement is true or false.

  1. Because it is more precise, quantitative research is more important than qualitative research.
  2. The list of ten types of research developed in this chapter forms a collectively exhaustive and mutually exclusive classification scheme.

Solution to Self-Test 33
Chapter 14

A. Recall (16 points each)   **B.** Inference (18 points each)
  1. a   **3.** c   **1.** False
  2. d   **4.** d   **2.** False

15

Sending Through
Oral Channels

In this chapter, turn from sending through written channels to sending through oral channels.

Because both the written and oral channels involve words, many of the suggestions in the preceding chapters on writing also apply to speaking. Extend and reinforce those suggestions as you review some principles for the oral channels. To do so, consider the different kinds of speaking at the interpersonal, medio, person-to-group, and mass levels of communication.

First, though, review the basic guidelines applied to the oral process.

GUIDELINES FOR SPEAKING

View the six guidelines from your role as a speaking communicator:

1. Define your purposes for speaking, the listener's purposes for listening, yourself, the listener, and the environment.
2. Identify the speaking channel.
3. Control the interference internal and external to you and the listener.
4. Select, encode, sometimes write, and speak the messages in light of the purposes, the participants, the environment, the channel, and the interference.
5. Use feedback from and to the listener.
6. Evaluate at each stage.

SPEAKING AT THE INTERPERSONAL LEVEL

Apply the principles of speaking to some specific interpersonal channels. The channels are (1) conversations, (2) dialogues, (3) interviews, and (4) small groups.

501

Conversation

You spend a great deal of your life—even of your business life—in informal conversation. Conversations allow for the exchange of information and for learning about other people and yourself through them.

The next sections on the dialogue, the interview, and speaking within the small group concentrate upon the structured, formal, highly purposive interpersonal situations. Therefore, consider the conversation to be relatively unstructured, informal, and nonpurposive.

Picture several topics for business conversations:

1. The due date of a report
2. The good or poor way a colleague made a presentation
3. Satisfaction or dissatisfaction with the way you just bid a contract
4. Progress on a project
5. The success or failure of a business trip
6. A request for help on a project
7. An offer to help on a project
8. Making an appointment
9. Discussion of an upcoming meeting, trip, audit, or other event
10. Basic exchanges about the health and well-being of family members
11. The latest company gossip
12. Current national and international news
13. Personal or business problems of you or a friend
14. The game, play, or program you or a friend saw the day before

Though many of the subjects in the list do not relate directly to business purposes, they nonetheless are important to smooth business functioning. Humans must interact as humans.

People cannot divorce their personal lives from their working lives. To the extent that the simple conversation helps them maintain good human relations and to reduce their personal problems, it improves their performance.

Apply the communication principles and guidelines to even the conversational channels. Take advantage of the immediacy of the feedback by raising questions to test and clarify your perceptions. Provide good feedback yourself. Listen actively, and observe nonverbal cues keenly. Use the common courtesies. Avoid defensiveness. Evaluate during and after the conversation.

Dialogue

The dialogue is a conversation with a purpose. Thus, the business dialogue is a conversation that takes place in a relatively structured formal setting. It has distinct, significant, and usually preannounced decision-making purposes.

Think of how two or three people in a business setting can open a dialogue with such purposes as to:

1. Decide on the details of a contract bid
2. Make all the decisions about a research proposal
3. Divide the work on a project
4. Develop a specific strategy for meeting with a contract client

5. Obtain your boss's approval of a two-year plan for executing a contract with a client
6. Discuss annual performance review
7. Meet with a lawyer to talk about a legal matter
8. Decide whether to hire or to dismiss someone
9. Make decisions about finance, production, marketing, and all other functions and areas of business
10. Write job description and job specifications

As a participant in a dialogue, bring all of the guidelines to bear. Make preliminary notes. During the dialogue contribute to the solution of the problem. Avoid defensiveness, and avoid arousing it in the other. Practice good human relations. Evaluate through mental processing alone, or use a written form.

Interview

The interview is a special type of dialogue, involving preset goals such as these:

1. Developing a job description and job specifications
2. Developing a performance review
3. Evaluating for promotion
4. Appraising an applicant for a job
5. Disseminating information to the media
6. Collecting information from an authority
7. Counseling for careers, personal problems, etc.
8. Reprimanding an employee
9. Applying grievance procedures
10. Complaining about work conditions

Consider the types of interviews and the roles of the participants in an interview.

Types

The interview involves at least some structure. Review the directive, nondirective, stress, and depth interviews.

Directive The directive interview puts the interviewer in relative command of the transaction. He or she sets the meeting time, determines the objectives, decides how to proceed, asks the questions, and controls the entire process. The interviewee plays the role prescribed by the interviewer. However, the interviewee is responsible for contributing to the success of the interview.

Nondirective The nondirective interview puts both parties into shared roles. Together they set the meeting time, determine the objectives, decide how to proceed, and take turns in leading the exchange.

Stress The stress interview is a special type of directive interview. It requires a highly qualified interviewer.

The stress interview is still used by some interviewers to determine how well the interviewee can handle emotion-laden and leading questions. An example of the type of question is, "When was the last time you stole anything from the company for which you were working?"

Depth   As the name implies, the depth interview involves an assertive, directive probe into a topic. It also requires a skilled interviewer.

The depth interviewer asks an open question and lets the interviewee respond in free fashion. Then the interviewer asks specific questions about the points introduced by the interviewee. The process continues until the interviewer gets to the bottom of the issues. The approach applies particularly well to motivational research.

Roles

You will act many times in your life as an interviewee and likely many times as an interviewer or shared-responsibility interviewer/interviewee. All three roles have important characteristics and responsibilities.

Interviewer   As the interviewer, prepare for the interview by defining purposes, participants, channel, interference, messages, feedback, and evaluation.

Make the interviewee comfortable. Tell the interviewee what your purposes are. Also ask what the interviewee would like to accomplish. Find a natural, common ground to open the discussion.

You may use a prestructured list of questions (a patterned interview) from which you read or which you have memorized. You also may use an unpatterned approach to the questioning.

Encode your questions to meet the educational level of the interviewee. Also avoid emotional symbols—unless you are conducting a stress interview. Use closed or open questions, all of them brief and clear.

You may want to take notes; if you do, avoid making a flourish of it. Proceed discreetly, and do not try to write every word.

Ask permission before you use a tape recorder. If you gain the permission, know how to use the equipment and have it in working order before meeting with the interviewee.

If you are going to interview an authority on some subject, you may want to send a list of questions ahead of time. If you do, avoid varying too much from the original list. Particularly avoid introducing anything controversial or demanding that is not on the list.

Listen and observe carefully. Ask questions to be sure you have understood the interviewee. Be particularly aware of the nonverbal elements of the situation. Watch the time as well as the interviewee. Dress appropriately. Adapt to the feedback you receive and evaluate.

Assume the responsibility for moving the interview in the direction you want it to go. Evaluate the process.

Interviewee   As an interviewee, prepare for the transaction just as fully as the interviewer. Define your purposes and try to define the interviewer's. Learn all you can about the interviewer and her or his operational framework.

Picture the interview. Think not only about the physical conditions, but about what the interviewer will ask and how you will answer.

Practice your answers aloud. However, do not make them sound mechanical. Maintain a natural and adaptable speaking style.

Prepare the questions you would like to ask. Memorize them so that you can avoid the negative appearance created by having to read them.

Anticipate the kinds of interference that may occur, and plan how you will overcome it.

Dress appropriately. Be on time.

Leave the control to the interviewer unless he or she indicates verbally or nonverbally that you may take control part of the time. However, contribute your part to making the interview a success.

Interviewer/interviewee   The nondirective interview requires joint resonsibilities for both parties.

To make such a joint venture successful, add to the points made in the preceding sections the suggestion that you exercise turn-taking fairly. Do not dominate a shared-responsibility interview. On the other hand, do your share to see that the other does not dominate either.

Case 2 illustrates the application of the guidelines to an interview.

Case Study 2

Appraisal and Promotion Interview

You work as a collection correspondent for a large firm. You have been in the position for nearly three years. Your job involves telephoning people whose payments are late and asking that they send them.

The manager of the collection department has notified you that you will have your annual performance-appraisal interview next week. You already have completed your self-appraisal form and met with the collection supervisor about it. You feel that the interview went well.

You know that the position of collection supervisor will be open for your area within the next few months. You plan to apply for it and thus want the appraisal interview with the manager to go particularly well.

You apply the guidelines.

1. You establish your purposes to be:
   a. To receive a higher composite appraisal rating than you did last year—already the highest in your area.
   b. To receive the highest step raise possible at your level from the annual merit appraisal.
   c. To have the manager record again this year your desire to become a supervisor and eventually to go into management.
   d. To have the manager record on the appraisal form three courses related to your work: Principles of Management, Credit and Collections, and Business Communication. (You took them at the local community college the past year.)
   e. To learn exactly how to activate your application for the supervisory position. (You already know the mechanics, but want to gain some additional information from the manager—and to fix in the manager's mind the seriousness of your intent.)

    f. To receive encouragement from the manager to apply for the supervisory position and the training program associated with it.
2. You decide that the manager's purposes are:
    a. To evaluate your performance correctly.
    b. To recommend the highest step raise only to the highest performer.
    c. To identify a person who is qualified and motivated to move into supervision.
    d. To submit the professed candidate for a supervisory position to some semi-stress interview techniques to determine whether he or she will be able to cope with the pressures of coordinating the activities of a collection operation.
    e. To encourage to apply for a supervisory position and associated training program only those people who are qualified in emotional makeup, education, and experience to perform well.
3. You define yourself in this context.
    a. Strengths.
       (1) A good age.
       (2) The highest performance record in area: have met or surpassed quota of collections for all but two weeks in the past year.
       (3) Satisfactory educational qualifications.
       (4) Good emotional stability.
       (5) Good communication ability.
       (6) Good relations with manager, supervisor, and all but one other correspondent in the area.
       (7) Highly motivated.
       (8) Good appearance.
       (9) Confident and assertive.
      (10) Personal life under control.
      (11) Good attendance record.
      (12) Good health.
      (13) Loyalty to the firm.
    b. Weaknesses.
       (1) Sometimes overbearing and zealous in arguing beliefs; put off some people.
       (2) Occasional temper flare-up.
       (3) One correspondent has obviously negative feelings toward you.
       (4) Lack of experience as a supervisor, though did supervise the area satisfactorily for three weeks during illness of supervisor.
4. You define the manager in this context.
    a. Strengths.
       (1) Conducts a skilled interview; allows time for input from interviewee.
       (2) Interested in finding the best people for jobs.
       (3) Professional attitude.
       (4) Does not hesitate to recommend pay increases when deserved.
    b. Weaknesses.
       (1) Seems to have some hesitancy about putting people of your sex in supervisory position.
       (2) Does not give praise easily.
       (3) Sometimes difficult to "read" for clues to feelings about employees' aspirations.
       (4) Somewhat wary of taking a risk by promoting an untested employee into a supervisory position.
5. You analyze the interview channel for its weaknesses and strengths.

6 You anticipate interference with the message and your purposes, and plan how to overcome it.

a. Possible interference from the manager.

b. Possible interference from you.

c. External interference (interruptions during interview, etc.).

7. You plan and practice how you will answer anticipated questions and what you want to volunteer.

a. You have been through the appraisal interview twice before, so you feel confident about answering the questions on the interview guide and form well. However, you decide on your self-ratings and answers to the questions.

b. You decide that the manager will probably ask some probing questions related to your professed interest in a promotion. You think about how you will answer in a manner that will be self-enhancing instead of self-effacing or bulldozing. Some of the questions and types of proposed answers are:

(1) "What makes you think that you are capable of being a supervisor?" You decide to cite your strengths in a confident, straightforward manner without bragging.

(2) "How do you expect to overcome your lack of experience?" You decide to suggest (a) that your three weeks' experience taught you a great deal; (b) that you have continued to think, read, and decide upon strategies through which you could have done even better; and (c) that you know that the training program is excellent and will help you overcome any weaknesses you have. You plan to describe some organizational experiences that show your leadership capabilities. You also will mention your college courses in management and related subjects and your plans to enroll in more.

(3) "How do you propose to overcome conflicts such as the one you already have with the correspondent in your area?" You decide to say that you will attempt to identify the source of the conflict, approach it directly, and work positively to overcome it.

(4) "I've noticed that you lose your temper—even with a customer—once in a while. What do you propose to do to overcome that problem?" You decide not to deny that the problem exists, but to state that you already have improved significantly (no flare-up at work in at least two months). You will also state that you are confident that you can control it, because you have identified practical and healthful alternatives to the outbursts. If asked what the alternatives are, you will mention that when you first sense that a situation is relentlessly propelling you toward a loss of self-control, you (a) remove yourself quickly but graciously from the situation; (b) turn a conversation from emotional to objective bases for disagreement; (c) diplomatically or overtly change a conversation subject entirely; (d) suggest that you would like more time to consider an issue and terminate a conversation to be taken up at a later time; (e) truly see another's view and say so; or (f) if impossible or improper to revise or avoid the situation, use mental force to remain calm as you state and explain your well-founded views without attacking the other's person.

(5) "Many people who are good at a job are not good at supervising that same job. What makes you think you are different?" Because this question is similar to the first and second questions, you decide that you will answer much as you would answer them. However, you also decide that you will stress that your abilities and goals from early childhood have related to leadership. You will point out that you have known people who are follow-

ers by nature, and that you are different. You have the capability to work on a team, to take directions from others, and to do your best in whatever position you serve. You will add that even though you have these capabilities, you believe that your best talents lie in management. If your manager does not seem to feel threatened by someone aspiring to the same position he or she holds, you will add that you want eventually to move into that level and even higher.

(6) "In the past I have placed two of your sex in a supervisory position, and neither worked out. Your present supervisor is not your sex and has been accepted well. Do you think you can overcome this problem?" You decide that you will react without becoming defensive. You will briefly allude to the fact that you did not know the two supervisors or why they did not succeed. You will then point out that you consider yourself quite able to deal diplomatically with any initial resistance to you on the basis of your sex alone, but that you are confident that your abilities will soon overcome even any initial resistance that might develop. You will add that you would like to be judged on your abilities and performance—the quality of which seemed to be acknowledged reasonably well by the majority of the other correspondents during the three-week period you took over for the supervisor.

8. Before and during the interview, you choose appropriate nonverbal messages.
   a. You dress and groom appropriately.
   b. You avoid tension-producing contacts prior to the interview.
   c. You arrive at the manager's office a few minutes ahead of time, announce your presence to the secretary, take a seat, and read, converse with the secretary, or sit in controlled silence.
   d. When the secretary tells you to enter the manager's office, you do so calmly and confidently, allowing the manager to cue your next move.
   e. You firmly shake the manager's hand if extended.
   f. You exchange pleasantries.
   g. You sit where the manager suggests. You establish good posture, but do not sit in a stiff, minimal-space style that shows a lack of confidence. Yet you do not sprawl in the chair and use so much space that you appear swaggeringly confident. Instead, you occupy a moderate amount of space—just enough to show strength of self-concept.
   h. You keep your hands still unless you use them in natural, positive gestures.
   i. You maintain eye contact and genuinely pleasant, controlled variations to express dynamism, but not nervousness.
   j. You let the manager take the lead in initiating, setting the direction of, and ending the interview.
   k. You listen and watch for nonverbal cues for appropriate turn-taking.
   l. If you use any materials, you put them in a clean folder and leave them in proper order on your lap or on the desk, removing, holding, and referring to them during the time you use them. Avoid shuffling or fingering them at other times.
9. During the interview, you select and transmit appropriate verbal messages in response to the manager's messages which you have observed and listened to carefully.
   a. You draw from your preplanning and practice. You fit your answers to the actual questions asked—even moving slightly beyond the original questions in order to say all you want to say.

b. If you receive any unanticipated questions, you remain calm, take a few seconds to think, and answer straightforwardly, thinking even as you speak.
10. You use feedback opportunities fully.
   a. You invite feedback.
   b. You take advantage of any invitations for feedback.
11. You interject self-enhancing questions and comments not introduced by the interviewer.
12. You evaluate.
   a. You evaluate continually during the interview. You adjust to the ebb and flow of the conversation in light of your purposes and the messages received from the manager.
   b. You conduct a thorough evaluation at the end of the interview. Because of the importance of the interview, you probably will choose to use an external form rather than trusting only to the haphazardness of some mental evaluations.
      (1) Decide whether you need a follow-up on any part of the interview.
      (2) Decide whether you were successful in attaining your objectives.
      (3) Decide where you might have improved your performance.
      (4) Decide what you will do differently in the next interview or dialogue in which you take part.

Small Group

Small-group communication is an eclectic type, with some characteristics of the interpersonal, medio, and person-to-group levels. However, the small-group channel retains the face-to-face, immediate-feedback, homogeneous-group features of the interpersonal.

The small-group channel is used extensively in the business setting. It provides the opportunity for many minds to contribute to the solutions and decisions that define business operations.

Consider the defining elements of size, location, time, topic, purpose, formality, designation, cohesion, methods, and roles.

Size

If conversations, dialogues, and interviews include no more than three people, then small groups begin with four. Once the size of a group gets past ten, discussion often becomes so difficult that the group may no longer be productive. Therefore, define a small group as one containing from four to ten people, with five to seven people probably representing the ideal sizes.

When a large group wants the advantages of small-group discussion, it breaks into small groups. The small groups function as described in this section. Each then summarizes its work and reports in person-to-group fashion to the reconvened larger group.

Location

The effective small group meets in a location convenient to the participants. The ideal room is relatively small, comfortable, and attractive. A round table is conducive to the work.

Time

Set a meeting time and honor it. Collectively keep the meeting moving so that the group does not waste time. Wasting time is one of the most serious complaints about group meetings.

Topic

The topics for small-group deliberations are often similar to those for conversations, dialogues, and interviews. The small group just changes the scenario somewhat by including more people.

Purpose

A major feature of the small-group meeting is that the meeting is for some well-defined purpose. The purpose usually relates to problem-solving and decision-making circumstances.

Formality

Meetings range in structure from the quite formal to the extremely informal and unstructured.

The formal, structured meeting may take on some of the characteristics of the person-to-group channel. It usually involves a previously designated chairperson. The chairperson sets the meeting time, prepares an agenda, appoints a recorder, and presides. He or she may deliver a monologue at the beginning of the meeting.

Once the discussion begins, however, even the formal chairperson usually acts only as a facilitator.

The informal, unstructured small-group session begins with no previously named chairperson or agenda. Instead, the recorder and leader emerge from the group—by consensus, election, or volunteerism.

If the group sets a second meeting, however, the members usually designate someone to coordinate the activities for the next time. That person may be called the chairperson, chair, coordinator, facilitator, or convener.

Designation

The groups and their meetings go by many different designations. The designations include task force, committee, team, work group, council, staff meeting, departmental meeting, and production meeting.

The task force is a particularly useful concept because it brings together a small group of specialists representing all of the major areas involved in addressing the issue. For example, a marketing strategy group could be comprised of specialists from marketing, advertising, research, finance, and production.

Cohesion

The good group unifies into a cohesive whole. The people work as one in their concentrated efforts toward attaining the established goal.

Though forging such a homogeneous group can be difficult, the organizer must try to do so. Whether leader or participant, every member of a group has a responsibility to the work of the group.

Working in whatever capacity, the members of a group should individually and collectively apply the principles and guidelines for good communication. They should establish not only the collective purpose for the group, but individual purposes for every member.

They should get to know each other and be able to depend on each other. They should know the unique environments in which each works. They should know the person to whom the results go.

They should understand the dynamics of the channel in which they are working—and employ them for best effect.

They should identify and overcome barriers.

They should carefully decide what they want to say during and at the conclusion of the meeting—and say it well.

They should invite and use feedback fully. They should use ongoing and terminal evaluation of the results of the small-group communication channel. Examples of evaluation forms for group discussion appear in Appendix B.

Methods

Consider four basic methods for conducting group meetings: (1) problem-solving, (2) educating, (3) brainstorming, and (4) role-playing.

Problem solving   Probably the most common pattern for business groups to follow, the problem-solving method introduces a scientific approach to accomplishing the objectives. When a group uses this method, the steps become:

1. Organize.
2. Define the problem and establish the objectives.
3. Analyze the problem.
4. Establish criteria for evaluating solutions.
5. Propose possible solutions.
6. Choose the best solution.
7. Communicate the solution.
8. Evaluate.

(1) To *organize*, decide upon a plan of action. Choose a strong leader. Also choose a recorder if desired. Establish the structure and rules of conduct.

(2) *State the problem* precisely. Write it on paper. *State the short-term objectives* for the first meeting. Also *state the long-term objectives* if the solution requires a series of meetings.

Classify problems as related to *fact, value,* or *policy.*

A *problem of fact* arises when the solution rests on the simple truth or falsity of a statement. If the problem is to determine whether one production line produces more units per hour than another, the problem is one of fact. The problem may be solved by counting. The results may be verified in the physical world.

A *problem of value* exists when the solution calls for a determination of the relative merits of qualitative information. Consider how these words introduce value judgments:

Good	Worthy
Bad	Unworthy
Superior	Reliable
Inferior	Unreliable
Effective	Safe
Ineffective	Unsafe

For example, assume your group wants to determine whether an authoritarian management style is superior to a permissive one. Even if you use some objective criteria and some quantitative data in your assessment, you still will not be able to verify the conclusion in the physical world. Therefore, the problem is based on judgment of values.

A *problem of policy* occurs when a group needs to decide what action the organization should take in the future. Identifying words are "shall" and "should."

For instance, suppose that a task force needs to determine where a firm shall build a plant. Because the decision relates to a future event, the problem concerns policy.

The results of decisions about policy cannot be verified. Whatever the decision about the location of the plant, the group will never know whether it was the best decision under the circumstances.

(3) *Analyze the problem* by considering every factor associated with it. Deal with the who, what, when, where, how, and why. Break the problem into its elemental parts. Think of every possible symptom, cause, effect, force, and variable. Study their relationships to the problem.

When the group has identified all possible factors, arrange them in the order of importance to the discussion. The brainstorming process works well for this part of the problem-solving sequence.

(4) *Establish criteria* for evaluation. Do so early in the process. This step fits well into the problem-defining, purpose-setting stage. Examples of problem-solving criteria include:

1. The solution will yield at least $2,000 more sales than at present.
2. The solution will stop the production of excessive numbers of defectives.
3. The solution will generate at least 50 new customers.
4. The solution will cost no more than the present problem.

(5) *Propose possible solutions* to the problem. Assess the effectiveness of each. Again, the brainstorming process can facilitate this step.

(6) *Choose the best solution* by applying the criteria to each suggested solution.

(7) *Communicate the solution* to the authorizing person, or put it into effect if you have authority to do so.

(8) *Evaluate* the problem-solving discussion. Such evaluation often must await some delayed application of the suggested solution. However, the group should establish a follow-up procedure to determine whether the solution met the criteria.

Educating   Some small-group meetings occur simply to share information or to educate the members. For such situations, the leader states or reads a new policy statement or similar message (person-to-group activity). Then he or she opens the floor to discussion (interpersonal activity). The leader and the members of the group may raise points for clarification, ask questions, give examples of applications, and tell what the message means to them.

Brainstorming   As introduced in the data-gathering section of Chapter 13, brainstorming is an important group device for generating ideas. As suggested in the coverage of the problem-solving method, it also may be used for other purposes.

The process of brainstorming involves these steps:

1. Organize. Even though the brainstorming method is not rigidly structured, some ground rules do apply. Therefore, the group should announce them and may need to designate someone to act as coordinator. The group may also name a recorder. The coordinator may use the chalkboard as the recorder uses pencil and paper. If everyone knows the rules for brainstorming, the leadership may emerge from the group—and may rotate among several participants during a session. The ground rules include:
   a. The group will not evaluate the contributions or reach a decision until the group has exercised the creative process fully. Some groups have an additional session before evaluating and deciding which ideas to use.
   b. Each group member should feel free and responsible to take an active part.
   c. No member may pressure any other member.
   d. No member may evaluate or criticize the contributions of another.
2. Define the task and establish the objectives. The task is the concept for which the ideas will be generated. The commonly felt need initiates the chain of expressions. For example, suppose a group holds a brainstorming session to identify the possible causes of shipping delays. The problem then becomes: What are the causes of shipping delays? The objectives of the session could then be to name every possible cause and then, afterwards, to evaluate and organize the suggestions into a list in order of importance as likely causes.
3. State the ideas as quickly as possible and record them on a chalkboard and/or paper. As soon as a member states one idea, another member immediately states another. The free-wheeling associations go forward without regard to whether the contributors or others support them or whether the ideas duplicate or overlap others already presented. The key is to think aloud without fear of being judged for the quality of the ideas. Feed upon each other. Chain the ideas. Reach into the recesses of the mind for even possibly ridiculous ideas. Even role-play the problem if that will help stimulate thinking. (The next section reviews role-playing.)
4. Organize the ideas. Reject duplications. Combine similar ideas under a single heading.
5. Arrange the ideas in the order of importance for resolving the original task or issue.
6. Act upon the listing or give the listing to the person authorizing the group to develop it.

Role-playing Another method sometimes employed by small groups is role-playing. Potter and Andersen state that in role-playing " . . . people act out problems containing human conflicts and then analyze their actions and reactions with the help of the other role-players and observers."[1]

Also according to Potter and Andersen, role-playing usually includes:

1. Selecting a problem that approaches reality as closely as possible—one that is steeped in meaning for the individuals portraying the roles or witnessing the

---

[1] David Potter and Martin P. Andersen, *Discussion in Small Groups: A Guide to Effective Practice,* 3d ed. (Belmont, Calif.: Wadsworth Publishing Company, Inc., 1976), p. 143.

unfolding of the action. Generally, the situation or plot is constructed in barest outline and is simply and clearly stated.

2. Structuring a problem only to the point where the problem is clear and the players have a mental picture of the roles that they are to portray. Usually no lines are written or memorized.
3. Choosing the role-players from within the group.
4. Instructing and, on occasion, "warming up" the players.
5. Instructing the observers.
6. Role-playing the problem situation; cutting or stopping the role-playing when the issues of the problem have been delineated.
7. Analyzing the role-playing in order to explore further the insights revealed and in order to put the behavior modifications suggested into practice.[2]

Roles

Three basic roles define group members. They are (1) participant, (2) leader, and (3) recorder.

Participant   Participants determine whether the process is successful or not. Not only do they bring their knowledge, arts, and skills to bear, but they also assume particular roles as they perform in the group. Theoreticians suggest that the behavior of members of a group may appear in three broad types of roles: (1) task-oriented roles, (2) process-oriented roles, and (3) destructive roles.

The *task-oriented roles* concentrate upon the subject matter of the meeting— the job to be done. The *process-oriented roles* concentrate upon the nature of the process—the human interactions. The *destructive roles* introduce activities counter- productive to both task- and process-oriented roles.

As you review some of the roles falling in each category, decide which com- binations you usually adopt. Try to improve your use of the positive task and process roles and reduce your playing of the negative roles.

1. For understanding *task-oriented behavior,* consider 11 roles:
   a. *Seeker of information.* The person who asks for factual data. This person understands and articulates the kind of data the group needs from knowledge, experience, and research.
   b. *Giver of information.* The person who provides factual data. This person draws heavily upon her or his own knowledge and experience and upon research. The person knows the material and provides it when needed.
   c. *Seeker of opinions.* The person who asks others to express their opinions. This person may not be secure and thus needs to know what others think before expressing her or his opinions. On the other hand, the seeker of opinions may be so secure that he or she asks others' opinions in order to learn more about the task.
   d. *Seeker of ideas.* The person who asks for ideas. This person is aware of the need for new ideas in given situations and stimulates the group to provide them.
   e. *Giver of ideas.* The person who provides ideas. This person is imaginative and contributes new ideas as needed.

---

[2]Ibid.

  f. *Giver of opinions.* The person who provides opinions. This person's contributions serve to clarify the task.

  g. *Starter.* The person who starts group activities. For both structured and unstructured situations, this person talks first, suggests procedures, and otherwise moves the group into the work.

  h. *Coordinator.* The person who clarifies ideas. This person paraphrases, explains, elaborates, connects, and suggests illustrations for the ideas of the group.

  i. *Expediter.* The person who keeps the group on the subject. This person notices when the members stray too far from the topic, and brings them back to it.

  j. *Analyzer.* The person who probes deeply into the subject. This person understands and applies logic and the scientific method to the task—and helps others do the same.

  k. *Summarizer.* The person who periodically summarizes the material to that point. This person helps the group by bringing the main ideas into sharp focus.

2. *Process-oriented roles* for members of groups take seven forms:

  a. *Climate maker.* The person who establishes a friendly, supportive atmosphere for the group.

  b. *Harmonizer.* The person who tries to reduce conflict and misunderstanding.

  c. *Gatekeeper.* The person who facilitates interactions by restraining dominant speakers and encouraging hesitant ones.

  d. *Setter of standards.* The person who acts as the role model for others by preserving objectivity, removing emotionalism, listening well, and maintaining momentum.

  e. *Leader of games.* The person who breaks monotony and tension by interjecting humor and other diversions into the work.

  f. *Compromiser.* The person who brings differing viewpoints together by suggesting minor adjustments to one or more of them.

  g. *Public-relations person.* The person who interacts well with entities external to the group.

3. Consider eight *destructive roles* often played by members of a group:

  a. *Withdrawer.* The person who retreats from the group activity and acts bored or indifferent.

  b. *Aggressor.* The person who tries to elevate herself or himself by criticizing and blaming others.

  c. *Competer.* The person who seems to be compelled to express differing views on every issue—simply for the sake of the attention and the competition.

  d. *Blocker.* The person who uses a wide variety of tactics to block the group from unifying on an issue, because he or she has some personal or work-related reason for resisting change.

  e. *Limited-idea person.* The person who repeats the same one or two ideas whatever the topic or whatever the group.

  f. *Clown.* The person whose relentless attempts to gain attention through clownish activities disrupts the interactions of the group.

  g. *Monopolizer.* The person who tries to convince the group of her or his prowess by dominating the discussion.

h. *Side-stepper.* The person who dodges issues by raising unrelated topics, dwelling on minor arguments, and otherwise avoiding responsibility.

In conjunction with the roles you play as a member of a small group, consider some summary suggestions for being a good participant:

1. Plan for the meeting by applying the guidelines.
2. Contribute actively to the discussion.
3. Select and play the appropriate positive roles; eliminate the negative roles.
4. Cooperate with and be friendly to the leader and other members.
5. Listen.
6. Accept new or different ideas.
7. Do everything you can to make the meeting successful.

Leader Just as participants tend to adopt certain roles as they interact with one another, leaders do the same. Three basic approaches to leadership define the types: (1) authoritarian, (2) democrat, and (3) permissive leader.

(1) The *authoritarian* is the leader who takes a dictatorial view toward the process. The authoritarian sets the rules, procedures, tasks, roles, and evaluative criteria. He or she tells people what to do and when, where, and how to do it.

The autocrat distributes a fixed agenda prior to the meeting and allows less participation by members than possible with other leadership styles. He or she evaluates the participants and the process.

The authoritarian meeting usually produces more work than either the democratic or permissive styles. Therefore, many situations require autocratic leadership.

When time and other variables allow, avoid the authoritarian approach. It seems to engender discontent, belligerence, dependence, and blind conformity.

The autocrat fits the problem-solving construct particularly well, and often fits the educating method. However, avoid the autocratic approach for a brainstorming session. The style likely will squelch the creativity necessary for it to function.

(2) The *democrat* takes a shared-participation view toward the process.

The democrat offers alternatives, but joins with the other group members to set the rules, procedures, tasks, roles, and evaluative criteria. The democratic leader and members together decide which people will do what, when, where, how, and why. Though the democrat may distribute an agenda ahead of time, he or she invites members to contribute items to it and to amend it once the meeting begins.

The democrat encourages and facilitates participation and evaluation by the members of the group.

The democratic meeting usually produces less work than the autocratic meeting. However, choose the democratic leader over the autocratic leader when the pressures of time and other variables do not dictate the autocratic style. The democracy tends to yield better creativity, motivation, positiveness, human relations, and cohesiveness than the autocracy.

The democratic style fits all three of the methods for meetings of groups. It is particularly adaptable to brainstorming and educating.

(3) The *permissive leader* takes a noninterference view toward the process. The permissive leader serves only to supply information—and then only when asked to do so.

The leader does not join with the other group members to set any rules, procedures, tasks, roles, and evaluate criteria. Without the participation of a leader, the members decide which people will do what, when, where, how, and why.

The permissive leader supplies no agenda. The members generate their own participation and conduct any evaluation that occurs.

The permissive meeting produces the least work of all three leadership styles. In effect, the persmissive leader is a nonleader, and the leaderless group tends to struggle aimlessly through an ineffective process.

Avoid the permissive style for all three patterns for meetings of groups—especially the problem-solving method. Use the permissive style only for rare circumstances: (a) Use it when the members of the group are so symbiotic that the group functions efficiently without any leader. (b) Use it when the situation requires some seemingly directionless exploration, even to find a basis upon which to select a leader. (c) Use it only until the group establishes enough of a structure that an appropriate leader emerges. (d) Use it when no one is capable of leading.

Leaders tend to have natural or adopted styles of leadership. Therefore, a group first should identify the style needed or desired for a given situation. Then it can select or allow to emerge someone who possesses that style. Otherwise, a group's productivity may suffer.

Picture the plight of a group as it tries to deal creatively with a delicate issue under the grinding heel of an autocrat. Picture also trying to analyze data and make a critical financial decision within a 15-minute period under the full-participation bent of a democrat or the noninvolvement of a permissive leader.

One person may be able to practice all of the three styles of leadership. However, the development of such a capability takes a great deal of effort and concentration.

Evaluate your own style. Are you more nearly an autocrat, a democrat, or a nonleader? Are you satisfied with your style?

If you determine that your present style is either extremely authoritarian or extremely permissive, you may want to move toward the relatively democratic middle ground.

If you fall rather firmly in any one of the three categories, try adopting some of the traits of the others. Even a democrat can learn to be dictatorial when conditions require it. Even an autocrat can learn to relax somewhat and allow others to participate when the work would be the better for it. Even a nonleader can learn to be assertive and to take the lead from time to time when the group needs that leadership.

A composite role for the effective leader includes these activities:

1. Create a positive climate for discussion. Tend to the physical setting, timing, and other nonverbal features of the discussion. Also tend to the psychological setting by using warmth, tension-reduction devices, tact, humor, formality, and informality as needed. Stimulate participation when desired or needed.
2. Establish or lead in establishing the outline or agenda and the ground rules for the session.
3. Arrange for and select or coordinate the selection of a recorder.
4. Introduce or stimulate the introduction of the members to one another—and to the audience if the discussion is to take place before one.
5. Introduce the subject of the discussion.
6. Guide the discussion. Keep the discussion on the subject and keep it moving. Diplomatically switch the discussion from the dominant members to the reticent ones. Encourage each member to talk to all of the others, not just to you and one or two others. Raise questions that spotlight the subject, reactivate the discussion,

and seek information and clarification. Even if operating in other than the brain-storming mode, change to brainstorming when the group reaches a stalemate. Introduce role-playing if it will help the discussion.

7. Supply appropriate transitions and intermediate summaries. Periodically pause to digest just what has transpired and to move forward to what needs to follow. Conduct any needed voting or consensus-taking.

8. Control the meeting. Take charge. Block the destructive members. Observe the rules established for the meeting so long as they contribute to progress. Be responsible for handling any event that may interfere with the meeting.

9. End the discussion efficiently. Conduct final voting or consensus-taking. Evaluate the work of the group in line with preestablished criteria. Make a final summary, including the findings of the group, the results of voting, and the evaluation. Conclude with a plan for the next step—be that step the dissemination of the results, the activation of a plan, or the establishment of another meeting.

Recorder Even small groups usually need someone to record the key points and results of the discussion. The brainstorming session demands that someone capture the ideas as they emerge.

The person who makes the record may be called the recorder or the secretary. The leader or group may select someone, or someone may volunteer. The person may be a member of the group or may be an outsider brought in to free all members of the group to participate fully.

The good recorder needs to be able to write quickly, summarize well, and think, listen, organize, and write all at the same time. Because the recorder usually prepares any report to be disseminated to others, he or she needs to be a good final-message writer as well.

SPEAKING AT THE MEDIO LEVEL

The second speaking level includes oral exchanges through some intermediary instrument. The most common oral medio transactions use the telephone, the private intercommunication system, the two-way radio, or the closed-circuit television (CCTV) as the mediating instrument.

In addition, though dictating messages to a transcriber or a machine does not qualify as a full-fledged one-to-one interaction, it is speaking that involves an intermediary. Therefore, because it certainly does not qualify either as interpersonal, person-to-group, or mass communication, dictating appears in this section on the oral medio level.

The intercom, the two-way radio, and the CCTV hookup may require a bit more involvement with equipment during role exchanges than does the telephone. However, the suggestions for using all four are essentially the same.

The major difference between the interpersonal and medio levels is the loss of important nonverbal feedback. Unless the setup involves phonovision or two-way video CCTV projection, the loss of the visual feedback is total. Even with phonovision and two-way video CCTV, the visual images are reduced, restricted, and often distorted. Although the vocal/aural portion of feedback always exists in oral medio transaction, it, too, can be incomplete and distorted.

Perhaps because of the loss of the visual components, the voice carries even more feedback in these channels than in face-to-face transactions. Therefore, if the voice carries some negative cues, the focus upon vocal nonverbal elements may intensify the negativism.

For example, have you not frequently been disturbed in medio conversations by voices that scream, drone, flatten, clip, whisper, twang, blur, quiver, gargle, growl, groan, break, wheeze, whine, slur, sputter, fade, mumble, pierce, or boom? Have you not also detected from the voice alone such emotional states as impatience, boredom, irritation, condescension, servility, hostility, agitation, tension, sadness, fear, and embarrassment?

Because the voice-only exchange amplifies the vocal nonverbal elements, it can also turn positive sounds into such exaggerated ones that even they have a negative effect. Raucous laughter, joyful shrillness, extreme bounciness, undue rapidity, slurred enunciation, and even a deep resonance can be misinterpreted.

The key to the correct medio voice, then, lies in moderation. Set your voice to fluctuate mildly around the golden mean in pitch, loudness, rate, rhythm, enunciation, inflection, and resonance.

Telephone, Intercommunication, Two-Way Radio, and Closed-Circuit Television

Consider some techniques for using the telephone, intercommunication system, two-way radio, and closed-circuit television.

Telephone

A telephone conversation involves rapid turn-taking between sender and receiver. Therefore, good listening (Chapter 2) is just as important as good speaking. However, because of the unified nature of the telephone transaction, consider skills for both sender and receiver here. Additional suggestions that may apply to conference calls appear in the preceding section on small groups.

Sending When you place a telephone call, you have the advantage over the receiver. You have at least some time to apply the guidelines and principles. During the planning, transacting, and evaluating stages, then, be sure to attend to the techniques which apply to most purposive transactions.

Select and identify the telephone channel on the basis of its strengths and weaknesses compared to the other channels. Consider its speed, turn-taking, feedback, cost, and acceptability.

Know precisely why you are going to make the call. Decide what you want the receiver to do as a result of it. Establish criteria for evaluating how well the receiver meets your objectives.

Learn all you can about the specific receiver, if possible, or about the type of receiver, if not. Try to decide what the receiver's reasons might be for receiving your call and for acting as you want her or him to act.

Picture the receiver and the environment as he or she reaches for the telephone.

Identify the potential interference inherent in the telephone channel, in the subject matter, in yourself and your environment, in the receiver and the receiver's environment, and in other external entities. Then plan your communication to overcome as much of it as possible.

For the telephone channel itself, the major sources of interference arise from (a) the somewhat restricted aural nonverbal feedback, (b) the lack of visual feedback, (c) the possibilities of poor transmission causing cutoffs, garbling, or low volume, and (d) time-zone differentials.

Select the messages carefully. Jot down your ideas and make a brief outline from them. Couch your messages in language correct for the occasion and the receiver. Leave space in your outline to record the information supplied by the receiver.

Paraphrase or repeat the receiver's words to be sure you understand.

Particularly plan how you will indicate the desired action and how you will overcome interference.

To begin transmission, establish your physical and mental position—one that is relaxed, but alert to the control you plan to exercise over the transmission. Visualize your receiver. Concentrate.

As soon as anyone answers, identify yourself and ask for the ultimate receiver. When the receiver answers, identify yourself again, exchange pleasantries if appropriate, and move quickly into the topic.

Follow your outline, but be adaptable to changes the receiver introduces.

Use your moderate voice pattern—moving toward the lower pitches, if you move in either direction at all. Adopt the positive and courteous approach.

Use all of the devices necessary to introduce appropriate vocal reinforcements such as emphasis, subordination, color, variety, and cordiality.

Listen carefully. Block interference. Stimulate feedback. End the conversation appropriately.

As the caller, you take leave first. Some communicators suggest that "Bye" and "Bye-bye" are inappropriate for business conversations. However, choose your leave-taking words for naturalness and appropriateness. Avoid abruptness, but convey a courteous finality.

Use feedback. Listen not only to the words, but to the nonverbal components as well. Adjust your messages according to your interpretations of the feedback as you receive it.

Evaluate as you converse and after completion. Determine whether the receiver's action meets your original criteria and purposes.

Receiving   Follow sound techniques for meeting the responsibilities of an initial receiver.

If you are the first to answer a business telephone, answer with the firm's name, followed by yours if appropriate. Do not just say, "Hello."

If someone else receives a call and transfers it to you, treat the initial receiver courteously, but switch to the sender immediately. Do not restate the firm's name; the initial receiver has done that. If the initial receiver has told you who is calling and you know that person, you may answer with something like: "Hello, Mr. Tompkins." However, if you do not know the person, you may answer with just your name: "Doris Turner."

Use relaxed, moderate, receptive tones. Avoid the drawn tones that often come from repeating a company name or your name many times a day. Keep the enunciation and attitude fresh.

If you take calls and transfer them to others, always explain each step that you take. Do not leave the caller on "hold" too long. Return frequently to explain delays. Offer to have the ultimate receiver return the call if a delay will be long. Offer to help the caller yourself.

Begin the conversation. Whether you answer first and then transfer a call, answer for yourself, or receive a transferred call, follow your identification with a question to start the exchange. Common phrases are: "May I ask who is calling," "May I help you?," "How are you?," "What may I do for you," "How may I help you?," and "How may I be of service?" However, you may move from such virtual clichés if you find some other approach more comfortable and natural for you and the caller. You may, of course, create custom phrases for senders whom you know.

Even as you answer a call and turn the conversation back to the caller, begin applying the guidelines. As quickly as you can, define the caller and her or his purposes and background. Define your own purposes.

Aid in using the channel to its fullest; help overcome interference. Let the sender speak fully, but interject enough feedback to let her or him know that you understand. Use paraphrasing and repetition to assure that you perceive correctly.

Whether or not your actions and responses coincide with those desired by the initiator, make them clear.

Use good vocal techniques and courtesy.

Write down the things you need for accuracy and storage on a pad kept near the telephone. Read them back to assure accuracy. Evaluate the ongoing stages of the transaction and adjust to them as necessary.

Allow the caller to close the conversation. Respond in kind to the sender's leave-taking words.

Evaluate after you close.

Two-way radio

The only differences between techniques for the telephone and those for the two-way radio lie in the natures of the channels themselves.

Mobile telephones are essentially two-way radios, but the use of the instrument remains basically the same as for the telephone.

With the two-way radio as a channel, however, you will need to learn to use a microphone well. Though you should hold the speaker of a telephone about one-half inch from your mouth, the distance varies among microphones.

Depending upon whether you use FM or AM channels for your transmission, you may need to learn some of the special jargon for the two-way radio. The AM channels require some of it, but its use is minimal for the FM channels. In both situations, use as natural a conversational style as you can while meeting the customs of other users.

Closed-circuit television

The most common use of CCTV is for one-directional transmission of both picture and sound to a selected group of people. However, if the system adds the capacity for vocal return by telephone (talk-back television) or two-way projection of both visual and vocal messages, it becomes a two-way medio transaction.

With talkback television, the speaker should solicit telephone feedback and respond to it quickly and naturally when it does come. The receiver who uses the telephone for feedback usually just lifts the receiver and talks. If you ever operate in such a situation, do not be hesitant to use the telephone. It adds an important dimension to the exchange.

If you choose a two-way video/audio television channel, try to look directly at the camera as if you are looking at the receiver. Speak and move naturally within the allowable space. Take advantage of the full range of nonverbal symbols to improve the interaction.

Techniques for Dictation

Dictating is an intermediate act in a chain leading to a written message. Consider your roles as both sender and receiver of dictated messages—with emphasis upon the sending act.

Sending

Apply the guidelines. Once you select a written-message channel that uses the dictating channel as an intermediary, the guidelines become:

1. Define the intermediate receiver (the word processor); the ultimate receiver; the purposes for you, the intermediate receiver, and the ultimate receiver; and the environment for you all.
2. Understand the characteristics of the channel. If you dictate to a live word processor (transcriber), you have greater opportunity to sense immediate feedback and make immediate adjustments in the message. If you dictate to a machine, you must learn how to use it correctly—how to start, stop, make corrections, and give instructions.
3. Understand the interference that can occur between you and the word processor and between you and the ultimate receiver. Try to control both.
4. To select and encode your messages, use the principles and procedures described for writing for the specific channel (letter, memorandum, etc.), and for the telephone. Plan ahead. Jot down ideas and organize them into an outline. Think through your message before you begin to speak. Once you speak, do so clearly. Concentrate on enunciation, pronunciation, a reasonably slow pace, a normal pitch, and sufficient volume. However, maintaining appropriate rhythm and resonance can help hold the attention of the word processor. Give clear and complete instructions at the beginning of the session. Supply all necessary data. Make corrections so that once you stop dictating, the message is ready to be transcribed into final form. Eliminate rough drafts. Through the entire sequence, picture your ultimate receiver. If you dictate to a live transcriber, speak to her or him as a substitute for the ultimate receiver. If you speak into a microphone, picture both the transcriber and the ultimate receiver—and adjust to the perceived needs of both.
5. With a live word processor, watch for and adjust to feedback as you dictate. Even solicit feedback if you are comfortable with receiving it. However, when you dictate to a machine, the feedback will be delayed. The transcriber will have to telephone you or ask in person for clarification or correction. Such contacts waste a great deal of time and money—and should be prevented through good initial dictation.

6. Evaluate how well you meet the needs of the transcriber, the ultimate receiver, and you. Also evaluate the performances of all three of you. Seek to improve your performance—whatever the role you take.

Receiving

If you ever take the role of a transcriber or word processor, you, too, have the responsibility for the oral part of the process.

If you take notes in the presence of the dictator, keep your interruptions to a minimum. You may, of course, ask for clarification, but do so when the natural flow of the composition halts. Listen carefullly. Know the language of the firm for which you work.

Give subtle nonverbal feedback during the dictation. If the dictator requests more overt suggestions about the messages, feel free to give them. Also be prepared to read segments of your notes to the dictator upon request.

Interpret the dictator's nonverbal messages as well as the verbal ones. Adapt to them.

Think of your purposes, those of the dictator, and those of the ultimate receiver. Such thoughts will help you make decisions during both the dictation and the transcription.

SPEAKING AT THE PERSON-TO-GROUP LEVEL

As a person-to-group speaker, you take only a short step from the interpersonal and medio-level exchanges. Basically, all you do differently is to dominate the exchange, increase the length of time you speak, reduce or eliminate the turn-taking, speak to many instead of one or a few, and control the process. Consider a speech (presentation) to be any monologue of any length made to any group from any location relative to that group.

If you fear the concept of "making a speech," just realize that you already have made hundreds of thousands of speeches in your life. You make many of them every time you talk with someone. You have the essential experience. All you need to do to become an effective person-to-group speaker is to make some minor adjustments to what you already know how to do—speak on a one-to-one basis and in small groups.

In reality, good interpersonal and medio transactions often demand more of you than good person-to-group ones. The one-to-one exchanges force you to engage many more human and communication arts and skills at a much more rapid pace than do most person-to-group situations.

The person-to-group level also has many disadvantages compared to the interpersonal and medio levels. They relate primarily to reduced feedback and associated evaluations and adjustments. They also relate to difficulties associated with analyzing the audience.

The disadvantages do not cripple the actual encoding and transmitting, however. They relate to the loss of richness and not to what many people seem to fear most—the speaking itself.

Consider person-to-group presentations classified first by content and purpose, then by style of transmission. Then consider some suggestions for applying the communication principles and guidelines.

Types of Speeches Classified by Content and Purpose

Recall that one traditional classification of communication is done according to three purposes: (1) to inform, (2) to persuade, and (3) to entertain. That classification, of course, implies one-directional communication, rather than actions and interactions between senders and receivers.

This book uses that traditional, convenient classification for oral presentations, simply extending it to four types of speeches: (1) informing, (2) persuading, (3) performing ritual functions, and (4) entertaining.

Informing

Speakers inform when they speak to groups to convey information to them. They may volunteer the information spontaneously or give it as the result of a request. They may supply it with or without completing extensive research into an assigned or unassigned topic. They may convey it formally or informally for two minutes or two hours. They may combine informative presentations with question-and-answer sessions with larger groups. They may make the presentations, break larger bodies into small groups for discussions, and reconvene the larger groups for summaries.

Consider these instances of speaking to inform:

1. Appearing before the members of an organization to notify them of changes in the laws that have an impact on the organization's constitution
2. Announcing to the members of a staff the dates of an upcoming audit
3. Reporting to the employees in a department about a recent business trip
4. Explaining the details of a written report on a research project to the president's council
5. Instructing a group on what they should do to prepare for the impending changeover in methods of production
6. Training people to write programs for the computer
7. Lecturing on the advantages and disadvantages of union membership
8. Briefing the department heads on the events in a department during the past month
9. Conducting a press conference and beginning with a statement
10. Reading a position paper (This presentation both informs and persuades)

When speaking to inform, collect and convey accurate information.

Begin with something the listeners already know, and build from that point. Select symbols that meet the listeners' abilities.

Solicit feedback, and use evaluative techniques that let you know whether the audience actually comprehends the information.

Persuading

You speak persuasive messages with the purpose of having the receiver act or accept—vote on your motion, buy your product, accept your suggestion.

To persuade, use facts. Use logical, psychological, and personal appeals to wants and needs. Provide clear avenues for acting upon the persuasion. Add nonverbal demonstrations to your verbal presentations. Show how acting in the manner you suggest will benefit the listener or solve some problem.

Techniques for persuasive written messages appear in Chapter 11. Most of the techniques work just as well for spoken messages. The APCA formula is particularly appropriate.

To gain attention, use words and nonverbal accompaniment that catch the listener's imagination, but relate to the topic. Use the amusing, the startling, the enveloping, the unusual, the familiar, the suspenseful, the dynamic.

Move smoothly and naturally into the perception of your topic in such a way that the listener becomes curious or interested enough to continue to listen.

Then develop your persuasive comprehension/conviction arguments. Supply the facts that convince the listener that you are right.

After completing development of the comprehension/conviction segment, stimulate the listener to take the action/acceptance that you suggest in the closing statement.

These situations represent persuasive speeches:

1. A member speaks in favor of or in opposition to a motion presented at a formal meeting.
2. An executive presents a position paper designed to bring others to a point of view.
3. A superior describes a dramatic potential change in the flow of paper work in a department and urges the group to adopt it.
4. A controller talks for 20 minutes on the merits of her proposed budget and ends with a plea for immediate adoption.
5. An insurance agent assures the members of an organization that they should change to his company's medical plan. He distributes literature and application blanks.
6. A sales representative speaks about and demonstrates a piece of equipment that she urges the listener/viewer to purchase. She leaves brochures and order forms.
7. An applicant speaks to the Executive Board of the local Chamber of Commerce to persuade the members that he should be the next Executive Director.
8. A citizen makes a presentation in support of a candidate for office.
9. A worker pleads her case before a grievance board and urges them to decide in her favor.
10. A manager praises the work of a social organization and asks for contributions to its work.
11. A department head gives a "pep talk" to the staff of a department whose sales are down.

Performing ritual functions

Business communicators often speak before groups to perform certain rites. Consider several such situations:

1. Introducing the speaker at a professional organization's annual awards banquet
2. Praising the qualities of the members who receive an organization's award of merit

3. Presenting the company's annual contribution to the local university's scholarship fund
4. Paying tribute to retiring employees at the annual retirement dinner
5. Describing the accomplishments of the Citizen of the Year and the Teacher of the Year and presenting plaques to them
6. Making a speech of acceptance for an award
7. Giving a eulogy at a funeral
8. Giving the welcoming speech to a group of visiting high-school students
9. Giving a welcome-to-the-city speech for the opening session of the annual national convention of a professional organization being held at a local hotel
10. Making the farewell speech to a long-time employee who is being transferred to another district
11. Giving the invocation and benediction for the spring dinner of a civic organization
12. Paying tribute at an inaugural ceremony

The kinds of rituals just described have traditional formats. However, still try to make them fresh. Think of the specific person about whom you speak. Think about your relationship to that person. Think about the audience to which you make the presentation. Find some original, creative way to tie the three together.

Match the presentation to the occasion. Avoid giddy, gushing, and overstated speeches. Instead, create a tone of sincerity and warmth. Offer honest praise. Concentrate upon the positive accomplishments of the honored person. However, you may want to acknowledge some small human foibles in a positive or humorous way.

Keep ceremonial presentations brief. However, make them dynamic. Apply the techniques for colorful, attention-getting messages.

Be sure to present accurate facts. Pronounce the name of the honored person correctly. Explain not only the accomplishments of the person, but the characteristics of any award or honor being bestowed.

When you introduce a speaker, present a brief sketch of the speaker and her or his background. However, also use your message to gain the attention of the audience and to merge the introduction into the speaker's topic. You then become a contributor to the development of the attention phase of the speaker's message.

For invocations and benedictions, respect the makeup of your audience. Such respect means that you usually need to use words that are neutral in terms of religious preference and gender of the deity. You may even suggest that those present meditate silently in their own way for a few moments. At the end of the silence, you might offer a neutral, but uplifting closing.

Write a ceremonial speech completely. However, practice it to the point that all you need is a note card containing a brief outline for the actual presentation.

Entertaining

Sometimes an entire speech has a core purpose of entertaining the listeners. At other times, entertaining messages serve as means for gaining attention or breaking tension within a speech for another purpose. Both require a special style.

Perhaps less can be done to help people learn an entertaining style than to teach them any other. However, everyone can develop some skills in this realm.

Entertainment   First, realize that the word "entertainment" includes much more than humor. Consider an entertaining piece to be one that:

Interests	Calms	Beguiles
Arouses curiosity	Excites	Creates enjoyment
Diverts	Brings pleased	Creates a pleasant
Takes away care	expressions, smiles,	state of mind
Amuses	chuckles, laughs, or	Agreeably occupies
	bemused groans	Holds attention

Business speakers usually limit the types of entertainment to humor, personal anecdotes, human experiences or foibles, suspense stories, unusual twists to ordinary happenings, and vivid descriptions. Above all, they create mental pictures that will hold audiences.

Drollery, witty sayings, jokes, puns, satire, irony, sarcasm, and ridicule fall into the realm of humor. However, as a business speaker, avoid the last two categories. If you attempt too much sarcasm and ridicule, your audience likely will become embarrassed, uncomfortable, and offended.

Humor   Avoid humor that disparages individual people or classes of people on the basis of nationality, race, ethnicity, sex, age, mental or educational level, geographic location, handicaps, or other stereotypes. While some few professional comedians can use such materials to hilarious effect, the risk is far too great for most speakers. Avoid "sick" jokes—or anything in bad taste.

Avoid the hackneyed, mechanical, "stock" joke. Also avoid telling a joke just because you think all speakers should tell jokes—at least at the beginning of every speech. Unless you can find a joke that naturally fits your subject, and unless you can tell it well, use some other entertaining or attention-getting device. Otherwise, you will appear clumsy and artificial.

Principles and guidelines   Apply the principles and guidelines for developing entertaining messages just as carefully as you do for developing any other type.

Be particularly careful to define your audience and your own capabilities. Set your objectives to reflect whether you want to receive only a sense of pleasant acceptance, flickers of smiles, polite laughter, or loud guffaws.

Also recognize how human-based interference is a serious factor affecting entertainment—particularly humorous entertainment. Obtaining a laugh from a resistant audience can be quite a difficult task.

Select, encode, and deliver entertaining messages to recognize the features of your audience. The inductive developmental style seems to be most appropriate for them. Use both verbal elements and nonverbal devices (good timing, in particular) to create the greatest impact in your transmission.

As you plan an entertaining opening for a speech with some other major purpose, be sure that the opening is brief and focused, relevant to the theme, and appropriate to the tastes of the audience. Practice it before a few people.

Use feedback from the audience wisely. If your material is not working, shift it. You may decide to skip some material you had planned simply because the audience does not respond favorably to some earlier material. On the other hand, you may find an audience warming to you so well that you will be able to create new enteraining messages on the spot.

Evaluate entertaining attempts just as you do others.

Types of Speeches Classified by Style of Transmission

Consider styles of transmission of person-to-group presentations in five major categories. They are: (1) written, (2) memorized, (3) extemporaneous, (4) impromptu, and (5) round-table.

Written

A speech transmitted from a written manuscript is not really speaking; it is reading. Therefore, avoid it. Use it if you must convey highly technical or formal information. Use it for direct quotations from the works of others. Use it if you must provide a copy of the presentation for publication or release to the media.

The oral presentation of a manuscript seriously limits your ability to (1) exhibit a natural style, (2) maintain eye contact, (3) observe and evaluate feedback, and (4) adjust the messages. Thus, the style effectively destroys most of the value of an oral presentation over a written one.

Never use the written style just out of fear of facing an audience, of forgetting the material, or of encoding messages improperly. You can overcome that fear through practice and experience, but not by hiding behind the written speech. Even if you do omit something or even construct a few clumsy sentences, the advantages of the contact with the audience far outweigh the disadvantages of such errors.

If the formality or technicality of an occasion demands the use of the manuscript, observe these important procedures:

1. Apply all the guidelines.
2. Write the speech according to sound writing principles, but stop short of putting it in final typewritten form.
3. Revise by reading the written speech aloud sentence by sentence and making adjustments necessary to convert a readable piece into a speakable piece.
4. Type the revised manuscript in double- or triple-spaced, wide-margined form on only one side of the paper, possibly all in capital letters.
5. Practice reading aloud at least three or four times before a videotape camera, friends, or a mirror. Analyze and improve delivery, eye contact, and other nonverbal transmissions each time.
6. Mark the points of some of your important pauses, phrases, emphases, and other nonverbal cues directly on the manuscript. Practice two or three more times.
7. When you appear before the audience, apply all of the suggestions for good verbal and nonverbal presentations.

Memorized

The memorized speech may lead to the poorest delivery of all.

Memorizing a presentation may seem to offer the opportunity for more eye contact than reading from a manuscript. However, the opportunity is often lost, or is offset by other problems. The speaker must concentrate so completely upon recalling the memorized material that he or she does not have the added capacity to make the contact and to observe, evaluate, and adjust to the feedback.

Additional flaws exist in the memorized-speech transmission. They include (1) the difficulty of memorizing more than a few paragraphs, (2) the possibility of forgetting material during the speech, (3) the difficulty of presenting a memorized speech in a nonmechanical manner.

Unless you have the rare talents to overcome the hazards inherent in the memorized-speech form of delivery, do not try it. Turn to the extemporaneous speech unless conditions require the manuscript type.

Extemporaneous

Choose the extemporaneous style over all of the others when you can do so appropriately. An extemporaneous delivery has the advantages of preparation, naturalness, flexibility, spontaneity, and full interaction with the audience.

Consider these suggestions for developing an extemporaneous speech:

1. Apply all of the guidelines.
2. Develop the speech by first writing and revising an outline. You may write a few key sentences—and perhaps the opening and the closing. However, do not write the sentences and paragraphs that complete the written message.
3. Place the outline or key words and phrases, possibly all in capital letters, on only one side of note cards. Leave plenty of space around and between lines.
4. Using the note cards only when necessary, practice speaking aloud several times before a videotape camera, friends, or a mirror. Analyze and improve delivery, sentence construction, eye contact, and other nonverbal transmissions each time.
5. Avoid practicing so much that you virtually set and memorize a fixed pattern of words. Practice only until you have enough experience to know that you will be able to say what you want to say in a coherent but spontaneous manner.
6. When you appear before the audience, apply all of the suggestions for good verbal and nonverbal presentations.

Impromptu

The impromptu speech is done on the spur of the moment, with little or no time for preparation. The speaker must apply the guidelines even as he or she speaks. Obviously, the reduced chances for analyzing the audience, organizing, encoding, and revising can lead to a weak presentation.

Avoid the impromptu speech when you can. However, when you must deliver one, use these suggestions:

1. The moment you have even a hint that you may be asked to speak, begin to apply the guidelines, even as you begin to walk or turn to face the audience.
2. Because the situation requiring the impromptu style usually occurs when you are already in session with a known group with a known general topic and purpose, move your planning directly to your specific topic and objectives. Write them on paper if you have the seconds necessary to do so.
3. Quickly decide on your key points. If you have a few extra seconds, jot them on paper.
4. When you face the audience, take a few seconds to form the first words silently before speaking them.
5. Listen to yourself as you speak. Watch for feedback to help you know when you need to repeat or clarify.

6. Restate your central theme if necessary to assure clarity.
7. Speak briefly, and conclude firmly.
8. If appropriate, ask if the group has questions about your presentation.

Round-table

Though the round-table discussion is not a delivery type absolutely distinct from the first four, it is sufficiently different to warrant this special treatment. Other names for and variations of the round-table discussion are the forum, panel, symposium, group discussion, lecture-discussion, film-discussion, debate, public dialogue, and public interview.

All the forms place groups of speakers before an audience. In addition, each has somewhat rigidly defined characteristics and rules of conduct. However, certain characteristics and rules are common to many of the types.

Features

Some of the features shared by most of the types include:

1. The participants sit or stand facing the audience, sometimes in a semicircle so that they also face each other.
2. A neutral moderator coordinates and controls the activities of the presentation.
3. Time limits control the stages of the presentation.
4. Each participant prepares at least a brief statement for delivery at the beginning of the presentation. The delivery may involve written, memorized, or extemporaneous techniques.
5. Each participant responds in an impromptu manner to the other participants' statements, to questions directed to her or him by the moderator, and/or to questions written or spoken by members of the audience.
6. Each participant makes a final statement.

The round-table presentation has the advantage of offering a variety of personalities and viewpoints to the audience. Thus, it may hold attention better than a single speaker. However, a major disadvantage is that the speakers rarely have enough time to develop their ideas fully. Audiences often feel cheated even if the session is longer than in a single-speaker setting.

To be a good member of a round-table group, combine the arts and skills applicable to extemporaneous, impromptu, and small-group speaking. Also apply the listening and other transactional techniques appropriate to small-group transactions. In addition, learn to interact with the other participants in the forum at the same time that you interact with the larger audience.

Suggestions for Making Good Speeches

Many techniques for effective speech-making appear throughout this section. However, review some of the key suggestions already made and learn a few new ones.

Place yourself in a position that faces the largest possible number of people in the audience.

Sweep the entire audience as you make eye contact. Make an extra effort to include the people who sit at the extreme right and left ends of wide rows near you.

The natural tendency is to make contact with a triangular or wedge-shaped group, with the narrowest point closest to you.

Avoid locking eyes with individual members of the audience. Brush past the eyes or look a little above them, and move on. Such a motion gives the impression of meeting them, yet does not distract you or the other person. You still will observe the general nonverbal signals of the audience well enough to evaluate and change your strategy if necessary.

Avoid turning for security to the most supportive of the nonverbal senders. Continue to include everyone in your sweeps.

If you move into a question-and-answer period and someone asks you a direct question, you may fix most of your response on that person. Even in such situations, however, still occasionally move your attention out to the others in the transaction.

Relax. You are a competent person or you would not be speaking. The audience likely will be with you. The people generally are friendly or neutral, not antagonistic.

For the written, memorized, and extemporaneous speeches, the best deterrent to stage fright is careful preparation and practice. Know your material, and know how to present it.

For the impromptu speech, you probably know your material; otherwise you would not volunteer or be asked to present it. Because it is an impromptu speech, the rules of evaluation are not as strict—whether you make the evaluation or another does.

Simply apply the suggestions for the impromptu speech, do the best you can under the circumstances, evaluate, decide how you might do better the next time, and forget it. Everyone in the audience has been in the same situation at one time or another—and understands it.

Observe the audience carefully. Evaluate all the feedback you receive—even if it seems to be negative. Adjust your presentation as much as you can to overcome any negative feedback. Continue to do what you had planned to do, making whatever small changes you can.

Avoid overemphasizing negative feedback, though. Oftentimes, what you read as negativity may be nothing more than neutrality or preoccupation. Even the most dynamic of speakers cannot hold the attention of everyone in the audience all of the time. Accept your losses for what they are and continue to speak confidently to those whom you do seem to be reaching.

Use appropriate nonverbal accompaniments. Avoid using those that distract.

Try stepping away from the speaker's stand. The first step away from the security of the speaker's stand can seem to be several yards long. However, once you taste success, the move becomes easier.

Use natural motions and gestures. Avoid tentative, off-rhythm, mechanical gestures; you would be better off not to gesture at all.

Stand or sit relatively erect, but occupy enough space to display appropriate confidence. Avoid shifting and shuffling on your feet and propping a foot on the base of the speaker's stand. Avoid plunging your hands in and out of pockets. Avoid rustling papers. Avoid twiddling with your hair, ears, or anything else; avoid rocking or swaying; control any other distracting motion.

Let your face come alive with pleasant, facile expressions, but avoid a false, Cheshire-cat smile. Women, some minorities, and some other people conditioned into lowered status tend to smile more frequently than conditioned high-status people. Therefore, they need to avoid the too-smiling appearance of fear and subservience. On the other hand, conditioned high-status people—often white males—need to be sure that their facial expressions do not offend by communicating an undesirable air of condescension and superiority.

Establish a moderate-to-low voice pattern for pitch, rate, and resonance. You may want to exaggerate enunciation, pronunciation, and rhythm somewhat—particularly for a large audience. Avoid the vocal segregates, and use the vocal differentiators guardedly.

Speak loudly enough to reach the persons sitting in the back row. You may even want to do a perception check by frankly asking those at the back of the room whether they can hear you.

If the room is so large that you must use a microphone, try to experiment with it prior to your speech. If you cannot, watch others ahead of you to learn proper distance for clarity of voice, how to change its position, and other features. Try not to allow the microphone to create a barrier between you and your audience.

If a fixed microphone is not sensitive, you may have to give up some of your nonverbal movements away from the speaker's stand. A voice that fades in and out can be quite disconcerting to an audience.

Even if you can hold the microphone in your hand or clasp it around your neck, you may not want to do so. Unless you have practiced with a portable microphone, you may feel uncertain about removing it from the stand or putting it back on, if not actually using it.

If you use audiovisual equipment, be sure it is in good working order. Have someone assist you with it unless it is simple to use and placed so that you can maintain contact as you operate it. Whether you or someone else operates it, practice the aids as you practice your presentation.

While referring to audiovisual presentations, keep eye contact with your audience. Do not speak as you face a chalkboard, screen, poster, flip chart, or other such visual aids.

With such visual aids, face the audience as you speak, turning between sentences just long enough to write or point to an item with a long pointer.

For the overhead projector, face the audience while you or another point to the transparency on the projector. Do not turn around to point to the screen. The opaque projector also has a pointer that allows the speaker to remain in contact with the audience.

Choose the correct style of transmission to fit the occasion, the content and purposes of the speech, and your abilities. You certainly would not choose the written speech for a greeting to a group of teenagers gathered for a pep rally. On the other hand, you would not choose the impromptu speech for presenting a research paper to a group of your peers at a convention.

Observe time limits set by the occasion. For most situations you know ahead of time what the limits will be. Prepare and practice the speech accordingly. Be particularly careful not to leave so much material in the presentation that you have to speak too rapidly.

Avoid saying "Thank you" at the end of the speech before the audience applauds. Find a means to close the speech so that the audience knows that the time for applause has arrived. On the other hand, take care not to leave the impression that you have come to the end before you actually have.

SPEAKING AT THE MASS LEVEL

 The major oral channels at the mass level are radio, television, and films. Business communicators sometimes speak on radio or television, but not often on movie film.

Many books and entire courses of study deal with the development of professional radio, television, and film skills. Therefore, the suggestions made in this book form only a minimal set for the nonprofessional person who rarely uses mass channels.

Television and Film

A nonprofessional on television—whether taped or live—or on film, usually appears in one of four modes. The four are the interview, the informative statement, the round-table discussion, and the speech. The basic characteristics, arts, and skills for the four modes essentially extend to their application to the mass media. However, some special suggestions may help make the application smooth:

(1) If a photographer tapes or films an appearance before a live audience, pretend he or she is not even there. Of course, perform at your peak, but do not look at the camera or acknowledge the photographer's presence in any way. Continue with your speech as you would if the camera were not there.

(2) If you make a statement or speech specifically for mass transmission, treat the camera as your audience. Maintain eye contact with it.

Restrict nonverbal messages to camera range. For example, you usually cannot move across a platform or into an audience as you might for a standard situation.

You may not even have a speaker's stand upon which to place notes. In such a situation, speak extemporaneously without them.

(3) If you appear as a panel member or interviewee, again pretend that the camera is not present. Talk to the moderator, another panel member, or the interviewer in a natural manner. Never adjust your position to look into the camera. If the camera operator shifts to pick up a direct shot of your face, still do not look at the camera. Continue to talk to the person as if the camera were not there. Try not to use note cards—and certainly not full-sized pages as you make such appearances. Speak extemporaneously from a memorized outline or use your impromptu skills well.

(4) Because you usually have much less time for a mass-media appearance than for a standard one, establish the key points you want to make. If the appearance involves an interview on a "talk show" or some other program, try to suggest or learn what questions might be asked. If you cannot (and you usually cannot), anticipate what they might be, and practice your answers.

(5) Dress professionally. Arrive at the suggested time. If appropriate, thank the interviewer, moderator, or director for the opportunity to appear—both on and off the air. Let the professionals control the appearance. They likely will talk with you briefly just before you move before the cameras. Learn as much as you can from that brief contact. Relax. Treat the transaction as naturally as possible. Be as formal or informal as the occasion requires.

(6) Apply the principles and guidelines. As you analyze the audience, you will realize that it includes a large number of people representing a wide variety of demographic factors. Therefore, keep your language at the lower range of educa-

tional ability. Avoid anything shocking or sarcastic. Adopt a middle-ground approach to your presentation; otherwise, you may offend or speak over the heads of some members of the audience. You usually will have no feedback from the larger audience, so you must trust your own abilities to assess what their reactions might be.

Radio

The radio appearance is a mediated experience similar to that before television or movie cameras, except that the visual components are missing. Therefore, place all of the weight of the presentation upon spoken words and nonverbal vocal qualities.

You still will have someone in the studio or on the other side of the microphone with whom to interact. Therefore, most suggestions for television and film also apply basically to radio appearances. Just think how best to employ them with microphones without cameras.

Again, the key to a good radio appearance lies in your ability to picture an audience and to speak naturally as if you were in their presence. Approach and complete the interview, panel, statement, or speech in a prepared and confident manner.

(703 words)
(test on page 539)

SUMMARY

The six communication guidelines for speaking are:

1. Define purposes, participants, and environment.
2. Select speaking channel.
3. Control interference.
4. Select, encode, sometimes write, and speak messages in light of purposes, participants, environment, channel, and interference.
5. Use feedback.
6. Evaluate.

Four channels—conversations, dialogues, interviews, and small groups—are the most used interpersonal channels.

Conversations are generally unstructured, informal, and slightly purposive. Conversations may not relate directly to business, but nonetheless contribute to smooth business functioning.

Dialogues are conversations with a purpose. Here the conversation is relatively structured and formal.

The *interview* is a special type of dialogue involving purposes such as appraising an applicant for a job or disseminating information to the media.

In the *directive interview*, the interviewer commands the transaction. In the *nondirective interview*, both parties are equally responsible for lending direction to the interview. The *stress interviewer* uses emotion-laden questions to determine how well the interviewee handles stress. The *depth interview* involves a directive probe into the topic.

As the interviewer, try to make the interviewee comfortable, tell her or him what your purposes are, and ask what he or she would like to accomplish. As an interviewee, prepare for the meeting just as fully as the interviewer.

Small groups include four to ten people. The more people, the more complicated the communication interaction is. Small groups usually meet for some well-defined purpose.

Problem-solving, educating, brainstorming, and *role-playing* are the four basic methods for conducting group meetings. You will serve basically in three roles—participant, leader, and recorder—in the groups in which you work.

As a *participant,* you take three broad types of roles: (1) *task-oriented roles,* (2) *process-oriented roles,* and (3) *destructive roles.* As a leader in a group, you can act as an *authoritarian leader, democratic leader,* or *permissive leader.* As the *recorder,* you must be able to write quickly, summarize well, and think, listen, organize, and write all at the same time.

The second speaking level, the medio level, often involves the use of the *telephone,* the *private intercommunication system,* the *two-way radio, closed-circuit television,* or *dictation* for word processing.

The major difference between the interpersonal and medio levels is the loss of important nonverbal feedback.

The *person-to-group level* has both advantages and disadvantages. However, it holds nothing to fear.

Four types of purposes for speeches exist: (1) to inform, (2) to persuade, (3) to perform ritual functions, and (4) to entertain. You *inform* when you speak to groups to convey information to them. You attempt to *persuade* when you develop your message with the purpose of having the receiver engage in the desired action/acceptance. You *perform ritual functions* when you do such things as introduce the speaker at an annual awards banquet or give the invocation or benediction for the spring dinner of a civic organization. When you seek to *entertain,* you may make an entire speech with the central purpose of entertaining your listeners, or you may use entertaining touches as a means for gaining attention or breaking tension during a speech for another purpose.

Person-to-group presentations fall into five categories defined by styles of transmission: (1) written, (2) memorized, (3) extemporaneous, (4) impromptu, and (5) round-table.

Try to avoid making a speech straight from a *written manuscript.* You will not be speaking; you will be reading aloud. When you cannot avoid speaking from a manuscript, make the presentation as seemingly extemporaneous as possible.

The *memorized* speech may lead to the poorest delivery of all. The speaker must concentrate so completely on the memorized material that he or she does not have the added capacity to make eye contact and to observe, evaluate, and adjust to the feedback.

The *extemporaneous* style of speaking is usually the best. The extemporaneous delivery has the advantages of preparation, naturalness, flexibility, spontaneity, and full interaction with the audience.

The *impromptu* speech allows little or no time for preparation, and forces the speaker to apply the communication guidelines even as he or she speaks.

The fifth style of transmission is the *round-table* speech. Other names include the panel, symposium, group discussion, lecture-discussion, and forum. All forms place groups of speakers before an audience. Each has defined characteristics and rules of conduct.

Suggestions for making good speeches include:

1. Place yourself in a position that faces the largest possible number of people in the audience.
2. Sweep the entire audience as you make eye contact.
3. Avoid locking eyes with individual members of the audience.
4. Relax.
5. Observe the audience carefully.
6. Use appropriate nonverbal accompaniments.
7. If you use audiovisual equipment, be sure it is in good working order.
8. Choose the correct style of transmission to fit the occasion, the content and purposes of your speech, and your abilities.
9. Observe time limits set by the occasion.
10. Wait to say "Thank you" at the end of the speech until the audience applauds.

When you speak at the mass level, know the special communication arts and skills associated with the major mass channels such as *radio, television,* and *film.*

Practice

1. [*Your professor will time the written part of this exercise.*] Prepare a three- or four-minute speech on vocal segregates (page 57). In the speech, define vocal segregates, give some examples, and explain why they are not necessary. Put the main points of your speech on cards. Practice the speech in front of a mirror. Now, meet with your group. You and each other group member stand and give the speech. Evaluate each of the speeches. Have one of your group members give her or his speech to the rest of the class.
2. Meet with your group. Choose four people to read this short play.

> *Dale:* I don't understand why we have to meet now. I have a lot of work to do.
> *Chris:* Well we have to decide whether or not to bid on the Warner contract this week, you know.
> *Lane:* We never get anywhere in these meetings.
> *Lou:* If we'd just . . .
> (*Dale interrupts.*)
> *Dale:* We don't get any help from management.
> *Lane:* Yeah. Did you hear that they fired old Rankin? They're trying to get rid of all of the good people.
> *Chris:* You're right. Lorner will be the next one to get canned.
> *Lou:* Probably. Listen, we'd better get back to the contract.
> *Lane:* Sure, Lou. But I don't think we have enough information to make a decision yet.
> *Lou:* Oldfield gave us this assignment six weeks ago!
> *Dale:* I'll bet he's the one who fired Rankin.
> (*Lou sighs.*)
>
> THE END

Discuss these questions as a group:
  a. What went wrong with Dale, Chris, Lane, and Lou's meeting?
  b. What could they have done to make the meeting more productive?
  c. How would you respond to Dale's "We don't get any help from management" statement?
  d. Is Lane's "lack of information" a valid excuse for not discussing the contract?
  e. Have you ever participated in a similar discussion? What, if anything, did you do to try to make it more productive?
  f. Was Dale, Chris, Lane, and Lou's meeting to have been a meeting to solve a problem, educate, or brainstorm?

3. Decide what role each of these people is taking.
  a. Ruth suggests a name for the potato chips your company is introducing.
  b. Ray politely asks the other group members to refrain from talking so that Nora can speak.
  c. Al says that Mona does not know what she is talking about.
  d. Liz always says "I believe that this is right" instead of "You are wrong" when expressing an opinion.
  e. Leonard says "Hey, this isn't *that* important" when Sheila and Stan begin a verbal battle over an issue.
  f. Leona suggets a script for the meeting.
  g. James says that he cannot work around women because he likes to look at them, thus he's distracted by them.
  h. Joanne says that labor unions are the problem, regardless of the issue.
  i. Harvey has an opinion on every subject. Some don't make much sense.
  j. Lisa listens intently to what other group members say and offers suggestions when people differ on an issue.
  k. Ron is an engineer. He provides technical information during meetings.
  l. Cathy makes lots of jokes. That's about all that she does.

4. Many communication and management specialists believe that authoritarian leadership is not appropriate in *any* business situation. Support or refute.

5. Exchange phone numbers with another class member. Call her or him and then have your partner call you to explain the important elements of making an entertaining speech or a speech punctuated with humourous anecdotes. When you initiate the call, evaluate yourself as a sender and your classmate as a receiver. Your classmate should also evaluate you as a sender and herself or himself as a receiver. Both of you should answer these questions:
  a. Did the sender know precisely why he or she was making the call?
  b. Did the sender make clear at the outset why he or she was calling and tell you his or her name?
  c. Did the sender speak clearly and at an appropriate volume?
  d. Was the sender's message well organized and concise?
  e. Did the sender solicit your comments during the call?
  f. Did you feel that the call was satisfactory in general? Why?
  g. What could have been done to make the call more productive?

6. Write one- or two-paragraph examples of each of the types of speeches (informing, persuading, performing ritual functions, and entertaining).

7. Meet with your group. Choose one group member to serve as the recorder. For a few minutes, discuss ways to best conduct problem-solving meetings. Now ask the recorder to read what he or she has written. Is the record of the meeting correct and complete? Choose another recorder and continue the discussion. Have the new recorder read her or his notes. Repeat the process until everyone in the group has served as the recorder.

8. Meet with your group. Your task is to hold a brainstorming session so that you can begin to write an informative, entertaining speech on the subject of different approaches to leadership. (Do not limit yourself to the three basic approaches listed in the book.) Pretend that one of you will give the speech at a meeting of the local Rotary Club. Do not write the speech. Just have a no-holds-barred idea session. Commit all of your ideas to paper, and have one group member read your ideas to the class.

9. Develop a five-minute extemporaneous speech on a business or economic topic of your choice, possibly the topic you chose for Exercise No. 6. Make the speech to inform, persuade, or entertain. Deliver the speech to the entire class or to your group—as your professor prescribes. Each member of the audience will complete an anonymous evaluation form in summary of your performance. You will get to see the completed forms. In addition, the group will discuss your performance with you orally.

10. Your professor will read a brief sketch of a case to the entire class. S/he will then ask for volunteers for or make assignments of the described roles to several in the group. The role-players will play the scene. Following the scene, the group at large will evaluate the solution of the case and the contributiveness or destructiveness of each of the roles.

11. Meet in groups of three. Take the roles of interviewer, interviewee, and observer. For just a few minutes simulate an interview between a supervisor and an employee about an alleged misuse of the expense-account privilege by the employee as the observer looks on. After the simulation, have the observer offer constructive criticism about the performances of both parties—paying attention to both the verbal and nonverbal aspects of the transaction. Change roles and repeat the process. Repeat one more time so that all three play all three roles. Convene the entire class and have one member of each three-member group summarize the findings of that group.

12. Your professor will assign a topic and lay down ground rules for a panel discussion to be conducted during a class meeting. Each member will prepare to be a member of the panel. On the day of the panel discussion, the professor will use a random method to select five members to serve on the panel, with the remainder of the class acting as audience/evaluators. Following the panel presentation the panel will interact with the audience in a question-and-answer period. Following the Q-and-A session, the entire class will engage in written and oral evaluations of the process.

13. Meet with your group. Role-play some randomly chosen leader and participant roles. To accomplish the randomization, first write the names of the types of leaders (authoritarian, democrat, and permissive leader) on three slips of paper, fold them, and place them in a container. Draw one and without looking at it, lay it aside. Then write the names of the 11 task-oriented participant roles on slips of paper and place them in a container. Draw a number of slips equal to about one-third of the size of your group. Lay the slip(s) with the one for leadership style. Repeat the process for the 7 process-oriented roles and then with the 8 destructive roles. (Draw only enough additional slips to bring the total of the selected slips to equal the number in your group and to contain at least one destructive role.) Then draw from the selected slips so that each member has one. Do not tell each other which role you drew. Take a few minutes to review the descriptions of your roles and to plan how you will play them. Reconvene. Have each person play her or his role during a five- to ten-minute simulation of a meeting to deal with this case:

> Absenteeism, tardiness, and lengthy coffee breaks and lunch hours have all increased among the workers this quarter. Your purpose is to find a way to overcome the problem without losing the goodwill and productiveness of the workers.

At the end of the simulation, try to identify which role each person played. (Each participant will either confirm the group's decision or name the role if not identified properly.) Evaluate the success of the meeting according to the contribution of (a) leadership style and (b) mixture of task-oriented, process-oriented, and destructive roles involved. If time allows, eliminate the roles used for the first simulation and repeat the process using the remaining roles.

14. Use your dictionary and thesaurus to create meanings for these words. Use the words when you think, write, and speak so that you feel comfortable using them.

a. Aural	**i.** Monologue
b. Bent (as noun)	**j.** Precede
c. Cohesive	**k.** Principal
d. Consensus	**l.** Principle
e. Eclectic	**m.** Purposive
f. Enliven	**n.** Spontaneity
g. Foible	**o.** Stalemate
h. Intermediary	**p.** Symbiotic

15. Take and score Self-Test 34 over the excerpt about speaking at the mass level.

Self-Test 34
Excerpt About Speaking at the Mass Level

A. Recall (33 points each). For each multiple-choice question, select the most accurate answer:

  1. If you make a statement or speech specifically for television, you should:
    a. Try not to look into the camera
    b. Read straight from your manuscript
    c. Treat the camera as your audience and maintain eye contact with it
    d. Always speak without notes
    e. Dress in bright colors and patterns

  2. The key to a good radio or television appearance is to:
    a. Picture your audience and speak naturally as if you were in their presence
    b. Avoid sounding the least bit frightened
    c. Have complete control over the technical side of the program
    d. Refrain from practicing beforehand so that your answers will be honest
    e. Avoid all controversial subjects

B. Inference (34 points). Indicate whether this statement is true or false.

When you appear on a television or radio program, you would do well to concentrate more on what you are saying than on trying to look and sound like a professional television or radio personality

---

Solution to Self-Test 34
Excerpt about Speaking at the Mass Level

A. Recall (33 points each)   **B.** Inference (34 points)

  1. c   **2.** a   True

---

16. Take and score Self-Test 35 over Chapter 15.

Self-Test 35
Chapter 15

A. Recall (25 points each). For each multiple-choice question, select the most accurate answer.

1. Which of these is *not* a true statement?
   a. You spend a great deal of your business life engaged in informal conversation.
   b. The stress interview is used to determine how well a person can handle emotion-laden and leading questions.
   c. As an interviewer, you should tell the interviewee what your purposes are for the interview.
   d. If you do not know much about the person who will interview you, you can do little to prepare for the interview.
   e. The nondirective interview requires joint responsibilities for both parties.

2. In a brainstorming meeting you want to avoid:
   a. Stating and recording the ideas as quickly as possible
   b. Allowing each group member to take an active part in the meeting
   c. Evaluating and criticizing the contributions of another person
   d. Offering too many ideas
   e. Such methods as role-playing

3. When you speak to persuade, you do *not:*
   a. Use logical, psychological, and personal appeals to wants and needs
   b. Provide clear avenues for acting upon the persuasion
   c. Show how acting as you suggest will benefit the actor or solve some problem
   d. Usually use the inductive method of development
   e. Try to stimulate the listener to take an action that you suggest in your closing statements

B. Inference (25 points). Indicate whether this statement is true or false.

A meeting cannot be successful without a leader.

Solution to Self-Test 35
Chapter 15

A. Recall (25 points each)		B. Inference (25 points)
1. d	**3.** d	False
2. c		

16

Sending Through Nonverbal Channels: Graphic Displays

Chapter 3 provides a general introduction to both the sending and receiving components of nonverbal communication, with emphasis on the personal components. This chapter on nonverbal sending concentrates upon sending nonpersonal nonverbal messages to accompany written and oral presentations.

Before turning to the two categories, however, consider the application of the specific guidelines to nonverbal sending.

GUIDELINES FOR SENDING NONVERBAL MESSAGES

These guidelines can greatly aid nonverbal sending:

1. Define your purposes for sending the nonverbal messages, the receiver's purposes for receiving the nonverbal messages, yourself, the receiver, and the environment.
2. Identify the nonverbal channel.
3. Control the interference internal and external to you and the receiver.
4. Select, encode, and transmit the nonverbal messages in light of the purposes, the participants, the environment, the channel, and the interference.
5. Use feedback from and to the receiver.
6. Evaluate at each stage.

DEVELOPING NONVERBAL MESSAGES
TO ACCOMPANY WRITTEN MESSAGES

Nonverbal messages often accompany written ones. Such messages include photographs, sketches, drawings, maps, blueprints, graphs, and tables. In addition, the stationery, format, envelopes, materials, colors, and the quality of the presentation carry nonverbal messages.

You studied many of the latter type of nonverbal contributions to written messages in the chapters on letters, memoranda, forms, and reports. Therefore, in this section, consider tables, graphs, and other illustrations.

Tables

Tables make excellent vehicles for presenting quantitative data or combinations of quantitative and qualitative data. Each type serves an important purpose.

In some ways, tables do not fit the definition of nonverbal messages. They involve only rows and columns of figures and words, rather than any elaborate nonverbal graphic techniques. However, because the table appears as a traditional design that does not follow a narrative pattern, it can safely be classified as a nonverbal channel.

Tables present information more accurately than graphs do. They include precise figures rather than pictorial representations of rounded estimates of them.

Types of tables

Two basic types of tables exist. They are the repository table and the analytical table.

Repository table   Repository tables simply store descriptive information in a form available for general use. Repository tables usually contain information collected by the person who puts it in the original form in which it appears. Therefore, repository tables usually contain *primary* data.

International, national, state, and local governments collect large amounts of the kinds of data that fill repository tables. Such data simply describe the observed universe in a simple summary of raw data. They do not attempt to move beyond that summary into any sort of analysis.

Governmental agencies usually disseminate their repository tables for the consumption of the general public. However, private entities also create repository tables available to rather narrowly defined groups. For example, each business firm regularly creates and stores records that serve as repositories of data for the firm. Staff members periodically draw from such repositories to perform the decision-making analyses necessary for meeting the ongoing purposes of the firm.

Figure 16–1 includes a repository table of information collected and reported by an agency of the United States government. Once the table is transferred from the original source, the information becomes *secondary*. It no longer appears in the exact form created by the original collectors.

Analytical table   An analytical table results from some sort of analysis performed upon the raw or organized data. The analysis may involve primary or secondary data. It may derive from repository tables or from the original, crude list of raw data collected by the analyst or by someone else.

Table 1. Employment status of the civilian noninstitutional population, January and July 1977

(Thousands of persons 16 years of age and over)

Employment status	1977	
	January	July
Total civilian		
noninstitutional population	155,248	156,547
Civilian labor force	94,704	99,314
Employed	86,856	92,372
At work	82,189	81,111
Full time	59,161	62,767
Part time	23,028	18,343
With a job but not at work .	4,667	11,261
On strike	52	138
On vacation	984	8,933
Bad weather	1,248	48
Temporary illness	1,515	1,296
Other	869	846
Unemployed	7,848	6,941
Looking for full-time work .	6,211	5,797
Looking for part-time work	1,637	1,144
Not in the labor force	60,544	57,234
Keeping house	34,642	34,740
In school	9,115	1,915
Unable to work	2,617	2,874
Other	14,169	17,706

Figure 16–1 Repository table

SOURCE: U.S. Department of Labor, Bureau of Labor Statistics, *How the Government Measures Unemployment*, BLS Rept. 505 (Washington, D.C.: Government Printing Office, 1977), p. 6.

Because of the analysis involved, the analytical table appears in comprehensive reports more often than in abbreviated ones.

The kinds of quantitative analysis that result in tables include the simple and the complex. The analysis may involve no more than the calculation of arithmetic means for several series. It may, however, involve the extensive calculations associated with multiple regression and correlation or analysis of variance.

Figure 16–2 is an analytical table. It represents the results of a research project involving a moderate level of quantitative analysis. Appendix G also includes an analytical table as part of the comprehensive report illustrated there.

Parts of a table

Figure 16–3 shows the breakdown of the parts of a table.

The standard table may contain many parts. They include the table number, title, subtitle, headnote, body, stub, stubhead, boxheadings, fields, source, footnotes, and other features.

Table number Unless the report contains only one or two tables, number each table. According to most style manuals, the table number appears first at the top of the table—even before the title.

When the title is short, center the table number in all-capital letters two lines above the title.

If the title occupies two or more full-width lines, however, you may move the title number to start at the extreme left position of the table itself and follow it by a period and a dash. The next section on the title includes an illustration of such an arrangement.

Most style manuals suggest the use of arabic numerals for tables. The order of the tables within the text of the report dictates the numbers for the tables themselves.

Consumer Price Index
Dallas/Fort Worth, Texas
Standard Metropolitan Statistical Area
(1967=100)
April 1980

GROUP	All Urban Consumers			Urban Wage Earners & Clerical Workers		
	Index	% Change From:		Index	% Change From:	
		4-79	2-80		4-79	2-80
All Items	251.4	19.1	4.0	249.6	18.1	3.6
Food and Beverages	245.6	7.4	1.3	246.4	6.8	1.4
Food	250.4	7.5	1.3	251.3	6.8	1.4
Food at home	238.4	5.1	1.5	241.5	5.5	1.7
Cereals and Bakery Prod.	238.9	12.7	4.8	240.5	13.6	2.7
Meats, Poultry, Fish, Eggs	223.0	-3.9	-0.8	229.2	-2.7	-0.9
Meats, Poultry, & Fish	230.2	-3.5	-1.1	236.4	-2.5	-1.5
Dairy Products	228.5	11.5	2.1	233.9	12.3	1.7
Fruits and Vegetables	222.6	1.5	2.6	222.9	-1.4	4.2
Other foods at home	281.4	10.7	1.6	281.3	12.2	3.2
Food away from home	286.3	12.1	1.1	283.0	9.4	0.8
Alcoholic Beverages	182.1	6.7	-0-	181.4	8.0	0.8
Housing	271.1	25.3	5.7	269.5	24.6	5.6
Shelter	305.8	31.5	7.2	306.8	31.3	7.1
Rent, Residential	186.4	9.6	1.2	186.4	9.6	1.2
Other Rental Costs	258.0	14.9	0.3	255.0	14.5	0.3
Homeownership	358.7	37.7	8.7	363.4	38.4	8.8
Fuel and Other Utilities	227.7	13.4	2.1	228.6	13.8	2.1
Fuels	292.7	18.0	3.0	294.2	18.6	3.0
Fuel Oil, Coal, & Bot. Gas1/	151.4	52.0	2.5	151.4	52.0	2.5
Gas (piped) & Electricity	290.1	16.7	3.1	290.3	16.8	3.0
Household Furnishings & Oper.	204.8	9.5	1.5	200.9	7.4	2.0
Apparel and Upkeep	181.2	5.7	1.6	181.1	8.0	2.4
Apparel Commodities	167.5	4.3	1.6	166.7	6.3	2.1
Men's and Boy's Apparel	180.0	5.4	0.7	181.2	7.9	3.5
Women's and Girl's Apparel	145.5	1.1	4.0	143.0	2.7	3.6
Footwear	196.7	8.8	4.0	197.5	12.4	1.8
Transportation	259.1	25.2	3.5	259.7	24.9	3.2
Private Transportation	260.2	25.0	3.5	260.5	24.8	3.2
Public Transportation	230.0	30.7	1.0	229.5	25.9	0.6
Medical Care	244.2	10.9	3.8	244.3	8.8	3.0
Entertainment	202.8	12.7	5.3	187.1	5.9	0.6
Other Goods and Services	215.1	10.1	0.7	214.4	11.0	0.5
Personal Care	224.6	11.8	1.3	227.4	14.3	1.0
All Items (1963=100)	271.7			269.9		

1/ Based to June 1978=100

The Dallas-Ft. Worth Consumer Price Index covers the counties of Collin,
Dallas, Denton, Ellis, Hood, Johnson, Kaufman, Parker, Rockwall, Tarrant, and
Wise.

Figure 16–2   Analytical table

SOURCE: U.S. Department of Labor, Bureau of Labor Statistics, Region 6, *Consumer Prices: April 1980*
(Dallas, Tex: Region 6), p. 2.

Always refer to a table by number within the text before inserting it into the material. Once you refer to a table, insert the table as soon after that paragraph as possible. However, wait until you have enough space to complete the table on a single page before starting it. If the table occupies more than one page, begin it at the top of the page following the first reference to it.

Always fill the space following the reference to a delayed table with narrative.

Sometimes a listing or tabulation is so simple that it does not need to be set aside with a number and a title. In that case, simply insert it immediately after the sentence that introduces it—even if not completed on that page.

Title   Center reasonably short titles in all-capital letters in the inverted-pyramid style. However, for a title that occupies two or more complete lines, begin the table

TABLE NUMBER

TITLE

(Subtitle)

(Headnote)

Stub Head	Boxheading	Boxheading	Boxheading	
stub	field	field	field	body of table

SOURCE

*Footnote

Figure 16–3 Parts of a table

number at the extreme left-hand edge of the table, follow it by a period and dash, and begin the title immediately. Complete the line to the right margin, and then begin the second line at the left margin and fill it to the right margin. Continue until you reach the last line. Center the last line if it does not fill it.

For full-width titles, begin only the first word and proper nouns with capital letters. Use lower-case letters elsewhere.

Consider this example of a long title and accompanying table number:

TABLE 7.—Residents of Oklahoma City, Oklahoma, classified by age, sex, occupation, religious preference, political party, and educational level

Once you select either the centered or full-width style for the number and title, use that style consistently throughout the report. Therefore, choose the style that matches the majority of the titles rather than switching back and forth from one to another. The good title should include the W's—at least the who, what, when, and where. It sometimes includes the how and even the why.

Subtitle Although a good title may include all the W's, some of them sometimes appear within a *subtitle* instead.

For instance, the example for the long title shown in the preceding section does not include a reference to when the classification was made. The time period could become part of the title itself. However, it could also appear in a subtitle. For the example a subtitle might be:

Annually for the period 198X–198X

Place a subtitle two lines below the last line of the title.

Headnote Another heading below the title shows such information as the units of measurements within the body of the table. Such a statement is called a headnote. In contrast to the footnote (described subsequently), the headnote refers to every item within the body.

Review these examples of headnotes:

(in percents)

(thousands of dollars)

(millions)

Place a headnote two lines below the last line of the title or subtitle. As shown, it often appears within parentheses, centered on the line.

Use mixed capitals or only capitalize the initial word and proper nouns, or use all lower-case letters. Make the capitalization fit the style of the major heading. For example, with an all-capitals centered title, mixed capitals fit well in a centered subtitle. Parentheses and all-lower-case letters fit any additional headnote.

Body   The body of a table is comprised of rows and columns of numerical information identified by titles. Rows are horizontal and columns are vertical. The body includes the stub, stubhead, boxheadings, and field.

Stub   The titles to rows of data are collectively called the stub. Each title may be called a stub item.

Use the stub items to establish mutually exclusive classes that identify the entries fully.

Stubhead   The title of the stub is the stubhead. It identifies the information contained in the stub itself. The stubhead is a special case of the boxheading.

Boxheadings   The titles for columns of data are designated boxheadings, column heads, or captions. If a boxheading overrides several individual column heads, it may be called a spanner heading.

As for the stub, make the boxheadings mutually exclusive and clearly descriptive.

Field   The actual data within the rows and columns constitute the field. Some writers call this collection the body.

The field contains the meat of the information. Therefore, be sure to present the numerical values within the field accurately. If the table includes totals or subtotals, use them to check the accuracy of the individual entries in a field during the proofreading.

Source   Unless you collected the information yourself, give credit to the source of the information. The source note often appears on the second line below the horizontal rule after the last line of the stub and field.

The format of a source note should parallel the style for the footnotes within the text of the message. However, it follows the word "SOURCE," which itself has a colon after it. In addition, it does not include a number.

Footnotes   Footnotes generally begin on the second line below the source note. A footnote refers to a specifically keyed entry within the field of information. In contrast, a headnote refers to all entries within the field.

Footnotes may add information, clarify an entry, explain why an omission occurs, define terms, or transmit other such messages about the individual values. In some elaborate tables footnotes may occupy as much space as the body itself.

To identify footnotes, you may use consecutive superior numbers or letters or asterisks (*, **, ***, ****). Avoid using asterisks for more than four footnotes.

Another system for identifying tabular footnotes includes a series of different symbols. One order for such a series includes the asterisk, dagger, double dagger, section mark, parallels, and number sign.

Choose a system that aids the reader. For example, if most of the footnotes refer to numbers within the field of data, avoid using superior numbers to identify the references. The reader might interpret such numbers as exponents rather than references to footnotes. In any case, the numbers would not be as obvious as would letters or symbols.

Other features Some of the most creative and nonverbal aspects of tables relate to spacing, ruling, and other features. Use all such elements to aid in readability and clarity.

As one suggestion, keep footnotes brief and to a minimum. A reader may be overwhelmed by masses of them.

Some latitude exists in acceptable tabular ruling. However, some general suggestions are:

1. For only two columns, omit all rules. Even on tables with many columns, you may omit vertical rules—if you provide liberal spacing between the columns.
2. When using rules, include a double rule above the boxheads and a single rule at the bottom of the field. Do not include rules at the sides.
3. Introduce rules within the table logically. For example, you might place a rule beneath the entire width of the area defined by a spanner heading, below captions, and below columns of figures for which you show totals.
4. As a general rule, leave space before and after rulings. Omission of such space may create the appearance of an underlined word or number.
5. Make double rules with the typewriter and single rules by hand. Place the two lines of a double rule close to one another.

Arrange the items in the stub, boxheadings, and field logically. For example, you may arrange them according to size, relationship, emphasis, importance, or interest. You may also arrange them alphabetically, chronologically, geographically, temporally, or simply according to custom.

Check a style manual for other features associated with tables. For example, you may need to continue a table on several pages or you may want to construct an unusually complex table.

Graphs

Graphs report the same kinds of data included in tables. However, they do so in pictorial form. Lines, bars, circles, stick figures, and maps characterize graphic presentations.

Before reviewing the types of charts, consider some general qualities and features.

Features

Cover these features of graphs and other illustrations: their placement, title and number, scales, and other elements.

Placement   Place a graph as close after the first mention of it as you can. Introduce it by number and/or title.

Do not begin a one-page figure on one page and continue it on another. Instead, first mention the figure in the text. Then insert the figure as soon as you can after that mention without splitting the figure unnecessarily. If a figure will not go on the page on which you introduce it, simply complete that page with narrative, and begin the figure at the top of the next page.

Title and number   Give interspersed illustrations arabic numbers in the order of their introduction. The word "figure" serves well as a label for them.

Though style-manual writers differ somewhat in their suggestions, you may refer to the figure in the narrative as "Figure 1," and write "Fig. 1" for the figure itself.

One acceptable placement for the figure number and title is on the second line beneath the figure itself. Center the number and title or write them in full-width lines. Place the figure number and title on the same line in either case. Capitalize only the first word and proper nouns in either case. Write the multi-lined title in sentence style the full width of the illustration. Review these examples of the two styles:

Fig. 7. Annual sales of Talent, Inc.

Fig. 9. Relationships among annual sales, advertising expenditures, and number of sales representatives for Sellebrity, Inc. for the period of 198X through 198X.

As in the case of titles of tables, select either the centered or sentence style and use it throughout the message. Unless the report has only a few figures with very brief titles, the choice usually will be the sentence style.

Scales   Make charts approximately square. Do so by establishing the scale on the X-axis first and then calculating an interval for the Y-axis scale that will make the height approximately the same as the width. If one dimension is greater than the other, generally make the height the greater of the two.

Recall certain basic concepts of the graphic grid. It contains four quadrants identified by the horizontal X-axis and the vertical Y-axis. Because business series tend to involve positive values on both axes, most business graphs fall into the first quadrant of the grid shown in Figure 16–4.

Many business and economic graphs include points in time along the X-axis. Therefore, the X-axis scale does not have to begin with zero. Just place the first period of time at the intersection of X and Y.

Certain business series do not need to show zero on the Y-axis. Index numbers and bivariate regression data are two examples.

Show zero on the Y-axis for most arithmetic series, though. When the smallest figure to be plotted on Y is quite large, simply begin Y with zero, break the axis, write the smallest value in the scale just above the break, and proceed.

A ratio scale on the Y-axis *cannot* begin with zero. Instead, it must begin with a positive number at the base of Y.

A ratio progression ordinarily combines with an arithmetic progression on X (usually time). Consequently, a ratio chart almost always fits on semilogarithmic paper (a logarithmic progression on Y and an arithmetic progression on X).

Subsequent sections on the various charts contain details for establishing scales for both arithmetic and ratio graphs.

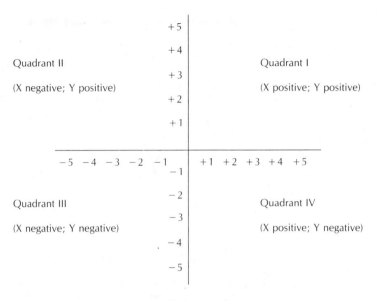

Figure 16–4 Grid showing four quadrants

Other features Check a style manual for information on other matters of style. It contains information on such things as turning a figure sideways on the page, using several pages for a single figure, or giving credit to the originator of an illustration.

Make graphic presentations clear, concise, complete, accurate, and attractive. The purpose of using graphic techniques is to transmit a striking message to engage the attention of the reader. Therefore, use the device to its fullest potential.

Introduce color when appropriate. Employ good artistic and drafting techniques. Be sure to include a clear legend to the information contained within the figure.

Use actual numbers to supplement bars, lines, and areas in pie charts and maps—if you can do so without cluttering the figure to the point of distraction.

Choose the type of illustration carefully. Consider some typical wise choices: (1) To feature the sweep and flow of data, choose the line chart. (2) To feature the differences among the sizes of the classes within a series, use the bar chart. (3) To feature both the total and relative sizes of the parts to the total, use the component line chart, the component bar chart, or the pie chart. (4) To show a series of changing totals, use line charts or bar charts; do not use a series of area charts. (5) To contrast amounts of difference or change, use an arithmetic scale. (6) To contrast rates of difference or change, use a ratio scale.

Types

Though a wide variety of types of graphs exist, concentrate here on just a few of them: (1) arithmetic line graphs, (2) logarithmic line graphs, (3) bar charts, (4) pie charts, (5) pictographs, and (6) maps.

Arithmetic line graphs Consider these types of arithmetic line graphs: (1) simple line graph, (2) frequency polygon, (3) "less than" cumulative frequency polygon, (4) "more than" cumulative frequency polygon, (5) multiple line graph, (6) component line graph, and (7) two-directional line graph.

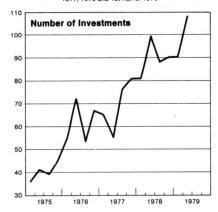

Figure 16–5   Simple arithmetic line graph

SOURCE: The Conference Board, *Worldwide Foreign Investment in Manufacturing,* Economic Road Maps, nos. 1862–1863 (New York: The Conference Board, September 1979), p. 4.

The *simple line graph* contains only one line. That line usually represents the movement of a series through time.

Figure 16–5 is a simple line graph constructed on arithmetic graph paper.

Two special types of line charts represent the graphic techniques for a frequency table. The two are the frequency polygon and the cumulative frequency polygon or ogive (pronounced "o-jive").

Use the set of data in Figure 16–6 as the basis for illustration of the frequency polygon and the two ogives possible from a frequency distribution.

HOURLY CHARGES FOR TELEVISION REPAIR
SYLVESTER, OHIO
MAY, 198X

Charges	f	"less than" CF	"more than" CF
$10 but under $15	2	2	114
15 but under 20	15	17	112
20 but under 25	25	42	97
25 but under 30	60	102	72
30 but under 35	12	114	12

Figure 16–6   Frequency table including frequency, "less than" CF, and "more than" CF columns for hypothetical data

The "f" is the symbol for "frequency." Thus, the f column indicates the number of cases that fall into each class for this continuous-data distribution. It forms the basis for the *frequency polygon* shown in Figure 16–7.

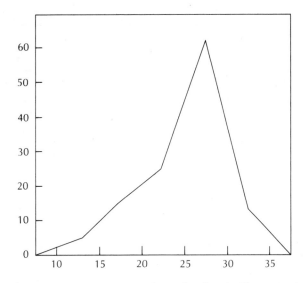

Figure 16–7   Frequency polygon for data in Figure 16–6

Observe these features of the frequency polygon:

1. Only the lower limits are placed along the X-axis, with the lowest lower limit beginning at least one-half an interval width to the right of the intersection of X and Y.
2. The Y-axis scale makes the graph approximately square.
3. The plots on the Y-axis are aligned with the midpoints of the classes on the X-axis.
4. The polygon is closed by showing zero frequency at the midpoints of the classes preceding and following the distribution.

The "less than" CF column in Figure 16–6 includes the cumulative frequencies read from upper limits of the classes. The "less than" cumulative-frequency figures result from accumulating the frequencies down the f column: Place 2 in the first row, add 15 to 2 to obtain 17 for the second row, add 25 to 17 to obtain 42 for the third row, and so forth.

To interpret the values in the "less than" CF column, simply perceive the accumulated number as the number (of hourly charges, in this example) having values less than the upper limit of that class (actually the lower limit of the succeeding class). For example, 42 of the cases have values less than $25, and 114 cases have values less than $35.

Observe the *"less than" cumulative frequency polygon (ogive)* shown in Figure 16–8. It contains both the "less than" CF values (left scale) and cumulative percentages (right scale).

Review these features as illustrated by Figure 16–8:

1. The X-axis scale begins at the intersection of the X and Y axes.
2. Only the lower limits of the classes appear along the X-axis.
3. The Y-axis scale makes the graph approximately square.

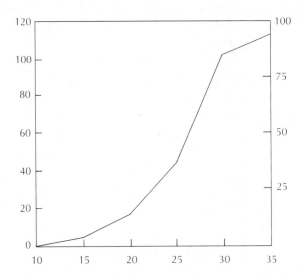

Figure 16–8 "Less than" cumulative frequency polygon (ogive) for data in Figure 16–6

4. The plots on the Y-axis are aligned with the upper limits (the same as the lower limits of the subsequent classes).
5. The ogive is closed by showing zero frequency at the upper limit of the class preceding the class in which a frequency is shown (the same as the lower limit of the first class). The zero on Y plotted at 10 on X shows that zero cases are less than $10.

The "less than" ogive takes the shape of the forward-bending lazy-S curve. The backward-bending lazy-S curve represents the "more than" cumulative frequency distribution.

The "more than" CF column in the frequency distribution develops by accumulating the values from the f column from the bottom up. Thus, for the frequency table in Figure 16–6, place the 12 in the last class. Then add 60 to the 12 to obtain the 72 in the class above it. The 97 results from adding 25 to 72. Find the other two cumulative values in the same manner.

Interpret the "more than" cumulative frequency in each class by relating it to the lower limit. However, include the lower limit in the interpretation. For example, 114 cases are equal to or more than $10, and 112 cases are equal to or more than $15.

The same rules apply to creating a "more than" ogive as apply to the "less than" ogive. However, the zero frequency class falls at the right-hand side of the graph instead of the left-hand side. Thus, for the example, zero frequencies are greater than or equal to $35—the lower limit of the class just higher than the last class in the series.

Figure 16–9 illustrates the *"more than" cumulative frequency polygon (ogive)*.

The two cumulative ogives may be plotted on the same chart. The point of their intersection identifies the value of the median on the X-axis.

The *multiple line graph* simply shows two or more series on the same graph. Figure 16–10 illustrates a multiple line graph with an arithmetic scale on the Y-axis. It also includes a bar chart and features a break in the Y-axis.

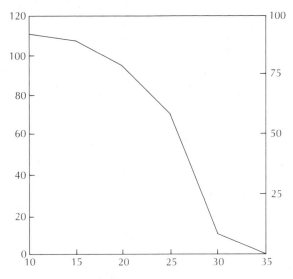

Figure 16–9   "More than" cumulative frequency polygon (ogive) for data in Figure 16–6

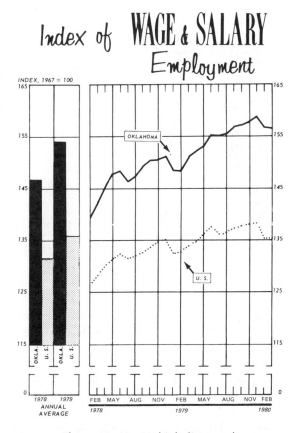

Figure 16–10   Multiple line graph

SOURCE: Oklahoma, *Oklahoma Labor Market,* March 1980, p. 26.

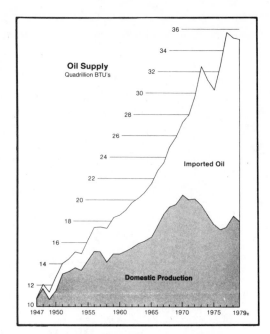

Figure 16–11   Component line graph

SOURCE: The Conference Board, *Long Term U.S. Energy Trends,* Economic Road Maps, nos. 1866–1867 (New York: The Conference Board, November 1979), p. 2.

The *component line graph* proves useful to show the movement of both a total series and its parts through time. Figure 16–11 provides an example on arithmetic graph paper.

A *two-directional line graph* illustrates the rise and fall of a series—usually through time. Thus, it is particularly adaptable to showing business cycles around a line of normalcy designated as zero.

Figure 16–12 shows the visual effect supplied by the two-directional line graph.

Logarithmic line graphs   To put information into a *simple line chart* with a *ratio scale* on the Y-axis, construct a logarithmic line graph.

The Y-axis on semilogarithmic paper is already constructed to convert the series into a logarithmic progression. You do not have to determine the logarithms of any numbers yourself.

Examine the one-cycle semilogarithmic paper illustrated in Figure 16–13. Though the blank graph paper contains numbers from 1 through 10 on the Y-axis, other sequences of positive numbers may replace them.

The top number in Figure 16–13 is ten times the size of the bottom number; the value of the top line of a cycle is always ten times that of the bottom line of a cycle. Therefore, a single cycle can handle a series such that the highest number is no more than ten times the smallest.

Also observe in Figure 16–13 that the same vertical distances represent the same rates of change. The easiest way to comprehend this fact is first to measure the distance between 1 and 2. That distance represents a 100-percent increase. There-fore, because the rate is constant, note that the distance between 1 and 2 is the same

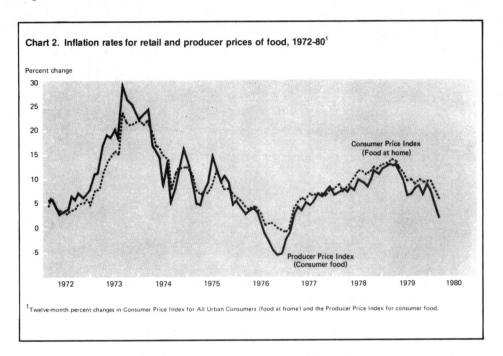

Figure 16–12 Two-directional line graph

SOURCE: *Monthly Labor Review* 103 (May 1980): 6.

as the distance between 2 and 4, between 3 and 6, between 4 and 8, and between 5 and 10.

Semilogarithmic paper also comes with more than one cycle. Figure 16–14 illustrates four-cycle paper. Again, the numbers on the Y-axis serve only to mark the break points (beginning anew with 1 at the base of each cycle). The actual scale used for the plotting replaces the numbers contained on the blank paper.

If the actual scale value at the base line of the first cycle is 1, then the increment for the first cycle is 1. The value of 10 at the top line of the first cycle is also the value at the base line of the second cycle. One zero would be added after the 1 at that point.

Because the value of the base line of the second cycle is 10, the increment for the scale through that cycle is also 10. Thus, the value at the top line (100) is ten times that at the base line. (The intermediate points would be 20, 30, 40, 50, 60, 70, 80, and 90.)

Likewise, the third cycle begins with 100, has an increment of 100, and ends with 1,000 (ten times 100), with intermediate values of 200, 300, . . . 900.

Because the fourth cycle begins with 1,000, each point on the scale is 1,000 more than the preceding point, and the top value is 10,000 (ten times 1,000). The intermediate points are 2,000, 3,000, . . . 9,000.

Any point in a given cycle is ten times the value at the same relative position in the preceding cycle. Thus, in the illustration, the 4,000 in the fourth cycle is ten times the 400 in that same position in the third cycle.

To plot a simple line graph on semilogarithmic paper, first decide on the number of cycles necessary to contain the series. To do so, divide the largest number

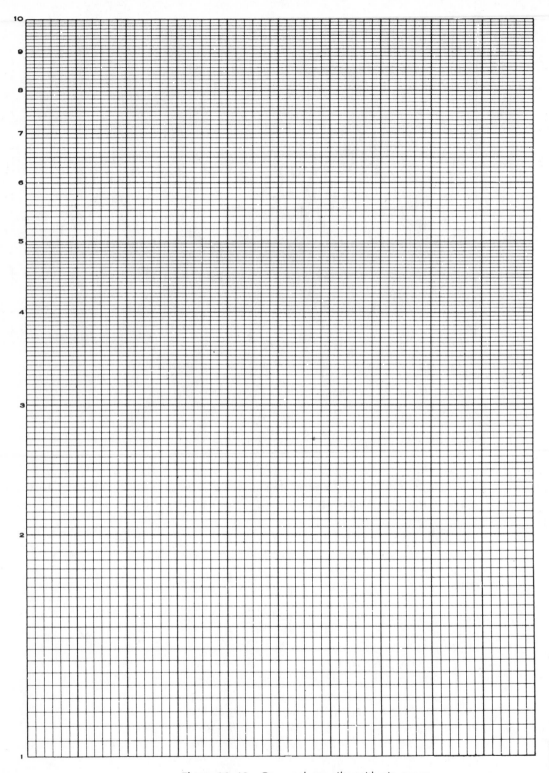

Figure 16–13 One-cycle semilogarithmic paper

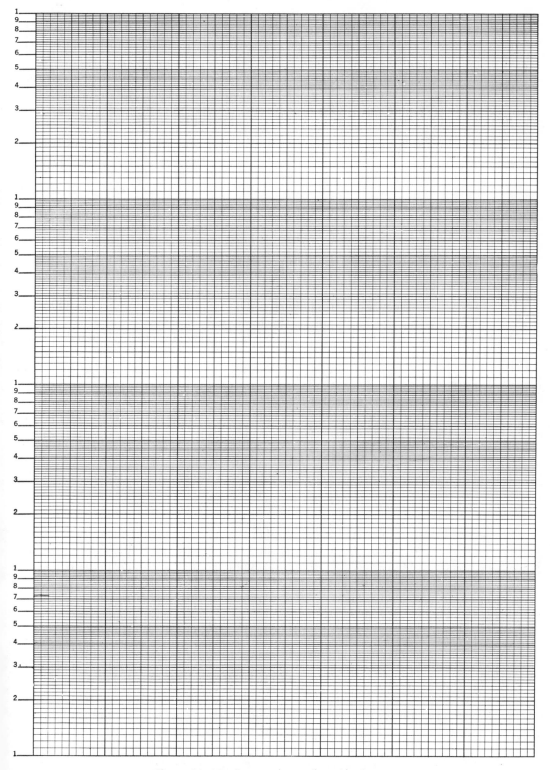

Figure 16–14 Four-cycle semilogarithmic paper

in the series by the smallest number in the series. The number of digits to the left of the decimal place in the quotient is the number of cycles needed.

Occasionally, the quotient is exactly 10, 100, 1,000, 10,000, . . . In such cases, use the number of cycles determined by subtracting 1 from the number of digits in the quotient. Thus, if the quotient is 10, use only one cycle, and if it is 100, use only two cycles.

To illustrate, assume you want to plot these data on semilogarithmic paper:

(in thousands)

1975	75
1976	9
1977	800
1978	789
1979	4,950
1980	700

Dividing 4,950 by 9 yields 550. Because 550 contains three digits, use three-cycle paper.

If 900 replaces 4,950 in the preceding series, use only two cycles (900/9 = 100). If 2,000 replaces 9, use two cycles (4,950/75 = 66).

Next, select the paper that contains the number of needed cycles and establish the scale on the X-axis.

To begin constructing the Y-axis scale, first place a round number equal to or smaller than the smallest number in the series on the base line of the first cycle. Work on scratch paper to determine the best choice for the base-line number.

For the preceding example, 9 could appear on the base line of the first cycle, in which case the values at the breaks between cycles would be:

9,000_____

900_____

90_____

9_____

However, placing 9 on the base line would yield a cumbersome scale. The first cycle would include 9, 18, 27, . . .; the second cycle, 90, 180, 270, . . .; and the third cycle, 900, 1,800, 27,000, . . . In addition a great deal of the third cycle would be wasted.

A 5 on the base line of the first cycle is the logical choice. The scratch-paper skeleton outline would become:

5,000_____

500_____

50_____

5_____

With this scale, the first cycle would progress 5, 10, 15, . . .; the second cycle, 50, 100, 150, . . .; and the third cycle, 500, 1,000, 1,500, . . . This scale is much more natural than the scale beginning with 9.

The scale could begin with 6, 7, or 8, but not with 3 or 4. However, the arguments in favor of a 5 at the first base line are compelling.

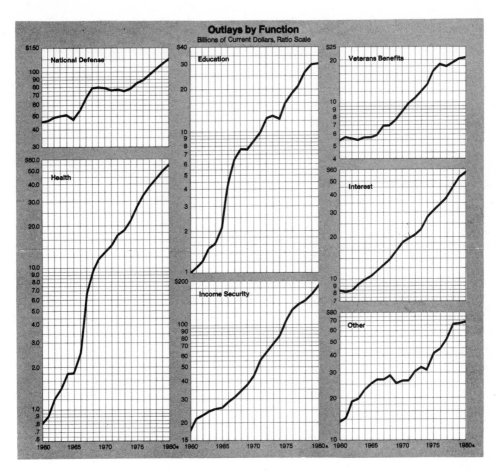

Figure 16–15   Series of simple line charts on ratio-scale paper

SOURCE: The Conference Board, *Federal Budget,* Economic Road Maps, nos. 1860-1861 (New York: The Conference Board, August 1979), p. 3.

Figure 16–15 includes a set of simple line charts with ratio scales on the Y-axes. It represents a series of federal budget outlays for different functions in billions of current dollars.

Some of the graphs in Figure 16–15 are much taller than wide—a fact necessitated in this case by keeping the graphs the same widths regardless of the number of cycles used on the Y-axis.

Also observe in Figure 16–15 that unused portions of the Y scale are deleted in order to conserve space. For example, for the series on health, notice that the base line of the first cycle obviously begins with .1. However, because the first plot falls at .8, the points from .1 through .5 do not appear. In addition, though the third cycle continues through 100.00, the scale stops at 60.00—just after the point of the highest value plotted on the chart.

What figure falls at the base line of the first cycle for national defense? for income security? for veterans benefits? for interest? Observe how the scales for

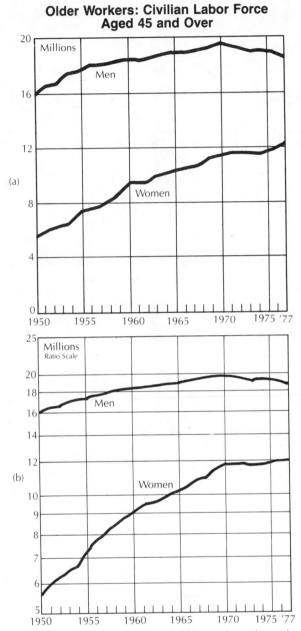

Figure 16–16   Multiple line chart on both arithmetic and semilogarithmic graph paper

SOURCE: The Conference Board, *Older Workers,* Economic Road Maps, no. 1835 (New York: The Conference Board, July 1978), p. 1.

national defense and income security show Y-axis points that fall between pairs of major points on the ten-point scale.

Nothing more clearly illustrates the strength of ratio scaling than does the *multiple line ratio graph.* Observe in Figure 16–16a how an arithmetic progression indicates that the numbers of older women in the labor force seem to be increasing at just about the same rate as the numbers of older men. However, Figure 16–16b (the same data on semilogarithmic paper) clearly shows that the *rate of increase* for women is much higher than that for men.

Observe also how the series of simple line charts in Figure 16–15 could be combined into a revealing multiple line chart. To compare the rates for the different federal-government outlays, just compare the slopes of the lines. Because equal vertical distances on semilogarithmic paper indicate equal rates of change, you may compare the lines directly—even though the charts have different Y scales.

Most business and economic series cannot properly use two scales on the same arithmetic chart, because equal vertical distances should represent equal *amounts* of dollars, tons, inches, or whatever is being observed. However, any ratio series may do so because it is concerned with equal *rates*. The scales may even involve different units of measurement (inches and pounds, for example) on the same chart.

As an example of using two scales on the same chart, Figure 16–17 includes the outlays for education and "other" outlays from Figure 16–15. The outlays for education correspond with the left scale. Other outlays correspond with the right scale.

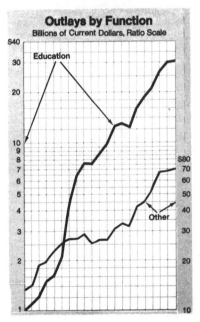

Figure 16–17   Multiple line chart on ratio-scale paper with two scales

SOURCE: Developed from data reported by The Conference Board, *Federal Budget*, Economic Road Maps, nos. 1860–1861 (New York: The Conference Board, August 1979), p. 3.

To find the number of cycles needed for plotting multiple line graphs, simply apply the procedure described earlier.

For a single scale, choose the highest and lowest numbers from all of the series combined. Illustrate by finding the number of cycles necessary to plot these data on semilogarithmic paper with only one scale:

Sellebrity, Inc.
Total and Regional Sales
(in ten thousands)

	Total	SW	NW	NE	SE
1976	$201	$108	$ 2	$57	$34
1977	313	168	22	75	48
1978	282	147	27	63	45
1979	298	159	37	65	37
1980	317	176	41	64	36

The plotting requires three cycles (317/2 = 158.5).

To use fewer cycles, but still put all of the lines on a single chart, use two scales. One scale will handle the total and the Southwest Region in one cycle, and another scale will handle the other three regions in two cycles. Thus, two-cycle paper could contain the series.

That arrangement would not only reduce the height of the chart, but bring the lines closer together for analytical purposes.

Bar charts   Consider four types of bar charts: (1) simple, (2) multiple, (3) component, and (4) two-directional. Because the concept of the ratio scale does not apply well to bar charts, review only arithmetic scales.

The *simple bar chart* involves the placement of a single bar at each point on the axis. The bars may be vertical or horizontal. The horizontal style works particularly well for qualitative identifying information. However, quantitative information often appears in the vertical style.

Arrange the bars in ascending or descending order when you can. Doing so highlights the kinds of contrast often desired in bar chart presentations.

Figure 16–18 illustrates a horizontal bar chart with the bars organized in order of size. Notice that the bars and the spaces between them maintain visually consistent and pleasant perspective in sizes. The bars are separated because of the qualitative nature of the data.

Figure 16–19 includes two simple vertical bar charts with time along the X-axis. The bars are separated. However, because they represent continuous data, they could be joined. Notice the break in the Y-axis.

The simple bar chart that corresponds ·with the frequency polygon is the *histogram*. Thus, the histogram is a vertical bar chart illustrating a frequency distribution. Figure 16–20 shows a histogram for the data in Figure 16–6 (page 550).

Observe these features of the good histogram:

1. A space the equivalent of at least one-half the horizontal increment is left at each end of the X-axis.
2. Because the data are continuous, only the lower limits of the frequency-distribution classes appear. For discrete data, show both the upper and lower limits.
3. No gaps appear between the bars because of the continuous data. For discrete data, show narrow gaps.
4. The chart is approximately square.

The *multiple bar chart* includes two or more bars at each point on the scale. The chart usually involves vertical bars. Figure 16–21 illustrates the concept.

Foreign Investments in the United States
1977, 1978 and 1st Half of 1979

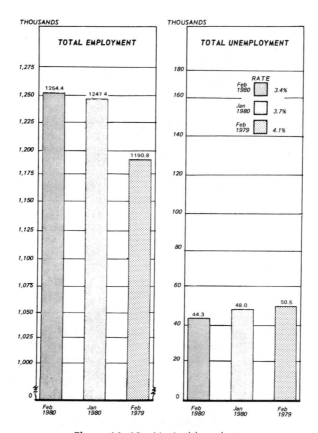

Figure 16–18   Horizontal bar chart

SOURCE: The Conference Board, *Worldwide Foreign Investment in Manufacturing,* Economic Road Maps, nos. 1862–1863 (New York: The Conference Board, September 1979), p. 4.

Figure 16–19   Vertical bar chart

SOURCE: Oklahoma, *Oklahoma Labor Market,* March 1980, p. 1.

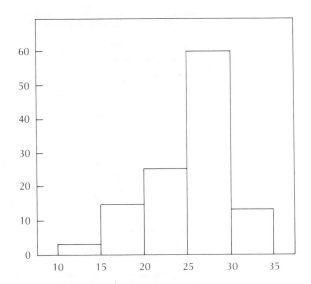

Figure 16–20   Histogram for data in Figure 16–6

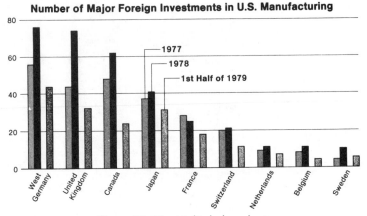

Figure 16–21   Multiple bar chart

SOURCE: The Conference Board, *Worldwide Foreign Investment in Manufacturing,* Economic Road Maps, nos. 1862–1863 (New York: The Conference Board, September 1979), p. 4.

A practical limit exists to the number of bars possible at a single point. There-fore, if you need to show more than three or four series, you may need to turn to the multiple line chart.

The *component bar chart* represents an excellent channel for showing wholes and the component parts of wholes. The bars may be vertical or horizontal, but often appear in vertical form. Figure 16–22 includes an example of such an approach.

The *two-directional bar chart*—either vertical or horizontal—provides an ex-cellent means for showing percentage changes. Such charts often show the changes in ascending or descending order. Figure 16–23 is an example.

Pie charts   Pie charts show the relative sizes of parts in a whole particularly well. However, do not use a series of different-sized circles to try to show different totals. The average viewer cannot grasp changes in areas or volumes well.

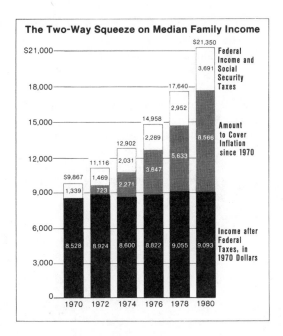

Figure 16–22   Component bar chart

SOURCE: The Conference Board, *The Two-Way Squeeze, 1980,* Economic Road Maps, nos. 1876–1877 (New York: The Conference Board, April 1980), p. 2.

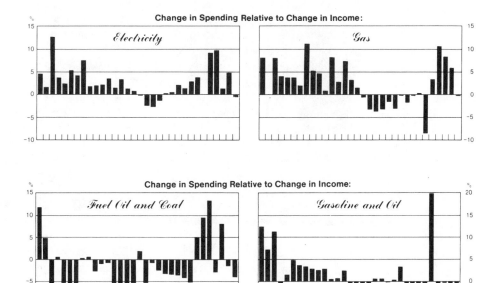

Figure 16–23   Two-directional bar chart

SOURCE: The Conference Board, *Long Term U.S. Energy Trends,* Economic Road Maps, nos. 1866–1867 (New York: The Conference Board, November 1979), p. 3.

To construct a pie chart, first determine a percentage distribution for the series. Then arrange the percents in order of size from largest to smallest—to be arranged in clockwise order beginning at twelve o'clock.

You may purchase paper with a circle divided into 100 equal parts. However, you may also use a compass and protractor to establish the circle and the parts of it. To calculate the degrees to assign to each wedge, multiple the percent represented by that wedge by 360°.

Figure 16–24 illustrates four coin-shaped pie charts.

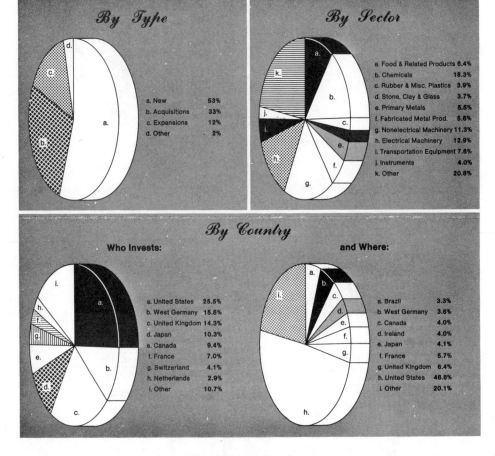

Global Foreign Investment in Manufacturing
(Number of Investments Announced in 1977, 1978 & First Quarter of 1979)

By Type

a. New   53%
b. Acquisitions 33%
c. Expansions   12%
d. Other   2%

By Sector

a. Food & Related Products 6.4%
b. Chemicals   18.3%
c. Rubber & Misc. Plastics 3.9%
d. Stone, Clay & Glass   3.7%
e. Primary Metals   5.5%
f. Fabricated Metal Prod. 5.6%
g. Nonelectrical Machinery 11.3%
h. Electrical Machinery   12.9%
i. Transportation Equipment 7.6%
j. Instruments   4.0%
k. Other   20.8%

By Country

Who Invests:

a. United States   25.5%
b. West Germany   15.8%
c. United Kingdom 14.3%
d. Japan   10.3%
e. Canada   9.4%
f. France   7.0%
g. Switzerland   4.1%
h. Netherlands   2.9%
i. Other   10.7%

and Where:

a. Brazil   3.3%
b. West Germany   3.6%
c. Canada   4.0%
d. Ireland   4.0%
e. Japan   4.1%
f. France   5.7%
g. United Kingdom   6.4%
h. United States   48.8%
i. Other   20.1%

Figure 16–24   Pie charts

SOURCE: The Conference Board, *Worldwide Foreign Investment in Manufacturing*, Economic Road Maps, nos. 1862–1863 (New York: The Conference Board, September 1979), p. 1.

Pictographs   Actually a special type of bar chart, the pictograph adds drama to a presentation by using figures to constitute the bars. The figures are all the same size, but combine to show a change in only one dimension—either vertical or horizontal.

Figure 16–25 includes a simple pictograph. Observe how the pictograph catches the attention better than traditional rectangular bars.

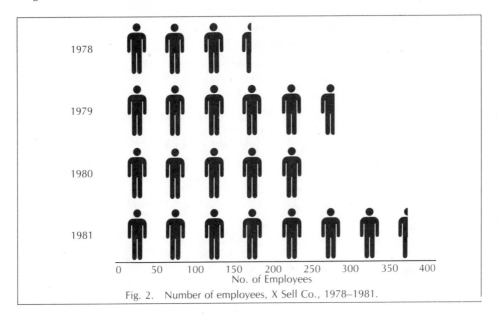

Fig. 2.   Number of employees, X Sell Co., 1978–1981.

Figure 16–25 Pictograph

Maps Information classified by geographical regions often takes the form of a map. With the mapping technique, choose the designations of such things as population density carefully. Also be sure to include a clear and complete legend to the information.

Figure 16–26 includes two informational maps.

DEVELOPING NONVERBAL MESSAGES
TO ACCOMPANY ORAL MESSAGES

Virtually all of the personal nonverbal messages described in Chapter 3 may accompany oral messages. In addition, many of the nonverbal messages used to accompany written messages may also accompany oral presentations. For example, tables and graphs may be put on slides, videotapes, posters, or transparencies for presentation to an audience.

Because of the overlapping types, therefore, consider the construction of only a few of the major nonpersonal vehicles for carrying nonverbal messages in conjunction with oral ones. The vehicles include: (1) transparencies; (2) posters and flip charts; (3) videotapes and movies; (4) audiotapes; and (5) slides, strip films, and photographs.

Transparencies

Transparencies shown on an overhead projector may complement an oral presentation. As the name implies, a transparency is a clear sheet of material con-

Executive Summary

Heating Degree-Days

Heating Degree-Days Accumulated from July 1 through April 27

Departure from last year

Departure from Normal

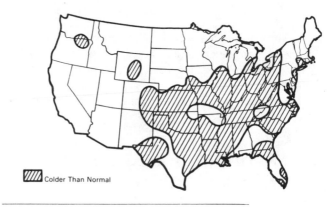

Source: • Department of Commerce — NOAA.

Figure 16–26   Maps

SOURCE: *Monthly Energy Review* (May 1980): 13.

taining information for projection upon a screen behind the speaker. Consider a few techniques for the development and use of transparencies:

1. Use large type or printing on transparencies.
2. Do not try to put too much on a single transparency.
3. Use transparencies primarily for well-constructed pictures, sketches, drawings, cartoons, charts, graphs, tables, and other nonverbal messages. Use them also for outlines of a few words. Put extensive numbers of words into printed form for distribution.
4. Bind transparencies if possible.
5. Number the transparencies in the order of presentation. Note in the outline of the speech the places for showing the numbered transparencies.

6. Do not try to show too many transparencies during a given session.
7. Leave a transparency on the overhead projector long enough for the viewers to study it and for the notetakers to outline the major points contained in it.
8. Use the transparencies as you practice the presentation. If another person will change the transparencies for you, practice once with her or him.
9. Whenever possible, practice in the actual room in which you will make the presentation.
10. On the day of the presentation, set up and test the equipment before beginning the presentation. Be sure both you and the audience can see each other and that the audience can see the screen and the information on the transparencies.
11. Whether you or someone else works the overhead projector, always face the audience. If you want to point to things on the transparencies, use a pointer—or have your companion use a pointer.
12. If you want to write on a transparency during a presentation, operate the overhead projector yourself. However, consider the advantages of preparing overlay transparencies that perform the same function as writing while in the presence of others.
13. If you must dim the lights during the showing of transparencies, have someone control the light switch unobtrusively; still maintain the semblance of visual contact.

Above all, make the transparency presentation a natural, integrated part of the whole. Do not allow it to become a distraction. In fact, if the shuffle of the transparencies overwhelms the oral elements of the presentation, you often would do better to omit them entirely.

Posters and Flip Charts

 Posters or flip charts often contribute to a presentation. Here are some suggestions for using them:

1. Make the messages large enough to be perceived by everyone in the room.
2. Do not crowd the area available on the poster or chart.
3. Use posters and charts primarily for well-constructed nonverbal messages, not for predominantly verbal ones. Engage a professional artist if necessary.
4. Select appropriate materials for the presentations. For example, if posters will have to stand on an easel or in a chalkboard tray, select a heavy card stock—one that will not buckle.
5. Organize the posters and flip charts in the order that you will display them.
6. Avoid showing too many posters/charts in a given session.
7. Show a poster/chart a long enough time to allow the viewers to study it and take notes from it. Then remove it from view.
8. Include the posters/charts in your practice sessions. Include any others who might aid in the presentation in at least one such session.
9. Whenever possible, practice in the room in which you will make the presentation.
10. Set up and test the posters or charts just before beginning the presentation. Be sure both you and the audience can see each other, and that the audience can see the posters/charts and the information on them.

11. Whether you or someone else controls the posters/charts, always face the audience without blocking the view of the materials. If you point to things on the posters/charts, use a long pointer—or have your companion use a pointer.

Just as for transparencies, make posters and flip charts an integral part of the oral presentation. Avoid allowing them to detract from it. Particularly take care not to use posters/charts as a crutch for avoiding oral and personal nonverbal contact with your audience.

Posters and flip charts may stand alone as message presenters. However, when you do place them on bulletin boards, easels, or walls, do not use too many, place them at eye level, and change them regularly. Such presentations soon make no more direct impact upon the receiver than the draperies. Think back to how invisible posters/charts become that stay in the same place day after day.

Videotapes and Movies

A few paragraphs here cannot create experts on presentations for the medio or mass media. However, even a few hints can help improve the simple presentations you may make.

Videotape and moving-picture film capture activity for presentation with or independently of a speech. Some general suggestions for the channels include:

1. Use good equipment. Engage a professional photographer if possible. Attend to all of the technical details associated with lighting, distance, focusing, etc.
2. Feature the kinds of activities that lend themselves to the visual/aural process. Using tape or film to show someone standing in one place and reading a speech hardly represents wise use of the medium.
3. Have the people or things being photographed do most of the moving. Move the camera between shots so as to avoid jerking the camera from one subject to another.
4. If you do include a panorama, move the camera steadily and slowly and only on distant subjects. If the subject of the panorama is moving, keep the subject centered.
5. Attend to everything that will be on the tape or film. Even a good sequence of the primary subject can be ruined by distractions in the background.
6. Vary the distances from the camera to the subject when possible. Use some close-ups along with distance shots. Use the zoom-lens technique when available.
7. Pay as much attention to the sound as to the picture.
8. Make naturalness of presentation a primary goal. When possible, shoot some candid scenes along with the necessary well-rehearsed ones.
9. Edit tape or film to remove unnecessary segments and create a unified whole.
10. When using tapes and films produced by others, view and analyze them before showing them.
11. Show videotape or film along with, not instead of, an oral presentation. Discuss the material before, after, and even during its showing (often as you stop the projector and turn up the lights).

12. Practice the oral presentation at least once with the media presentation itself—preferably in the room in which you will speak.
13. Be sure that everyone in the audience can see and hear well.

(890 words)
(test on page 576)

Audiotapes

Because of the expense of videotapes and movies, you likely will use more audiotapes than either of them. Though losing a great deal of communication power available from audiovisual techniques, audiotapes still create fine reinforcements to oral presentations. Some hints for using them include:

1. Use good equipment and tape. Attend to all of the technical details.
2. Feature the kinds of activities that fit the aural mode particularly well. Introduce music, sound effects, and other such complementary messages in addition to voices.
3. Choose good voices for audiotape creations.
4. Make the presentation as natural as possible. When you can, capture some candid situations along with the necessary well-rehearsed scenes.
5. Introduce variety into the presentation by using many different voices, different distances, different speeds, and built-in interaction with the audience.
6. Edit tape to remove unnecessary segments and create a unified whole.
7. When using tapes produced by others, listen to and analyze them before playing them for an audience.
8. Play audiotape along with, not instead of, an oral presentation. Discuss the material before, after, and even during its playing.
9. Practice the oral presentation at least once with the media presentation itself—preferably in the room in which you will speak.
10. Be sure that everyone in the audience can hear well.

Slides, Strip Films, and Photographs

Slides, strip films, and photographs make good companions for oral presentations. Though the suggestions for producing and using them parallel those for several of the other channels, review a few here:

1. Use good equipment; engage a professional photographer if possible. Attend to all of the technical details associated with the process of photography.
2. Spotlight the kinds of activity that belong to the still-shot category. Establish a sense of activity even as you produce still shots.
3. Choose subjects carefully.
4. Vary the shots in terms of distances, angle, etc.
5. Add an audiotape if possible.
6. Seek a natural presentation. Shoot some candid scenes along with the necessary well-staged scenes.
7. Edit slide, strip-film, or photograph presentations in order to remove unnecessary scenes and create a unified whole.

8. Number the slides or photographs in the order of presentation.
9. When using slides, strip films, or photographs produced by others, view and analyze them before you show them.
10. Show slides, photographs, or strip films along with, not instead of, an oral presentation. Discuss the material before, after, and even during its showing (often as you stop any projection involved and turn up the lights).
11. Practice the oral presentation at least once with the media presentation itself—preferably in the room in which you will speak.
12. Be sure that everyone in the audience can see well.

SUMMARY

The guidelines for nonverbal sending are:

1. Define purposes, participants, and environment.
2. Identify nonverbal channel.
3. Control interference.
4. Select, encode, and transmit nonverbal messages in light of purposes, participants, environment, channel, and interference.
5. Use feedback.
6. Evaluate.

Because Chapter 3 covers personal nonverbal sending as well as receiving, this chapter deals with nonpersonal nonverbal messages to accompany written and oral messages.

Tables and graphs are more nonverbal than verbal. Tabular and graphic techniques represent a broad range of nonverbal types of messages.

One basic type of table is the repository table. The *repository table* stores descriptive information in a form available for the general use of interested people. Repository tables usually contain primary data. The other type of table, the *analytical table*, results from some sort of analysis performed upon the raw or organized data. The data may be *primary* or *secondary*.

When a report contains more than two tables, number and give a title to each. Also, arrange the data in a coherent, readable form. If you did not collect the information for the table yourself, list the source, and place the footnotes under the source note.

The traditional table has most of these parts: number, title, subtitle, headnote, stub head, stub, boxheadings, field, source note, and footnotes.

Graphs report the same kind of data contained in tables, but in more pictorial and less accurate form.

Place a graph as close after the first mention of it as possible. If it occupies more space than is available after it is introduced, complete the page with narrative, and start the figure at the top of the next page. Give a graph a title and a number. The usual designation for a graph or other illustration is "figure."

Make charts approximately square. Always begin the Y-axis with 0 on arithmetic graph paper. On semilogarithmic graph paper, begin with any positive number at the base line of the first cycle.

Some of the most-used graphs are line graphs, bar charts, pie charts, pictographs, and maps.

The four types of *line graphs* are *simple, multiple, component,* and *two-directional*.

The *semilogarithmic (ratio) line chart* features rates of change on the Y-axis instead of the amounts of change featured by the *arithmetic scale*.

The ratio-scale graph is particularly useful for multiple line charts because it compares rates of unlike series. It can also include two different scales on the same chart.

Two special types of line charts represent the graphic techniques for a frequency table: the frequency polygon and the cumulative frequency polygon (ogive). The *frequency polygon* includes the plots of the frequencies at the midpoints of the classes. The *"less than" cumulative frequency polygon* has the cumulative plots at the upper limits of the classes. The *"more than" ogive* has the cumulative plots at the lower limits.

The four types of *bar charts* are also *simple, multiple, component,* and *two-directional*. The *histogram* is the bar chart for a frequency table.

Pictographs are actually a special type of bar chart in which the figures constitute the bars. *Maps* report many types of statistical data for geographical regions.

The nonverbal messages that accompany oral messages can involve the use of *transparencies, posters* and *flip charts, videotapes* and *movies, audiotapes,* and *slides* and *photographs*. All of these studio and visual aids must be prepared and presented carefully.

Practice

1. This table could be made to look and read better in another form. A title of some sort would also make it better. Put the table into another form and give it a title.

PRODUCT	GROSS SALES (In Thousands)							
	1974	1975	1976	1977	1978	1979	1980	1981
Hair Dryers	$200	$220	$180	$250	$255	$260	$240	$175
Heating Pads	$185	$190	$195	$190	$190	$185	$180	$180
Can Openers	$105	$110	$110	$115	$120	$125	$120	$100

2. You are writing a report for your boss at Feather Corporation. You have gathered some data that you want to put into table or graph form. Put the data into the form that you think is appropriate. Label the table or graph with a number and a title.

    a. In 1970 the annual turnover rate among upper and middle managers at Feather Corporation was 15 percent. It was 22 percent in 1971, 23 percent in 1972, 28 percent in 1973, 27 percent in 1974, 36 percent in 1975, 41 percent in 1976, 31 percent in 1977, 30 percent in 1978, and 31 percent in 1979.

    b. The turnover rate among line supervisors at Feather Corporation was 18 percent in 1970, 25 percent in 1971, 29 percent in 1972, 28 percent in 1973, 44 percent in 1974, 59 percent in 1975, 57 percent in 1976, 41 percent in 1977, 37 percent in 1978, and 36 percent in 1979.

    c. The turnover rate among staff professionals at Feather Corporation was 22 percent in 1970, 24 percent in 1971, 28 percent in 1972, 28 percent in 1973, 37 percent in 1974, 38 percent in 1975, 61 percent in 1976, 59 percent in 1977, 32 percent in 1978, and 33 percent in 1979.

    d. The turnover rate among clerical personnel at Feather Corporation was 25 percent in 1970, 29 percent in 1971, 27 percent in 1972, 35 percent in 1973, 44 percent in 1974, 45 percent in 1975, 72 percent in 1976, 71 percent in 1977, 64 percent in 1978, and 47 percent in 1979.

3. Write a short (two- or three-minute) statement about the four types of line graphs. Pretend that you will give this lecture at your company's workshop on nonverbal communication. Meet with your group. You and each other group member deliver the statements orally. Answer these questions immediately after each of the statements.

    a. Did the speaker speak at an appropriate pitch, rate, and volume? Why?

    b. Did the speaker use body movements that added to or detracted from her or his speech?

    c. Was the speaker's facial expression appropriate?

    d. In general, what nonverbal messages supported what the speaker said? What nonverbal messages contradicted what the speaker said?

    e. What did the speaker do well? What could be improved?

4. [*This is a dictation exercise.*] Because most of your colleagues at work use transparencies during their speeches, you have been asked to write a one-page memorandum on the use of transparencies. Your colleagues are particularly interested in practical suggestions. Prepare an outline of the memorandum. Now meet with your group. You and each other group member dictate the memorandum from the outline. Discuss these questions after each performance.

    a. Did the speaker dictate clearly?

    b. Did the speaker dictate at an appropriate pitch, rate, and volume?

    c. Was the speaker able to dictate a complete, understandable memorandum from her or his outline?

    d. Did the speaker give the transcriber adequate instructions?

    e. In general, what did the speaker do well? What needs more practice?

5. Given these sales data for CDE Company and three of its eight territories:

	CDE Company	Southeast	South Central	Northwest
1976	$ 995,600	387,100	10,400	135,200
1977	1,033,500	385,400	12,900	134,800
1978	998,700	388,200	13,100	136,100
1979	1,122,100	391,600	20,200	139,200
1980	1,118,500	390,800	24,500	138,900

    a. Plot all four series on arithmetic graph paper.

    b. Plot all four series on a single sheet of semilogarithmic paper of the correct number of cycles. You may plot all four series on one scale, or you may use two scales.

    c. Interpret both charts and contrast what they show.

6. Given this frequency distribution:

Hourly Wages	No. of Workers
$5.00 but under $5.50	38
5.50 but under 6.00	78
6.00 but under 6.50	114
6.50 but under 7.00	189
7.00 but under 7.50	62
7.50 but under 8.00	7

    a. Construct a frequency polygon.
    b. Construct a histogram.
    c. Construct a "less than" cumulative frequency polygon.
    d. Construct a "more than" cumulative frequency polygon.
    e. Interpret and contrast the meanings of the four charts.
7. Construct a pie chart from these data:

	Sales ($000)
Department A	38
Department B	182
Department C	12
Department D	59
Department E	203

8. Given this distribution of departmental sales for three years (in thousands of dollars):

	Dept. A	Dept. B	Dept. C	Dept. D	Dept. E
1979	38	182	12	59	203
1980	50	180	22	54	210
1981	47	168	25	62	228

Construct a single graph containing a component bar chart for departmental sales for each of the three years.
9. For the data in No. 8, construct a component line chart.
10. Meet with your group. Develop, rehearse, and tape-record or videotape a ten-minute presentation on some aspect of tabular and graphic communication. Play each group's production for the class. Evaluate each production.
11. Develop a poster or a series of flip charts to illustrate the concepts associated with the frequency distribution and its associated graphics. Display them for the evaluation of the class.
12. Develop a series of transparencies to illustrate the construction of a semilogarithmic chart. Prepare a five-minute oral presentation to accompany the transparencies. Make the presentation to the class. Evaluate.
13. Interview a photography professor about some hints for the non-professional photographer. Prepare an interview guide ahead of time. Write a two-page report of the interview.
14. Use your dictionary and thesaurus to create meanings for these words. Use the words when you think, write, and speak so that you feel comfortable using them.

a. Allude		**h.**	Inertia
b. Behest		**i.**	Logarithm
c. Codify		**j.**	Nebulous
d. Component		**k.**	Prowess
e. Cumulative		**l.**	Reticent
f. Deter		**m.**	Spatial
g. Discern		**n.**	Temporal

15. Take and score Self-Test 36 over the excerpts about posters, flip charts, videotapes, and movies.

Self-Test 36
Excerpts about Posters, Flip Charts,
Videotapes, and Movies

A. Recall (33 points each). For each multiple-choice question, select the most accurate answer.

1. Posters and flip charts should *not*:
   a. Be organized in the order that you will display them
   b. Contain a great deal of detailed information
   c. Be used primarily for well-constructed nonverbal messages
   d. Contain messages large enough to be viewed and read by everyone in the room
   e. Be used during a practice run of the speech

2. Which of these message situations least warrants the use of the videotape or moving-picture medium?
   a. Your manager wants to read her annual state-of-the-company speech to your company's 48 centralized employees.
   b. You want to show potential employees the manufacturing operations at your six foreign plants.
   c. You wish to teach all of your company's mechanics how to overhaul your new fleet of delivery trucks. Your company employs over 600 mechanics at a dozen plants across the nation.
   d. This is your company's 25th anniversary. You want to relate your company's most notable accomplishments to your 25,000 employees.
   e. Because your company is concerned about air pollution, you, a communications specialist, have been asked to try to convince your company's employees to ride the bus, join a car-pool, walk, or ride a bicycle to work. You know that most of your employees do not like to read memoranda or listen to speeches.

B. Inference (34 points). Indicate whether this statement is true or false.

A presentation or speech is always made more interesting with the use of flip charts, posters, or film.

Solution to Self-Test 36
Excerpts About Posters, Flip Charts,
Videotapes, and Movies

A. Recall (33 points each)   B. Inference (34 points)

1. b   2. a   False

16. Take and score Self-Test 37 over Chapter 16.

Self-Test 37
Chapter 16

A. Recall (25 points each). For each multiple-choice question, select the most accurate answer.

1. If you want to feature the sweep and flow of data, you should use a:
   a. Pictograph
   b. Bar chart
   c. Arithmetic scale
   d. Ratio scale
   e. Line chart

2. Which one of these statements is true?
   a. Charts are more accurate than tables.
   b. Governmental agencies supply more analytical tables than repository tables.
   c. Rows are horizontal arrangements of data.
   d. When a table will not fit on the page on which it is introduced, leave the rest of that page blank and start at the top of the next page.
   e. A footnote refers to all items in the body of a table.

3. Which one of these statements is true?
   a. Given this series of data for the Y-axis: 18; 7; 200; 8,983; 46; 299. A semi-logarithmic chart would require three-cycle graph paper.
   b. The Y-axis plots for a frequency polygon appear at the lower limits of the classes.
   c. The intersection of the two ogives identifies the mean of a series.
   d. The Y-axis of both arithmetic and logarithmic data must begin with zero.
   e. A major advantage of the overhead projector is that the speaker may face the audience while using it.

B. Inference (25 points). Indicate whether this statement is true or false.

Nonpersonal nonverbal communication is less important to business than is personal nonverbal communication.

Solution to Self-Test 37
Chapter 16

A. Recall (25 points each).   B. Inference (25 points).

   1. e   3. e   False
   2. c

Part d

SEEKING
EMPLOYMENT

17

Employment: Career Planning, Résumé, Application Letter

No situation calls more upon the full range of your communication abilities than does the campaign for employment.

The campaign involves the written, the oral, and the nonverbal. It requires both sending and receiving. It involves some routine activity and a great deal of creative and persuasive activity. It requires formality and informality. It calls upon abilities to be both forceful and retiring. It depends upon skills as both a collector and supplier of information. Above all, a campaign for employment requires skillful application of the communication principles and guidelines.

The treatment of the search for a position, then, provides a perfect opportunity to summarize, review, and integrate virtually every aspect of the communication process covered in the previous chapters. At the same time, practical and valuable information is applied to a vital topic in this discussion of job seeking.

This chapter covers the guidelines, planning for a career, planning for a job, the résumé, and the letter of application. Chapter 18 deals with other written messages, oral messages, nonverbal messages, and communication as a career field.

GUIDELINES FOR POSITION-SEARCH COMMUNICATION

The generic guidelines provide the foundation for playing all communication roles in the position-search process:

1. Define your purposes, the other participants' purposes, yourself, the other participants, and the environment.
2. Identify the channel.
3. Control the interference internal and external to you and the other participants.

4. Select, encode, decode, and transceive the messages in light of the purposes, the participants, the environment, the channel, and the interference.
5. Use feedback to and from the other participants.
6. Evaluate at each stage.

Define Purposes, Participants, and Environment

Not only must you know yourself, the others, and the environment in general terms, but you must fit and expand that knowledge in terms specific to the circumstances. First, consider your purposes and those of the others in proposed position-search transactions.

Define your purposes

Your purposes vary somewhat with the stages of your position-search or career-establishment process. However, when aligned into short-, intermediate-, and long-term goals, all stages blend together into one coherent whole.

Begin by setting long-term career goals. Then set the intermediate-term and short-term goals.

Try engaging in this process whatever your current status of employment. Even a person who has worked for many years can benefit from periodically establishing, reviewing, or revising career and employment goals.

In addition to setting career goals, also set criteria for evaluating attainment of them. Such criteria often exist within the goals themselves. For example, if you set obtaining a certain managerial position in five years as your goal, the criterion is simple. You either have the position then, or you do not.

Because career planning forms such a significant part of the employment process, consider it as a distinct topic. Discussion of it follows this coverage of the guidelines.

Define others' purposes

Even as you develop your own career and position-campaign goals, objectives, and plans, try to understand the purposes of the others involved in the process. Some of the other participants include family, friends, educators, trainers, counselors, employment agencies, publishers, government agencies, personnel officers, superiors, peers and subordinates, and former employers.

At each stage, try to define the motives of the sender or receiver in the particular transaction. Once you define them, see how well they mesh with yours. When the motives complement one another, your actions are easier to complete successfully than when they do not. However, even when your and the others' purposes appear to be at odds, you usually can find some common ground upon which to build your campaign.

Consider some examples of the purposes of others.

Family and friends   Family and friends usually have purposes that support yours. However, their purposes may oppose yours.

For example, they may want you to remain in one location when your career plans call for mobility. They may want or require you to be mobile when your career plans call for stability.

Educators, trainers, and counselors   The purposes of educators, trainers, and counselors usually blend well with yours. However, even here, some of them may have a theoretical bent when you want a practical one, or the reverse. They may be more interested in research or money than in your growth.

Employment agencies   The personnel at employment agencies certainly want to place you; their fees depend upon such placement. In addition, they want both you and the firm to be satisfied with the arrangement. However, they may not care as much about your long-term career plans as they do for the money gained by an immediate placement.

Publishers   Publishers of information about education, training, counseling, careers, and specific jobs usually publish to make a profit. However, generally, they must satisfy their clients and readers in order to do so. Thus, their purposes usually match yours.

Government agencies   Government agencies with an impact on career planning may be employment agencies, the Equal Opportunity Commission, or other agencies. Their purposes relate to the action undertaken by you when you approach them.

Government employment agencies usually provide free services, but may not provide the kinds of broad services provided by private employment agencies. Because they do not operate for a profit, government employment offices may not be quite as purposive as a private agency in trying to match employer to employee. On the other hand, the lack of a profit motive may allow them to provide more human-centered counseling.

If you approach an Equal Employment Opportunity office as an employee making a complaint, the purposes will be different than those of an employer who is the object of the complaint.

Personnel officers   Most personnel officers have as their major purposes the retention of their jobs. They usually retain them by locating people who will do the described work well. Therefore the purposes of personnel officers usually complement yours. Thus, try to match yourself and the requirements of the job and then to convince the personnel officer of the perfection of that match.

Superiors   When someone is a superior to you in a hiring or promoting sequence, he or she usually has purposes similar to those of a personnel officer. Again, the superior's success often depends in part on how well he or she chooses people to fill positions.

Peers or subordinates   When someone in a career situation is in the position of a peer or subordinate to you, he or she may have purposes supportive of or contrary to yours. One such situation arises when your promotion is the topic of a transaction. If a peer or subordinate with purposes antagonistic to yours communicates with the person(s) who will make the decision, your purposes may not be well served.

Previous employers   Prospective employers often communicate with someone for whom you have worked previously. If those people support your application, your and their purposes complement each other. However, if you are at cross purposes with such people, you must try to anticipate and counter the effects their messages may have on your purposes.

Define participants and environment

While defining your and the other participants' purposes, also define yourself, the other, and the environment.

The unit on career planning deals significantly with self-definition. Therefore, concentrate here upon defining the others and the environment. Think particularly about the potential employer and her or his environment.

To define an employer with which you plan to make application, learn about the organization itself and about the key personnel within it.

Organization   First, go to the literature to read about the firm and/or to people who know personally about the organization to talk about it.

Look at such publications as annual reports and stock-market reports.

In addition, review such sources as:

Annual Guide to Business Opportunities
Business Periodicals Index
Career: The Annual Guide to Business Opportunities
College Placement Annual
College Placement Directory
Dun & Bradstreet
Guide to American Directories
Journal of College Placement
Moody's Industrial Manual
Moody's Manuals of Investment
Poor's Register of Directors and Executives; United
    States and Canada
Public Affairs Information Service
Standard and Poor's Manuals
Thomas' Register of American Manufacturers
World Trade Directory Reports
World Wide Chamber of Commerce Directory

Try to learn:

1. How it rates financially
2. How it treats personnel
3. What benefits it provides for personnel
4. What its public image is
5. What its products and services are
6. Its organizational structure
7. Its standing in the industry
8. Whether it is conservative or progressive in its production, marketing, and financial activities
9. Its emphasis upon the specific field in which you are interested.

Key personnel   Try to learn about the personnel manager, the president, the chair of the board, and the vice president and line managers in the branch for which you are applying. Try to get to know their philosophies and styles of management. Also try to learn the personal styles, tastes, and characteristics of the people you hope to meet face to face in the process of applying and interviewing.

As discussed in previous chapters, you may not have access to much detailed information about key people. Therefore, you may have to work with some generalities and prepare yourself for a wide range of possibilities.

Particularly when you face your first interview, mentally work through how you will interact with as many possible personalities as you can. Try to picture the scene. Above all, project yourself into that scene as a confident person.

Identify Channel

Recall the theory and applications associated with channel choice and definition. Particularly recall the advantages and disadvantages of each general level (interpersonal, oral medio, and written medio, especially) and of each specific type within the levels.

Some flexibility in format and approach exists for the letter of application, for it is basically a persuasive message. However, rather traditional forms exist for the résumé (personal data sheet, data sheet, vita). Of course, oral exchanges may be either quite structured or relatively unstructured.

More about the features of the specific channels appears in the sections on encoding the messages. The sections discussing the encoded examples form the latter part of this chapter.

Protocol

Observe protocol as you select or mold your approach to the various kinds of channels. For example, even though the interpersonal and oral medio channels are richer, you rarely would use the face-to-face or telephone channels for your initial contact with the person(s) who will make the decision about whether to hire you. Instead, usually begin with the written medio form—the letter of application accompanied by a résumé and/or a completed application blank.

Creativity

The preceding warning is not intended to squelch creativity. An analysis of a particular situation may show that your only chance to be noticed is to ignore custom and proceed in some unorthodox, warm-channel manner. In such a case, forget protocol and take the risk. A great deal of your position-search success depends upon your ability to make just such decisions.

Responses

If you do take the traditional approach, once you submit the written materials, you become the hopeful receiver of either a written or telephone response asking you to come in for an interview. If you receive a written call for the interview, you may respond and set up the interview by mail or telephone—but usually by telephone. Encode either type of message carefully so that it uses the strengths of the chosen channel.

Interview

Once you face an interview situation, analyze the features, strengths, and weaknesses of it. Prior to the interview, mentally project yourself into the situation and carefully rehearse your part of it. Envision and rehearse for a variety of circumstances and interview styles. Decide the image you want to create in each.

Follow-up

While the interviews themselves are oral, the follow-up stages usually are written. Immediately after an interview and sometimes again after a certain length of time, you may write a letter to reinforce your strengths for the position. However, some follow-up messages may be transmitted by telephone—but rarely in person.

Offer and response

The employer may make the offer of a position in any of the three modes—by letter, by telephone, or in person. Thus, you may respond in kind. However, even when you respond orally, you should affirm that response in writing—be the response one of acceptance or rejection of the offer.

Nonverbal messages

For all of the written and oral stages, try to attend to the nonverbal messages integral to them. Pay particular attention to the nonverbal messages you transmit during oral interchanges.

Recall the importance of these nonverbal elements to any oral exchange: face, eyes, voice, movement, touch, appearance, space, time, and environment. Also recall how a larger proportion of social messages flow through the nonverbal channels than through the verbal ones.

Nonverbal messages are critical to oral transactions; they are equally crucial to written ones. A letter of application or résumé containing an error or smudge may cause a reader to dismiss you as an incompetent—no matter how good the verbal contents of the message may be.

A "package" must be complete, and completeness requires the proper integration of the verbal and nonverbal.

Control Interference

Every kind of interference that can occur in oral and written exchanges can occur in exchanges associated with employment. Recall that the major interference with messages emanates from within the people involved. However, external forces also become sources of interference.

Select, Encode, Decode, and Transceive Messages

Once you define purposes, the participants, the environment, the channel, and the interference, you are ready to send and receive messages in light of them. The latter part of this chapter deals primarily with sending position-search messages. However, receiving messages about employment is also important to the process.

The suggestions for effective listening, reading, and observation of nonverbal cues apply fully. Analyzing and interpreting received information can be just as important as sending it.

Use Feedback

Stimulate, receive, analyze, evaluate, and send employment feedback well.

Your receiving and analytical skills play a large part in using feedback to your advantage. Concentrate upon all the information returned from a receiver—whether in written, oral, or nonverbal form.

When you initiate employment messages, encourage feedback action through verbal persuasion. Not only encourage it, but be sure to make the feedback easy. Provide your telephone number and mailing address. In addition, indicate the times you will be available. However, tradition suggests that you do *not* include an addressed, stamped envelope with a letter of application as you do with many other persuasive messages.

When you receive a message, analyze and evaluate it fully; reply promptly and skillfully. Select and use channels for feedback as carefully as you do channels for original messages. Interruptions in the transactional spiral do nothing but irritate the very person you want to impress.

Evaluate

Evaluation of employment messages is tied closely to both purposes and feedback. For the career-planning and position-search processes, test feedback against pre-established criteria at each stage of an exchange. To the extent possible, adjust the exchange to reflect what you have learned from the evaluation.

For example, assume a letter of response shows that you have applied to the wrong person for a job. Assume that, in addition, the writer notes that he or she has forwarded your materials to the proper person—and gives the name and address of that person. Your adjustment to such feedback might be to encode a supplemental message for the proper person and transmit it to arrive soon.

Treat carefully the final evaluation of how well you attained the ultimate goal for a particular transaction. Not only assess whether you were successful or unsuccessful in meeting the criteria you established, but why you did or did not succeed.

PLANNING FOR A CAREER AND A JOB

Many workshops, courses, and programs are devoted to career planning. You may already have participated in some of them. However, in case you have not—or want some reminders about the process—review some of the basic principles and techniques associated with planning for a career.

As you do, consider setting goals and conducting self-evaluations. Such acts are necessary for success in the long-term career development itself. However, they are also necessary for creating the kinds of communication transactions that will yield desired results as you build a career.

Planning for a Career

Consider an outline of the stages of career planning:
1. Assess your current status
   a. Present employment
   b. Education and training
   c. Experience
   d. Intelligence and knowledge
   e. Attitudes, beliefs, values, interests, and aptitudes
2. Establish what you would like your career status to be:
   a. 20 years from now
   b. 10 years from now
   c. 5 years from now
   d. 3 years from now
   e. 1 year from now
3. Identify barriers to the attainment of the levels listed in No. 2
   a. Internal
   b. External
4. Determine what you need to do to reach each level specified in No. 2
   a. Education and training
   b. Experience
   c. Strengths
   d. Weaknesses
   e. Barriers
5. Establish a precise plan and a time schedule for accomplishing the stages listed in No. 4
6. Activate the plan
7. Review and revise the plan periodically

Tests

The completion of the assessment and goal-setting stages just described in the outline can take a great deal of time. The assessment may involve taking some evaluative tests at a counseling or testing center. Such tests may measure intelligence, achievement, values, aptitude, personality, and interest.

Publications

One way to learn about available careers, employers, and positions is to conduct a search of the literature on jobs and careers. Such a search might involve the publications about specific organizations listed on page 584. Some additional general sources include:

> Career Information Service
> Career Planning
> Careers Research Monographs
> Dictionary of Occupational Titles
> Occupational Literature
> Occupational Outlook Handbook
> Reality and Career Planning: A Guide for Personal Growth (Weiler)

Interviews and counseling

In addition to searching the literature, you may want to talk with people who presently occupy positions in the career paths in which you are interested. You also may want to participate in some career counseling—either on an individual basis or as part of a group.

Timing

To set the timing for goals in a satisfactory manner, try to combine realism and optimism. Above all, understand the need to retain some flexibility in the plan. To do so, establish a schedule for reassessing the plan periodically. Also take account of the fact that many jobs become obsolete as conditions change.

Education, training, experience, and strengths

To gain the education, training, experience, and strengths necessary to reach goals, identify people and institutions to help you.

The search for good educational and training institutions can be quite demanding, particularly for specialized fields. However, libraries, counseling centers, and other sources provide information on how to proceed in such a search.

You may want to mount a campaign to receive scholarships and grants. Such a process involves many of the same techniques used to find jobs.

To obtain the appropriate experience, seek to identify and be hired for the kinds of positions that yield it. Therefore, at each stage of application for a position or promotion, look at your overall career-plan goals. Then establish specific plans and objectives to fit the larger goals.

Barriers

Gaining the needed education, training, experience, and strengths overcomes many weaknesses and barriers to goals. However, try to identify and attack barriers directly in order to surmount as many of them as possible.

Identify barriers early, set strategies for overcoming them, and employ your strategies with perseverance and a positive attitude.

Realistically, you may not be able to surmount every barrier. Therefore, adopt an attitude that allows for a revision of plans. Try to make the attitude one that permits you to retain self-confidence when you do have to revise goals.

That attitude is born of the understanding that some things in life lie beyond control, but that the lack of control does not reduce you as a worthy person. Many seeming failures bring about a revised course of action as good as or better than the original.

In addition, no aborted plan is ever a waste. Growth in experience and knowledge occur as a result of establishing and applying it. Such growth often increases the chances for success in a revised plan.

Above all else, avoid letting the existence of barriers and chance effects cause you to avoid planning for a career and setting life goals. Many people move through an all-too-short life being nudged here and there by forces they do not even try to control.

Barriers may exist within or without you.

Internal   Most barriers to success probably lie within the person's mental, emotional, and physical being. Consider some examples of such obstacles to career growth:

1. Hesitation to take risks because of the fear of failure
2. Hesitation to advance because of a fear of success
3. Lack of the mental ability needed for a given discipline
4. Lack of application to the study or job
5. Lack of the will to work hard
6. Value system that runs counter to the operational reality of a chosen field
7. Lack of the physical size and strength necessary to do the desired work
8. Lack of interest
9. Allowing the opinions and attitudes of others to have undue influence

As a specific instance of how internal barriers occur, assume that you have not conquered the mathematics necessary for the career level and field you want, yet you must get a job immediately.

To overcome the barrier, you might decide to work at any job you can get as you continue to learn the mathematics necessary for the originally desired field and level. You might decide to be satisfied with a different level in the same field permanently. You might decide to change fields entirely.

If traditional educational methods will not overcome internal barriers, you may need to:

1. Counsel with experts
2. Work with groups in order to practice such things as interpersonal relations and receive constructive criticism about them
3. Join organizations or seminars that give experience in speaking before groups
4. Participate in assertive training
5. Obtain advice about the dress and appearance appropriate for the business scene

External   Some external barriers to employment include:

1. General unemployment may be high.
2. Unemployment in a specific field may be high.
3. Personal economic conditions may prohibit obtaining the needed education.
4. The country may be at war and require military service.
5. Personal biases, grudges, or even vendettas exercised by people in positions of power.
6. Attitudes of others about race, ethnic origin, sex, physical being, religion, or age.
7. Years of service and accompanying benefits at one firm or in one field that prevent a desired shift.
8. Unfair legal or policy requirements for physical and mental abilities for certain kinds of work.

Overcome or accept such barriers as you do internal ones.

(1063 words)
(test on page 614)

Planning for a Job Campaign

After setting general career goals and plans, set your plans for a specific job campaign. Establish objectives that reflect the appropriate stage of the career plan.

A job campaign usually involves a series of objectives and associated criteria. The final objective of a campaign may be to be hired by a given firm at a given salary by a given date under a given set of conditions. However, other objectives build to that one:

1. To learn everything possible about the firm and the people within it
2. To develop and test a résumé and letter of application specific to the firm
3. To send the letter and résumé to arrive at the office of the appropriate officer at a time beneficial to your campaign
4. To receive a notice that the personnel officer wants an interview
5. To perform so well in the interview that the firm calls back for the second interview
6. To perform so well in that interview that you receive the offer of the position at the desired salary by the desired time with the desired conditions
7. To encode a message of acceptance that convinces the firm of its wise choice

Applicants rarely deal with just one firm at a time. When a job campaign does involve several firms, expand the objectives to include appropriate priorities and actions. Establish your objectives to include alternatives reflecting how such actions relate to one another and to your preferences.

Focus objectives carefully at each stage of a job campaign, even as the stages fit into a greater whole.

Also maintain a flexibility that will take advantage of positive events and overcome negative ones. Without the flexibility, your vision may be restricted so tightly to one narrow course that you miss an opportunity for even greater success than that which you sought.

WRITTEN MESSAGES AND ACCOMPANYING NONVERBAL MESSAGES

Career and position-search plans often require written messages. Of course, nonverbal messages always accompany the verbal ones.

Always typewrite résumés, letters, and most other employment messages. When possible, even use the typewriter to complete application blanks. When an application form requires handwriting or when a typewriter is not available for completing it, write legibly and neatly.

Some applicants have résumés printed by professional printers. However, readers sometimes gain the impression that such applicants might be broadcasting résumés indiscriminately.

Also attend to the nonverbal aspects of written messages. Such aspects include format, color, weight of paper, texture of paper, size and style of type, underlining, use of upper-case and lower-case letters, neatness, and placement of parts of the page.

Two of the major types of written/nonverbal messages are the résumé and the letter of application.

Résumé

The résumé (personal data sheet, data sheet, vita) forms the backbone of the communication process for gaining a desired position. It is a message that contains the key information about the applicant's qualifications for employment.

Because the résumé forms the foundation of the employment search, develop it before developing any of the other messages. Use it to accompany application letters. Give it to any employment agencies or bureaus you use. Have it put in your placement-office file.

Construct the résumé as the informational core of your persuasive process. Make your résumé itself an informational piece—yet inherently persuasive as well. Like the research proposal, the résumé accomplishes most of its persuasion through the quality of the contents and their presentation, rather than through any overt techniques.

Arrange the contents of the résumé in an order that emphasizes the features you want to emphasize. Basically, then, begin and end with your strongest points, and place the others between. However, custom sometimes runs counter to the rules of emphasis, particularly in the placement of the names of references at the end of the résumé.

Develop the résumé as part of the self-assessment, goal-setting, and subsequent states of your career-planning process. You may need to develop several forms of your résumé in order to feature the different elements of your background to fit a variety of positions.

A specific position search often calls for a custom-made résumé. As time passes, revise your basic résumé to account for the changes in your history.

Though the résumé is typically a rather formal channel, you may add some creativity and flair—particularly if your preparation and the position you seek fall into the creative realms.

The well-written résumé, then, usually includes a persuasively arranged summary of such components as:

Heading
Objectives
Education and training
Experiences
Research and publications
Activities and accomplishments
Memberships
Honors and awards
Personal information
Hobbies and interests
Desired action
References

The components may carry different names or fall in a different order; some of the components, of course, might not be relevant to your background, and thus should not be included.

Figures 17–1, 17–2, 17–3, and 17–4 provide examples of résumés. The résumé in Figure 17–1 takes a traditional format and style of language. Figure 17–2 illustrates some variation in a still-traditional style. Figures 17–3 and 17–4 introduce some flair even as they retain the traditional components.

Heading

The heading of the résumé serves as an introductory title. It should include your name, the type of work or position you want, and perhaps some identifying word such as "qualifications," "credentials," "assets," or "strengths." Do not use the words "résumé," "personal data sheet," "data sheet," or "vita" in the heading.

Objectives

A brief statement of objectives often follows the heading. Use the statement to continue the persuasion begun with the heading. Use this emphatic (early) position to illustrate enthusiasm for the position or type of work cited in the heading.

Education and training

Include a recitation of education and training early in a résumé.

Order of listing   List the latest educational or training level first and work chronologically backward from there. Be sure to account for any significant gaps between major educational training events. Include your degree or diploma, major field, institution, and date of attainment for each level.

Courses and grades   You may list and group the courses that you have had that relate to the position or field you want to enter. Put them in descending order of importance. Use titles that explain the content. If you include individual grades, use letters or some generally accepted and understood system.

You may show grade-point averages for total programs, your major, or a block of courses. However, if you do, be sure to state the numerical base for the average. In many schools 4.0 = A. However, other schools use different bases.

Related experiences   Include citations of related educational and training experiences. Usually such experiences either did not result from traditional or formal settings or did not result in a diploma or degree.

Examples of such experiences include participation in seminars, workshops, practicums, study groups, retreats, and even audited courses. Such programs may be offered by local libraries, military personnel, traveling consultants, in-service-training personnel of a firm, or educational institutions. They may cover such general topics as leadership, supervisory and managerial functions, assertiveness, self-awareness, human relations, or communication (oral and written). They may also cover any topic related to a career field (C.P.A. review, law review, insurance workshops, banking seminars, etc.).

When you do include a list of such learning experiences, indicate the who, what, when, and where of each activity. If it resulted in some sort of recognized

MILTON A. ROSEN

Candidate for Bachelor of Science Degree in Management
University of Dillon, Dillon, Utah

OBJECTIVE: A challenging position of responsibility as a
personnel director, personnel specialist, or
organization development specialist in private
industry anywhere in the United States

FULL NAME: Milton Aaron Rosen

PERMANENT ADDRESS: 3641 Alvin Elber Drive
Salt Lake City, Utah 33113

SCHOOL ADDRESS: 400 Skinner Street, Apartment 14B
Dillon, Utah 33129

TELEPHONE: (555) 322-8963 School
(555) 331-3110 Home

DATE AND PLACE OF BIRTH: September 25, 1959, Boise, Idaho

MARITAL STATUS: Single

HEALTH: Excellent

EDUCATION:

Bachelor of Science in Management, University of Dillon, Dillon,
Utah—May, 1981 (expected month of graduation)

Organization Development Certificate, Wyler Institute of
Management, Dillon, Utah—August, 1980 (completed 320-hour
summer program in organization development)

UNDERGRADUATE CONCENTRATION (in semester hours):

Management—22 hours; Marketing—12 hours; Accounting—6
hours; and Finance—6 hours

Figure 17–1 Traditional résumé for soon-to-be graduated student

documentation of your participation (a certificate, for example), report it. Also indicate the number of hours actually spent in the contact.

Be sure that the activity was significant enough in your preparation to include it. Also be sure that reporting it contributes to your indirect persuasion. Do not fill valuable space with the citation of events that will not substantially persuade the reader of your abilities for the specified career or position.

Certification   Consider certain kinds of certification either as education and training

MILTON A. ROSEN 2

WORK EXPERIENCE:

Tutor (part-time), University of Dillon Study Center—1978-present (tutor undergraduates in both management and marketing subjects)

Typist (full-time), University of Dillon Library—summer of 1977 (typed overdue notices and order forms)

UNIVERSITY ACTIVITIES:

President, Kramer Dormitory—1977-1978

Member, Management Club—1978-1981

Editor, Business School Weekly—1980-1981

UNIVERSITY AWARDS AND HONORS:

Dean's Honor Roll—1979-1981

Chamber of Commerce Scholarship—1980-1981

PROFESSIONAL ORGANIZATIONS:

Member, Management Society of Utah—1980-present

Member, Dillon Business Association—1980-present

REFERENCES (permission obtained from all references):

Alice Symington, Ph.D., Professor of Management,
School of Business, University of Dillon, Dillon, Utah 33129;
phone—(555) 322-8666

Edward Winters, M.S., Assistant Professor of Marketing,
School of Business, University of Dillon, Dillon, Utah 33129;
phone—(555) 322-8667

Deborah Wechsler, Ed.D., Director, Study Center,
University of Dillon, Dillon, Utah 33129;
phone—(555) 322-8680

Delbert Irving, B.Ed., Supervisor, Library Business Office,
University of Dillon, Dillon, Utah 33129;.
phone—(555) 322-8770

Figure 17–1 (continued)

or as forming a distinct category. Such certification involves not only extensive education, but also significant testing by an agency independent of educational institutions. Examples include testing for the designations of Certified Public Accountant, Chartered Life Underwriter, and Certified Professional Secretary. Admission to the bar in a given state is a similar type of educational testing category.

You may include the appropriate acronym for such certification after your name at the top of the page—either in place of or in addition to featuring it in a listing. Thus, a name might be written "Y. R. Self, CFA."

JANET E. SMITH

2332 Pine Road   555-721-6231 (home)
Anthony, Idaho 44662   555-721-4992 (message)

Objectives

A challenging position, with opportunities for promotion, in
financial planning, financial management, or investment
counseling.

Education

Master of Business Administration degree in Finance, Anthony University (3.42 grade point average, based on 4-point scale)	1980
Bachelor of Science degree in Finance, Anthony University, Anthony, Idaho (academic scholarship student)	1979
Associate of Science degree in Business Administration, Linwood Community College, Linwood, Idaho	1977

Experience

Investment Assistant, DiRenzio and Barber, Inc., Anthony, Idaho (full-time)	Summers of 1978 and 1979

Assisted two investment counselors in preparing investment
folders on major Idaho corporations. Also worked as an
investment counselor on several occasions.

Carpenter, Leland and Daughters Construction Company, Anthony, Idaho (full-time)	Summers of 1976 and 1977

Built kitchen and bathroom cabinets in new homes and new
office buildings.

Figure 17–2 Traditional résumé for recent graduate

Experience

Include any experiences you have had that will contribute to success in the work or career you seek. Such experiences usually relate to civilian work for which you have been paid. However, they also may relate to the military, sometimes to significant volunteer work with a not-for-profit-organization, or sometimes even to positions of responsibility in major professional organizations.

List everything you have done since graduation from high school or college—depending upon the status of your career—but distinguish between full- and part-time work.

Activities

Panelist, Women in Management Workshop, Anthony University	1978
Vice President, Anthony University Finance Club	1978-1979

Memberships

Member, Finance Association of America	1978-present
Member, Anthony Downtown Business Club	1979-present

Honors and Awards

Outstanding Business Student Award, Linwood Community College	1977
Elizabeth Blanchard Scholarship, Anthony University	1977-1978
Susan Stanton Finance Award, Anthony University	1978

Personal Information

Married, two children, excellent health

Hobbies and Interests

Cross-country skiing, furniture building, and reading

References

References provided upon request

Figure 17–2   (continued)

Cite experiences in logical groupings—and generally in reverse order within the groupings. Thus, the latest position you held in a particular grouping will appear at the top of the list.

Give dates, names of organizations for which you worked, job titles, and a summary of responsibilities. Spotlight the work that shows the most valuable and related experiences.

If you include such experiences as internships, consulting, and self-employment, you may want to treat them in a separate section. However, you may combine all such types under a single heading.

```
4321 Vine Street                          555-666-1319 (home)
Boston, Massachusetts 99496               555-666-3422 (message)
```

Qualifications of

MARIA E. MARTINEZ

for a career in training and development

Employment Goal

I seek an extremely challenging position as the training and development
director for a major United States corporation.

Summary of Qualifications

Training and Development
- 2 years of experience as the training and development manager for
  Adams and Ross, Inc., Boston
- 12 semester hours in graduate training and development courses
  (earned a perfect—4.0—grade point average in these courses)
- 9 semester hours in undergraduate training and development courses
  (perfect—4.0—grade point average)
- 2 years of experience in teaching undergraduate training and
  development courses

Organization Development
- 2 years of experience as an organization development planner for
  Darmer Real Estate, Danville, West Virginia
- 12 semester hours in graduate courses in organization development
  (perfect—4.0—grade point average)
- 3 years of experience in conducting organization development
  workshops and seminars for professional groups

General Business
- 60 semester hours of graduate work in business (earned a 3.9 out of
  4.0 grade point average)
- 45 semester hours of undergraduate work in business (earned a 3.75
  out of 4.0 grade point average)
- 1 year of experience in teaching undergraduate accounting courses

Experience

Manager, Training and Development   Adams and Ross, Inc.
March 1, 1978-April 15, 1980   Systems Management Group
                                           Boston, Massachusetts

I began the first training and development programs at Adams and Ross.
When I left, 75 percent (380) of the company's professional and managerial
employees were voluntarily participating in the 15 training and
development sequences that I developed. As the first manager of training
and development, I hired and supervised a staff of 10 training and
development associates and 8 clerical workers.

Figure 17–3 Résumé for person who has professional experience.

Experience (continued)

Organization Development Planner   Darmer Real Estate
January 1, 1976-February 20, 1978   Danville, West Virginia

As the only planner in the three-person organization development
department, I developed and implemented the two organization development
programs that were in themselves responsible for a 16 percent reduction in
the turnover rate among all Darmer personnel. I also conducted a number of
group dynamics and team building workshops for both the managers and
salespersons.

Education

I earned the Master of Business Administration degree in June, 1980, from
the Boston Business Institute. I completed 60 semester hours in graduate
courses at the institute, and I earned a 3.9 out of 4.0 grade point average.

I was graduated from the University of Danville, Danville, West Virginia,
with a Bachelor of Business Administration degree in December, 1975. I
completed 124 semester hours of coursework, and I earned a 3.6 out of 4.0
grade point average.

Publications

Organization Development: Developing Socio-Technical Systems.
    Boston: Business Books Press, 1979.

"Training the Professional Systems Manager," Training Digest 12
    (October 1978): 112-119.

Professional Affiliations

Member, Training Society of Boston, 1979-present
Member, Association of Organizational Developers, 1976-present

Personal

I am married, and I am willing to relocate.

References

I will furnish references upon request.

Figure 17–3   (continued)

13 Walker Avenue
Argyle, Maine 22914
(555) 231-9964

                                        LEE WU'S

                            qualifications for the position of

                                      SALESPERSON

OBJECTIVE   To secure a challenging position as a salesperson for
                            a major, growing pharmaceutical company

EDUCATION AND   Bachelor of Arts degree in business, with a major in
TRAINING   selling, from the University of Argyle, Argyle, Maine,
                            1981
                            Twelve semester hours of selling and marketing
                            courses at the Claire Moran Sales Institute, Argyle,
                            Maine, 1980-1981

SELLING AND   Selling
MARKETING   Basic Personal Selling—A
COURSES   Advanced Personal Selling—A
AND GRADES   Salespersonship—A
                            Selling Problems—A
                            Managing Sales Districts—A
                            Marketing
                            Basic Marketing Management—A
                            Managing the Marketing Function—B
                            Consumer Behavior—A
                            Marketing Reseach—A

Figure 17–4   Résumé for salesperson

Research and publications

A recitation of research projects and publications sometimes relates to the work and shows the quality of the applicant's background. If the position featured in the résumé involves research, such a section is mandated. Even if it does not require research, but is supported by it, you may still want to include the section.

The section on research and publication provides evidence of additional effort that some kinds of employers respect. Applicants for positions in universities often include such a section, as do applicants for certain kinds of positions in business.

LEE WU'S   PAGE 2

SELLING   Full-time chemical salesperson for the Argyle
EXPERIENCE   Chemical Company, summers of 1977-1980.
                     Responsible for entire Vermont sales district.
                     Always exceeded monthly sales quotas.

                     Part-time clothing salesperson at the Argyle
                     Department Store, school years of 1977-1981.
                     Responsible for boys' department. Exceeded sales
                     quotas most every month.

UNIVERSITY   President, Salespersons' Club, 1980-1981
ACTIVITIES   Member, Argyle Business Students' Club, 1980-1981
                     Coordinator, Salespersonship Workshop, 1979

PROFESSIONAL   Member, Salespersons of America, 1979-present
ACTIVITIES   Member, Argyle Selling Association, 1980-present

PERSONAL   Age 21, single, perfect health

REFERENCES   Ann Sleth, Ph.D., Professor of Marketing
(by permission)   University of Argyle
                     Argyle, Maine 22914

                     Richard Mackin, Ed.D., Professor of Salespersonship
                     University of Argyle
                     Argyle, Maine 22914

                     Carol Dimitri, Marketing Director
                     Argyle Chemical Company
                     6231 North Wayne Road
                     Argyle, Maine 22914

                     Warren Ochoco, Manager
                     Argyle Department Store
                     18 North Broadway Street
                     Argyle, Maine 22914

Figure 17–4   (continued)

Suppose a listing of research and publications is longer than a half page. In that case, include a section in the body of the résumé that features a few of your major works, but refers the reader to a complete listing attached as an appendix to the résumé itself.

If you do not think you should include a complete listing in either the body or an appendix, you might use a heading indicating that you are reporting selected research and publications. You might also include a sentence that indicates the volume of other research projects and/or publications that you do not include in the résumé.

Observe the organization of the part on publications which is presented in Figure 17–3.

Activities and accomplishments

Some major activities and accomplishments do not fit well into the other, more traditional categories. Yet if these endeavors have prepared you for the career or position which you seek, include them as a separate category.

Examples Here are examples of the kinds of activities that do not quite "belong" elsewhere:

1. Speeches or panels
2. Workshops and seminars for organizations, civic groups, or programs at public schools and colleges
3. Volunteer counseling for people in the community
4. Supervision of business-school interns who worked for your firm for a period of time
5. Tutoring of people in the field for which you are applying
6. Service in a major capacity for some professional organizations—officer of a local, regional, or national unit
7. Work without pay in a businesslike position for a not-for-profit organization (sometimes listed as part of experience)
8. Extensive travel or residence in a foreign country in which a firm has holdings
9. Speaking the language of a foreign country in which a firm has holdings
10. Nonremunerated consulting work that provided valuable related experience (sometimes listed as part of experience)

Relevancy In a section on activities and accomplishments, include only those relevant to the objectives and significant enough to add support to your persuasive thrust.

Unless you are just out of high school, do not include high-school activities here unless they show substantial maturity, responsibility, or relevancy to the position for which you apply. Do not list such activities as cheerleading, social fraternities and sororities, pep clubs, sports, choirs, and other musical groups unless they relate directly to your objectives or exemplify significant leadership abilities.

Once you complete a post-secondary degree, drop all high school activities from your résumé. Until you establish some experience after completion of a degree, you may include some collegiate activities. However, again, do not include activities unless they exhibit leadership or relate closely to your career field. Certainly do not include the kinds of activities listed in the preceding paragraph.

Include an activities section only when pertinent activities do not fit naturally into the other sections. Do not feel that you have to include one.

Figures 17–1, 17–2, and 17–4 contain sections on activities.

Memberships

Some of the types of activities and accomplishments suggested for the previous section relate to memberships in professional, honorary, and civic organizations. Therefore, a single section may show a combination of activities and affiliations with such organizations.

Whether combined or separated, however, a listing of pertinent organizational memberships and participation belongs in many résumés.

Put in the list only those organizations that represent current educational and career status. Include only the names of those active organizations of which you are currently a dues-paying or paid-up member. Thus, you may include active honorary organizations here, but leave the inactive ones for the subsequent section on honors.

Honors and awards

When significant honors and awards relate to your career plan, report them in your résumé.

High school If you have not been out of high school long, you may include significant honors from your high-school career. Appropriate honors include such earned recognitions as who's who, honor societies, valedictorian, salutatorian, and scholarships awarded upon graduation. Appropriate honors do *not* include such designations as kingships, queenships, beauty-pageant titles, sweethearts, class favorites, or "most-popular" designations.

Sometimes honors such as being named "most likely to succeed," "outstanding business student," or "outstanding athlete" may qualify as preparation for a career. However, many readers consider them unrelated to the serious pursuance of a career.

College Once you receive a degree from a college or university, drop the high-school honors, and add those gained during the collegiate years.

Appropriate to include in the post-secondary listing are such honors as Phi Beta Kappa, Rhodes Scholar, Mortar Board, who's who, scholarships, valedictorian, salutatorian, class marshall, *summa cum laude, magna cum laude, cum laude,* and awards for outstanding scholarship in special fields of study. Inappropriate are the same kinds of designations cited for high-school listing.

Post-college As soon as you have built some career experience, drop all of the collegiate honors and awards except those that carry a lifetime of meaning. The Phi Beta Kappa and *laude* designations are examples of those that can be retained.

As you drop collegiate honors and awards, replace them with professional ones: outstanding man/woman of the year; leading a city, region, or the nation in annual sales; or some other kind of recognized achievement.

Consider carefully whether to include some of the "who's who" publications. Many of them have reached the point that almost anyone may be listed if he or she just completes a form and buys a copy of the publication. Some personnel officers have begun to dismiss them as meaningless affectations by those who do list them in their résumés.

The further you are past the completion of your education, the less likely it is that you will include an honors section in your résumé. Experience and accomplishments take the place of honors.

Personal information

Somewhere in your résumé you should include a brief summary of the personal characteristics you deem pertinent to your objectives. The traditional résumé includes these characteristics as the first component. However, many applicants now recognize that such data do not deserve that emphasized location.

Personal information includes sex, marital status, race, ethnic background, age, religion, physical characteristics, state of health, physical handicap, and a photograph.

Decide carefully what you want to include in this section. A critical psychology is associated with your decision.

For instance, laws and rulings state or at least suggest that you need not provide virtually any personal information. In the same vein, you do not have to include the photograph so common to the résumé of a few years ago.

While personal information cannot be required, some employment decision-makers like to know of it. On the other hand, some people do not even want it, lest they be accused of allowing it to influence their decisions.

Your solution, of course, is, first, to try to learn what the receiver prefers, next, to decide what you think is reasonable, and, finally, to take some sort of middle ground on the issue.

A middle-ground approach might be simply to include your mailing address(es), telephone number(s), and times when you can be reached at each. You might omit the photograph and any of the personal characteristics that you believe might hurt your chances of being treated fairly. However, include some of the information that will not lead to prejudice against you. For example, giving your family status (married or single, children or no children, etc.) sometimes has no impact upon the reader except to suggest something about you as a human being. Similarly, the inclusion of such physical characteristics as height, weight, and general health may help create a nonprejudicial personal sketch.

If you include a photograph, do not fix it permanently to the page. The reviewers may want to remove it for their own purposes.

The inclusion of a statement of interests and hobbies can serve to replace some of the questionable personal items.

Figures 17–1 through 17–4 illustrate some different treatments of the personal sections of résumés. Analyze them in light of your own preferences.

Hobbies and interests

Sometimes a résumé includes a part that lists hobbies and interests. However, with the movement away from revealing much personal information, this section may gradually become the major portion of the personal section. It may no longer exist as a distinct one.

Briefly naming and describing some of your personal hobbies, pleasures, and interests often provides a good relief from the heaviness of the other information in a résumé. Introduce such a listing if you believe it will do so. In any case, such a listing does not take much space and usually is innocuous enough that it introduces no risk.

Observe how the writer treats the sections on hobbies and interests in Figure 17–2.

Desired action

Though creating controversy, a section on desired action now occasionally appears in a résumé. The controversy exists because the classical résumé contains no persuasion other than that inherent in the content of the message. Persuasive statements usually appear in the letter of application that accompanies the résumé. In fact, many communication writers suggest that directly persuasive statements have absolutely no place in a résumé.

A résumé sometimes must stand alone, however. For example, if you have a résumé put in a placement- or employment-office folder, you cannot write a letter of application that will satisfy any but a general situation. Therefore, you may want to allow the résumé to stand as a self-contained preliminary document of your persuasive attempt to be hired.

If you do elect to include some sort of closing persuasive call to action, keep it brief. Make it fit the format and style of the preceding sections. For example, if you have used no complete sentences previously, do not use them in the closing action section either. Also create a heading for the action section that parallels the previous structure.

Introduce overt persuasion into a résumé cautiously. Most decision-makers probably still expect the traditional factual style. They might tend to reject anything that departs too much from that expectation.

References

References usually occupy the final position in a résumé. As suggested earlier, they do so out of custom, not out of any realistic consideration for emphasizing the most important component.

If you list the names, titles, addresses, and telephone numbers of references, be sure to obtain their permission to do so prior to completing the résumé. Indicate on the résumé that you did obtain the permissions.

Carefully choose the people whom you include as references. Try to select people with knowledge representing the range of the various facets of your career and professional talents and experiences. Because you usually will list no more than five or six, do not include character references unless specifically requested.

Writers often omit a list of references in the résumé. However, they do include the reference section and simply note that the references will be provided upon request. Figures 17–2 and 17–3 include such notations.

Application Letter

A letter of application usually accompanies a résumé. Begin a review of the characteristics of the letter of application by skimming Figures 17–5 through 17–8. Observe that they represent a variety of circumstances and styles.

As the examples show, letters of application may be solicited or unsolicited, general or specific, formal or informal, and inherently or overtly persuasive. Whatever the approach and style, though, the letter of application must develop a strong effort to persuade the reader to action.

Format and style

Use the basic letter format for the application message. However, you may want to include some of the colorful variations made possible by the persuasive nature of the transaction. (See Figure 17–8.)

Always adapt the style to fit your analysis of the receiver and her or his environment. For example, if you write an unsolicited message, you may have to

400 Skinner Street, Apt. 148
Dillon, Utah 33129
April 15, 1981

Ms. Lee Wong, Human Relations Manager
Mariel Lumber Company
15 Mariel Way
Frilen, Washington 99432

Dear Ms. Wong:

I have taken more courses in organization development than have most of
my contemporaries. As an entry-level specialist in your organization
development program, I could put my excellent training and extensive
knowledge to work for you and for Mariel Lumber Company.

The 320-hour program that I completed at the prestigious Wyler Institute of
Management afforded me the opportunity to fully explore the world of
organization development that I had begun to explore as a management
major at the University of Dillon. My training would allow me to make
meaningful contributions to your brilliant organization development
program, the program I read about in the March issue of Human Resources
Monthly. Your program is the most perfectly planned and ambitious
program that I have ever seen.

I am confident that I could perform in a variety of roles in your program
because of my unique training as an organization development specialist,
because of my two years of experience as a management tutor, and because
of my solid general training in business and the arts and sciences at the
University of Dillon.

Because I know my unique training would be an asset to your top-notch
program, I am eager to become a part of your organization development
team, Ms. Wong. I will be available for work on May 15, a week after I
complete my Bachelor of Arts degree in business at the University of Dillon.

By referring to the enclosed résumé and contacting the people I list as
references, you will be able to acquire an overall picture of my specialized
qualifications.

Please call me or write me soon because I am eager to have a personal
interview with you. I will be able to come to Frilen at your convenience.

Sincerely,

Milton A. Rosen

Milton A. Rosen

Enclosure

Figure 17–5   Letter of application that accompanies Milton A. Rosen's résumé

2332 Pine Road
Anthony, Idaho 44662
June 1, 1980

Mr. Eric Hendricksen, Personnel Director
Shapiro, Hart & Wenner, Inc.
Willtoe, Nevada 33963

Dear Mr. Hendricksen:

As the daughter of two farmers, I learned the meaning of hard work at an early age. The lessons I learned on the farm have been invaluable, and I have devoted all of my energy to every job, project, or school course that I have ever undertaken.

Your advertisement in the May 29 edition of the Daily Nevadan asked for an energetic, hard-working person. Your advertisement also asked that the job applicant be a competent investment counselor.

My two degrees in finance and my experience as an investment assistant make me a competent investment counselor. My years on the farm and the fact that I paid my own way through rigorous, expensive undergraduate and graduate finance programs make me a hard working, competent investment counselor. As you will notice on the enclosed résumé, my work at DiRenzio and Barber, Inc., involved both investment planning and investment folder preparation.

I want to use my farm-hand energy and common sense, my excellent training in finance, and my considerable intelligence to give your Shapiro, Hart & Wenner clients sound investment advice. I can begin work for you immediately.

May I please hear from you soon concerning a personal interview? You can contact me at my home address, at 555-721-6231, or at 555-721-4992.

Sincerely,

Janet E. Smith

Janet E. Smith

Enclosure: Résumé

Figure 17–6 Application letter that accompanies Janet E. Smith's résumé

4231 Vine Street
Boston, Massachusetts 99496
August 3, 1980

Ms. Linda Kelsoe, Industrial Relations Manager
Quarel Foods, Inc.
13904 Industrial Triangle Drive
Boston, Massachusetts 09498

Dear Ms. Kelsoe:

My extensive training and valuable experience in training and development
make me confident that I could competently and creatively perform as the
training and development manager at your firm.

As my resume indicates, I have four years of full-time experience in training
and development and organization development. Perhaps my most notable
accomplishment in the training field was the extremely successful training
and development program that I developed and implemented at Adams and
Ross, Inc., a systems management group. By the time that I left Adams and
Ross, 75 percent of the managerial and professional employees were
voluntarily participating in my program's 15 training sequences.

While earning the B.B.A. and M.B.A. degrees in management, I took 33
semester hours of training and development and organization development
courses, and I earned a perfect—4.0—grade point average in those courses.
The Boston Business Institute, the institution from which I earned my
M.B.A. degree, is well known for its excellent training and development
courses.

Because I am familiar with your Quarel Foods, Inc., operation, I know your
industrial relations department is most impressive. I would very much like
to be a part of the food manufacturing industry and of your fine department
as the manager of training and development at Quarel Foods. Your interest
in team building is an interest that I share, and the team-building workshops that I conducted at Darmer Real Estate were both successful and
enjoyable.

Please call me at 666-1319 so that I can answer any of your questions.
Sometime during the next two weeks I would like to meet with you at your
convenience. I am eager to discuss my many training and development ideas
with you.

Sincerely,

Maria E. Martinez

Maria E. Martinez

Enclosure

Figure 17–7   Application letter that accompanies Maria E. Martinez's résumé

13 Walker Avenue
Argyle, Maine 22914
August 15, 1981

Personnel Director
Waygo Pharmaceuticals, Inc.
333 East Main Street
Silverton, New Hampshire 33692

YOUR COMPANY COULD PUT AN ENERGETIC,
SUCCESSFUL SALESPERSON LIKE ME
TO WORK IMMEDIATELY.
AND YOU'D GET FANTASTIC RESULTS!

HERE'S WHY:

1. For the four summers that I managed the entire Vermont
   sales district for the Argyle Chemical Company, I exceeded
   my sales quota every month.

2. While working my way through the University of Argyle, I
   was a top part-time salesperson for the Argyle Department
   Store.

3. My major at the University of Argyle was selling, and I
   earned my Bachelor of Arts degree in business. Twenty-
   seven quarter term hours in selling and marketing made up
   a significant portion of my coursework.

As my résumé notes, a challenging position as a salesperson for
a major, growing pharmaceutical company like yours is my
objective. Remember, both my selling experience and business
education would allow you to put me to work immediately. You
could have me exceeding sales quotas for you every month of
the year.

Selling is the thing I do best. Please call me at (555) 232-1194
so that I can begin work for you immediately.

Sincerely,

Lee Wu

Lee Wu

Enclosure

Figure 17–8 Application letter that accompanies Lee Wu's résumé

add some flair in order to gain the desired attention. On the other hand, you may
need to retain a moderate approach so that you will not risk alienating the receiver
because of an unusual style. Your decision depends upon a careful analysis of the
circumstances and the probable nature of the receiver.

Even if you add persuasive touches of color and informality to application
messages, preserve most of the amenities. Typewrite the letter using correct basic

format and mechanics. Use good-quality paper. Include your return address properly positioned. Include the inside address. Include or omit the salutation depending upon the choice of style. Use subject and attention lines if appropriate. Except for the simplified style, include an appropriate complimentary close. Use the signature block to establish your name and desired courtesy title. Use the enclosure notation to acknowledge your résumé and any other enclosure. Always refer to the résumé in the body of the letter as well.

Address the envelope correctly, and fold and insert the letter and other materials properly. If the mailing is bulky, use an envelope large enough to hold the materials without having to fold them.

Whenever possible, write each letter of application uniquely and personally to the appropriate person(s) at the firm for which you want to work. If you simply cannot obtain that information, include in the inside address and salutation a traditional title. One such title is "Personnel Director." Figure 17–8 illustrates the approach.

If you decide to omit the unknown name, title, and thus the salutation, you may replace the salutation with the kinds of attention-getting phrases and statements used for any persuasive letter. Observe such an approach in the example in Figure 17–8.

Use the basic APCA plan of development. Apply the principles for gaining attention; establishing perception and interest; developing comprehension, conviction, and desire; and securing acceptance and action. Apply all of the other suggestions relating to such features as emphasis, tone, vocabulary, active voice, transition, and coherence. Even retain the "you" attitude. Appeal to the reader's needs. Try to convince the reader that hiring you will benefit her or him.

Even with the "you" attitude, you will have to use the first person pronouns. However, try not to overuse them, and space them well through the message.

Whatever the circumstances of the transaction, apply the guidelines and principles particularly carefully. Never will you be in a situation that requires you to sell anything more important—for you are essentially selling yourself.

Techniques for successful application letters

Gootnick lists 13 techniques for developing successful messages of application:

1. Be positive and confident, but not presumptuous or arrogant.
2. Talk of key credentials to fulfill the job requirements.
3. Show interest in working for the company.
4. Show knowledge of the company.
5. Show knowledge of the job requirements.
6. Prove that your capabilities and experience fulfill key requirements.
7. Be forthright in seeking the interview, but still respectful.
8. Compliment the firm's work or reputation but avoid obvious or insincere flattery.
9. Refer to the résumé for evidence of your qualifications.
10. Avoid any negative remarks about yourself, others, and the company.
11. Use the letter opening to excite the reader about you and to let the reader know what you want, namely the job. You capture attention and build interest by mentioning such things as
    a. the job-ad source
    b. a person well known to the reader

    c. a person of fame

    d. a comment that assures reader agreement

    e. a significant accomplishment of the firm

    f. an accomplishment of the reader

    g. an award or honor of the reader

    h. a significant change in the field

    i. an important and felt need of the firm

    j. a personal qualification currently in need by the firm

12. Use the letter middle to create desire. Prove, in this part, that you have what it takes to excel in the job. Whet the reader's interest by highlighting key capabilities and by using the enclosed résumé as a reservoir of key accomplishments to prove your strengths. If you have prepared a nutshell summary in the résumé, be certain that this part of the letter is phrased or slanted somewhat differently.

13. Use the letter ending to request the interview and stimulate action.[1]

Even as you try to include all of these elements, however, try to limit your letters to one page. Carefully develop the theme, the key points, and tie them together in a warm, but concise package.

Analyze Figures 17–5 through 17–8 to determine how well you think they met the criteria. Would the recipients read the résumés? Would they invite the writers for interviews? Would they acknowledge receipt of the material even if an opening does not exist? Would they hand them to someone else for consideration? Would they simply file them?

As you review the figures, also notice how the general-search letter (Figure 17–8) lacks some of the precision and zest possible in the specific letters (Figures 17–5, 17–6, and 17–7). Similarly, notice how the response to an advertisement (Figure 17–6) cannot include the focus on a specific theme that is possible when the writer has more detailed information about the firm. The contrast between that letter and Figures 17–5 and 17–7 illustrates the difference in what can be achieved.

The key to developing a successful letter of application is to retain a basic honesty running through a message that reflects a sound application of the principles and guidelines for good communication. Let your personal style emerge even as you meet the requirements that custom and good form impose.

SUMMARY

The campaign for employment involves sending and receiving written, oral, and nonverbal messages. The generic guidelines provide the foundation for playing all roles in that campaign:

1. Define purposes, participants, and environment.
2. Identify channel.
3. Control interference.
4. Select, encode, decode, and transceive messages in light of purposes, participants, environment, channel, and interference.
5. Use feedback.
6. Evaluate.

---

[1]David Gootnick, *Getting a Better Job* (New York: McGraw-Hill Book Company, 1978), p. 85.

Planning for a career requires several steps: (1) Assess your current status. (2) Establish what you would like your career status to be by selected points in time in the future. (3) Identify barriers to the attainment of the career-status goals. (4) Determine what you need to do to reach the specified career-status goals. (5) Establish a precise plan and time schedule. (6) Activate the plan. (7) Review and revise the plan periodically.

To aid in career planning, you may want to take *tests,* consult *publications, interview* or *counsel* with knowledgeable people, use both *optimism* and *realism* in setting *time schedules,* and identify and set strategies to *overcome internal and external barriers.*

After setting career goals and plans, set them for a specific *job campaign.* The goals and plans relate to such aspects of the campaign as learning about the firm, developing and testing a résumé and letter of application, interviewing well, and receiving the job offer.

Many written messages characterize a job search. Two of the major types are the résumé and letter of application.

The *résumé*—also called a personal data sheet, data sheet, or vita—is the message that contains information about you and your qualifications for employment. Arrange the contents of the résumé in an order that emphasizes the features you want to emphasize. When possible, tailor résumés to the positions for which you are applying. The résumé may include as many as 12 parts.

The *heading* may include your name and type of work you want, but not such words as "résumé" or "personal data sheet."

Use the opening position for *objectives* that illustrate enthusiasm for the desired position or type of work indicated in the heading.

In the section on *education and training,* list the latest educational and training experiences first. If you list courses and grades, organize them as they relate logically to the position. Include descriptive titles.

Be sure that the listed *experiences* fit the position campaign. You may include special kinds of certification at this point. Cite experiences in logical groupings, with the most recent listed first.

List *research and publications* if they are associated with the position for which the application is made.

The section on *activities and accomplishments* may include such things as speeches, supervision of interns, or service in a major capacity for professional organizations. Do not include irrelevant activities. As you climb the career ladder, drop the high-school and even collegiate activities.

In the section on *memberships* list only those active and honorary memberships that are pertinent to the application.

Include only significant, current *awards and honors.*

Reveal the kinds of *personal information* that you feel will not compromise your principles, but will help portray you as a good candidate for the position. You need not include a photograph.

You might want to include a brief section on *hobbies and interests*—either as part of the personal-information section or as a section unto itself.

Though not a conventional practice, some people include a brief section on *desired action* in the résumé.

The section on *references* usually occupies the final position. Be sure to obtain permission from the references named. You may, instead of listing the references, state that you will provide a listing upon request.

The *letter of application* is a relatively formal, but persuasive message. Adapt the *format* and *style* to fit your personality and the circumstances of the application. Apply the writing principles and communication guidelines fully and carefully.

Some of the techniques for a successful letter of application are: (1) Be positive and confident. (2) Talk of key credentials. (3) Show interest and knowledge. (4) Refer to the résumé. (5) Avoid negative remarks. (6) Use the opening and closing positions for gaining attention and soliciting action. (7) Try to contain the letter on one page.

Practice

1. You stand a good chance of getting hired at Aldridge, Inc., if you can get an interview with Alice Rogers, a very powerful Aldridge vice president. The normal procedure is to send an application to the personnel department, but you know that few people make it past the personnel department. Write a letter directly to Rogers. Try to persuade her to grant you an interview. Remember that Rogers will not be following the normal employment procedure if she decides to interview you.

2. [*Your instructor will time this exercise.*] You just learned that a position opened up at the firm for which you want to work. The opening is for an entry-level marketing associate who will develop marketing plans for small toys. The toys will be sold only in the local area. You have already prepared a résumé that emphasizes your abilities as a marketer. Now write a one-page letter of application that you will send with your marketing résumé. Address the letter to:

   Mr. Arnold Benner, Personnel Director
   Dorn Marketing Group
   2233 Fisher Lane
   Savelle, Mississippi 26919

3. Prepare your own résumé. Do not tailor it to any specific position, but do emphasize your best qualities in a traditional form. Try to include all of the résumé components listed on page 592 except for the section on desired action.

4. Convert your conventionally designed résumé (No. 3) into a résumé with creativity and flair. Include a section on desired action. Meet with your group to discuss and evaluate both forms of the résumés. Decide whether you think prospective employers generally would react more favorably toward the conventional or creative résumé in each case— and why. Choose a member to report the group's decision and reasons to the class.

5. You plan to apply for a position as an accountant at a local accounting firm. You have been told that you are to send only your résumé; the firm wants no letters of application. You decide that because your résumé must stand alone, you should include a section that makes explicit the action that you desire. Write the desired-action paragraph.

6. Meet with your group. Use the brainstorming technique to identify the interpersonal strengths and weaknesses of each member of the group. Allow each person to participate in her or his own analysis. After the brainstorming, allow each member to discuss her or his list—questioning the validity of it if desired. Summarize any strengths or weaknesses common to the members of the group. Choose one member to report the findings to the class.

7. Select a career field which you would like to enter upon graduation. Check the literature to learn all you can about it. Write a two-page paper reporting your findings.

8. Identify and analyze an actual firm in the career field selected in No. 7. Write a letter of application for a desired position within that firm.

9. Complete for yourself the first five stages of career planning outlined on page 588.

10. Develop a schedule of how and when you will activate, review, evaluate, and possibly revise the career plan you developed in No. 9. Make the plan a practical one that you actually will use.

11. Visit the testing/counseling center on your campus. Learn what services, tests, etc., are available to help in your personal career planning. Write a one- or two-page paper summarizing your findings and indicating which of the services and tests you plan to use. Include an actual time schedule for that use.

12. Meet with your group. Develop an interview guide for interviews with businesspeople to learn what they consider to be the major mistakes made by applicants for positions with their firms. Have each member select a businessperson who has contact with applicants, schedule and complete the interview, and report the findings in a one- or two-page paper. Reconvene the group to summarize the papers. Select a group member to report the summary to the class.

13. Interview representatives of a private employment agency and a government employment office. Develop an interview guide before doing so. Write a report comparing the findings of the two interviews.

14. Use your dictionary and thesaurus to create meanings for these words. Use the words when you think, write, and speak so that you feel comfortable using them.

a. Cardinal   h. Orientation
b. Characterize   i. Peer
c. Coherent   j. Perceive
d. Defuse   k. Protocol
e. Evolve   l. Remuneration
f. Exemplify   m. Scenario
g. Innocuous   n. Unorthodox

15. Take and score Self-Test 38 over the excerpt about planning for a career.

Self-Test 38
Excerpt about Planning for a Career

A. Recall (33 points each). For each multiple-choice question, select the most accurate answer.

1. The first step in planning your career is to:
   a. Find several references
   b. Prepare your résumé, letters of application, and placement files
   c. Identify all of the jobs available in your city
   d. Assess your current status in employment, education and training, experience, intelligence and knowledge, and attitudes and interests
   e. Visit an employment agency

2. Which of these is a career barrier over which you have some control?
   a. You do not have the education necessary for the jobs that you want.
   b. Unemployment in your field is high.
   c. You simply cannot find a job that will pay enough to allow you to get the education that you need.
   d. General unemployment is high.
   e. You are the "wrong" sex or race, have the "wrong" ethnic background, belong to the "wrong" church, or have some physical limitations.

B. Inference (34 points). Indicate whether this statement is true or false.

When you engage in careful career planning, you exercise more control over your life.

Solution to Self-Test 38

Excerpt about Planning for a Career

A. Recall (33 points each)   **B.** Inference (34 points)

1. d   **2.** a   True

16. Take and score Self-Test 39 over Chapter 17.

Self-Test 39

Chapter 17

A. Recall (25 points each). For each multiple-choice question, select the most accurate answer.

1. Which of these is probably the best channel to use for your initial job contact?
   a. Telephone
   b. Letter
   c. Face-to-face interview
   d. Telegram
   e. a and b

2. Which of these entries does *not* belong on a résumé that you will use to secure a position as a financial analyst?
   a. Member, Finance Club
   b. M.B.A. in Accounting, University of Arizona
   c. Baton Twirler, Del Ray High School
   d. B.A. in Journalism, University of Kansas
   e. Salesperson, Alling Pharmaceutical Company

3. Which one of these statements is true?
   a. The guidelines for position-search communication are significantly different than those for other types of communication.
   b. The résumé usually is overtly persuasive.
   c. Letters of application generally allow for more creativity and persuasion than do résumés.
   d. Nonverbal messages have no impact on the written parts of the employment process.
   e. The most important information in a résumé or letter of application should be placed in the middle (body) of the message.

B. Inference (25 points). For the multiple-choice question, select the most accurate answer.

Which one of these statements is *false?*
   a. Exercise modesty about listing post-college honors and awards in a résumé.
   b. No universal suggestions exist for the content of the personal information section of the résumé.
   c. A résumé may take on some of the features usually reserved for the letter of application.

     d. The inclusion of a list of references in a résumé is declining.
     e. The closing part of a letter of application may be used to stimulate the reader
        to contact you about an interview.

Solution to Self-Test 39
Chapter 18
(Careful Reading)

A. Recall (25 points each)   **B.** Inference (25 points)

   1. b   **3.** c   a
   2. c

18

Employment: Other Written Messages, Interviews, Appearance, Communication Careers

Chapter 18 completes the coverage of employment messages. The first section deals with additional written messages. Subsequent sections cover interviews, appearance and dress, communication and careers, and business as a communication-centered operation.

ADDITIONAL WRITTEN MESSAGES

The résumé and the letter of application are the two major written messages of an employment process. However, several other written messages often enter into that process. Such messages include letters of follow-up, acceptance, rejection, delay and thanks, application blanks, and other messages.

Letter of Follow-up

Sometimes an application process calls for messages as follow-ups to others. Such messages may follow an initial application or an initial contact from a prospective employer.

Initial application

Sometimes an initial application message elicits no response, or at best a routine one. Such a situation arises more often for an unsolicited application than for a solicited one.

   In routine-response or nonresponse circumstances, then, you may want to write a follow-up letter. Such a letter serves the purpose of initiating or intensifying interest in the application.

13 Walker Avenue
Argyle, Maine 22914
August 30, 1981

Personnel Director
Waygo Pharmaceuticals, Inc.
333 East Main Street
Silverton, New Hampshire 33692

YOU HIRE SUCCESS IF
YOU HIRE ME!

Perhaps you haven't had time to respond to my first letter? As I
wrote in that letter, I am an experienced, educated, and
extremely successful salesperson who would like to sell for you
at Waygo.

My bachelor's degree is in business—with a major in selling.
More important, I have four years of solid experience as a
quota-bursting salesperson. My resume tells my success story
well, so I enclosed another one for your convenience.

Though I am eager to work for you, I have a number of offers to
consider. You could give me a chance to accept yours. I could
come for an interview almost any time next week.

Please call me at (555) 232-1194. You'll get an energetic,
successful salesperson on the line.

Hire immediate success.

Sincerely,

Lee Wu

Lee Wu

Enclosure

Figure 18–1   Lee Wu's follow-up letter

Make the follow-up message brief and persuasive. While reinforcing some of
the key points included in the original message, try to stimulate the reader to review
the original. Use the attention and action segments as particular sources of that
stimulation.

You might send two or three such letters, or even move to the richer telephone
channel. However, after a few follow-up contacts, dismiss that company and move
on to another strategy.

Figure 18–1 illustrates a follow-up letter written after the application letter
received no reponse.

13 Walker Avenue
Argyle, Maine 22914
September 7, 1981

Ms. Wenoma Drum, Sales Manager
Waygo Pharmaceuticals, Inc.
333 East Main Street
Silverton, New Hampshire 33692

Dear Ms. Drum:

Thank you so much for taking some time out of your busy
Thursday to discuss selling opportunities at Waygo with me. The
advice you gave me was most informative.

The prospect of selling for Waygo Pharmaceuticals, Inc., still
interests me very much. I am confident that I could bring
success to one of the three entry-level sales positions we
discussed.

As I pointed out, I know how to sell, and I enjoy selling
immensely. Your Waygo sales quotas would be barriers that I
could cross in no time; at Argyle Chemical I never let a sales
quota go unsurmounted. Also, my bachelor's degree in
business—with a major in selling—gave me a solid educational
background from which I can continually create both new
selling approaches and innovative distribution techniques.

Now that I've had a chance to discuss the Waygo operations
with you, Ms. Drum, I am absolutely convinced that I want to
work for you as a Waygo salesperson.

Again, I so appreciate the time you spent with me.

Sincerely,

Lee Wu

Lee Wu

Figure 18–2   Lee Wu's post-interview follow-up letter

Initial contact from prospective employer

Another stage of the application process that may call for a follow-up letter comes
after successful completion of a substantial contact with a potential employer. In one
such case, a nonroutine letter or telephone call by the prospective employer may
follow an initial application. In another case, it may follow an initial interview. In
both cases, either you or the prospective employer may decide that you need to
supply additional information or develop an idea introduced in the first transaction.

The follow-up letter in Figure 18–2 shows how messages at this stage may
continue to build the persuasion toward action. Observe how it employs the same

13 Walker Avenue
Argyle, Maine 22914
September 25, 1981

Ms. Wenoma Drum, Sales Manager
Waygo Pharmaceuticals, Inc.
333 East Main Street
Silverton, New Hampshire 33692

Dear Ms. Drum:

I most definitely accept your offer to join Waygo as an
entry-level salesperson in the Vermont sales district. My
familiarity with Vermont will allow me to seek out new
customers as well as provide excellent service to your
established clients.

The $14,500 annual salary and the sales commission schedule
are most satisfactory. Your $500 salary advance will make it
much easier for me to move to Silverton before Monday, October
15, the day that you want me to report to work. I will come to
your office at 9 A.M. on that Monday, as you asked.

Thank you for making me a part of your Waygo sales team. You
will get excellent work from me every day that I sell for you.

I look forward to meeting with you on October 15.

Sincerely,

Lee Wu

Lee Wu

Figure 18–3   Lee Wu's letter of acceptance

basic techniques introduced for the initiating application messages. The APCA plan simply advances to a higher, more focused level of activity.

Letter of Acceptance

A prompt response should follow an offer of a position. The response may be an acceptance.

Write a letter of acceptance in a straightforward style. Write it to convey satisfaction at receiving the offer, to indicate the intent to accept it, and to reinforce confidence in your abilities to do the job.

Because the letter of acceptance is basically a good-news letter, use the deductive style of writing. Keep the message direct and brief.

Figure 18–3 provides an example of a letter of acceptance.

13 Walker Avenue
Argyle, Maine 22914
September 25, 1981

Ms. Wenoma Drum, Sales Manager
Waygo Pharmaceuticals, Inc.
333 East Main Street
Silverton, New Hampshire 33692

Dear Ms. Drum:

Thank you for your generous job offer. I realize that the
Vermont sales district is a plum, and I think that your sales
department is one of the best that I have seen.

The Morey Drug Company just offered me the job of heading its
entire Pacific sales district. I would supervise the district's
thirty salespersons, and I would also travel extensively. Because
the sales manager acts as a salesperson, manager, and world
traveler all at once, I have decided to join the Morey Drug
Company staff.

Again, thank you for taking the time to discuss your company
with me. And more important, thank you for the appealing job
offer.

I am sure that this will be a record-breaking sales year for you,
and I hope that I'll be fortunate enough to meet you again
someday.

Sincerely,

Lee Wu

Lee Wu

Figure 18–4   Lee Wu's letter of rejection

Letter of Rejection

The letter of rejection is more difficult to write than the letter of acceptance. It is
basically a bad-news message because it usually involves rejecting an actively
sought position.

Because of the negative nature of the repsonse, select the inductive developmental method for the letter of rejection. Build to the rejection by citing the reasons
for it. Retain courtesy and the "you" attitude throughout.

Figure 18–4 illustrates a letter of rejection. It uses the positive sandwich in
order to deliver the bad news.

2332 Pine Road
Anthony, Idaho 44662
June 10, 1980

Mr. Alvin Swagner, Personnel Manager
Scanlon Investment Services, Inc.
326 West Ninth Avenue
Dariel, Tennessee 72221

Dear Mr. Swagner:

Your offer to have me join Scanlon Investment Services, Inc., as
a financial analyst is most appealing. The job sounds both
interesting and challenging.

I have not yet completed interviews with three other investment firms; my last interview will take place early next week.
Because I want to base my career decisions on as much information as possible, I would like to respond to your offer by
phone next Friday, June 24, after my last interview. If June 24
is not satisfactory, please call or write me so that we can
discuss a more convenient time for you.

I was very impressed with both Scanlon Investment Services
and the city of Dariel when I visited you last week. As a
financial analyst in your international division, I know that I
could make sound contributions to your fine company.

Sincerely,

Janet E. Smith

Janet E. Smith

Figure 18–5 Janet E. Smith's letter of delay

Letter of Delay

A letter of delay asks for a postponement on the decision of whether to accept a job
offer.

The need to delay may arise when an offer comes from a firm before completion of other interviews. The need may also arise because the offer comes from a
lower-priority firm, although it could serve if a preferred offer does not materialize.
Requests to delay a decision about an offer may also arise from personal reasons or
external circumstances.

The letter of delay is a combination of bad-news and persuasive messages.
Thus, use the positive sandwich to accompany the inductive development style. Be

2332 Pine Road
Anthony, Idaho 44662
June 21, 1980

Ms. Mary Shapiro, Partner
Shapiro, Hart & Wenner, Inc.
Willtoe, Nevada 33963

Dear Ms. Shapiro:

Thank you so much for taking the time to discuss the bright
future of your investment firm with me. Your five-year plan
takes into account every conceivable economic change.

I am even more interested in working as an investment
counselor for Shapiro, Hart & Wenner, Inc., now that I have
talked with you, Ms. Shapiro. The company is in very good
hands.

Again, thank you for the fine interview. Please let me know if
you have any questions.

Sincerely,

Janet E. Smith

Janet E. Smith

Figure 18–6   Janet E. Smith's thank-you letter

relatively direct, but diplomatically persuasive. Logically support the request for action—the receiver's agreement to the delay.

Figure 18–5 shows an example of a request for postponement of the decision in response to an offer of a position.

Letter of Thanks

Sometimes an employment-seeking process calls for thank-you messages. For example, a thank-you message may acknowledge an interview with an important prospect. It will show thoughtfulness, fix the application in the mind of the interviewer, and reinforce the persuasion.

Follow the traditional rules for writing a routine thank-you message. However, insert just enough information to support your original application purposes.

Figure 18–6 is an example of a thank-you message appropriate to an employment sequence.

Application Blank

The application blank represents another major type of application message. The ability to complete one satisfactorily often has a great deal to do with the success of an application.

The attainment of many entry-level jobs—particularly jobs in the trades or jobs with minimal requirements—depends entirely upon proper completion of an application form.

Consider these suggestions for completing application forms:

1. Keep your résumé up to date, and carry a copy of it (or a skeleton outline of the key points of it) with you any time you expect to be asked to complete an application form.
2. Read the instructions on the form carefully before beginning to complete it. Follow them precisely.
3. If the instructions specify that you are to print or handwrite your responses, do whichever is required. Otherwise, use the style that creates the better nonverbal impression.
4. Complete every blank on the form—even if you insert such entries as "None," "Not applicable," "0," or "—."
5. Complete the form correctly and neatly. Carry a small dictionary with you if you need it to spell words correctly.
6. For open-end questions, organize your thoughts carefully and write a draft of the answer on a piece of scratch paper before transferring it to the form.
7. Answer questions as accurately and honestly as possible—but in a manner that will emphasize strengths, not weaknesses.
8. As suggested for the résumé, consider carefully whether to include or omit answers to questions that you may not be legally required to answer.
9. If the form includes a question about what salary you expect to receive, you may write an actual figure or range of figures if you have made such a decision. Otherwise, you may write something like:
   a. The typical salary paid for the position to someone of my ability
   b. To be discussed during interview
   c. Negotiable
   d. Open for discussion
10. Once you have completed the form, review your entries for completeness and accuracy.

The major purpose for completing an application form well is to obtain a desired position. However, another purpose for doing so arises from the fact that it may become a permanent part of a personnel file.

Figure 18–7 stands as an example of a completed application form.

Other Messages

Additional written messages in an employment series may be routine or special in nature. Consider two examples: (1) tests and (2) placement- and employment-office files.

Tests

Many firms require applicants to complete employment tests. Of course, completing them is similar to completing an academic test. However, the stakes may be much higher when performance may determine whether you obtain a desired position—a position necessary to your career plan.

Anticipate and review the kinds of questions that may be asked in a given situation. Obtain sample tests and take them.

As in the case of completing any form, read test instructions and follow them carefully. Try to relax. Take account of the time factor involved. Answer open-end questions particularly carefully; they show not only knowledge, but the ability to write.

Placement- and employment-office files

A campus placement office or an employment agency sometimes aids your search for a position. Either type of service usually requires the same kinds of messages that one prepares for an independent job search.

Carefully make the decision about whether to mark recommendation forms "confidential" or "nonconfidential." If you mark them "confidential," the persons recommending you may feel freer to write frankly. The reader, then, in turn, may feel that the information holds more meaning than does a nonconfidential recommendation. If you mark the forms "nonconfidential," you do have the right to review them. Thus, you can make sure that no one has included some false information—or some information that may militate against your opportunities to obtain jobs.

Most directors of placement offices recommend marking the forms "confidential." However, the choice is yours.

INTERVIEWS

The search for a position or a career involves many oral transactions. Examples of such transactions include:

> Telephone conversations
> Face-to-face conversations with receptionists and other personnel in company and employment-agency offices.
> Informal conversations over lunch or coffee with personnel from an interviewing firm
> Introductions to potential co-workers
> Interviews

The interview, however, forms the hub of the application process.

The first interview usually occurs with a professional interviewer from a personnel office. The second interview usually occurs with one or more of the superiors who must approve offers and hirings.

The interview is a verbal and nonverbal sales presentation you must make, but in a rather formal and subdued setting. To a great extent, that setting falls under the control of the interviewer.

SHAPIRO, HART & WENNER, INC., Willtoe, Nevada 33963

General Information

Date ___June 6, 1980___ Job wanted ___Investment Counselor___ Salary wanted ___$18,000/year___

Full name ___Janet Ellen Smith___

Address ___2332 Pine Road, Anthony, Idaho 44662___

Message phone ___(555) 721-4992___ Home phone ___(555) 721-6231___

Social Security number ___448-000-000___

Of what country are you a citizen? ___U.S.A.___

Equal Opportunity Information

You are not obligated to complete this section. Your decision will not affect your chances for a job.

Sex ___Female___ Age ___31___ Race ___Black___ Are you handicapped? ___No___

Legal Information

Have you ever been convicted of a felony? ___No___

Have you ever had your driver's license suspended? ___No___

If you answered "yes" to one or both of the above, explain the circumstances here: _____
_____ Not applicable _____

Educational Information

Name the high schools, colleges, and other training institutions that you attended. Include the school's address, the degree you received, and the dates that you attended.

1. ___Linwood High School, Linwood, Idaho 44621___

   ___High school diploma.___

   ___From September, 1972, through May, 1975.___

2. ___Linwood Community College, Linwood, Idaho 44621___

   ___Associate of Science degree in Business Administration.___

   ___From September, 1975, through May, 1977___

3. ___Anthony University, Anthony, Idaho 44662___

   ___Bachelor of Science degree in Finance.___

   ___From September, 1977, through May, 1979.___

4. ___Anthony University, Anthony, Idaho 44662___

   ___Master of Business Administration in Finance.___

   ___From June, 1979, through May, 1980.___

Figure 18–7 Janet E. Smith's completed application blank

Employment Information

List your current or last positon first.

Firm's name ___DiRenzio and Barber, Inc.___

Supervisor's name ___Kathryn Barber___

Address ___98 East Fourth Street, Anthony, Idaho 44662___

Phone ___(555) 721-4999___ Starting salary ___$650/month___ Ending salary ___$710/month___

Period worked ___June 5, 1978 & June 5, 1979___ to ___Sept. 5, 1978 Sept. 5, 1979___ Part-time _____ Full-time ___X___

Title ___Investment Assistant___

Duties ___Prepared investment folders and counseled clients___

Reason for leaving ___Went back to school___

Firm's name ___Leland and Daughters Construction Company___

Supervisor's name ___Carolyn Leland___

Address ___46 Dayfield Plaza, Anthony, Idaho 44662___

Phone ___(555) 721-4332___ Starting salary ___$4/hour___ Ending salary ___$6/hour___

Period worked ___June 1, 1976 & June 1, 1977___ to ___Sept. 1, 1976 Sept. 5, 1977___ Part-time _____ Full-time ___X___

Title ___Carpenter___

Duties ___Built kitchen and bathroom cabinets in new homes and office buildings.___

Reason for leaving ___Went back to school___

References

Give the names, addresses, occupations, and phone numbers of three references. Do not name the supervisors you listed in the employment section.

1. ___Sidney Lewis, Ed.D., 32 Farley Hall, Anthony University___

   ___Anthony, Idaho 44662—professor.___   Phone: (555) 721-1343

2. ___Denise Flanagan, 462 Albert Place___

   ___Anthony, Idaho 44662—investment counselor.___   Phone: (555) 721-3368

3. ___Wallace Erickson, 16 Avell Road___

   ___Linwood, Idaho 44621—banker.___   Phone: (555) 821-9175

The information I have given is to the best of my knowledge correct and complete.

Janet E. Smith   7/5/1981
Signature   Date

Figure 18–7   (continued)

627

Review four elements associated with the interview: (1) techniques, (2) style, (3) content, and (4) types of questions.

Techniques

Chapter 15 contains general descriptions and suggestions for interviews. However, consider these techniques for a successful employment interview:

1. If possible, become an anonymous and unobtrusive observer of the interview site a day or so before the interview. Observe both the people and the environment.
2. Arrive for an interview about ten minutes ahead of time—well rested and calm, but alert.
3. Announce your presence and the time of your appointment to the person in the outer office.
4. Remove your coat and leave it in the outer office.
5. Follow the lead of the interviewer, of course, but generally shake hands with her or him. Make the handshake firm.
6. Enter the office with confidence.
7. Remain standing until the interviewer invites you to be seated.
8. Establish the proper posture, and command the desired amount of territory as you sit. Minimal occupation of space communicates passivity and weakness, but maximum occupation of space communicates a power status that may threaten an interviewer.
9. Do not have gum, candy, a mint, a cough drop, a cigarette, a cigar, or a pipe in your mouth in either the outer or inner office.
10. Avoid the negative messages associated with fidgeting with hair, clothing, jewelry, handbag, briefcase, papers, or something on the interviewer's desk.
11. Use facial expression properly. Too much smiling transmits weakness and servility, but too little smiling may threaten the interviewer.
12. Use your voice as an instrument for establishing the desired level of confidence and enthusiasm.
13. Make good eye contact with the interviewer. If you continually look away, the interviewer may attribute unwarranted negative traits to you.
14. Carry only small briefcases, handbags, and folders. Place all loose articles in them before entering the interviewer's office. Place the items in your lap or on the floor rather than on the interviewer's desk. Do locate a pen or pencil and a note pad within easy reach.
15. If the interviewer has not seen your résumé ahead of time, give her or him time to read it as you sit quietly and organize your thoughts.
16. Let the interviewer take the lead in the interview, but contribute your part by answering questions with more than a mere "Yes" or "No."
17. If you take notes, do so quickly and quietly. Do not be disturbed if the interviewer also takes notes.
18. Do not use profanity even if the interviewer does.

19. Do not tell jokes, but do exchange pleasantries when the interviewer establishes that pattern.
20. Always use "Mr.," "Ms.," or other preferred title, never the first name of the interviewer.
21. Avoid the servile attitude exhibited by overuse of "ma'am" or "sir."
22. If the interviewer receives a telephone call during the interview, just remain seated and quietly look through some of your material. Try not to listen; at least give the impression that you are not listening.
23. If the interviewer receives a caller while you are in the office, remain seated and facing the original direction. However, if the interviewer introduces you to the caller, rise, shake hands, and interact appropriately.
24. Avoid a show of anger toward the interviewer—even if the line of questioning is improper. Use a controlled, reasoned approach if you must stop such a line of questioning.
25. Never look at your watch during an interview. The interviewer will end the interview when he or she wants to do so. However, be sensitive to nonverbal cues that the interview is nearing an end.
26. Never part with a question like "Do I get the job?" Instead, say, "I am very interested in the position; when do you think I might hear from you about your decision?" or "When might I call?"
27. As you leave, express appreciation for the interview.
28. Immediately after the interview, record any notes you want to make. Also analyze and evaluate your performance. Decide what you might do to improve the next interview.

Style

Interviewers make countless decisions on the basis of style (charisma) rather than substance—particularly when the qualities of several candidates are roughly equal.

Style alone probably does not often lead an interviewer to hire an incompetent candidate. However, style often does lead the decision-maker to choose a slightly less qualified person over a more highly qualified one. Such a choice may be subconscious—and may occur more often than interviewers realize or will admit. Particularly at the managerial level, the tendency is to choose someone whose "chemistry" is right.

If you think your personal style may harm your chances, analyze and try to improve it.

Content

These suggestions may help you effectively communicate the content you desire in an interview:

1. Review the analysis of the firm and the particular job just before the interview.
2. Review your self-analysis and résumé just before the interview.

3. Anticipate the kinds of questions the interviewer might ask. Rehearse your responses to them.

4. Make a list of the information you want to be sure to give—even if the interviewer does not ask for it. Rehearse how you might insert it by making a smooth transition from the specific answers to a question into the volunteer information.

5. Develop and memorize the questions you want to ask; rehearse them.

   a. Generally, do not talk about salary until the interviewer introduces the topic—usually in a post-offer interview.

   b. Generally, do not talk about fringe benefits until the interviewer introduces the topic.

6. Answer and introduce questions in clear, concise, and specific terms. However, avoid being curt.

7. Tell the interviewer the truth, but couch negative messages in positive-sandwich terms—without being defensive or self-deprecating.

8. Maintain a natural, conversational style, but avoid using slang and jargon.

9. State your qualifications in straightforward language, but avoid leaving the impression that you are bragging.

10. Avoid undue criticism of your present employer. The interviewer may wonder whether you are just a critical person—particularly of management.

11. Observe and listen carefully to the content of the messages the interviewer sends. Adjust your messages accordingly.

12. Feature your strengths, and subordinate your weaknesses.

13. Speak in grammatically correct and complete sentences. Avoid run-on sentences that do not allow the interviewer to interject comments.

14. Understand and adapt to the circumstances that define your relative chances of being hired. If you are in a strong bargaining poisition, interview differently than if you are in a weak one.

15. Learn and apply the techniques of negotiation on employment issues such as salary and location. Understand that everyone must win something for negotiation to be successful.

16. As soon as you sense that the interview is nearing its end (usually after twenty to forty minutes), be sure to transmit the information that you want to introduce in this emphatic position. Finish strong.

Types of Questions

Review a few of the potentially difficult interview questions. Also review some ways to deal with them.

General questions

Some of the general statements/questions that interviewers may use include:

(1) *Tell me about yourself.* Take this opportunity to present the rehearsed persuasive exposition of your key qualities and your interest in and understanding of the firm.

(2) *What kind of work do you want to do?* Stress capabilities and determination related to the work for which you are applying. Also indicate your ambition to advance beyond the level of the particular job for which you are applying.

(3) *What are your weaknesses (faults)?* Indicate that you know that everyone has flaws either in innate ability, personality, education, experience, or in other factors that go into defining a good employee. Stress that you have analyzed both your strengths and weaknesses and have found that your strengths far outweigh your weaknesses.

State that you have already conquered some of the weaknesses and have a strategy for overcoming the remainder. Possibly cite one or two minor weaknesses along with evidence of your strategy to overcome them.

End on a positive note—solutions and strengths rather than problems and weaknesses.

(4) *Why have you chosen this career (position, company, etc.)?* Use this question to express knowledge about the topic. In addition, use it to emphasize the strength of your interest in it. Incorporate your central persuasive thrust into it.

(5) *What makes you think you are qualified for this position?* Convert this question from one that could make you defensive into one that lets you feature your qualifications. Stress the education, training, experience, and personal abilities that specifically fit you to the position.

(6) *What do you do in your leisure time?* Answer honestly about some of your less serious activities. Interviewers are interested in your ability to relax—to lead a balanced life. However, if you spend some of your leisure time in the pursuit of additional education, training, or experience, report that too.

(7) *Why are you leaving your present job?* Stress the reasons that place you in the best light. Do not criticize your employer, no matter how justified the criticism may be.

(8) *What salary do you expect?* During a first interview, try to dodge this question. Suggest that you would prefer to await a job offer, but that you know that the salary should be based upon your ability to contribute to the firm's goals.

If the interviewer in a first interview presses you, or if you receive an offer, then meet the salary question directly. Negotiate from a realistic assessment of your bargaining position.

Try to get the interviewer to state the first figure. Then, if your position is strong, you may ask for more—but still probably within the range you have learned most people at this position receive.

If your bargaining position is poor, you may have to be satisfied with the offer—or only slightly higher than it. You may even have to be satisfied with a salary at the low end of the usual range.

(9) *Tell me about your family.* Straightforwardly describe your home life. Do not show photographs. Avoid directing too much attention away from the purpose of the meeting—your qualifications for the work for which you apply. Show a realistic concern for family responsibilities, but leave the clear impression that they will not interfere with your duties in the position you desire.

If you prefer not to discuss marital status, children, living arrangements, and other such features, phrase your declining statement carefully. Though you have a legal right not to discuss these matters, you may lose ground with the interviewer by not responding.

(10) *Do you smoke? drink? use drugs?* Avoid an emotional reaction if the interviewer asks this question.

You may choose to answer. If so, if you smoke, say so. If you consume alcoholic beverages, indicate that you do so in moderation and for social reasons.

When speaking of the other drugs, tread lightly. For example, even if you believe that marijuana should be legalized, the interview is not the place to express such views.

The decision about how to handle this question is extremely difficult. Basically, answer truthfully, but also protect yourself from adverse reactions if you have tried drugs.

One option is to state that you consider such matters to be private. Add that if you do use any of the three substances, their use in no way impairs your ability to perform the job. Make such statements forthrightly, and without a show of irritation.

(11) *Though we cannot require it, would you agree to take a polygraph test?* If you agree, you may be giving up some of your rights. If you disagree, you may irritate the questioner—and even arouse suspicions. If you disagree, explain that you have nothing to hide, but that your principles do not permit you to submit to the test.

(12) *Have you ever stolen anything from a store or from a former employer (padded an expense account)?* The question on drugs and this question on stealing are the kinds that are often used in conjunction with a polygraph test or stress interviews.

You may decide that you do not want to work for a firm badly enough to answer such probing, personal, possibly self-incriminating questions. However, do not answer in an irritated fashion or leave in a huff. Instead, give the kind of answer that shows strength combined with control.

One strong response is: "Though I have nothing to hide, I do not choose to answer this sort of question. I believe my record of education and experience establish my competency to perform the work for which I am applying."

Just such an answer may be what the interviewer wants to hear as evidence of your maturity. You may not risk losing the job at all. You may actually improve your chances of getting it.

Another way to handle such a stress question is to answer somewhat candidly. Show no surprise and use words something like these: "Oh, I took some candy a couple of times as a child and have taken my share of pencils and paper clips from the office where I worked. That was generally accepted practice there. However, I more than replaced the value of any office supplies I ever took. I worked overtime many times for no pay. I occasionally used my own car (car fare) to run errands for the firm without being reimbursed. If a firm has a strict rule against using its supplies for an occasional personal purpose, I can certainly abide by such a rule."

(12) *What do you expect your salary to be in three years? five years? ten years?* Answer to show knowledge of your chosen career field and of the salaries paid in it. Also answer to show confidence in your ability, but not to show outright conceit by stating an unrealistically high figure. Use ranges or approximations. Try to cite an actual published source of the information you report.

(13) *What kinds of working conditions do you like best?* Stress the satisfaction you feel when you do your job well and when you meet challenges. Also stress the

importance of contributing to the solution of problems and working with talented and cooperative people.

Omit or subordinate any mention of such insecure feelings as the need "to be appreciated" or "to be treated well."

Avoid any emphasis upon salary and benefits at this point.

Establish a clear picture of yourself as one who is self-motivated, but who enjoys working with others of the same kind. Emphasize the environment only as it contributes to your doing your job—not for your personal benefit.

(14) *What are your strengths?* List in a forthright manner the education, experience, and personal characteristics that portray you as one capable of occupying the prospective position. In addition, feature the strengths that show that you can grow beyond that position rapidly.

(15) *Why should XYZ Corporation hire you?* Reinforce your understanding of the firm, of your qualities, and of how the two match. Impress the interviewer with your realistic confidence and adaptability.

(16) *Aren't you overqualified for this job?* If you are overqualified, yet need the job, indicate how your additional qualifications will help you perform the work in superior fashion. Through such an approach, persuade the interviewer that your additional qualifications do not constitute overqualification in the traditional sense. Assure the interviewer that you have the ability to function productively at many levels without being bored, condescending, or dissatisfied.

Stereotyped questions

An interviewer may ask anyone the preceding types of questions. However, some questions show evidence of stereotypes and the biases associated with them. The stereotypes run the gamut of those that society uses to define people—race, ethnic origin, sex, marital status, age, religion, cultural heritage, and handicap, for example.

Review here some samples of questions that relate to only one of the major classes—sex. First consider the kinds of questions often directed to women. Then consider them for men.

Women   Stereotyped questions that might be asked of a woman are:

1. I observe that you prefer the courtesy title "Ms." You're not one of those "women's libbers," are you?
2. Who will take care of your children?
3. What will you do when your children are sick?
4. Don't you think a mother's place is in the home?
5. What if we hire you, and then in a year or so your husband is transferred?
6. I see you're not married. Do you live with a man?
7. Do you ever plan to get married?
8. Are you a divorcée?
9. Do you plan to have children? What birth-control method do you use?
10. This job requires a great deal of travel. Do you think women should travel with men?
11. You have listed volunteer work on your résumé. Do you actually think that volunteer work will help you in the real business world?
12. Is your work attendance record better than most women's?

13. Can you control your emotions?
14. Do you type? (To an applicant for a nontyping position)
15. Most people don't like to work for women. Why do you think you're the exception?
16. You're an attractive woman. Do you think your looks will be a distraction to the men in the office?
17. Do you really think you will be able to be a boss and get along with the men you supervise?
18. At meetings with the other supervisors (all male), will you be willing to serve coffee and take notes?
19. What do you think about all this flurry about alleged sexual harrassment on the job? You don't really mind a little kidding and fun between the sexes, do you?
20. You seem to be rather aggressive. Do you think aggressiveness is attractive in a woman?
21. Do you think you can do this job and retain your femininity?
22. What does your husband think about your wanting to work? Would the pressure of your work be a strain on your marriage?
23. Does your husband let you work overtime (travel, attend company functions alone, etc.)?
24. I see you were graduated from college in 19XX, worked only two years, and have been out of the job market for 20 years. How can you claim you are qualified to apply for a supervisory position?
25. Have you ever filed a claim against a company on the basis of sexual discrimination or sexual harrassment?
26. The women we hire usually start in a secretarial position. You would be willing to start there, wouldn't you?
27. Do you think that affirmative action requirements are fair to firms?

Many of these questions will not be asked directly; many are illegal. However, if you are a woman, you should be prepared to answer them directly or to insert the "answers" to them in an indirect way as you build your persuasion.

Develop responses that:

1. Enhance your image as one capable of doing the job for which you apply
2. Do not betray other women
3. Do not show aggressiveness, servility, or passivity
4. Separate your private life from your company life
5. Indicate that you are assertive, strong, courageous, and capable, but that femininity does not preclude such abilities
6. Do not show a negative, reactionary defensiveness to the questions
7. Briefly explain why you choose not to answer certain questions

Men   The presence of men in the higher ranks of business has been and still is the norm. Therefore, the list of questions unique to men is much briefer than the list unique to women:

1. I see you're not married. You probably know that we like our executives to have wives who can do some of the entertaining for the corporation—and to accompany their husbands to important functions. How do you propose to overcome this problem?

2. I see you're married and have children. We have found that our single executives are freer to transfer and to travel than are married ones. Will family responsibilities cut down on your flexibility? (This one is similar to some of the questions for women.)
3. Have you gotten your military obligations out of the way? (This question comes and goes as the draft comes and goes. At the time of the publication of this book, the question has always applied to men. However, it may eventually apply to women as well.)

As a man, answer these questions just as women do those aimed stereotypically at them. Answer in a self-enhancing manner. Be straightforward and composed. Try not to react defensively or in a negatively reactionary way. If you choose not to respond, briefly explain why.

(2,200 words)
(test on page 645)

APPEARANCE AND DRESS

Dress and appearance form only a part of the nonverbal messages transmitted during an interview. However, many of the other nonverbal components directly associated with the interview itself received treatment in the preceding section. Therefore, consider dress and appearance as a distinct nonverbal category here.

Chapter 3 covers dress and appearance in general terms. However, review some summary suggestions for dress and appearance for the interview in particular: (1) general suggestions, (2) special suggestions for men, and (3) special suggestions for women.

General Suggestions

Some suggestions for good appearance apply to men and women alike. The overriding one is to follow all of the standard rules for good grooming and cleanliness.

An anonymous visit to the site of an interview ahead of time allows for the observation of the appropriate manner of dress. However, an applicant cannot always be as casual as can those already working in an office.

As an alternative to an anonymous visit to the site, check similar offices or read into the literature about the dress appropriate to the position. If doubts remain, lean toward conservatism.

Some other general suggestions include:

1. Wear fingernails at a short to medium length. Have them clean and well manicured.
2. Choose a haircut and style that fits the standard for the work. Have it cut a week or so before the interview.
3. Have freshly cleaned and pressed clothing—including overcoats and raincoats.
4. Use a minimum amount of shaving lotion, cologne, or perfume.
5. Choose shoes in a calf leather, dark color, and traditional style. Be sure they show no wear and are well cleaned and shined.

6. Choose clothing reasonably appropriate for the season. However, do not choose unusually lightweight or lightly colored clothing even in the summer.
7. Choose styles that enhance your personal characteristics.
8. Choose clothing that fits comfortably.
9. Avoid wearing obviously brand-new, untested clothing.
10. Just before you go into the outer office of the interviewer, check your clothing and grooming—preferably somewhere that you will not be seen.
11. Once in the office, forget your clothing and appearance. Do not shift and adjust clothing, check hair, or do any of the myriad of other things that indicate improper preoccupation with and nervousness about such elements.
12. Wear a minimum of jewelry. Be sure what you do wear is tasteful. Do wear a watch.

Special Suggestions for Men

Though overlapping with the general suggestions, these suggestions apply specifically to a man:

1. If you have facial hair, be sure that it is cut in an acceptable style. Have it well trimmed and groomed.
2. Wear a traditional two- or three-piece business suit in a dark, solid color in a hard-finished fabric. Do not wear a leisure suit.
3. Choose a conservative shirt, tie, socks, belt, and shoes to coordinate properly with the color and style of the suit.
4. Even if you wear a necklace during your leisure hours, leave it off for the interview.
5. Carry an unworn billfold or wallet in a traditional style. Remove all unnecessary bulk from it.
6. Have a cleanly laundered handkerchief in a pocket.
7. Remove all unnecessary keys, change, and other items from your pockets.
8. If you wear a hat, be sure that it is well cleaned and blocked. Leave it in the outer office with your coat.

Special Suggestions for Women

These special suggestions apply to women:

1. Wear a two-piece, below-the-knee, skirted business suit or a simple, tailored dress in a dark, solid color and a hard-finished fabric. Do not wear a vest, pants, or pants suit, sheer fabrics, flimsy fabrics, tight-fitting jacket or skirt, low-cut dress, short or unusually long skirt, or any high-fashion clothing..
2. Choose a conservative, medium- to high-cut blouse coordinated properly with the suit. Do not choose a low-cut, sheer, or clinging blouse or a sweater.
3. Choose medium-colored, sheer stockings. Do not choose opaque or high-fashion stockings.
4. Choose closed-toed, closed-heeled, low- to medium-heeled pumps in a dark-colored kid or suede leather coordinated with your suit. Do not choose high heels, sandals, open toes, open heels, boots, white or other light colors, or patent leather.

5. Wear little or no jewelry. Do not wear large-looped or dangling earrings.
6. Be sure that a full-length winter coat or raincoat is longer than your skirt.
7. Choose a hair style that will convey moderation and confidence. Avoid high-fashion or out-of-date styles—particularly the highly sprayed, backcombed, beehive styles.
8. Use conservative makeup.
9. If you use nail polish, choose a medium-toned color.
10. Carry a small, dark-colored, leather handbag that coordinates with your suit and shoes. Carry nothing in it that you do not absolutely need. Be sure to close it before entering the office.
11. Never use compact or lipstick in either the outer or inner office.
12. Choose accessories such as scarves, belts, gloves, and hats to show moderate taste and an understanding of acceptability for that office. Be sure to put any removable items such as gloves in your coat pocket or purse before being called into the interviewer's office.

COMMUNICATION AND CAREERS

To complete both a section on careers and employment and a book on business communication, consider the two in tandem—communication and careers. First review some careers in the field of business communication. Then conclude the book with a summary of the importance of communication to any business career.

"Communication . . . is the growth area of the next decade—bringing with it tremendous career possibilities."[1] So writes O'Connell, who cites four reasons for such a claim: (1) technical advances and the accompanying information explosion, (2) interdependence and the resultant need for integration of activities through communication, (3) legislation leading to requirements for more—and better—communication, and (4) the growth in employee communication.[2]

Giersbach echoes O'Connell's claim:

The field of business communications has come into its own. Gone are the days when a multi-million dollar corporation relied on an under-budgeted, unattractive "house organ" and called it communications. . . .

The growth in internal and external business communications means that you need not leave the field to continue climbing the career ladder.[3]

Though small firms often have one or two professional communicators, the best opportunities lie with large corporations or independent consulting. Some of the positions available to the career communicator are:

Vice president for communication (responsible for all company publications, advertising and promotion, and employee training in communication)

---

[1]Sandra E. O'Connell, "Communication: Growth Field of the Seventies," *Journal of Business Communication* 15 (Spring 1978): 37.

[2]Ibid., pp. 37–39.

[3]Walter F. Giersbach, *Sell Yourself As a Pro. Communicator* (New York: New York Business Communicators, 1979), p. 12.

Director or manager of
   Employee relations
   Customer or consumer relations
   Public relations
   Corporate relations
   Government relations
   Administrative/office services
   Communication
   Credit and collections
   Word processing
Administrative assistant or other staff position, such as
   Interviewer
   Editor
   Writer
   Counselor
   Photographer
   Designer
   Audiovisual specialist
   Trainer
Self-employed consultant
College teacher

Preparation for a business communication career should include work in both written and oral communication, business, and human behavior. O'Connell suggests that "... written communications—publications and management newsletters—are the foundation of corporate communication."[4] However, she also found in a survey that:

> ... business was conducted primarily by oral communication. Print was used for documentation, followup, and with large audiences. Clearly, the key to business transactions is in oral communication, face-to-face and over the phone. This results, of course, in a need for training: presentation skills, interviewing, negotiation, performance review discussions, and participation in meetings.[5]

O'Connell summarizes the abilities needed by the communication professional in this paragraph:

> ... you need to fulfill four criteria: 1) be knowledgeable in a broad range of communication processes; 2) be well grounded in theory—the whys and complexities of the communication process; 3) possess the ability to bridge the gap between theory and application and move between these two worlds; and 4) have some understanding of the business environment.[6]

O'Connell suggests that a career communicator needs to obtain education and experience related to the four areas just reported, get an entry level job, and set career goals.

---

[4]O'Connell, "Communication: Growth Field," p. 41.

[5]Ibid.

[6]Ibid., p. 44.

As a final admonition, she writes that though communication is a growth field, not many organizations send recruiters to campuses to find communication professionals. Instead, people interested in the area will need to take responsibility for their own careers, seek out potential employers, and take the initiative in selling their own abilities.[7]

BUSINESS AS A COMMUNICATION-CENTERED OPERATION

In historical surveys, respondents have consistently ranked communication as the most important or among the most important of the business arts and skills. In addition, they have tended to assign more importance to oral communication than to written communication.

The Importance of Communication Compared to Other Business Skills

In 1971, Bennett sent questionnaires to top executives in the 58 California-based corporations listed among *Fortune's* 500 largest U. S. Industrial Corporations. With a 60 percent return, Bennett reported:

> Every one of the respondents felt that effective business communication skills had played a part in their advancement to a top executive position in their company. Sixty-six percent of the respondents indicated that "effective communication skills" had played a "major part" in their advancement while only 34 percent indicated "some part" in their advancement.[8]

Penrose conducted a survey of businesspeople in Austin, Texas, in 1976. The 157 respondents rated 11 business-related abilities from "1" (Very Valuable) to "7" (Not Valuable). The mean responses for all respondents form this array: public relations (1.84), marketing (1.92), accounting (1.96), finance (2.25), business speaking (2.32), business writing (2.34), mathematics (2.35), office administration (2.39), business law (3.03), statistics (3.46), computer methods (4.01), and government (4.06).[9] Thus, the research places public relations and marketing (both highly communication-related fields), business speaking, and business writing in the top half of the array.

In affirmation of the importance of communication to management, Mintzberg writes:

> We need to pay particular attention in our management development programs to the development of verbal [oral] skills. In fact, we should develop methods to train management students in the use of all the managerial media. The telephone, the scheduled and

[7]Ibid., pp. 44–45.

[8]James C. Bennett, "The Communication Needs of Business Executives," *Journal of Business Communication* 9 (Spring 1971): 8.

[9]John M. Penrose, "A Survey of the Perceived Importance of Business Communication and Other Business-Related Abilities," *Journal of Business Communication* 13 (Winter 1976): 21.

unscheduled meetings, the tour, and the mail are the manager's prime tools. We should train the student systematically in their use.[10]

The Relative Importance of
Various Communication Skills

The preceding excerpt from Mintzberg's book revives interest in the relative importance of the types of channels. Mintzberg emphasizes the oral as the primary vehicle for managerial communication, even as he acknowledges the necessity for the written. To understand his argument—based upon his review of the literature and his own research involving observation of managers at work—consider another excerpt:

> The manager uses five basic media: the mail (documented communication), the telephone (purely verbal), the unscheduled meeting (formal face-to-face), and the tour (visual). . . . Documented communication requires the use of a formal subset of the language, and involves long feedback delays. All verbal [oral] media can transmit, in addition to the messages contained in the words used, messages sent by voice inflection and by delays in reaction. In addition, face-to-face media carry information transmitted by facial expression and by gesture.
>   . . . managers demonstrate very strong attraction to the verbal [oral] media. Virtually every empirical study of managerial time allocation draws attention to the great proportion of time spent in verbal [oral] communication . . . . My own findings bear this out. . . . verbal [oral] interaction accounted for 78 percent of the . . . managers' time and 67 percent of their activities.[11]

Notice how Mintzberg's findings confirm the proportions of time spent in the various sending and receiving activities reported in Chapter 2 (45 percent—listening; 30 percent—speaking; 16 percent—reading; and 9 percent—writing). Together they show that the components associated with oral communication occupy more time than the written ones.

In a survey of businesspeople in 1974, Weinrauch and Swanda found slightly different proportions, but similar results:

> Generally, listening consumes from one-fourth to one-third of a practitioner's time spent in communication.
>   . . . Speaking was found generally to be the second significant form of communication by business personnel. It consumed about one-fifth to one-fourth of the business practitioner's time. Writing was the least relevant form. It was utilized between one-eighth and one-sixth of the time spent in communication. An interesting side-light to this study is that the respondents were engaged about 20 percent of the time in indirect communication activities [planning messages and the mental activity associated with preparing messages].[12]

In research conducted among businesspeople, Cox found similar proportions. He reported estimates of the percentages of job time spent on activities in an average

---

[10]Mintzberg, *The Nature of Managerial Work,* pp. 190–191.

[11]Ibid., p. 38.

[12]J. Donald Weinrauch and John R. Swanda, Jr., "Examining the Significance of Listening: An Exploratory Study of Contemporary Management." *Journal of Business Communication* 13 (Fall 1975): 31.

month to be: "Listening, 29 percent; speaking, 26 percent; writing, 25 percent; reading, 20 percent."[13]

Huegli and Tschirgi conducted research in 1974 to determine communication skills needed by entry-level business employees. Of 13 skills listed, the first four ranks represented oral skills, the next five, writing skills, and the final four, oral skills. Converted to combined percentages of frequency of use very often and occasionally, 64 percent involved oral communication and 36 percent involved written.[14]

During 1974-1976, a committee of the American Business Communication Association (ABCA) conducted a survey to determine evaluations of the basic collegiate business communication course. The committee sent questionnaires to 151 graduating students in 1974. Eighty-five responded. Of the 85 receiving the follow-up questionnaire in 1975, 49 responded. Of the 49 receiving the follow-up questionnaire in 1976, 36 responded.

In summary of the consistent findings for the three years, the study reports:

1. The course time spent on letter writing and long-report writing should be *decreased*.
2. The time spent on memoranda, speaking, interpersonal and small-group communication, interviewing, listening, nonverbal communication, barriers to communication, and psychology of communication should be *increased*.
3. The time spent on short report writing, dictating, job applications, communication theory and semantics, and other topics should be *maintained*.
4. The course time spent on lectures should be *decreased*.
5. The time spent on group activities should be *increased*.
6. The largest proportions of communication time on the job are spent in nonwriting activities.[15]

With minor exceptions, two important communication facets—the intrapersonal and the nonverbal—have received little, if any, attention in the reported research.

The indirect communication activities cited by Weinrauch and Swanda hint at the intrapersonal. However, it is only the intrapersonal associated with the multihuman levels of communication.

The ABCA survey indicates the need to increase the coverage of nonverbal communication in the collegiate business communication course. However, though all the researchers undoubtedly intended to imply that the proportion of time spent on each of the stated skills includes the nonverbal, that implication is difficult to draw.

The purpose for delineating some of the research about the relative importance of the communication arts and skills lies in the need for a balanced view. Unfortu-

---

[13]Homer Cox, "The Voices of Experiences: The Business Communication Alumnus [sic] Reports," *Journal of Business Communication* 13 (Summer 1976): 37.

[14]Jon M. Huegli and Harvey D. Tschirgi, "An Investigation of Communication Skills Application and Effectiveness at the Entry Job Level," *Journal of Business Communication* 12 (Fall 1974): 25.

[15]American Business Communication Association *Ad Hoc* Committee, Bobbye Persing, Chairperson, "The 1976 ABCA Followup Evaluation of the Course Content, Classroom Procedures, and Quality of the Basic Course in College and University Business Communication," *ABCA Bulletin* 40 (March 1977): 18–24.

nately, business communication is often equated with writing—particularly letter writing and report writing.

Though writing remains as an indispensable tool in the communication kit, listening, speaking, reading, and their nonverbal accompaniments must be added to that kit. In addition, theory should join practice in order that each may grow.

Everyone employed in the field of business is a business communicator. Thus, whether planning to function in business as a communication specialist or in some other capacity, develop the full spectrum of arts, sciences, and skills that define the communication process. Whatever your specialty, you can serve your career—and your life—no better than to meet the requirements of the ultimate binder of business and living—communication.

SUMMARY

Chapter 18 completes the coverage of employment messages by dealing with additional written messages, interviews, appearance and dress, communication and careers, and business as a communication-centered operation.

A *follow-up letter* reminds a prospective employer of your keen interest in a job. The follow-up letter should reinforce some of the key points made in the résumé and the letter of application. The follow-up letter may also reinforce important statements made during an interview.

Following the offer of a job, write a letter of acceptance, a letter of rejection, or a letter of delay.

In the *letter of acceptance*, convey your satisfaction at receiving the offer. Also write that you intend to accept the job and that you are confident that you can do the work well.

The *letter of rejection* is essentially a bad-news message calling for the inductive developmental method. Just build to the rejection by listing the reasons for it.

A *letter of delay* asks for additional time in which to make a decision about whether to accept or reject an offered position. The time may be needed to complete other interviews or needed as a result of personal or external circumstances.

A *letter of thanks*—particularly for an interview—provides the opportunity to retain the momentum of the job-search sequence.

Carry your résumé with you during a job search to aid in completing *application blanks*. Take great care to be neat, accurate, and persuasive when completing the blanks. Some prospective employers look at nothing else.

Tests and *placement- and employment-office files* often enter into a position search. Decide carefully whether you want recommendations to be confidential or nonconfidential.

Before an *interview*, learn as much as possible about the firm and the people who will be interviewing you. Apply self-enhancing techniques as you prepare for and participate in interviews. Develop the content of the interview to improve the chances for success.

Anticipate and practice answering the general and special questions you may be asked, particularly the difficult ones.

Establish *appearance and dress* appropriate to the occasion of the interview. Lean toward conservatism.

Careers in business communication may well be the growth field of the eighties. Some of the positions in the field are vice president for communication, director, manager, administrative assistant, self-employed consultant, and college teacher.

Whatever the career field, it may well require communication skills above all others. Such abilities must cover written, oral, and nonverbal communication—with particular emphasis upon the oral and nonverbal aspects of the process.

Practice

1. You applied for the position of personnel manager at the local telephone company. It represents the job that you really want. A bank to which you applied has offered you the position of assistant personnel manager. You would like to wait for a response from the telephone company before committing yourself to the bank. Write a letter of delay to the bank president. Make up the necessary names, addresses, and other information.

2. [*Your professor will time this exercise.*] Karen Creek just interviewed you for the position of insurance salesperson at Creek & Fuller Insurance, Inc. Creek, a co-owner of the firm, took you to lunch. She also gave you a great deal of information about the insurance industry. Write a thank-you letter to her. Use your imagination to create addresses and to add information.

3. You sent a letter of application and your résumé to an insurance company over a month ago. The company, which had been advertising for salespeople, has not responded to your letter. Write a follow-up letter that briefly emphasizes your general competence, your selling abilities, and your interest in working for the company. Create the company name, address, and other needed information.

4. Alice Snedley, the owner of the small hardware store that you want to manage, will interview you next week. You have taken great pains to learn about the store, Snedley Hardware, and Snedley herself. Here is what you have discovered:
   a. Snedley's mother built the store 50 years ago. The mother died, and Snedley has been managing the store herself for the last 35 years.
   b. Snedley employs five salespeople, all of whom have been working at the store for at least 10 years. None of the employees has a college degree. Nor does Snedley.
   c. Snedley is now 65 years old. She is hiring a manager so that she can go into semi-retirement.
   d. Snedley, a Democrat, opposes labor unions, supports both minority rights and women's rights, and dislikes what she terms "giddy, giggly people."
   e. Snedley once said that she finds aggressive, creative people very interesting.
   f. Snedley has always worked over 15 hours a day, Monday through Saturday.
   g. Snedley Hardware has not been in the black since the new suburban shopping center was built two years ago.
   Make a list of the questions that you believe Ms. Snedley might pose during the interview. Develop answers for all of the questions. Which of the questions do you consider difficult?

5. Apparently Snedley (question No. 4) was impressed with you because she just called you and wants to hire you. First write a letter of acceptance. Now assume that you do *not* want the job, and write a letter of rejection. You do not want the job because you have been offered a better-paying job at the hardware store in the new suburban shopping center.

6. Meet with your group. Have one group member play the role of an interviewer, and have another group member act as the job applicant. Have them conduct a short interview

while the other group members evaluate the interviewer's and applicant's performances. Have the interviewer ask at least one difficult or stressful question in the process of the interview. Continue the interviews until everyone in your group has played both roles. Discuss both performances immediately after each interview.

7. Obtain and complete an application blank for a firm. Analyze the form and your ability to answer the questions in a self-enhancing manner.

8. Meet with your group. Design a simple survey. Design the instrument to determine whether the firms to which you will submit it have any career positions in the field of business communication. Pool the designs of all the groups. Divide the work among the class members. Compile the results. Have each member of the class write a brief report of the research.

9. Based upon the literature and/or observation, write a brief paper about the mode of dress and appearance appropriate for the position you want to hold.

10. Meet with your group. Briefly discuss any or all of these topics. After the discussion, a spokesperson for each group will report to the class.
    a. The issue of open files and whether to mark recommendation forms confidential or nonconfidential
    b. Hints about taking employment tests
    c. Handling interview questions about drugs, theft, and other difficult subjects
    d. Responding to a leading question; e.g., "You don't like . . ., do you?"
    e. Developing a good personal style

11. Visit your campus placement office to learn its procedures for aiding people to obtain jobs. Also obtain copies of any forms used as part of those procedures. Evaluate both the procedures and the forms and write a one-page paper summarizing the evaluation. Meet with your group to discuss and summarize the independent evaluations of the group members. Designate one person to present the group's summary to the class. After the presentations from all of the groups, the class may want to establish a team to develop a set of written and oral recommendations to be presented to the placement office. If you are nearing graduation, you may want to complete your placement-office file at this time.

12. You were interviewed last week by Elton Ables of the X. Acting Corp. in your city for a position as a personnel officer. You received a call today from one of Ables' assistants indicating that Ables would like to have a written statement about the salary you would expect to receive if you join the firm. He needs the statement within two days. The assistant did not say that Ables wants to see you again at this point. Write the statement, supplying any additional information you may need. Indicate how you would transmit the statement to arrive within the specified two days.

13. Recall (without looking, if you can) the six guidelines for effective communication. Write a two- or three-page paper explaining how you would apply each of the guidelines to the transactions associated with your career planning and search for employment.

14. You are scheduled to be interviewed by Donna Lofgren, President of the small accounting firm for which you wish to work. The Lofgren firm is the only accounting firm in town, and you know that competition is stiff for jobs there. Describe how you will apply the six communication guidelines for next week's interview. Summarize the application in a one- or two-page paper.

15. Use your dictionary and thesaurus to create meanings for these words. Use the words when you think, write, and speak so that you feel comfortable using them.

a. Aggressive	i. Obsolete
b. Aptitude	j. Preoccupation
c. Assertive	k. Raucous
d. Belligerent	l. Self-deprecating
e. Entity	m. Self-incriminating
f. Facile	n. Servility
g. Impasse	o. Strategy
h. Militate	p. Succinct

16. Take and score Self-Test 40 over the excerpt about types of interview questions.

Self-Test 40
Excerpt about Types of Interview Questions

A. Recall (25 points each). For each multiple-choice question, select the most accurate answer.

1. Which one of these questions involves a stereotyped approach to interviewing?
   a. What are your weaknesses?
   b. Tell me about your family.
   c. Will you be able to travel?
   d. Are you married?
   e. Has your husband given you permission to work?

2. Which one of these statements is true?
   a. When asked about the salary you expect to receive, always state some figure.
   b. When asked about personal matters, tell the interviewer, "It's none of your business."
   c. If you choose not to answer certain questions, briefly and assertively explain why.
   d. Never refuse to answer a question.
   e. Avoid reciting your qualities, honors, or awards; the interviewer will think you are conceited.

3. Which one of these approaches is correct?
   a. By using a positive answer, try to turn a negative question to your favor.
   b. When asked why you are leaving your present employer, be sure to describe the employer's flaws to the interviewer.
   c. Use a question about leisure time to report only serious activities.
   d. Always agree to take a polygraph test; otherwise the interviewer will think you have something to hide.
   e. When asked about the kind of working conditions you like, be sure to emphasize salary and benefits.

B. Inference (25 points). For the multiple-choice question, select the most accurate answer.

You are interviewing for the position of loan officer at a bank. The interviewer asks you what you think of the military draft. Which answer would most likely allow you to be true to your beliefs and avoid a disagreement at the same time?
   a. I think all able-bodied people should be drafted.
   b. I am opposed to the draft, aren't you?
   c. *I* certainly don't want to go to war, but I do think the draft is a good thing.
   d. What does your question have to do with the job?
   e. I've heard a number of interesting discussions on both sides of the question. The draft is certainly a complex issue.

Solution to Self-Test 40
Excerpt about Types of Interview Questions

A. Recall (25 points each)

   1. e   **3.** a

   2. c

B. Inference (25 points)

   e

17. Take and score Self-Test 41 over Chapter 18.

Self-Test 41
Chapter 18

A. Recall (20 points each). For each multiple-choice question, select the most accurate answer.

  1. A letter of follow-up:

    a. May have the purpose of initiating or intensifying interest in a previously submitted application

    b. Should be long and comprehensive

    c. Must not be repeated

    d. Should not include additional information

    e. Must not include any persuasion

  2. When an employer uses the mail to offer you a position with a firm,

    a. Always wait several days before responding

    b. Write a response of acceptance in the inductive style

    c. Write a response of rejection in the deductive style

    d. Include no reasons in a response asking for more time to make a decision

    e. Treat a letter asking for a delay as a combination of persuasive and bad-news messages

  3. Before and during an interview, you should *not:*

    a. Ask such questions as: "Are you going to give me this job?" or "Will you give me a decent salary?"

    b. Arrive for the interview ten minutes ahead of time

    c. Remain standing until the interviewer invites you to be seated

    d. Make good eye contact with the interviewer

    e. Let the interviewer take the lead

  4. Which one of these statements is true?

    a. You need not complete every blank on a questionnaire.

    b. Always mark recommendation forms "confidential."

    c. Show photographs of your family at the first interview to indicate allegiance to your family.

    d. High-fashion clothing impresses the interviewer because it shows that you are up to date.

    e. Whether in a business communication career or another career in business, written, oral, and nonverbal communication arts and skills are critically important to it.

B. Inference (20 points). For the multiple-choice question, select the most accurate answer.

Which one of these statements is *false?*

  a. Even though careers in business communication are expanding, a business-communication major would be wise to prepare in a second field.

  b. Most interviewers are unaware of the impact that interviewees' personal styles have on them.

  c. The first impression created by dress and appearance may override many other of the interviewee's characteristics.

  d. An interviewee is hypocritical if he or she does not deliberately state views on controversial issues.

  e. Business-communication students tend to believe that the proportion of class time devoted to group activities, speaking, and discussion should be increased.

Self-Test 41
Chapter 18

A. Recall (20 points each)

1. a   **3.** a

2. e   **4.** e

B. Inference (20 points)

d

Appendix A

Date	Material Read (Page No., Self-Test No., or Other ID)	No. of Words	No. of Seconds	Words a Minute (w.a.m.) $\dfrac{\text{No. of Words} \times 60}{\text{No. of Seconds}}$	Comprehension Test Score (c.t.s.)	Reading Efficiency Score (r.e.s.) w.a.m. × c.t.s.

RECORD OF SPEED

CAREFUL READING

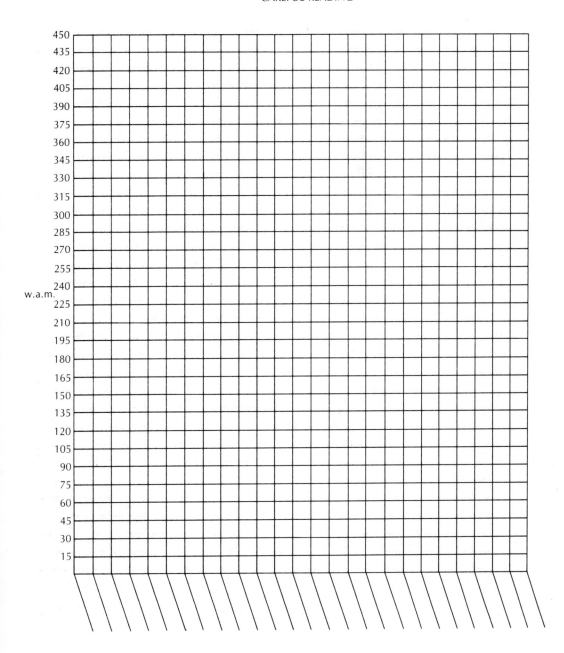

w.a.m.

Date

RECORD OF READING EFFICIENCY SCORE

CAREFUL READING

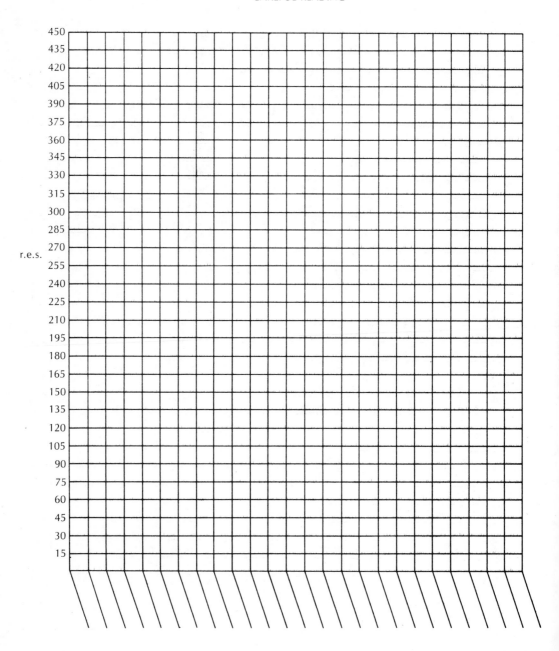

r.e.s.

Date

RECORD OF READING EFFICIENCY
RAPID READING

Date	Material Read (Page No., Self-Test No., or Other ID)	No. of Words	No. of Seconds	Words a Minute (w.a.m.) No. of Words × 60 / No. of Seconds	Comprehension Test Score (c.t.s.)	Reading Efficiency Score (r.e.s.) w.a.m. × c.t.s.

RECORD OF SPEED
RAPID READING

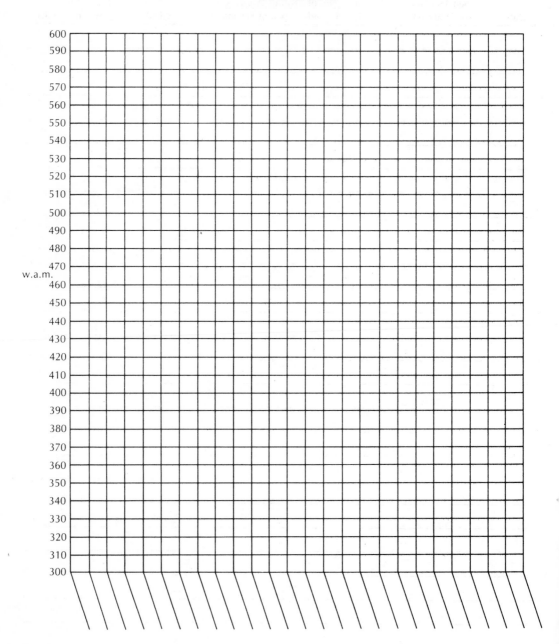

Date

RECORD OF READING EFFICIENCY SCORE
RAPID READING

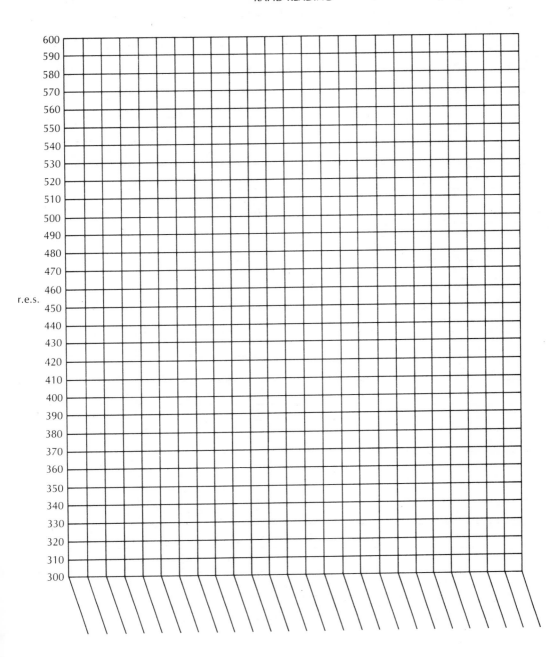

Date

RECORD OF READING EFFICIENCY
SKIMMING

Date	Material Read (Page No., Self-Test No., or Other ID)	No. of Words	No. of Seconds	Words a Minute (w.a.m.) $\dfrac{\text{No. of Words} \times 60}{\text{No. of Seconds}}$	Comprehension Test Score (c.t.s.)	Reading Efficiency Score (r.e.s.) w.a.m. × c.t.s.

RECORD OF SPEED

SKIMMING

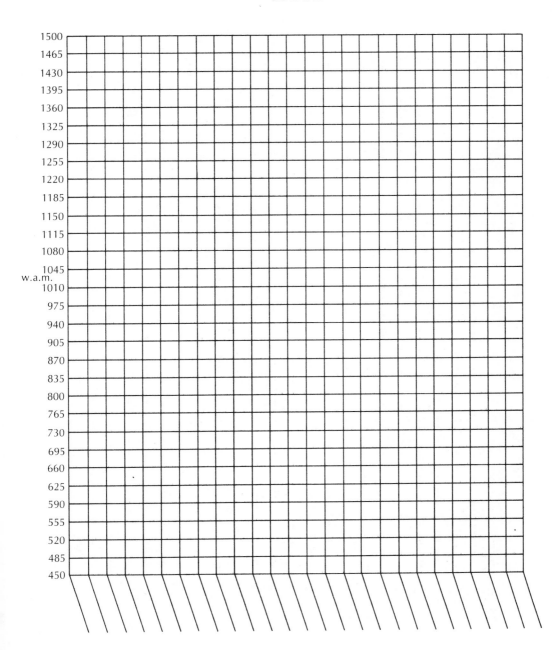

Date

RECORD OF READING EFFICIENCY SCORE
SKIMMING

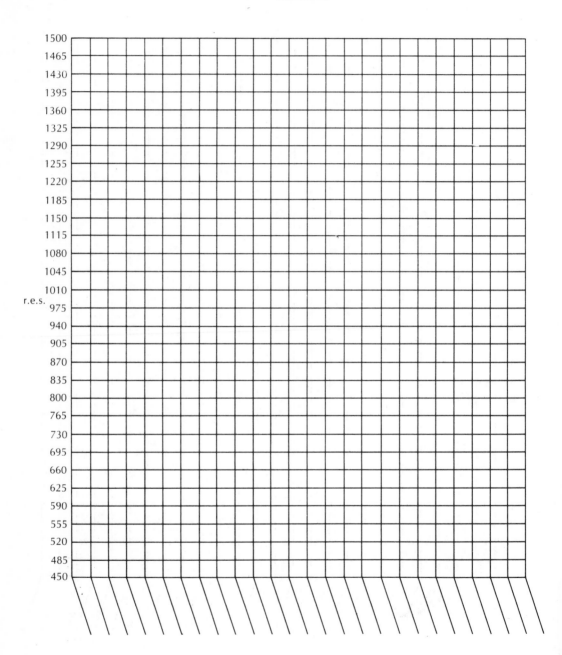

Date

RECORD OF READING EFFICIENCY
SCANNING

Date	Material Read (Page No., Self-Test No., or Other ID)	No. of Words	No. of Seconds	Words a Minute (w.a.m.) $\dfrac{\text{No. of Words} \times 60}{\text{No. of Seconds}}$	Comprehension Test Score (c.t.s.)	Reading Efficiency Score (r.e.s.) w.a.m. $\times$ c.t.s.

RECORD OF SPEED

SCANNING

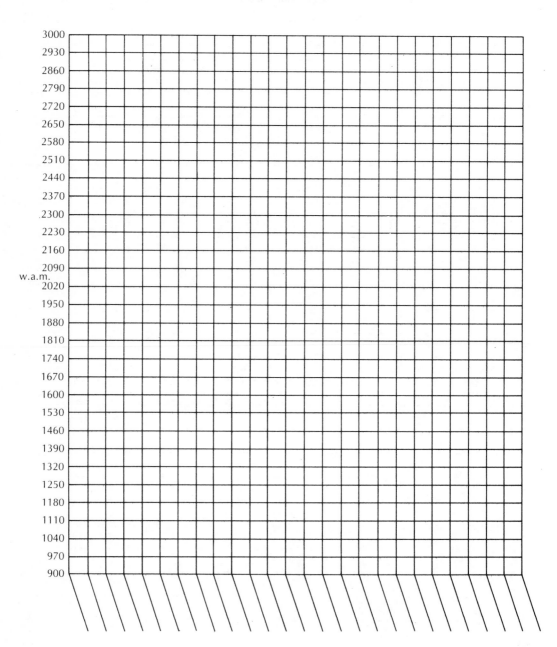

Date

RECORD OF READING EFFICIENCY SCORE

SCANNING

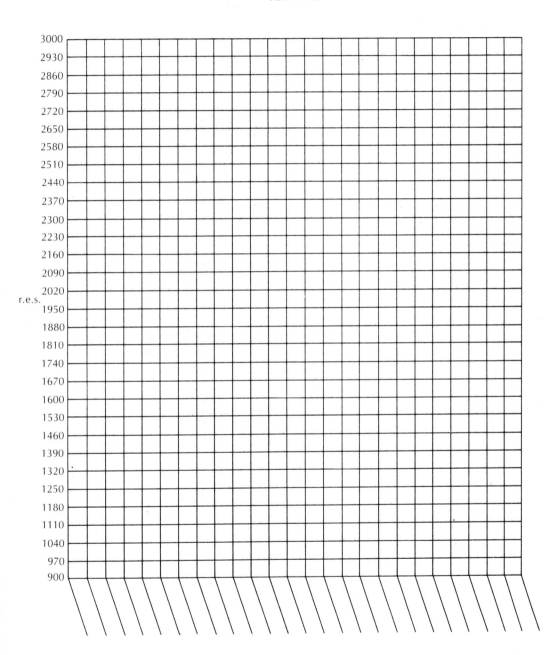

Date

Appendix B

NAME _____ DATE _____

NUMBER OF PEOPLE IN GROUP _____ WHAT WAS THE PURPOSE OF YOUR

MEETING? _____

1. Do you feel that your group stayed with the topic(s) you had planned to discuss? ____ If yes, write a summary of the discussion. If no, explain what was discussed and why you think the group did not discuss what was planned.

2. Did all group members participate in the discussion? Who participated the most? The least? If someone dominated the discussion, was he or she asked to allow others a chance to speak? If not, why?

3. What, specifically, could be done to make your group work better in the future? If you were satisfied with the discussion, what made it go well?

GROUP DISCUSSION
GENERAL EVALUATION QUESTIONNAIRE

NAME _____ DATE _____

NUMBER OF PEOPLE IN GROUP _____ WHAT WAS THE PURPOSE OF YOUR

MEETING? _____

_____

	Strongly Agree	Agree	Neutral	Disagree	Strongly Disagree
1. All group members were prepared for the meeting.	_____	_____	_____	_____	_____
2. The purposes and/or goals of the meeting were clear.	_____	_____	_____	_____	_____
3. The purposes and/or goals of the meeting were met.	_____	_____	_____	_____	_____
4. All group members participated in the meeting.	_____	_____	_____	_____	_____
5. The quality of discussion was high.	_____	_____	_____	_____	_____
6. Group members seemed to feel satisfied with their contributions to the meeting.	_____	_____	_____	_____	_____
7. Group members seemed to feel satisfied with the meeting.	_____	_____	_____	_____	_____
8. The meeting was very productive.	_____	_____	_____	_____	_____
9. The meeting was satisfactory.	_____	_____	_____	_____	_____
10. The meeting might as well not have been held.	_____	_____	_____	_____	_____
11. I look forward to meeting with the group again.	_____	_____	_____	_____	_____

GROUP DISCUSSION
PERSONAL STRENGTHS AND WEAKNESSES
EVALUATION FORM

NAME _____ DATE _____

NUMBER OF PEOPLE IN GROUP _____ WHAT HAD YOU PLANNED TO DISCUSS?

_____

_____

1. My contributions to the group discussion included:

   a. Identifying goals   _____   g. Responding to questions   _____
   b. Relating information   _____   h. Asking questions   _____
   c. Identifying problems   _____   i. Clarifying   _____
   d. Solving problems   _____   j. Taking notes   _____
   e. Explaining   _____   k. Other _____
   f. Planning   _____   _____

2. My contributions to the group process included:

   a. Lending support   _____   e. Defending a group member
   b. Mediating conflicts   _____   under attack   _____
   c. Reminding group members of   f. Evaluating the group
      the purpose of the meeting _____   process   _____
   d. Asking quiet members   g. Other _____
      for suggestions   _____   _____

3. My weaknesses in the group discussion included:

   a. Remaining quiet   _____   l. Not preparing for the
   b. Getting angry   _____   meeting   _____
   c. Fidgeting   _____   m. Talking too much   _____
   d. Arguing too much   _____   n. Shaking when I spoke   _____
   e. Ignoring   _____   o. Giving inadequate or
   f. Acting silly   _____   inaccurate information   _____
   g. Daydreaming   _____   p. Using bad grammar   _____
   h. Not listening   _____   q. Using sexist or other
   i. Not taking notes   _____   discriminatory language   _____
   j. Not being forceful   r. Using words with which few
      enough   _____   people were familiar   _____
   k. Not staying on the   s. Other _____
      subject   _____   _____

GROUP DISCUSSION
STRENGTHS AND WEAKNESSES OF OTHER GROUP MEMBERS
EVALUATION FORM

NAME OF GROUP MEMBER YOU ARE EVALUATING _____

YOUR NAME _____ DATE _____

NUMBER OF PEOPLE IN GROUP _____ WHAT HAD YOU PLANNED TO DISCUSS?

_____

1. Her or his contributions to the group discussion included:

   a. Identifying goals _____   g. Responding to questions _____
   b. Relating information _____   h. Asking questions _____
   c. Identifying problems _____   i. Clarifying _____
   d. Solving problems _____   j. Taking notes _____
   e. Explaining _____   k. Other _____
   f. Planning _____   _____

2. Her or his contributions to the group process included:

   a. Lending support _____   e. Defending a group member
   b. Mediating conflicts _____   under attack _____
   c. Reminding group members of   f. Evaluating the group
      the purpose of the meeting _____   process _____
   d. Asking quiet members   g. Other _____
      for suggestions _____   _____

3. Her or his weaknesses in the group discussion included:

   a. Remaining quiet _____   l. Not preparing for the
   b. Getting angry _____   meeting _____
   c. Fidgeting _____   m. Talking too much _____
   d. Arguing too much _____   n. Shaking when he or she spoke _____
   e. Ignoring _____   o. Giving inadequate or
   f. Acting silly _____   inaccurate information _____
   g. Daydreaming _____   p. Using bad grammar _____
   h. Not listening _____   q. Using sexist or other
   i. Not taking notes _____   discriminatory language _____
   j. Not being forceful   r. Using words with which few
      enough _____   people were familiar _____
   k. Not staying on the   s. Other _____
      subject _____   _____

Appendix C

English Review

GRAMMAR

When people make grammatical errors in their writing, speaking, and thinking, they usually make one or more of the mistakes described in this section. Study the examples that illustrate each of the grammatical rules so that you can avoid making these errors.

1. **MISTAKE:** *The subject and the verb in a sentence or clause do not agree. In other words, the subject is singular and the verb is plural, or the subject is plural and the verb is singular.*

   SOLUTION: When the subject is plural, its associated verb should be plural. When the subject is singular, its associated verb should be singular. The subject and verb must agree regardless of the number of words separating them.

   HINT: When several words separate the subject and the verb, mentally remove them so that they do not confuse your thinking. For example, if a sentence such as "The person for the Higgs and Suggs accounts is Daren" is confusing, just think of the sentence as "The person is Daren" for a moment. Clearly both the subject and the verb are singular in this instance, though "accounts" is plural. Again, just put mental parentheses around the words that separate the subject and its associated verb.

   EXAMPLES

INCORRECT	CORRECT
The manager (of the shoe and hosiery departments) are absent.	The manager (of the shoe and hosiery departments) is absent.
They was at the meeting.	They were at the meeting.
The number (of times the books is used) are inconsequential.	The number (of times the books are used) is inconsequential.
Neither (Frank nor Alice) were asked back for another interview.	Neither (Frank nor Alice) was asked back for another interview.
If either (Rachel or Lane) go, I will write the report.	If either (Rachel or Lane) goes, I will write the report.
If either Ms. Baum or the Fabers joins us, we will have to order more coffee.	If either Ms. Baum or the Fabers join us, we will have to order more coffee.

   (Note: Here the subject closest to the verb determines whether the verb is singular or plural. "Fabers" is plural, so the verb "join" is plural.)

2. **MISTAKE:** *"Each," "everyone," "everybody," "anyone," and "anybody" are used as if they were plural.*

   SOLUTION: "Each," "everyone," "everybody," "anyone," and "anybody" are singular. Use them as such.

664

EXAMPLES

INCORRECT	CORRECT
Everybody and their parents will attend.	Everybody and her or his parents will attend.
Each of the accountants are working on the audit.	Each of the accountants is working on the audit.
We want everyone to have their chance.	We want everyone to have her or his chance.
Each of the department heads will contribute their time, and all of the employees are planning to donate old clothes.	Each of the department heads will contribute her or his time, and all of the employees are planning to donate old clothes.

3. **MISTAKE:** *"Us" is used in the subjective case and "we" is used in the objective case.*
   SOLUTION: Always use "we" as part of the subject and "us" as part of the direct or indirect receiver of the subject's action.
   HINT: When trying to decide whether to use "us" or "we," think of the sentence without the word or words following "us" or "we." For example, say the sentences in the first example without the word "employees." "Us want a better grievance system" sounds odd, but "We want a better grievance system" sounds, and is, correct.

EXAMPLES

INCORRECT	CORRECT
Us employees want a better grievance system.	We employees want a better grievance system.
The manager gave the new guidelines to we salespeople.	The manager gave the new guidelines to us salespeople.
The report that us board members want should be ready tomorrow.	The report that we board members want should be ready tomorrow.

4. **MISTAKE:** *"I" is used in the objective case and "me" is used in the subjective case.*
   SOLUTION: Use "I" as the subject and "me" as the direct or indirect receiver of the subject's action.

EXAMPLES

INCORRECT	CORRECT
Fred gave the presentation to Laura and I.	Fred gave the presentation to Laura and me.
Him and me share an office.	He and I share an office.
It is me.	It is I.
The party was given for Adam and I.	The party was given for Adam and me.

5. **MISTAKE:** *"Who is used as an object and "whom" is used as a subject.*
   SOLUTION: Use "who" in the subjective case and "whom" in the objective case.
   HINT: Substitute "he," "she," or "we" for "who," and substitute "her," "him," or "us" for "whom" when you are confused.

EXAMPLES

INCORRECT	CORRECT
Rhoda Sills, whom works for us, will make the trip.	Rhoda Sills, who works for us, will make the trip.
You will be giving the raise to who?	You will be giving the raise to whom?
Who are you talking about?	Whom are you talking about?

(Note: Here, you can restate the sentence as "You are talking about her?," which sounds, and is, correct.)

Whomever wrote this knows her or his subject.	Whoever wrote this knows her or his subject.

PUNCTUATION

Because numerous punctuation rules exist, the treatment of the rules in this appendix is by no means exhaustive. However, some of the important rules do appear here.

1. **THE PERIOD, THE EXCLAMATION POINT, AND THE QUESTION MARK:** *The period, exclamation point, and the question mark are used to end sentences.* A sentence, of course, is a complete thought which includes at least a subject and a verb, such as: "Mr. Skibbs is the manager." A sentence can also be a command, such as "Sit!," where the subject, you, is understood. *A period is used to end most sentences. An exclamation point is used to end a command or a sentence expressing great excitement, grief, or something of extraordinary significance. A question mark ends sentences that are questions.*

INCORRECT	CORRECT
If I could write well. I would write more.	If I could write well, I would write more.
Please send me a sample copy of *City Executive!*	Please send me a sample copy of *City Executive.*
Congratulations, Forrest. *(You want to express excitement.)*	Congratulations, Forrest!
I plan to look for a job after I go to Europe I want to teach business writing my strengths are in punctuation and spelling.	I plan to look for a job after I go to Europe. I want to teach business writing. My strengths are in punctuation and spelling.

2. **THE COMMA:** *Commas are used within sentences to cause the reader to pause, and then continue reading.* Commas make sentences more readable. When you are trying to decide whether to use a comma, say the sentence out loud. Often you will need to put commas in the places where you paused when speaking the sentence. Commas serve a number of functions, most of which are described in this section.

   a. *Commas set off introductory and parenthetical words, and commas signal a direct reference to the reader.*

INCORRECT	CORRECT
Curiously Jane and Felix refused to finish the project.	Curiously, Jane and Felix refused to finish the project.
Even so I will talk to Ms. Rames.	Even so, I will talk to Ms. Rames.
Given that the reorganization plan should be written by a third party.	Given that, the reorganization plan should be written by a third party.
The Simmons Plan I believe is due on Wednesday.	The Simmons Plan, I believe, is due on Wednesday.
The candidate I chose however speaks very well.	The candidate I chose, however, speaks very well.
I am pleased to inform you Ms. Blue Sky that you will receive your certificate at the employees' luncheon.	I am pleased to inform you, Ms. Blue Sky, that you will receive your certificate at the employees' luncheon.

   b. *Commas set off introductory clauses and phrases.*

INCORRECT	CORRECT
If I choose a company outside of Omaha it must be located in the San Francisco area.	If I choose a company outside of Omaha, it must be located in the San Francisco area.
The company I choose, must be located in the San Francisco area.	The company I choose must be located in the San Francisco area.

| When Mr. Li makes a speech most people listen. | When Mr. Li makes a speech, most people listen. |
| Because the offices are too crowded now the Roy Company will move to a new building. | Because the offices are too crowded now, the Roy Company will move to a new building. |

    c. *Commas connect two complete sentences joined by a conjunction.*

INCORRECT	CORRECT
I fully intend to complete the appendices on time and I plan to begin preparing the index next week.	I fully intend to complete the appendices on time, and I plan to begin preparing the index next week.
I do hope that you are pleased with your first Bilmark Briefcase and I do want you to visit our store soon so that you can receive your free gift.	I do hope that you are pleased with your first Bilmark Briefcase, and I do want you to visit our store soon so that you can receive your free gift.
Ms. Dorn did quite well in her interview and Ms. Ross was impressed by Mr. Schapp's credentials.	Ms. Dorn did quite well in her interview, and Ms. Ross was impressed by Mr. Schapp's credentials.

    d. *Commas set off nonrestrictive clauses.* Nonrestrictive clauses give additional information, but do not provide information essential to the sentence.

INCORRECT	CORRECT
Sharon who is a C.P.A. is the head of the Accounting Department.	Sharon, who is a C.P.A., is the head of the Accounting Department.
The five-year plan I wrote is sixty pages long which is twice the length of the plan Wellings wrote in 1979.	The five-year plan I wrote is sixty pages long, which is twice the length of the plan Wellings wrote in 1979.
The Lansing office which is located in Farmer Michigan had an extremely high turnover rate last year.	The Lansing office, which is located in Farmer, Michigan, had an extremely high turnover rate last year.

    e. *Commas set off longer introductory prepositional phrases.*

INCORRECT	CORRECT
To everyone but Sam Alice was the best marketing manager in the history of the firm.	To everyone but Sam, Alice was the best marketing manager in the history of the firm.
For reasons only he knew the new orders were canceled.	For reasons only he knew, the new orders were canceled.
In response to Faye's letter Tom withdrew his proposal.	In response to Faye's letter, Tom withdrew his proposal.

    f. *Commas set off words or phrases in a series.*

INCORRECT	CORRECT
Dan ordered paper clips pencils and rubber bands.	Dan ordered paper clips, pencils, and rubber bands.
I reviewed the report attended a meeting wrote a memorandum and discussed a problem with Mona.	I reviewed the report, attended a meeting, wrote a memorandum, and discussed a problem with Mona.
Check the progress report for errors type the report and then give the report to me.	Check the progress report for errors, type the report, and then give the report to me.

    g. *Commas set off two or more words that modify a noun.*

INCORRECT	CORRECT
An intelligent articulate financial analyst is easy to find in this town.	An intelligent, articulate financial analyst is easy to find in this town.
No company should be without a reliable inexpensive phone system.	No company should be without a reliable, inexpensive phone system.
The first, preliminary report was both informative and interesting.	The first preliminary report was both informative and interesting.

h. Commas set off words that emphasize differences.

INCORRECT	CORRECT
The person for the job should have experience in the private not public sector.	The person for the job should have experience in the private, not public, sector.
We assumed that Pam not David would do the honors.	We assumed that Pam, not David, would do the honors.

i. Commas set off clauses beginning with "but," "yet," "or," "nor," and "for."

INCORRECT	CORRECT
I answered the phone but the caller said nothing.	I answered the phone, but the caller said nothing.
She received excellent performance ratings yet was never considered for promotion.	She received excellent performance ratings, yet was never considered for promotion.
The supervisors did not cross the picket lines nor did the janitors clerks or mechanics.	The supervisors did not cross the picket lines, nor did the janitors, clerks, or mechanics.

j. Commas set off academic degrees, titles, parts of personal names, cities, states, countries, dates, and "Inc." and "Ltd."

INCORRECT	CORRECT
Arnold Schwartz Jr. Ed.D. will give the major address at the production managers' conference in Kansas City Missouri on Monday February 6, 198X.	Arnold Schwartz, Jr., Ed.D., will give the major address at the production managers' conference in Kansas City, Missouri, on Monday, February 6, 198X.
Stella Vale Vice President is married to an artist.	Stella Vale, Vice President, is married to an artist.
Conway Inc. is a wholly-owned subsidiary of Lentek Ltd. of London England.	Conway, Inc., is a wholly-owned subsidiary of Lentek, Ltd., of London, England.

k. Commas set off direct quotations.

INCORRECT	CORRECT
John asked me "Who are you to disagree?"	John asked me, "Who are you to disagree?"
What she said was "All of the employees in my department have equal rights and responsibilities."	What she said was, "All of the employees in my department have equal rights and responsibilities."

3. THE COLON: *The colon marks the beginning of a series of words. The colon also introduces descriptions, long quotations, and lists.*

INCORRECT	CORRECT
Joan Elliott, an expert on motivation and work behavior, said	Joan Elliott, an expert on motivation and work behavior, said:
No employee should have to view herself or himself as a nobody. The manager should tell the employee that she or he is an important part of the organization and then behave in a manner that supports, not contradicts, the employee's feeling of importance.	No employee should have to view herself or himself as a nobody. The manager should tell the employee that she or he is an important part of the organization and then behave in a manner that supports, not contradicts, the employee's feeling of importance.

Six people are being considered for the job Joe, Louise, Fred, Martha, Henry, and Rita.

Please answer these questions
  1. What is your name?
  2. What is your job title?
  3. What is your home address?
  4. What is your home telephone number?
  5. What amount do you wish to donate?

Six people are being considered for the job: Joe, Louise, Fred, Martha, Henry, and Rita.

Please answer these questions:
  1. What is your name?
  2. What is your job title?
  3. What is your home address?
  4. What is your home telephone number?
  5. What amount do you wish to donate?

4. THE SEMICOLON: *The semicolon serves to cause a more definite pause than the comma.* The most important uses of the semicolon are described in this section.

   a. *Semicolons connect two complete sentences.* Here, the sentences must be related, and no conjunction is used to separate them.

INCORRECT	CORRECT
I was the first person to voice an opinion James was the first person to take offense.	I was the first person to voice an opinion; James was the first person to take offense.
Dave has worked for the firm for six years his work record is exemplary.	Dave has worked for the firm for six years; his work record is exemplary.

   b. *Semicolons connect two main clauses, the second of which begins with a conjunctive adverb.*

INCORRECT	CORRECT
Good health contributes to good learning however, not every healthy person is a quick learner.	Good health contributes to good learning; however, not every healthy person is a quick learner.
You have sold more merchandise than any other salesperson, consequently you have been named Shoe City Salesperson of the year.	You have sold more merchandise than any other salesperson; consequently, you have been named Shoe City Salesperson of the Year.

   c. *Semicolons separate long or complex items or phrases in a series, including phrases or clauses that contain commas.*

INCORRECT	CORRECT
These people participated in the workshop: Susan Morris, marketing, Randy Fein, accounting, Lisa Foo, typing pool, and Walter Nern, editorial services.	These people participated in the workshop: Susan Morris, marketing; Randy Fein, accounting; Lisa Foo, typing pool; and Walter Nern, editorial services.
Marilyn DiRicci volunteered to write the training plan, including the training schedule, to talk to Joe Byrne about the marketing, accounting, and payroll problems, to call Anna Friend, and to conduct the next meeting.	Marilyn DiRicci volunteered to write the training plan, including the training schedule; to talk to Joe Byrne about the marketing, accounting, and payroll problems; to call Anna Friend; and to conduct the next meeting.

5. THE DASH: *Dashes mark a major shift in the structure of a sentence, enclose some words of significance, or set off explanatory words that contain commas.*

INCORRECT	CORRECT
Albert takes the time to talk to his employees and believe me they are pleased with the attention.	Albert takes the time to talk to his employees — and, believe me, they are pleased with the attention.
The district five states Kansas, Nebraska, Missouri, and Arkansas were slow to adopt our new dog food, Doggie Palace.	The district five states — Kansas, Nebraska, Missouri, and Arkansas — were slow to adopt our new dog food, Doggie Palace.

6. QUOTATION MARKS: *Quotation marks are placed before and after the unaltered words of a speaker or writer. Quotation marks also enclose titles of newspaper or magazine articles, reports, songs, short poems, and other short pieces of writing.* Remember that commas and periods go inside the quotation marks, and colons and semicolons are placed outside the quotation marks. If a quotation is a question or an exclamation, the question or exclamation point should be placed inside the quotation marks. If the entire sentence is a question or an exclamation, the question mark or exclamation point should be placed outside the quotation marks. *Also, quotation marks can be used to enclose slang or unusual words, words used sarcastically, and words used to mean something other than their dictionary meaning. Finally, words that you are describing should be enclosed in quotation marks.*

INCORRECT	CORRECT
Ms. Wane said, Every human being has a right to food and shelter.	Ms. Wane said, "Every human being has a right to food and shelter."
How to Organize Your Day, an article in *Business First,* was quite helpful.	"How to Organize Your Day," an article in *Business First,* was quite helpful.
Mr. French thinks that cool has something to do with temperature.	Mr. French thinks that "cool" has something to do with temperature.
I, you, he, she, it, we, and they are pronouns in the subjective case.	"I," "you," "he," "she," "it," "we," and "they" are pronouns in the subjective case.

7. THE HYPHEN: *Hyphens connect words that modify the same noun, connect compound words, and divide words too long to fit at the end of a line.*

INCORRECT	CORRECT
The half written paper was of no use to me.	The half-written paper was of no use to me.
The instructions were self explanatory.	The instructions were self-explanatory.

8. PARENTHESES: *Parentheses suggest that the words they enclose are not critical to the sentence.* The words in parentheses are usually explanatory words, "aside" words that do not flow well in the sentence. Avoid overusing parenthetical structures.

INCORRECT	CORRECT
The current interest rate, too high, I think, is the topic of my finance paper.	The current interest rate (too high, I think) is the topic of my finance paper.
I wrote, remember how poorly I wrote in high school, a report that will be read before the commission.	I wrote (remember how poorly I wrote in high school?) a report that will be read before the commission.

9. ITALICS AND UNDERLINES: Italics are used in printed material for words that are underlined in typewritten material. *Italics and underlines are used to emphasize words, signal foreign words that are not generally used, and set off titles of books, pamphlets, magazines, newspapers, plays, operas, movies, and long poems.*

INCORRECT	CORRECT
I "do not" want my name to be used.	I do *not* want my name to be used.
Elaine considers herself a member of the bourgeoisie.	Elaine considers herself a member of the *bourgeoisie.*
The article in "Newsweek" was reprinted in "Professional Secretary."	The article in *Newsweek* was reprinted in *Professional Secretary.*

10. THE APOSTROPHE: *The apostrophe is used to make words possessive, to form contractions, and to make some abbreviations, letters, and words plural.*

a. *Apostrophes make nouns and indefinite pronouns possessive. In most cases, you make a singular noun or pronoun possessive by adding an apostrophe followed by an "s." An apostrophe is placed after the "s" in plural nouns and indefinite pronouns.*

INCORRECT	CORRECT
The managers office is imposing.	The manager's office is imposing.
(Note: Only one manager occupies the office.)	
The manager's offices are located on the fifth floor.	The managers' offices are located on the fifth floor.
(Note: Several managers occupy the offices.)	
The manager's will meet in my office.	The managers will meet in my office.

(Note: If a word is plural but not possessive, no apostrophe is needed. In this example, the managers do not own or possess anything, so "managers" is not possessive.)

INCORRECT	CORRECT
Davids home is in the suburbs.	David's home is in the suburbs.
She has six months experience in computer programming.	She has six months' experience in computer programming.
She has six months' of experience in computer programming.	She has six months of experience in computer programming.
The Liss son is one of the applicants.	The Liss's son is one of the applicants.
Carol and Johns paper is excellent.	Carol and John's paper is excellent.
(Note: Here both Carol and John wrote the paper.)	
Robert and Nancys papers are late.	Robert's and Nancy's papers are late.
(Note: Here Robert and Nancy wrote separate papers.)	
The door handle was broken.	The door's handle was broken.
They had a years worth of food.	They had a year's worth of food.

b. *Put apostrophes in the place of missing letters in contractions.*

INCORRECT	CORRECT
I have'nt finished the report.	I haven't finished the report.

(Note: Here the apostrophe goes between the "n" and the "t" in place of the missing "o.")

INCORRECT	CORRECT
Its enough to be here.	It's enough to be here.
Is'nt the chart ready?	Isn't the chart ready?
Wer'e on our way.	We're on our way.

(Note: Here the apostrophe goes between the "e" and the "r" in place of the missing "a.")

c. *Apostrophes make plural both abbreviations and letters.*

INCORRECT	CORRECT
Lonnie made two Aes and three Bes.	Lonnie made two A's and three B's.
	or
	Lonnie made two As and three Bs.
Always put "ss" after the apostrophe in singular nouns and pronouns that are possessive.	Always put "s's" after the apostrophe in singular nouns and pronouns that are possessive.
The accountants had three Ph.D.s among them.	The accountants had three Ph.D.'s among them.

d. *Apostrophes can be used to make numbers, years, and symbols plural. Also, words that are referred to in a sentence can be made plural with an apostrophe and an "s."*

INCORRECT	CORRECT
Things were calm in the 1970es.	Things were calm in the 1970's.
Six "7es" appeared in the sentence.	Six 7's appeared in the sentence.
Do not overuse "howevers" and "therefores."	Do not overuse "however's" and "therefore's."
Put "%s" after the numbers in column three.	Put "%'s" after the numbers in column three.

SPELLING AND PRONUNCIATION

The best way to learn to spell and pronounce words correctly is to practice the troublesome words until you have them committed to memory. When the least bit unsure about how to spell or pronounce a word, check a dictionary. Recall, however, that the order of pronunciations in a dictionary does not indicate the order of correctness or preference.

This section lists words that are often misspelled and mispronounced.

WORDS THAT ARE OFTEN MISSPELLED AND MISPRONOUNCED
(Second column alphabetized correctly)

INCORRECT	CORRECT
abscent	absent
accomodate	accommodate
accounant	accountant
acknowledgement	acknowledgment
accross	across
ajust	adjust
administrate	administer
advise (for advice)	advice
adviseable	advisable
advice (for advise)	advise
alright	all right
all most	almost
anlysis	analysis
analyse	analyze
anxous	anxious
arguement	argument
asteriks	asterisk
athalete	athlete
athaletics	athletics

(Note: "Athlete'" has only two syllables; "athletics" has only three.)

attendence	attendance
atitude	attitude
attornies	attorneys
auxilary	auxiliary
batchler	bachelor
babtise	baptize
bargan	bargain
begining	beginning
believeable	believable
beleiving	believing
benefical	beneficial
bookeeper	bookkeeper
bullitin	bulletin

WORDS THAT ARE OFTEN MISSPELLED AND MISPRONOUNCED
(Second column alphabetized correctly)

INCORRECT	CORRECT
burocracy	bureaucracy
busyer	busier
bussiness	business
calender	calendar
campane	campaign
catagory	category
changable	changeable
chargable	chargeable
colesterol	cholesterol
chose (for choose)	choose
choose (for chose)	chose
commited	committed
commitee	committee
companys	companies
compatant	competent
concieve	conceive
congradulate	congratulate
consientous	conscientious
concious	conscious
controled	controlled
convience	convenience
corelate	correlate
correspondant	correspondent
couragous	courageous
curteus	courteous
criteria (for criterion)	criterion
curiousity	curiosity
data (for datum)	datum
deficent	deficient
dependant	dependent
discribe	describe
desireable	desirable
desert (for dessert)	dessert
developement	development
discrete (for discreet)	discreet
discrepency	discrepancy
eficent	efficient
elgible	eligible
embarass	embarrass
inclose	enclose
envirorment	environment
equiped	equipped
excape	escape
expecially	especially
excede	exceed
excelent	excellent
excitment	excitement
exersize	exercise
exausted	exhausted

WORDS THAT ARE OFTEN MISSPELLED AND MISPRONOUNCED
(Second column alphabetized correctly)

INCORRECT	CORRECT
existance	existence
extention	extension
familar	familiar
famos	famous
feasability	feasibility
feasable	feasible
Febuary	February
financialy	financially
finnish	finish
forcable	forcible
formost	foremost
forseen	foreseen
gambel	gamble
goverment	government
grammer	grammar
grievence	grievance
garuntee	guarantee
gilt (for guilt)	guilt
habet	habit
handleing	handling
happyness	happiness
harras	harass
half to	have to
heighth	height
hygene	hygiene
illigitimate	illegitimate
inaguration	inauguration
incidently	incidentally
indispensible	indispensable
insistance	insistence
inteligent	intelligent
interferred	interfered
introduceing	introducing
irrevelant	irrelevant
jelousy	jealousy
jewls	jewels
journies	journeys
legable	legible
liesure	leisure
liason	liaison
lisence	license
maintainence	maintenance
managment	management
medium (for median)	median
median (for medium)	medium
momento	memento
memorandem	memorandum
merchent	merchant
miscelanious	miscellaneous

WORDS THAT ARE OFTEN MISSPELLED AND MISPRONOUNCED
(Second column alphabetized correctly)

INCORRECT	CORRECT
mispelled	misspelled
morale (for moral)	moral
moral (for morale)	morale
naturel	natural
neccessary	necessary
negetive	negative
negociate	negotiate
niether	neither
nuetral	neutral
nineth	ninth
noticable	noticeable
nucular	nuclear
numberous	numerous
obveous	obvious
ocassion	occasion
ocurred or occured	occurred
ocurrence	occurrence
origenal	original
oweing	owing
pamplet	pamphlet
paralell	parallel
preform (for perform)	perform
permanant	permanent
personell	personnel
prespiration	perspiration
preceed	precede
preceeding	preceding
presise	precise
prefered	preferred
prevelent	prevalent
priveledge	privilege
proceedure	procedure
procede	proceed
proposel	proposal
psycology	psychology
quanity	quantity
questionaire	questionnaire
rasberry	raspberry
realator	realtor
realaty	realty
recieve	receive
reccommend	recommend
referrence	reference
refered	referred
reguard	regard
revelant	relevant
rediculous	ridiculous
runaway (for runway)	runway
sells (for sales)	sales

WORDS THAT ARE OFTEN MISSPELLED AND MISPRONOUNCED
(Second column alphabetized correctly)

INCORRECT	CORRECT
scrutany	scrutiny
seperate	separate
sherbert	sherbet
silance	silence
simalar	similar
solvant	solvent
spaded	spayed
stastistics	statistics
suficient	sufficient
summery	summary
supercede	supersede
tacktics	tactics
tenative	tentative
tho	though
thoughtfull	thoughtful
thru	through
tonite	tonight
tradgedy	tragedy
transfered	transferred
transfering	transferring
truely	truly
unlikly	unlikely
useage	usage
wif	with
witholding	withholding
writting	writing

WORD USAGE

People sometimes use words incorrectly or confuse them with words that have similar spellings. Some of the words that give people trouble appear in this section.

1. **ACCEPT AND EXCEPT:** When you *accept* something, you receive it. When you *except* something, you leave it out—you exclude it. Remember, when you accept, you receive; when you make an exception, you exclude something.

INCORRECT	CORRECT
I excepted the job because I have wanted to be an executive secretary all of my life.	I accepted the job because I have wanted to be an executive secretary all of my life.
Everyone accept Johnny has a degree in business.	Everyone except Johnny has a degree in business.
All of the computers excepted the data accept the computer programmed in BASIC.	All of the computers accepted the data except the computer programmed in BASIC.

2. **ADAPT, ADEPT, AND ADOPT:** When you *adapt* something, you make an adjustment so that it will work or fit. When you are *adept* at something, you are very good at it. Finally, when you *adopt* something, you take it and use it as your own.

INCORRECT	CORRECT
Recent graduates often find that it takes several weeks to adopt themselves to a fulltime job.	Recent graduates often find that it takes several weeks to adapt themselves to a fulltime job.
Rose was adapt at both writing and speaking.	Rose was adept at both writing and speaking.
The committee adepted the guidelines listed in Fran's proposal.	The committee adopted the guidelines listed in Fran's proposal.

3. **ADVERSE AND AVERSE:** Something is *adverse* when it is quite hostile or unfavorable. You are *averse* to something when you are opposed to it or are reluctant to face it.

INCORRECT	CORRECT
The averse publicity forced the company to withdraw its Sugar Fun Cereal from the market.	The adverse publicity forced the company to withdraw its Sugar Fun Cereal from the market.
A person is said to be risk-adverse when he or she carefully avoids risks.	A person is said to be risk-averse when he or she carefully avoids risks.
I am adverse to aversity.	I am averse to adversity.

4. **AFFECT AND EFFECT:** When you *affect* something, you bring about a change in it. When you *effect* something, you make it happen. Also, an *effect* is a result.

INCORRECT	CORRECT
The recent staff changes will effect morale.	The recent staff changes will affect morale.
If a person is to affect changes in this organization, he or she must be willing to take some risks.	If a person is to effect changes in this organization, he or she must be willing to take some risks.
What affect will the move have on the regional vice presidents?	What effect will the move have on the regional vice presidents?

5. **ALL READY, ALREADY, ALL TOGETHER, AND ALTOGETHER:** When something is *all ready,* it is prepared or completely done. When something is *already* done, it was done previously. Things that are *all together* are things that are together in one group. When you are *altogether* something, you are entirely something.

INCORRECT	CORRECT
She was all ready late.	She was already late.
The packages were already for shipping.	The packages were all ready for shipping.
They were altogether in the conference room.	They were all together in the conference room.
He was not all together wrong in his assessment of the situation.	He was not altogether wrong in his assessment of the situation.

6. **APPRAISE AND APPRISE:** When you *appraise* something, you evaluate it or estimate its worth. When you *apprise* someone of something, you inform her or him.

INCORRECT	CORRECT
The insurance company sent a woman to the garage to apprise the value of the damaged car.	The insurance company sent a woman to the garage to appraise the value of the damaged car.
Six people were chosen to appraise the affected employees of the reasons for the changes in the salary structure.	Six people were chosen to apprise the affected employees of the reasons for the changes in the salary structure.

7. **ANXIOUS AND EAGER:** When you are *anxious,* you are worried about something that may happen. When you are *eager,* you look forward to something or want something to happen.

INCORRECT	CORRECT
I am eager about the probable cut in my pay.	I am anxious about the probable cut in my pay.
I am anxious to meet all of you.	I am eager to meet all of you.

8. CAPITAL AND CAPITOL: A *capital* is a city, and the *capitol* is the main government building in the capital. *Capital* is also money or property.

INCORRECT	CORRECT
We went to Oklahoma's capitol, Oklahoma City, to take a tour of the capital.	We went to Oklahoma's capital, Oklahoma City, to take a tour of the capitol.
We do not have enough capitol to incorporate.	We do not have enough capital to incorporate.

9. CITE, SIGHT, AND SITE: You *cite* a person when you quote her or him or when you commend her or him for good service. You *sight* a person when you locate her or him with your eyes. A *site* is the place where something was, is, or is to be located.

INCORRECT	CORRECT
The attorney sited Marks v. Lainer.	The attorney cited Marks v. Lainer.
We last cited Don and Meyer in the park.	We last sighted Don and Meyer in the park.
We need to find a suitable sight for the new insurance office.	We need to find a suitable site for the new insurance office.

10. COMPLEMENT, COMPLIMENT AND COMPLIMENTARY: Something *complements* something else when it completes it or perfects it. Someone *compliments* someone else when he or she gives praise or expresses admiration. Something is *complimentary* when it is given at no charge as a courtesy.

INCORRECT	CORRECT
The chair compliments the desk.	The chair complements the desk.
She rarely gives complements.	She rarely gives compliments.
A complementary drink is given to every passenger.	A complimentary drink is given to every passenger.

11. CONFIDANT AND CONFIDENT: Your *confidant* is a trusted friend. You are *confident* when you are relatively sure about someone or something.

INCORRECT	CORRECT
Sally is my confident; I tell her everything.	Sally is my confidant; I tell her everything.
I am confidant that I will be promoted to group leader.	I am confident that I will be promoted to group leader.

12. CONSCIENCE AND CONSCIOUS: Your *conscience* is what distinguishes between right and wrong. You are *conscious* when you are aware of something about yourself or about your environment.

INCORRECT	CORRECT
My conscious was bothering me because I had neglected my family.	My conscience was bothering me because I had neglected my family.
I was conscience of your problem, but not of Milt's.	I was conscious of your problem, but not of Milt's.

13. CONTINUAL AND CONTINUOUS: Something that happens *continually* happens often. Something that takes place *continuously* takes place without interruption.

INCORRECT	CORRECT
Harry continuously stayed after closing time.	Harry continually stayed after closing time.
The continual buzz of the clock distracts me.	The continuous buzz of the clock distracts me.

14. COUNCIL, COUNSEL, COUNCILOR, AND COUNSELOR: A *council* is a group of people. You *counsel* someone when you discuss something with her or him. You are a *councilor* when you are a member of a council. You are a *counselor* when you act as an adviser.

INCORRECT	CORRECT
I am a member of the city counsel.	I am a member of the city council.
I council my clients to invest in money market certificates.	I counsel my clients to invest in money market certificates.
I was a city counselor for sixteen years.	I was a city councilor for sixteen years.
I am a career councilor at Synne High School.	I am a career counselor at Synne High School.

15. CREDIBLE AND CREDITABLE: You are *credible* when you are preceived to be honest and knowledgeable. When you do good work, your work is *creditable*.

INCORRECT	CORRECT
I would not quote him because most people do not consider him a creditable source.	I would not quote him because most people do not consider him a credible source.
The work you did on the sales campaign is credible.	The work you did on the sales campaign is creditable.

16. DISINTERESTED AND UNINTERESTED: When you are *disinterested*, you are unbiased or impartial. When you are *uninterested*, you are simply not interested in the subject.

INCORRECT	CORRECT
Most circuit court judges are said to be uninterested because they are impartial.	Most circuit court judges are said to be disinterested because they are impartial.
Claudine seemed disinterested in my book about Australian wheat.	Claudine seemed uninterested in my book about Australian wheat.

17. EVERY ONE, EVERYONE, ANY ONE, AND ANYONE: "Of" usually follows the words "*every one*" and "*any one*." "*Everyone*" means everybody and "*anyone*" means anybody.

INCORRECT	CORRECT
Everyone of you is responsible.	Every one of you is responsible.
I want every one to have a chance to speak.	I want everyone to have a chance to speak.
Anyone of you could be the next chairperson.	Any one of you could be the next chairperson.
Any one caught divulging company secrets will be suspended.	Anyone caught divulging company secrets will be suspended.

18. FARTHER AND FURTHER: "*Farther*" is a greater distance in space that can be measured in such units as inches or miles. "*Further*" usually refers to a distance in space or time that cannot be measured in standard units or refers to a greater degree for a qualitative factor. "*Further*" also refers to advancing something.

INCORRECT	CORRECT
My new car can go further on a gallon of gasoline than my old car.	My new car can go farther on a gallon of gasoline than my old car.

The farther I get into this project, the more I like it.

The completion of my degree will farther my career.

The further I get into this project, the more I like it.

The completion of my degree will further my career.

19. **FOREWORD AND FORWARD:** A *foreword* is a preface or introduction. You move toward the front when you move *forward*. Also, if you are aggressive, you might be considered *forward*.

INCORRECT	CORRECT
The forward of the book was too long.	The foreword of the book was too long.
I sometimes wonder why he is not moving foreward in his career.	I sometimes wonder why he is not moving forward in his career.

20. **FORMALLY AND FORMERLY:** You do something in a formal way when you do something *formally*. You were something or did something *formerly* when you were something or did something previously.

INCORRECT	CORRECT
Carnes will formerly hand over the reigns of power at the banquet.	Carnes will formally hand over the reigns of power at the banquet.
Louise Frankel, formally of Biggs and Weinberg, will direct all research projects.	Louise Frankel, formerly of Biggs and Weinberg, will direct all research projects.

21. **ITS AND IT'S:** "*Its*" is used as a possessive pronoun. "*It's*" is used as the contraction of "it is" or "it has."

INCORRECT	CORRECT
The agency applied for it's license after the deadline.	The agency applied for its license after the deadline.
Its unfortunate that the company will not allow it's employees to have flexible work hours.	It's unfortunate that the company will not allow its employees to have flexible work hours.

22. **LAY AND LIE:** You place something on a surface when you *lay* it down. You yourself rest or recline on a surface when you *lie* down. Objects *lie* after they have been placed on a surface. The past tense of *lie*, however, is *lay*.

INCORRECT	CORRECT
Please lie down your papers so that you can write on the board.	Please lay down your papers so that you can write on the board.
The books just laid there unused for a week.	The books just lay there unused for a week.

23. **LEAD AND LED:** You *lead* if you are directing, guiding, or conducting something or someone now or in the future. You *led* if you directed, guided, or conducted something or someone in the past. *Lead* is also a metallic substance.

INCORRECT	CORRECT
I lead a fund drive last summer.	I led a fund drive last summer.
The type bars are made of led.	The type bars are made of lead.

24. **LOOSE AND LOSE:** Something is *loose* when it is not tight. When you *lose* something, you are unable to find it or you do not win it.

INCORRECT	CORRECT
The drawer handle is lose.	The drawer handle is loose.
If we loose the contract, we will be in financial trouble.	If we lose the contract, we will be in financial trouble.

25. PASSED AND PAST: *"Passed"* is the past tense of *"pass." "Past"* is an adjective that refers to something that has gone by or something that is no longer current.

INCORRECT	CORRECT
We past the school on the way to work.	We passed the school on the way to work.
The bill is passed due.	The bill is past due.
What happened in the passed is of no concern to me.	What happened in the past is of no concern to me.

26. PERSECUTE AND PROSECUTE: You *persecute* someone when you purposely harm her or him. You *prosecute* someone when you bring a legal action against her or him.

INCORRECT	CORRECT
We aren't giving you suggestions for the purpose of prosecuting you.	We aren't giving you suggestions for the purpose of persecuting you.
Do you intend to persecute the person who altered your firm's books?	Do you intend to prosecute the person who altered your firm's books?

27. PERSONAL AND PERSONNEL: Something that is *personal* is something that is yours. The employees of an organization are its *personnel*.

INCORRECT	CORRECT
I try to keep my personnel life separate from my life at work.	I try to keep my personal life separate from my life at work.
We offer an excellent package of benefits to our personal.	We offer an excellent package of benefits to our personnel.

28. PERSPECTIVE AND PROSPECTIVE: Your *perspective* is your point of view. *"Perspective"* also refers to the relationship of the parts to each other and to the whole. A *prospective* something is an expected something.

INCORRECT	CORRECT
Your prospective on the matter seems to differ from mine.	Your perspective on the matter seems to differ from mine.
The perspective client wants us to give her a presentation.	The prospective client wants us to give her a presentation.

29. PRACTICAL AND PRACTICABLE: Something that is *practical* is something that is useful or something that is acquired through action, not through theory. Something that is *practicable* is something that is capable of being put into use. Though *"practical"* can refer to both things and people, *"practicable"* refers to only things.

INCORRECT	CORRECT
Because he wears clothes that are both stylish and functional, I consider him to be practicable.	Because he wears clothes that are both stylish and functional, I consider him to be practical.
The plan for modifying the computer network is most likely practical.	The plan for modifying the computer network is most likely practicable.

30. PRECEDE AND PROCEED: When something *precedes* something, it comes before that something. You *proceed* when you continue.

INCORRECT	CORRECT
The foreword proceeds the chapters in the book.	The foreword precedes the chapters in the book.
I told Ms. Wong to precede with her work on the financial reporting requirements.	I told Ms. Wong to proceed with her work on the financial reporting requirements.

31. **PRINCIPAL AND PRINCIPLE:** A *principal* something is the most important something. A person who is a *principal* is the head of a school or is an important person in some organization or activity. *"Principal"* can also refer to the amount of a loan before interest. A *principle* is a law, rule, assumption, or fundamental truth. *"Principle"* is used only as a noun.

INCORRECT	CORRECT
The principle of Waller High School is Sharon Kline.	The principal of Waller High School is Sharon Kline.
The principle reason I chose to become an accountant is that I have always liked to work with numbers.	The principal reason I chose to become an accountant it that I have always liked to work with numbers.
Most of the money we pay each month goes to pay off the interest, not the principle, of our loan.	Most of the money we pay each month goes to pay off the interest, not the principal, of our loan.
The examination covered basic accounting principals.	The examination covered basic accounting principles.

32. **SALES AND SELLS:** *"Sales"* is a noun. You hold a sale. You make a sale. Your sales for the year are high. *"Sells"* is a verb. A person sells something.

INCORRECT	CORRECT
Jane, who sales vitamins to health food stores, made more sells in December than the other four sellspeople combined.	Jane, who sells vitamins to health food stores, made more sales in December than the other four salespeople combined.

33. **SOME TIME AND SOMETIME:** When you refer to a period of time, you use *"some time."* When you refer to an occasion, you use *"sometime."*

INCORRECT	CORRECT
I will need sometime to drive to my appointment in Jersey City.	I will need some time to drive to my appointment in Jersey City.
I will call you some time.	I will call you sometime.

34. **STATIONARY AND STATIONERY:** You do not move when you are *stationary*. You write letters on *stationery*.

INCORRECT	CORRECT
I exercise on the stationery bicycle in the family room.	I exercise on the stationary bicycle in the family room.
When I write letters to prospective employers, I use my best stationary.	When I write letters to prospective employers, I use my best stationery.

35. **TACK AND TACT:** When you use a certain plan of action, you take a certain *tack*. When you know how to act in a socially appropriate manner, you are said to have *tact*.

INCORRECT	CORRECT
The correct tact is not always obvious.	The correct tack is not always obvious.
A public relations person should have tack.	A public relations person should have tact.

36. **THEIR, THERE, AND THEY'RE:** *"Their"* is a possessive form of "they." *"There"* refers to a place. *"They're"* is the contraction of "they are."

INCORRECT	CORRECT
There office is located on the seventh floor.	Their office is located on the seventh floor.
There office is located over their.	Their office is located over there.
Their due here in an hour.	They're due here in an hour.

38. TRACK AND TRACT: A *track* is some sort of mark or path. A *tract* is either a piece of land or a propaganda paper.

INCORRECT	CORRECT
The visitors left muddy tracts in my office.	The visitors left muddy tracks in my office.
The right-wing political party's track was written by a college professor.	The right-wing political party's tract was written by a college professor.

39. USE AND UTILIZE: Though both *"use"* and *"utilize"* mean practically the same thing, *"utilize"* sounds stilted and is usually not necessary. *"Utilize"* should be used only when referring to something rather technical or formal, such as "The Facilities Utilization Plan," where *"utilization"* means the profitable and efficient use of the facilities. *"Utilized"* is used too frequently.

INCORRECT	CORRECT
When I write, I utilize my pen or pencil.	When I write, I use my pen or pencil.
Turn off the typewriter after you utilize it.	Turn off the typewriter after you use it.

40. WHO'S AND WHOSE: *"Who's"* is a contraction of "who is." *"Whose"* is the possessive form of "who" and "which."

INCORRECT	CORRECT
Whose going to lunch with her?	Who's going to lunch with her?
Mr. Farias, who's daughter is an electrical engineer, plans to go back to college to finish his degree in business.	Mr. Farias, whose daughter is an electrical engineer, plans to go back to college to finish his degree in business.

41. YOUR AND YOU'RE: *"Your"* is the possessive form of "you." *"You're"* is the contraction of "you are."

INCORRECT	CORRECT
You're department is more productive than mine.	Your department is more productive than mine.
Your one of the finest employees I have had the good fortune to know.	You're one of the finest employees I have had the good fortune to know.

SENTENCE STRUCTURE

Eight major types of errors in sentence construction receive treatment in this section. Examples illustrate incorrect and correct sentence construction. English grammar and style books supply additional suggestions for controlling sentence structure.

1. **MISTAKE:** *Commas are put in places where they do not belong.* The result is a sentence that does not flow well.
    SOLUTION: Review the section on commas in the Punctuation section of this appendix. Note just when and where commas *are* used. Remember that a sentence *without* the necessary commas usually reads better than a sentence *with* unnecessary commas.

HINT: As suggested in that section of the appendix, read your sentence out loud. If you do not pause, the sentence probably does not need a comma. If you do pause somewhere in the sentence, you probably need a comma there.

INCORRECT	CORRECT
Mr. Wince is, a valuable employee.	Mr. Wince is a valuable employee.
She would like to apply, for a promotion.	She would like to apply for a promotion.
Danny, Christine, and Mary won, scholarships.	Danny, Christine, and Mary won scholarships.

2. **MISTAKE:** *Commas are placed between two complete, distinct sentences.* This mistake is often called a *comma splice.*

   SOLUTION: Commas link two sentences only if they are related, if they are relatively simple, and if the comma precedes a conjunction such as "and" or "but." Remember that most complete sentences are *not* linked by commas or semicolons.

   HINT: If you wish to put a comma between two complete sentences, put "and," "but," "or," "nor," "for," or "yet" after the comma. If you are at all confused, however, just end each sentence with a period.

INCORRECT	CORRECT
Carol uses the communication guidelines whenever she writes, speaks, or communicates nonverbally, Arnold uses the guidelines too.	Carol uses the communication guidelines whenever she writes, speaks, or communicates nonverbally. Arnold uses the guidelines too.
	OR
	Carol uses the communication guidelines whenever she writes, speaks, or communicates nonverbally; Arnold uses the guidelines too.
She wants to work for an investment firm, I want to be a real estate broker.	She wants to work for an investment firm, and I want to be a real estate broker.
When he studies, he tries to find a quiet room, he also likes to take frequent exercise breaks.	When he studies, he tries to find a quiet room. He also likes to take frequent exercise breaks.
Sheila is doing well, she just got a job at the marketing firm.	Sheila is doing well. She just got a job at a marketing firm.
	OR
	Sheila is doing well because she just got a job at a marketing firm.
George seems quite capable, however his performance is inconsistent.	George seems quite capable; however, his performance is inconsistent.

3. **MISTAKE:** *Incomplete thoughts are used as sentences.* In other words, the sentences do not contain both a subject and a verb. Incomplete sentences are often called *sentence fragments.* Sentence fragments are used sometimes as attention getters; however, they are not usually employed in formal writing.

   SOLUTION: Check your writing to make sure that all of your sentences are complete thoughts. Complete thoughts include both a subject and a verb.

INCORRECT	CORRECT
Of course. You are going to get a raise!	Of course you are going to get a raise!
For the reasons I cited in my letter. I plan to pursue a career in teaching.	For the reasons I cited in my letter, I plan to pursue a career in teaching.
What do you plan to do? With that book?	What do you plan to do with that book?
She will join the staff in February. Which is two months after Herman is scheduled to leave.	She will join the staff in February, which is two months after Herman is scheduled to leave.

| When you are not sure about the spelling of a word. Look it up in the dictionary. | When you are not sure about the spelling of a word, look the word up in the dictionary. |

4. **MISTAKE:** *Two or more sentences that should be separated by a punctuation mark are not separated at all.* These sentences are referred to as *run-on sentences*.
   SOLUTION: Two or more complete thoughts must be separated by a period, a question mark, an exclamation point, a semicolon, or a comma followed by a conjunction, whichever is appropriate.
   HINT: Read the sentences out loud. You likely will need to end a sentence where you pause *longer* than briefly. Commas or semicolons are usually needed at the places where you pause *only* briefly.

INCORRECT	CORRECT
Karen is the very antithesis of an authoritarian manager she studied under Katherine Ingalls, Ph.D., the author of *Employees Deserve Respect*.	Karen is the very antithesis of an authoritarian manager. She studied under Katherine Ingalls, Ph.D., the author of *Employees Deserve Respect*.
When he receives an assignment he quickly writes down everything that he knows about the subject he then goes back to organize the material.	When he receives an assignment, he quickly writes down everything that he knows about the subject. He then goes back to organize the material.
She wrote the report Don typed the bibliography I designed the cover.	She wrote the report, Don typed the bibliography, and I designed the cover.
We hope that you will order the desk, an order form is enclosed.	We hope that you will order the desk. An order form is enclosed.

5. **MISTAKE:** *Words that are intended to modify certain other words are put in the wrong place in the sentence.* As a result, the wrong words are modified.
   SOLUTION: Always place the modifying words directly before or directly after the words they are intended to modify.
   HINT: Think about the sentences you write or speak. Do they say what you intended them to say?

INCORRECT	CORRECT
The man prepared the minutes with a degree in secretarial science.	The man with a degree in secretarial science prepared the minutes.
	OR
	The man who has a degree in secretarial science prepared the minutes.
She bought a hamburger at the cafeteria with cheese, lettuce, tomatoes, and mayonnaise on it.	She bought a hamburger with cheese, lettuce, tomatoes, and mayonnaise on it at the cafeteria.
He received a letter from a financial analyst with résumé attached.	He received a letter with a résumé attached from a financial analyst.
The person will write the newsletter who wins the writing competition.	The person who wins the writing competition will write the newsletter.

6. **MISTAKE:** *A modifying phrase or a modifying word does not modify anything in the sentence.* This modifier is called a *dangling modifier* because it relates to nothing in the sentence.
   SOLUTION: Put words of modification in the *same* sentence as the words they modify.

INCORRECT	CORRECT
Without any warning, who will attend the staff meeting?	If given no warning, will anyone attend the staff meeting?

Having no knowledge of the problem, the door was shut in my face.	Because he had no knowledge of my problem, he shut the door in my face.
Without any brakes, I took it to the garage.	Because my car had no brakes, I took it to the garage.
Born to a wealthy family, the university was the most expensive in the area.	Born to a wealthy family, she was able to attend the most expensive university in the area.

7. **MISTAKE:** *The sentence contains nonparallel phrases or mixed phrases.*
   SOLUTION: Always make sure that your sentences do not arbitrarily mix active voice and passive voice, infinitives and gerunds, and infinitive phrases and relative clauses. You want the phrases and clauses in a sentence to be similar, or parallel, in construction.

INCORRECT	CORRECT
He likes writing, to read, and cross-country ski trips.	He likes writing, reading, and cross-country skiing.
She decided to buy a machine that can collate and to print on both sides of the paper.	She decided to buy a machine that collates the pages and that prints on both sides of the paper.
Obviously, the report was written by Sara and Dan typed it.	Obviously, Sara wrote the report and Dan typed it.
Not only is the vice president involved, but the president did it too.	Not only is the vice president involved, but the president is involved as well.

8. **MISTAKE:** *A verb, preposition, conjunction, or noun is omitted in the second and subsequent phrases or clauses in a sentence.* Such an omission is not necessarily a grammatical error.
   SOLUTION: In order to make the meaning of a sentence more clear, include the appropriate verb, preposition, conjunction, or noun in all parts of the sentence.

SOMETIMES UNCLEAR	CORRECT
She was hired as a management analyst, and he as a financial assistant.	She was hired as a management analyst, and he was hired as a financial assistant.
They are and always will be hard workers.	They are hard workers and always will be hard workers.
The first report will be typed by Frances, and the second by Albert.	The first report will be typed by Frances, and the second report will be typed by Albert.

OTHER MECHANICS

In this section, some of the mechanics of writing and speaking that were not covered elsewhere are described. The topics include numbers, possessives, syllabication, capitalization, abbreviations, contractions, footnotes, and the bibliography.

1. **NUMBERS:** Style manuals contain many rules for writing numbers. Consider 12 of them here.

   a. *Always spell out numbers that begin a sentence.*

INCORRECT	CORRECT
60 pages were missing.	Sixty pages were missing.

   b. One set of rules has you *spell out numbers one through ten* when no larger numbers are part of the same sentence. *If larger numbers appear in the sentence, however, use figures for all the numbers.*

INCORRECT	CORRECT
I want 3 copies of *Small Business Week* and 9 copies of *Maryland Executive*.	I want three copies of *Small Business Week* and nine copies of *Maryland Executive*.
He ordered six company bowling shirts, nine trophies, and 105 programs for the bowling awards banquet.	He ordered 6 company bowling shirts, 9 trophies, and 105 programs for the bowling awards banquet.

   c. *When two numbers come together in a sentence, write out the smaller number.*

INCORRECT	CORRECT
She requested 2 48-inch typing tables.	She requested two 48-inch typing tables.
They forgot to deliver the twelve 3-pound postage scales.	They forgot to deliver the 12 three-pound postage scales.

   d. *Spell out one- or two-word approximate numbers.*

INCORRECT	CORRECT
He invited about 60 people to the reception.	He invited about sixty people to the reception.
Approximately six hundred and fifty people attended the strike rally.	Approximately 650 people attended the strike rally.

   e. *A person's age, when given in years, is spelled out.* If the person's exact age (years, months, and days) is given, use figures without commas separating them.

INCORRECT	CORRECT
The chairwoman will be 54 years old on Friday.	The chairwoman will be fifty-four years old on Friday.
John's daughter, Emily, is one year, two months, and eleven days old.	John's daughter, Emily, is 1 year 2 months and 11 days old.

   f. *Figures precede "A.M." and "P.M." Words precede "o'clock."*

INCORRECT	CORRECT
The meeting is scheduled to begin at eight A.M.	The meeting is scheduled to begin a 8 A.M.
She never leaves before 6 o'clock.	She never leaves before six o'clock.

   g. *Always use figures when referring to distance, cents, dollars, percents, page numbers, weights, and heights. When a dollar amount is even, use no zeros or decimal points. Commas separate millions, thousands, and hundreds in the same figure.*

INCORRECT	CORRECT
He will be reimbursed for eighty miles of travel.	He will be reimbursed for 80 miles of travel.
Just pay the driver eighty cents.	Just pay the driver 80 cents.
We presented him with $25.00.	We presented him with $25.
Please send a check for $1416982.24.	Please send a check for $1,416,982.24.
Meetings take up at least ninety percent of my time.	Meetings take up at least 90 percent of my time.
Please begin on page three.	Please begin on page 3.
The carton weighs two pounds.	The carton weighs 2 pounds.
A police officer must be at least five feet three inches tall.	A police officer must be at least 5 feet 3 inches tall.

   h. *When no other numbers appear in a sentence, spell out fractions. When a whole number and a fraction are part of the same number, write them as figures.*

INCORRECT	CORRECT
He wrote ¼ of the memorandum.	He wrote one-fourth of the memorandum.
Multiply the number by one and one-fourth.	Multiply the number by 1¼.
	or
	Multiply the number by 1.25.

    i. When the month precedes the day, do not add a "th," "d," "nd," "rd," or "st" to the number of the day. However, when the day precedes the month, use words or figures with "th," "d," "nd," "rd," or "st," whichever one is appropriate. Remember always to write out the month in a sentence.

INCORRECT	CORRECT
The conference begins on September 25th.	The conference begins on September 25.
The 23 of October is the date of the school party.	The 23rd of October is the date of the school party.
She will meet us in the lobby on Dec. sixth at 3 o'clock.	She will meet us in the lobby on December 6 at three o'clock.

    j. Use figures for house numbers 11 through infinity. Street numbers one through ten usually are written out. Use figures for all other street numbers.

INCORRECT	CORRECT
She will be at 1 Delano Street.	She will be at One Delano Street.
Please send the brochure to Sixteen Rodriguez Avenue.	Please send the brochure to 16 Rodriguez Avenue.
Andrew lives on 8th Street.	Andrew lives on Eighth Street.
Joyce once lived on Sixty-fourth Avenue.	Joyce once lived on 64th Avenue.

    k. When numbering a list, use figures.

INCORRECT	CORRECT
Please answer these questions:	Please answer these questions:
One. Are you satisfied with your job?	1. Are you satisfied with your job?
Two. What are your career plans?	2. What are your career plans?
Three. Do you plan to go back to school?	3. Do you plan to go back to school?

    l. When completing forms, use numbers.

INCORRECT

CATALOGUE NUMBER	NAME	QUANTITY
Sixteen	pencils	one hundred sets
Forty-seven	rubber bands	thirty-six boxes

CORRECT

CATALOGUE NUMBER	NAME	QUANTITY
16	pencils	100 sets
47	rubber bands	36 boxes

  2. POSSESSIVES: A possessive noun or pronoun is someone or something that owns or possesses someone or something else in the sentence. *You usually make a singular noun or pronoun possessive by adding an apostrophe and an "s." You usually make a plural noun or pronoun possessive by adding an apostrophe after the "s."* Take care to not confuse possessives with plurals. Plural words that are not possessive do not need an apostrophe.

a. Apostrophes make singular nouns and indefinite nouns possessive. *An apostrophe and an "s" follow singular possessive words.*

INCORRECT	CORRECT
Joans husband is a salesperson.	Joan's husband is a salesperson.
Alberts children live in Bristow.	Albert's children live in Bristow.
The boss work philosophy differed from mine.	The boss's work philosophy differed from mine.

b. *An apostrophe followed by an "s" makes plural nouns that do not end in an "s" possessive.*

INCORRECT	CORRECT
The childrens' goals were numerous.	The children's goals were numerous.
The peoples' requests are written here.	The people's requests are written here.

c. *Place an apostrophe after the "s" in other plural nouns in order to make them possessive.*

INCORRECT	CORRECT
We value our employees suggestions.	We value our employees' suggestions.
Our clients questions were easy to answer.	Our clients' questions were easy to answer.
My daughters-in-laws careers are as important as my son-in-laws career.	My daughters-in-law's careers are as important as my son-in-law's career.
The suburban branches roles vary.	The suburban branches' roles vary.
He had six years experience in the U.S. Navy.	He had six years' experience in the U.S. Navy.
My book's were stacked in the bookcase's.	My books were stacked in the bookcases.

d. *An apostrophe and an "s" make an abbreviation possessive.*

INCORRECT	CORRECT
An M.B.A.s first job is usually a good one.	An M.B.A.'s first job is usually a good one.
The C.P.A.s convention is held in Houston once a year.	The C.P.A.'s convention is held in Houston once a year.

3. **SYLLABICATION:** Several rules govern how words are divided in written communication. Some rules and examples that illustrate the rules appear in this section.

a. *A word should be divided between syllables.* A dictionary shows where the syllables begin and end.

INCORRECT	CORRECT
He had no knowled- ge of the problem.	He had no knowl- edge of the problem.

b. *Do not divide a one-syllable word.*

INCORRECT	CORRECT
She was a sta- unch supporter.	She was a staunch supporter.
The figures were bas- ed on data from 1968.	The figures were based on data from 1968.

c. *Do not divide words that contain fewer than five letters.*

INCORRECT	CORRECT
He was ver- y capable.	He was very capable.
He makes ov- er $39,000 a year.	He makes over $39,000 a year.

d. *Divide hyphenated words at the hyphens.*

INCORRECT	CORRECT
He is self-ef- facing.	He is self- effacing.

e. *Do not divide numbers, names, contractions, or abbreviations.*

INCORRECT	CORRECT
The plan is for 19- 90 and after.	The plan is for 1990 and after.
Her name is Dor- othy Jensen.	Her name is Dorothy Jensen.
He said that he wo- n't worry.	He said that he won't worry.
He will earn an M.- B.A. in finance.	He will earn an M.B.A. in finance.

f. *Do not separate one- or two-letter prefixes, suffixes, or syllables from the rest of the word.*

INCORRECT	CORRECT
He is an ex- pert in his field.	He is an expert in his field.
She has never been a complain- er.	She has never been a complainer.

g. *Do not divide words between double vowels, except when one of the vowels is part of another syllable.*

INCORRECT	CORRECT
He wants to be a bookke- eper.	He wants to be a book- keeper.
There is no agre- eing with Marvin.	There is no agree- ing with Marvin.
Reading, skii- ng, and running are my hobbies.	Reading, ski- ing, and running are my hobbies.

h. *Words can be divided between their double consonants.*

INCORRECT	CORRECT
I was a boo- kkeeper.	I was a book- keeper.
They were committ- ing errors.	They were commit- ting errors.

i. *Divide a word that contains a one-letter syllable after the one-letter syllable.*

INCORRECT	CORRECT
I would elim- inate the chart. Running is exhil- arating.	I would elimi- nate the chart. Running is exhila- rating.

j. *Do not divide the word at the end of the last line on a typewritten page. Also, do not divide the last word in a paragraph.*

k. *Do not divide words in two consecutive lines, if possible. Divide no more than three words on a page.*

l. *Do not divide a word in a place that confuses the reader.*

INCORRECT	CORRECT
She is com- passionate. The young soldier re- signed in May.	She is compassionate. The young soldier re-signed in May.

4. **CAPITALIZATION:** Selected rules for capitalizing words constitute this section.

a. *Capitalize a person's title when it directly precedes her or his name.* Do not capitalize the title when it follows the person's name.

INCORRECT	CORRECT
vice president Sue Anders	Vice President Sue Anders
aunt Kathleen	Aunt Kathleen
Ron Rames, President, will speak to his company's employees.	Ron Rames, president, will speak to his company's employees.

b. *A title used in place of a name is not capitalized.* The President of the United States is always capitalized even when it is used alone.

INCORRECT	CORRECT
My Aunt wrote to me.	My aunt wrote to me.
The Vice President wrote the letter.	The vice president wrote the letter.
Our nation's president will give a speech.	Our nation's President will give a speech.

c. *Always capitalize a person's title when it is part of an address or signature block.*

INCORRECT	CORRECT
Ms. Alice Foine, president Lexington Manufacturing, Inc. 666 Olive Avenue Sother, Nevada 11111	Ms. Alice Foine, President Lexington Manufacturing, Inc. 666 Olive Avenue Sother, Nevada 11111

d. *Capitalize the complete names of organizations.* Do not capitalize such words as "company," "university," or "firm" when used instead of the full name of the organization. Also, do not capitalize "federal," "government," "navy," "army," or "air force," when used alone.

INCORRECT	CORRECT
Bysar products, inc., is located in Waynesberg.	Bysar Products, Inc., is located in Waynesberg.
The Company makes bathroom fixtures.	The company makes bathroom fixtures.

| The Federal Government and Navy offices are located in Washington. | The federal government and navy offices are located in Washington. |

e. *When you are writing about your own company's departments, it is correct to capitalize them.* Do not capitalize the names of other company's departments, though.

INCORRECT	CORRECT
Our finance department is made up of six analysts.	Our Finance Department is made up of six analysts.
I hope to work in an Organization Development Department.	I hope to work in an organization development department.

f. *Capitalize the official names of courses, but not general areas of study.*

INCORRECT	CORRECT
She is taking calculus II.	She is taking Calculus II.
He wants to take a Shorthand course.	He wants to take a shorthand course.

g. *Capitalize all of the words in the titles of publications except for the articles, prepositions, and coordinate conjunctions. Always capitalize the first and final words in a title, however.*

INCORRECT	CORRECT
"What are your Goals In Life?," an article in this month's *Wealth For The Masses*, is worth reading.	"What Are Your Goals in Life?," an article in this month's *Wealth for the Masses*, is worth reading.

h. *Days of the week, months, holidays, and very special events or periods in history should be capitalized.*

INCORRECT	CORRECT
She is a world war II veteran.	She is a World War II veteran.
Please read a book on the industrial revolution.	Please read a book on the Industrial Revolution.

i. *Capitalize the official names of places.* Do not capitalize general references to places.

INCORRECT	CORRECT
They live on rockhound street.	They live on Rockhound Street.
We visited the Mountains in Idaho this weekend.	We visited the mountains in Idaho this weekend.

j. *Capitalize regions of the country.* Do not capitalize directions when they modify other words.

INCORRECT	CORRECT
She was born in the south.	She was born in the South.
She lives South of here.	She lives south of here.
They went to Northwestern Wyoming.	They went to northwestern Wyoming.

k. *Capitalize the adjectival forms of countries and other proper names.*

INCORRECT	CORRECT
I bought a chinese vase.	I bought a Chinese vase.
Their jewish heritage is very important to them.	Their Jewish heritage is very important to them.

l. *Capitalize most nouns that precede numbers.*

	INCORRECT		CORRECT

<table>
<tr><td>INCORRECT</td><td>CORRECT</td></tr>
</table>

INCORRECT
The data are part of table 6.
The meeting will be held in room 14C.

CORRECT
The data are part of Table 6.
The meeting will be held in Room 14C.

5. **ABBREVIATIONS:** *Avoid using many abbreviations in formal writing.* The rules in this section illustrate the most common uses of abbreviations.

a. These abbreviations appear in *both formal and informal writing.*

SINGULAR	PLURAL
A.D.	——
B.A.	B.A.s or B.A.'s
B.C.	——
B.S.	B.S.s or B.S.'s
CPA; C.P.A.	CPAs or CPA's; C.P.A.s or C.P.A.'s
Dr.	Drs.
M.B.A.	M.B.A.s or M.B.A.'s
M.D.	M.D.s or M.D.'s
Mr.	Messrs.
Mrs.	Mesdames
Ms.	Mses.
U.S.	——

b. These abbreviations are used in *informal writing.*

SINGULAR	PLURAL
apt.	apts.
B.t.u.	B.t.u.'s
c.o.d.	c.o.d.'s
dept.	depts.
f.o.b.	f.o.b.'s
ft. (foot)	ft. (feet)
g (gram)	g (grams)
gal.	gals.
hwy.	hwys.
in. (inch)	in. (inches)
Inc.	——
L (liter)	L (liters)
lb.	lbs.
Ltd.	——
mgr.	mgrs.
mo.	mos.
oz. (ounce)	oz. (ounces)
p. (page)	pp. (pages)
qt.	qts.
yd.	yds.
yr.	yrs.

c. *Spell out addresses in most formal writing. The two-letter state abbreviation can be used in an address, however.*

INCORRECT
Ms. Meredith Wiley
16 N. 6th St.
Tulsa, Okla. 73000

CORRECT
Ms. Meredith Wiley
16 North Sixth Street
Tulsa, OK 73000

6. **CONTRACTIONS:** *A contraction is one word that represents a longer word or two words.* A contraction always contains an apostrophe. The apostrophe usually replaces one or several of the missing letters. The missing letters are often vowels. The apostrophe never goes between the original two words, but does replace a letter or letters in the second word. Study the incorrect and correct versions of the list of contractions so that you do not make the common error of putting the apostrophe in the wrong place. Remember that contractions do not belong in formal writing.

COMPLETE WORDS	CONTRACTIONS INCORRECT	CORRECT
are not	are'nt	aren't
cannot	ca'nt	can't
have not	have'nt	haven't
he will	h'ell	he'll
I am	Im	I'm
is not	is'nt	isn't
it is	its	it's
she will	sh'ell	she'll
there is	theres	there's
they are	the'yre	they're
they will	the'yll	they'll
we are	w'ere	we're
we will	w'ell	we'll
were not	were'nt	weren't
will not	wo'nt	won't
you are	yo'ure	you're

7. **FOOTNOTES:** *When you write another person's written or spoken words, you have the responsibility to identify the person you have cited.* You need not identify the person, however, if what he or she said is common knowledge. (If you write that Washington, D.C., is the nation's capital, you need not cite a source of that information.) When you do use someone's work, though, consult a style manual for information on how to identify the cited material. These are examples of footnotes that you may find helpful:

a. *You cite from a book with one author.*

[6]Ann Grico, *Statistics for Business and for Life* (New York: Oro Press, 198X), pp. 81-82.

b. *You cite from a book with two authors.*

[1]Edna G. Grown and Robert Frank, *Business Writing for Children* (London: Smythe and Waco Publishing Co., 1976), p. 251.

c. *You cite from a book with three authors.*

[5]Albert Fox, Marsha Wiler, and Nancy Toledo, *Always Writing* (Kansas City, Mo.: PRA Co., 1976), p. 11.

d. *You cite from a book with more than three authors.*

[3]Simon Wales et al., *Accounting in America* (San Francisco: Wechsler Press, 198X), p. 314.

e. *You cite from a book with no author.*

[9]*Business, Money, and Ethics* (Eugene, Oreg.: Davlyn Press, 198X), p. 92.

f. *You cite from a book with an editor acting as the author.*

[2]Susan Woodell, ed., *Women in Business and Industry* (Corning, Tex.: Corning University Press, 1968), pp. 460-461.

g. *You cite from a report with one, two, or three authors.*

    [3]Elizabeth Hart, Mark Tunis, and Irene Perez, *Report on Foreign Exchange Rates* (Portland, Oreg.: Floridian Investments, Inc., 1978), p. 8.

h. *You cite from an article in a journal.*

    [4]Wayne Limone, "Writing Without Fear," *Journal of American Communication* 61 (August 198X): 47.

i. *You cite from an article in a magazine.*

    [9]Lucille Phillips, "Organizations Cannot Survive the Decade," *Business Digest*, September 198X, p. 137.

j. *You cite from a newspaper article.*

    [4]"Allensnapco Raises Prices," *McKenzie Times*, 16 February 198X, sec. B., p. B17.

8. **THE BIBLIOGRAPHY:** The bibliography lists all of the sources of material cited, consulted, or recommended. Place the bibliography at the end of the paper. Again, consult a style manual for a detailed treatment of the preparation of bibliographies. The footnotes used as examples in the preceding section of this appendix are in bibliographical form in this section. Note that the author's names are reversed and that the form of the entry differs from that of the footnote.

a. *Your bibliography includes a book with one author.*

    Grico, Ann. *Statistics for Business and for Life.* New York: Oro Press, 198X.

b. *Your bibliography includes a book with two authors.*

    Grown, Edna G., and Frank, Robert. *Business Writing for Children.* London: Smythe and Waco Publishing Co., 1976.

c. *Your bibliography includes a book with three authors.*

    Fox, Albert; Wiler, Marsha; and Toledo, Nancy. *Always Writing.* Kansas City, Mo.: PRA Co., 1976.

d. *Your bibliography includes a book with more than three authors.*

    Wales, Simon; Deutsch, R. F.; Michaelson, Denise P.; and Wendstrom, Gloria S. C. *Accounting in America.* San Francisco: Wechsler Press, 198X.

e. *Your bibliography includes a book with no author.*

    Business, Money, and Ethics. Eugene, Oreg.: Davlyn Press, 198X.

f. *Your bibliography includes a book with an editor acting as the author.*

    Woodell, Susan, ed. *Women in Business and Industry.* Corning, Tex.: Corning University Press, 1968.

g. *Your bibliography includes a report with one, two, or three authors.*

    Hart, Elizabeth; Tunis, Mark; and Perez, Irene. *Report on Foreign Exchange Rates.* Portland, Oreg.: Floridian Investments, Inc., 1978.

h. *Your bibliography includes an article from a journal.*

    Limone, Wayne. "Writing Without Fear." *Journal of American Communication* 61 (August 198X): 44-50.

i. *Your bibliography includes an article from a magazine.*

    Phillips, Lucille. "Organizations Cannot Survive the Decade." *Business Digest*, September 198X, pp. 135-141.

j. *Your bibliography includes a newspaper article.*

    "Allensnapco Raises Prices." *McKenzie Times*, 16 February 198X, sec. B, p. B17.

Appendix D

Guidelines for Nonsexist Communication

Sexist communication may be defined as any communication that precasts people on the basis of their sex. Though other discriminatory communication exists, sexism is the most pervasive. Therefore, consider some guidelines to help you communicate without it.

In an appendix to my book *The Nonsexist Communicator*[1] I include general guidelines, specific guidelines, and a comprehensive listing of sexist words and phrases along with nonsexist alternatives for them. The guidelines include examples as well as references to explanatory material throughout the six chapters in the book. However, this appendix cites only the guidelines.

GENERAL GUIDELINES FOR NONSEXIST COMMUNICATION

1. Commit yourself to remove sexism from all of your communication.
2. Practice and reinforce nonsexist communication patterns until they become habitual. The ultimate test lies in the ability to carry on a nonsexist private conversation and to think in nonsexist terms.
3. Set a nonsexist communication example and direct or persuade others to adopt your example.
4. Use familiar idiom whenever possible, but if a choice must be made between sexism and the unfamiliar, use the unfamiliar until it becomes the familiar.
5. Take care not to create negativism in the receiver by using awkward, cumbersome, highly repetitious, or glaring revisions. A sufficiently wide variety of graceful, controlled, sex-positive, dynamic revisions are available so that the nonsexist communicator can avoid entirely the use of bland or offensive construction.
6. Use the full range of techniques for correction of sexist communication, including reconstruction, substitution, and omission.
7. Check roots and meanings of words to be sure that the words need to be changed before changing them.
8. Check every outgoing message—whether written, oral, or nonverbal—for sexism before "sending" it.[2]

SPECIFIC GUIDELINES FOR NONSEXIST COMMUNICATION

The sexist pronoun

1. Use female and male pronouns only when they refer to specific females and males.
2. Instead of male pronouns as generic pronouns (pronouns that refer to an indefinite person) and instead of female and male pronouns in stereotypes (The truck driver . . . he . . . and the elementary school teacher . . . she):

---

[1] Bobbye Sorrels Persing, *The Nonsexist Communicator* (East Elmhurst, N.Y.: Communication Dynamics Press, 1978.)

[2] Ibid., p. 117.

    a. Use, sparingly, female and male pronoun pairs such as "he and she," "his or her," "her or him," "herself or himself," "he/she," "hers/his," "him/her," "herself/himself," and the written combined form "s/he."

    b. Use something other than the male-first procedure for listing female and male pronoun pairs.

       (1) Alphabetize the pronouns.

       (2) Alternate the pronoun order, but maintain nonstereotyped reference.

       (3) Maintain pronoun order when sets of referents are to the same generic individual.

    c. Change from singular to plural form.

    d. Repeat the noun if a number of words intervene.

    e. Use a different noun or pronoun when repeating, including such sex-neutral words as "person" and "one."

    f. When direct address is appropriate, use the second-person or "you" style.

    g. Reword in order to omit the pronouns or replace them with other words such as "the," "a," "an."

    h. Use, occasionally, the passive voice instead of the active voice.

    i. Use, occasionally, "it" or "there" as an expletive.

    j. Alternate the female and male pronouns throughout the narrative, but maintain nonstereotyped references.

    k. Use, only in informal circumstances and only if acceptable to the communication receiver/s, the plural pronoun instead of the singular masculine pronoun for reference to an indefinite person.

    l. Use either the female or male pronouns as generic and state, before beginning the narrative and repeatedly throughout the narrative, that only one set of pronouns—either female or male—is used and the set is intended to refer to both males and females. This device should be used only when no other solution is possible and must provide for equality of alternation between male pronouns and female pronouns in extensive passages and for nonstereotyped reporting. Thus, in a lengthy report, one major section would reflect the female forms and the next would reflect the male forms as the generic pronouns. In a book or manual, one chapter would reflect the male forms and the next would reflect the female forms as the generic pronouns. If this alternative is chosen, *in no case* must it be used as an excuse to return to the exclusive use of the male pronouns as the generic pronouns, or the stereotypical use of pronouns, as some guidelines recommend.

    m. Write sentence fragments initiated by verb forms for job information instruments.

The "-ess," "-ette," and "-ix" word endings

1. Omit the "-ess" ending from words for which it is used to denote a female (directress, authoress, poetess). Three "-ess" words are so ingrained that they will be difficult to eradicate in the short run: "waitress," "hostess," and "actress." However, if you retain any of the three, do not introduce the sexism of using the plural of the basic word to include the female. For example, if "actress" is used, do not use "actors" to include "actresses"; use "actors and actresses" instead.

2. Omit the "-ette" ending from words for which it is used to denote a female (bachelorette).

3. Omit the "-ix" ending from words for which it is used to denote a female.

The "-man" word compounds

Revise words including the syllable "man" when it is used to denote both males and females.

1. Use "person" instead of "man."

2. Use syllables other than "person" to replace "man."

3. Change the word structure in order to avoid "man."

4. Omit "man" from word.

5. Change "man" to "woman" for female if, during transitional period, "man" is retained

for male. Do not pair "man" for a man with "person" (or other neutral form) for a woman.
6.   Use neutral words for plurals of the original "man" words.

The "Gentlemen," "Dear Sirs," and "My dear Sirs" organizational salutations

Use sex-neutral organizational salutations. (Although "Dear Sirs" and "My dear Sirs" are incorrect even when sexism is not an issue, they are still used and thus require nonsexist alternatives.)

1.   Use variations of "Ladies and Gentlemen," "Gentlemen and Gentlewomen," and "Mesdames and Sirs."
2.   Omit the salutation or substitute a conversational lead-in or subject line for it.
3.   Address the letter to an individual or position title in the organization instead of to the organization itself. When this device is invoked, maintain nonsexism in the salutation. Nonsexism in salutations for messages directed to individuals is covered in the two following guidelines.

The "Dear Sir" and "My dear Sir" salutations

Use sex-neutralizing alternatives to "Dear Sir" and "My dear sir" when a letter is addressed to an individual whose sex is unknown or to a position title in an organization.

1.   Use the "Madam or Sir" or "Sir or Madam" format.
2.   Use a nonsexist subistitute for "Sir."
3.   Omit the salutation or substitute a conversational lead-in for it.

The courtesy title problem

1.   Use "Mrs.," "Miss," and "Mrs. John Jones" format only for those who demand it, only as a last resort, only for extraorganizational addresses, and only for the short run. A sufficient number of alternatives are described in this manual that the sexist courtesy titles need to be used only in the most extreme circumstances.
2.   Use "Ms." for all women except in the extreme circumstances just described.
3.   Introduce "Mrd." (pronounced "murd") and "Mngl." (pronounced "mingle") or similar designations for married and single men, respectively, if "Mrs." and "Miss" retained for women.
4.   Omit courtesy titles for both men and women.
5.   Substitute position or status title for traditional courtesy title.
6.   Use "M." for dealing with names which do not clearly suggest gender, or in the case of given and middle initials only.
7.   Control the potential sexism in courtesy titles for addresses derived from mailing lists—generally sexist because households are represented in them by a male's name.
     a.   Use the male name in conjunction with words that indicate that you know that others may reside at the same address.
     b.   Use inclusive terms instead of males' names.
     c.   Omit courtesy titles instead of assuming that those listed are males.

The sexism in names

In addition to the rules related to the sexism in reporting names covered in other specific guidelines, some rules related to the names themselves are included.

1.   Use woman's given and married surname (or given, middle, birth surname and married surname) and not the "Mrs. John Jones" style of reporting in employee publications.
2.   Establish sex-fairness as parents by practicing positive naming of daughters. (The problems related to naming sons are also sexist toward females because of the negativism toward "effeminate" names for males.)

3. Act upon and tell daughters and other women of the right to retain birth names upon marriage.
4. Adopt the compound surname style in which birth and married surnames are joined with a hyphen.
5. Apprise people of the sexism in the "-son" and "-man" surnames and establish that little can be done about them—unless, in rare cases, people change them. Much as with the recognition of the fact that slavery existed, the person grows by simply understanding what happened even if nothing can be done about it.

The institutionalization of sexism in communication by academia

1. Write and speak to academia whenever you can. Write and speak in nonsexist form about nonsexist communication.
2. Speak up in academic classes if you attend them.
3. Write to authors of sexist academic books and articles calling for the removal of sexist references.

The male-first order of reporting names

1. Use the "male-first" order only for those who indicate it or demand it, only as a last resort, only for extraorganizational addresses, and only for the short run. A sufficient number of alternatives are described in this manual that the sexist order need be used only in the most extreme circumstances. If a woman and man sign a letter by using both names and "Ms." or no courtesy title for the woman, they are expressing a nonsexist act and have probably thought about the order of the names as well.
2. Base the order of names on something other than sex.
    a. Arrange alphabetically by last names if different and by first names if the last name is the same.
    b. Alternate between woman-first and man-first order by using a formal or informal method for keeping the name rotation 50/50 between the names.
    c. Observe rank if it takes precedence over consideration of sex-order fairness for names.

The inconsistency or nonparallelism in paired references to females and males

1. Omit the courtesy titles for both males and females or include them for both.
2. Omit the parenthetical titles in the typewritten name in the signature block for both women and men or include them for both women and men. As long as courtesy titles are used, the inclusion of the parenthetical notation is logical, for many names are neither clearly female or male.
3. Use first names consistently.
4. Use "Ms." for both married and single women.
5. Pair "gentleman" with "lady."
6. Use pairs of words that consistently do or do not include syllables that indicate gender.
7. Maintain the parallelism of "husband and wife."
8. Pair "man" with "woman."
9. Report age-referent pairs of words for females and males consistently.
10. Introduce nonsexist ordering of pairs involving both sexes.

The male as the norm

1. Use neutral words to refer to groups that include both females and males.
2. Maintain the sex-neutrality of words.
3. Vary references to remove the male-as-norm imagery.
4. Use words positive to males; male-as-norm words are not always so.

The stereotyping of females

1. Portray females in roles other than "housewife" and mother in sales messages and other imagery.
2. Portray females in roles other than sex object.
3. Portray females in other than servant roles and, when so, in a positive way.
4. Use humanizing, nongeneralizing words for females.

The stereotyping of males

1. Portray males in roles as household worker and father.
2. Portray males in roles other than womanizer.
3. Portray males in other than dominant roles and, when so, in a positive way.
4. Portray males in roles other than working drudge, head of household, "baby-like" when ill, insurance purchaser, strong hero-type, etc.
5. Use humanizing, nongeneralizing words for males.

The sexism in animal and other subhuman references and names

1. Use something other than the generic masculine pronouns to refer to generalized animals.
   a. Refer to the animal as "it."
   b. Alternate between female and male pronouns.
   c. Use the paired pronouns.
2. Use nonsexist words to refer to the female of the animal species.
3. Remove the sexism that occurs because of the less serious impact of the animal references on males compared to females.
4. Remove the sexism that occurs because of the less serious impact of other subhuman references on males compared to females.
5. Use nonstereotyped sex references to inanimate subhuman forms.
   a. Use feminine forms to indicate strength and activity half of the time.
   b. Use masculine forms to indicate weakness and passivity half of the time.
   c. Vary the sex references to things like hurricanes by alternating within each year or between years.
   d. Use references other than sexist clichés.
   e. Replace "Miss" with "Ms." if femininity is assigned to qualities.

The sexism in excerpts and names of organizations

1. Summarize or paraphrase sexist excerpts.
2. Use only nonsexist titles and organizational names if possible; if sexist ones must be used, place them only in the footnotes and bibliography. [Place "*sic*" in brackets after sexist expression.]
3. Use substitutes for sexist organization names in the body of the instrument.

The absence of positive words for females

1. Recast sentences to convey positive qualities of females.
2. Use a series of descriptive words for communicating that a woman is stripped of her woman-defining human qualities; no equivalents to "emasculated" and "castrated" exist.

The sexist adjective

Establish parallelism in the use of adjectives for males and females.

The problems of being "womanly," "effeminate," "womanish," "female," "feminine"

As covered previously, no words exist to name women as possessors of high human qualities. To call a man "manly" implies strength and control; to call a woman "womanly" implies weakness and frailty. To call a man "masculine" creates images of straightforwardness and bravery; to call a woman "feminine" creates images of pink, frilly clothing and mindlessness.

The women's section

Eliminate the concept of a "women's section," "women's news," "society page," and journalistic reporting style from all communication including employee news letters and magazines.

The sexism in religious communication

Understand the male bias of the patriarchal culture out of which the Judeo-Christian religions came, and use nonsexist religious language.

The sexism in monarchial references

Use monarchial references only if they are nonsexist.

The special problems of oral communication

1. Think before speaking so that sexism is not present in words that cannot be erased.
2. Use positive words in conversation instead of negative words which "creep in."
3. Avoid the sexism in the Robert's-Rules-of-Order approach to formal meetings.
4. Discard sexist "humor" and do not laugh at the sexist "humor" of others.
5. Use nonsexist methods in conducting interviews.

The special problems of nonverbal communication

1. Cultivate postures, gestures, movements, respect for territory, and touches that are sex-positive.
2. Cultivate nonsexist facial expressions, eye movements, voice patterns, and nonverbal vocal sounds.
3. Create pictures that represent nonstereotyped roles for females and males.
4. Develop and support nonsexist attitudes and actions about dress and appearance.
5. Cultivate sensitive listening and feedback-monitoring skills in order to develop awareness of sexist practices. Use the awareness to eliminate sexist practices.

The negative imagery associated with the wife and mother

Treat the wife-and-mother imagery with the same respect as the husband-and-father imagery.[3]

---

[3]Ibid., pp. 117–136.

Appendix E

Sampling

Researchers cannot always observe every elementary unit in the universe under study. Time, money, inaccessibility, destructiveness of observation techniques, and other factors often prevent them from doing so. In such cases, researchers must turn to sampling. However, because of the soundness of correct sampling procedures, researchers draw samples even when the cited factors do not require them.

The two broad categories of samples are probability samples and nonprobability samples. Probability sampling uses random processes to give every item equal opportunity of being selected. Only chance enters into the process.* With nonprobability sampling, elements other than chance affect the selection procedures.

Nonprobability samples are drawn arbitrarily, judgmentally, or conveniently. Thus, bias (unrepresentativeness) may enter into the data. Unless validated through careful procedures, the researcher cannot safely infer to a universe from the observations of a nonprobability sample.

Because of the necessity for unbiased inferences, this appendix includes coverage of only probability samples. Before considering the types of probability samples, however, review the characteristics that define them.

CHARACTERISTICS OF GOOD PROBABILITY SAMPLES

A sound inductive process depends upon drawing adequate and representative samples.

Adequate Size

A sample of adequate size meets the researcher's requirements and those of the chosen analytical approach. Unfortunately, such a statement does not offer any magical numbers; no such magical numbers exist. However, the size of a sample does not depend upon whimsical decisions either. Objective criteria do exist. The nature of such criteria depends upon the nature of the research.

Qualitative data

If research involves the description and analysis of qualitative (nonquantitative) information, calculations cannot yield an optimum sample size. Instead, the sample size depends upon the researcher's store of knowledge, the literature, and the views of authorities. The resulting sample size meets traditional or acceptable numbers of observations appropriate to the research.

For example, suppose the purpose of research is to describe from direct observation the

---

*For statistical sampling methods, the word "random" carries a special meaning. It does *not* denote haphazardness. Instead, it denotes a carefully designed and controlled process through which chance is the only determinant of items within the sample.

kinds of architectural designs evident in the dwelling units located in New York City. Obviously, no mathematical formula exists to yield the number of houses to be inspected.

Ultimately, the establishment of the sample size for qualitative research evolves from decisions made by the researcher. Because of the character of some kinds of qualitative research, the decisions may not even be made before going into the field to make the observations.

Quantitative data

Establishment of sample sizes for quantitative research is much more objective—and thus easier—than for qualitative data. Therefore, convert the qualitative into the quantitative whenever the conversion can meet the original purposes of the research. Quantification of criteria also aids in evaluating transactions.

This brief section cannot cover all of the details of sampling adequacy for quantitative research. Statistics and research books supply them. However, it does include some of the major points associated with the topic.

First, the purpose of quantitative research does not always involve inference from a sample to the population from which the sample was drawn. For example, assume a researcher wants to know the mean expense-account expenditure of the 953 sales representatives of a firm for the past week. The researcher could observe and record the 953 expenditures, total them, and divide the total by 953. Because the 953 sales representatives form the population, not a sample, no sample size is involved.

Suppose, however, that the researcher decides to draw a sample, describe the sample (calculate the mean weekly expenditure for it), and make an inference from that description to all 953 people. In this case, he or she should calculate the sample size necessary to accomplish the goals. The calculation should take place before beginning to select the actual figures to be included in the calculation of the sample mean.

The appropriate sample size for inferential quantitative research depends upon the tool to be used for the analysis. The tools fall into two broad classes: nonparametrics and parametrics.

Nonparametric tools Nonparametric tools relate to distribution-free analyses—analyses free of assumptions about the distribution of the parent universe. The choice of a nonparametric tool is based upon many considerations described in statistics and research books on the subject.

A nonparametric tool has certain requirements for its applications. Those requirements usually include a minimum sample size. The sample size may be as much larger as time, money, and other such factors allow.

Parametric tools Parametric analyses involve data from parent populations with known distributions and characteristics. The normal curve is, of course, the best-known parametric distribution.

To calculate the optimum sample size for a given piece of parametric research, choose from among the many formulas available. Again, books on statistical and research methods supply the theory and details for this concept.

For purposes of the example of the expense-account analyses, consider the formula for calculating the sample size for estimating the universe mean when the universe size is known:

$$n = \frac{1}{\left(\dfrac{e}{\sigma z}\right)^2 + \dfrac{1}{N}}$$

Where: n = sample size; e = allowable error (one-half of desired confidence interval); σ = standard deviation of the universe (estimated by taking a pilot sample and calculating, using a standard deviation from a similar study, or dividing the range by 6); z = standard normal deviate; N = universe size

For the example, assume that you make these decisions or estimates:

1. You decide that you want the final interval to be no more than $10 from lower limit to upper limit; e = $10/2 = $5
2. You estimate the standard deviation for the universe to be $30, found by dividing the known range of weekly expenditures by 6; ($240 − $60)/6 = $30
3. You decide to use the .90 level of confidence; z = 1.65
4. You know that the universe size is 953; N = 953

Once you have these figures, the calculation of the sample size for the restrictions you have set becomes:

$$n = \cfrac{1}{\left(\cfrac{5}{30(1.65)}\right)^2 + \cfrac{1}{953}}$$

$$= \cfrac{1}{\cfrac{25}{2450.25} + .0010493}$$

$$= \cfrac{1}{.010203 + .0010493}$$

$$= \cfrac{1}{.0112523} = 88.87 = 89$$

Of course, different values would change the sample size from 89 to some other number. Thus, the precalculated sample size is clearly a function of your decision, estimates, and actual values.

The formula for calculating the sample size for estimating a universe mean also is appropriate for a one-sample-mean test of significance.

Figure 9-23 (page 293) includes an illustration of the calculation of the sample size for estimating a universe proportion or conducting a one-sample-proportion test of significance. It also includes examples of how the size of the sample varies as the decisions and estimates vary.

Representativeness

Representativeness is the quality of a sample that makes it a miniature replica of the population from which it came. The best way to assure representativeness is to draw a probability sample.

Four basic methods define probability samples: (1) simple random sampling, (2) systematic sampling, (3) stratified sampling, and (4) cluster sampling.

Simple random sampling

Simple random sampling requires that the population be finite and numbered in some unbiased fashion. Once each item in the population has its own unique number, enter a table of random numbers at random and proceed through it systematically until identifying the desired number of usable numbers. Then pull those numbered items from the population for observation on the defined dimension.

For the continuing example, then, first number the sales representatives from 1 through 953. Then enter a table of random numbers randomly (letting only chance determine the first number). If the first number falls between 1 and 953, it is usable; include it as one of the 89 numbers. If it is not between 1 and 953, move down (across, up) the column one line at a time until identifying a usable number. Continue this process to identify 89 usable numbers. Then use the records to determine the expense-account expenditure for each salesperson whose number appears in the list of 89.

Systematic sampling

Systematic sampling also has the potential of creating representative samples. The systematic sampling technique works best when the universe is represented by some pre-existing, unbiased compendium including all items in the universe.

To draw a systematic sample from such a compendium, first calculate the value of k by dividing the universe size by the sample size (N/n). Then, enter the compendium at random and include the first item so selected as the first item in the sample. Then proceed to select each kth-numbered item from that first point of entry until exhausting the compendium and drawing the predetermined number of items.

If a universe can be represented by a telephone directory or a city directory, each forms the type of compendium appropriate to systematic sampling. Any sort of catalog or listing of items does so.

For example, suppose that 953 folders are arranged alphabetically in file drawers. In that situation, the systematic procedure described in the letter in Figure 9–23 applies.

Stratified sampling

Another probability technique involves selecting the sample by a stratified method. To use the stratified sampling procedure efficiently, apply it to a population comprised of clearly identifiable, mutually exclusive classes that collectively exhaust the items in the universe.

For instance, all of the students enrolled at a university at one time form at least one natural stratification. The stratification is defined by classification as first-year, second-year, third-year, fourth-year, and graduate students. Because the classification depends upon earned credit hours, the stratification is quantified—and thus a particularly easy one to apply.

Many other possibilities for stratification exist. The determinants of the stratification may be qualitative or quantitative. However, the differences among the determinants should be so sharp that each item falls into one and only one stratum—a stratum heterogeneous to all other strata.

Occupation, sex, age, income, educational level, experience in a given field, political and other organizational affiliations, religion, physical features (height, weight, color of eyes)—all are examples of potential qualitative and quantitative bases for stratification of human beings. Similar characteristics exist for nonhuman populations—stratifications based on classes of measurements, counts, and qualities.

Use a probability method to select items from each stratum. Simple random sampling and systematic sampling usually work well.

Proportional   For proportional stratified sampling, the number selected from each stratum is a function of the predetermined size of the sample, the size of the stratum, and the size of the universe. Decide how many to choose from each stratum by dividing the sample size by the universe size (n/N) and multiplying the result by the number of items in each stratum.

Nonproportional   In nonproportional stratified sampling, deliberately choose disproportionate numbers from the strata—for reasons associated with the research. So long as chance is the only determinant of the items selected from each stratum, the sample still retains its probability status. However, for calculations based upon nonproportional samples, weight the calculations to bring the results back to proportional representativeness.

Example   Return to the continuing example of the expense-account research to review an example of stratified sampling. Suppose that the firm classifies sales representatives by ranges of the previous year's sales and maintains lists accordingly. Thus, one list would include the names of all salespeople with previous-year sales of $500,000 and higher, another the names of all salespeople with sales between $450,000 and $500,000, etc. Suppose the numbers falling in each category take the frequency distribution shown in the first two columns of this table:

Last Year's Sales	No. of Salespersons in Universe	No. of Salespersons in Sample
Under $250,000	62	6
$250,000 up to $300,000	98	9
$300,000 up to $350,000	204	19
$350,000 up to $400,000	276	26
$400,000 up to $450,000	182	17
$450,000 up to $500,000	78	7
$500,000 and over	53	5
	953	89

For a proportional stratified sample, divide 89 by 953 and obtain a factor of .0933892. Multiply the factor by the number in each layer. The results appear in the third column of the preceding table.

Next, turn to the list for that cell and take a systematic sample from it.

As an example for the list of those with sales under $250,000, first divide 62 by 6 (N/n) and obtain k = 10.33 = 10. Then choose the first name at random. That name will be the first name in the sample. Then move to the next name on the list after the first name in the sample. Count it as 1, count the next name as 2, and continue counting until reaching 10. The tenth name will be the second name in the sample. Move to the next listed name after the second name in the sample. Count it as 1 and continue until reaching 10. The tenth name will be the third name in the sample. Continue this process through the end of the list and back through any of the list ahead of the first randomly chosen name. Because k = 10 is a rounded number, the gap will not be exactly 10 names between the sixth name chosen and the first one chosen. However, the sample will contain exactly 6 names from that stratum, with chance the only factor in their selection.

After selecting the desired number of names from each stratum, make the observations of the expense-account figures for each. Then proceed with the analysis.

The analysis in this case first involves finding the mean weekly expenditure for the sample. Therefore, for a proportional sample, simply sum the values of the 89 weekly expenditures and divide by 89. Then calculate the standard deviation and establish the confidence-interval estimate of the universe mean.

For the sample of 89 drawn on a nonproportional basis, introduce the appropriate weights during the calculations of the mean and standard deviation. For example, to do so for the weighted mean, first calculate the mean for each stratum for the sample number observed in that stratum. Then weight each stratum's mean by multiplying it by the actual number of population items in that stratum. Then sum all of the weighted means and divide the sum by the number in the population. The result would make the sample mean representative of the population from which it came.

Cluster sampling

The cluster sampling method applies to a universe of homogeneous parts — clusters that are alike in the key factors defining them. Because the clusters are alike, one randomly chosen cluster may constitute the sample.

The cluster method is particularly appropriate for sampling large geographic areas such as the United States. After dividing a large area into homogeneous regions, randomly choose one or more regions from which to make the observations. Because the regions are equivalent, the inference to the whole of the area involves a probability process.

Sample within a cluster by using any of the probability sampling techniques that apply: simple random sampling, systematic sampling, stratified sampling, or cluster sampling.

To use cluster sampling within a cluster, divide the cluster into equivalent subclusters, select one or more at random, and again select the sampling method to be used within the subcluster(s).

The major hazard in the clustering method is the difficulty of establishing homogeneous clusters. Picture the immensity of the chore of defining regions in the United States that are identical—even on only one or two dimensions.

For example, even with median family income as the only criterion for defining homogeneity, the task can be difficult.

To help identify the severity of the chore, think of the problems associated with trying to establish equivalent election districts within a state. The only factor is population—quite a simple one compared to others established for business research.

In spite of the difficulties associated with cluster sampling, it is used extensively. For instance, national marketing researchers must depend upon the cluster design. Simple random sampling, systematic sampling, and stratified sampling simply do not provide the vehicles necessary for sampling under the factorial, temporal, and economic constraints of the research.

To apply the cluster-sample method to the continuing example of the expense accounts, assume that the sales representatives are assigned to six regions in the United States. Also assume that no significant differences exist in the patterns formed by the sales activities in the six regions.

Number the six regions, place six disks in a bowl, mix them, and draw one without looking. That number is the number of the region to be used as a sample.

Then use some probability process to select 89 weekly expense figures from that one region. The simple random or systematic processes likely would apply well to lists of names or personnel files within the region.

Appendix F

Proposal

RAYLYNNE CO.

785 Crays Boulevard   *Shraft, CO 77777*   *888–88–888*

January 12, 1981

Ms. Cindy Melsa
Credit Manager

Dear Ms. Melsa:

Here is the proposal for the collection-series research we discussed last week. I believe
the proposed research could help to answer some of the questions the executive
committee raised about the decline in the rate of collections.

The proposed research will require minimal expenditure of time and money—
particularly if it helps to solve such a serious problem.

Because the work must begin in February in order to complete the research during the
period March-May, I should appreciate having your response by next week. If you would
like to discuss the proposal, I shall be glad to meet with you.

Sincerely yours,

Y. R. Self

Y. R. Self
Research Specialist

YRS:aa

Enclosure

THE DIFFERENCES BETWEEN TWO COLLECTION SERIES IN

PROPORTIONS AND MEANS OF PAYMENTS RECEIVED

BY RAYLYNNE CO. IN MARCH-MAY, 1981

PROPOSAL

Prepared for

Ms. Cindy Melsa
Credit Manager
Raylynne Co.

Prepared by

Y. R. Self
Research Specialist
Raylynne Co.
January 12, 1981

THE DIFFERENCES BETWEEN TWO COLLECTION SERIES IN

PROPORTIONS AND MEANS OF PAYMENTS RECEIVED

BY RAYLYNNE CO. IN MARCH-MAY, 1981

During 1979 and 1980 the rates of collection for delinquent accounts at Raylynne Co. declined significantly. Though inflation and recession undoubtedly explain the major portion of the decline, the age of the collection series may have contributed to rates lower than would have been experienced with a more modern series.

Raylynne Co. created and began to use the presently used Series 17G2 in 1978. Series 17G2 seemed to produce good results that year. However, as shown in this table, 1979 and 1980 do not reflect good collection rates—not even as good as those experienced in 1975 and 1976 with Series 17G1.

ANNUAL RATES OF COLLECTION

RAYLYNNE CO., 1975-1980

Year	Percent of Outstanding Dollars Collected After Three Letters	Percent of Outstanding Dollars Collected After All Six Letters
1975	68.5	83.6
1976	68.8	82.3
1977	69.1	83.1
1978	71.7	86.1
1979	64.5	78.2
1980	60.4	72.6

THE PROBLEM

The general problem is the decline in the rate of collections during 1979 and 1980. Thus, the purpose of the proposed research is to find whether a new series of collection letters increases the rate of collections.

1

Research Problem

The specific problem for the proposed research is to determine whether the collections for a new series—Series 17G3—are significantly greater than the collections for Series 17G2 for the period March through May, 1981.

To establish appropriate controls, the outstanding accounts will be randomly divided into two groups. Group O will receive Series 17G2, and Group N will receive Series 17G3. The primary determination will be made for the totals for all six letters. However, determinations also will be made for each of the six letters.

Two factors will form the basis for the analysis. They are (1) the proportions of people who make payments within two weeks of the mailings, and (2) the mean sizes of the payments received.

The scope of the delimited research problem, then, is to determine during the period March-May, 1981, whether Group N and Group O differ in:

1. The proportions of payments received after the first letter

2. The proportions of payments received after the second letter

3. The proportions of payments received after the third letter

4. The proportions of payments received after the fourth letter

5. The proportions of payments received after the fifth letter

6. The proportions of payments received after the sixth letter

7. The proportions of payments received for all six letters

8. The mean payments received after the first letter

9. The mean payments received after the second letter

10. The mean payments received after the third letter

11. The mean payments received after the fourth letter

12. The mean payments received after the fifth letter

13. The mean payments received after the sixth letter

14. The mean payments received for all six letters

Limitations

The random division of outstanding accounts into two groups will control such extraneous variables as economic conditions, seasonality, volume of credit, cost of credit, and volume of sales. However, some limitations to the proposed research do exist.

First, a longer period of time might give more valid results. However, the seriousness of the collection-rate problem necessitates taking no more than three months for the initial test of the new series.

Another limitation will arise if the collection staff does not keep accurate records of the added information necessary for the research. For people already pressed to meet their own job requirements, the additional work could add the type of burden that leads to carelessness. The section on personnel training includes suggestions for preventing this limitation.

Still another potential limitation rests with the nature of the research design: If the proportions of responses after the first letter are significantly greater for the new series, the proportion of remaining delinquent accounts for the new series will be smaller than the proportion for the old series. Thus, the group receiving the new series likely would have a larger proportion of the "hard-core" delinquents than the group receiving the old series. Such an effect could continue through the remainder of the six letters as well. If such an effect does occur, the analysis after the first letter and after all six letters may be the only two valid tests.

Another limitation will arise if the sizes of the samples reduce after successive collections to the point that they do not meet the criteria for applying two-sample proportions tests. An examination of previous collection cycles shows that the samples will probably hold at least through the analysis of the fifth letter.

Hypotheses

So that the statements of hypotheses in this section will not conflict with those necessary for the quantitative analysis, they take the null form:

1. For the first letter, the proportion of payments received from Group N is less than or equal to the proportion received from Group O.

2. For the second letter, the proportion of payments received from Group N is less than or equal to the proportion received from Group O.

3. For the third letter, the proportion of payments received from Group N is less than or equal to the proportion received from Group O.

4. For the fourth letter, the proportion of payments received from Group N is less than or equal to the proportion received from Group O.

5. For the fifth letter, the proportion of payments received from Group N is less than or equal to the proportion received from Group O.

6. For the sixth letter, the proportion of payments received from Group N is less than or equal to the proportion received from Group O.

7. For all six letters, the proportion of payments received from Group N is less than or equal to the proportion received from Group O.

8. For the first letter, the mean payment received from Group N is less than or equal to the mean payment received from Group O.

9. For the second letter, the mean payment received from Group N is less than or equal to the mean payment received from Group O.

10. For the third letter, the mean payment received from Group N is less than or equal to the mean payment received from Group O.

11. For the fourth letter, the mean payment received from Group N is less than or equal to the mean payment received from Group O.

12. For the fifth letter, the mean payment received from Group N is less than or equal to the mean payment received from Group O.

13. For the sixth letter, the mean payment received from Group N is less than or equal to the mean payment received from Group O.

14. For all six letters, the mean payment received from Group N is less than or equal to the mean payment received from Group O.

RELATED RESEARCH

Because of its relationship to circumstances specific to Raylynne Co., the precise topic of the proposed research receives no treatment in the literature. However, two reports were located that do relate to the general subject matter.

Roland reports on research associated with the instigation of a new collection process (including a new mail collection series) for the Cella Co. in 1977. Though she did not assess the impact of the collection series as an isolated variable, she did suggest:

> The improvement in the rate of collection after the establishment of the new process likely depends a great deal upon the modernized series of five collection letters. Though not tested directly, the new series led the collectors to comment that the new letters brought an obviously improved rate of response.[1]

Similarly, Novick conducted research and concluded: "The 1974 collection series led to a significantly greater average collection than did the 1973 series."[2] However, Novick's research seems to have one major flaw: He did not hold any sort of control over the other factors that might have related to an increased average. He simply took the mean dollar value of collections for a firm for each of the years and tested to determine whether the means differed significantly. Thus, the increase in 1974 could have been explained by any number of variables other than the collection series.

---

[1]Jennifer Roland, "The Collection Process Does Matter," The Collectors' Monthly 22 (February 1978): 26.

[2]Walter Novick, "Mean Dollar Collections for the Alabaster Corp. before and after Revision of the Written Collection Series, 1973-1974," Collection Management 95 (Summer 1975): 5.

DEFINITIONS OF TERMS

These definitions may expedite reading this proposal:

Group N—The group receiving the new collection series (17G3)

Group O—The group receiving the old collection series (17G2)

$N_1, N_2 \ldots N_6$—First new-series letter, second new-series letter ... sixth new-series letter

$O_1, O_2 \ldots O_6$—First old-series letter, second old-series letter ... sixth old-series letter

Payment—Payment made within two weeks of mailing of letter

METHODOLOGY

The methodology of the proposed research will involve collection, organization, and analysis of the data.

Collection

These steps will accomplish the collection of the data:

1. Beginning February 2, 1981, design the six letters of series 17G3, and put them into word processing system.

2. On March 2, pull the cards for the accounts to be started on the collection series. Leave the cards in alphabetical order. Number the cards. Use a table of random numbers to choose the first card. Assign that card the old collection series, the next card the new series, the next card the old series, etc., until all cards have an assignment. Repeat the process with each new scheduled cycle for collection follow-up.

3. For each cycle and each letter, complete the form illustrated as the attachment to this proposal.

Organization

At the end of the three-month period, the organizational stage will involve counting the numbers who have made payments for each of the letters and for all six letters for both Group O and Group N. In addition, it will involve finding the mean payments received from each of the two groups. Letters for which the two-week response period has not expired will be eliminated from the analysis. Tables and charts will illustrate the organization.

Analysis

The analysis of the comparative proportions of people who make payments will proceed from the grand total for the six letters and for each of the six letters. The totals will be converted into proportions—the proportion who make payments in response to $O_1, O_2 \ldots O_6$, to $N_1, N_2 \ldots N_6$, and to the totals for all six letters.

This part of the analysis will take the form of one-tailed tests of hypotheses for two-sample proportions. The test for each letter and for the total will determine whether the proportion of payments for the new series is less than or equal to the proportion for the old series.

A one-tailed, two-sample-mean test will determine whether the mean payment from Group N for each of the six letters is less than or equal to the mean payment from Group O for all six letters. The same tests will apply to the means for the payments for the totals for all six letters.

All 14 tests will be conducted at the .05 and .01 levels of risk. Each test will lead to a rejection or an acceptance of the associated null hypothesis.

From the decisions will come the conclusions and recommendations.

If a test leads to a rejection of the null hypothesis, Series 17G3 will have been successful in improving the rate of collections or the mean size of the payment received.

PLANS FOR REPORTING

At the end of the three-month period, the researcher will prepare a complete report of the research. The report will include a review of the sections included in this proposal as well as a summary of the findings of the collection, organization, and analysis of the data. It will also include the conclusions and recommendations drawn from the analysis.

The reports will be submitted to Credit Manager Cindy Melsa and Collection Supervisor Ken Edah for their desired use and distribution.

SCHEDULE OF TIME AND WORK

The schedule for the work is:

1. Beginning early in February, 1981, Melsa and Edah develop Series 17G3.

2. Late in February, Self, Melsa, and Edah conduct one-hour workshop for collectors.

3. From Monday, March 2, through Friday, March 29, 1981, collectors record data.

4. During the week of June 1, analyze data and prepare report.

5. On June 8, submit report to Melsa and Edah.

PERSONNEL AND TRAINING

Though the research will require no additional personnel, the existing personnel will take on some additional work and will need some brief training and some motivational development.

To accomplish the training and the motivation, the researcher will schedule and conduct a one-hour session in February for all 26 collectors. They will learn how to divide the delinquents into Group O and Group N and how to complete the forms. Melsa and Edah will also be present to encourage the employees to take the few minutes needed each day to collect the information for it.

A great deal of the responsibility for day-to-day coordination of activities and summarization of the information will fall upon Edah. He will work closely with both the researcher and the collectors.

ATTACHMENT

THE DIFFERENCES BETWEEN TWO COLLECTION SERIES IN
PROPORTIONS AND MEANS OF PAYMENTS RECEIVED
BY RAYLYNNE CO. IN MARCH-MAY, 1981

FORM FOR RECORDING DATA

Date of Mailing _____, 1981 Letter No. _____

Collector _____ Group O or N? _____

Surname on Delinquent Account	Account Number	Amount Owed	Date of Payment	Amount of Payment
1.				
2.				
3.				
4.				
5.				
6.				
7.				
8.				
9.				
10.				
11.				
12.				
13.				
14.				
15.				

Appendix G

Final Report of Research Project

THE DIFFERENCES BETWEEN TWO COLLECTION SERIES IN

PROPORTIONS AND MEANS OF PAYMENTS RECEIVED

BY RAYLYNNE CO. IN MARCH-MAY, 1981

Report of Research

Prepared for

Ms. Cindy Melsa
Credit Manager
Raylynne Co.

Prepared by

Y. R. Self
Research Specialist
Raylynne Co.
June 8, 1981

RAYLYNNE CO.

785 Crays Boulevard   *Shraft, CO 77777*   *888–88–888*

January 26, 1981

Mr./Ms. Y. R. Self
Research Specialist

Dear Mr./Ms. Self:

The Executive Committee met last Wednesday to consider your proposal for research
into the power of a new collection series to increase the rate of collections. In addition, I
met privately with Vice President Allen to discuss it.

As a result of the two meetings, we have decided to proceed with your proposed research
as you have designed it.

Mr. Edah and I would like to meet with you this week to begin the development of the
new collection series and to make plans for the workshop for the collectors. I will be out
of town Wednesday.

Whether we determine that the new series increases the collection rate or not, we need a
new series. We also need to know whether we must search for other factors to explain
the declining rate. If a change in the series does not make a difference, we might
consider an experiment involving telephone collection instead of collection by mail.

Sincerely,

Cindy Melsa

Cindy Melsa
Credit Manager

CM:bb

RAYLYNNE CO.

785 Crays Boulevard　　　　　*Shraft, CO 77777*　　　　　*888–88–888*

June 8, 1981

Ms. Cindy Melsa
Credit Manager

Dear Ms. Melsa:

This report summarizes the collection-series research you authorized on January 26. It confirms the findings reported in the preliminary report sent to you on April 17: The new collection series does lead to a significantly improved rate of collection.

As suggested in the recommendations section of the report, we may want to begin exclusive use of the new series, but also conduct research to determine whether a telephone collection process might improve the rate even more. I shall be glad to prepare a proposal for such research if you would like.

Thank you for the opportunity to complete the research—and for all of the aid and support that you provided.

Sincerely,

Y. R. Self

Y. R. Self
Research Specialist

YRS:aa

CONTENTS

ILLUSTRATIONS

Figure

TABLES

ABSTRACT

During 1979 and 1980 the rates of collection for delinquent accounts at Raylynne Co. declined significantly. This research involved tests to determine whether a new collection series (17G3) might yield a higher rate of collection and a higher mean collection than Series 17G2.

For the period March-May, 1981, the outstanding accounts were randomly divided into two groups. Group O received the six letters of Series 17G2, and Group N received the six letters of Series 17G3.

One-tailed tests of two-sample proportions covered five hypotheses—one each for the proportions of payments made within two weeks after each of the first four letters, and one for the proportions for all six letters. The samples were not large enough to test Letter Nos. 5 and 6.

One-tailed tests of two-sample means covered seven hypotheses—one each for the means of payments made within two weeks after each of the six letters, and one for the means of the payments received for all six letters.

The analysis yielded these conclusions:

1. Compared to Series 17G2, Series 17G3 significantly improved the proportions of payments received after the first and fourth letters, and for the total of all six letters.

2. Only the first letters showed a significant difference in the mean payments, with Group N having a significantly larger mean than Group O.

3. Though not tested for significance, the proportion of outstanding dollars after all six letters is less for Group N than for Group O.

4. Series 17G3 clearly improves the rate of payments and reduces the amount of outstanding accounts.

Recommendations flowing from the research include:

1. Change from Series 17G2 to Series 17G3 for all collections.

2. Revise and test the second and third letters in Series 17G3 to try to improve the
   proportions of responses.

3. If deemed important to test the fifth and sixth letters for proportions of
   responses, continue the research on the two letters until the sample sizes are
   large enough to conduct the tests.

4. Authorize the development of a proposal to conduct research into the possibility
   of using telephone collections in conjunction with or in addition to mail
   collections.

THE DIFFERENCES BETWEEN TWO COLLECTION SERIES IN

PROPORTIONS AND MEANS OF PAYMENTS RECEIVED

BY RAYLYNNE CO. IN MARCH-MAY, 1981

During 1979 and 1980 the rates of collection for delinquent accounts at Raylynne Co. declined significantly. Though inflation and recession undoubtedly explain the major portion of the decline, the age of the collection series may have contributed to rates lower than would have been experienced with a more modern series.

Raylynne Co. created and began to use the present series (17G2) in 1978. Series 17G2 seemed to produce good results that year. However, as shown in Table 1, 1979 and 1980 do not reflect good collection rates—not even as good as those experienced in 1975 and 1976 with Series 17G1.

TABLE 1

ANNUAL RATES OF COLLECTION

Raylynne Co., 1975-1981

Year	Percent of Outstanding Dollars Collected After Three Letters	Percent of Outstanding Dollars Collected After All Six Letters
1975	68.5	83.6
1976	68.8	82.3
1977	69.1	83.1
1978	71.7	86.1
1979	64.5	78.2
1980	60.4	72.6

THE PROBLEM

The general problem of the research was the decline in the rate of collections during 1979 and 1980. Thus, the purpose of the research was to find whether a new series of collection letters increases the rates of collections.

Research Problem

The specific problem of the research was to determine whether the collections for a new series (17G3) were significantly greater than the collections for the old series (17G2) for the period March through May, 1981.

To establish appropriate controls, the outstanding accounts were randomly divided into two groups. Group O received Series 17G2, and Group N received Series 17G3. The primary determinations were made for the totals for all six letters. However, other determinations were made for each of the six letters.

Two factors formed the basis for the analysis. They are (1) the proportions of people who made payments within two weeks of the mailings and (2) the mean sizes of payments received within two weeks of the mailings.

The scope of the delimited research problem, then, was to determine during the period March-May, 1981, whether Group N or Group O differed in:

1. The proportions of payments received after the first letter

2. The proportions of payments received after the second letter

3. The proportions of payments received after the third letter

4. The proportions of payments received after the fourth letter

5. The proportions of payments received after the fifth letter

6. The proportions of payments received after the sixth letter

7. The proportions of payments received for all six letters

8. The mean payments received after the first letter

9. The mean payments received after the second letter

10. The mean payments received after the third letter

11. The mean payments received after the fourth letter

12. The mean payments received after the fifth letter

13. The mean payments received after the sixth letter

14. The mean payments received for all six letters

Limitations

The random division of outstanding accounts into two groups controlled such extraneous variables as economic conditions, seasonality, volume of credit, cost of credit, and volume of sales. A simple test of significance showed that no significant difference existed between the mean values of outstanding accounts for Group O and Group N at the beginning of the test.

A period longer than three months probably would have given more valid results. However, the seriousness of the collection-rate problem necessitated completing the analysis in as brief a time as possible.

No limitations seemed to arise from the activities of the collectors. Examination of randomly selected samples of completed forms showed no errors or inaccuracies in recording.

Potential limitations in inappropriate sample sizes materialized for letters 4 and 5. Therefore, the hypotheses for proportions of payments for the two letters could not be tested for such small proportions.

Hypotheses

So that the statements of hypotheses in this section would not conflict with those necesary for the quantitative analysis, they took the null form:

1. For the first letter, the proportion of payments received from Group N is less than or equal to the proportion received from Group O.

2. For the second letter, the proportion of payments received from Group N is less than or equal to the proportion received from Group O.

3. For the third letter, the proportion of payments received from Group N is less than or equal to the proportion received from Group O.

4. For the fourth letter, the proportion of payments received from Group N is less than or equal to the proportion received from Group O.

5. For the fifth letter, the proportion of payments received from Group N is less than or equal to the proportion received from Group O.

6. For the sixth letter, the proportion of payments received from Group N is less than or equal to the proportion received from Group O.

7. For all six letters, the proportion of payments received from Group N is less than or equal to the proportion received from Group O.

8. For the first letter, the mean payment received from Group N is less than or equal to the mean payment received from Group O.

9. For the second letter, the mean payment received from Group N is less than or equal to the mean payment received from Group O.

10. For the third letter, the mean payment received from Group N is less than or equal to the mean payment received from Group O.

11. For the fourth letter, the mean payment received from Group N is less than or equal to the mean payment received from Group O.

12. For the fifth letter, the mean payment received from Group N is less than or equal to the mean payment received from Group O.

13. For the sixth letter, the mean payment received from Group N is less than or equal to the mean payment received from Group O.

14. For all six letters, the mean payment received from Group N is less than or equal to the mean payment received from Group O.

RELATED RESEARCH

Because of its relationship to circumstances specific to Raylynne Co., the precise topic of the proposed research receives no treatment in the literature. However, two reports were located that do relate to the general subject matter.

Roland reports on research associated with the instigation of a new collection process (including a new mail collection series) for the Cella Co. in 1977. Though Roland did not assess the impact of the collection series as an isolated variable, she did suggest:

> The improvement in the rate of collection after the establishment of the new process likely depends a great deal upon the modernized series of five collection letters. Though not tested directly, the new series led the collectors to comment that the new letters brought an obviously improved rate of response.[1]

Similarly, Novick conducted research and concluded: "The 1974 collection series led to a significantly greater average collection than did the 1973 series."[2] However, Novick's research seems to have one major flaw: He did not hold any sort of control over the other factors that might have related to an increased average. He simply took the mean dollar value of collections for a firm for each of two years and tested to determine whether the means differed significantly. Thus, the increase in 1974 could have been explained by any number of other variables.

DEFINITIONS OF TERMS

These definitions may expedite reading this report:

Group N—The group receiving the new collection series (17G3)

---

[1] Jennifer Roland, "The Collection Process Does Matter," The Collectors' Monthly 22 (February 1978): 26.
[2] Walter Novick, "Mean Dollar Collections for the Alabaster Corp. before and after Revision of the Written Collection Series, 1973-1974," Collection Management 95 (Summer 1975): 5.

Group O—The group receiving the old collection series (17G2)

$N_1, N_2 \ldots N_6$—First new-series letter, second new-series letter $\ldots$ sixth new-series

      letter

$O_1, O_2 \ldots O_6$—First old-series letter, second old-series letter $\ldots$ sixth old-series letter

Payment—Payment made within two weeks of mailing.

METHODOLOGY

The design of the investigation included collection, organization, and analysis.

Collection

These steps accomplished the collection of the data:

1. During February, Melsa and Edah developed the six letters of 17G3 and put them

   into the word processing system.

2. Beginning on March 2, 1981, the collectors pulled the cards for the accounts to

   be started on the collection series and left them in alphabetical order. They

   numbered the cards, used a table of random numbers to choose the first card, and

   assigned it to Series 17G2. They then assigned the next card to Series 17G3, the

   next card to Series 17G2, etc., until all cards had an assignment. They repeated

   the process with the other cycles beginning during the period.

3. For each cycle and each letter, the collectors completed the form illustrated as

   the attachment to this report.

Organization

At the end of the period, the organizational stage involved counting the numbers

who made payments for each of the letters and for all six letters for both Group O and

Group N. In addition, it involved finding the mean payments received from each of the

two groups for the six letters combined and for each letter. Letters for which the

two-week response period had not expired were eliminated from the analysis. Tables and charts in the next section illustrate the organization.

Analysis

The analysis of the comparative proportions of payments and of the mean payments proceeded from the data for each of the six letters and for the totals for all six letters. One-tailed tests of significance were made at the .05 and .01 levels of risk. The results of the tests appear in the next section.

RESULTS

The results of the collection and analysis fall naturally into the two major categories of that analysis: proportions of payments and means of payments.

Proportions of Payments

Figure 1 shows the numbers of payments made by both Groups O and N. In addition, it shows the parts contributed by each of the letters to the totals for both groups.

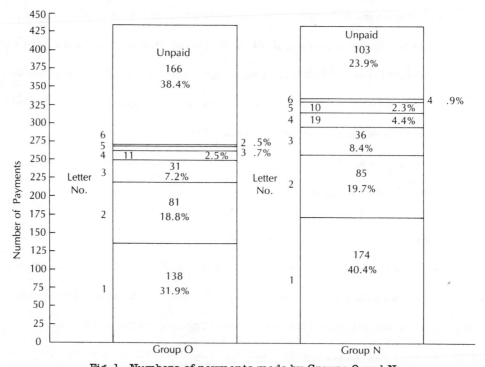

Fig. 1. Numbers of payments made by Groups O and N.

The numbers of delinquent accounts in Groups O and N are virtually identical (432 and 431, respectively). Thus, Figure 1 shows that the number of payments by Group N represents .761 of the total, while the number of payments by Group O represents .616 of the total.

Table 2 contains a detailed summary of the comparative proportions of the payments received from the two groups. The values of z reported in the last column result from the calculations of the differences between the two sample proportions for each designated test. As indicated in the section on limitations, z values for letters 5 and 6 could not be calculated because the sample sizes do not meet the criteria for proportions testing.

For the one-tailed, normal-distribution tests reflected by the z scores, the critical points of rejection are 1.64 for the .05 level of risk and 2.33 for the .01 levels of risk. Compared to the critical points, then, three values of z lead to a rejection of the associated null hypotheses—with all three rejections at the .01 level of risk. Thus, for Letter Nos. 1 and 4, and for the combined data for all six letters, Group N made significantly greater proportions of payments than did Group O. For Letter Nos. 2 and 3 the tests do not establish that Group N made higher proportions of payments. However, though not calculated here, the Type II probabilities do exist. They are the probabilities that the tests lead to an acceptance of false hypotheses—the hypotheses that the proportions for Group N are less than or equal to the proportions for Group O.

Means of Payments

Figure 2 illustrates the schedule of payments by amounts. It shows for both Groups O and N the total dollars outstanding on March 2, the amounts paid after each letter, the total amount paid during the period March through May, the amount outstanding at the end of the period, and the proportions paid and unpaid.

TABLE 2

COMPARISON OF PROPORTIONS WHO MADE PAYMENTS
IN RESPONSE TO THE TWO COLLECTION SERIES

Raylynne Co., March-May, 1981

Letter No.	No. in Group O	No. of Payments from Group O	Proportion of Payments from Group O	No. in Group N	No. of Payments from Group N	Proportion of Payments from Group N	Calculated Value of z
1	432	138	.319	431	174	.404	2.600**
2	294	81	.276	257	85	.331	1.404
3	213	31	.146	172	36	.209	1.621
4	182	11	.060	136	19	.140	2.415**
5	171	3	.018	117	10	.086	NA***
6	166	2	.012	107	4	.037	NA***
1-6	432	266	.616	431	328	.761	4.598**

**Significant at .01 (critical ratio = 2.33)
***Not available because sample sizes too small to calculate ratios for proportions this small

9

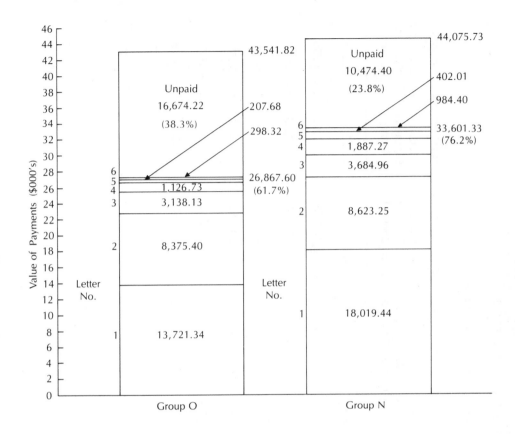

Fig. 2. Amounts of payments made by Groups O and N.

As the bar chart shows, the total number of dollars collected from Group N is larger in amount and in proportion than the total from Group O.

Table 3 summarizes the detail of the schedule of the dollar amounts of payments and the mean sizes of payments. The final column of z and t values shows the results of the tests of the seven null hypotheses comparing two sample means.

As might be expected, the means sizes of the payments tended not to be significantly different—subject, of course, to the Type II error. Only in the case of the mean payments after the first letter were the mean sizes of the payments significantly different—with the mean larger for Group N than for Group O at the .01 level. Thus, the only null hypothesis about means rejected through the analysis is Hypothesis No. 8.

TABLE 3

COMPARISON OF MEAN PAYMENTS IN RESPONSE
TO TWO COLLECTION SERIES

Raylynne Co., March-May, 1981

Letter No.	No. of Responses from Group O	Value of Payments Received from Group O	Mean Payment for Group O	No. of Responses from Group N	Value of Payments Received from Group N	Mean Payment for Group N	Calculated Value of z or t
1	138	$13,721.34	$ 99.43	174	$18,019.44	$103.56	z = 2.446**
2	81	8,375.40	103.40	85	8,623.25	101.45	z = -0.956
3	31	3,138.13	101.23	36	3,684.96	102.36	z = 0.237
4	11	1,126.73	102.43	19	1,887.27	99.33	t = -1.845
5	3	298.32	99.44	10	984.40	98.44	t = -0.177
6	2	207.68	103.84	4	402.01	100.50	t = -1.773
1-6	266	26,867.60	101.01	328	33,601.33	102.44	z = 1.316

**Significant at the .01 level (critical ratio = 2.33)

Table 4 provides an informational extension to the results. It simply shows the proportions of outstanding dollars remaining after each of the six letters.

PROPORTIONS OF OUTSTANDING DOLLARS AFTER
LETTERS IN TWO COLLECTION SERIES

Raylynne Co., March-May, 1981

Letter No.	No. of Dollars Outstanding for Group O	Proportion of Dollars Outstanding for Group O	No. of Dollars Outstanding for Group N	Proportion of Dollars Outstanding for Group N
1	$43,541.82	1.000	$44,075.73	1.000
2	29,820.48	.685	26,056.29	.591
3	21,445.08	.493	17,433.04	.396
4	18,306.95	.420	13,748.08	.312
5	17,180.22	.395	11,860.81	.269
6	16,881.90	.388	10,876.41	.247
1-6	16,674.22	.383	10,474.40	.238

CONCLUSIONS AND RECOMMENDATIONS

The conclusions and recommendations flow naturally from the results of the analysis.

Conclusions

The logical conclusions drawn from the research include:

1. Compared to the old collection series, the new collection series significantly improves the proportions of payments received after the first and fourth letters, and for the total of all six letters.

2. No essential difference exists in the mean payments for all six letters for Group O and Group N.

3. After six letters the proportion of outstanding dollars is less for Group N than for Group O.

4. Compared to the old collection series, the new collection series improves the rate of payments and reduces the amount of outstanding accounts.

Recommendations

In light of the conclusions and the interpretation of them, these recommendations seem to be in order:

1. Change from Series 17G2 to Series 17G3 for all collections.

2. Revise and test the second and third letters in Series 17G3 to try to improve the proportions of responses.

3. If deemed important to test the fifth and sixth letters for proportions of responses, continue the research on the two letters until the sample sizes are large enough to conduct the tests.[3]

4. Authorize the development of a proposal to conduct research into the possibility of using telephone collections in conjunction with or in addition to mail collections.

---

[3]The required sample sizes vary with the sizes of the proportions. Thus, if the test is continued, the Research Department has a table of required sample sizes keyed to sizes of the proportions being tested.

ATTACHMENT

THE DIFFERENCES BETWEEN TWO COLLECTION SERIES IN
PROPORTIONS AND MEANS OF PAYMENTS RECEIVED
BY RAYLYNNE CO. IN MARCH-MAY, 1981

FORM FOR RECORDING DATA

Date of Mailing _____, 1981 Letter No. _____

Collector _____ Group O or N? _____

Surname on Delinquent Account	Account Number	Amount Owed	Date of Payment	Amount of Payment
1. _____				
2. _____				
3. _____				
4. _____				
5. _____				
6. _____				
7. _____				
8. _____				
9. _____				
10. _____				
11. _____				
12. _____				
13. _____				
14. _____				
15. _____				

SELECTED BIBLIOGRAPHY

Novick, Walter. "Mean Dollar Collections for the Alabaster Corp. before and after Revision of the Written Collection Series, 1973-1974." Collection Management 95 (Summer 1975): 3-8.

Roland, Jennifer. "The Collection Process Does Matter." The Collectors' Monthly 22 (February 1978): 23-29.

Sources

Articles

ABCA Bulletin 38 (December 1975). (Contains 14 articles on communication for employment.)

Almaney, Adnan. "The Effect of Message Treatment on Feedback in Business Communication." *Journal of Business Communication* 9 (Spring 1972):19–23.

American Business Communication Association *Ad Hoc* Committee, Bobbye Persing, Chairperson. "The 1976 ABCA Followup Evaluation of the Course Content, Classroom Procedures, and Quality of the Basic Course in College and University Business Communication." *ABCA Bulletin* 40 (March 1977):18–24.

Bennett, James C. "The Communication Needs of Business Executives." *Journal of Business Communication* 8 (Spring 1971):5–11.

Cox, Homer. "The Voices of Experiences: The Business Communication Alumnus [sic] Reports." *Journal of Business Communication* 13 (Summer 1976):35–46.

Ekman, Paul, and Friesen, Wallace V. "The Repertoire of Nonverbal Behavior: Categories, Origins, Usage, and Coding." *Semiotica* 1 (1969):49–93.

Fisher, Jeffrey D.; Rytting, Marvin; and Heslin, Richard. "Hands Touching Hands: Affective and Evaluative Effects on Interpersonal Touch." *Sociometry* 39 (1976):416–421.

Flesch, Rudolf. "A New Readability Yardstick." *Journal of Applied Psychology* 32 (June 1948):221–233.

Holland, Winford E.; Stead, Bette Ann; and Leibrock, Robert C. "Information Channel/Source Selection as a Correlate of Technical Uncertainty in a Research and Development Organization." *IEEE Transactions on Engineering Management* EM–23 (November 1976):163–167.

Huegli, Jon M., and Tschirgi, Harvey D. "An Investigation of Communication Skills Application and Effectiveness at the Entry Job Level." *Journal of Business Communication* 12 (Fall 1974):24–29.

Johnson, H. G.; Ekman, Paul; and Friesen, Wallace V. "Communicative Body Movements: American Emblems." *Semiotica* 15 (1975):335-353.

O'Connell, Sandra E. "Communications: Growth Field of the Seventies." *Journal of Business Communication* 15 (Spring 1978):37–46.

Pauly, John. "The Case for a New Model of Business Communication." *Journal of Business Communication* 14 (Summer 1977):11–23.

Penrose, John M. "A Survey of the Perceived Importance of Business Communication and Other Business-Related Abilities." *Journal of Business Communication* 13 (Winter 1976):17–24.

Persing, Bobbye Sorrels. "Search and Re-search for Solutions to Communication Problems." *Journal of Business Communication* 16 (Winter 1979):13–25.

_____."Sticks and Stones *and* Words: Women in the Language." *Journal of Business Communication* 14 (Winter 1977):11–19.

Rogers, Carl R., and Roethlisberger, F. J. "Barriers and Gateways to Communication." *Harvard Business Review* 30 (July–August 1952):46ff.

Weinrauch, J. Donald, and Swanda, John R., Jr. "Examining the Significance of Listening: An Exploratory Study of Contemporary Management." *Journal of Business Communication* 13 (Fall, 1975): 31.

"Who Is the Real Family?" *Ms.*, August 1978, p. 43.

Books

Agee, Warren K.; Ault, Phillip H.; and Emery, Edwin. *Introduction to Mass Communications.* 5th ed. New York: Harper & Row, 1976.

American Business Communication Association Research Committee, C. Glen Pearce, Chairperson. *Guidelines for Research in Business Communication*. Urbana, Ill.: American Business Communication Association, 1977.

Andersen, Kenneth E. *Introduction to Communication Theory and Practice*. Menlo Park, Calif.: Cummings, 1977.

Berlo, David K. *The Process of Communication: An Introduction to Theory and Practice*. New York: Holt, Rinehart and Winston, 1960.

Berne, Eric. *Games People Play*. New York: Random House, Inc., Grove Press, 1964.

Blake, Reed H., and Haroldsen, Edwin O. In *A Taxonomy of Concepts in Communication*. Humanistic Studies in the Communication Arts. Edited by George N. Gordon. New York: Communication Arts Books, Hastings House, 1975.

Blumer, Hubert. "Symbolic Interaction: An Approach to Human Communication." In *Approaches to Human Communication*, pp. 401–419. Edited by Richard W. Budd and Brent D. Ruben. Rochelle Park, N.J.: Spartan Books, Hayden, 1972.

Bonner, William H. *Better Business Writing*. Homewood, Ill.: Richard D. Irwin, 1974.

Bonner, William H., and Voyles, Jean. *Communicating in Business: Key to Success*. Houston, Tex.: Dame Publications, 1980.

Bowman, Joel P., and Branchaw, Bernadine. *Successful Communication in Business*. New York: Harper & Row, 1980.

Branchaw, Bernadine P. *English Made Easy*. New York: Gregg Division/McGraw-Hill, 1979.

Brendel, Leroy A.; Donnelly, Frank P.; and Peterson, John C. *Communication Word Power: Vocabulary and Spelling Mastery*. New York: Gregg Division/McGraw-Hill, 1968.

Brennan, John. *The Conscious Communicator: Making Communication Work in the Work Place*. Reading, Mass.: Addison-Wesley, 1974.

Brooks, William D. *Speech Communication*. 4th ed. Dubuque, Iowa: Wm. C. Brown, 1981.

Brown, Leland. *Communicating Facts and Ideas in Business*. 2d ed. Englewood Cliffs, N.J.: Prentice-Hall, 1970.

Brusaw, Charles T.; Alred, Gerald J., and Oliu, Walter E. *The Business Writer's Handbook*. New York: St. Martin's Press, 1976.

Butera, Mary C.; Krause, Ruthetta; and Sabin, William A. *College English: Grammar and Style*. New York: Gregg Division/McGraw-Hill, 1967.

Campbell, James H., and Hepler, Hal W. *Dimensions in Communications: Readings*. 2d ed. Belmont, Calif.: Wadsworth, 1970.

Clover, Vernon T., and Balsley, Howard L. *Business Research Methods*. 2d ed. Grid Series in Management. Columbus, Ohio: Grid, 1978.

Cornwell, Robert C., and Manship, Darwin W. *Applied Business Communication*. Dubuque, Iowa: Wm. C. Brown, 1978.

Damerst, William A. *Resourceful Business Communication*. Harcourt, Brace and World, 1966.

Dance, Frank E. X. "Toward a Theory of Human Communication." In *Human Communication Theory: Original Essays*, pp. 288–309. Edited by Frank E. X. Dance. New York: Holt, Rinehart and Winston, 1967.

Dance, Frank E. X., and Larson, Carl E. *Speech Communication: Concepts and Behavior*. New York: Holt, Rinehart and Winston, 1972.

Dartnell's Glossary of Word Processing Terms. Chicago: Dartnell, 1975.

Dawe, Jessamon, and Lord, William Jackson, Jr. *Functional Business Communication*. 2d ed. Englewood Cliffs, N.J.: Prentice-Hall, 1974.

Ekman, Paul, and Friesen, Wallace V. *Unmasking the Face*. Englewood Cliffs, N.J.: Prentice-Hall, 1975.

Fabun, Don. *Communications: The Transfer of Meaning*. Beverly Hills, Calif.: Glencoe Press, 1968.

Fast, Julius. *The Body Language of Sex, Power, and Aggression*. New York: M. Evans and Company, 1977.

Felber, Stanley B., and Koch, Arthur. *What Did You Say?* 2d ed. Englewood Cliffs, N.J.: Prentice-Hall, 1978.

Flesch, Rudolf. *The Art of Readable Writing*. 25th anniv. ed. New York: Harper & Row, 1974.

Freeman, Michael J. *Writing Résumés, Locating Jobs, and Handling Job Interviews*. Homewood, Ill.: Richard D. Irwin, 1976.

Gootnick, David E. *Even You Can Give a Talk*. East Elmhurst, N.Y.: Communications Dynamics Press, 1975.

_____. *Getting a Better Job*. New York: McGraw-Hill, 1978.

Gunning, Robert. *More Effective Writing in Business and Industry*. Boston, Mass.: Industrial Education Institute, 1963.

_____. *The Techniques of Clear Writing*. Rev. ed. New York: McGraw-Hill, 1968.

Hall, Edward T. *The Silent Language*. Garden City, N.Y.: Anchor Press/Doubleday, Anchor Books, 1959.

Haney, William V. *Communications and Interpersonal Relations*. 4th ed. Homewood, Ill.: Richard D. Irwin, 1979.

Harris, Thomas A. *I'm OK—You're OK*. New York: Harper & Row, Avon Books, 1969.

Hatch, Richard. *Communicating in Business*. Chicago: Science Research Associates, 1977.

Hayakawa, S. T., in consultation with Arthur Asa Berger and Arthur Chandler. *Language in Thought and Action*. 4th ed. New York: Harcourt Bruce Jovanovich, 1978.

Henley, Nancy M. *Body Politics: Power, Sex, and Nonverbal Communication*. Englewood Cliffs, N.J.: Prentice-Hall, 1977.

Henley, Nancy, and Thorne, Barrie, comps. *She Said/He Said: An Annotated Bibliography of Sex Differences in Language, Speech, and Nonverbal Communication*. Pittsburgh, Pa.: Know, Inc., 1975.

Himstreet, William C., and Baty, Wayne Murlin. *Business Communications*. 6th ed. Belmont, Calif.: Wadsworth, 1981.

Howard, C. Jeriel; Tracz, Richard Francis; and Thomas, Coramae. *Contact: A Textbook in Applied Communications*. 3d ed. Englewood Cliffs, N.J.: Prentice-Hall, 1979.

Huseman, Richard; Lahiff, James; and Hatfield, John. *Business Communication: Strategies and Skills*. New York: Dryden Press, 1980.

Huseman, Richard C.; Lahiff, James M.; and Hatfield, John D. *Interpersonal Communication in Organizations*. Boston, Mass.: Holbrook, 1976.

International Association of Business Communicators. *Without Bias: A Guidebook for Nondiscriminatory Communication*. Edited by Judy E. Pickens, Patricia Walsh Rao, and Linda Cook Roberts. San Francisco, Calif.: International Association of Business Communicators, 1977.

Jacobus, Lee A. *Improving College Reading*. 3d ed. New York: Harcourt Brace Jovanovich, 1978.

Janis, J. Harold. *Writing and Communicating in Business*. 3d ed. New York: Macmillan 1978.

Knapp, Mark L. *Nonverbal Communication in Human Interaction*. 2d ed. New York: Holt, Rinehart and Winston, 1978.

Korzbski, Alfred. *Science and Sanity: An Introduction to Non-Aristotelian Systems and General Semantics*. Lancaster, Pa.: Science Press, 1933.

Larson, Charles U. *Communication: Everyday Encounters*. Belmont, Calif.: Wadsworth, 1976.

_____. *Persuasion: Reception and Responsibility*. 2d ed. Belmont, Calif.: Wadsworth, 1979.

Leedy, Paul D. *Practical Research*. 2d ed. New York: Macmillian, 1980.

Leonard, Donald J. *Shurter's Communication in Business*. New York: McGraw-Hill, 1979.

Lesikar, Raymond V. *Basic Business Communications*. Homewood, Ill.: Richard D. Irwin, 1979.

_____. *Business Communication: Theory and Application*. 4th ed. Homewood, Ill.: Richard D. Irwin, 1980.

_____. *Report Writing for Business*. 6th ed. Homewood, Ill.: Richard D. Irwin, 1980.

Level, Dale A., Jr., and Galle, William P. Jr. *Business Communications: Theory and Practice*. Dallas, Tex.: Business Publications, 1980.

Lewis, Phillip V., and Williams, John. *Readings in Organizational Communication*. Grid Series in Management. Columbus, Ohio: Grid, 1980.

McCabe, Helen M., and Popham, Estelle L. *Word Processing: A Systems Approach to the Office*. New York: Harcourt Brace Jovanovich, 1977.

McGough, Elizabeth. *Your Silent Language*. New York: William Morrow and Company, 1974.

McIntosh, Donal W. *Techniques of Business Communication*. 2d ed. Boston, Mass.: Holbrook Press, 1977.

Mangieri, John N., and Baldwin, R. Scott. *Effective Reading Techniques: Business and Personal Applications*. New York: Harper & Row/Canfield Press, 1978.

Maslow, Abraham H. *Motivation and Personality*. 2d ed. New York: Harper & Row, 1970.

Mehrabian, Albert. *Silent Messages*. Belmont, Calif.: Wadsworth, 1971.

Menning, J. H.; Wilkinson, C. W.; and Clarke, Peter B. *Communicating Through Letters and Reports*. 6th ed. Homewood, Ill.: Richard D. Irwin, 1976.

Michulka, Jean H. *Let's Talk Business*. Cincinnati, Ohio: South-Western, 1978.

Miller, Casey, and Swift, Kate. *Words and Women*. Garden City, N.Y.: Anchor Press/Doubleday, 1976.

Mintzberg, Henry. *The Nature of Managerial Work*. New York: Harper & Row, 1973.

Montagu, Ashley, and Matson, Floyd. *The Human Connection*. New York: McGraw-Hill, 1979.

Murphy, Herta A., and Peck, Charles E. *Effective Business Communications*. 3d ed. New York: McGraw-Hill, 1980.

National Lexicographic Board. *The New American Roget's College Thesaurus in Dictionary Form*. New York: World, 1962.

Pearsall, Thomas E., and Cunningham, Donald H. *How to Write for the World of Work*. New York: Holt, Rinehart, and Winston, 1978.

Persing, Bobbye Sorrels. *The Nonsexist Communicator*. East Elmhurst, N.Y.: Communication Dynamics Press, 1978.

Poe, Roy W., and Fruehling, Rosemary T. *Business Communication: A Problem-Solving Approach*. 2d ed. New York: Gregg Division/McGraw-Hill, 1978.

Potter, David, and Andersen, Martin P. *Discussion in Small Groups: A Guide to Effective Practice*. 3d ed. Belmont, Calif.: Wadsworth, 1976.

Robert, General Henry M. *Robert's Rules Newly Revised*. Edited by Sarah Corbin Robert. Glenview, Ill.: Scott, Foresman, 1981.

Ruesch, J., and Kees, W. *Nonverbal Communication: Notes on the Visual Perception of Human Relations*. Los Angeles, Calif.: University of California Press, 1956.

Schneider, Arnold E.; Donaghy, William C.; and Newman, Pamela Jane. *Organizational Communication*. New York: McGraw-Hill, 1975.

Shannon, Claude E., and Weaver, Warren. *The Mathematical Theory of Communication*. Urbana, Ill.: The University of Illinois Press, 1964.

Sheridan, Donald H. *Basic Communication Skills*. Columbus, Ohio: Charles E. Merrill, 1971.

Sigband, Norman B. *Communication for Management and Business*. 2d ed. Glenview, Ill.: Scott, Foresman, 1976.

Sigband, Norman B., and Bateman, David N. *Communicating in Business*. Glenview, Ill.: Scott, Foresman, 1981.

Simon, Julian L. *Basic Research Methods in Social Science: The Art of Empirical Investigation*. New York: Random House, 1969.

Stewart, Daniel K. *The Psychology of Communication*. New York: Fund & Wagnalls, 1968.

Stewart, Marie M.; Lanham, Frank W.; Zimmer, Kenneth; Clark, Lyn; and Stead, Bette Ann. *Business English and Communication*. 5th ed. New York: Gregg Division/McGraw-Hill, 1978.

Swindle, Robert E. *The Business Communicator*. Englewood Cliffs, N.J.: Prentice-Hall, 1980.

Thayer, Lee. *Communication and Communication Systems*. Homewood, Ill.: Richard D. Irwin, 1969.

Treece, Malra. *Communication for Business and the Professions*. Boston: Allyn and Bacon, 1978.

_____. *Successful Business Writing*. Boston: Allyn and Bacon, 1980.

Turabian, Kate L. *A Manual for Writers of Term Papers, Theses, and Dissertations*. 4th ed. Chicago: The University of Chicago Press, Phoenix Books, 1973.

University of Chicago Press. *A Manual of Style*. 12th ed., rev. Chicago: The University of Chicago Press, 1969.

Vardaman, George T., and Vardaman, Patricia Black. *Communication in Modern Organizations*. New York: John Wiley & Sons, 1973.

Verderber, Kathleen S., and Verderber, Rudolph F. *Inter-Act: Using Interpersonal Communication Skills*. 2d ed. Belmont, Calif.: Wadsworth, 1980.

Verderber, Rudolph F. *Communicate!* Belmont, Calif.: Wadsworth, 1975.

Weitz, Shirley, ed. *Nonverbal Communication: Readings with Commentary*. 2d ed. New York: Oxford University Press, 1979.

Wells, Walter. *Communications in Business*. 3d ed. Belmont, Calif.: Wadsworth, 1981.

Whalen, Doris H. *Handbook for Business Writers*. New York: Harcourt Brace Jovanovich, 1978.

Wittenberg, Mary Alice, and Voiles, Price R. *Modern Business English: A Text-Workbook for Colleges*. 6th ed. New York: Gregg Division/McGraw-Hill, 1979.

Wolf, Morris Phillip: Keyser, Dale R.; and Aurner, Robert R. *Effective Communication in Business*. 7th ed. Cincinnati, Ohio: South-Western, 1979.

Wolf, Morris Phillip, and Stead, Bette Ann. *Easy Grammar: A Programmed Review*. Dubuque, Iowa: Kendall/Hunt, 1970.

Zall, Paul M., and Franco, Leonard N. *Practical Writing in Business and Industry*. North Scituate, Mass.: Duxbury Press, 1978.

Zelko, Harold P., and Dance, Frank E. X. *Business and Professional Speech Communication*. 2d ed. New York: Holt, Rinehart and Winston, 1978.

Other

Conference Board. *Federal Budget*. Economic Road Maps, nos. 1860–1861. New York: The Conference Board, August 1979.

_____. *Long Term U.S. Energy Trends*. Economic Road Maps, nos. 1866–1867. New York: The Conference Board, November 1979.

_____. *Older Workers*. Economic Road Maps, no. 1835. New York: The Conference Board, July 1978.

_____. *The Two-Way Squeeze, 1980*. Economic Road Maps, nos. 1876–1877. New York: The Conference Board, April 1980.

_____. *Worldwide Foreign Investment in Manufacturing*. Economic Road Maps, nos. 1862–1863. New York: The Conference Board, September 1979.

Giersbach, Walter F. *Sell Yourself as a Pro. Communicator*. New York: New York Business Communicators, 1979.

Guidelines for Creating Positive Sexual and Racial Images in Educational Materials. New York: McGraw-Hill, 1972.

Klare, George R. *A Manual for Readable Writing*. Glen Burnie, Md.: R E M, 1975.

Lipman, Michel, and Joyner, Russell. *How to Write Clearly*. San Francisco: International Society for General Semantics, 1979.

Massey, Morris E. "What You Are, Is Where You Were When." Videotape. Boulder, Colo.: University of Colorado, 1978.

Monthly Energy Review (May 1980):13.

Monthly Labor Review 103 (May 1980):6.

Oklahoma. *Oklahoma Labor Market*. March 1980, pp. 1 and 26.

Oklahoma Natural Gas Company 1979 Annual Report, p. 17.

Rainey, Bill G. *Writing Business Proposals: A Teaching Unit.* Ada, Okla.: East Central State College, 1971.

Trager, G. L. "Paralanguage: A First Approximation." *Studies in Linguistics* 13 (1958): 1-12.

U.S. Department of Labor, Bureau of Labor Statistics. *How the Government Measures Unemployment.* BLS Rept. 505. Washington, D.C.: Government Printing Office, 1977.

U.S. Department of Labor, Bureau of Labor Statistics, Region 6. *Consumer Prices: April 1980.* Dallas, Tex.: Region 6.

U.S. Department of Labor, Manpower [*sic*] Administration, *Job Title Revisions to Eliminate Sex- and Age-Referent Language from the Dictionary of Occupational Titles, Third Edition*, Washington, D.C.: Government Printing Office, 1975.

U.S. Postal Service. *Domestic Postage Rates, Fees, and Information.* Notice 59 (June 1979).

U.S. Postal Service. *Mailroom Addressing for Automation.* Customer Services Dept. Notice 23–C (October 1977).

Index

DATE DUE

GAYLORD			PRINTED IN U.S.A.